Risk Management and Corporate Governance

Routledge Advances in Management and Business Studies

For a full list of titles in this series please visit http://www.routledge.com

13 **Rethinking Public Relations**
The Spin and the Substance
Kevin Moloney

14 **Organisational Learning in the Automotive Sector**
Penny West

15 **Marketing, Morality and the Natural Environment**
Andrew Crane

16 **The Management of Intangibles**
The Organization's Most Valuable Assets
A. Bounfour

17 **Strategy Talk**
A Critique of the Discourse of Strategic Management
Pete Thomas

18 **Power and Influence in the Boardroom**
James Kelly and John Gennard

19 **Public Private Partnerships**
Theory and Practice in International Perspective
Stephen Osborne

20 **Work and Unseen Chronic Illness**
Silent Voices
Margaret Vickers

21 **Measuring Business Excellence**
Gopal K Kanji

22 **Innovation as Strategic Reflexivity**
Edited by Jon Sundbo and Lars Fuglsang

23 **The Foundations of Management Knowledge**
Edited by Paul Jeffcutt

24 **Gender and the Public Sector**
Professionals and Managerial Change
Edited by Jim Barry, Mike Dent and Maggie O'Neill

25 **Managing Technological Development**
Hakan Hakansson and Alexandra Waluszewski

26 **Human Resource Management and Occupational Health and Safety**
Carol Boyd

27 **Business, Government and Sustainable Development**
Gerard Keijzers

28 **Strategic Management and Online Selling**
Creating Competitive Advantage with Intangible Web Goods
Susanne Royer

29 **Female Entrepreneurship**
Implications for Education, Training and Policy
Edited by Nancy M. Carter, Colette Henry, Barra Ó Cinnéide and Kate Johnston

30 **Managerial Competence within the Hospitality and Tourism Service Industries**
Global Cultural Contextual Analysis
John Saee

31 Innovation Diffusion in the New Economy
The Tacit Component
Barbara Jones and Bob Miller

32 Technological Communities and Networks
International, National and Regional Perspectives
Dimitris G. Assimakopoulos

33 Narrating the Management Guru
In Search of Tom Peters
David Collins

34 Development on the Ground
Clusters, Networks and Regions in Emerging Economies
Edited by Allen J. Scott and Gioacchino Garofoli

35 Reconfiguring Public Relations
Ecology, Equity, and Enterprise
David McKie and Debashish Munshi

36 The Pricing and Revenue Management of Services
A Strategic Approach
Irene C. L. Ng

37 Critical Representations of Work and Organization in Popular Culture
Carl Rhodes and Robert Westwood

38 Intellectual Capital and Knowledge Management
Strategic Management of Knowledge Resources
Federica Ricceri

39 Flagship Marketing
Concepts and Places
Edited by Tony Kent and Reva Brown

40 Managing Project Ending
Virpi Havila and Asta Salmi

41 AIDS and Business
Saskia Faulk and Jean-Claude Usunier

42 The Evaluation of Transportation Investment Projects
Joseph Berechman

43 Urban Regeneration Management
International Perspectives
Edited by John Diamond, Joyce Liddle, Alan Southern and Philip Osei

44 Global Advertising, Attitudes, and Audiences
Tony Wilson

45 Challenges and Controversies in Management Research
Edited by Catherine Cassell and Bill Lee

46 Economy, Work, and Education
Critical Connections
Catherine Casey

47 Regulatory Governance and Risk Management
Occupational Health and Safety in the Coal Mining Industry
Binglin Yang

48 Risk Management and Corporate Governance
Edited by Abol Jalilvand and A.G. Malliaris

Risk Management and Corporate Governance

Edited by Abol Jalilvand and
A.G. Malliaris

Routledge
Taylor & Francis Group
NEW YORK LONDON

First published 2012
by Routledge
711 Third Avenue, New York, NY 10017

Simultaneously published in the UK
by Routledge
2 Park Square, Milton Park, Abingdon, Oxon OX14 4RN

Routledge is an imprint of the Taylor & Francis Group, an informa business

Typeset in Sabon by IBT Global.
Printed and bound in the United States of America on acid-free paper by IBT Global.

Library of Congress Cataloging-in-Publication Data

Risk management and corporate governance / edited by Abol Jalilvand and A.G. Malliaris. — 1st ed.
p. cm. — (Routledge Values in Business ; 1)
Includes bibliographical references and index.
1. Risk management. 2. Corporate governance. I. Jalilvand, Abol. II. Malliaris, A. G.
HD61.R56886 2011
658.15'5—dc22
2011008272

ISBN: 978-0-415-87970-5 (hbk)
ISBN: 978-0-203-80498-8 (ebk)

Contents

Figures

Tables

APPENDIX TABLES

Preface

In this book, we introduce a series of fifteen chapters selected from the 2009 annual conference "Risk Management and Corporate Governance" sponsored by the Center for Integrated Risk Management and Corporate Governance at Loyola University Chicago. The book provides a good opportunity for academics and practitioners alike to take stock of the state of risk management and corporate governance research in an international setting. Collectively, the selected chapters overlay the areas of risk management and corporate governance on both financial and operating decisions of a firm while treating legal and political environments as externalities to decisions undertaken.

Funding for the conference and this book was provided by the Loyola University and its School of Business Administration. In addition, much of the work of the Center, including this conference, has been made possible through the generosity of the Chicago Mercantile Exchange (CME) Trust.

This is the second volume in a series of monographs on the topics of integrated risk management and corporate governance. The first volume, *Corporate Boards: Managers of Risk, Sources of Risk*, was edited by Robert W. Kolb and Donald Schwartz and published by Wiley-Blackwell. We wish to thank Routledge for collaborating with us to produce this volume.

We acknowledge the competent assistance of Ron MacDonald in compiling and editing numerous versions of the submitted chapters and keeping the production on course and on time. We are, of course, responsible for any errors remaining.

Abol Jalilvand
A.G. Malliaris

Introduction

Abol Jalilvand and A.G. Malliaris

In a recent article, Adams, Hermalin, and Weisbach (2010), offer a detailed conceptual framework for understanding and evaluating the role of boards of directors in corporate governance. The fundamental question most often asked about the role of boards is: "What determines their actions?" There appears to be a puzzling asymmetry: senior management makes numerous day-to-day decisions giving the impression that corporate boards do not matter; yet, when problems and failures arise, corporate boards become the center of attention. Witness the recent hearings at the Financial Crisis Inquiry Commission chaired by Phil Angelides, who served from 1999 to 2007 as California's state treasurer. You may recall that the Financial Crisis Inquiry Commission is a ten-member bipartisan panel created by Congress and charged with examining the causes of the nation's financial crisis and reporting its findings to the president and Congress by December 2010. During the week of April 5, 2010, two former top-ranking Citigroup officials apologized to the nation for taking the banking giant to the brink of extinction. Former CEO Charles Prince and ex–board member and chairman of the board Robert Rubin offered repentance before the Financial Crisis Inquiry Commission.

Ex-Citi CEO Charles O. "Chuck" Prince ran the company from 2003 through 2007. During much of his tenure, Citigroup ran up billions of dollars in losses, eventually causing the U.S. government to spend $45 billion to prevent its collapse. "I'm sorry," said Prince, "that our management team, starting with me, like so many others, could not see the unprecedented market collapse that lay before us." Rubin offered regrets but refused to accept responsibility for the day-to-day operations that created the Citigroup debacle. This asymmetry of responsibilities between management and corporate governance both for day-to-day operations and the board's monthly or quarterly review and evaluation remains an unresolved challenge.

At Loyola University Chicago's School of Business Administration, the Center for Integrated Risk Management and Corporate Governance has chosen the area of risk management as one of the central and critical domains that boards of directors must possess as their own responsibility.

Put differently, Loyola's Center for Integrated Risk Management and Corporate Governance has identified expertise in the area of risk management as a fundamental requirement for effective corporate governance, if not by all, certainly by some board members. This means that along with board committees such as "compensation," "audit," "strategy," and several others, "risk management" committees must be established to monitor the likelihood of certain events that may cause the collapse of the firm.

It is in this niche that we have both organized the conference and selected the chapters in this volume. Risk management is an art as well as a highly technical skill and it addresses both national and global risks.

The book is divided into three parts preceded by individual summaries that discuss the importance of the area and the questions it focuses on, how the chapter makes a contribution to this area, and what we do and do not know about the area. The four chapters that constitute Part I examine the performance effects of risk management and corporate governance from several perspectives that illustrate how systemic decisions and individual behavior are determinates of firm performance. In the following four chapters that constitute Part II, technical models and laboratory experiments are used to communicate information about risk and managing it, primarily, through the use of targeted financial instruments. The chapters in Part III focus on global risk management and corporate governance. They particularly address how the current global financial crisis has affected global banks' management of risk. They further discuss the effectiveness of voluntary mechanisms for companies to pursue better corporate governance practices. In the wake of the last decade's high-profile corporate scandals and the current financial crisis, fervent debate has arisen regarding regulation, corporate compliance, and the rights of shareholders among other topics. In the final part, we turn our focus toward the timely issues of legal and regulatory compliance in risk management and corporate governance.

BIBLIOGRAPHY

Adams, Rene, Benjamin Hermalin, and Michael Weisbach. 2010. "The Role of Boards of Directors in Corporate Governance: Conceptual Framework and Survey." *Journal of Economic Literature* 48 (1): 58–107.

Part I

The Performance Effects of Risk Management and Corporate Governance

Recent studies have documented that efforts in managing the firm's overall risk do create shareholders' value by mitigating and managing financial and operating imperfections and enhancing its opportunities (see, for example, Rene Stultz (2008) and Smithson & Simkins, (2005)). In fact, the recent global financial crisis has clearly demonstrated that certain banks that took risk management seriously and diversified appropriately, such as J.P. Morgan, performed much better than others who did not such as Citi Corp. Although both the approach to risk management and the tools utilized continue to evolve, it appears reasonable to argue that a focus on managing the firm's overall risk, also known as Enterprise-Wide Risk Management (ERM), has taken off and created a new paradigm which is devoid from fragmentation where every major department managed its risks following a silo approach. Furthermore, the new paradigm also moves away from selectivity and ad hoc approaches to risk management where risk was managed when division managers judged it necessary. Also, risks were narrowly defined to include insurable risks and risks from interest rate and currency exposures. The new paradigm emphasizes an integrated, enterprise-wide coordinated and continuous process that addresses all possible financial, business and strategic risks and opportunities.

Firms employ various mechanisms of corporate governance and risk management to bolster their shareholders' assurance of fair returns on their investments. Without such mechanisms, only the cash flow and assets of businesses could finance their operations and investments, making adequate economic performance unlikely. Even when implemented, risk management and corporate governance mechanisms cannot guarantee optimized economic performance, for firms' choices regarding risk and governance affect the performance of the individuals who are charged with their oversight. The five chapters that constitute Part I examine the performance effects of risk management and corporate governance from several perspectives that illustrate how systemic decisions and individual behavior are determinates of firm performance.

Chapter 1 explores how enterprise risk management practices can affect firm performance with regard to regulatory compliance. In "The Role of Enterprise Risk Management in Determining Audit Fees: Complement or Substitute," Kurt Desender and Esteban Lafuente use a sample of pharmaceutical firms to explore how their adoption of enterprise risk management practices influences their external audit fees. Is the hiring of a Chief Risk Officer enough for these firms to keep audit fees low? Or, must they rely more heavily on risk management throughout the enterprise to keep down audit fees? These are two of the key questions addressed in the authors' research. The authors hope that similar studies of other industries will occur.

Recent corporate governance research shows that board independence is linked to improvements in decision making, such as structuring efficient executive compensation arrangements. Adding to the literature are authors Yu Flora Kuang and Bo Qin. In Chapter 2, "Performance Based Equity Grants and Corporate Governance Choices," the authors examine the relationship between a board's degree of independence and its use of performance targets for equity compensation. Their findings provide valuable insight into matters of incentivizing managers to promote shareholder value, monitoring agency problems, and attracting and retaining talent.

In his Chapter 3 essay, "A Theoretical Framework for Voluntary Corporate Governance," Rodrigo Zeidan focuses on voluntary mechanisms for companies to pursue better corporate governance practices. Zeidan argues that a firm's decision to adopt better governance is complex and cannot be explained by market forces alone. Instead, he posits, one must consider the different contexts in which a given firm operates. Zeidan develops a decision framework that, at its foundation, separates market and non-market mechanisms. A corollary argument of the essay holds non-market mechanisms to be most relevant in developing countries. By classifying the mechanisms and developing a theoretical framework for explaining companies' decisions, the author hopes that his research can aid in the design of regulatory policies in capital markets worldwide.

Chapter 4 and Chapter 5 examine managerial behavior. In "Managers' Behavior when Governance is Weak," Ralf Steinhauser examines whether under slack governance, managers seek to minimize the risks associated with costly and difficult decisions. Steinhauser argues that in such situations, managers might wish to raise their levels of personal happiness through increasing the firm's focus on issues of corporate social responsibility, usually at the expense of profit maximization. Steinhauser uses a unique dataset to test his hypotheses. His findings may prove useful in both reassessing studies of the causes of socially responsible behavior and informing the design of policy and regulation enforcement for corporate governance.

In "Stock Repurchase Programs and Corporate Governance: Ethical Issues and Dilemmas," Richard McGowan breaks from the current literature that seeks to establish why stock repurchase programs have begun to replace dividend payments as management's preferred method of cash disbursement. McGowan, instead, uses an econometric model to determine whether or not any of the established motivations of managers for implementing repurchase programs correlate to the size of the repurchases. McGowan believes that if such correlations exist, it is necessary to examine the ethical implications for corporate governance. It is boards of governors, after all, who are responsible for the approval of stock repurchase plans. And with many conflicting interests, boards face ethical decision making challenges in approving stock repurchase plans.

REFERENCES

Stultz, Rene M. 2008. "Risk Management Failures: What Are They and When Do They Happen?" *Journal of Applied Corporate Finance*, 20(4): 39–48.

Smithson, Charles W., & Betty J. Simkins. 2005. "Does Risk Management Add Value? A Survey of the Evidence", *Journal of Applied Corporate Finance* 17(3): 8–17.

1 The Role of Enterprise Risk Management in Determining Audit Fees

Complement or Substitute

Kurt Desender and Esteban Lafuente

INTRODUCTION

The clear implication for corporate governance from an agency theory perspective is that adequate monitoring or control mechanisms need to be established to protect shareholders from management's conflict of interest (Fama and Jensen 1983). In that sense, external statutory auditors attest that all shareholders are equally treated and that financial statements are in conformity with contractual commitments. Therefore, audit quality may improve the confidence of investors in financial reporting, facilitate the assessment of the objective situation of the firm, and finally increase fund-raising possibilities. The Enron failure, together with other high-profile corporate collapses, has led to a debate concerning the efficiency and the role of corporate governance and external auditors. Companies have suffered astonishing losses as a result of poor decisions leading to excessive risk taking. Massive gaps in both the understanding and communication of a company's risk appetite and exposure have been identified in postmortem reviews. The corporate governance failures culminated in the passage of the Sarbanes-Oxley Act on July 30, 2002, which emphasized the importance of enterprise risk management (ERM) in preventing fraudulent reporting. Section 404 of the Sarbanes-Oxley Act of 2002 required U.S. publicly traded corporations to utilize a control framework in their internal control assessments (e.g., the Committee of Sponsoring Organizations of the Treadway Commission [COSO] Internal Control Framework). In addition, new guidance issued by the Public Company Accounting Oversight Board (PCAOB) in 2007 placed increasing scrutiny on top-down risk assessment and included a specific requirement to perform a fraud risk assessment (PCAOB 2007). In addition, the emerging regulatory capital framework, Basel II, leading the reform of banking supervision, endorsed enterprise risk management as an umbrella notion that can accommodate the techniques required for bank capital adequacy calculation: "integrated firm-wide approaches to risk management should continue to be strongly encouraged by the regulatory and supervisory community" (BIS 2003, 11–12). In response to these requirements, companies and financial institutions are embracing ERM to manage risks across the entity. Rating agencies, such as Standard and Poor's and Moody's, are examining how managers are controlling and tracking the risks facing their enterprises (Samanta, Azarchs, and Martinez 2005; Standard and Poor's 2005). These rating agencies have publicly reported their explicit focus on ERM activities in the financial services, insurance, and energy industries.

In addition to the recommendations about risk management, the regulatory reforms have tried to reinforce the independence of the external auditors. Whereas initial literature has looked at firm characteristics related with ERM implementation, little is known about how ERM influences the external audit fees. The objective of this chapter is to explore how the level of ERM and the presence of a chief risk officer (CRO) influence the audit fee. This chapter contributes mainly to the field of corporate governance by providing new evidence on the relationship between the external audit and ERM. The results show that ERM and the external audit effort are substitutes. Specifically, we find that the mere presence of a CRO does not exert any significant impact on external audit fees. However, a different picture emerges when we take into account the different risk management practices adopted by firms. In this case, those firms that heavily rely on ERM report significantly lower audit fees. This finding is especially relevant as it signals that the presence of an integrated system of internal controls and risk management practices not only creates the conditions for better internal monitoring, but it also facilitates external auditor's work, which implies a reduction in the number of hours required by these external auditors. In what follows, we discuss the prior research and hypothesis development. Afterwards, we focus on the sample description and the research method. Finally, we describe the results and formulate the conclusions and limitations of this research.

PRIOR RESEARCH AND HYPOTHESES DEVELOPMENT

Existing agency theory proposes a series of mechanisms that seek to reconcile the interests of shareholders and managers, including the utilization of internal control mechanisms such as monitoring by nonexecutive directors (Fama and Jensen 1983), monitoring by large shareholders (Shleifer and Vishny 1986), the incentive effects of executive share ownership (Jensen and Meckling 1976), and the implementation of internal controls (Matsumura and Tucker 1992). An additional instrument of shareholder monitoring is the statutory audit whereby independent auditors report annually to shareholders on the appropriateness of the financial statements prepared by management (Watts and Zimmerman 1986).

THE EXTERNAL AUDITOR

An extensive body of literature has emerged examining the level and nature of audit fees in organizations (e.g., Hay, Knechel, and Wong 2006; O'Sullivan 2000; Carcello et al. 2002; Abbott et al. 2003). Research on the drivers of audit fees has traditionally explained the determinants of audit fees from a production-based view. The stream of literature shows that audit fees are influenced by factors related to the size of the organization, complexity, inherent risk, and litigation risk amongst others. More hours will be put into an audit to ensure the accounting numbers presented reflect reality, leading to a higher audit fee when a company is large, complex, and has a high risk of accounting errors. Recently, studies focusing on the relationship between audit fees and corporate governance have introduced a new approach. Following a production-based approach, good corporate governance, such as the existence of independent board members, is expected to improve the control mechanisms and reduce the need for external auditing, leading to lower audit fees. However, Hay and Knechel (2004) highlight the importance of the demand effect, which may lead to the opposite result: independent directors may demand more auditing in order to fulfill their responsibilities, protect their reputations, and discharge their responsibility of due diligence. Specifically, Hay and Knechel (2004) argue that the demand for auditing is a function of the set of risks faced by individual stakeholders in an organization (management, shareholders, creditors, etc.) and the set of control mechanisms available for mitigating those risks. Because individual decisions concerning control processes and procedures may shift both benefits and costs across groups of stakeholders, the net investment in auditing may increase (Knechel and Willekens 2006). Empirical research has confirmed the importance of the demand effect for audit by the board of directors (Hay, Knechel, and Wong 2006; Carcello et al. 2002).

The demand for auditing is also expected to be influenced by the portfolio of control mechanisms available to mitigate risk. The agency literature suggests that some control mechanisms may be substitutable so that there could be a trade-off among various sources of control available to individual stakeholders, including external assurance (Jensen and Meckling 1976). In this chapter, we examine the role of ERM in the determination of audit fees. Using data collected from a sample of publicly listed pharmaceutical companies in the U.S., we consider the possible relationship between the level of the audit fee and the level of ERM, as well as the presence of a CRO.

Enterprise Risk Management

Risk management has evolved from a narrow, insurance-based view to a holistic, all-risk-encompassing view, commonly termed ERM. In September 2004, COSO issued *Enterprise Risk Management—Integrated Framework* to provide a model framework for ERM. That framework defines ERM as "a process, effected by an entity's board of directors, management and other personnel, applied in strategy setting and across the enterprise, designed to identify potential events that may affect the entity, and manage risks to be within its risk appetite, to provide reasonable assurance regarding the achievement of entity objectives" (p. 8).

Whereas ERM has numerous sources feeding the same basic idea, the COSO (2004) version has become a world-level template for best practice over a short period of time (Power 2007). COSO stands for the Committee of Sponsoring Organizations of the Treadway Commission, an "organizing organization" (Ahrne and Brunsson 2006) or coalition of the main accounting and finance trade associations in the U.S. and formed in light of concerns about fraudulent financial reporting in the mid-1980s. The Treadway Commission reported its findings in 1987 and COSO published guidance on internal control in 1992. This guidance provides the antecedent conceptual building blocks for the 2004 framework for ERM; hence, a direct line of influence on ERM can be traced to an accounting conception of internal control, itself a product of broader engineering conceptions of control theory. So the ERM model is strongly, if not exclusively, influenced by accounting and auditing norms of control, with an emphasis on process description and evidence.

Two streams of research have been developed around ERM. One stream focuses on the influence of ERM on firm performance (e.g., see Lam 2001; COSO 2004; Nocco and Stulz 2006; Hoyt and Liebenberg 2009), whereas the other stream studies the determinants of ERM (e.g., Kleffner, Lee, and McGannon 2003; Liebenberg and Hoyt 2003; Beasley, Clune, and Hermanson 2005; Desender and Lafuente 2009; Desender 2010). A general argument gaining momentum in the literature is that the implementation of an ERM system will improve firm performance. The findings by Hoyt and Liebenberg (2009), for example, based on data from the insurance industry and using Tobin's Q as the measure of performance, support this argument. The fact that many firms have adopted ERM lends additional support to the view that ERM will improve firm performance. Nevertheless, empirical evidence confirming this relation between ERM and firm performance is quite limited and is not based on a robust measure of ERM.

The External Auditor and Enterprise Risk Management

External auditors can rely on the work of internal auditors in many respects in carrying out their external audit duties as both auditors are concerned that proper controls are in place. ERM can assist external auditors to understand the internal control system that has been set up before any compliance or substantive work has been carried out. Reliance on the work of the ERM should have the potential to reduce the audit hours that need to be spent on the audit and thus help to reduce the audit fee that needs to be paid—of particular importance in view of the upwards pressure on external audit fees, not least due to a progressive tightening of the audit requirement in the wake of Enron and other corporate debacles. Empirically, Knechel and Willekens (2006) find that audit fees are lower when a company discloses a relatively high level of compliance risk, but higher when a company discloses a relatively high level of financial risk. In addition, Goddard and Masters (2000) find a negative relationship between audit fees and improved internal controls in the presence of audit complexity. We therefore formulate our first hypothesis:

> *H1: There is a negative relationship between external audit fees and the level of ERM.*

In addition to the level of ERM, the presence of a CRO could influence the demand for audit. Liebenberg and Hoyt (2003) used CRO appointments to examine the determinants of ERM adoption. The authors found that companies appointing a CRO had higher leverage. Furthermore, Beasley, Clune, and Hermanson (2005), Desender and Lafuente (2009), and Desender (2010) show that the presence of a CRO is associated with the level of ERM adoption. CROs have strategic and risk-related responsibilities, giving the company a more risk-based approach during strategic decision making. CROs may therefore be able to influence the demand for external audit, also. From this argument emerges our second hypothesis:

> *H2: There is a negative relationship between external audit fee and the presence of a CRO.*

THE BOARD OF DIRECTORS AND THE OWNERSHIP STRUCTURE

To study the relationship between audit fees and ERM, we also need to consider other corporate governance aspects. We consider the composition of the board and its audit committee and the ownership structure. Hay and Knechel (2004) argue that an independent board will be more concerned about discharging its monitoring role and, therefore, will put pressure on management to enhance the external audit function. Furthermore, independent board members reduce their responsibilities, without bearing the costs (Carcello et al. 2002). This suggests that companies with greater board independence will seek a more comprehensive audit. Several studies have reported a positive relationship between the independence of the board and the demand for external audit, as measured by the audit fees (O'Sullivan 2000; Carcello et al. 2002; Hay and Knechel 2004). This leads us to formulate our third hypothesis:

> *H3: There is a positive relationship between external audit fee and board independence.*

Another aspect of the board of directors that has been studied extensively is the CEO duality, which is generally perceived as compromising the independence of the board, because one individual possesses a great amount of power and authority (Jensen 1993). Because the audit report can be considered to be an instrument of supervision over the managers, the latter may be assumed to have powerful incentives to limit this external supervision exercised by the auditors. This is especially the case when the opinion of the auditors may indicate inefficiencies or irregularities in the managers' performance with respect to the use of company resources. Therefore, managers may impose limits on the supervision by the auditors, restricting the scope of the auditors' investigations and scrutiny. From this argument comes our fourth hypothesis:

> *H4: There is a negative relationship between external audit fee and CEO duality.*

The relationship between audit committees and external audit is a complex one, stemming from both the demand for audit services by the client and the supply of audit services by the external auditor (Collier and Gregory 1996). From the demand side, the presence of an audit committee might lead to an increase in audit fees because the committee should ensure that audit hours are at a level that does not compromise the quality of the audit (Cadbury Report 1992). Additionally, Abbott et al. (2003) suggest that an effective committee should reduce the threat of auditor dismissal, thereby strengthening the auditor's bargaining position during fee negotiations. From the supply side, the audit committee's involvement in strengthening internal controls might lead the external auditor to reduce the assessed level of control risk, resulting in less substantive testing and, hence, a lower audit fee (Collier and Gregory 1996). The results of prior studies examining the relation between audit fees and audit committee effectiveness have, however, been inconsistent. Carcello et al. (2002), using U.S. data from the early 1990s, find that board characteristics rather than audit committee characteristics are associated with higher audit fees. In contrast, Abbott et al. (2003) and Knechel and Willekens (2006) report a significant positive association between audit committee characteristics and audit fees. We therefore formulate our fifth hypothesis:

> *H5: There is a positive relationship between external audit fee and size of the audit committee.*

Finally, we are interested in examining to what extent the presence of large shareholders affects decisions linked to external auditing. It is often argued that ownership concentration mitigates free-riding problems of corporate control associated with a scattered principal. Likewise, large investors have the incentive to exercise a closer oversight and control of management, in order to reduce agency costs and increase their monitoring role in the companies where they invest. Demsetz and Lehn (1985) argue that within firms facing more uncertain environments, insiders' actions are less observable and thus the benefits of ownership are greater. For example, if information asymmetry is an increasing function of the uncertainty, it would suggest a positive relationship between business risk taking and ownership concentration. Nevertheless, large shareholders also have a strong preference for control, and this could lead to the expropriation of minority shareholders' wealth. This implies that ownership concentration can also create costs within the firm that may outweigh its benefits over some intervals of the distribution of ownership concentration (De Miguel, Pintado, and De la Torre 2004). Therefore, higher levels of audit could be used to signal the absence of expropriation of minority shareholders by controlling shareholders.

Empirically, Mitra, Hossain, and Deis (2007) find evidence of a significantly positive relationship between diffused institutional stock ownership (i.e., having less than 5 percent individual shareholding) and audit fees, and a significantly negative relationship between institutional blockholder ownership (i.e., having 5 percent or more individual shareholding) and audit fees, for a sample of U.S. firms. The authors also document a negative relationship between managerial stock ownership and audit fees. For a sample of UK listed companies, O'Sullivan (2000) shows that audit fees are negatively related to the proportion of equity owned by executive directors, but finds no evidence that ownership by large blockholders (institutional or otherwise) has a significant impact on audit fees. Therefore, our last hypothesis emerges:

H6: There is a negative relationship between external audit fee and ownership concentration.

DATA AND METHOD

We focus our study on one particular industry to maximize comparability between firms in terms of business environment, degree of competition, and risk. The sample is composed entirely of pharmaceutical firms (SIC code: 2834—pharmaceutical preparations), an industry that has also been used in previous corporate governance research (Robb, Single, and Zarzeski 2001; Macher and Boerner 2005). The attractiveness of this industry becomes clearer when considering that firms operating in this sector are faced with the same array of risks and seem to display a sufficient amount of variation in earning management practices. The pharmaceutical companies are capital intensive and mainly rely on the stock market to finance their R&D projects. Furthermore, it is a competitive industry, with pressure to perform, generating incentives to cut corners if results are not satisfactory. In fact, the SEC enforcement list contains several pharmaceutical companies that manipulated numbers in response of bad results. Therefore, we believe that this industry is ideal to study ERM and its relationship to audit fees. The original data set comprises information for one hundred pharmaceutical firms randomly chosen (out of a population of 213 firms) for 2004. All selected firms are listed on AMEX, NYSE, or NASDAQ. However, to ensure a rigorous methodology, three observations were dropped as we want to include in the final sample only those firms for which a complete data set of the dependent and independent variables can be clearly identified.

Consistent with recent studies on audit fees (e.g., Craswell, Francis, and Taylor 1995; Carcello et al. 2002; Hay and Knechel 2004), we use the natural log of audit fees as a dependent variable. The variable considers the total fee paid to all auditors for both audit and nonaudit services. In our final sample, pharmaceutical firms pay on average 5.50 million U.S. dollars to external auditors (Table 1.1). In addition, from Tables 1.1 and 1.2 it can be noticed that the resources given to external auditing firms vary greatly, and that the mean audit fees range from 67.3 U.S. dollars (at the bottom quartile of the distribution of external audit fees) to over 20.5 million U.S. dollars (at the upper quartile of the distribution of external audit fees; Table 1.2).

With respect to our set of independent variables, data was collected for 2004 from the company's annual reports. Descriptive statistics are presented in Tables 1.1 and 1.2. We first consider firm size. Since the pioneering article by Simunic (1980) on this subject, as well as other international studies (e.g., see Craswell, Francis, and Taylor 1995; Simon and Francis 1988; Carcello et al. 2002), company size appears to be a key factor when studying audit fees. This relation is rather intuitive,

Table 1.1 Descriptive Statistics for the Selected Variables

	Mean	*Standard deviation*	*Minimum*	*Maximum*	*Obs.*
External audit fee in million of US$	5.50	16.57	0.0135	93.1368	97
Total assets in million of US$	8,022.76	20,274.16	2.19	117,271.20	97
Chief Risk Officer	0.3918	0.4907	0.0000	1.0000	97
Enterprise Risk Management	0.3273	0.1584	0.0200	0.9500	97
Leverage	0.1935	0.2370	0.0000	0.8800	97
Board independence	0.7582	0.1270	0.1400	1.0000	97
CEO – Chairman duality	0.4330	0.4981	0.0000	1.0000	97
Size of audit committee	3.4536	0.9016	2	6	97
Top external audit firm	0.6289	0.4856	0.0000	1.0000	97
Stake held by the largest shareholder	0.1446	0.0895	0.0490	0.5570	97
Stake held by the three largest shareholders	0.2561	0.1198	0.0752	0.6825	97

because auditors' fees are paid according to the amount of time spent completing a given job. Larger companies are involved in a greater number of transactions that necessarily require longer hours for an auditor to inspect. As a result, we introduce size in our analysis and this variable is measured by total assets. In our sample, firms report on average 8,022.76 million U.S. dollars on assets, and company size varies from a minimum of 19 million U.S. dollars to a maximum of 117,271 million U.S. dollars (Table 1.1).

We use two variables to measure ERM. Similar to Liebenberg and Hoyt (2003) and Desender and Lafuente (2009), we introduce a single event like the presence of a CRO to proxy ERM. This dummy variable takes the value of one if the pharmaceutical firm has a CRO in the year 2004, and zero otherwise. From Table 1.1 we observe that, in our final sample, 39.18

Table 1.2 Descriptive Statistics at Different Points of the Distribution of the Selected Variables

			Mean values at different quartiles of the distribution of External Audit Fees		
	Obs.	*Overall*	*Bottom quartile*	*Middle quartiles*	*Top quartile*
External audit fee in million of US$	97	5.50 (16.57)	0.0673 (0.0327)	0.7496 (0.7332)	20.6351 (28.7548)
Total assets in million of US$	97	8,022.76 (20,274.16)	193.16 (288.17)	804.04 (1,429.78)	30,590.57 (31,699.64)
Chief Risk Officer	97	0.3918 (0.4907)	0.3333 (0.4815)	0.3469 (0.4809)	0.5417 (0.5090)
Enterprise Risk Management Index	97	0.3273 (0.1584)	0.3242 (0.1042)	0.2920 (0.1358)	0.4025 (0.2163)
Leverage	97	0.1935 (0.2370)	0.0792 (0.1614)	0.2231 (0.2521)	0.2475 (0.2393)
Board independence	97	0.7582 (0.1270)	0.7604 (0.1266)	0.7420 (0.1430)	0.7892 (0.0842)
CEO – Chairman duality	97	0.4330 (0.4981)	0.8750 (0.3378)	0.3265 (0.4738)	0.2083 (0.4149)
Size of audit committee	97	3.4536 (0.9016)	2.8333 (0.4815)	3.4490 (0.7654)	4.0833 (1.0598)
Top external audit firm	97	0.6289 (0.4856)	0.5000 (0.5108)	0.6531 (0.4809)	0.7083 (0.4643)
Stake held by the largest shareholder	97	0.1446 (0.0895)	0.1756 (0.1138)	0.1349 (0.0796)	0.1333 (0.0770)
Stake held by the three largest shareholders	97	0.2561 (0.1198)	0.2870 (0.1496)	0.2540 (0.1030)	0.2295 (0.1165)

percent of firms report the presence of a chief risk manager in 2004. In addition, we observe from Table 3.2 that the proportion of firms with a chief risk manager increases when comparing the results for the first (33.33 percent) and the fourth (54.17 percent) quartiles of the distribution of audit fees paid by firms in our sample.

At this point, an important qualification is in order. This dummy variable only reflects the presence of a risk manager, rather than the number of practices related to risk management implemented by firms. This is a major concern in this study, as we are interested in examining the extent to which variables that are linked to the adoption of risk management practices help to explain the audit fees. As a result, we use the COSO (2004) ERM framework, which has become a world-level template for best practice over a short period (Power 2007), as well as prior work by Knechel (2002) to identify those variables that best reflect relevant control and risk management procedures, in order to derive an aggregate measure of ERM.

We used a three-step methodology to construct our ERM index. First, we obtained an initial list of 254 items related to ERM, derived from the recommendations made in the COSO (2004) ERM framework. Second, we asked five senior auditors to evaluate the original list and select those items that they consider as the most relevant to measure the degree of ERM. Based on their assessment, we retained all components that were selected by at least three different auditors. The final list consists of 108 ERM components, scoring zero (absence) or one (presence). Third, we added to our ERM index the eight dimensions of ERM that are indicated in the COSO (2004) ERM framework: (a) internal environment, (b) objective setting, (c) event identification, (d) risk assessment, (e) risk response, (f) control activities, (g) information and communication, and (h) monitoring.

Having determined the composition of our ERM index, information about ERM practices was obtained from public sources (10-K's, proxy statements, annual reports, and the company website). Similar to Knechel (2002), we expect that the disclosure of control and risk management practices indicates that the organization is more sensitive to the need to identify and manage those specific risks. Furthermore, it is reasonable to expect that firms with elaborated risk management practices want to signal this to the market. The ERM index in this study is the same measure used by Desender and Lafuente (2009) and is similar to the measure adopted by Desender (2010). We introduce the value of our ERM index (weighted average of the eight ERM dimensions mentioned earlier) in the regression analysis. The full list of ERM items considered in this study is presented in Appendix 3.1. From the descriptives we notice that firms in our sample have adopted on average 32.73 percent of the ERM practices considered in our index (Table 1.1). Additional descriptives presented in

Table 1.2 indicate a dissimilar adoption of ERM practices in our sample of pharmaceutical firms. Whereas firms paying low audit fees (bottom quartile) adopted 32.42 percent of the ERM practices considered in our index, firms with audit fees in the top quartile of the distribution of this variable (external audit fees) adopted 40.25 percent of the practices. In addition, firms that are positioned in the middle-quartile range (according to the audit fees they pay) adopted on average 29.20 percent of ERM practices. These results should be interpreted with some caution, as it only indicates that the ERM index is unevenly distributed along the different quartiles of the distribution of audit fees.

We also consider two variables linked to the board composition. First, in line with O'Sullivan (2000), Carcello et al. (2002), and Hay and Knechel (2004), we identify the proportion of independent directors, measured as the number of nonexecutive board members divided by the total number of board members. Adams and Ferreira (2007) highlight the importance of board independence for the quality of monitoring, as more independent boards are more likely to exert a more diligent monitoring over management, leading the CEO to disclose partial information about the firm. To the contrary, those boards dominated by executives might be friendlier and exert a more relaxed monitoring. In line with these arguments, Hay and Knechel (2004) remark that independent boards will be more supportive to the external audit function because they seek to reduce their responsibility and liability and obtain more accurate information about the course of action of the firm, and because they do not bear the cost of the audit. From the descriptive statistics we observe that boards in our sample are highly independent (on average, 75.92 percent of board members are nonexecutives), and board independence remains high irrespective of whether the firm pays low or high external audit fees (Table 1.2).

The second variable related to board composition is the leadership structure (CEO duality). As mentioned earlier, CEO duality is generally perceived as compromising the independence of the board as one individual possesses a great amount of power and authority (Jensen 1993). In the presence of a dominant CEO, nonexecutives are expected to face difficulties in effectively monitoring management. Previous literature (Jensen 1993; Fama and Jensen 1983; Cadbury Report 1992) emphasizes that boards lose power to management when the positions of CEO and chairman are vested in the same person. Thus, in the presence of a dominant CEO, nonexecutives are expected to face difficulties in effectively monitoring management. In our analysis, we include a dummy variable, taking the value of one if the positions of chairman and CEO are vested in the same person, and zero otherwise. In the final sample 43.30 percent of firms report a one-tier leadership structure (Table 1.1). Also, the proportion of firms with a unified leadership structure monotonically decreases along the different quartiles of the distribution of audit fees: from 87.50 percent for firms with low audit fees (lowest quartile) to 20.83 percent for firms with the highest (top quartile) audit fees (Table 1.2).

We consider two variables closely related with the audit process: the size of the audit committee and the type of external auditor. Similar to previous literature (e.g., Abbott et al. 2003; O'Sullivan 2000), we define audit committee size as the total number of audit committee members. We control for the audit committee size because research suggests that a large audit committee tends to enhance the audit committee's status and power within an organization (Kalbers and Fogarty 1993). In our sample, audit committees have on average 3.45 members, and the number of members of these committees ranges from two to six members (Table 1.1). We also notice from Table 1.2 that the size of the internal audit committee increases as the firm affords higher external audit fees. For firms paying low audit fees (bottom quartile) the internal audit committee has on average 2.83 members, whereas this figure stands at 4.08 for firms paying high external audit fees (top quartile). With respect to the second element, we introduce a dummy variable, taking the value of one if the firm has a Big Four external auditor (Deloitte Touche Tohmatsu, KPMG, PWC, and Ernst & Young), and zero otherwise. Higher audit fees are expected when an auditor is recognized to be of superior quality to other firms (Hay, Knechel, and Wong 2006). From Table 1.1 we observe that for nearly 63 percent of the pharmaceutical firms in our sample, the external auditor is a Big Four company. Similar to the descriptive results for the size of the audit committee, the proportion of firms for which the external auditor is a Big Four company increases along with the distribution of the external audit fees (Table 1.2). This descriptive result is not surprising, as one may expect that Big Four auditors charge higher audit fees to firms.

Data availability allows us to identify two measures that capture ownership concentration: the stake held by the largest and by the three largest shareholders. In our sample, the largest shareholder controls on average 14.46 percent of shareholders' equity, whereas this figure stands at 25.61 percent in the case of the three largest shareholders (Table 1.1). In addition, the results in Table 1.2 show that firms that pay higher external audit fees have a more dispersed ownership structure.

Finally, we introduce leverage as a control variable. This variable, measured as the ratio of long-term debt divided by total assets, proxies both the capital structure of the firm and the agency costs between a company and its outside debt holders (Watts and Zimmerman 1986).

To corroborate our hypotheses about the different factors that drive firms to face higher external audit fees, and given the characteristics of our dependent variable, we adopt OLS regression as our methodological approach. The full model to be estimated follows:

$$\begin{aligned}\text{External Audit Fees}_i = {} & \delta_0 + \delta_1\text{Size}_i + \delta_2\text{ERM}_i + \delta_3\text{Board Independence}_i \\ & + \delta_4\text{CEO} - \text{Chairman}_i + \delta_5\text{Internal audit committee}_i \\ & + \delta_6\text{Big} - 4\text{ audit firm}_i + \delta_7\text{Ownership concentration}_i \\ & + \delta_8\text{Leverage}_i + \varepsilon_i\end{aligned}$$

In Equation [1] δ_0 is the constant term δ_i refers to the vector of parameter estimates for the *jth* independent variables, and $\mathcal{E}_i$ is the normally distributed disturbance term for the *ith* firm. The dependent variable is the natural log of external audit fees, and ERM refers to the variables capturing risk management: the presence of a CRO and our index to measure ERM. It is important to remark that for greater robustness of our estimation, we examined the properties of the errors derived from the different model specifications. In all regressions, results for the Jarque-Bera test indicate that error terms are normally distributed. As an additional measure of goodness of fit, we estimated the variance inflation factor and, in all model specifications, the mean result reported for this measure is below the threshold value of ten, confirming that our approach to external audit fees is appropriate.

RESULTS

This section presents the empirical findings. The first set of three columns in Table 1.3 presents the results when the presence of a chief risk manager is used as proxy for ERM, whereas the second set of model specifications introduces our ERM index. The first model in every set does not take into consideration ownership structure in the analysis. The second model adds to the analysis of the stake held by the largest shareholder, whereas specification three considers the impact of ownership concentration by the three largest shareholders upon external audit fees.

The results for firm size indicate that, throughout the different model specifications applied to our sample, larger firms pay higher external audit fees (Table 1.3). This result is consistent with previous evidence that has used similar variables (Simunic 1980; Simon and Francis 1988; Craswell, Francis, and Taylor 1995; Carcello et al. 2002).

As for the key findings of our study, we observe that, in our sample, the mere presence of a CRO does not exert a significant impact on external audit

Table 1.3 Regression Results: Impact of Enterprise Risk Management on External Audit Fees

	Model 1	*Model 2*	*Model 3*	*Model 1*	*Model 2*	*Model 3*
Ln total assets	0.5120 ***	0.5261 ***	0.5191 ***	0.5335 ***	0.5391 ***	0.5325 ***
	(0.0606)	(0.0574)	(0.0556)	(0.0592)	(0.0582)	(0.0575)
Chief Risk Officer	−0.4916	−0.5257	−0.5318			
	(0.3302)	(0.3302)	(0.3296)			
Enterprise Risk Management Index				−2.0277 **	−1.8662 **	−1.8530 **
				(1.0271)	(0.9411)	(0.9425)
Leverage	1.5167 **	1.2911 *	1.4102 **	1.4254 **	1.2612 **	1.3630 **
	(0.6680)	(0.6825)	(0.6610)	(0.6832)	(0.6997)	(0.6806)
Board independence	0.0311	0.1026	0.0210	−0.0092	−0.0125	−0.0881
	(0.8732)	(0.8488)	(0.8396)	(0.9057)	(0.8785)	(0.8822)
CEO – Chairman duality	−0.7611 **	−0.7828	−0.7603	−0.7495	−0.7865 ***	−0.7700 ***
	(0.3118)	**(0.3030)	**(0.3069)	**(0.2917)	(0.2844)	(0.2872)
Size of audit committee	0.4212 **	0.3398 *	0.3446 **	0.3634 **	0.2963 *	0.3006 *
	(0.1719)	(0.1738)	(0.1710)	(0.1707)	(0.1768)	(0.1731)
Top external audit firm	0.3976	0.5037 *	0.5674 *	0.4459	0.5137 *	0.5632 *
	(0.2974)	(0.3022)	(0.3087)	(0.2987)	(0.3000)	(0.3049)
Stake held by the largest shareholder		−2.6527 *			−2.1973	
		(1.3971)			(1.3943)	
Stake held by the three largest shareholders			−2.0984 *			−1.7264
			(1.0774)			(1.0726)
Intercept	5.1704 ***	5.5956 ***	5.8164 ***	5.5700 ***	6.0045 ***	6.1948 ***
	(0.9552)	(0.9526)	(1.0026)	(0.8496)	(0.8583)	(0.9098)
F – test	34.53 ***	31.78 ***	31.73 ***	39.38 ***	35.63 ***	35.04 ***
Adjusted R2	0.6514	0.6605	0.6615	0.6601	0.6651	0.6656
Jarque Bera Test	4.575	4.386	4.585	4.861	4.922	4.956
Average Variance Inflation Factor	1.43	1.42	1.42	1.40	1.39	1.40
RMSE	1.2187	1.2028	1.2009	1.2034	1.1945	1.1935
Number of observations	97	97	97	97	97	97

Robust standard errors are presented in brackets. *, **, *** indicate significance at the 10%, 5% and 1%, respectively.

fees. However, a different picture emerges when we take into account the different risk management practices adopted by firms. In this case, results from the second set of regressions indicate that those firms that heavily rely on ERM report significantly lower levels of external auditing. This finding is especially relevant, as it signals that the presence of internal control systems and the adoption of risk management practices not only create the conditions for better internal monitoring, but also facilitate the external auditor's work, which implies a reduction in the number of hours required by these external auditors. This finding, which is similar to that reported by Goddard and Masters (2000) and Knechel and Willekens (2006), confirms our first hypothesis (H1), which proposes a negative relation between the level of ERM and external audit fees. When we introduce the variable linked to the presence of a CRO, results show that parameter estimates for this variable are negative, as hypothesized. However, they are not statistically significant, and this leads us to reject our second hypothesis (H2).

Concerning board composition, our results indicate on the one hand that board independence is not a factor explaining external audit fees. Therefore, we cannot confirm our third hypothesis (H3), which states that firms with more independent boards pay higher external audit fees. However, this result should be read with caution because the lack of significance in the parameter estimates could be a consequence of the characteristics of the board in our sample. From the descriptive we know that the rate of nonexecutive board members is nearly 76 percent, and this rate is highly homogenous along the distribution of external audit fees. In addition, the interaction between the board of directors and the external auditor could be partially delegated to the audit committee. On the other hand, we consistently report a significantly negative relation between the presence of a unified leadership structure and external audit fees paid by firms, indicating that external audit fees are significantly lower in firms where the CEO also serves as chairman (i.e., CEO duality). This result is consistent with our fourth hypothesis (H4), and it reinforces our argument that the incentives to exert diligent monitoring over managers are lower in boards dominated by the CEO.

Concerning the size of the audit committee, our results indicate that this variable exerts a significantly positive effect on external audit fees. This result is consistent throughout our model specifications, and it is in accordance with previous results by Abbott et al. (2003) and Knechel and Willekens (2006). Here, our findings indicate that internal audit committees foster a larger audit scope in order to ensure an appropriate level of quality of internal controls. These results provide support for hypothesis five (H5).

The results for the relationship between ownership concentration and audit fees is only weakly significant, when the independent variable linked to ERM is the presence of a CRO. The result is, however, insignificant when we introduce our ERM index. As a result, we cannot confirm our hypothesis six, which proposes a negative relation between ownership concentration and external audit fees (H6). Finally, as for the presence of a Big Four audit firm, we only find weak evidence that the presence of Big Four audit firms increases the external audit budget.

CONCLUSIONS

The efficiency and the role of corporate governance and external auditors have been subject to heavy debate, following the Enron-failure. While excessive risk taking at the firm level has led shareholders to suffered astonishing losses, massive gaps in the understanding of a firm's risk appetite and exposure have been identified in postmortem reviews. In a response to the corporate failures, the Sarbanes-Oxley Act of 2002 has strongly emphasized the importance of ERM in preventing fraudulent reporting and has tried to reinforce the independence of the external auditors. The objective of this chapter is to explore how the level of ERM and the presence of a CRO influence the audit fees.

As for the key findings of our study, we observe that, in our sample, the mere presence of a CRO does not exert any significant impact on audit fees. However, a different picture emerges when we take into account the different risk management practices adopted by firms. In this case, those firms that heavily rely on ERM report significantly lower audit fees. This finding is especially relevant, because it signals that the presence of internal control systems and the adoption of risk management practices not only create the conditions for better internal monitoring, but it also facilitate the external auditor's work, which implies a reduction in the number of hours required by these external auditors.

Concerning the other corporate governance mechanisms, we find that the board independence and ownership concentration are not significantly related to audit fees. However, our analysis shows that external audit fees are significantly lower in firms where the CEO also serves as chairman. Furthermore, the size of the audit committee is found to be positively related to the external audit fees. This result is consistent throughout our model specifications, and it is in accordance with previous results by Abbott et al. (2003) and Knechel and Willekens (2006).

We acknowledge limitations in our research approach. First, we use publicly available data to proxy for the degree of ERM implementation. To the extent that annual report or other company information does not reflect the true state of control and risk management practices, our results are limited. To cope with this limitation, we tested our hypotheses using an alternative proxy for ERM. Second, this study focuses on a single industry. Therefore, our results may not be generalized for other industries. Finally, there may be other organizational characteristics of ERM deployments that were not reflected in this study. As a consequence, further research should attempt not only to replicate a similar analysis in a different industrial context, but also to enrich the content of the model as well as its longitudinal perspective.

APPENDIX 1.1

Table 1.4 Dimensions and Average Values of Enterprise Risk Management

	Dimensions of Enterprise Risk Management	*Average*
	Internal Environment	32%
1	Is there a charter of the board?	34%
2	Information on the code of conduct/ethics?	64%
3	Information on how compensation policies align interest of managers with shareholders?	38%
4	Information on individual performance targets?	18%
5	Information on procedures for hiring and firing of board member and management?	31%
6	Information on remuneration policy of board members and management?	56%
7	Information on training, coaching and educational programs?	24%
8	Information on training in ethical values?	11%
9	Information on board responsibility?	34%
10	Information on audit committee responsibility?	23%
11	Information on CEO responsibilities?	11%
12	Information on senior executive responsible for risk management	24%
13	Information on supervisory and managerial oversight	44%
	Objective Setting	52%
14	Information on company's mission?	65%
15	Information on company's strategy?	95%
16	Information on company's business objectives?	68%
17	Information on adopted benchmarks to evaluate results?	26%
18	Information on approval of the strategy by the board?	6%
19	Information on the link between strategy, objectives and shareholder value	50%
	Event Identification	54%
	Financial Risk	
20	Information on the extent of liquidity?	84%
21	Information on the interest rate?	82%
22	Information on the foreign exchange rate?	67%
23	Information on the cost of capital?	56%
24	Information on the access to the capital market	46%
25	Information on long-term debt instruments?	69%

(continued)

Table 1.4 (continued)

	Dimensions of Enterprise Risk Management	*Average*
26	Information on default risk?	42%
27	Information on solvency risk?	49%
28	Information on equity price risk?	64%
29	Information on commodity risk?	57%
	Compliance Risk	
30	Information on litigation issues?	85%
31	Information on compliance with regulation?	88%
32	Information on compliance with industry codes?	58%
33	Information on compliance with voluntary codes?	11%
34	Information on compliance with recommendation of Corporate Governance?	45%
	Technology Risk	
35	Information on data management?	19%
36	Information on computer systems?	36%
37	Information on the privacy of information held on customers?	24%
38	Information on software security?	19%
	Economical risk	
39	Information on the nature of competition?	89%
40	Information on the macro-economic events that could affect the company?	61%
	Reputational Risk	
41	Information on environmental issues?	69%
42	Information on ethical issues?	23%
43	Information on health and safety issues?	76%
44	Information on lower/higher stock or credit rating?	41%
	Risk Assessment	51%
45	Risk assessment of the extent of liquidity?	84%
46	Risk assessment of the interest rate?	82%
47	Risk assessment of the foreign exchange rate?	67%
48	Risk assessment of the cost of capital?	56%
49	Risk assessment of the access to the capital market	46%
50	Risk assessment of long-term debt instruments?	69%
51	Risk assessment of default risk?	38%
52	Risk assessment of solvency risk?	43%

(continued)

Table 1.4 (continued)

	Dimensions of Enterprise Risk Management	*Average*
53	Risk assessment of equity price risk?	56%
54	Risk assessment of commodity risk?	50%
55	Risk assessment of litigation issues?	85%
56	Risk assessment of compliance with regulation?	88%
57	Risk assessment of compliance with industry codes?	58%
58	Risk assessment of compliance with voluntary codes?	11%
59	Risk assessment of compliance with recommendation of Corporate Governance?	45%
60	Risk assessment of data management?	19%
61	Risk assessment of computer systems?	36%
62	Risk assessment of the privacy of information held on customers?	24%
63	Risk assessment of on software security?	11%
64	Risk assessment of the nature of competition?	89%
65	Risk assessment of environmental issues?	69%
66	Risk assessment of ethical issues?	23%
67	Risk assessment of health and safety issues?	76%
68	Risk assessment of lower/higher stock or credit rating?	35%
69	Information on techniques used to assess the potential impact of events combining	18%
	Risk Response	28%
70	General description of processes for determining how risk should be managed?	8%
71	Information on written guidelines about how risk should be managed?	11%
72	Response to the liquidity risk?	47%
73	Response to the interest rate risk?	51%
74	Response to the foreign exchange rate risk?	39%
75	Response to the risk related to cost of capital?	26%
76	Response to the access to the capital market	29%
77	Response to long-term debt instruments?	28%
78	Response to litigation risk?	67%
79	Response to default risk?	24%
80	Response to n solvency risk?	28%
81	Response to equity price risk?	31%
82	Response to commodity risk?	23%

(continued)

Table 1.4 (continued)

	Dimensions of Enterprise Risk Management	*Average*
83	Response to compliance with regulation?	55%
84	Response to compliance with industry codes?	28%
85	Response to compliance with voluntary codes?	8%
86	Response to compliance with recommendation of Corporate Governance?	27%
87	Response to data risk?	6%
88	Response to computer systems risk?	2%
89	Response to the privacy of information held on customers?	6%
90	Response to risk of software security?	9%
91	Response to the risk of competition?	64%
92	Response to environmental risk?	38%
93	Response to ethical risk?	22%
94	Response to health and safety risk?	38%
95	Response to risk of lower/higher stock or credit rating?	14%
	Control Activities	21%
96	Information on sales control?	29%
97	Information on review of the functioning and effectiveness of controls?	37%
98	Information on authorisation issues?	13%
99	Information on documents and record as control?	11%
100	Information on independent verification procedures?	22%
101	Information on physical controls?	10%
102	Information on process control?	24%
	Information and communications	28%
103	Information on verification of completeness, accuracy and validity of information?	49%
104	Information on channels of communication to report suspected breaches of laws, regulations or other improprieties?	11%
105	Information on channels of communication with customers, vendors and other external parties?	23%
	Monitoring	20%
106	Information on how processes are monitored?	24%
107	Information about Internal audit?	32%
108	Information about the budget of the Internal Audit?	3%

BIBLIOGRAPHY

Abbott, L., J.S. Parker, G.F. Peters, and K. Raghunandan. 2003. "An Empirical Investigation of the Audit Fees, Nonaudit Fees, and Audit Committees." *Contemporary Accounting Research* 20 (2): 1–21.

Adams, R., and D. Ferreira. 2007. "A Theory of Friendly Boards." *Journal of Finance* 62:217–250.

Ahrne, G., and N. Brunsson. 2006. "Organizing the World." In *Transnational Governance: Institutional Dynamics of Regulation*, ed. M.-L. Djelic and K. Sahlin-Andersson, 74–94. Cambridge: Cambridge University Press.

Beasley, M.S. 1996. "An Empirical Analysis of the Relation between the Board of Director Composition and Financial Statement Fraud." *Accounting Review* 71:443–465.

Beasley, M.S., R. Clune, and D. Hermanson. 2005. "Enterprise Risk Management: An Empirical Analysis of Factors Associated with the Extent of Implementation." *Journal of Accounting and Public Policy* 24 (6): 521–531.

BIS (The Basel Committee on Banking Supervision). 2003b. *Trends in risk integration and aggregation*. Available from www.bis.org.

Cadbury Report. 1992. *Report of the Committee on the Financial Aspects of Corporate Governance*. London: Gee and Co.

Carcello, J.V., D.R. Hermanson, T.L. Neal, and R.R. Riley Jr. 2002. "Board Characteristics and Audit Fees." *Contemporary Accounting Research* 19 (Fall): 365–384.

Collier, P., and A. Gregory. 1996. "Audit Committee Effectiveness and the Audit Fees." *European Accounting Journal* 5 (2): 177–199.

Committee of the Sponsoring Organizations of the Treadway Commission. 2004. *Enterprise Risk Management, Integrated Framework (COSO-ERM Report)*. New York: AICPA.

Craswell, A., J. Francis, and S. Taylor. 1995. "Auditor Brand Name Reputations and Industry Specializations." *Journal of Accounting and Economics* 20:297–312.

De Miguel, A., J. Pintado, and C. De la Torre. 2004. "Ownership Structure and Firm Value: New Evidence from Spain." *Strategic Management Journal* 25:1199–1207.

Demsetz, H., and K. Lehn. 1985. "The Structure of Corporate Ownership: Causes and Consequences." *Journal of Political Economy* 93:1155–1177.

Desender, K. 2010. "On the Determinants of Enterprise Risk Management Implementation." In *Handbook of Research on Enterprise IT Governance, Business Value and Performance Measurement*, ed. Solomon Shi Nan Si and Gilbert Silvius, 87–100. Singapore: IGI Global.

Desender, K., R. Crespi, M. Garcia-Cestona, and R. Aguilera. 2009. "Board Characteristics and Audit Fees: Why Ownership Structure Matters?" Working Paper, University of Illinois at Urbana-Champaign.

Desender, K., and E. Lafuente. 2009. "The Influence of Board Composition, Audit Fees and Ownership Concentration on Enterprise Risk Management." Working Paper. Available at www.ssrn.com.

Fama, E., and M. Jensen. 1983. "Agency Problems and Residual Claims." *Journal of Law and Economics* 26 (2): 327–349.

Goddard, R.A., and C. Masters. 2000. "Audit Committees, Cadbury Code and Audit Fees: An Empirical Analysis of UK Companies." *Managerial Auditing Journal* 15 (1): 358–371.

Goyal, V.K., and C.W. Park. 2002. "Board Leadership Structure and CEO Turnover." *Journal of Corporate Finance* 8:49–66.

Hay, D., and R. Knechel. 2004. "Evidence on the Association among Elements of Control and External Assurance." Working Paper, University of Auckland.

Hay, D., R. Knechel, and N. Wong. 2006. "Audit Fees: A Meta-Analysis of the Effect of Supply and Demand Attributes." *Contemporary Accounting Research* 23(1): 141–191.

Hermalin, B., and M. Weisbach. 2003. "Board of Directors as an Endogenously Determined Institution: A Survey of the Economic Literature." *FRBNY Economic Policy Review* 9:7–26.

Hoyt, R.E., and A.P. Liebenberg. 2009. "The Value of Enterprise Risk Management." Working Paper. Available at www.ssrn.com.

Jensen, M. 1993. "The Modern Industrial Revolution, Exit, and the Failure of Internal Control Systems." *Journal of Finance* 48:831–880.

Jensen, M., and W. Meckling. 1976. "The Theory of the Firm: Managerial Behavior, Agency Costs and Ownership Structure." *Journal of Financial Economics* 3:305–360.

Kalbers, L.P., and T.J. Fogarty. 1993. "Audit Committee Effectiveness: An Empirical Investigation of the Contribution of Power." *Auditing: A Journal of Practice and Theory* 12 (1): 24–49.

Kleffner, A., R. Lee, and B. McGannon. 2003. "The Effect of Corporate Governance on the Use of Enterprise Risk Management: Evidence from Canada." *Risk Management and Insurance Review* 6 (1): 53–73.

Knechel, R. 2002. "The Role of the Independent Accountant in Effective Risk Management." *Journal of Economics and Management* 47 (1): 65–86.

Knechel, R., and M. Willekens. 2006. "The Role of Risk Management and Governance in Determining Audit Demand." *Journal of Business Finance and Accounting* 33 (9–10): 1344–1367.

Lam, J. 2001. "The CRO Is Here to Stay." *Risk Management* 48 (4): 16–22.

Liebenberg, A., and R. Hoyt. 2003. "The Determinants of Enterprise Risk Management: Evidence from the Appointment of Chief Risk Officers." *Risk Management and Insurance Review* 6 (1): 37–52.

Macher, J., and C. Boerner., C.S. 2005. "Development and the boundaries of the firm: A knowledge-based examination in drug development." The Center for Business and Public Policy, Georgetown University.

Matsumura, E., and R. Tucker. 1992. "Fraud Detection: A Theoretical Foundation." *Accounting Review* 67 (Fall): 753–782.

Milgrom, P., and J. Roberts. 1992. *Economics, Organization and Management.* London: Prentice Hall.

Mitra, S., M. Hossain, and D.R. Deis. 2007. "The Empirical Relationship between Ownership Characteristics and Audit Fees." *Review of Quantitative Finance and Accounting* 28:257–285.

Nocco, B., and R. Stulz. 2006. "Enterprise Risk Management: Theory and Practice." *Journal of Applied Corporate Finance* 18 (4): 8–20.

O'Sullivan, N. 1997. "Insuring the Agents: The Role of Directors' and Officers' Insurance in Corporate Governance." *Journal of Risk and Insurance* 64 (3): 545–556.

———. 2000. "The Impact of Board Composition and Ownership on Audit Quality: Evidence from Large UK Companies." *British Accounting Review* 32 (December): 397–414.

Pagach, D., and R. Warr. 2007. "An Empirical Investigation of the Characteristics of Firms Adopting Enterprise Risk Management." Working Paper, North Carolina State University.

Power, M. 2007. *Organized Uncertainty: Designing a World of Risk Management.* Oxford: Oxford University Press.

Public Company Accounting Oversight Board. 2007. *Auditing Standard No. 5: An Audit of Internal Control Over Financial Reporting That Is Integrated with An Audit of Financial Statements.* Available at www.pcaobus.org.

Robb, S., L. Single, and M. Zarzeski. 2001. "Nonfinancial Disclosures across Anglo-American Countries." *Journal of International Accounting, Auditing and Taxation* 10:71–83.

Samanta, P., T. Azarchs, and J. Martinez. 2005. *Credit Policy Update: S&P Expands Review of Trading Risk Management within Financial Institutions.* New York: ERM Commentaries, Standard and Poor's.

Sarbanes-Oxley Act. 2002. *Public Law No. 107–204.* Washington, DC: Government Printing Office.

Shleifer, A., and R. Vishny. 1986. "Large Shareholders and Corporate Control." *Journal of Political Economy* 94 (3): 461–488.

Simon, D.T., and J.R. Francis. 1988. "The Effects of Auditor Change on Audit Fees: Tests of Price Cutting and Price Recovery." *Accounting Review* 63 (April): 255–269.

Simunic, D. 1980. "The Pricing of Audit Services: Theory and Evidence." *Journal of Accounting Research* 18 (Spring): 161–190.

Standard & Poor's. 2005. *Enterprise Risk Management for Financial Institutions: Rating Criteria and Best Practices, Standard & Poor's, Inc., New York, NY.* Available at www.standardandpoors.com.

Stoh, P.J. 2005. "Enterprise Risk Management at United Health Group." *Strategic Finance* 87 (July): 26–35.

Walker, P.L., W.G. Shenkir, and T. Barton. 2002. *Enterprise Risk Management: Putting It All Together.* Altamonte Springs, FL: Institute of Internal Auditors Research Foundation.

Watts, R.L., and J. Zimmerman. 1986. *Positive Accounting Theory.* Englewood Cliffs: NJ: Prentice Hall.

Willekens, M., and P. Sercu. 2005. *Corporate Governance at the Crossroad.* Antwerp, Belgium—Oxford: Intersentia.

2 Performance-Based Equity Grants and Corporate Governance Choices

Yu Flora Kuang and Bo Qin

INTRODUCTION

The last decade has witnessed a series of reforms on executive compensation.[1] One of the latest developments is to condition managerial benefit from equity compensation (i.e., stock and stock options) upon the achievement of predetermined performance targets (Bettis et al. 2010; Gerakos, Ittner, and Larcker 2007).[2] From a perspective of corporate governance choices, this chapter investigates the determinants of performance-based equity grants in an effort to shed some light on the implications of such rewards on managerial behavior.

Equity compensation provides opportunities for managers to share the increase of firm-value with shareholders. However, undesired consequences of equity compensation have been discussed in the compensation literature (Kuang 2008; Bergstresser and Philippon 2005; Cheng and Warfield 2005; Burns and Kedia 2003; Johnson, Ryan, and Tian 2009). For example, in a market where stock prices increase over time (i.e., a bull market), managers' payoff from equity compensation might merely reflect the general improvements in market prices, rather than managerial personal effort or firm economic performance (Bebchuk, Fried, and Walker 2002). The managerial effort–irrelevant benefits provide no economic value to the firm but increase compensation cost that shareholders have to bear. Thus, such windfall gains transferred to managers are not desired by shareholders and a call for compensation reforms has been increasingly voiced from market regulators, activist shareholders,[3] public media, and academics. Starting from high-profile companies, attaching performance hurdles (i.e., accounting and/or market based) to executive equity grants has been adopted to tighten up the link between executive pay and shareholder value. Advocated by market regulators and consulting firms (e.g., PWC), such incentive instruments met with great implementation. In FTSE top 250 nonfinancials, 90 percent included performance targets to executive option compensation in 2003 (Kuang and Suijs 2006).[4] In the U.S., half of top one hundred corporations were rewarding their executives with performance-based equity in 2006, mentioned by Peter Chingos, head of the U.S. executive-compensation practice at Mercer.

Performance-based equity compensation is deemed to restrain managers from reaping effort-irrelevant profits and provide them with incentives to execute shareholders' best interest. However, prior studies yield mixed evidence on the implications of such rewards on managerial behavior. On the one hand, some theoretical studies indicate that performance-based equity compensation (e.g., performance-vested stock options) stretches effort from managers (Kuang and Suijs 2006) and motivates managers to promote shareholders' wealth (Johnson and Tian 2000). On the other hand, managerial power perspective contends that executive compensation may lead to rather than alleviate agency problems (Bebchuk and Fried 2004; Bebchuk, Fried, and Walker 2002). Earlier evidence shows that if they possess substantive influence on the design of their own compensation, managers will exert their discretion on the grants of performance-based equity (Buck et al. 2003). The process of setting performance targets may simply provide an additional opportunity for managers to design the compensation in their own favor (Jensen 2003). Instead of mitigating agency problems and improving shareholder value, firms may symbolically reward managers with performance-based equity compensation so as to palate shareholders who advocate compensation reforms.

It is a widely held belief in regulatory bodies and the corporate world that shareholders' interest can be best promoted in well-governed firms, which suggests that executives' exercise of excessive power will be effectively constrained and controlled by board directors operating independent of the management. In a similar vein, if firms with superior corporate governance structures reward managers more performance-based equity compensation, such rewards are likely employed as incentive instruments for higher managerial effort and firm economic performance; in contrast, if the usage of such compensation is linked to weak corporate governance, managers likely utilize the grants to seek rents from the organization.

This chapter tackles incentive effects of performance-based equity compensation by examining the association between such rewards and corporate governance features. More specifically, two corporate governance features are investigated: managerial power in influencing firm decisions and independent directors' position in supervision. In line with the general belief in corporate governance codes (e.g., Combined Code in the UK), we expect that superior corporate governance effectively constrains managerial excessive power and maintains independent directors' position at firm decisions.

Using a data set of 2,986 yearly observations on executive directors from 1999 to 2004, we find that the intensity of performance-based equity grants increases with the number of independent directors and their proportion in the boardroom; executives with longer tenure will receive less performance-based equity. These results suggest that better governed firms will rely more intensively on performance-based equity to motivate managers. Because shareholders' interest can be best promoted within good corporate governance structures, the findings are supportive of our conjecture that performance targets attached to equity grants mitigate agency problems and provide managers with incentives to implement shareholder value. In addition, economic determinants play a role in explaining the intensity of performance-based equity grants. More specifically, firms adopt such incentive vehicles in hopes of better performance and raise managerial risk preference. Firms in great need of managerial talents will reward managers with more performance-based equity. Moreover, such an incentive device is employed to retain chief executives and extend their decision horizons.

The contribution of the current study to the literature is twofold: First, this study is among the first to investigate the incentive effects of performance-based equity compensation that has already been widely adopted. Our sample consists of companies in the UK where firms have a relatively long history of applying this incentive pay (Conyon et al. 2000). Therefore, our results reveal valuable insights compared with prior studies that focus on firms in the U.S. where the application of such an incentive vehicle is still sparse (Bettis et al. 2010; Gerakos et al. 2007).[5] Second, we examine the incentive effects from a perspective of corporate governance choices and thus add to the growing evidence on the influence of corporate governance on firm-compensation practices.

The reminder of the chapter consists of following sections. The next section briefly reviews the institutional background of British corporate governance codes. The third section provides a literature review and develops our hypotheses. The fourth describes measurement choices and sample selection procedure. Empirical results are presented in the fifth section. The sixth reports results from additional analysis and conclusions are made in the final section.

DEVELOPMENT OF BRITISH CORPORATE GOVERNANCE CODES

During the late 1980s and the early 1990s, a number of high-profile companies in the UK (e.g., Maxwell and Polly Peck) engaged in severe corporate scandals. In an attempt to restore investors' confidence to the market and improve the reliability of firm reporting, British regulatory bodies started much earlier than the regulators in other countries with building up best corporate governance provisions, as to provide guidelines for firm practices in corporate governance. At present, researchers and public media believe that the development of corporate governance regulations in the UK has reached a high degree of maturity and firms in the UK in general have obtained a sound quality of corporate governance arrangements.[6]

Influential corporate governance codes such as codes of best practices issued by the Cadbury (1992), Greenbury (1995), and Hampel (1998) committees, delineate the general framework of corporate governance in the UK. Combined Code, revised in 2003, has incorporated provisions of best practices outlined in prior corporate governance codes and defined the system by which companies are directed and controlled. In particular, all listed firms are required to report their compliance against the Code and should explain areas of noncompliance. The theme embedded in the Code is that firms should deliberately maintain the balance of the boards and rigidly control excessive managerial power over company decisions. For instance, Principle A of the Code (the *Combined Code* 2003) states that:

> [t]he board should include a balance of executive and non-executive directors . . . such that no individual or small group of individuals can dominate the board's decision making; no one individual should have unfettered powers of decision.

The theme of balanced boards is implemented by detailed provisions of best corporate governance in the Code. For instance, from a managerial power perspective, firms are suggested to follow a dual strategic leadership pattern and split the roles of CEO and the chairman of the board (Higgs 2003)[7]; executive directors are not allowed to dominate the nomination, removal and succession planning of senior management; neither can they design their own compensation portfolios (see the Combined Code 2003). In addition, top executives are subject to an annual performance review at shareholder annual general meetings (AGMs). Reelections of senior managers take place at regular intervals of no more than three years and extensions of their employment contracts require approvals from the board's nomination committee and the shareholders.

Independent directors' substantive position in supervision and monitoring is established by the codes. For instance, the Cadbury Report (1992) states that remuneration committee should be made up entirely or mainly of nonexecutive directors. Similar recommendations have been found in the Higgs Report (2003) with respect to the composition of nomination committees. In addition, independent directors' position in monitoring has been further enhanced by the structural suggestion in the Combined Code (2003) that at least half of the board should comprise independent directors. Further, in an effort to reduce the dependence or other forms of bond between management and independent directors, candidates for director selections should be drawn from a wide pool and frequent turnover of the independent directors is recommended (Combined Code 2003).

Remarkably, managerial equity compensation in UK firms is in general subject to performance hurdles. Companies started introducing these constraints into executives' compensation portfolios in the middle of the 1990s, as a response to the Greenbury Code (1995).[8] Nowadays, the majority of boards in the UK are attaching performance criteria to executive equity rewards (Kuang and Suijs 2006; Conyon, Core, and Guay 2011).

LITERATURE REVIEW AND HYPOTHESIS DEVELOPMENT

There is mounting evidence supportive of an association between corporate governance quality and the design of top management compensation. The first cluster of studies demonstrates a positive association between corporate governance quality and firm performance outcomes (Larcker, Richardson, and Tuna 2007; Bhagat and Bolton 2008; Gompers, Ishii, and Metrick

2003; Bushman and Smith 2001; Shleifer and Vishny 1997). Executive payment is usually linked to firm performance and thus a positive association is expected between managerial compensation and corporate governance quality. The second cluster of studies explicitly examines the association between corporate governance structures and managerial compensation (Jensen et al. 2004; Hermalin and Weisbach 2003; Core, Holthausen, and Larcker 1999; Daily et al. 1998; Hallock 1997; Boyd 1994; Lambert, Larcker, and Weigelt 1993). It argues that improvements on corporate governance quality and effectiveness of control and supervision will reduce information asymmetry on managerial real effort. Under the assumption that executive compensation is the product of arm's-length bargaining between managers and shareholders (or their representatives in the boardrooms) aiming to solve agency problems, managerial compensation becomes less dependent upon firm performance (Hart and Holmstrom 1987).

More recently, the arm's-length bargaining assumption has been subject to severe challenges. Bebchuk and Fried (2004) and Bebchuk, Fried, and Walker (2002) propose to examine executive compensation from a managerial power perspective, where executive compensation reflects agency problems (rather than a remedy to the problems) and weak corporate governance structures will result in an inefficient design of compensation contracts. Growing evidence shows that powerful managers will self-serve during compensation contracting and influence the design of their own compensation in a way that is favorable to themselves (Sautner and Weber 2011; Buck et al. 2003; Bertrand and Mullainathan 2001). For example, firms may symbolically adopt compensation elements that are recommended by external stakeholders. The purpose is to gain support from the public and protect the organization from having its compensation schemes questioned (Gerakos, Ittner, and Larcker 2007; Zajac and Westphal 1995; Westphal and Zajac 1994, 1998).

Economic incentive hypothesis and rent extraction hypothesis provide two plausible explanations to firms rewarding managers with performance-based equity compensation. From an economic incentive perspective, equity grants with performance targets give managers stronger incentives to improve performance and outperform competitors (Kuang and Suijs 2006; Johnson and Tian 2000). The improvements on firm performance are in line with shareholders' interest. Because shareholders' interest can be best promoted in good corporate governance structure (Jensen, Murphy, and Wruck 2004; Bebchuk, Fried, and Walker 2002; Core, Holthausen, and Larcker 1999; MacAvoy and Millstein 1998, 2003), our first hypothesis predicts a positive association between performance-based equity grants and corporate governance quality. In contrast, the rent extraction hypothesis suggests that firms may symbolically comply with recommendations on compensation reforms (Gerokas et al. 2007). Granting performance-based equity compensation may merely reflect significant managerial power over executive pay. Our second hypothesis conjectures a negative association between performance-based equity grants and good corporate governance structures. In what follows, we develop our hypotheses from the economic incentive perspective and the rent extraction perspective, respectively.

Performance-Vested Equity Compensation and Economic Incentive Hypothesis

By granting equity compensation, shareholders share an increase of a firm's net profits with managers and it is in the interest of both managers and shareholders to promote firm market performance (see Nagar, Nanda, and Wysocki 2003; Warfield, Wild, and Wild 1995; Jensen and Murphy 1990, among others). One of the major concerns pertains to the effort-irrelevant windfall benefits that managers might reap from equity grants. Such gains may merely mirror general improvements at market prices instead of increases on firm economic performance or managerial personal effort (Gerakos, Ittner, and Larcker 2007). As a result, attaching performance targets to equity grants has been recommended as a remedy to insufficient effort-exerting incentives associated with traditional equity compensation (Bettis et al. 2010; Kuang and Suijs 2006).[9]

The managerial benefits arising from general market improvements provide no economic value to the firm but increase the compensation cost that shareholders have to bear. Performance targets attached to equity grants, however, filter out marketwide (sectorwide) noise in compensating managers and provide an extra degree of freedom for firms to pose performance hurdles. Adding additional signals that are informative of unobservable managerial effort increases the precision in inferring managerial hidden actions based on observed firm performance (Holmstrom 1979). Managers who used to shirk but still receive windfall gains will miss the targets and receive nothing if they keep the original effort level. Thus the performance hurdles yield direct effort implications and motivate managers to exert higher effort and promote shareholder interest (Kuang and Qin 2009). To the extent that weak corporate governance features will result in an inefficient design of managerial compensation contracts, good corporate governance structures will lead to superior managerial pay practices and in turn better advance shareholders' interest (Jensen, Murphy, and Wruck 2004; Bebchuk and Fried 2004; Bebchuk, Fried, and Walker 2002). Therefore, we conjecture that grants of performance-based equity compensation are associated with good corporate governance structures. Our hypothesis states that:

> *Ha*: Other things equal, performance-based equity grants are associated with good corporate governance structures.

Performance-Based Equity Compensation and Rent Extraction Hypothesis

Interests of managers and shareholders are not inherently aligned. It is well documented that managers have significant power over firm decisions on operations and controls, and they are apt to exert such discretion for their own personal benefits and extract rents from the firm at the cost of shareholders (Jensen 2003; Shleifer and Vishny 1997; Baiman 1982). Following this line of argument, managers will utilize their influence during the setting of compensation contracts to have the contracts designed in a way that is favorable to themselves (Buck et al. 2003; Bertrand and Mullainathan 2001).

Studies have examined the adoptions of performance-based incentive pay that has been recommended by external stakeholders or public press with the purported aim to execute shareholders' best interest (e.g., performance-based cash compensation, performance-based stock and stock option plans). Consistent with the rent extraction hypothesis, empirical findings suggest that firms may window-dress and symbolically adopt the incentive instruments in order to minimize public scrutiny on managerial power over the design of compensation contracts and protect managers from having compensation decisions questioned (Gerakos, Ittner, and Larcker 2007; Zajac and Westphal 1995; Westphal and Zajac 1994, 1998). Therefore, rather than improving firm performance and stretching managerial effort, performance-based equity grants may be employed to camouflage significant managerial control over their own compensation and justify excessive executive pay associated with performance-based equity grants.[10]

The weaker the corporate governance constructed, the greater managerial power to influence compensation contracting in his/her own favor (Bebchuk and Fried 2004; Bebchuk, Fried, and Walker 2002). To the extent that performance-based equity grants may reflect managerial control over the design of their own compensation, we predict that grants of performance-based equity compensation are associated with weak corporate governance. In contrast to Ha, our alternative hypothesis states that:

> *Hb*: Other things equal, performance-based equity grants are associated with weak corporate governance structures.

METHODOLOGY AND SAMPLE SELECTION

This section describes the definitions of our proxies for the conceptual variables and the method we employed to examine our hypotheses. Sample selection procedure is also explained.

Measurements of Variables

Grants of Performance-Based Equity Compensation

The dependent variable is the intensity of performance-based equity compensation grants, proxied by the ratio of the annual grants of performance-based equity to the base salary of the year for an individual executive. All compensation elements are valued at the end of the year. Black-Scholes fair value models[11] are employed to estimate the value of performance-vested stock options. Because managers are only eligible to benefit from performance-based equity compensation after performance targets are achieved, the probability of realization could be smaller than one. The probability is not incorporated in the valuation models. In the spirit of prior literature (Kuang and Suijs 2006; Conyon, Core, and Guay 2011), we perform robustness checks by adjusting the value of performance-based equity compensation at various discount rates.[12]

Quality of Corporate Governance

An unsolved issue in corporate governance studies is how to appropriately measure the quality of the governance. As there is no consensus on this issue (Larcker, Richardson, and Tuna 2007), we ground our measurements on the theme embedded in the Combined Code (2003) that effective corporate governance is to implement policies and mechanisms to discipline managerial behavior and protect shareholders' wealth. More specifically, we measure quality of corporate governance from two angles[13]: managerial power and board independency.

Managerial power in influencing boardroom decisions is measured by the number of committee roles the executive serves, the number of years the executive sits on the board, and the number of other boards the executive serves. The first two measurements capture managerial entrenchment in the company (Ryan and Wiggins 2004; Berger, Ofek, and Yermack 1997). The longer the executive sits on the board and/or the more committee roles he/she serves in the company, the more power he/she maintains in determining corporate strategies and the higher probability of rent extraction. The number of other boards the executive serves measures his/her influence on other companies' decisions. Studies show that managers who cross-sit on each other's boards may indirectly affect their own compensation contracts (Collins and Clark 2003). Thus, the power to influence other companies' decisions will eventually be translated into substantial influence on the decisions of their own companies. The more managerial power, the less likely that corporate policies and mechanisms will discipline managerial behavior, and the weaker corporate governance is in turn expected.

Independent directors act as "professional referees" and represent shareholders' interest in boardrooms. They have incentives to take actions that maximize firm wealth due to their concerns about their reputation at human capital market (Fama and Jensen 1983). Following prior literature and provisions in corporate governance codes, we employ the independence of board to capture the efficiency of the board in controlling managerial opportunism and monitoring the design of executive compensation. The board independency is measured by the number and proportion of independent directors on the board. We expect that the quality of corporate governance increases with the board independency.

Economic Determinants

Economic determinants (Core, Holthausen, and Larcker 1999) are controlled for when examining the association between performance-based equity grants and corporate governance quality. Standard agency models suggest that design of executive compensation depends on firm performance. Thus, we incorporate the measures of firm performance into our models. Firm performance is measured from an accounting perspective (i.e., sales) as well as from a market perspective (i.e., market returns). Firms usually justify the grants of performance-based equity compensation by claiming that the incentive pay will provide managers with stronger incentives to improve the firm's economic performance (Gerakos, Ittner, and Larcker 2007). Accordingly, a negative association is predicted between performance-based equity grants and firm prior performance. In a similar vein, incentive for risk taking is also controlled for (i.e., volatility of return on equity in prior five years and volatility of monthly market return in last year). Because analytical findings (Camara 2001; Johnson and Tian 2000) suggest that performance-based equity grants provide managers with stronger incentives to undertake risky capital investment projects, we expect the grants of performance-based equity compensation to be negatively associated with firm risk in the prior period.

We also control for growth opportunities of the firm. Following Core, Holthausen, and Larcker (1999), we measure growth opportunity with the firm's year-end market-to-book ratio averaged over the previous five years. Evidence suggests that performance-based equity grants are used as a device to sort managerial talent and attract capable employees (Bettis et al. 2010). Firms with high growth opportunities are in great demand for managerial talents. Thus, we expect a positive association between the performance-based equity grants and the firm's growth opportunities. Finally, industry dummies (first two-digit SIC codes) and year dummies are included to control for unobservable industry and year fixed effects.

Other Control Variables

A number of variables measured at both the executive and the firm level are included. Managerial horizon affects their decisions. Instead of maximizing long-run firm-value, managers may make decisions to serve their personal interest within their tenure. We include the number of years to retirement to control for the managerial horizon effects. Further, earlier evidence illustrates a difference between CEO and non-CEO executive directors in terms of compensation contracts (Conyon, Core, and Guay 2011). Thus, a dummy variable is incorporated, equaling one if the executive is CEO of the company and zero otherwise, so as to control for the potential difference. In addition, managerial ownership is controlled for. By holding company shares, managers share the firm's value increases with shareholders and thus are expected to be better motivated. We expect that managerial ownership is negatively associated with performance-based equity grants, given the substitution relationship between executive share holdings and equity new grants.

With regard to firm-level variables, firm size is controlled for, measured by the company's market value at the end of year. We also incorporate leverage ratio to control for the effects of "free cash flow." Jensen (1986) shows that due to the commitments to repaying interests and principal, leverage may play a role in mitigating conflicts between managers and shareholders caused by managerial discretions over free cash flows. Moreover, blockholder ownership is employed to proxy large shareholders' control over the design of compensation contracts. We expect that the control increases with the blockholder ownership.

Empirical Models

To identify the association between the cross-sectional variations in performance-vested equity grants and the quality of corporate governance, we employ the following Tobit model:

$$perf\_EG_{i,j,t} = f(CG_{i,j,t}, CG_{j,t}, EcoD_{j,t-1}, \overrightarrow{CONTROL_t}) + \varepsilon_{i,j,t}$$

Where:

$perf\_EG_{j,t}$ = the ratio of performance-based equity compensation granted to executive i during year t to his/her annual salary of that year in firm j.

$CG_{i,j,t}$ = executive level corporate governance measures of executive i at the end of year t in firm j, including the number of functional roles the executive serves, the number of years the executive sits on the board, and the number of other boards the executive serves.

$CG_{j,t}$ = firm level corporate governance measures at the end of year t in firm j, including the number of independent directors on the board, and the proportion of independent directors on the board.

$EcoD_{j,t-1}$ = economic determinants, including sales of year t-1 scaled by total assets in that year, stock return of year t-1, standard deviation of annual stock returns for the prior five years, and year-end market-to-book ratio averaged over the five years ended in year t-1.

$CONTROL$ = other control variables, including natural logarithm of firm's market value at the end of year t; leverage ratio measured as total liability over the sum of total liability and market value of equity at the end of year t; years to retirement measured at the end of year t; dummy variable indicating a CEO, and the ratio of the individual executives' share holdings to market capitalization measured at the end of year t; and total blockholder (with ownership at least 5 percent) ownership at the end of year t.

$\varepsilon_{i,j,t}$ = error terms.

A Tobit model is employed because the dependent variable perf_EG is nonnegative and truncated at zero (Tobin 1958), where the application of ordinary least square (OLS) could generate biased results (Amemiya 1985, 1973). Table 2.1 summarizes variable definitions and our predictions.

Table 2.1 Variable Definitions and Predictions

Panel A: Definitions of Variables	
Variable Name	*Descriptions*
Dependent variables:	
perf_EG	The ratio of value of performance-based equity pay granted during the current year to annual salary, where performance-vested stock options are valued by Black-Scholes models and all compensation elements are valued at the end of the year
Explanatory variables: *Corporate governance*	
#Roles	The number of committee roles the executive serves
Tenure	The number of years the executive sits on the board
#Other_boards	The number of other boards the executive serves
#Independent_dir	The number of independent directors on the board
%Independent_dir	The proportion of independent directors on the board
Economic determinants	
MtB	Year-end market-to-book ratio averaged over the five years ended prior year
RET	Stock return of the prior year
Vol_RET	Standard deviation of annual stock return for the prior five years
Sales	Sales of prior year scaled by total assets in that year
Other control variables:	
Debt	The ratio of total liability to the sum of total liability and market value equity at the end of the year
LnMV	The natural logarithmic of market value equity at the end of the year
Year_retirement	The length of time, stated in years to retirement, based on the company's retirement age.
Variable Name	Descriptions
DummyCEO	A dummy variable, equaling 1 if the executive is CEO of the firm and 0 otherwise
%Ownership	The ratio of individual executive's share holdings to market capitalization at the end of the year
Blockholder_ownership	Blockholder (with ownership at least 5%) ownership

(continued)

Table 2.1 (continued)

Panel B: Theoretical Predictions

Variables	*Ha*	*Hb*
	perf_EG	*perf_EG*
Corporate governance		
#Roles	--	+
Tenure	--	+
#Other_boards	--	+
#Independent_dir	+	--
%Independent_dir	+	--
Economic determinants		
MtB	+	+
RET	--	--
Vol_RET	--	--
Sales	--	--
Other control variables		
Debt	?	?
LnMV	?	?
Year_retirement	?	?
DummyCEO	?	?
%Ownership	--	--
Blockholder_ownership	?	?

Sample Selection and Data Sources

Our sample starts with the top 350 nonfinancial firms in the UK, based on the company equity value in 2004. Compared with the firms elsewhere (e.g., in the U.S.), British firms have a relatively longer history of rewarding managers with performance-based equity compensation and thus possess more experience regarding the implications of the incentive instrument on managerial behavior. The results will provide new insights regarding the effects of the incentive mechanism and the implications on managerial behavior in a mature application environment. Moreover, all listed firms in the UK are required to include audited remuneration reports in their annual reports, which fully disclose firm practice in compensating executive directors.[14] The information facilitates our empirical examinations. The final sample consists of 2,986 executive-year observations[15] for 1,373 executives from 245 firms from 1999 to 2004. Data on managerial compensation and corporate governance structures are collected from BoardEx database. Information on firm accounting performance is from Compustat Global, capital market performance from Datastream, and ownership information from Amadeus.

EMPIRICAL RESULTS

Figure 2.1–2.5 exhibit the changes of executive compensation, board composition, and managerial power from 1999 to 2004. As shown in Figures 2.1 and Figure 2.2, a steady increase in managerial annual compensation has been observed since 2000, accompanied with more incentive pay, including bonuses and performance-based equity. Although fixed salary comprises an important part in annual payments, its weight in total compensation has decreased over time. These results suggest that by following the best corporate governance provisions (e.g., Greenbury Code 1995) firms increasingly link managerial paychecks with performance so as to motivate their top managers.

In spite of a decrease in its usage during 2000 to 2002, equity-linked compensation overweighed fixed salary in annual compensation across the sample period. A closer investigation of the composition of equity compensation shows that the weight of performance-based equity grants has increased steadily during the observation period, suggesting that firms attach performance targets to equity compensation and this may be intended to limit windfalls reaped by managers and induce higher managerial effort (Kuang and Suijs 2006). Figure 2.3 exhibits that the weight of performance-vested stock options in total performance-based equity has increased sharply since 1999 and accounted for nearly 70 percent of performance-based equity grants in 2001. Although the usage has declined pronouncedly since 2001, it remains an important element in executive pay, comprising over 40 percent of performance-based equity grants.

EXECUTIVE DIRECTORS' COMPENSATION, BOARD COMPOSITION, AND MANAGERIAL POWER

Figure 2.4 shows the evolvement of board structure during the sample period. Firms in general comply with the recommendations by the governance codes (such as the Combined Code 2003). First, on average company board has downsized. Second, the number of independent directors has remained stable. As a result, the proportion of independent directors in the boardroom has increased over time and in 2004 about 54 percent of the board directors are independent members. The slightly decreased managerial tenure as shown in Figure 2.5 implies an increase in the competition at management human capital market and the mobility of top talents. Further, top managers are not active in taking roles in the company committees. Neither are they active in serving other boards.

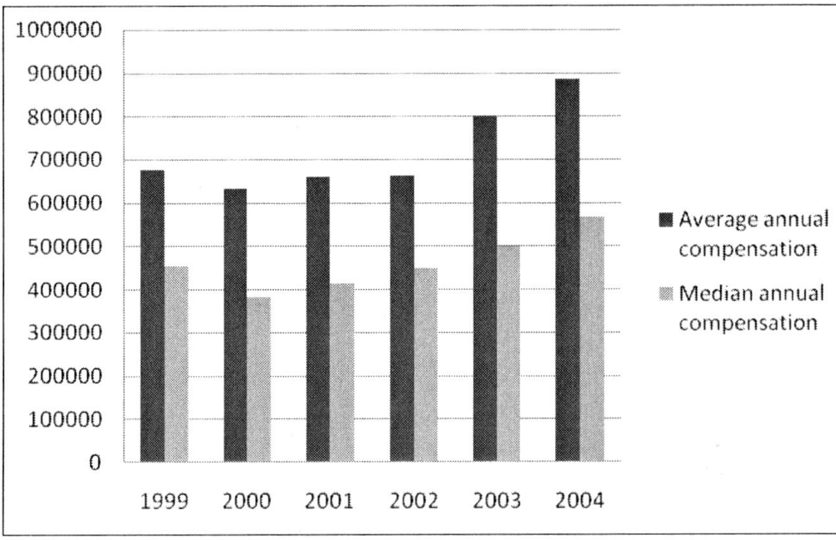

Figure 2.1 Annual compensation from 1999 to 2004 (in £s).

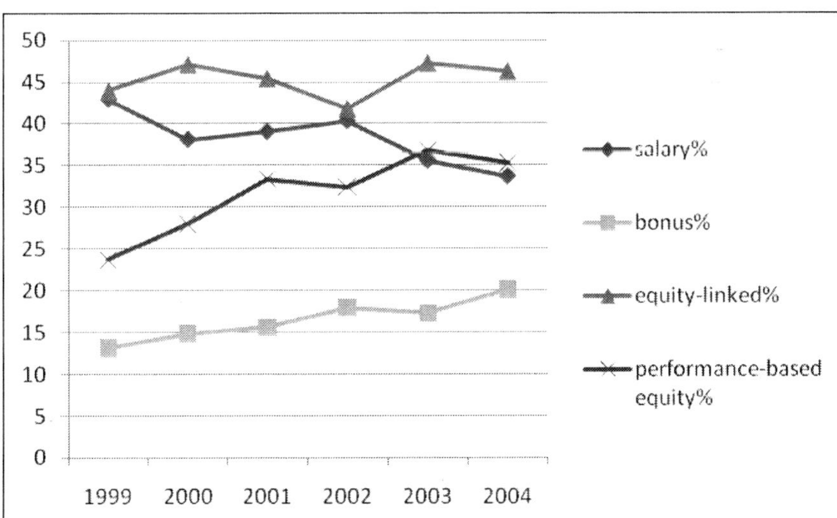

Figure 2.2 Components of annual compensation from 1999 to 2004.

Note: Salary% is the proportion of salary in total annual compensation; bonus% is the proportion of cash bonus in total annual compensation; equity-linked% is the proportion of annual equity grants in total annual compensation; performance-based equity% is the proportion of performance-based equity grants in annual equity grants.

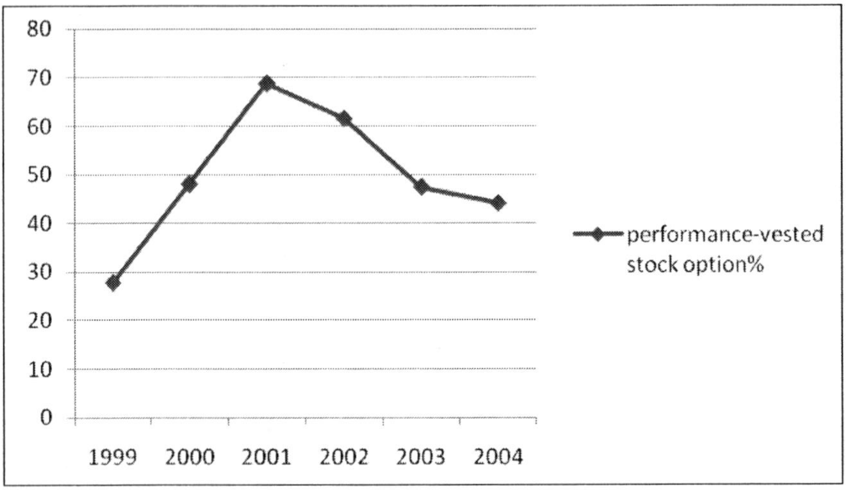

Figure 2.3 Proportion of performance-vested stock options in annual performance-based equity grants from 1999 to 2004.

Note: performance-vested stock option% is the proportion of performance-based stock option grants in total performance-based equity granted during that year.

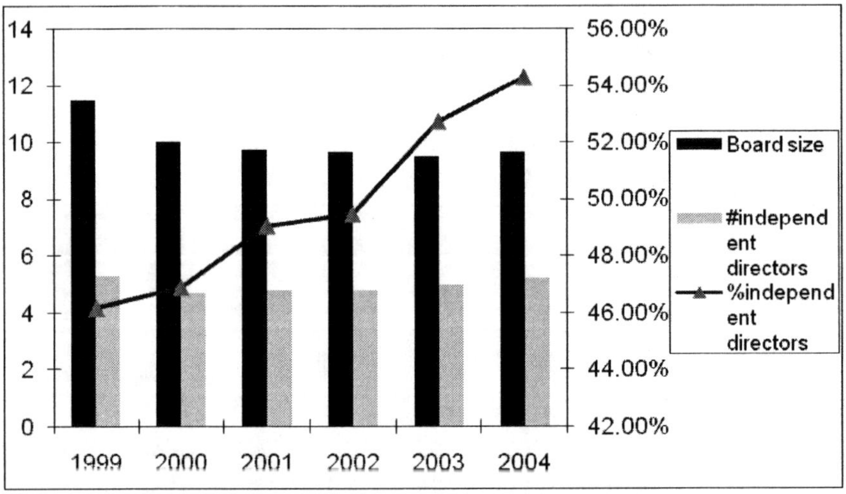

Figure 2.4 Composition of company boards from 1999 to 2004.

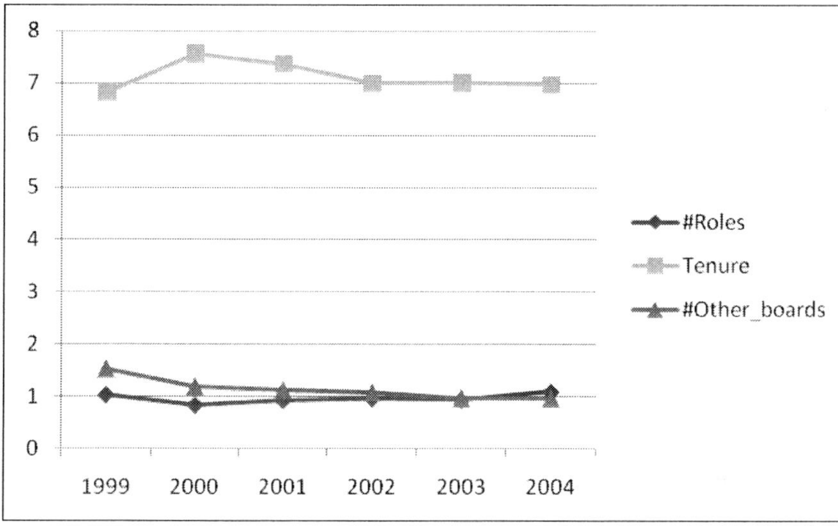

Figure 2.5 Executive tenure, #roles, and #other boards served from 1999 to 2004.

Descriptive Statistics

Table 2.2 presents managerial annual compensation in detail. Statistics confirm prior findings (Bettis et al. 2010) that managers are compensated for bearing the additional risk from the performance-based equity grants. More specifically, the compensation comes in two forms: managers will receive more cash-based payment; meanwhile, they are also compensated by receiving more equity rewards.

Table 2.3 provides summary statistics for variables employed in following analyses. The dependent variable, performance-based equity compensation grants, perf_EG, is truncated at zero (median = 0), which justifies the adoption of Tobit regressions to handle the potential bias associated with OLS.

Statistics on corporate governance measurements indicate that firms in our sample on average comply well with the best practice provisions in corporate governance codes. For example, on average, independent directors comprise half of the board, consistent with the provisions on board balance and independence (Combined Code 2003). Besides current company, an executive director also serves another board (of a quoted or private company), as code provisions limit full-time executive directors taking on nonexecutive directorship in other companies (i.e., no more than one nonexecutive directorship in a FTSE 100 company). On average, executive directors are hardly taking on any role in board committees (i.e., remuneration committee, nomination committee, or audit committee) and they have served about seven years on the company board. Large institutional owners

Table 2.2 Difference of Means (Medians) between Firms Granting Performance-Based Equity and Firms without such Grants (in Thousand £s)

Compensation	*Group*	*Mean*	*Std. Dev.*	*Median*	*t-test (t-statistics)*	*Mann-Whitney U test (Z-values)*
Salary and bonus						
	perf_EG=0	343	250	280		
	perf_EG>0	448	340	362	-9.571***	-14.847***
Total direct compensation						
	perf_EG=0	391	296	314		
	perf_EG>0	507	385	410	-9.240***	-15.498***
Equity-linked compensation						
	perf_EG=0	150	442	8		
	perf_EG>0	465	1,054	232	-10.512***	-32.732***
Total annual compensation						
	perf_EG=0	493	615	337		
	perf_EG>0	912	1,285	628	-11.258***	-24.488***

This table reports mean comparisons between firms that grant performance-based equity and firms that do not include such reward in managerial annual payments. *, **, and *** indicate a significant difference between two groups' means at the 10%, 5%, and 1% significance levels (two-tailed) respectively.

on average hold 14.6 percent of the company's stake. Consistent with prior work, we find the distribution of executive directors' ownership is right-skewed, with the mean (median) executive ownership approximates 1.2 percent (0.1 percent) of the outstanding equity.

Company-level variables show that our sample covers from traditional industries (as indicated by low MtB and low Vol_RET) to high-growth industries (high MtB and high Vol_RET), from equity-financed to heavily debt-financed firms (high Debt), and from loss makers (negative RETs) to profit winners (positive RETs).

Correlation coefficients between variables are presented in Table 4.4. An important observation is that the results tend to be consistent with the economic incentive hypothesis (Ha) as the indicators for good corporate governance are in general positively correlated to the grants of performance-based equity. In addition, correlations between performance-based equity compensation and firm-level economic determinants are in line with our

Table 2.3 Descriptive Statistics

Variable Name	*Mean*	*Std. Dev.*	*1%*	*25%*	*Median*	*75%*	*99%*
perf_EG	0.696	2.118	0	0	0	0.800	7.320
Corporate governance							
#Roles	0.275	0.745	0	0	0	0	3
Tenure	7.151	6.194	1	2.800	5.100	9.400	28.900
#Other_boards	1.089	1.233	0	0	0	1	10
#Independent_dir	4.927	1.941	2	4	5	6	11
%Independent_dir	0.500	0.127	0.200	0.416	0.500	0.571	0.818
Economic determinants							
MtB	4.176	16.981	0.325	1.282	1.985	3.288	28.876
RET	0.163	0.829	-0.711	-0.144	0.095	0.339	1.754
Vol_RET	0.472	0.819	0.052	0.23	0.324	0.488	3.375
Sales	1.161	0.714	0.057	0.651	1.054	1.504	3.524
Other control variables							
Debt	0.415	0.186	0.022	0.287	0.413	0.553	0.820
LnMV	6.703	1.468	4.298	5.534	6.496	7.65	10.266
Year_retirement	14.497	6.905	0	9	14	20	30
DummyCEO	0.291	0.454	0	0	0	1	1
%Ownership	0.012	0.058	0	0	0	0.001	0.263
Blockholder_ ownership	0.146	0.188	0	0	0.073	0.215	0.801

This table reports descriptive statistics for variables used in the analysis. perf_EG is the ratio of value of performance-based equity pay granted during the current year to annual salary, where performance-vested stock options are valued by Black-Scholes models and all compensation elements are valued at the end of the year; #Roles is the number of committee roles the executive serves; Tenure is the number of years the executive sits on the board; #Other_boards is the number of other boards the executive serves; #Independent_dir is the number of independent directors on the board; %Independent_dir is the proportion of independent directors in the board; MtB is the year-end market-to-book ratio averaged over the five years ended in prior year; RET is market return of the prior year; Vol_RET is the standard deviation of annual stock return for the prior five years; Sales is the sales of prior year scaled by total assets in that year; Debt is the ratio of total liability to the sum of total liability and market value of equity at the end of the year; LnMV is the natural logarithm of market value equity at the end of the year; Year_retirement is the number of years to executive retirement; DummyCEO equals 1 if the executive is CEO of the firm and 0 otherwise; %Ownership is the ratio of individual executive's share holdings to market capitalization at the end of the year; and Blockholder_ownership represents the aggregate ownership of blockholders who hold at least 5% of the company total shares.

Table 2.4 Pearson Correlation Matrix

	(1)	(2)	(3)	(4)	(5)	(6)	(7)	(8)	(9)	(10)	(11)	(12)	(13)	(14)	(15)
(1) perf_EG	1														
(2) #Roles	-0.042***	1													
(3) Tenure	-0.088***	0.212***	1												
(4) #Other_boards	0.006	0.138***	0.078***	1											
(5) #Independent_dir	0.137***	0.021	-0.195***	-0.127***	1										
(6) %Independent_dir	0.112***	-0.045***	-0.221***	-0.084***	0.719***	1									
(7) MtB	0.027*	0.002	-0.010	-0.013	0.050***	0.028*	1								
(8) RET	0.022	0.010	0.014	0.033*	0.021	0.020	0.226***	1							
(9) Vol_RET	0.003	0.002	-0.046***	-0.031*	-0.027	0.024	0.107***	0.331***	1						
(10) Sales	-0.040**	-0.050***	0.034**	-0.090***	-0.193***	-0.121***	0.063***	0.015	-0.107***	1					
(11) Debt	-0.149***	-0.053***	-0.091***	0.035**	0.177***	0.106***	-0.282***	-0.092***	-0.220***	0.021	1				
(12) LnMV	0.1979***	0.072***	-0.130***	0.168***	0.600***	0.291***	0.106***	-0.010	-0.081***	-0.241***	-0.105***	1			
(13) Year_retirement	0.071***	-0.242***	-0.355***	-0.128***	-0.082***	0.012***	0.039**	0.046***	0.142***	0.001	-0.089***	-0.129***	1		
(14) DummyCEO	0.051***	0.473***	0.277***	0.128***	-0.002	0.113***	-0.009	0.006	-0.002	0.007	-0.029*	-0.025	-0.172***	1	
(15) %Ownership	-0.045***	0.127***	0.366***	0.087***	-0.125***	-0.148***	-0.009	0.007	0.009	0.122***	-0.011	-0.151***	-0.024	0.229***	1
(16) Blockholder_ownership	-0.060***	-0.028*	0.006	0.037**	-0.093***	-0.085***	-0.023	0.005	-0.074***	0.089***	0.018	-0.106***	0.019	-0.027*	-0.038**

This table presents Pearson correlation statistics computed for the variables employed in the analysis. perf_EG is the ratio of value of performance-based equity pay granted during the current year to annual salary, where performance-vested stock options are valued by Black-Scholes models and all compensation elements are valued at the end of the year; #Roles is the number of committee roles the executive serves; Tenure is the number of years the executive sits on the board; #Other_boards is the number of other boards the executive serves; #Independent_dir is the number of independent directors on the board; %Independent_dir is the proportion of independent directors in the board; MtB is the year-end market-to-book ratio averaged over the five years ended in prior year; RET is market return of the prior year; Vol_RET is the standard deviation of annual stock return for the prior five years; Sales is the sales of prior year scaled by total assets in that year; Debt is the ratio of total liability to the sum of total liability and market value of equity at the end of the year; LnMV is the natural logarithm of market value equity at the end of the year; Year_retirement is the number of years to executive retirement; DummyCEO equals 1 if the executive is CEO of the firm and 0 otherwise; %Ownership is the ratio of individual executive's share holdings to market capitalization at the end of the year; and Blockholder_ownership represents the aggregate ownership of blockholders who hold at least 5% of the company total shares. *, **, and *** correspond to 10%, 5%, and 1% significance levels (two-tailed).

predictions. The managerial power proxies are positively correlated with each other at statistically significant levels, indicating a satisfactory level of coherence in these measures capturing managerial power. Further, the proxies for managerial power are in general negatively correlated with those for board independency, suggesting that the two sets of proxies capture two counter-affected mechanisms in corporate governance. A high correlation (0.719 with p-value < 0.01) is observed between the number of independent directors and their proportion on company boards. To prevent the results from being contaminated by potential multicollinearity, we include either variable into the regressions in the following analysis.

Tobit Regression Results of Full Sample

Within one company, executive directors' compensation might be similarly constructed. To deal with the clustered observations within firms, we adjust standard errors for autocorrelation and heteroskedasticity. Table 2.5

Table 2.5 Tobit Regression Results of Full Sample

Variables	*perf_EG* (1)	*perf_EG* (2)
Corporate governance		
#Roles	0.115	0.109
	(1.08)	(1.04)
Tenure	-0.064***	-0.063***
	(-3.19)	(-3.13)
#Other_boards	-0.035	-0.036
	(-0.63)	(-0.65)
#Independent_dir	0.091*	
	(1.53)	
%Independent_dir		1.366**
		(1.67)
Economic determinants		
MtB	0.101***	0.101***
	(5.05)	(5.07)
RET	-0.012	-0.014
	(-0.12)	(-0.13)
Vol_RET	-0.254***	-0.255***
	(-2.73)	(-2.74)
Sales	-0.288***	-0.293**
	(-1.65)	(-1.68)

(continued)

Table 2.5 (continued)

Variables	*perf_EG* (1)	*perf_EG* (2)
Other control variables		
Debt	-2.471***	-2.392***
	(-4.04)	(-4.04)
LnMV	0.269***	0.299***
	(2.85)	(3.74)
Year_retirement	0.020	0.018
	(1.31)	(1.22)
DummyCEO	0.644***	0.595***
	(2.99)	(2.74)
%Ownership	-1.281	-1.085
	(-0.58)	(-0.51)
Blockholder_ownership	-1.394**	-1.498***
	(-1.89)	(-2.04)
industry dummies	yes	Yes
year dummies	yes	Yes
# of obs	2,986	2,986
chi-square	4,414	4,427
prob>chi2	<0.01	<0.01

This table presents results of Tobit regressions examining the association between performance-based equity grants and corporate governance features for full sample. The dependent variable in each regression is perf_EG, the ratio of value of performance-based equity pay granted during the current year to annual salary, where performance-vested stock options are valued by Black-Scholes models and all compensation elements are valued at the end of the year; #Roles is the number of committee roles the executive serves; Tenure is the number of years the executive sits on the board; #Other_boards is the number of other boards the executive serves; #Independent_dir is the number of independent directors on the board; %Independent_dir is the proportion of independent directors in the board; MtB is the year-end market-to-book ratio averaged over the five years ended in prior year; RET is market return of the prior year; Vol_RET is the standard deviation of annual stock return for the prior five years; Sales is the sales of prior year scaled by total assets in that year; Debt is the ratio of total liability to the sum of total liability and market value of equity at the end of the year; LnMV is the natural logarithm of market value equity at the end of the year; Year_retirement is the number of years to executive retirement; DummyCEO equals 1 if the executive is CEO of the firm and 0 otherwise; %Ownership is the ratio of individual executive's share holdings to market capitalization at the end of the year; and Blockholder_ownership represents the aggregate ownership of blockholders who hold at least 5% of the company total shares. t-statistics are reported in the brackets. Significance levels are based on one-tailed tests where there is a prediction of the sign of and coefficient and based on two-tailed tests otherwise. *, **, and *** correspond to 10%, 5%, and 1% significance levels.

provides a summary of the regression results with full sample. Column 1 reports the results from the basic Tobit regression, where #Independent_dir is included, whereas Column 2 reports the results with percentIndependent_dir included instead. Chi-square statistics show that both models are significant at $p < 0.01$, indicating explanatory variables are statistically significant in explaining the variance of the dependent variable, perf_EG.

The results are supportive of Ha on economic incentives of performance-based equity compensation. First, proxies for managerial power have significantly negative associations with the grants of performance-based equity. The coefficient on tenure is negative and significant at $p < 0.01$, which suggests that the longer the executive director sits on the company board and the more power he/she accrues, the less performance-based equity compensation will be granted to the director. We also find that the measurements for board independency are positively associated with performance-based equity grants. More specifically, the coefficients on the number of independent directors (#Independent_dir) and their proportion in the total number of board members (percentIndependent_dir) are positive and significant. Overall, the results suggest the grants of performance-based equity are associated with good corporate governance.

Turning to economic determinants, results are consistent with our predictions. The average market-to-book ratio (MtB) in the prior five years captures the firm's investment opportunities. The positive coefficient on MtB suggests that firms with more growth opportunities will grant more performance-based equity to their top managers, aiming to reduce agency problems arising from the increasing information asymmetry on managerial behavior accompanied with the growth. Firms' prior performance (Sales) and risk (Vol_RET) are negatively association with performance-based equity rewards (perf_EG), consistent with the numerical results from Johnson and Tian (2000), which implies that performance-based equity grants provide strong incentives to improve firm performance and increase firm risk.

Other control variables also exhibit significant explanatory power. The coefficient on Debt is negative and significant at p-value < 0.01. This is consistent with "free cash hypothesis" (Jensen 1986) that precommitments to cash flow required by leverage provide managerial "discipline," which substitutes for incentive pay in mitigating agency problems. Firms larger in size, as measured by market value of equity (LnMV), grant more equity compensation with performance targets. This finding coheres with the observation that performance-based equity compensation is more intensively used in companies subject to greater public scrutiny. Company CEOs are compensated with more performance-based equity as the coefficient on DummyCEO is positive and significant at p-value < 0.01. This is in line with the prediction based on tournament theory that firms need to enlarge the difference between winning and losing for managers who sit on the top of organizational hierarchy (i.e., CEOs) because they have zero expected value regarding development within the company and thus lack of incentives for competing and exerting high effort (Lambert, Larcker, and Weigelt 1993; Rosen 1986, 1982; Calvo and Wellisz 1979). The results also demonstrate blockholders' significant impact on executive-compensation design. The coefficient on Blockholder_ownership is negative and significant at p-value < 0.05, suggesting that blockholder ownership mitigates agency problems and thus makes it less necessary to align the interests between managers and shareholders via incentive pay.

To summarize, performance-based equity grants are positively associated with the quality of corporate governance, which is reflected in the measures of managerial power and board independency. The findings are consistent with our conjecture from an economic incentive perspective. Rewarding managers with performance-based equity compensation is to stretch managerial effort and promote shareholder value rather than to justify excessive managerial pay.

Tobit Regression Results of CEO Subsample

Next, we focus on a subsample consisting of CEO yearly observations. The reason of examining CEO observations is twofold: (a) prior literature mainly focuses on compensation schemes of CEOs; and (b) the design of CEO compensation is among the major issues drawing increasing attention from public media, investors, regulators, and practitioners. Regression results of the CEO subsample are provided in Table 2.6.

Table 2.6 Tobit Regression Results of CEO Subsample

Variables	*perf_EG*	*perf_EG*
	(1)	(2)
Corporate governance		
#Roles	0.084	0.036
	(0.57)	(0.49)
Tenure	-0.081***	-0.075***
	(-3.07)	(-2.83)
#Other_boards	-0.028	-0.015
	(-0.35)	(-0.18)
#Independent_dir	0.435***	
	(4.42)	
%Independent_dir		5.045***
		(4.01)
Economic determinants		
MtB	0.180***	0.179***
	(4.09)	(4.06)
RET	-0.106	-0.096
	(-0.45)	(-0.42)
Vol_RET	-0.486***	-0.439***
	(-2.63)	(-2.38)
Sales	-0.502**	-0.528***
	(-2.10)	(-2.21)

(continued)

Table 2.6 (continued)

Variables	*perf_EG*	*perf_EG*
	(1)	(2)
Other control variables		
Debt	-2.957***	-2.312***
	(-3.36)	(-2.65)
Other control variables		
LnMV	0.302**	0.513***
	(2.23)	(4.31)
Year_retirement	0.091***	0.082***
	(3.56)	(3.23)
%Ownership	-5.732***	-4.236***
	(-2.75)	(-2.09)
Blockholder_ownership	-0.734	-0.915
	(-0.64)	(-0.79)
industry dummies	Yes	Yes
year dummies	Yes	Yes
# of obs	866	866
Chi-square	1,182	1,179
prob>chi2	<0.01	<0.01

This table presents results of Tobit regressions examining the association between performance-based equity grants and corporate governance features for CEO subsample. The dependent variable in each regression is perf_EG, the ratio of value of performance-based equity pay granted during the current year to annual salary, where performance-vested stock options are valued by Black-Scholes models and all compensation elements are valued at the end of the year; #Roles is the number of committee roles the executive serves; Tenure is the number of years the executive sits on the board; #Other_boards is the number of other boards the executive serves; #Independent_dir is the number of independent directors on the board; %Independent_dir is the proportion of independent directors in the board; MtB is the year-end market-to-book ratio averaged over the five years ended in prior year; RET is market return of the prior year; Vol_RET is the standard deviation of annual stock return for the prior five years; Sales is the sales of prior year scaled by total assets in that year; Debt is the ratio of total liability to the sum of total liability and market value of equity at the end of the year; LnMV is the natural logarithm of market value equity at the end of the year; Year_retirement is the number of years to executive retirement; %Ownership is the ratio of individual executive's share holdings to market capitalization at the end of the year; and Blockholder_ownership represents the aggregate ownership of blockholders who hold at least 5% of the company total shares. t-statistics are reported in the brackets. Significance levels are based on one-tailed tests where there is a prediction of the sign of and coefficient and based on two-tailed tests otherwise. *, **, and *** correspond to 10%, 5%, and 1% significance levels.

CEO subsample consists of 886 CEO yearly observations. Statistics of chi-squares show that the models are significant at p-value < 0.01 in explaining the variation of performance-based equity grants to CEOs. We find the results consistent with prior evidence that the better corporate governance constructed, the more intensively CEOs will be compensated by performance-based equity. More specifically, tenure has a significant and negative association with perf_EG, suggesting that the longer the CEO stays in the current board, the greater power he/she accrues to impact firm decisions and his/her own compensation, and the smaller proportion of performance-based equity in his/her annual compensation.

The measurements of board independency (i.e., #Independent_dir and percentIndependent_dir) are positively related to the grants of performance-based equity, suggesting that the scrutiny from independent directors increases the use of performance targets in managerial equity compensation.

Economic determinants and other control variables exert significant power in explaining performance-based equity grants and the results in general corroborate with prior findings. However, Blockholder_Ownership loses its significance. This suggests that blockholders may have insignificant influence on the design of CEOs' compensation schemes. The coefficients on percentOwnership turn out to be negative and significant, which implies that incentive pay is redundant for CEOs who have already accumulated a large stake in their firms. Further, Year_retirement has a significantly positive association with perf_EG, suggesting that performance-based equity grants are systematically higher for CEOs new in the tenure, thus extending their decision horizons.

ADDITIONAL ANALYSIS

Plausible Alternative Explanation

A plausible alternative explanation for the negative association between performance-based equity grants and tenure is that managers who have long tenure may be holding more performance-based equity than those who have been newly appointed. Prior literature documents that managerial incentives are subject to optimal levels, which suggests that long-tenured managers will receive fewer performance-based equity grants. To explore this plausible alternative explanation, we control for managers' holdings of performance-based equity at the end of t-1 (i.e., the proportion of performance-based equity holdings in total managerial equity holdings at the end of the year t-1) and replicate the prior analyses. Untabulated results show a negative association between the new grants and prior year's holdings of performance-based equity compensation, whereas the main results stay unchanged.

Different Model Specifications

Interdependency among managers, especially for those in the same company, may result in similarity in their compensation contracts. We therefore employ multilevel modeling and allow for firm- and industry-level fixed effects in our sample. Untabulated results are in line with our prior findings and supportive of the economic incentive hypothesis.

We also perform Heckman 2SLS procedure and examine whether firms' self-selection in granting performance-based equity affects the prior results. In the first stage selection model, we include all explanatory variables used in the prior analyses. In the second stage Heckman regression, the inverse Mill's ratio is not statistically significant, suggesting that the self-selection bias from ignoring the decision on grant or not grant performance-based equity does not severely affect the coefficients in the one-pass Tobit models.

Different Measurements for Incentives

As mentioned in Sub-section Measurements of Variables, performance criteria attached to equity grants decrease the probability that managers benefit from those grants. Therefore, standard estimation models (i.e., Black-Scholes fair value model) might overestimate the value of the options. Following prior literature, we discount performance-based equity grants at various rates and replicate previous analyses. Results show that prior findings do not depend on the estimation assumptions.

Performance-Based Stock Options vs. Performance-Based Shares

Stock and stock option compensations have different incentive mechanisms in the sense that managers start to benefit from stock options only after market price exceeds exercise price whereas there is no such price constraint upon stock compensation. So we partition our sample into performance-based stock grants versus performance-based stock option grants and examine the association between corporate governance features and the equity grants within each subsample. Relative to performance-based stock compensation, stock option compensation with performance targets is more extensively rewarded in our sample firms. In particular, 39.27 percent of executive directors were compensated with performance-based stock options whereas only 21.23 percent received performance-based stocks during the investigation period. Empirical results presented in Table 2.7 are in general supportive of economic incentive hypothesis. In particular, long-tenured managers receive less performance-based stocks as well as less performance-based stock options. The grants of both types of equity compensation increase with the number and proportion of independent directors on the board. Differences are observed on control variables. Volatility of prior stock returns and prior sales lose their significance in explaining the variance of performance-vested stock option grants, which is consistent with earlier evidence (Gerakos, Ittner, and Larcker 2007). Further, blockholders' significant influence on equity grants is observed in performance-based stock grants but not in stock option grants. Likewise, the proxy for managerial risk aversion (i.e., Year_retirement) exhibits a significant association with performance-based stock (but not stock option) grants.

Table 2.7 Tobit Regression Results of Stock vs. Stock Option Subsamples

Variables	*perf_SO*	*perf_SO*	*perf_S*	*perf_S*
	(1)	*(2)*	*(3)*	*(4)*
Corporate governance				
#Roles	-0.003	-0.008	0.029	0.022
	(-0.05)	(-0.15)	(0.29)	(0.22)
Tenure	-0.044**	-0.024*	-0.038*	-0.036*
	(-2.26)	(-1.32)	(-1.50)	(-1.39)
#Other_boards	-0.020	-0.015	-0.079	-0.075
	(-0.38)	(-0.30)	(-1.04)	(-1.00)
#Independent_dir	0.105**		0.178**	
	(1.73)		(2.13)	
%Independent_dir		0.954*		2.117**
		(1.27)		(1.92)
Economic determinants				
MtB	0.050**	0.036**	0.150***	0.149***
	(2.57)	(1.97)	(4.55)	(4.53)
RET	-0.036	-0.023	0.106	0.108
	(-0.32)	(-0.24)	(0.44)	(0.44)
Vol_RET	-0.051	-0.021	-0.733***	-0.728***
	(-0.556)	(-0.24)	(-3.69)	(-3.70)
Sales	-0.019	0.029	-1.580***	-1.561***
	(-0.12)	(0.19)	(-6.24)	(-6.10)
Other control variables				
Debt	-1.469***	-10.791*	-0.909*	-0.636
	(-2.63)	(-1.54)	(-1.29)	(-0.94)
LnMV	0.126	0.168**	0.382***	0.473***
	(1.45)	(2.40)	(3.40)	(4.76)
Year_retirement	-0.001	0.003	0.054***	0.051***
	(-0.03)	(0.18)	(2.74)	(2.60)
DummyCEO	0.485**	0.288	0.475*	0.403
	(2.22)	(1.39)	(1.74)	(1.46)
%Ownership	-0.519	-0.065	-2.409	-1.810
	(-0.26)	(-0.04)	(-1.10)	(-0.84)

(continued)

Table 2.7 (continued)

Variables	*perf_SO*	*perf_SO*	*perf_S*	*perf_S*
	(1)	*(2)*	*(3)*	*(4)*
Blockholder_ ownership	-0.593	-0.291	-1.137**	-1.278*
	(-0.85)	(-0.45)	(-1.91)	(-1.56)
industry dummies	Yes	Yes	Yes	yes
year dummies	Yes	Yes	Yes	yes
# of obs	2,987	2,987	2,987	2,987
chi-square	4,315	4,062	2,463	365.31
prob>chi2	<0.01	<0.01	<0.01	<0.01

This table presents results of Tobit regressions examining the association between performance-based equity grants and corporate governance features in performance-based stock option grants versus performance-based stock grants. The dependent variable in Columns (1) and (2) is perf_SO, the ratio of value of performance-vested stock options granted during the current year to annual salary, where performance-vested stock options are valued by Black-Scholes models and all compensation elements are valued at the end of the year; the dependent variable in Columns (3) and (4) is perf_S, the ratio of value of performance-based stocks granted during the current year to annual salary, where all compensation elements are valued at the end of the year; #Roles is the number of committee roles the executive serves; Tenure is the number of years the executive sits on the board; #Other_boards is the number of other boards the executive serves; #Independent_dir is the number of independent directors on the board; %Independent_dir is the proportion of independent directors in the board; MtB is the year-end market-to-book ratio averaged over the five years ended in prior year; RET is market return of the prior year; Vol_RET is the standard deviation of annual stock return for the prior five years; Sales is the sales of prior year scaled by total assets in that year; Debt is the ratio of total liability to the sum of total liability and market value of equity at the end of the year; LnMV is the natural logarithm of market value equity at the end of the year; Year_retirement is the number of years to executive retirement; DummyCEO equals 1 if the executive is CEO of the firm and 0 otherwise; %Ownership is the ratio of individual executive's share holdings to market capitalization at the end of the year; and Blockholder_ownership represents the aggregate ownership of blockholders who hold at least 5% of the company total shares. t-statistics are reported in the brackets. Significance levels are based on one-tailed tests where there is a prediction of the sign of and coefficient and based on two-tailed tests otherwise. *, **, and *** correspond to 10%, 5%, and 1% significance levels.

CONCLUSIONS

Attaching performance targets to managerial equity compensation and thus conditioning their equity benefits upon the achievement of prespecified performance hurdles helps to tighten up shareholder value with managerial paychecks. This compensation vehicle is deemed to be consistent with provisions of best practices outlined in various corporate governance codes. But literature on institutional theories shows that firms have incentives to window-dress and adopt token incentive elements that are desired and advocated by external shareholders.

This chapter examines the effectiveness of performance-based equity grants from a perspective of corporate governance choices. Economic incentive hypothesis predicts a positive association between the use of performance-based equity compensation and good corporate governance structures; rent extraction hypothesis, however, conjectures a negative association. Our empirical results are consistent with the prediction of economic incentive hypothesis. We find that indicators for good corporate governance structures, such as larger influence of independent directors and weaker managerial impact on board decisions, are associated with a greater intensity of performance-based equity compensation. Furthermore, economic determinants play a significant role in explaining firms' practice in managerial compensation. We find that the use of performance-based equity compensation is higher in firms with more growth opportunities, suggesting that such rewards are utilized to retain talents. Consistent with prior literature (Bettis et al. 2010), we also find that this incentive device is used to retain chief executives and extend their decision horizons. Empirical results also suggest that firms rely on the performance-based incentives to improve performance and upscale managerial risk appetite.

As with other studies in corporate governance and managerial compensation, this chapter could be subject to endogeneity problem. Correlated omitted variables may also bias the results. In robustness tests, we adopt multilevel modeling and use industry- and firm-level fixed effects to address the problems. Standard Black-Scholes fair value model may overestimate performance-based option value. Although we employ various discount rates to adjust for the upward bias, the estimation issue may still remain. In addition, because there is no consensus regarding the measurement for corporate governance quality, we ground our measurements on the provisions of best practices outlined in corporate governance codes and focus on governance mechanisms inside the corporations. However, our proxies could still be subject to measurement errors. Future research can further explore these issues.

NOTES

1. For instance, as promoted in the Sarbanes-Oxley Act (2002), the Combined Code (2003), the Tabaksblat Code in the Netherlands (2004), the German Corporate Governance Code (2002), etc.
2. "US Boards Tie CEO Pay to Results," *Wall Street Journal*, February 22, 2006.
3. For example, American Federation of State, County and Municipal Employees' Pension Fund.
4. The usage will be higher if also considering performance-based share plans.
5. Alan Levinsohn (2001) finds that only 5 percent of the 250 largest publicly traded companies condition option vesting upon realized performance during the investigation period.
6. "Better Run U.K. Firms Beat Peers, Study Says," *Wall Street Journal*, February 28, 2008.
7. More than 90 percent of the firms in our sample have split the roles of CEO and the chairman of the board. Due to the lack of variation, the factor of

duality is not included in the analysis. The same applies to gender because more than 97 percent of the executives in our sample are males.

8. The Code strongly suggests that firms improve executive equity compensation schemes by making managers' benefits conditional on "challenging performance criteria," to reduce windfall gains made by the executives and to compensate delivered performance.
9. "Emerging Trends in Corporate Governance 2006," PricewaterhouseCoopers.
10. "Mr. Levin's Stock Options," *Wall Street Journal*, October 12, 2007.
11. Volatility is measured using daily stock return volatility of the last three months. We take the dividend yield of the current year. Risk-free rate is the yield on a treasury security with approximately the same maturity as the years remaining until maturity for the stock options.
12. Conyon, Core, and Guay (2011) discount performance-based equity compensation at 80 percent for evaluation purposes whereas Kuang and Suijs (2006) show that the optimal vesting rate for performance-vested stock options should be higher than 71 percent.
13. Using single indicator for corporate governance is subject to severe measurement error problems and then may bring about inconsistent results (Larcker, Richardson, and Tuna 2007).
14. Listed firms in the U.S. are not subject to requirements of such kind.
15. Executives with temporary employment (i.e., less than three years) are excluded because their compensation contracts might be designed differently.

BIBLIOGRAPHY

Amemiya, T. 1973. "Regression Analysis When the Dependent Variable Is Truncated Normal." *Econometrica* 41:997–1016.

———. 1985. *Advanced Econometrics*. Oxford: Basil Blackwell.

Baiman, S. 1982. "Agency Research in Managerial Accounting: A Survey." Journal *of Accounting Literature* 1:154–213.

Bebchuk, L., and J. Fried. 2004. *Pay without Performance: The Unfulfilled Promise of Executive Compensation*. Cambridge, MA: Harvard University Press.

Bebchuk. L., J. Fried, and D. Walker. 2002. "Managerial Power and Rent Extraction in the Design of Executive Compensation." *University of Chicago Law Review* 69:751–846.

Berger, P., E. Ofek, and D. Yermack. 1997. "Managerial Entrenchment and Capital Structure Decisions." *Journal of Finance* 52:1411–1438.

Bergstresser, D., and T. Philippon. 2006. "CEO Incentives and Earnings Management." *Journal of Financial Economics* 80:511–529.

Bertrand, M., and S. Mullainathan. 2001. "Are CEOs Rewarded for Luck? The Ones without Principals Are." *Quarterly Journal of Economics* 116:901–932.

Bettis, C., J. Bizjak, J. Coles, and K. Swaminathan. 2010. Stock and Option Grants with Performance-based Vesting Provisions. *Review of Financial Studies* 23: 3849–3888.

Bhagat, S. and B. Bolton. 2008. Corporate Governance and Firm Performance. *Journal of Corporate Finance* 14:257–273.

Boyd, B. 1994. "Board Control and CEO Compensation." *Strategic Management Journal* 15:335–344.

Buck, T., A. Bruce, B. Main, and H. Udueni. 2003. "Long Term Incentive Plans, Executive Pay and UK Company Performance." *Journal of Management Studies* 40:1709–1727.

Burns, N., and S. Kedia. 2006. "The Impact of Performance-Based Compensation on Misreporting." *Journal of Financial Economics* 79:35–67.

Bushman, R., and A. Smith. 2001. "Financial Accounting Information and Corporate Governance." *Journal of Accounting and Economics* 32:237–334.

Cadbury, A. 1992. *Report of the Committee on the Financial Aspects of Corporate Governance.* London: Gee.

Calvo, G., and S. Wellisz. 1979. "Hierarchy, Ability and Income Distribution." *Journal of Political Economy* 87:991–1010.

Camara, A. 2001. "The Pricing of Relative Performance Based Incentives for Executive Compensation." *Journal of Business, Finance and Accounting* 28:1149–1188.

Cheng, Q., and T. Warfield. 2005. "Equity Incentives and Earnings Management." *Accounting Review* 80:441–476.

Collins, C., and K. Clark. 2003. "Strategic Human Resource Practices, Top Management Team Social Networks and Firm Performance." *Academy of Management Journal* 46:740–751.

Combined Code. 2003. *The Combined Code on Corporate Governance.* London: Financial Reporting Council.

Conyon, M., J. Core and W. Guay. 2011. Are US CEOs Paid More than UK CEOs? Inferences from Risk-Adjusted Pay. *Review of Financial Studies* 24:402–438.

Core, J., R. Holthausen, and D. Larcker. 1999. "Corporate Governance, Chief Executive Officer Compensation, and Firm Performance." *Journal of Financial Economics* 51:371–406.

Daily, C, J. Johnson, A. Ellstrand, and D. Dalton. 1998. "Compensation Committee Composition as a Determinant of CEO Compensation." *Academy of Management Journal* 41:209–220.

Fama, E., and C. Jensen. 1983. "Separation of Ownership and Control." *Journal of Law and Economics* 26:301–325.

Gerakos, J., C. Ittner, and D. Larcker. 2007. "The Structure of Performance Stock Option Grants." In *Essays in Accounting Theory in Honour of Joel S. Demski*, ed. R. Antle, P. Liang, and F. Gjesdal, 227–250. New York: Springer.

Gompers, P., J. Ishii, and A. Metrick. 2003. "Corporate Governance and Equity Prices." *Quarterly Journal of Economics* 118:107–155.

Greenbury, R. 1995. *Directors' Remuneration: Report of a Study Group Chaired by Sir Richard Greenbury.* London: Gee.

Hallock, K. 1997. "Reciprocally Interlocking Boards of Directors and Executive Compensation." *Journal of Financial and Quantitative Analysis* 32:331–344.

Hart, O., and B. Holmstrom. 1987. *The Theory of Contracts, in Advances in Economic Theory. Fifth World Congress.* Cambridge: Cambridge University Press.

Hermalin, B., and M. Weisbach. 2003. "Boards of Directors as an Endogenously Determined Institution: A Survey of the Economic Literature." *Economic Policy Review* 9:7–26.

Higgs, D. 2003. *Review of the Role and Effectiveness of Non-Executive Directors.* London: DTI.

Holmstrom, B. 1979. "Moral Hazard and Observability." *Bell Journal of Economic* 10:74–91.

Jensen, M. 1986. "Agency Costs of Free Cash Flow, Corporate Finance, and Takeovers." *American Economic Review* 76:323–329.

———. 2003. "Paying People to Lie: The Truth about the Budgeting Process." *European Financial Management* 9:379–406.

Jensen, M., and W. Meckling. 1976. "Theory of Firm: Managerial Behavior, Agency Costs and Ownership Structure." *Journal of Financial Economics* 4:305–360.

Jensen, M., and K. Murphy. 1990. "Performance Pay and Top-Management Incentives." *Journal of Political Economy* 98.225–264.

Jensen, M., K. Murphy, and E. Wruck. 2004. "Remuneration: Where We've Been, How We Got to Here, What Are the Problems, and How to Fix Them." Working

Paper, Harvard Business School, Marshall School of Business—University of Southern California, and Econalytics.
Johnson, S., H. Ryan and Y. Tian. 2009. Managerial Incentives and Corporate Fraud: The Sources of Incentives Matter. *Review of Finance* 13:115–145.
Johnson, S., and Y. Tian. 2000. "The Value and Incentive Effects of Nontraditional Executive Stock Option Plans." *Journal of Financial Economics* 57:3–34.
Kuang, Y. 2008. "Performance-Vested Stock Options and Earnings Management." *Journal of Business, Finance and Accounting* 35:1049–1078.
Kuang, Y., and B. Qin. 2009. "Performance-Vested Stock Options and Interest Alignment." *British Accounting Review* 41:46–61.
Kuang, Y., and J. Suijs. 2006. "Incentive Effects of Performance-Vested Stock Options." Working Paper, VU University Amsterdam and Tilburg University.
Lambert, R., D. Larcker, and K. Weigelt. 1993. "The Structure of Organizational Incentives." *Administrative Science Quarterly* 38:438–461.
Larcker, D., S. Richardson, and I. Tuna. 2007. "Corporate Governance, Accounting Outcomes, and Organizational Performance." *Accounting Review* 82:963–1008.
Levinsohn, A. 2001. "A Garden of Stock Options Helps Harvest Talent." *Strategic Finance* 82:81–85.
MacAvoy, P., and I. Millstein. 1998. "The Active Board of Directors and Performance of the Large Publicly Traded Corporation." *Columbia Law Review* 98:1283–1321.
———. 2003. *The Recurrent Crisis in Corporate Governance*. New York: Palgrave.
Nagar, V., D. Nanda, and P. Wysocki. 2003. "Discretionary Disclosure and Stock-Based Incentives." *Journal of Accounting and Economics* 34:283–309.
Rosen, S. 1982. "Authority, Control and the Distribution of Earnings." *Bell Journal of Economics* 13:311–323.
———. 1986. Prizes and Incentives in Elimination Tournaments. *The American Economic Review*, 76: 701–715.
Ryan, H., and R. Wiggins III. 2004. "Who Is in Whose Pocket? Director Compensation, Board Independence, and Barriers to Effective Monitoring." *Journal of Finance* 73:497–542.
Sarbanes-Oxley Act. 2002. One Hundred Seventh Congress of the United States of America, Second Session.
Sautner, Z. and M. Weber. 2011. Corporate governance and the design of stock option programs. Working paper. University of Amsterdam and University of Mannheim.
Shleifer, A., and R. Vishny. 1997. "A Survey of Corporate Governance." *Journal of Finance* 52:737–783.
Tobin, J. 1958. "Estimation for Relationships with Limited Dependent Variables." *Econometrica* 26:24–36.
Warfield, T., J. Wild, and K. Wild. 1995. "Managerial Ownership, Accounting Choices, and Informativeness of Earnings." *Journal of Accounting and Economics* 20:61–91.
Westphal, J., and E. Zajac. 1994. "Substance and Symbolism in CEOs' Long-Term Incentive Plans." *Administrative Science Quarterly* 39:367–390.
———. 1998. "The Symbolic Management of Stockholders: Corporate Governance Reforms and Shareholder Reactions." *Administrative Science Quarterly* 43:127–153.
Zajac, E., and J. Westphal. 1995. "Accounting for the Explanations of CEO Compensation: Substance and Symbolism." *Administrative Science Quarterly* 40:283–308.

3 A Theoretical Framework for Voluntary Corporate Governance

Rodrigo Zeidan

INTRODUCTION

One of the cornerstones of corporate governance research is the idea that better corporate governance practices are a source of competitive advantage, either through lower capital costs or higher stock prices. Anand (2005, 19) is an example of such a view: "companies have a strong incentive to institute corporate governance practices voluntarily in order to deter or prevent investors from devaluing the company." Assuming this is true irrespective of company or market characteristics, market competition would lead companies to adopt better corporate governance practices and would result in dynamic positive feedback, and there wouldn't be any need for best corporate governance codes or any form of stringent regulations.

In this chapter I argue that the incentives to pursue voluntary corporate governance are much more complex than simple market mechanisms, and also depend on the institutional framework and endogenous and exogenous mechanisms faced by companies in different contexts. Here I implicitly follow the skepticism of Shleifer and Vishny (1997) regarding competition as the main driver of voluntary corporate governance—the authors argue:

> While we agree that product market competition is probably the most powerful force toward economic efficiency in the world, we are skeptical that it alone can solve the problem of corporate governance. One could imagine a scenario in which entrepreneurs rent labor and capital on the spot market every minute at a competitive price, and hence have no resources left over to divert to their own use. But in actual practice, production capital is highly specific and sunk, and entrepreneurs cannot rent it every minute. (738)

Especially relevant to this discussion is geography: the structure of capital markets varies significantly around the world, and thus there are different incentives dependent on each particular market for companies to adopt better governance practices. Whereas the American market probably presents the best structure in terms of market incentives for companies to reduce information asymmetry through the adoption of better corporate governance practices, that is not true in many markets around the world, especially in emerging markets. In this chapter I try to derive a theoretical framework that encompasses different possible capital market structures in the search of a model that maps the incentives for the voluntary adoption of better corporate governance.

CAPITAL MARKET STRUCTURE AND CORPORATE GOVERNANCE

There are two basic contexts or paradigmatic models to classify international environments of corporate governance. First is the Anglo-Saxon model, where property is dispersed and the stock market has an important role in allowing liquidity and facilitating the exit of shareholders. Variations in stock prices reflect the amount of agreement, by market players, with the strategies traced by the publicly listed companies and the evaluation of their performance. The control systems of corporate governance are strongly influenced by the negotiation of shares and takeovers.

In the second context, known as the Japanese-German model, the ownership is concentrated in banks or economic groups (or in family-owned companies in many emergent countries), and there are cross holdings, with frequent involvement of workers and representatives of society on the boards of directors. This concentration of ownership fosters the use of internal instruments of control exercised by shareholders.

These two models can also be classified as exit and voice (Buck et al. 1999). In the Anglo-Saxon model, or exit, the behavior of managers is constrained by the threat of shareholders to sell their shares and leave the company. In the Japanese-German model, or voice, there is greater involvement of shareholders in the business decisions and controlling mechanisms, including the participation of nonshareholders, like employees, on the board.

The definition of these models helps to establish paradigmatic assumptions about the existence of links between economic, social, cultural, and institutional development of a country and, in particular, the methods of financing companies and adoption of corporate governance practices. There are important research questions regarding the identification of particular forms of ownership in a country or region. This identification problem can arise from two kinds of pressure: exogenous and endogenous pressures.

In analyzing an endogenous perspective, Demsetz and Lehn (1985) argue that the ownership is the outcome of decisions made by shareholders in order to maximize their profits. That means the ownership structure is an endogenous outcome of share trading by profit-maximizing shareholders (Kapopoulos and Lazaretou 2007). In a later study, Demsetz and Villalonga (2001) argued that the ownership structure should be modeled simultaneously as an amalgam of shareholdings owned by persons with different interests, including managers. In their words, "persistent diffuseness of a company's ownership structure plausibly serves the company's shareholders better than would a concentrated ownership structure, even if more diffuseness of ownership would allow professional management to divert more of the company's resources to serve its own narrow interests" (216).

However, the endogenous model is unable to answer the structure of family-owned companies in many countries. A business structure based on state-owned and family enterprises does not appear to be one that solely seeks to maximize profits. Thomsen and Pedersen (1996), following an exogenous perspective, place two hypotheses for investigation. First, what they call the industry effect—corporate ownership patterns will vary across industries beyond what differences in company size can explain. Second, the nation effect—that is, political, institutional, and cultural differences between nations will have an independent impact on corporate ownership patterns beyond what differences in industrial structure can explain. They found nation-specific differences in the ownership structures of companies in Europe, and also found that economic conditions like industry and company size influence those structures.

This exogenous perspective can also be associated with the issues of culture and institutional environment. La Porta, Lopez-de-Silanes, and Shleifer (1998) related ownership dispersion and the system of law, and found that in countries where the judicial system does not present good protection for investors there is a high concentration of ownership as a substitute for the weak protection. An example of costs associated with this concentrated ownership structure is that these companies "probably face difficulty raising equity finance, since minority investors fear expropriation by managers and concentrated owners" (1151).

We arrive then at the situation that voluntary corporate governance is the result of two different pressures: the structure of capital markets (either voice or exit) and institutional and cultural national idiosyncrasies. Countries with exit models, like the United States, present the best environment for competition to enhance the benefits of voluntary corporate governance, whereas the reverse is true in countries where voice is more relevant—the possibilities of gains through concentrated ownership are higher and thus there is less benefit in adopting higher standards of corporate governance.

Besides the main structure of capital markets—exit or voice—institutional and cultural idiosyncrasies would also change the cost-benefit ratio of voluntary corporate governance for companies in different countries. This would allow for a continuum of different incentives for the adoption of corporate governance best practices, and the ultimate companies' decision would also be based on the internal factors that would translate the different incentives to a particular decision-ruling mechanism. Because different environments change the incentives for companies to adopt better corporate governance practices, and in many cases render market competition ineffective as a driver of voluntary corporate governance, I turn to ask: which internal factors to the companies would yield better corporate governance practices, even in an environment where companies have few external incentives to do so, like in the case of many countries that follow the voice model? Here I depart from the literature, which aside from some papers that deal with cross-country examples and empirical investigations (Drobetz, Schillhofer, and Zimmermann 2003 for Germany; Black, Jang, and Kim 2006 for Korea; de Jong et al. 2002 for the Netherlands; Beiner et al. 2004 for Switzerland; Leal and Carvalhal-da-Silva 2005 for Brazil; Black 2001 for Russia; Bauer, Guenster, and Otten 2004 and 2008 for Europe; and Bauer et al. 2008 for Japan), mainly focus on corporate governance issues in the U.S. market, where there are enough market incentives that competition is a major driver of governance best practices.

INTERNAL DETERMINANTS OF VOLUNTARY CORPORATE GOVERNANCE

The idea that market competition is the only driver of voluntary corporate governance is insufficient to explain the patterns of voluntary corporate governance around the world. Looking at the company as the decision unit, market considerations are only one class of variables to be taken into consideration in the decision to adopt better corporate governance practices. Here I will try to analyze each component of the decision vector, trying to develop a theoretical framework that encompasses the decision model irrespective of the structure of each country's capital markets. In this way, companies in countries in capital markets with the Anglo-Saxon structure (exit) would be more affected by market competition variables than companies in the countries with the Japanese-German (voice) structure. The main theoretical division is then between market and nonmarket variables influencing the companies' decisions.

Market Variables

There are three ways in which market mechanisms can influence the companies' decisions to adopt better governance practices: market value, lower capital costs, and realized positive feedback. The first two are self-explanatory and are the focus of most papers on corporate governance practices. The positive feedback argument is related to the two paradigmatic models, exit and voice. In the Anglo-Saxon model, companies have the incentive to pursue better corporate practices just because all other companies are acting in the same way. This incentive is already realized by past market developments, and deviation can be severely punished. This would be translated in a special case of realized path dependence. Companies with poor governance are readily devalued, and arguments like the one advanced by Anand (2005) hold. One of the main changes happening in many markets around the world is the development of capital markets to induce positive feedback. This is being done through new regulations and codes of conduct, or even the creation of higher corporate governance standards markets, like the Neuer Markt for technology shares in Germany and the Novo Mercado in Brazil. Even though some authors (one example is Corbett and Jenkinson 1996) have questioned the foundations of the Anglo-Saxon model, arguing that self-financing is more important than market funding, there is clear evidence of peer pressure in the corporate governance decisions of companies in the U.S. and UK markets, and some countries are trying to emulate that by trying to create incentives that will trigger positive feedbacks in the adoption of better corporate governance practices by local companies.

Nonmarket Variables

Controlling shareholders have a strong incentive to maintain a poor governance structure in many countries. An anecdotal example shows this: after the crisis of 2008, a listed company from the phone sector in Brazil with excess cash holdings announced a record dividend payment of R$3.07 per share, when the share was at R$31. The reason for this record dividend of almost 10 percent of the company's value was that the controlling shareholder was another company that suffered a strong liquidity squeeze during the crisis and used the excess cash of the phone company to ease the liquidity pressure of the parent company. Small shareholders were of course appalled by the dividend payment and many tried to stop the company from disbursing an amount of cash that made the company much less liquid to pursue new projects. When faced with possibilities like this many companies would rather maintain a poor governance structure than choose better practices, even if those practices come with higher market value and lower capital costs. In fact, many agency problems that are prevalent in the American market disappear in a context where companies have owners that can single-handedly decide all strategies and have a vested interest in the managers' decisions.

In markets where companies with controlling shareholders are the norm, like in many countries with voice models, what are the reasons that may give companies incentives to pursue better corporate governance practices—which incentives can supplant the many benefits from ownership? I give four reasons for a comprehensive model of voluntary corporate governance that deals with nonmarket variables: exit via liquidity, the role of institutional investors, conflict resolution, and path dependence.

Exit

The necessity of controlling shareholders to exit via the market may make companies search for better corporate governance practices—what Aguilera and Jackson (2003) call liquidity, or "the ability of owners to exit by selling their stakes without a loss of price" (451). Controlling shareholders can exit through selling the controlling shares as a block or via the market. Usually the first is preferred, but many reasons can make exit via the market attractive, such as periods of market boom, overvaluation of the company, or even capital market imperfections—there may not be any agent with the ability to raise enough capital to purchase the whole block of controlling shares. In exiting via the market good corporate governance practices can enhance the liquidity of the company's shares, and reduce information asymmetry that will make the company more attractive for investors—the same information asymmetry that allows controlling shareholders to pursue expropriation strategies.

Institutional Investors

Many institutional investors, like pension funds, public investment banks, and others, have important stakes in publicly listed companies. Pension funds, particularly, are active shareholders and usually try to promote corporate governance best practices as part of their long-term strategies (for a comprehensive analysis of shareholders activism and its importance in promoting governance best practices, see Gillan and Starks 2000). In many countries that follow the Japanese-German model institutional investors are the leading agents of corporate governance transformation. One such example is Brazil, where companies like Previ and Petros (both pension funds) and BNDES (one of the biggest public investment banks in the world) are active promoters of changes in the governance structure of companies in which they have significant voice.

Conflict Resolution

Conflict between controlling shareholders or between shareholders and management can lead to better governance practices by turning implicit strategies in explicit company policies. Ingley and Van-Der Walt (2004) explored this idea in the American context, with recommendations for changing the architecture of boards of directors. In the concentrated ownership structure of many countries conflicts between shareholders and the board are rare, because controlling shareholders can just change the board to align their interests with management. Even so, conflicts between shareholders with big stakes are much more common, and sometimes result in periods of power vacuums that can be explored by management to enforce better corporate governance practices with the objective of more board independence.

Path Dependence

Although initial conditions for capital markets structure are an important reason for differences between capital markets in the world and are a main source of the theoretical separation between the Anglo-Saxon and Japanese-German models, they are also a source of convergence as markets develop. Bebchuk and Roe (1999) have shown the relevance of path dependence in shaping capital markets, and corporate governance as a result. As markets develop, there should be a natural process of convergence on corporate governance practices around the world, even if only as a result of enough companies going through changes that would lead them to, at one point in time, adopt better governance practices. Because reversing such practices is costly, the amount of companies adopting improved practices should be increasing at all times and positive feedback should ensure a better governance environment in the future. However, differently from the market mechanism of positive feedback, this is a tentative path dependence, because as Schmidt and Spindler (2002) have argued, there is a possibility of 'inefficient convergence,' in which bad governance practices are reinforced over time. Even so, and especially in emergent markets that want to rapidly increase the relevance of national capital markets, mechanisms that enhance efficient convergence are procured as a way to enhance markets' liquidity. Adding to that, the development of capital markets can change one of the more important characteristics of capital markets in emerging markets, that of ownership culture. In many countries there is a cultural preference to concentrated ownership, and family-owned companies are the norm. One such example is Brazil, where the property culture is so prevalent that the number of companies with dispersed ownership is very small. Zeidan and Fontes Filho (2008) present a historical perspective that shows that path dependence is changing this cultural landscape, but at a slow pace.

FINAL CONSIDERATIONS

The idea that corporate governance stems from agency problems is central to the Anglo-Saxon model, but is insufficient to explain the patterns of corporate governance practices around the world. Instead of codes and rules of conducts, here I focus on voluntary mechanisms for companies to pursue better governance practices. I separate the mechanisms in market and nonmarket mechanisms, and argue that whereas market mechanisms may be sufficient to explain the voluntary decision in companies located in markets with exit characteristics, for companies in emergent markets and other places with Japanese-German characteristics, nonmarket mechanisms can play a large role in the decision to voluntarily adopt better governance practices.

I classify the nonmarket mechanisms as four: exit, institutional investors, conflict resolution, and path dependence. These four mechanisms have been explored in the literature, and here what I try to achieve is to formalize a theoretical framework that can explain companies' decisions irrespective of capital markets' structures. Understanding which variables are relevant to the companies' decisions is particularly relevant for the design of public policy that can try to foster an environment conducive to self-determination of better corporate governance practices, complementing the top-down approach of codes of conduct and other kinds of regulation.

BIBLIOGRAPHY

Aguilera, R.V., and G. Jackson. 2003. "The Cross-National Diversity of Corporate Governance. Dimensions and Determinants." *Academy of Management Review* 28:447–465.

Anand, A.I. 2005. "Voluntary vs. Mandatory Corporate Governance: Towards an Optimal Regulatory Framework." Bepress Legal Series, Paper 566.

Bauer, R., N. Guenster, and R. Otten. 2004. "Empirical Evidence on Corporate Governance in Europe. The Effect on Stock Returns. Firm Value and Market Performance." *Journal of Asset Management* 5:91–104.

Bauer, R., B. Frijns, R. Otten, and A. Tourani. 2008. "The Impact of Corporate Governance on Corporate Market performance: Evidence from Japan." *Pacific-Basin Finance Journal* 16(3):236–251.

Bebchuk, L., and M.J. Roe. 1999. "A Theory of Path Dependence in Corporate Ownership and Governance." *Stanford Law Review* 52:127–170.

Beiner, S., W. Drobetz, F. Schmid, and H. Zimmermann. 2004. "An Integrated Framework of Corporate Governance and Firm Valuation. Evidence from Switzerland." ECGI Paper 34/2004.

Black, B.S. 2001. "The Corporate Governance Behavior and Market Value of Russian Firms." *Emerging Markets Review* 2:89–108.

Black, B., H. Jang, and W. Kim. 2006. "Predicting Firms' Corporate Governance Choices. Evidence from Korea." *Journal of Corporate Finance* 12:660–691.

Buck, T., I. Filatotchev, M. Wright, and V. Zhukov. 1999. "Corporate Governance and Employee Ownership in an Economic Crisis: Entrepreneurial Strategies in the Former USSR." *Journal of Comparative Economics* 27 (3): 459–474.

Corbett, J., and T. Jenkinson. 1996. "The Financing of Industry. 1970–1989: An International Comparison." *Journal of the Japanese and International Economies* 10 (1): 71–96.

de Jong, A., D.V. Dejong, G. Mertens, and C. Wasley. 2005. "The Role of Self-Regulation in Corporate Governance. Evidence and Implications from the Netherlands." *Journal of Corporate Finance* 11:473–503.

Demsetz, H., and K. Lehn. 1985. "The Structure of Corporate Ownership: Causes and Consequences." *Journal of Political Economy* 93:1155–1177.

Demsetz, H., and B. Villalonga. 2001. "Ownership Structure and Corporate Performance." *Journal of Corporate Finance* 7:209–233.

Drobetz, W., A. Schillhofer, and H. Zimmermann. 2003. "Corporate Governance and Expected Stock Returns. Evidence from Germany." Working Paper No. 02/03, WWZ, Department of Finance, University Basel, Switzerland.

Gillan, S., and L. Starks. 2000. "Corporate Governance Proposals and Shareholder Activism: The Role of Institutional Investors." *Journal of Financial Economics* 57:275–305.

Ingley, C., and N.T. Van-Der Walt. 2004. "Institutional Investors and Conflicts of Interest." *Corporate Governance: An International Review* 12 (4): 534–551.

Kapopoulos, P., and S. Lazaretou. 2007. "Corporate Ownership Structure and Firm Performance: Evidence from Greek Firms." *Corporate Governance: An International Review* 15 (2): 144–158.

La Porta, R., F. Lopez-de-Silanes, and A. Shleifer. 1998. "Law and Finance." *Journal of Political Economy* 106(6):1113–1155

Leal, R., and A. Carvalhal-da-Silva. 2005. "Corporate Governance and Value in Brazil and Chile." Working Paper, Inter-American Development Bank/Latin American Research Network.

Schmidt, R., and G. Spindler. 2002. "Path Dependence. Corporate Governance and Complementarity." *International Finance* 5 (3): 311–333.

Shleifer, A., and R. Vishny. 1997. "A Survey of Corporate Governance." *Journal of Finance* 52:737–783.

Thomsen, S., and T. Pedersen. 1996. "Nationality and Ownership Structures: The 100 Largest Companies in Six European Nations." *Management International Review* 36:149–166.

Zeidan, R.M., and J.R. Fontes Filho. 2008. "Corporate Governance and Industrialization: An Historical Approach." Paper presented at the 12th Annual Conference of the European Society for the History of Economic Thought, Prague, Czech Republic, May 15–17.

4 Managers' Behavior When Governance Is Weak

Ralf Steinhauser

INTRODUCTION

It is well established that managers' personal interests and therefore their incentives can differ from those of the firm owners.[1] Managers in charge of firms' operations bear little direct financial cost when pursuing their own goals rather than maximizing shareholder value.[2] Corporate governance mechanisms are used to better align the incentives of managers with shareholders. These mechanisms include legal protection of shareholders, effective boards of directors, regulations in firm charters, performance-dependent compensation for managers, and takeover threats from the market, all of which can be found in today's firm structures. The strength of corporate governance in a corporation determines the strength of the profit constraint in managers' decision making. For example, if managers fear losing their jobs after a hostile takeover, they may be more inclined to maximize shareholder profits and put their other personal interests aside.

But what are managers' personal interests? When governance weakens, what do managers do with their newly gained freedom? Understanding managers' preferences is important to designing corporate governance mechanisms and to predicting impacts of changes in government policy toward corporate governance on firm outcomes, such as the environmental or social performance of the firm. The changes in governance rules by the Securities and Exchange Commission as a result of the 2002 Sarbanes-Oxley Act highlight the need for a better understanding in this regard.[3] The act covers issues such as auditor independence, corporate governance, and enhanced financial disclosure. The new regulations are aimed at strengthening firms' governance in order to avoid accounting scandals. My research shows that firms' environmental or social performance might also be affected.

The existing literature on the effect of weaker governance on managers' behavior consistently finds evidence that managers pursue personal interests when given more freedom. Bertrand and Mullainathan (1999) find that higher protection raises CEO compensation. Looking at plant-level outcomes, Bertrand and Mullainathan (2003) find that workers' wages increase with weak governance and that there are fewer plant openings and closings. Garvey and Hanka (1999) look at firms' leverage and find that managers with more protection reduce their use of debt. Finally, Gompers, Ishii, and Metrick (2003) conclude that weaker governance leads to lower firm performance, whereas capital expenditure and acquisitions increase. My research contributes to this literature and expands our understanding of managerial behavior to the domain of social and environmental preferences.

My study is unique as I merge two previously distinct firm-level data sets. Corporate governance data on antitakeover provisions from the Investor Responsibility Research Center is combined with data on firms' Corporate Social Responsibility (CSR) performance from KLD Research & Analytics. Data on firms' social and environmental performance offer a way to observe outcomes as a result of specific management decisions. How much charitable giving a firm does, or how strong its voluntary pollution prevention programs are, is decided by the firm's management.[4] Other firm characteristics are obtained from Compustat North America, resulting in a large longitudinal panel. The combination of the three data sets allows me to observe how changes in corporate governance affect managers' behavior with regards to social preferences, conditional on other firm characteristics such as size and earnings. The large number of social and environmental indicators in the KLD data allows me to look at a variety of decisions that reflect managers' diverse ethical principles.

My results suggest that managers with more protection engage in stronger pollution prevention, give more money to charity, promote employment and equal opportunities for women and minorities, implement progressive gay and lesbian policies, and improve benefits to workers. I also find that managers with weak governance neglect some of their core duties so that the firm incurs more environmental fines and regulatory problems and produces fewer profitable innovations.

I connect two areas of literature in my chapter that have traditionally been fairly separated. One is the management literature that looks at causes and effects of CSR. The second is the literature on antitakeover provisions (ATPs). There are a few studies that have looked at the link between different measures of corporate governance and CSR. Coffey and Wang (1998) find that more managerial control is linked with higher charitable giving, and Mahoney and Thorne (2005) find that Canadian firms have less environmental problems when managers have a long-term compensation plan. McGuire, Dow, and Argheyd (2003) argue that increased long-term salary incentives lead to a decrease in negative social performance. These past studies employ cross-sectional data or short panels, which results in them not being able to properly control for some of the unobserved heterogeneity between firms. I contribute to this part of the literature by looking at the effect of corporate governance in the form of ATPs on CSR employing much longer and wider panel data. My use of panel data allows me to control for unobservable time invariant firm heterogeneity. My theory reconciles the seemingly contradictory findings in the existing literature that weaker governance leads to an increase in CSR but that stronger governance can also lead to an increase in CSR. I show that it is important to understand the relative preferences of managers and shareholders based on the costs and benefits of individual CSR measures.

The second literature on ATPs is spread across the fields of law, management, and finance, and looks at the effectiveness of ATPs in protecting the interests of shareholders. ATPs are takeover defenses in the form of bylaws or amendments to the charter that restrict shareholder rights.[5] Their aim is to make unwanted takeovers by raider firms more difficult. The popularity of ATP adoptions was a response to an increased threat of hostile takeovers driven by the rise of the junk bond market in the 1980s. When putting an ATP in place, the potential harm of a hostile takeover is traded off against increased manager freedom. The empirical literature on the link between ATPs and shareholders' wealth finds mixed results and leaves the question open as to whether the main effect of ATPs is a higher takeover premium or greater managerial entrenchment at shareholders' expense.[6] My findings support the view that ATPs lead to a costly entrenchment of managers from the shareholders' perspective. More resources are allocated to social and environmental projects with uncertain benefits for shareholder value, whereas other unambiguously important manager duties get neglected. Overall, my results suggest an increase in environmental and social performance of firms under weaker governance, but I also find for some types of CSR a shift to a lower performance.

CORPORATE GOVERNANCE AND MANAGERS' BEHAVIOR

As discussed earlier, the existing literature on manager behavior under weak governance finds managers to behave rather opportunistically with regard to shareholder interests. Bertrand and Mullainathan argue that their observations can be explained by a "quiet life" model of manager behavior. Managers with slack governance prefer to avoid difficult decisions and costly efforts. This is supported by their findings of fewer plant openings and closings when takeover laws are in place. They also observe higher wages for workers, even though total factor productivity goes down. This, they argue, is a way for the manager to avoid trouble with employees and unions. Additional support for the "quiet life" hypothesis comes from Malmendier and Tate (2005), who find that CEOs who win awards subsequently write more books and underperform as managers while getting higher compensations.

In this chapter, I suggest that managers seek something more than simply a "quiet life." I propose that managers seek a "good life" in which they will raise their subjective well-being through a combination of quiet life and good deeds. According to my hypothesis, when governance constraints are relaxed, managers will put more effort and resources into environmentally and socially responsible projects, which were restricted under profitability constraints to a lower level than the manager would prefer.

For example, managers could prefer to spend more of the firms' money on charitable giving or strong pollution prevention than is economically optimal, or they would like to raise workers' benefits to a level where the firm will not experience an equivalent increase in worker productivity. Most of the CSR indicators in the data I use fall into this category, where managers prefer a higher level of CSR than shareholders do.

My second hypothesis predicts that managers reduce the effort and resources put into projects that are part of their core duties, such as avoiding fines and penalties for pollution or other violations, when governance is slack. For these types of CSR, the profit-maximizing level will be higher than the managers' preferred level of CSR implementation. In such cases, the effort needed to be put into these core duties to get to the optimal level from the shareholders' perspective might outweigh the "warm glow" managers receive from it.

There are two cases apart from the perfect alignment of managers' and shareholders' interests. The manager could prefer a higher or a lower level of CSR compared to the shareholders' optimum. The case in which the manager prefers a higher level of a given type of CSR I will refer to as "type I" CSR. This will particularly be the case for voluntary actions of the firm that have an ambiguous effect on shareholder value at high levels, but give the manager a strong feeling of doing something good. This will also be true for CSR that has a "quiet life" component where the manager can avoid conflict situations.

The second case is when the manager prefers a lower level of CSR compared to the profit-maximizing level. As discussed earlier, this might be the case for core duties that require great effort, which outweighs the relatively small "warm glow" the manager gets from the implementation of the higher, profit-maximizing level of CSR. Under strong governance, we will be at the optimal level from the shareholders' point of view where the manager implements the profit-maximizing level of CSR. With a weakening in governance, the manager will have more freedom to follow his personal goals and we would expect to see a decrease in such a type of CSR, which I will refer to as "type II" CSR.

To sum up the theoretical motivation, managers with more governance slack may devote less of their personal energy and company resources to core or profit maximization (type II) kinds of CSR and will shift their efforts into voluntary ethical projects such as helping the needy or protecting the environment (type I CSRs). Thus, my two main testable hypotheses are:

Hypothesis I: When governance is slack, managers increase environmental and social performance on indicators that are less profitable and give the manager a "warm glow."

Hypothesis II: When governance is slack, managers decrease environmental and social performance on indicators that are profitable and give the manager a relatively small "warm glow."

DATA AND METHODOLOGY

Data Sources

The main data source used in this chapter is CSR ratings by KLD Research & Analytics, Inc.[7] The KLD data is the most comprehensive data source for CSR ratings and is the dominant data used in the CSR research literature. Each firm is identified by name, ticker symbol, and Committee on Uniform Securities Identification Procedures (CUSIP) code and is rated on about one hundred indicators.[8] The indicators are grouped in qualitative issue categories. The relevant categories for this study that cover the set of environmental and social preferences are community relations, diversity issues, employee relations, and environmental performance. This leaves me with thirty-three specific types of CSR rated for each firm. Each of those four categories has multiple strengths and concerns, which refer to outstanding positive types of CSR or outstanding negative CSR, respectively. KLD rates indicators as "one" if firms show a certain outstanding performance and "zero" if the particular strength or concern doesn't apply to a firm. I will refer to those binary strength and concern ratings as *indicators*. For example, in the community category, "charitable giving" is one of the strength indicators, and firms are rated with "one" if they give at least 1.5 percent of their net earnings before taxes to charity. A concern indicator in the same category, "negative economic impact," is rated as "one" if the firm's actions resulted in major controversies concerning its economic impact on the community. A list of all indicators sorted by categories with a short description is included in Table 4.2.

Data on ATPs comes from the Investor Responsibility Research Center (IRRC), which collects data biennially on ATPs. The data cover twenty-two typical antitakeover defenses commonly adopted by firms.[9] Also included in the data is the Gompers-Ishii-Metrick index on weak governance, which counts all antitakeover amendments a firm has adopted or laws put in place in the firm's state of legislation, such that a *larger* number in the index is an indicator for *weaker* shareholder rights or higher management power. I will focus my research on a subset of six ATPs that Gompers, Ishii, and Metrick (2003) classify as manager protections whose adoptions by the firm will lead to a clear weakening in corporate governance.[10] These amendments, which were specifically designed to insure directors and top managers against job related liability or to compensate them in case of job termination, are summed to an index that I will refer to as "manager protection" throughout the chapter.

I combine both data sets with Standard & Poor's Compustat North America. I match all three data sets by CUSIP number and supplement it by checking by hand.[11] Summary statistics for my matched sample of 2,230 firms with 12,896 firm-year observations are reported in Table 4.1 for the first year (1991) as well as the last year (2005) in my sample. It is worth pointing out that the number of firms in my matched panel increased sharply over the period from 572 to 1,702. The mean market capitalization of firms in my matched sample has increased from just under $5 billion to over $8 billion over the sample period, whereas the firms' return as a percentage of assets has been fairly constant at a mean of around 4.5 percent. There is a large variation across firms, ranging from small firms with a market capitalization of under $40 million to large firms with over $350 billion for the year 2005.[12] Average manager protection falls from 1991 to 2005 in the extended sample by about one-half to two protection provisions for each corporation.

Table 4.1 Summary Statistics

Variables	1991				2005			
	Mean (std)	*Std*	*Min*	*Max*	*Mean (std.)*	*Std*	*Min*	*Max*
Market Capitalization ($ mill.)	4,819	8,980	14	75,605	8,254	23,368	37	367,473
Total Assets ($ mill.)	10,635	24,144	90	216,922	16,344	82,048	60	1,494,037
Return on Assets	0.044	0.067	-2.67	0.41	0.046	0.089	-1.27	0.39
Manager Protections (6)	2.57	1.22	0	6	2.07	1.16	0	5
Weak Governance Index (24)	9.64	2.71	1	16	9.08	2.59	2	18
Community Strength (6)	0.37	0.62	0	3	0.16	0.53	0	5
Community Concerns (4)	0.03	0.17	0	1	0.11	0.34	0	2
Diversity Strength (8)	0.25	0.55	0	3	0.80	1.17	0	7
Diversity Concerns (3)	0.04	0.18	0	1	0.35	0.50	0	2
Employment Strength (7)	0.23	0.49	0	3	0.28	0.60	0	5
Employment Concerns (5)	0.12	0.37	0	2	0.53	0.69	0	4
Environment Strength (7)	0.23	0.46	0	2	0.14	0.48	0	4
Environment Concerns (7)	0.40	0.80	0	5	0.28	0.74	0	5
Number of firms		572			1,702			

The table provides summary statistics for the matched sample of firms for the years 1991 and 2005. The units of variables are in brackets. The numbers in brackets after the governance and CSR categories indicate the total number of indicators in each category in the year 2005 stating the maximum number of points possible in each category. The weak governance index refers to the Gompers-Ishii-Metrick (2003) index where higher values refer to weaker shareholder rights and where the maximum is twenty-four, whereas the manager protections refer to the subset of provisions designed to insure officers and directors against job-related liabilities or to compensate them in case of termination.

Definition of Variables

I take a disaggregated approach and make use of the full information of the KLD data, running separate regressions for each CSR indicator as a dependent variable to identify governance effects on type I and type II indicators of CSR. It is important to stress the conceptual difference between CSR strength and CSR concern indicators. Strength indicators have a straightforward natural interpretation. A rating of "one" for a strength indicator implies a positive outcome on some social or environmental dimensions. Furthermore, if certain strengths are more profitable in nature, we expect them to be a type II case, predicting a decrease under weak governance. On the other hand, a rating of "one" for a concern indicator implies that the firm performs very badly on some social or environmental dimension. Therefore, an increase in a concern indicator signals a decrease in a firm's social or environmental performance. Nevertheless, if we have a concern that the shareholders would like to get rid of due to its harmful effect on the profitability of the firm (such as "having problems with environmental regulation and paying substantial fines"), we have a case of a type I CSR and predict a shift towards more of this type of CSR if governance is slack. Remember that more of this concern category CSR indicator actually means less social responsibility.

In accordance with my hypotheses, I have categorized each CSR indicator on the basis of the short descriptions given by KLD into a type I CSR, a type II CSR, or an ambiguous type for which it is unclear if the manager's desired level of CSR is higher or lower than the profit-maximizing level. Indicators are marked with (I), (II), or (?) accordingly and the categorization is marked next to the indicator name in Table 4.2. For instance, I categorize "charitable giving," "employment of disabled," "(exceptional) union relations," and "(notably strong) pollution prevention" as type I CSRs. These have a less profitable character but a strong potential for a "warm glow" on the manager's side. Therefore, we would expect to see the manager implementing a higher level of CSR than is optimal for shareholders. On the other hand, indicators like "(deriving revenue from) environmental products and services," "employee involvement (e.g., stock ownership)," and "climate change concern (i.e., substantial revenues from the sale of coal and oil)" are directly linked to maximizing a firm's profit and are categorized as type II CSRs. The type I and type II CSR categories that I have created are clearly subjective and might be debatable in some cases. However, these categories represent my best and objective ex ante attempt at categorizing according to my theoretical structure.

Empirical Methodology

The basic regression specification used to analyze the effect of weaker governance on the different dimensions of CSR can be defined as follows:

$$CSR_{jt} = \alpha_t + \alpha_s + \alpha_i + \beta X_{jt} + \delta MP_{jt-1} + \varepsilon_{jt} \quad (1)$$

where CSR_{jt} is the firm *j*'s performance score of some CSR measure, *s* indexes the state of incorporation of a company, *t* indexes time, and *i* is the index for the firm's industry; α_t, α_s, and α_i are year, state, and industry dummies. X_{jt} is a vector of control variables such as firm size and returns. MP_{jt-1} are the manager protections in place in firm *j* in year $t-1$; ε_{jt} is an error term. Including year fixed effects allows controlling for common changes over time. The industry fixed effects control for industry-specific heterogeneity of firms like specific advertising practices in some industries or different distances in the supply chain to the end consumer. This is particularly important because some of KLD's CSR indicators are very industry specific. State fixed effects additionally allow controlling for local economic differences or differences in other local governance regulation. For my main analysis of all thirty-three individual binary CSR indicators, I will use logit regression models given the binary nature of the dependent variables.
Every regression specification is estimated twice, once as a pooled specification controlling for industry and state effects with α_s and α_i, and once as a regression across time where I include firm fixed effects to control for unobserved time invariant firm heterogeneity. In the latter case α_s and α_i are not included and instead I will use firm-specific dummies α_j in my regression specification. Both specifications have their advantages and disadvantages. Although the firm fixed effect regression allows me to control for all unobserved characteristics, such as a firm's internal culture or how qualified or harmonious the management team is, it leads to a loss of degrees of freedom and a loss of power for any test statistics. I also lose an enormous amount of data in these regressions as all firms that do not ever have a rating of one for a certain CSR indicator drop out. Therefore, these regressions only identify the effect of manager protections among a subset of firms that have a rating change for the CSR at some point in time.

The cross-sectional approach has the advantage of a much bigger sample set, but I don't control for unobservable heterogeneity on the firm level. This specification, however, allows me to add additional time invariant firm-level controls. Besides time dummies, firm size, and instrumented returns, I also control for heterogeneity across different industries and for the different state laws firms are facing by including a dummy for the state of incorporation. These controls will account for a large part of firm heterogeneity when we don't include firm dummies. I further cluster the standard errors from those regressions by firm ID to avoid a downward bias estimate of the variance due to the remaining heterogeneity.

In order to avoid simultaneity bias in my main regressions, where I define returns on assets (ROA) as a control variable, I instrument for returns in a first-stage regression. In the first stage, I project ROA onto all other (exogenous) variables in my main regression and the first three lags of ROA:

$$ROA_{jt} = \delta_t + \delta_s + \delta_i + \phi X_{jt}(without\ ROA) + \varphi_1 ROA_{jt-1} + \varphi_2 ROA_{jt-2} + \varphi_3 ROA_{jt-3} + \eta_{jt} \quad (2)$$

The fitted values for ROA from the preceding projection serve as instrumental variables for my second-stage regression defined in Equation 1, replacing the contemporaneous ROA variable.

RESULTS

For each CSR indicator, I estimate a logit model as specified in Equation 1. Table 1.2 summarizes the results of these sixty-six individual logit regressions. The indicators, which represent the changing dependent variables, are ordered by category. In each category the strength indicators are followed by the category's concern indicators, which are marked by an italic font. [13] I will go through the findings in the table by category. The first three columns of Table 1.2 present the regressions results from the pooled specification where we control for state of incorporation and industry fixed effects. Columns four through six present the according results for each indicator where the logit regressions are specified as cross time regressions using firm fixed effects. For each regression I report the main coefficient of interest on management protection, the number of firm-year observations included in the regression, number of firms as well as the log likelihood value, and the regressions' pseudo R^2.

These are logit regression where the dependent variables are KLD indicators. The categorization is marked in parentheses, (I) for type I indicator where the manager prefers a higher level of CSR relative to shareholders, (II) for a type II CSR indicator where managers prefer a relative lower level, and (?) indicators, which are not categorized into either group. Regressions also include a constant, an instrument for returns on assets, logged assets, and year dummies as well as either state dummies and three-digit industry dummies in the left column or firm dummies in right column. The data is for 1991 through 2005. Standard errors in parentheses are clustered by firms; stars represent significance levels *** $p < 0.01$, ** $p < 0.05$, * $p < 0.1$.

Table 4.2 Main Results—Logit Regressions of Individual CSR Indicators on Manager Protection

	Logit regression with:	*Year, State, and Industry FE*			*Year and Firm FE*		
	Dependent Variable + short description	*Manager Protection (s.e.)*	*Number of Observations [Firms]*	*Log Likelihood [Pseudo R2]*	*Manager Protection (s.e.)*	*Number of Observations [Firms]*	*Log Likelihood [Pseudo R2]*
COMMUNITY	**Charitable Giving (I)**	**0.039**	8,357	-2023	**0.144**	2,195	-841.3
	Notably generous, s.a. giving 1.5% of net earnings	(0.075)	[1,396]	[0.21]	(0.111)	[188]	[0.04]
	Innovative Giving (I)	**0.053**	7,471	-1613	**-0.189**	1,581	-569.2
	Giving to NGOs, promoting self-sufficiency, permitting giving drives in workplace	(0.086)	[1,287]	[0.36]	(0.144)	[133]	[0.12]
	Support for Housing (I)	**0.156***	6,495	-1748	**0.181**	1,527	-595.8
	Prominent participant in partnerships supporting housing	(0.089)	[1,127]	[0.33]	(0.127)	[153]	[0.08]
	Support for Education (I)	**0.167***	5,881	-1389	**0.213**	1,062	-409
	Notably innovative support, job-training program for youth	(0.098)	[1,141]	[0.39]	(0.167)	[108]	[0.08]
	Investment Controversies (II)	***-0.111***	2,478	-494	***-0.716******	558	-185
	Lending or investment led to controversies	(0.125)	[560]	[0.39]	(0.249)	[76]	[0.18]
	Negative Economic Impact (?)	***0.353******	5,733	-1061	***0.110***	1,356	-431
	Major controversies, s.a. contamination, water rights dispute	(0.100)	[1,041]	[0.37]	(0.146)	[116]	[0.27]
	Tax Disputes (I)	***0.255*****	5,654	-748	***0.077***	1,095	-318
	Major tax disputes with authorities	(0.124)	[979]	[0.39]	(0.183)	[106]	[0.22]

ENVIRONMENT	**Beneficial Products and Services (II)**	**0.072**	3,659	-916	**-1.115********	799	-261.4
	Substantial revenues from environmental products or services	(0.117)	[550]	[0.29]	(0.269)	[68]	[0.18]
	Pollution Prevention (I)	**0.100**	5,422	-1057	**0.255***	1,325	-539.3
	Notably strong pollution-prevention programs	(0.107)	[902]	[0.32]	(0.145)	[103]	[0.03]
	Recycling (?)	0.000	3,494	-661	**0.297**	687	-242.7
	Substantial user of recycled material, major factor in recycling industry	(0.138)	[545]	[0.42]	(0.242)	[57]	[0.04]
	Clean Energy (I)	**0.261****	5,178	-927	**0.153**	1,177	-428.7
	Significant use of renewable energy, commitment outside its operations	(0.11)	[898]	[0.53]	(0.14)	[113]	[0.02]
	Communications (I)	**0.369***	2,393	-421	**-0.695***	318	-108.2
	Substantive environmental report, internal communication CERES principles	(0.197)	[683]	[0.41]	(0.403)	[44]	[0.15]
	Hazardous Waste (I)	0.239***	6,806	-1641	0.141	1,700	-600.2
	Liabilities for hazardous waste > $50 million, substantial fines	(0.081)	[1,131]	[0.51]	(0.115)	[146]	[0.10]
	Regulatory Problems (I)	0.153**	7,495	-2035	0.443***	2,427	-887.5
	Substantial fines for violation of env. regulation	(0.067)	[1,294]	[0.42]	(0.105)	[218]	[0.10
	Substantial Emission (I)	0.077	6,384	-1446	-0.036	1,977	-703.4
	Emissions highest among all companies	(0.075)	[1,110]	[0.42]	(0.106)	[180]	[0.12]
	Agricultural Chemical (II)	0.050	1,192	-227.9	-0.054	212	-77

(continued)

Table 4.2 (continued)

	Logit regression with:	*Year, State, and Industry FE*			*Year and Firm FE*		
	Dependent Variable + short description	*Manager Protection (s.e.)*	*Number of Observations [Firms]*	*Log Likelihood [Pseudo R2]*	*Manager Protection (s.e.)*	*Number of Observations [Firms]*	*Log Likelihood [Pseudo R2]*
	Substantial producer of agricultural chemicals	(0.219)	[191]	[0.53]	(0.293)	[18]	[0.15]
	Contributing to Climate Change (II)	***-0.077***	1,074	-426.8	***-0.021***	155	-55
	Substantial revenues from sale or indirect combustion of fuel	(0.160)	[253]	[0.41]	(0.513)	[28]	[0.12]
DIVERSITY	**Promotion (I)**	**0.027**	11,078	-5232	**0.141****	5,018	-1984
	Notable progress in promotion of women and minorities	(0.040)	[1,944]	[0.16]	(0.071)	[533]	[0.07]
	Board of Directors (I)	**0.173****	8,538	-2413	**0.112**	2,739	-742.9
	Women or minorities hold > 4 seats or 1/3 of less then 12 seats	(0.070)	[1,428]	[0.28]	(0.117)	[257]	[0.36
	Work/Life Benefits (I)	**0.115**	7,777	-2191	**0.302**	1,674	-432.8
	Outstanding employee benefits, e.g., child care, flextime	(0.085)	[1,395]	[0.37]	(0.187)	[144]	[0.40]
	Women & Minority Contracting (I)	**0.104**	7,443	-1521	**-0.042**	1,816	-627.2
	Strong record of purchasing or contracting with minority-owned business	(0.088)	[1,257]	[0.34]	(0.117)	[149]	[0.16]
	Employment of the Disabled (I)	0.057	5,,831	-813.2	**0.023**	1,192	-389.6
	Superior reputation as employer of disabled	(0.096)	[1034]	[0.40]	(0.140)	[94]	[0.15]
	Gay & Lesbian Policies (I)	**0.226*****	8,052	-2333	**0.530*****	2,944	-355
	Notably progressive policies for gay and lesbian employees	(0.065)	[1,695]	[0.39]	(0.200)	[370]	[0.72]

	Diversity Controversies (I)	***-0.020***	8,306	-1807	***-0.153***	2,170	-709
	Paid substantial fine or major involvement in affirmative action controversy	(0.074)	[1,484]	[0.29]	(0.117)	[209]	[0.20]
	Nonrepresentation (II)	***-0.172******	10,206	-3911	***-0.129***	3,400	-1001
	No women on board or among senior managers	(0.051)	[1,996]	[0.23]	(0.119)	[547]	[0.22]
EMPLOYEE RELATIONS	**Union Relations (I)**	0.447*	1,384	-220.7	**1.216*****	210	-73.78
	Exceptional effort to treat union workforce fairly	(0.259	[216]	[0.44]	(0.382)	[18]	V0.20]
	Cash Profit Sharing (?)	**0.029**	8,827	-2975	**0.227****	2,158	-873.5
	Cash profit-sharing program for majority of workforce	(0.070)	[1,515]	[0.21]	(0.110)	[202]	[0.04]
	Employee Involvement (II)	**-0.093**	9,153	-3484	**0.030**	2,595	-1000
	Strongly encourages worker involvement and ownership	(0.060)	[1,587]	[0.17]	(0.102)	[256]	[0.11]
	Retirement Benefits Strength (I)	**-0.004**	7,895	-2080	**-0.153**	2,259	-855.3
	Notably strong retirement benefits	(0.075)	[1,360]	[0.18]	(0.100)	[214]	[0.04]
	Poor Union Relations (I)	***0.067***	5,603	-1047	***0.063***	1,139	-420.7
	History of notably poor union relationship	(0.106)	[865]	[0.29]	(0.131)	[100]	[0.06]
	Health and Safety Concern (I)	***0.047***	6,808	-1209	***0.118***	1,711	-531
	Paid substantial fine or major health and safety controversies	(0.089)	[1,157]	[0.31]	(0.137)	[159]	[0.15]
	Workforce Reductions (II)	***0.077***	8,829	-2135	***0.053***	2,303	-719.8
	Significant reduction in workforce in recent years	(0.060)	[1,568]	[0.23]	((0.122)	[282]	[0.18]
	Retirement Benefits Concern (II)	***0.028***	11,091	-4440	***-0.200*****	5,637	-1550
	Inadequate or underfunded retirement program	(0.040)	[2,055]	[0.16]	(0.089)	[701]	[0.30]

In the first category in Table 4.2, Community Relations, I find that although there is no significant effect of manager protection on charitable giving or innovative giving, manager protection has a positive significant effect on a firm's performance for support of housing and support for education. I will connect the findings in this category directly to my hypotheses to help understand how my theory integrates with my empirical analysis. Housing and education indicators are categorized as type I CSRs. The increase of these CSR indicators under slack governance follows the predictions of my theory and support hypothesis I. I further find a strong negative effect of weak governance on investment controversies, which means that firms have fewer investment controversies in the community when managers have more slack. According to my categorization, "investment controversies" is a type II CSR and so we expect to see a downward shift in the indicator. This result is therefore also in support of hypothesis I. The last two concern indicators in the Community Relations category indicate that managers with more protection from shareholders tend to neglect their tax duties, but also assert more negative externalities on the community such as an environmental contamination or water right disputes. Whereas I categorize the negative economic impact as ambiguous given the diverse issues mentioned in KLD's description that enter into the rating, I categorize the tax duties as a type I CSR, which, according to my hypothesis, predicts the observed increase in the indicator under a weakening in corporate governance.

The last finding is similar to what we see in the Environmental Concerns category, a neglect of the firm's core duties such as complying with environmental regulations. A manager who is more entrenched in the firm will incur more fines and penalties for both hazardous waste and pollution offences. This result is especially strong as it is consistent looking across firms and also across time when including firm fixed effects. Although managers with more slack behave recklessly with regards to the environment by neglecting core duties, they also engage in proactive pollution prevention. Firms with more protections for managers also commit themselves to clean energy policies even outside their own operations. The CSR indicator for Environmental Communication shows how different the identification for the effect of manager protections can be in pooled regression compared to the firm fixed effect regression. Whereas I find a positive correlation with protections in accordance with my hypothesis in the pooled regression, looking at the small subsample of firms that have had a change in this CSR rating, we observe a negative correlation. As the sample in the fixed effect regressions is reduced, we identify the effect of changes in corporate governance using far fewer firms. The effect is particularly strong for this indicator, as the total number of observations is rather small to start with. The variable has only half the observations in addition to a very exclusive rating in which only 3 percent of all firms get rated as "one." This reduces the number of firms used to identify the manager protection coefficient in the fixed effect regression to only forty-four, which makes the regression results less robust to individual firm influences. The results on beneficial products and services show a case where, in accordance with my hypothesis II, managers neglect a type II CSR. Further, I find that managers' freedom has no effect on firms' core business, such as producing agricultural chemicals or selling oil and gas. This is not surprising as these are screening indicators that evaluate what the firm's business is rather than how they conduct it.

The Diversity Issue section consists of much more homogenous indicators. Across indicators, I find that managers with weak governance support minorities. This is in accordance with my theory assuming that outstanding performance on diversity types of CSR do not generate a positive return to shareholders but give managers a warm glow; therefore, managers will have a preference for relatively higher support for minorities, as stated in hypothesis I. I find that entrenched managers promote more women and minorities in positions of responsibility and support progressive policies for gay and lesbian workers. Firms with more manager protections also have more women on the board of directors and in top management.

Among Employee Relations indicators I find a general increase in support for worker interests under weaker governance. Managers have better union relationships, which is in accordance with hypothesis I and supports the findings that managers do more for their workers when they have more protections in place. I also observe more profit sharing with workers. This is in support of my theory because it is a type I CSR according to the profit regression where I find a negative effect of profit sharing with next period's accounting profits. The very last result of Table 4.2 suggests that managers increase efforts in retirement benefits programs when profit constraints are relaxed. This finding gives further support for my first hypothesis—judged by KLD's description of the indicator more benefits are not in the interest of shareholders.

Overall, I find strong support in favor of my hypotheses, which validates my theory. Out of all thirty-three indicators, eighteen are statistically significant. Of these only one is not in accordance with my hypotheses and the categorization based on KLD's description. The deviating indicator is the negative effect of manager protections on the Environmental Communications CSR. As I pointed out earlier, this particular result from the firm fixed effect regression, which is the opposite of the across firm regression result, needs to be taken with care as we identify a very small subsample in this low data CSR category.

SUMMARY AND CONCLUSION

The separation of ownership from control in modern corporations leads to a potential conflict of interest for the manager of the firm. A manager is hired to represent the interest of the shareholders of the firm but also has his own preferences and goals he would like to pursue. Corporate governance mechanisms try to align the incentives of both parties. Scandals in big firms like Enron, WorldCom, and Tyco International have put the topic of corporate governance back at the top of politicians', administrators', and managements' agendas. The Sarbanes-Oxley Act of 2002 aims to strengthen corporate governance as a result of these scandals. In my research, I examine the potential effects of changes in governance on no-financial firm outcomes in the social and environmental domain. I infer managers' preferences from the response of corporate social performance to changes in takeover defenses. A better understanding of managers' preferences is important to integrate the corporate governance debate into the broader fields of compliance and enforcement of regulation, corporate philanthropy, and corporate citizenship.

I argue for a "good life" theory of managers' behavior that extends the existing "quiet life" theory that managers simply try to avoid difficult decisions and costly efforts. I argue that the "warm glow" managers get from implementing social and environmental programs motivates them to spend more of the firm's resources and put in more personal effort. Thus, social responsibilities that are relatively unprofitable will receive more attention by mangers when the profitability constraint of the manager's actions is relaxed due to an increase in governance slack.

My theory also implies that a manager's core duties will be more often neglected when he is protected from shareholders. This holds true even if they concern positive social or environmental aspects.

Employing a unique data set, I test whether my findings provide support for my testable hypotheses. I find that managers increase benefits to workers when they are more protected from shareholders, as both the "good life" and the "quiet life" theory predict. The data also confirm that managers with more slack tend to neglect core duties, such as compliance with pollution regulations. This is consistent with managers' preference to avoid costly efforts. Additionally, my results show that managers under weaker governance put more effort into environmental performance, give more money to charity, and support women and minorities in the workforce. These results support my hypothesis that top managers implement higher levels of socially responsible corporate programs once they are more entrenched, which in turn reflects their social and environmental preferences.

In terms of the debate on the overall effect of takeover preventions, my results support the view that ATPs lead to entrenchment of management in ways that are costly from the shareholders' perspective. More resources are allocated to social and environmental projects with ambiguous benefits on shareholder value, whereas some unambiguously important manager duties are neglected.

Finally, my study sets the stage for future work. The longitudinal data on corporate social responsibility and the disaggregated methodology could prove fruitful in reassessing earlier studies of the causes and effects of corporate social responsibility. In light of my results on pollution violations, future studies should look at the effects of corporate governance on compliance in different fields of regulation. Results from such studies could provide additional guidance for the design of regulation enforcement and policy rules on corporate governance.

NOTES

1. The idea of management undertaking projects for their own benefits that may not be in the interest of shareholders goes back to Smith (1776) and Berle and Means (1933). Revived in the 1960s by Baumol (1959), Marris (1964), and Williamson (1964), this phenomenon is now explained in most microeconomics textbooks.
2. For managers in the United States, Ofek and Yermack (2000) report a median ownership of 0.06 percent and a mean of 0.75 percent of stocks.
3. The Sarbanes-Oxley Act of 2002 is a U.S. federal law passed in response to a number of major corporate and accounting scandals including those affecting Enron, Tyco International, and WorldCom. The legislation is wide ranging and establishes new or enhanced standards for all U.S. public company boards, management, and public accounting firms. The act contains eleven sections ranging from additional corporate board responsibilities to criminal penalties, and requires the Securities and Exchange Commission to implement rulings on requirements to comply with the new law.
4. Galaskiewicz (1997) concludes in his study that managers have a big influence on the amount of firms' charitable giving.
5. Whereas the ATPs are aiming to restrict takeovers by raider firms and therefore sometimes explicitly restrict the rights for new shareholders (e.g., unequal voting rights), most of them restrict the rights for shareholders in general (e.g., supermajority voting requirements for mergers or giving managers golden parachutes).
6. An overview of the empirical literature on links between ATPs and shareholder wealth can be found in Comment and Schwert (1995) and Mahoney and Mahoney (1993). Sundaramurthy (2000) summarizes and extends the theoretical background about if and when ATPs benefit shareholders.
7. The KLD stands for Kinder, Lydenberg, and Domini. KLD Research & Analytics, Inc., is a social investment advisory firm, which rates firms on more than one hundred indicators related to CSR.
8. The CUSIP code is a unique identifier for company, issues, and the type of security consisting of up to nine digits.
9. A complete list of all antitakeover amendments with a short description can be found in Appendix I of Gompers, Ishii, and Metrick (2003) or at the IRRC website in the glossary under www.irrc.com/resources/glossary.htm.
10. Manager protection ATPs give the management more protection from the shareholders by securing benefits in case of a change in control or by limiting liability to their conduct. These six amendments are: Compensation Plans, Contracts, Golden Parachutes, Indemnification, Liability, and Severance.
11. After an automated matching of most firms, checking each unmatched entry individually was necessary because neither ticker symbol nor CUSIP number are permanent identifiers of a firm and change over time, a feature that made matching with the correct Compustat firm record rather tedious.
12. Citicorp is the largest firm in the sample in terms of market capitalization and assets.

13. This is done to distinguish concern indicators in each category more clearly form the strength indicators given the very different interpretation of results.

BIBLIOGRAPHY

Baumol, W.J. 1959. *Business Behavior, Value and Growth*. New York: Macmillan.

Berle, A.A., and G.C. Means. 1933. *The Modern Corporation and Private Property*. New York: Macmillan.

Bertrand, M., and S. Mullainathan. 1999. "Is There Discretion in Wage Setting? A Test Using Takeover Legislation." *Rand Journal of Economics* 30 (3): 535–554.

———. 2003. "Enjoying the Quiet Life? Corporate Governance and Managerial Preferences." *Journal of Political Economy* 111 (5): 1043–1075.

Coffey, B.S., and J. Wang. 1998. "Board Diversity and Managerial Control as Predictors of Corporate Social Performance." *Journal of Business Ethics* 17 (14): 1595–1603.

Comment, R., and G.W. Schwert. 1995. "Poison or Placebo-Evidence on the Deterrence and Wealth Effects of Modern Antitakeover Measures." *Journal of Financial Economics* 39 (1): 3–43.

Galaskiewicz, J. 1997. "An Urban Grants Economy Revisited: Corporate Charitable Contributions in the Twin Cities, 1979–81, 1987–89." *Administrative Science Quarterly* 42 (3): 445–471.

Garvey, G.T., and G. Hanka. 1999. "Capital Structure and Corporate Control: The Effect of Antitakeover Statutes on Firm Leverage." *Journal of Finance* 54 (2): 519–546.

Gompers, P., J. Ishii, and A. Metrick. 2003. "Corporate Governance and Equity Prices." *Quarterly Journal of Economics* 118 (1): 107–155.

Mahoney, J.M., and J.T. Mahoney. 1993. "An Empirical-Investigation of the Effect of Corporate Charter Antitakeover Amendments on Stockholder Wealth." *Strategic Management Journal* 14 (1): 17–31.

Mahoney, L.S., and L. Thorne. 2005. "Corporate Social Responsibility and Long-Term Compensation: Evidence from Canada." *Journal of Business Ethics* 57 (3): 241–253.

Malmendier, U., and G. Tate. 2009. "Superstar CEOs." *Quarterly Journal of Economics*, 124(4): 1593–1638.

Marris, R.L. 1964. *The Economic Theory of Managerial Capitalism*. Glencoe, IL: Free Press of Glencoe.

McGuire, J., S. Dow, and K. Argheyd. 2003. "CEO Incentives and Corporate Social Performance." *Journal of Business Ethics* 45 (4): 341–359.

Ofek, E., and D. Yermack. 2000. "Taking Stock: Equity-Based Compensation and the Evolution of Managerial Ownership." *Journal of Finance* 55 (3): 1367–1384.

Smith, A. 1776. *Wealth of Nations, Great Minds Series*. Buffalo, NY: Prometheus Books.

Sundaramurthy, C. 2000. "Antitakeover Provisions and Shareholder Value Implications: A Review and a Contingency Framework." *Journal of Management* 26 (5): 1005–1030.

Williamson, O.E. 1964. "The Economics of Discretionary Behavior: Managerial Objectives in a Theory of the Firm." PhD thesis, Prentice-Hall Carnegie Instite of Technology.

5 Stock Repurchase Programs and Corporate Governance

Ethical Issues and Dilemmas

Richard McGowan

INTRODUCTION

The first section of this chapter will discuss the myriad reasons hypothesized to motivate corporate managers to repurchase stock. Topics discussed include: the preferential tax treatment of capital gains versus ordinary income, the ability to adjust leverage and capital structure balances through via a share repurchase, the financial flexibility of share repurchases in comparison to dividend programs, the extent to which executives are compensated with stock options, the information conveyed by share repurchases, the opportunity for firms to profit through the acquisition of undervalued stock, the avoidance of common equity dilution arising from the issuance of compensatory stock options, the volatility of current and expected earnings and cash flows, the prevention of hostile acquisitions, the desire to expropriate value from bondholders, a lack of available positive NPV investment opportunities, and the avoidance of misguided overinvestment by management in negative NPV projects. The remaining part of this section will provide an analysis and statistical evaluation of the extent to which each of these factors drives the size of share repurchase programs implemented by U.S. industrial firms.

The second section of the chapter will explore how the statistical results could affect the decision-making process of the directors of a corporate board. What factors ought the board take into account when they are deciding whether or not to approve a stock repurchase program? Who are the stakeholders that should play the greatest role in determining a stock repurchase program by a board of directors?

STOCK REPURCHASES: THE MECHANICS, RATIONALES, AND ANALYSIS

History of Stock Repurchases

Stock repurchase programs came into vogue as a means of distributing cash to investors in the early 1980s and have become significantly more popular since. In the early 1980s, share repurchase program announcements by U.S. industrial firms amounted to less than $10 billion per year and fewer than one hundred firms commanded the managerial and financial expertise to implement this method of cash dispersal. As corporate financial management practices became more sophisticated over the following decade, however, the frequency and size of share repurchase programs announced by U.S. firms grew dramatically. Between 1985 and 1996, the number of open-market repurchase program announcements by U.S. industrial firms increased 650 percent from 115 to 755 and their aggregate announced value increased 750 percent to $339 billion. Between 1992 and 1996, share repurchase programs represented an average of 25.6 percent of the total cash distributed by Industrial firms in the United States compared to just 7.1 percent in 1980. By 1999, more than 4,000 U.S. firms announced share repurchase programs totaling more than $550 billion.[1] This torrid growth in the frequency and size of share repurchase programs shows the rapidly increasing popularity of share repurchases as a means of distributing cash to shareholders. Much of this growth in popularity of share repurchase programs has come at the expense of more traditional dividend programs. This is evidenced by the fact that dividend payouts by industrial firms listed on CompUSA increased by a factor of just over two between 1980 and 2000 from $67.6 billion to $141.7 billion.[2] These findings, in addition to the subsequent conclusions drawn by this chapter, convincingly demonstrate that share repurchase programs have become an increasingly important and essential vehicle for U.S. industrial firms to disperse cash.

Dividends vs. Share Repurchases: The Basics

Empirical evidence shows that mangers utilize stock repurchase programs and dividends as a means to disseminate excess cash to stockholders for very different reasons. Dividends represent an ongoing payout commitment and are used to distribute cash flows deemed to be permanent in nature and arising from a firm's normal business operations. Dividend programs implicitly commit firms to maintain or increase cash dispersions for the indefinite future. Any cancellation of a dividend program or reduction in dividend yield, no matter how slight, portends significant unexpected near-term cash flow and profitability declines and causes a firm's stock price to decline significantly. Several studies have statistically demonstrated that dividend reductions precipitate an immediate average stock price decline of approximately 6 percent.[3] Thus, in the interest of maintaining the integrity of their stock price, corporate managers avoid, at all costs, committing any current or future cash flows to dividend programs that cannot be permanently sustained.

Repurchase programs, on the other hand, are most often financed by nonpermanent cash flows arising from nonoperating activities such as onetime windfalls resulting from the sale of assets or gains on investments. Repurchase programs are singular, one-off initiatives understood by the investment community to be nonrecurring. Stock repurchase programs do not involve the same level of future financial commitment as dividend programs and can be reduced or canceled at any time without negatively impacting the company's stock price. Thus, repurchase programs afford managers an element of financial flexibility that dividend programs do not. The financial flexibility inherent to stock repurchase programs has been highlighted in several academic studies as a leading and empirically verifiable reason why management propensity to favor stock repurchases over dividends has increased so dramatically over the past thirty years.[4]

Share Repurchase and Dividend Payout Growth Rates

Analyzing the historical growth trends of dividend and share repurchase program volumes provides additional telling insight into the motivations driving each cash dispersal method. Over the past thirty years, the level of annual share repurchases by U.S. firms has been highly volatile, varying considerably in a positively correlated fashion with the business cycle. Firms increase repurchase activity during boom times when they have larger than usual amounts of excess cash on hand from operating and nonoperating activities and reduce them during recessions when earnings, profitability, and cash flows wane.[5] Over this same thirty-year period, dividend payout rates in the United States have demonstrated a smooth, highly unvarying upward grow trend and have not been affected in a statistically significant way by the vagaries of the business cycle. The highly stable nature of dividend payout growth lends credence to the argument that dividend programs are financed with persistent cash flows generated by firms' stable and continuing operations.

Shareholders' Right to Tender

Tendering (selling) shares upon the announcement of a stock repurchase program is a voluntary decision by individual shareholders. Shareholders are not obligated to tender shares and, thus, have the choice to receive a cash payout or keep their investment capital committed to the equity market. This choice affords individual investors a great benefit in that they have complete discretion over the balance of equity versus cash in their investment portfolio. Dividend payments, on the other hand, are involuntary and obligate investors to take a cash payment. Receiving a dividend is not ideal for investors who wish to maintain an investment portfolio that is fully committed to the equity markets as they must pay expensive broker and transaction fees to recommit their cash dividend to the equity markets and attain their personally ideal asset allocation profile.

Stock Price Integrity

Share repurchase programs afford managers a means to distribute cash to shareholders without adversely affecting their company's stock price. When a company goes ex dividend, its firm-value and stock price decline as the number of total shares outstanding remains constant but the total value of the firm is reduced by the size of the cash dividend payout. This reduction in stock price, however, does not happen when a firm distributes cash via a share repurchase program. To illustrate this point, consider a firm worth \$100 with ten shares outstanding seeking to distribute \$10 of cash. If this firm issues a \$1 dividend, it will have an ex dividend value of \$90 and each of the ten shares still outstanding will be worth \$9, a 10 percent value reduction that is manifest in a commensurate decline in the price of the stock. If the firm, however, distributes the \$10 via the repurchase of one outstanding share, it will still have an ex-cash distribution value of \$90, but will only have nine shares outstanding, thus preserving the \$10 value and price of each outstanding share.[6] This simple example demonstrates that share repurchases allow managers to both distribute excess cash to shareholders and maintain the integrity of their company's stock price. The stock value preservation component of share repurchase programs has been a significant driving force in the increased popularity of share repurchase programs over the past thirty years and represents a compelling motive for managers to select share repurchases over dividends as a means of cash distribution.

Methods of Transacting a Share Repurchase Program

There are three primary methods companies use to repurchase stock. Firms most commonly buy back shares through an open-market transaction that affords the firm the opportunity to repurchase stock from tendering shareholders in the open market over a specified time at the prevailing market price. In a Fixed-Price or Dutch Auction tender offer, firms purchase shares directly from tendering shareholders at a set price and moment. A less commonly utilized method of stock repurchase is a Private Placement transaction. A firm privately negotiates the terms of the share repurchase with a select number of individual shareholders. This method is most often used as a poison pill to mitigate the threat of a takeover by a hostile bidder.

THEORETICAL RATIONALES FOR REPURCHASING STOCK

Literature examining the panoply of philosophical and financial factors that motivate managers to implement stock repurchase programs abounds in finance academia. The following section presents a discussion of the most commonly accepted of these factors and how each is thought to contribute to the cash distribution decisions of U.S. corporate managers.

Stock Price Undervaluation Hypothesis

The theory most commonly attributed to the implementation of repurchase programs is the Stock Price Undervaluation Hypothesis. This hypothesis is based on the premise that information asymmetry between a company and the market about a firm's future earnings and cash flow prospects may cause a firm's stock to be mispriced. When a company perceives its stock to be undervalued, repurchasing shares serves as a means of passing on the value of this asymmetrical inside information to current shareholders.[7] The market interprets the repurchase as an indication that the stock is undervalued and promptly corrects it's assumptions about the firms future prospects that underlie its current valuation and drive the price of the company's stock up to its fair value. This generates a swift capital gain for residual shareholders and increases the future earnings per common share of common equity (EPS) of the repurchasing company.[8]

Instances of stock price undervaluation typically occur when a company experiences abnormal or unexpected earnings declines precipitated by difficult economic conditions or unusual, nonrecurring company-specific problems. Bereft of publically available information about the underperforming firm's future earnings and cash flow prospects, the market assumes that the company's current subpar performance levels will persist in future periods and uses underestimates of the firm's future earnings and cash flows in modeling the company's stock price. These misguided and incorrect estimates cause the company's stock to trade at a discount to its fair or intrinsic value.

Prospective investors who are privy to the fact that a company's stock is mispriced seek to purchase shares for less than they are worth. In so doing, these investors enjoy a swift and often significant positive return on investment when the market corrects its valuation of the stock and drives the stock's price up to its fair value. Because the equity market is thought to be perfectly efficient, an acquirer of undervalued shares can expect that the market will almost immediately realize its valuation mistake and drive the price of his shares up to their intrinsic value. When this happens, the investor enjoys a capital gain that he can monetize by selling his now fairly valued shares in the open market. Because a company's management team has inside information about the current and future health and profitability of its firm, it can easily identify when the market has undervalued its stock. If the firm has excess uncommitted cash or the ability to assume incremental debt, it can act as the aforementioned prospective investor and purchase shares of its own stock from current shareholders at a market price that is below the intrinsic value of these shares.

Repurchasing undervalued shares affords a company the ability to create significant value for shareholders in several ways. First, decreasing the number of common equity shares outstanding allows the company to reduce its ownership base and distribute future profits and cash flows across a smaller number of outstanding shares. Assuming that the company can at least sustain its current level of profitability, this reduction in outstanding shares necessarily increases the company's future EPS. Residual equity investors that hold shares following the repurchase own a larger proportional stake of the company than they did before the repurchase and, therefore, receive an increased percentage of the company's total profits and payouts. Because EPS is the main fundamental driver of a company's stock price, the increase in EPS associated with a share repurchase program is the primary reason a repurchasing company's stock price rises following the implementation of a share repurchase program.

The second way in which a share repurchase program could generate value for equity investors is associated with the program's implication about a firm's future performance. Companies that announce share repurchase programs convey to the market a sense of confidence in their future earnings and cash flow prospects. The company would not want to increase its ownership stake by repurchasing shares if it did not think that future earnings would surpass the levels currently anticipated by the market. This positive information signal, discussed in depth later in the chapter, causes the market to adjust its expectations about the firm's future profitability, which results in an almost immediate increase of the company's stock price, thus generating value for residual shareholders.

The third way in which share repurchases generate shareholder value is that they provide an efficient, inexpensive, and profitable way for investors to terminate their investment in a company's stock. To entice investors to tender their shares, many firms offer to repurchase shares at a significant premium to the prevailing market price. Share repurchase programs, thus, allow investors already desiring to sell their shares to do so while collecting an often significant premium as an added bonus.

Most empirical evidence corroborates the undervaluation hypothesis. Several studies have shown a significant negative correlation between repurchase program announcements and stock performance in periods preceding the announcement and a strong positive correlation between repurchase announcements and stock returns in periods subsequent to the announcements.[9] The stocks of companies that implement share repurchase programs demonstrate abnormal returns ($-\alpha$) below the market of -0.35 percent per month in the year prior to the announcement of a repurchase program. In the three years following the announcement, however, repurchasing firms outperform the market and achieve positive abnormal stock returns (α) of 0.59 percent per month.[10] Such poor preannouncement performance and subsequent market outperformance present a strong case for Stock Price Undervaluation Hypothesis as a significant motive for repurchasing stock. These findings also suggest that managers confident that their company's future earnings and cash flows will exceed market expectations trade strategically to capitalize on their mispriced stock to generate value for shareholders.

Leverage and Capital Structure Hypothesis

Share repurchase programs have become popular as a means for companies to swiftly, efficiently, and inexpensively achieve desired capital structure balances and drive increases in EPS and return on equity (ROE). When a firm repurchases stock, it reduces the amount of common equity outstanding, thus increasing the firm's debt-to-equity profile. This "levering-up" of the capital structure facilitates higher future EPS and ROE, assuming the firm can maintain its current level of profitability following the necessary reduction in cash and assets associated with financing the share repurchase program. An equal or increased level of profits is distributed across a reduced number of equity shares outstanding, leaving each residual equity share remaining after the share repurchase with a larger proportional ownership stake in the company's future profits.

Provided a firm has sufficient means to service additional debt, it can finance a stock repurchase program via a commensurate debt issuance. Financing stock repurchase programs with debt instead of cash is tantamount to a direct debt-for-equity exchange and facilitates an even more pronounced increase in capital structure leverage than a repurchase program financed with cash.[11] ROE, EPS, and firm-value increase proportionally more after a debt-financed share repurchase program as the additional debt concurrently reduces the equity base without depleting the firm's valuable cash reserves.

Provided the repurchasing firm's preannouncement debt-to-equity level was below its optimal level, its after-tax firm-value will increase for two reasons. First, firm-value will increase due to the tax subsidy generated by the interest payments made to service the incremental debt issued to finance the repurchase program. Firm-value is unaffected by capital structure composition in a tax-free world.[12] Absent taxes, debt and equity capital sources are valued equivalently and neither affords a company an advantage in achieving a higher firm-value. However, because debt-servicing interest payments are tax deductible, a firm employing leverage realizes a significant advantage insofar as it can apply debt-servicing interest payments against taxable net income.[13]

Repurchasing companies also enjoy an increased firm-value because of a decrease in the firm's weighted average cost of capital that accompanies the implementation of a stock repurchase program. Because debt is more senior than equity in the capital structure, the cost of debt is lower than the cost of equity. Thus, because share repurchase programs increase the proportion of debt to equity in a firm's capital structure, the weighted average cost of capital logically declines after a share repurchase. This cost of capital argument holds as long as the repurchasing firm's pre- and postrepurchase debt-to-equity levels are at or below the firm's optimal level. This benefit does not hold if the firm's postrepurchase debt-to-equity ratio raises above the optimal level as inordinately high debt levels portend higher probabilities of default and insolvency, which increase the risk profile of the company, lead to higher costs of debt and equity, and, therefore, reduce overall firm-value.

Stock Options—Executive Wealth Preservation Hypothesis

The extension of stock options has become an increasingly popular means of executive compensation over the past thirty years. Stock option compensation aligns individual managers' motives with those of the company and efficiently ensures that managerial decisions are made honestly and with the best interests of shareholders and the future viability and prosperity of the company in mind.

In relation to managerial cash distribution decisions, however, stock option compensation can cause a breakdown in this motive alignment. Because the value of in-the-money stock options declines when a stock goes ex dividend, executives who own unexercised in-the-money stock options have a selfish motive to avoid paying dividends as doing so would erode the value of their option portfolio. Thus, executives seeking to preserve their personal wealth or soon exercise outstanding options have an incentive to avoid dividend payments even if this decision violates their fiduciary responsibility to shareholders.

This Executive Wealth Preservation Hypothesis is another widely accepted explanation of why corporate managers choose to repurchase stock instead of pay out dividends. Because stock repurchases cause a company's stock price to rise and, thus, increase the value of outstanding in-the-money stock options, managers that are largely compensated with options have a personal incentive to pursue this cash distribution option. This theory is statistically corroborated by the fact that the value of unexercised in-the-money stock options owned by decision-making executives is more than twice as high for firms that implement repurchase programs than it is for firms that initiate or increase dividend programs.[14]

To quantify the significance of the Executive Stock Option Value Preservation Hypothesis, consider the following. In 1993, the average executive at a repurchasing firm had at stake $345,000 in making the decision to repurchase stock or pay a dividend. This meant that had the firm decided to distribute cash via a dividend payment, the value of the average executive's personal stock option portfolio would have declined by $345,000 due to the equity dilution caused by the dividend payment.[15] The present-day value of the average executive option portfolio at risk at the time of a repurchase program announcement is likely significantly larger than $345,000 as stock option compensation has increased considerably as a proportional component of managerial pay over the past two decades. This extensive amount of executive wealth exposed to destruction at the time of a cash disbursement decision clearly demonstrates why the level of executive stock option ownership seems to so strongly influence corporate cash distribution decisions.

A consideration of the dramatic growth of open-market share repurchases and stock-based compensation over the past thirty years in combination with the concurrent deceleration in dividend payout growth over the same period lends additional credence to the Executive Wealth Preservation Hypothesis and further demonstrates that as managers become more heavily compensated by stock options, they increasingly favor share repurchases over dividends as a means of cash distribution. In their study examining the relationship between cash distribution decisions and executive stock option ownership, Jagannathan, Weisbach, and Stephens (2000) demonstrate that there exists a strong negative relationship between dividends and the value of unexercised in-the-money stock options owned by company executives.[16] The study found that one standard deviation increase in the value of in-the-money stock options owned by company executives reduces dividend yields by a statistically significant thirty-eight basis points. This study also showed an ancillary statistically significant positive relationship between the level of corporate share repurchases and the value of unexercised in-the-money stock options owned by company executives.[17] These findings provide significant support for the notion that the rise in popularity of share repurchases by U.S. firms that has come at the expense of traditional dividend programs over the past three decades was motivated, at least partially, by the incentive of corporate executives to preserve their personal wealth and the value of their option portfolio at the time of a cash distribution decision.

Whenever the personal interests or wealth of executives is at all affected by a managerial decision, agency problems abound. The preceding discussion and statistical corroboration of the Executive Wealth Preservation Hypothesis clearly demonstrates that corporate executives' personal motives shape their cash distribution decisions. Executives who own an option portfolio of appreciable value will always have a personal incentive to distribute cash via nondividend alternatives. As such, additional incentive alignment measures must be implemented by companies that rely on stock options for executive compensation to ensure that there is not a breakdown in executives' fiduciary responsibilities to shareholders when cash distribution decisions are made.

Stock Options—Common Equity Dilution Prevention Hypothesis

Preventing common equity dilution caused by the extension of compensatory stock options is another motivation commonly associated with share repurchase programs. When issuing stock options as compensation to employees, managers often concurrently repurchase a number of shares outstanding equivalent to the number of new shares they issue to employees in order to avoid diluting their firm's equity base. Issuing stock options as compensation increases the number of common equity shares outstanding and decreases EPS. As discussed earlier, any decrease in EPS, no matter the magnitude, places downward pressure on a firm's stock price. The primary goal underlying all managerial decisions is the maintenance and improvement of their company's stock price. Thus, managers have a vested interest and obligation to ensure that their employee compensation decisions do not adversely affect the overall valuation of the firm and destroy value for current shareholders. When buying back stock to offset the dilutive effects of a stock issuance, a manager is even willing to pay a premium to entice current shareholders to tender their shares because the additional price paid to repurchase the shares represents only a small fraction of the overall value that would be destroyed if he allowed the stock options to dilute the current equity base and drive down the price of his company's stock. The propensity of managers to implement share repurchase programs concurrently with the issuance of compensatory stock options increases as the number of stock options extended increases in proportion to the number of common equity shares outstanding.

Cash Flow Volatility Hypothesis

The Cash Flow Volatility Hypothesis maintains that firms are inclined to distribute excess cash via a share repurchase program rather than a dividend when the value of financial flexibility is highest, i.e., when there is a high likelihood that the cash flows being paid out are temporary or nonpersistent. Such temporary cash flows arise when a firm's overall cash flow is comprised of a proportionally higher level of nonoperating income relative to operating income, when a firm's earnings volatility in periods preceding the repurchase is high, or when the firm's future cash flows are expected to decline. Share repurchases preserve financial flexibility relative to dividends for firms because they do not explicitly commit the firm to maintain any sort of cash distribution program in future periods and can be reduced or cancelled at any time without consequence. Thus, when companies generate excess nonpersistent cash flows, it benefits them to distribute this cash via stock repurchases rather than dividends. If, however, a firm commits an unusually high level of nonpersistent cash flows to a dividend program that is expected to be maintained for an indefinite amount of time, the firm will likely have to reduce the size of the dividend payment in a subsequent period when these nonrecurring cash flows disappear. Given that dividend payment reductions and cancelations project significant negative connotations about a firm's future viability and are accompanied by an average stock price decline of approximately 6 percent,[18] it is clear why managers favor share repurchases as the primary means of distributing unsustainable nonoperating cash flows.

For similar reasons, firms with highly volatile operating cash flows also seek to distribute cash to shareholders via share repurchases. Ghosh and Woolridge (1988) demonstrate that the standard deviation of the operating cash flow for firms that implement share repurchase programs is approximately twice as high as it is for firms that initiate or increase dividend payments.[19] These findings suggest that the cash flows of repurchasing firms are substantially more variable than they are for dividend paying firms and corroborate the theory that firms use repurchases to payout nonoperating cash flows that have been and are projected to continue to be highly volatile and dividends to pay out permanently sustainable operating cash flows.

An analysis of the growth trends of dividends and share repurchases over the past thirty years lends further credence to the Cash Flow Volatility Hypothesis and strongly suggests that each cash distribution vehicle is employed at different times and by different types of firms. Dividend payments by American companies have historically demonstrated slow and steady growth.[20] Aggregate dividends paid by U.S. industrial firms listed on CompUSA have increased steadily over the past three decades. Total cash distributions by U.S. industrial firms, however, have demonstrated a highly volatile growth trend over this same period. The majority of this year-to-year variation is attributable to share repurchases that are highly pro-cyclical[21] and have historically fluctuated significantly with the business cycle.[22] Because share repurchases are generally financed with cash generated by one-off windfalls and nonpersistent nonoperating business activities,[23] it is logical that firms increase their repurchases disproportionately relative to dividends during boom times when cash flows are abnormally high and reduce them proportionally more during recessions when cash flows are abnormally low.[24]

Given the preceding, a number of conclusions can be made about the cash flow profile of companies that choose to repurchase stock. Firms uncertain about their ability to maintain current levels of operating cash flows can be expected to utilize repurchases to a greater extent than dividends to distribute cash to shareholders. Also, firms with high levels of nonoperating cash flow are much more likely to repurchase stock than initiate or increase a dividend program. Finally, because repurchases are more likely to reflect temporary, nonpersistent cash flow windfalls, it can be reasonably assumed that firms that repurchase stock will have lower levels of future distributable cash than firms that initiate or increase their dividend programs.

Negative NPV Investment of Free Cash Flow Hypothesis

This hypothesis suggests that companies with cash flows in excess of their available investment opportunities are likely to invest in value-destroying negative NPV projects that reduce the firm's value. Shareholders wary of this agency problem can actively manage the amount of cash at the disposal of company management by demanding that the firm repurchase stock. In so doing, equity holders prevent the further or continued unprofitable investment in negative NPV endeavors.[25]

This scenario typically occurs when a company transitions from its growth phase to its maturity phase. When a firm is in its growth phase, it generally has many positive NPV projects available that command high levels of capital expenditure and deplete cash flows. However, when the firm's growth slows and competition infiltrates the market, the number of available positive NPV investment opportunities declines and cash flows accumulate. As these investment opportunities decline and management struggles to identify profitable uses for its mounting cash reserves, the likelihood of overinvest by management in nonprofitable negative NPV projects increases significantly. Demanding the firm to repurchase stock, therefore, is a way for shareholders to ensure that management does not apply available investment capital to value-destroying investment endeavors.

The reduction in agency-related costs associated with a share repurchase initiated by a firm with waning positive NPV investment opportunities is another likely explanation of why the market views share repurchases so favorably. The market would much rather see firms repurchase shares with excess cash than unprofitably invest it.

Tax Advantage Hypothesis

Corporations do not experience any tax advantage by repurchasing stock rather than issuing a dividend. The U.S. tax code treats stock repurchases and dividends the same at the corporate level. Share repurchases, however, do present a tax advantage relative to dividends for individual investors at the personal tax level. Dividend payments are direct cash payments and are taxed at the ordinary income tax rate. Share repurchases, on the other hand, result in an increase of the company's stock price, which creates an unrealized capital gain. If a shareholder wishes to monetize this capital gain after the implementation of a repurchase program, he must sell his shares in the open market. The realized monetary gains enjoyed by investors that tender their shares subsequent to the implementation of a repurchase program are taxed at the capital gains rate.[26] The tax rate imposed on capital gains has historically trailed the ordinary income tax rate by roughly 50 percent. This preferential tax treatment of capital gains is meant to incentivize public investment in the equity market and is a major reason why investors, especially those in high tax brackets, prefer stock repurchases to dividends. Thus, corporations seeking to maximize investment returns and value for their shareholders often choose share repurchases as a favored vehicle for cash distribution.

Information Signaling Hypothesis

Modigliani and Miller suggest that when markets are incomplete and information is asymmetrical, firms can implicitly lend insight about their future cash flow and profitability prospects through changes in payout policy.[27] Subsequent investigations into the information content of stock repurchases have corroborated Modigliani and Miller's original thesis and demonstrated that corporate cash distribution decisions are not actions that simply happen to provide signals about a firm's future health and viability, but rather are explicit signals that portend specific information about a firm that is presently unknown by the market.[28] A firm's decision to distribute cash via dividend payments, corporate acquisitions, or stock repurchases each communicate different information about a firm's future earnings, cash flow, and cash distribution profile.

That share repurchase program announcements precipitate positive stock price appreciation in subsequent periods has been vigorously discussed in the preceding sections and at this point is considered a given. What then of the specific information communicated by a company's decision to disseminate cash via this distribution vehicle? Historically, most share repurchase program announcements have been followed by relatively immediate positive news about the firm's future profitability and cash flow prospects. Most repurchasing firms also enjoy abnormal increases in EPS and market-outperforming stock returns in following periods. As share repurchase programs have become increasingly popular as a means of cash distribution, it has become nearly universally accepted that firms that repurchase stock realize subsequent market-outperforming stock returns and positive future earnings and cash flows in the intermediate term. Repurchasing firms know that these positive prospects and market outperformance are expected and, thus, do not initiate repurchase programs unless they are able to achieve performance results consistent with the expectations associated with share repurchase announcements.

The fact that managers repurchase stock at a premium to the prevailing market price also lends credence to the Information Signaling Hypothesis. Managers should only be willing to repurchase shares above the current market price if they think that the market unjustifiably undervalues the future profitability and cash flow assumptions that underlie their stock's current valuation. Assuming this is true, companies that buy back outstanding shares at a premium to the current market price signal positive information about the future growth prospects and earnings expectations of their company not currently recognized by the market. Thus, in addition to validating any speculation that a company's stock might be underpriced, a share repurchase program that offers a premium for tendered shares conveys a very strong positive message about the firm's future earnings and cash flows expectations.

Furthermore, the fact that companies are not legally required to announce their intention to repurchase stock presents another viable and convincing argument that strengthens the credibility of information signaling as a motive for managers to implement share repurchase programs. Firms may repurchase shares of their own stock in the open market at any time without publically announcing their intention to do so. Virtually all share repurchase programs, however, are accompanied by widely proliferated and costly public announcements. These public announcements suggest that repurchasing firms desire the public to know of their intention to repurchase shares and represent a concerted effort by management to intentionally communicate positive asymmetrical information about their company's future profits, cash flows, and viability to which the market is not currently privy.

Several studies, such as the one conducted by Grullon and Michaely (2004), have recently been unable to statistically demonstrate any evidence that repurchasing firms actually achieve appreciably increased stock returns and profitability in the several years following the implementation of a repurchase program. Some studies have actually demonstrated that the profitability and stock returns of repurchasing companies in several industries actually decline in periods subsequent to a stock repurchase.[29] These conflicting findings suggest that even though information signaling is often cited by company managers as a reason for implementing a share repurchase program, it is far from the primary factor motivating managers to buy back stock.

Bondholder Value Expropriation Hypothesis

Stock repurchases expropriate value from bondholders in several ways. First, repurchasing stock reduces the assets of the company, and therefore the value of the claims of bondholders. Unexpected share repurchase programs that were not anticipated by the market result in a decline in the value of outstanding bonds as the reduced level of company assets is factored into the price of the bonds. When this unexpected value expropriation occurs, wealth is transferred directly from bondholders to equity holders whose shares enjoy an increase in price and a larger proportional ownership stake in the profits and future cash flows of the repurchasing company after the announcement of the repurchase program.

Share repurchases also expunge value from bondholders in that they increase balance sheet leverage and reduce the amount of cash and assets available to service future debt obligations. These consequences of share repurchase programs enhance the risk profile of the repurchasing company and greatly increase the probability that the repurchasing company will default on outstanding bonds or suffer a value-destroying credit rating downgrade on its outstanding debt.

Bond ratings downgrades, which cause the value of outstanding bonds to decline significantly, have been shown to be twice as likely after the announcement of the repurchase program.[30] To quantify the magnitude of bondholder value destroyed when a company's debt is downgraded, consider the historical spread (price) differential between A and AA and B and BB rated bonds. The average spread between the AA and A rated bonds has historically been between ten and twenty basis points. The spread between BB and B rated bonds has been between seventy and one hundred basis points.[31] These spread differentials clearly demonstrate how even a slight change in credit rating can erode significant bondholder value.

Bondholder value expropriation may motivate managers to repurchase stock when they have a significant equity stake in the firm or a vested personal interest in preserving value for equity investors over debt investors. Because repurchasing stock transfers wealth from bondholders to equity investors, executives that own a large number of outstanding shares or whose option portfolio is valuable might be inclined to repurchase stock to increase their personal wealth. This agency problem is important to consider in an analysis of the factors that motivate corporate stock repurchases, but is likely an insignificant explanation of why executives repurchase stock. Credit downgrades and an increased probability of debt default not only erode bond value but also negatively impact the market's perception and valuation of the firm as a whole. Thus, actions that result in credit downgrades or increase the likelihood of insolvency are generally avoided at all costs by managers, regardless of the size of their equity stake in the firm or personal interest in preserving value for equity investors. Therefore, although considerable, the Bondholder Value Expropriation Hypothesis is not a robust explanation of why executives repurchase stock.

Hostile Acquisition Prevention Hypothesis

The Hostile Takeover Defense Hypothesis posits that firms at risk of becoming takeover targets are more likely to repurchase stock.[32] This theory is rooted in the facts that share repurchases increase the takeover cost of the targeted firm and often transfer significant additional voting power to company managers seeking to maintain the independence of the firm for which they work.

The relatively immediate stock price appreciation precipitated by a share repurchase makes it ideal for use as a poison pill to block hostile takeover attempts by corporate raiders. Share repurchases swiftly increase the lowest price for which a company's stock is available for purchase and, if properly implemented, can cause the targeted company to become too expensive for the hostile raider to afford and significantly diminish the returns he seeks.

Share repurchases are also attractive and logical poison pill options for targeted companies as they significantly reduce the amount of noncommitted excess cash on the targeted company's balance sheet. Companies with large cash balances are attractive takeover targets because this cash can be applied to the overall consideration needed by the hostile raiders and significantly reduce the amount of personal capital he must bring forward to consummate the acquisition. Companies with large cash balances that fear takeover by a hostile raider are well advised to deploy some of their excess cash to repurchase shares as doing so reduces the amount of attractive cash on its balance sheet and increases the amount of personal consideration required of the hostile investor to successfully complete the acquisition.

Another way in which share repurchases efficiently deter hostile takeovers is that they transfer a larger proportion of voting rights to current management. If company executives, who typically possess significant equity stakes in the company for which they work, repurchase a large enough number of outstanding shares, the proportional voting power of their shares may become large enough to vote down the hostile takeover attempt in a proxy battle. A similar argument states that privately negotiated share repurchases remove those equity investors with the lowest reservation price, leaving only those investors requiring a significant premium to tender their shares. These high-reservation investors will also vote their shares against the hostile raider if his offer price falls short of the price they demand.[33]

Though theoretically sound, the Hostile Takeover Prevention Hypothesis has been shown to work to varying degrees over the past thirty years and does not seem to be an applicable predictor of repurchase program size. For this reason, and because none of the share repurchases analyzed for this chapter were flagged by CompUSA as takeover defense initiatives, this hypothesis is not considered in the final regression analysis of this chapter.

STATISTICAL ANALYSIS

This chapter seeks to statistically determine the primary financial and psychological factors that drive the size of share repurchase programs implemented by U.S. industrial firms. To test the hypothesized theories discussed in the preceding, testable data from several sources were compiled from several sources. The M&A application on the Securities Data Company (SDC) database provided robust information about all share repurchases programs announced by U.S. industrial sector firms during between January 1, 1997, and December 31, 2006. SDC provided the name of the repurchasing company, the date of the transaction, the size of the announced repurchase program, as well as a wealth of other data crucial to the research for this chapter. To supplement the data provided by SDC, several applications within the CompUSA database supported by the WRDS platform were used. The Fundamentals Annual component of CompUSA provided afforded key valuation and performance metrics for the repurchasing companies analyzed. The

Execucomp application of CompUSA provided all necessary relevant information about the executive stock option holdings of the repurchasing firms analyzed for this chapter. Only those firms with data listed in all three of these databases were retained for inclusion in the final quantitative analysis and regression tested conducted in this chapter. SDC initially provided information on 517 repurchase programs announced by U.S. industrial firms during the test period. Of these 517 repurchase announcements, only 261 also had relevant data listed on the Fundamentals Annual and Execucomp databases. Thus, for the purposes of the regression analysis that follows, only data from these 261 repurchase announcements were retained. Exhibit I lists the name of the repurchasing companies considered in the chapter as well as the date and dollar value of each repurchase announcement.

HYPOTHESIS AND EXPLANATORY VARIABLE DISCUSSION

Based on an analysis of the prevailing literature regarding corporate share repurchases, the hypotheses discussed in the following section are likely to have the most significant effect on the size of share repurchase programs implemented by U.S. industrial firms. To statistically test the ability of each of these hypotheses to predict the size of share repurchase programs, one or more independent variables representing each hypothesis is included in an initial regression model. This model is intended to demonstrate the extent to which each of the theories presented in this chapter drives the size of share repurchase programs implemented by U.S. industrial firms. The following sections provide a discussion and justification of each independent variable included in the initially hypothesized regression model.

Stock Price Undervaluation

The Price-to-Earnings (P/E) multiple is included in the regression model to test for the effects of stock price undervaluation on share repurchase size. A low P/E multiple often signals that a company is unjustifiably undervalued in relation to its peers and that its shares can be purchased relatively cheaply in comparison to the shares of competing firms its peer group. Companies trading at lower P/E multiples likely repurchase a larger proportion of their total shares outstanding to take advantage of their undervalued shares and generate value for shareholders. If this variable proves not to be correlated to the size of share repurchase programs implemented by U.S. industrial firms, it will likely be because low P/E multiples also often reflect the market's expectation of poor or volatile earnings performance in future periods. If a company's future performance is correctly thought to be subpar or highly volatile, its low valuation multiple may actually reflect a fair valuation, meaning that the company is not undervalued, and a share repurchase initiated on the basis of stock price undervaluation would not be warranted or prudent.

Leverage and Capital Structure Management

To model the effects of leverage and capital structure management on the size of share repurchase programs announced by U.S. industrial firms, the debt-to-equity ratio of each repurchasing firm is included in the initial regression model. As discussed earlier, one of the most commonly cited motivations for enacting a share repurchase program is the ability of a company to increase balance sheet leverage to attain a "more optimal" capital structure balance. Firms repurchase shares to decrease the amount of total equity outstanding and, thus, increase their overall debt-to-equity ratios. It can be expected that a firm's debt-to-equity ratio will be negatively correlated with the size of its share repurchase program. Firms with lower debt-to-equity ratios will be inclined to repurchase a greater extent of their total equity outstanding to bring their debt-to-equity ratio up to its optimal level and align their capital structure with those of competing firms.

Preservation of Executive Option Portfolio Value

To test for the effects of executive option portfolio value on the size of share repurchases implemented by U.S. industrial firms, the aggregate value of the unexercised in-the-money stock options held by each company's top three executives as reported by Compustat's Execucomp database is included in the initial regression model. The aggregate option holdings of top executives is likely positively correlated to repurchase program size as executives with larger amounts of personal wealth at stake at the time of a share repurchase decision will theoretically be inclined to repurchase a larger proportion of outstanding equity in an attempt to preserve as much of their personal option portfolio value as possible.

Volatility of Cash Flows

To model the effects of cash flow volatility on the size of share repurchase programs announced by U.S. industrial firms, the average annual change in each tested company's EBITDA over the four-year period preceding the share repurchase is included in the initial regression model. This metric captures the extent to which each firm's cash flows fluctuate year over year and allows for a meaningful assessment of the Cash Flow Volatility Hypothesis. It is likely that firms with more volatile positive EBITDAs seek to repurchase a larger portion of outstanding equity and firms with less volatile or negative EBITDAs seek to repurchase a smaller portion of total outstanding equity.

Proportion of Total Cash Flows Derived from Nonoperating Activities

Firms with larger levels of cash flows from nonoperating activities will be likely to implement proportionally larger share repurchase programs as it would be unwise to commit this nonrecurring cash flow stream to a dividend program. To test this hypothesis, the amount of each tested company's nonoperating cash flows as a percentage of its total cash flows in the year prior to the repurchase is included in the initially hypothesized regression model. There will likely be a positive correlation between the amount of cash flow a company derives from nonoperating activities and the size of its share repurchase program as firms traditionally distribute nonpersistent, nonoperating cash flows via share repurchase programs.

Negative NPV Investment Prevention

To test for the effects of negative NPV investment prevention on the size of share repurchases implemented by U.S. industrial firms, the Price/Book Value of Equity ratio (P/B), EBITDA/Total Assets ratio (EBITDA/TA), and balance sheet cash balance (Cash Balance) of each repurchasing firm considered in this chapter is included in the initially hypothesized regression model. All three of these variables explain how well firms have used past cash flows to generate value for shareholders through the identification and implementation of positive NPV projects. Companies with high P/B and EBITDA/TA values have done well in investing in profitable, value creating projects and, thus, can be reasonably expected to continue making wise investment decisions in the future that will not prompt shareholders to demand the implementation of a repurchase program. A large accumulated cash balance implies that a company may have had trouble identifying positive NPV projects and, thus, may be pressured by shareholders to divest of a large portion of this accumulated cash through a share repurchase program to prevent the unprofitable investment of this excess cash in value-destroying negative NPV projects.

Companies with low P/B and EBITDA/TA values, on the other hand, have not been successful in identifying profitable investment projects and will likely face a continuing dearth of positive NPV opportunities in future periods. These companies are also more likely to face shareholder pressure to repurchase shares. Companies with low cash balances are not at risk of investing in negative NPV projects and are unlikely to implement a share repurchase program as they do not have the capital means to do so. Thus, it can be expected that P/B, EBITDA/TA, and Cash Balance value will be negatively correlated to share repurchase program size.

Initially Hypothesized Regression Model

The following variables will be included in an initially hypothesized regression model that seeks to predict the size of share repurchase programs implemented by U.S. industrial firms:

Y: Repurchase Value/Market Value of Equity (RepoVal/MktVal)

X_1: Price/Earnings (P/E)

X_2: Debt/Equity (D/E)

X_3: Aggregate value of option holdings of top three company executives (Option Value)

X_4: Four-year average change in Cash Flow (CF Volatility)

X_5: Nonoperating Cash Flow/Total Cash Flow (NOCF/Total CF)

X_6: Price/Book Value of Equity (P/B)

X_7: EBITDA/Total Assets (EBITDA/TA)

X_8: Balance Sheet Cash Balance (Cash Balance)

The complete regression model used to test the preceding hypotheses follows:

$$\left(\frac{RepoVal}{MktVal}\right) = fn\left(\left(\frac{P}{N}\right) + \left(\frac{D}{E}\right) + (OptionValue) + (CFVolatility) + \left(\frac{NOCF}{Total\ CF}\right) + \left(\frac{P}{B}\right) + \left(\frac{EBITDA}{TA}\right) + (CashBalance)\right)$$

REGRESSION ANALYSIS RESULTS

Before running a regression model to test the extent to which each of the variables in the model drives share repurchase program size, it was necessary to first develop a correlation matrix. A correlation matrix provides two key insights. First, it demonstrates the extent to which each tested variable is correlated with the dependent variable and whether that correlation is statistically significant. The correlation matrix also shows the extent to which each of tested independent variables is correlated with the other independent variables being considered and whether these correlations are statistically significant. The correlation matrix in Table 2.1 yields the following conclusions:

None of the variables tested is statistically significantly correlated with the dependent variable at an acceptable 0.05 level of significance. From this, it can be concluded that even though myriad managers and academics have cited each of the preceding tested hypotheses as a reason for implementing a share repurchase programs, there does not seem to be one prevailing motive that drives the size of all share repurchase programs initiated by U.S. industrial firms.

Table 5.1 Correlations

		RepoVal_MktVal	CFVolatility	EBITDA_TA	NOCF_TotalCF	D_E	CashBalance	P_E	P_B	OptionValue
RepoVal_MktVal	Pearson Correlation	1.000	.013	.001	-.056	.048	-.056	-.096	-.110	.073
	Sig. (2-tailed)		.834	.982	.371	.437	.370	.124	.076	.241
	N	261.000	261	261	261	261	261	256	261	261
CFVolatility	Pearson Correlation	.013	1.000	-.048	.163**	.197**	-.044	-.112	-.042	-.021
	Sig. (2-tailed)	.834		.442	.008	.001	.475	.073	.499	.738
	N	261	261.000	261	261	261	261	256	261	261
EBITDA_TA	Pearson Correlation	.001	-.048	1.000	.013	-.173**	-.171**	-.105	.245**	.135*
	Sig. (2-tailed)	.982	.442		.836	.005	.006	.093	.000	.030
	N	261	261	261.000	261	261	261	256	261	261
NOCF_TotalCF	Pearson Correlation	-.056	.163**	.013	1.000	.040	-.099	-.010	-.033	.027
	Sig. (2-tailed)	.371	.008	.836		.520	.111	.870	.597	.665
	N	261	261	261	261.000	261	261	256	261	261
D_E	Pearson Correlation	.048	.197**	-.173**	.040	1.000	-.046	.271**	.246**	-.114
	Sig. (2-tailed)	.437	.001	.005	.520		.456	.000	.000	.066
	N	261	261	261	261	261.000	261	256	261	261
CashBalance	Pearson Correlation	-.056	-.044	-.171**	-.099	-.046	1.000	.004	-.003	-.041
	Sig. (2-tailed)	.370	.475	.006	.111	.456		.955	.962	.514
	N	261	261	261	261	261	261.000	256	261	261
P_E	Pearson Correlation	-.096	-.112	-.105	-.010	.271**	.004	1.000	.222**	-.079
	Sig. (2-tailed)	.124	.073	.093	.870	.000	.955		.000	.207
	N	256	256	256	256	256	256	256.000	256	256
P_B	Pearson Correlation	-.110	-.042	.245**	-.033	.246**	-.003	.222**	1.000	-.043
	Sig. (2-tailed)	.076	.499	.000	.597	.000	.962	.000		.493
	N	261	261	261	261	261	261	256	261.000	261
OptionValue	Pearson Correlation	.073	-.021	.135*	.027	-.114	-.041	-.079	-.043	1.000
	Sig. (2-tailed)	.241	.738	.030	.665	.066	.514	.207	.493	
	N	261	261	261	261	261	261	256	261	261.000

CONCLUSION

The fact that none of the variables tested in this chapter can statistically significantly predict the size of share repurchase programs implemented by U.S. industrial firms at .05 confidence level suggests that firms repurchase shares for a vast number of reasons and are not consistently driven by any single motive to repurchase their stock. It is likely that many if not all of the hypotheses considered in this chapter contribute, at least to some extent, to the determination of the size of share repurchase programs; however, none seems to consistently inform the decision made by U.S. industrial firms about the size of their share repurchase programs.

Also, the fact that all of the variables tested in this chapter are statistically insignificant predictors of share repurchase program size is likely the reason why there currently exists a dearth of academic literature seeking to determine the motives that drive share repurchase program size. Literature abounds that discusses, analyzes, and statistically proves why managers repurchase stock; however, there have been no academic breakthroughs that have been able to demonstrate which factors consistently inform managerial decisions about the size of share repurchase programs.

So, given these results, what criteria should a board of directors employ as they wrestle with the decision of whether or not to approve a stock repurchase programs? Clearly, some of the criteria are in the stockholders interests; some favor higher management whereas some might endanger the long-term viability of a firm, which would clearly not be in the interest of employees. There are, of course, other stakeholders, such as financial analysts and government officials who could influence the board's decision-making process in determining the appropriateness of a stock repurchase. Is there any way of delineating how the board ought to view the possible contributions that these various stakeholders?

Stakeholder Analysis

> The fact that the businessman's work, although conducted as his private enterprise is nevertheless something which affects all members of the community. . . . express it permits us to relationship to government as that of a surrogate, a deputy.[34]

This certainly describes the situation that a board finds itself in deciding whether or not to approve a stock repurchase. Epstein (1969) provides examples in his work of this surrogateship (e.g., firms operate basic transportation, communications) and argues: "surrogateship is a fundamental ingredient of an interdependent capitalistic order" (208). Essentially, Epstein makes the case that corporations often act in the place of government and perform necessary functions for the overall good of society.

Surrogateship implies, if not demands, that the "deputy" knows what those they are representing want and that the deputy is in some level of communication with those they are representing. How does one assess the validity of such claims? One clear measure is how does the person/organization/government that is being represented act with regards to the deputy? Those who are being represented by a deputy can repudiate the actions of the deputy or note that one (or more) surrogates are their "true" representative.

There is, however, a subtle distinction that can be made here, in that the deputy can "assume" they know what those they are representing want and act on that assumption. If this last relationship is not true, than the party(ies) that the deputy is supposedly acting for can repudiate the actions of the deputy as not representing their interests as noted earlier.

However, this surrogateship, it could be argued, is not always as direct as Epstein's work implies. Indeed, government attempts to get business to bend to its will (and the last eighteen months of deepening government involvement in the automotive industry, investment banking, commercial banking, health care, and the mortgage and credit risk business is ample evidence of these influence attempts) can be direct, subtle, and a combination of direct and subtle tactics. However, government's strategies and tactics to "impose" surrogateship on business often take the form of regulations and the actions of regulatory agencies (again look at the current ongoing dispute between Treasury and the Federal Reserve as to who will best oversee and protect the consumer on issues of credit).

Epstein's original view of surrogateship allows for a different conception of stakeholders. The underlying argument for the existence of stakeholders is that they have a "stake" in the organization or in the issue at hand. What if a "stakeholder's" interest in an issue is not based on the organization or on the issue itself, but rather on their serving as a deputy or agent for the public interest or some other organizational set?

The best example that can be offered of this independent surrogateship relationship can be found in the actions of public interest groups. Public interest groups argue that they are acting in behalf of their membership—but the membership rarely knows what positions and actions the interest group is taking on their behalf, and the interest groups rarely seek approval from the broad base of membership. The reasonable question here is: is the public interest group actually representing the interests of all of its members, of the majority of its members, or their *interpretation* of what they think the members want?

So when a board of directors is playing the role of a surrogate/deputy in deciding whether or not to approve a stock repurchase, who are the potential stakeholders and how should they be evaluated? For a stock repurchase decision, there are five types of stakeholders that the surrogate must take into account:

1. issue/substance-based stakeholders
2. process-based stakeholders
3. industry- based stakeholders
4. ideological-based stakeholders
5. opportunistic-based stakeholders

At the outset, it is entirely possible that a given stakeholder could be in all five categories, but highly unlikely. It is more the case that a given stakeholder could be based in multiple categories noted in the preceding, but not all. It should also be clear that organizational response to stakeholders, if successful, will recognize whom and what the stakeholder is representing.

Issue/substance-based stakeholders are the easiest to address and tend to be the most researched in the literature. These are stakeholders who are focused on a narrow set of issues and concerned with the substantive aspects of those issues and their resolution. Stakeholders in this category are focused on the implication of a stock repurchase on the future of the firm. They are knowledgeable of the substance of the issue, are aware of the history surrounding the issue (legislative, judicial, public action, etc.), and are cognizant of the limits to which they can push a solution. The typical issue/substance stakeholders would be unions and towns and cities where a firm is located.

Process-based stakeholders are more concerned with the process by which issues are resolved and less concerned with the substantive aspects of the concerns. These stakeholders may be totally neutral with regards to which outcome is the "best" or "optimal" but are deeply concerned with the process by which a resolution is achieved. Their concerns are with access to due process, with the rules and equity and fairness by which a resolution is achieved. It should be immediately clear that a surrogate who treats issue/substance stakeholders and process-based stakeholders the same is going to face some challenges in achieving a solution. It is, as noted, quite possible that a stakeholder can be concerned with both substance and process—but what they are representing is quite different. The issue/substance stakeholders concern themselves with the substantive concerns around a repurchase of stock whereas the process stakeholder sees itself as a "deputy" to the process under which the repurchase takes place. The SEC and other governmental agencies would constitute this type of stakeholder.

Industry-based stakeholders are just what the name implies, stakeholders who have a narrow-based interest centered on a given industry. The best examples here are Wall Street brokers and others who specialize in a given industry. They represent their investors in those industries and track them very closely. Their "stake" in the industry is financial performance for their investors. They are less concerned with substantive or process-based issues except in how they impact on financial performance and return to investors. In most cases, their sole concern with a stock repurchase is: will this repurchase lead to a long-term increase in the price of the stock?

Ideological stakeholders pose a particular problem for a surrogate or deputy. Ideological stakeholders are committed to a specific course of action and a predetermined solution—there are no negotiations, there are no "middle grounds" for a resolution, and there is no compromise. These stakeholders represent an ideological position, usually in the case of a stock repurchase of a public interest group that is determined to change the conduct of a firm. They would usually oppose the stock repurchase on the grounds that it will make the corporation less responsive to their reforms. For example, suppose that Philip Morris proposed a stock repurchase; it would most likely be opposed by antismoking groups.

Any stakeholder can be "opportunistic." It is possible for a stakeholder to get involved in issues or situations because they see opportunities for advancement of the stakeholder in the issue—and the resolution of the issue is of secondary importance. In the case of a stock repurchase, if management's motivation to increase a stock's price lies solely with a stock option compensation plan, it appears that the primary motivation is strictly to preserve personal wealth, not in any of other stakeholder's long-term interests. Obviously the other "opportunistic" stakeholders could be the board itself as well as large holders of the stock who stand to gain from a repurchase of stock.

Nonetheless, a skeptical reader should be concerned with two aspects of this commentary. The fierce independence of governmental regulatory agencies such as the Federal Reserve and the SEC seems to suggest that the clarity of surrogateship remains muddled. In any event, looking more deeply at surrogateship from both a theoretical and practical perspective seems warranted, especially in regards to any controversy surrounding a stock repurchase program. Second, if the concept of surrogateship is pushed a bit, then one can act as a deputy not only to organizations, but to substance, to process, to ideology, to industry, and to opportunistic situations. This would suggest, then, that a board member's knowledge of an organization must be extensive. Whether or not this is feasible or could be required is something that also needs to be further studied.

NOTES

1. Jagannathan, Weisbach, and Stephens (2000).
2. Ibid.
3. Ghosh and Woolridge (1988); Denis and Kadlec (1994).
4. Jagannathan, Weisbach, and Stephens (2000).
5. Ibid.
6. Masulis (1980).
7. Vermaelen (1981).

8. Ibid. See also Comment and Jarrell (1991).
9. Vermaelen (1981); Ikenberry, Lakonishok, and Vermaelen (1995).
10. Ikenberry, Lakonishok, and Vermaelen (1999).
11. Vermaelen (1981).
12. Shoven (1986).
13. Miller and Modigliani (1961).
14. Jolls (1998).
15. Ibid.
16. Jagannathan, Weisbach, and Stephens (2000).
17. Ibid.
18. Ghosh and Woolridge (1988); Denis and Kadlec (1994).
19. Jagannathan, Weisbach, and Stephens (2000).
20. Lintner (1956).
21. Jagannathan, Weisbach, and Stephens (2000).
22. Ibid.
23. Ibid.
24. Ibid.
25. Grossman and Hart (1982); Jensen (1986).
26. Vermaelen (1981).
27. Miller and Modigliani (1961).
28. Grullon and Michaely (2004).
29. Ibid.
30. Maxwell and Stephens (2003).
31. Ibid.
32. Bagwell (1991).
33. Ibid.
34. Epstein (1969).

BIBLIOGRAPHY

Asquith, Paul, and David W. Mullins Jr. 1983. "The Impact of Initiating Dividend Payments on Shareholders' Wealth." *Journal of Business* 56:77–96.

Bagwell, Laurie S. 1991. "Share Repurchase and Takeover Deterrence." *Rand Journal of Economics* 22:72–88.

Bartov, Eli. 1991. "Open-Market Stock Repurchases as Signals for Earnings and Risk Changes." *Journal of Accounting and Economics* 14:275–294.

Benartzi, Shlomo, Roni Michaely, and Richard H. Thaler. 1997. "Do Changes in Dividends Signal the Future or the Past?" *Journal of Finance* 52:1007–1034.

Berk, Jonathan B., Richard C. Green, and Vasant Naik. 1999. "Optimal Investment, Growth Options, and Security Returns." *Journal of Finance* 54:1553–1607.

Bhattacharya, Sudipto. 1979. "Imperfect Information, Dividend Policy, and 'The Bird in the Hand' Fallacy." *Bell Journal of Economics* 10:259–270.

Boehme, Rodney, and Sorin M. Sorescu. 2002. "The Long-Run Performance Following Dividend Initiations and Resumptions: Underreaction or Product of Chance?" *Journal of Finance* 57:871–900.

Brav, Alon, John R. Graham, Campbell R. Harvey, and Roni Michaely. 2003. "Payout Policy in the 21st Century." Working Paper, Duke University.

Comment, Robert, and Gregg A. Jarrell. 1991. "The Relative Signaling Power of Dutch Auction and Fixed-Price Self Tender Offers and Open Market Share Repurchases." *Journal of Finance* 46:1243–1271.

Constantinides, George M., and Bruce D. Grundy. 1989. "Optimal Investment with Stock Repurchase and Financing as Signals." *Review of Financial Studies* 2:445–465.

Dann, Larry Y., Ronald W. Masulis, and David Mayers. 1991. "Repurchase Tender Offers and Earning Information." *Journal of Accounting and Economics* 14:217–251.

DeAngelo, Harry, Linda DeAngelo, and Douglas J. Skinner. 1996. "Reversal of Fortune: Dividend Signaling and the Disappearance of Sustained Earnings Growth." *Journal of Financial Economics* 40:341–371.

Denis, David J. 1990. "Defensive Changes in Corporate Payout Policy: Share Repurchases and Special Dividends." *Journal of Finance* 45 (5): 1433–1456.

Denis, David J., and Gregory B. Kadlec. 1994. "Corporate Events, Trading Activity, and the Estimation of Systematic Risk: Evidence from Equity Offerings and Share Repurchases." *Journal of Finance* 49:1787–1811.

Dittmar, Amy K. 2000. "Why Do Firms Repurchase Stock?" *Journal of Business* 73 (3): 321–356.

Epstein, E.M. 1969. *The Corporation in American Politics*. Englewood Cliffs, NJ: Prentice Hall.

Fama, Eugene F., and Kenneth R. French. 1993. "Common Risk Factors in the Returns on Stocks and Bonds." *Journal of Financial Economics* 33:3–56.

Fenn, George W., and Nellie Liang. 2001. "Corporate Payout Policy and Managerial Stock Incentives." *Journal of Financial Economics* 60:45–72.

Ghosh, Chinmoy, and Randal J. Woolridge. 1988. "An Analysis of Shareholder Reaction to Dividend Cuts and Omissions." *Journal of Financial Research* 11 (4): 281–295.

Grossman, Sanford J., and Oliver D. Hart. 1982. "Corporate Financial Structure and Managerial Incentives." in *The Economics of Information and Uncertainty*, ed. John McCall. Chicago: University of Chicago Press.

Grullon, Gustavo, and Roni Michaely. 2002. "Dividends, Share Repurchases, and the Substitution Hypothesis." *Journal of Finance* 57:1649–1684.

———. 2004. "The Information Content of Share Repurchase Programs." *Journal of Finance* 59:651–680.

Grullon, Gustavo, Roni Michaely, and Bhaskaran Swaminathan. 2002. "Are Dividend Changes a Sign of Firm Maturity?" *Journal of Business* 75:387–424.

Hausch, Donald B., and James K. Seward. 1993. "Signaling with Dividends and Share Repurchases: A Choice between Deterministic and Stochastic Cash Disbursements." *Review of Financial Studies* 6:121–154.

Hertzel, Michael, and Prem C. Jain. 1991. "Earnings and Risk Changes around Stock Repurchase Tender Offers." *Journal of Accounting and Economics* 14:253–274.

Ikenberry, David, Josef Lakonishok, and Theo Vermaelen, 1995. Market Underreaction to Open Market Share Repurchases." *Journal of Financial Economics* 39:181–208.

———. 1999. "Stock Repurchases in Canada." *Journal of Fianance*, 55(5): 2373–2397.

———. 2000. "Stock Repurchases in Canada: Performance and Strategic Trading." *Journal of Finance* 55:2373–2397.

Jagannathan, Murali, and Clifford P. Stephens, 2003. "Motives for Multiple Open-Market Repurchase Programs." *Financial Management* 32:71–91.

Jagannathan, Murali, Michael S. Weisbach, and Clifford P. Stephens. 2000. "Financial Flexibility and the Choice between Dividends and Stock Repurchases." *Journal of Financial Economics* 57:355–384.

Jensen, Michael C. 1986. "Agency Costs of Free Cash Flow, Corporate Finance, and Takeovers." *American Economic Review* 76:323–329.

Jolls, Christine. 1998. "Stock Repurchases and Incentive Compensation." *National Bureau of Economic Research*. Working Paper No. 6467.

Kalay, Avner, and Uri Loewenstein. 1986. "The Informational Content of the Timing of Dividend Announcements." *Journal of Financial Economics* 16:373–388.

Lie, Erik. 2000. "Excess Funds and Agency Problems: An Empirical Study of Incremental Cash Disbursements." *Review of Financial Studies* 13:219–247.

———. 2001. "Detecting Abnormal Operating Performance: Revisited." *Financial Management* 30:77–91.

Lintner, John. 1956. "Distribution of Incomes of Corporations among Dividends, Retained Earnings, and Taxes." *American Economic Review* 46:97–113.

Masulis, Ronald W. 1980. "Stock Repurchase by Tender Offer: An Analysis of the Causes of Common Stock Price Changes." *Journal of Finance* 35 (2): 305–319.

Maxwell, William F., and Clifford P. Stephens. 2003. "The Wealth Effect of Repurchases on Bondholders." *Journal of Finance* 58 (2): 895–919.

Miller, Merton H., and Franco Modigliani. 1961. "Dividend Policy, Growth and the Valuation of Shares." *Journal of Business* 34:411–433.

Miller, Merton H., and Kevin Rock. 1985. "Dividend Policy under Asymmetric Information." *Journal of Finance* 40:1031–1051.

Nohel, Tom, and Vefa Tarhan. 1998. "Share Repurchases and Firm Performance: New Evidence on the Agency Costs of Free Cash Flow." *Journal of Financial Economics* 49:187–222.

Ofer, Aharon R., and Anjan V. Thakor. 1987. "A Theory of Stock Price Responses to Alternative Corporate Cash Disbursements Methods: Stock Repurchase and Dividends." *Journal of Finance* 42:365–394.

Penman, Stephen H. 1983. "The Predictive Content of Earnings Forecasts and Dividends." *Journal of Finance* 38:1181–1199.

Persons, John C. 1997. "Heterogeneous Shareholders and Signaling with Share Repurchases." *Journal of Corporate Finance* 3:221–249.

Shoven, John B. 1986. "New Developments in Corporate Finance and Tax Avoidance: Some Evidence." *National Bureau of Economic Research*, Working Paper No. 2091.

Shoven, John B., and Laurie B. Simor. 1987. "Share Repurchases and Acquisitions: An Analysis of Which Firms Participate." *National Bureau of Economic Research*, Working Paper No. 2243.

Vermaelen, Theo. 1981. "Common Stock Repurchases and Market Signaling: An Empirical Study." *Journal of Financial Economics* 9:139–183.

———. 1984. "Repurchase Tender Offers, Signaling and Managerial Incentives." *Journal of Financial and Quantitative Analysis* 19:163–181.

Weisbenner, Scott J. 1998. "Share Repurchases in the 1990s: What Role Do Stock Options Play?" Federal Researve Board Working Paper, Washington DC.

Part II

Theoretical and Experimental Approaches to Risk Management

Before we describe the contributions made by the selected authors in this part of the book, we wish to offer two broad methodological remarks. First, risk management and corporate governance are truly complex subjects and any analysis of these topics is by necessity selective. Second, firms and individual traders alike require mechanisms to quantify and disseminate the levels of risk present in both financial and non-financial institutions. Risk management is, by nature, heavily quantitative since it requires measurement and thus subject to numerous approaches driven by traditional as well as new mathematical techniques. These two aspects are carefully and extensively discussed in two recent surveys by Jorion (2010) and Golub and Crum (2009). The four chapters that constitute Part II feature technical models and laboratory experiments that communicate information about managing risk, primarily, with targeted financial instruments.

In "Board Risk Oversight, Hedging Intensity, and the Idiosyncratic Risk of U.S. Banks," authors Fogel, Shao, and Yeager question whether the complexity of the risk environment makes effective risk management by banks' boards impossible. The authors attempt to answer that question by examining the intensity of a bank's interest-rate risk and foreign exchange hedging, as specific mechanisms through which corporate governance affects bank risk. The authors hope that these mechanisms and others identified in further research will serve as indicators of board quality for investors.

In "Tail Dependence of Major U.S. Stocks," Long Kang and Simon Babbs fill a gap in the literature related to methods of asset allocation and risk management in an extreme environment. Kang and Babbs argue that financial market volatility makes tail dependence, a non-normal property of multiple asset returns, a crucial tool for effectively managing risk and making asset allocation decisions. Because tail dependence measures the dependence structure of random variables in an extreme environment, it is necessary, they argue, to precisely quantify tail dependence of considered assets and find a proper model which well captures different tail dependence patterns in a multivariate setting. To do so, the authors review estimation methods of the tail dependence coefficient (TDC), simulating their finite-sample performance. Using semi-parametric and non-parametric estimators, they estimate TDCs of major U.S. stocks.

"Investors' Cognitive Profile and Herding," by Beatriz Fernández, Teresa Garcia-Merino,Rosa Mayoral Valle Santos, and Eleuterio Vallelado seeks to unravel complexities that lead to the phenomenon of investor herding. The authors use an experiment to observe and analyze subjects' behavior in a variety of settings that mimic the informational uncertainty present in financial markets, while taking into account the subjects' cognitive profiles. In a call for further research on the topic, the authors point to the need to better measure an investor's cognitive profile and its interaction with information processing in financial markets.

An investor making an optimal decision needs to know the true parameters underlying its distribution of asset returns. But the true parameters are unknown by the decision maker and have to be estimated. Under Markowitz's mean variance framework (1952), an investor cares only about expected returns and volatility of the static portfolio that should hold for the tangency portfolio on the efficient frontier. Following Tobin and Sharpe, the optimal portfolio for an investor is the mix between the tangency portfolio and the risk-free asset. To implement this portfolio in practice, one needs to estimate both expected returns and the covariance matrix from the time series. The standard estimators used by practitioners and academics are the sample mean for the expected returns and the sample covariance matrix. However, several empirical studies have pointed out that the assumption of normality does not hold for modeling assets returns. Thus, the sample tangency portfolio obtained from the standard portfolio model, due to estimation errors in the sample mean and sample covariance matrix produces extreme weights that fluctuate substantially over time and perform poorly out-of-sample. The paper by Ghislain Yanou on "Sample Tangency Portfolio, Representativeness and Ambiguity: Impact of the Law of Small Numbers" addresses these issues and provides a novel technique for improving the estimation.

REFERENCES

Golub, Bennett W. and Crum, Conan C., "Risk Management Lessons Worth Remembering from the Credit Crisis of 2007-2009 (October 31, 2009)". Available at SSRN: http://ssrn.com/abstract=1508674

Jorion, Philippe, "Risk Management (December 2010)", Annual Review of Financial Economics, Vol. 2, pp. 347-365, 2010. Available at SSRN: http://ssrn.com/abstract=1707921

6 Board Risk Oversight, Hedging Intensity, and the Idiosyncratic Risk of U.S. Banks

Kathy Fogel, Yingying Shao, and Timothy Yeager

INTRODUCTION

Can the board of directors of U.S. banks provide effective risk oversight in today's complex risk environment? The answer, according to Robert Rubin, former director of Citigroup, is no, because "[t]he board as a whole is not going to have a granular knowledge [of operations]."[1] If this view is representative of U.S. banks generally, it raises concerns about the strength of corporate governance in the banking industry and its impact on the risk management of these institutions. Intensity of risk management in turn affects the riskiness of bank stocks and, ultimately, the survival of the individual banks and the stability of financial markets.

This chapter also investigates the linkage between corporate governance and idiosyncratic risk of U.S. banks. Whereas other studies have tested similar hypotheses, we go further by trying to identify a specific mechanism through which corporate governance affects bank risk. The mechanism we examine is a bank's interest-rate risk and foreign exchange hedging intensity. Within this framework, we are able to test several hypotheses. The first hypothesis is that hedging intensity is positively correlated with better governed banks. Second, we hypothesize that better governed banks have lower idiosyncratic risk. The third hypothesis is that a firm's corporate governance characteristics fully explain a bank's hedging intensity. Support of the last hypothesis suggests that hedging intensity is a proxy for the firm's risk management such that corporate governance and hedging are best viewed as substitutes. Rejection of the hypothesis suggests that hedging and corporate governance are best viewed as complements.

We collect data on the characteristics of the board of the directors, focusing on the size (number of directors), structure (staggered or not), and independence of the board (percentage of outside board members). We also add CEO duality (whether CEO simultaneously serves as chairman of the board) and the index of managerial entrenchment.

We show that tighter corporate control by the board of directors is correlated with larger hedging positions. Banks with smaller and unstaggered boards and more outside directors tend to hedge more, controlling for an array of bank characteristics. This is consistent with prior literature such as

Lel (2009) and Dionne and Triki (2005) that relates strong board monitoring to larger hedging positions. Banks where CEOs also serve as chairmen tend to hedge more, possibly suggesting that the information advantage that management possesses outweighs agency concern (Brickley, Cole, and Jarrell 1997).

We also show that, in general, tighter corporate control reduces idiosyncratic risk. Banks with more outside directors and CEO duality have lower idiosyncratic risk. Hedging, however, lowers idiosyncratic risk by statistically significant amounts even after controlling for board characteristics. Taken together, these results suggest that board characteristics and hedging activity are best viewed as complements to risk management, not substitutes.

The rest of the chapter will proceed as follows. The next section provides an overview of the literature on corporate governance of financial institutions, and establishes the connection between board characteristics, intensity and effectiveness of risk management, and a bank's idiosyncratic risk. The third section describes the data used in the empirical investigation. Econometric analysis and discussion of the results are detailed in the fourth section. Finally, the fifth section concludes.

BOARD CHARACTERISTICS AND HEDGING INTENSITY IN FINANCIAL INSTITUTIONS

Whereas regulators ponder the colossal failure of the current regulatory infrastructure,[2] more attention has focused on the effectiveness of internal control mechanisms at U.S. banks. Has the board of directors satisfied its fiduciary duty of monitoring and controlling strategic managerial decisions such as containing and managing risks? Although board members cannot (and should not) be directly involved in the actual day-to-day risk management operations, directors should at least assure themselves that a proper risk management process is functioning and opportunistic risk taking is contained within a prespecified range.

The boards of financial institutions should be concerned about risk management more than their counterparts in limited liability companies of all other industries because the assets banks accumulate are largely financial assets that bear interest-rate, currency, default, liquidity, and general economic risk. Although the protection of the federal deposit insurance may reduce the bank's incentive to hedge, Whidbee and Wohar (1999) show that deposit insurance implies that a certain class of debt holders does not bear downside risk, and therefore the payoff to equity holders is even more convex than other industries. Diamond (1991) shows that risk management of financial intermediaries reduces bankruptcy costs and preserves bank charter values.

The theoretical predictions and empirical findings of the effect of corporate governance on hedging practice are multifaceted. One strand of research emphasizes a positive relation between stronger board control and larger hedging propensity. For example, Lel (2009) demonstrates that strong monitoring by the board and large shareholders has a major impact on a firms' use of derivatives. Dionne and Triki (2005) show that firms with independent boards and financially knowledgeable audit committees have larger hedge ratios.

Another strand of research focuses on the role of minority shareholder protection and advocacy in corporate governance. In this case, better corporate governance is correlated with more risk taking to maximize shareholder wealth. Due to career concerns or to preserve large private benefits from on-the-job consumption, entrenched insiders tend to be overly conservative in their investment decisions (John, Litov, and Yeung 2008). On the other hand, diversified minority shareholders tend to benefit more from risk taking. It therefore follows that stronger outside investor rights should related to higher risk raking (Esty 1998).[3]

Although the very act of "hedging" cannot be interpreted as the exact opposite of risk taking, we argue (and empirically demonstrate) that larger hedging positions relate to lower bank idiosyncratic risk. Froot, Scharfstein, and Stein (1993) theorize that hedging reduces the variability of cash flows, hence reducing the probability of financial distress. Smith and Stulz (1985) further show that hedging reduces the volatility of taxable cash flow in the real world with progressive tax rate schemes. The risk-reduction effect of hedging could further be translated to greater firm-value, as shown in Allayannis and Weston (2001) and others.

Furthermore, hedging allows better information flows to outside investors and other market participants and this reduces information asymmetry between insiders and outsiders. DeMarzo and Duffie (1991) argue that hedging mitigates information asymmetry between corporate insiders and outside investors, thereby reducing firm-specific risk. DeMarzo and Duffie (1995) investigate the role of managerial career concerns in determining corporate financial hedging policy. A reduction in information asymmetry facilitates the transformation of a signal of management ability. Guay, Haushalter, and Minton (2002) show that information asymmetry proxied by the errors and dispersion in analysts' forecasts is significantly correlated with unexpected shocks in earnings, and that the firm's hedging strategies are related to this earnings uncertainty. Finally, DaDalt, Gay, and Nam (2002) add to the evidence that the use of derivatives is associated with lower asymmetric information.

We fully recognize our limitations. Bank executives might have different motivations to hedge their interest rate, exchange rate, or other exposures; however, unable to observe those motivations directly, we cannot distinguish between "prudence" and "conservatism." We simply argue that, particularly during market crashes and financial crises, hedging reduces the potential for extreme losses and improves a bank's chance of survival.

In summary, board oversight is critically related to a firm's risk management practice, financial health, and survival. We hypothesize that one channel through which strong board oversight reduces firm idiosyncratic risk is sound risk management practice. We therefore adopt a three-step panel regression approach, starting by signing the relations between hedging intensity and firm idiosyncratic risk. We then investigate various aspects of corporate control and their effect on risk management practices. Finally, we use the kitchen-sink technique to connect corporate governance, hedging intensity, and the idiosyncratic risk of U.S. banks.

DATA AND VARIABLES

Our sample includes 143 publicly traded bank holding companies (BHCs) with total assets greater than $5 billion for the period from 1995 to 2008.

The major risk exposures of large BHCs are interest-rate risk, credit risk, and foreign exchange risk for multinational banks. Therefore, we focus on interest-rate derivatives and foreign exchange derivatives as hedging instruments. The data are from the Federal Reserve Bank's FR Y-9C reports. Hedging intensity is measured as the notional amount of derivatives reported under "contracts held for non-trading purposes" divided by the total assets of the bank at the end of each quarter.[4]

Our variables on board characteristics are hand collected from the annual proxy statement through SEC EDGAR, and include information on the size, structure, independence of the board of directors, CEO/chairman duality, and an index measuring board/executive entrenchment, the E-index. *Board Size* is the number of the directors on the board of directors. *Classified* is a dummy variable that equals one if the terms of board members are staggered and zero otherwise. *Outside* is the proportion of independent directors on the board. *Duality* is a dummy variable that equals one if the CEO is also the chairman of the board and zero otherwise. *E-Index* is the entrenchment index defined by Bebchuk, Cohen, and Farrell (2009) with higher values indicating more entrenchment.

Our measure of idiosyncratic volatility follows Morck, Yeung, and Yu (2000) and is defined as the natural logarithm of $(1-R^2)/R^2$, where R^2 is derived from the market model:

$$r_{it} = \alpha_i + \beta_i (r_{mt} - r_{ft}) + \varepsilon_i \tag{1}$$

r_{it} is the excess return for stock i on day t, and $(r_{mt}-r_{ft})$ is the market risk premium. Based on equation (1), the relative bank-specific idiosyncratic risk, defined as the ratio of idiosyncratic variance to total variance, is precisely $1 - R^2_{it}$. Given the bounded nature of R^2_{it}, we use a logistic transformation of $1 - R^2_{it}$

$$\psi_{it} = \log(\frac{1 - R_{it}^2}{R_{it}^2}) \quad (2)$$

Thus, the variable ψ_{it} measures bank-specific idiosyncratic risk relative to systematic risk.

We first explore the role of board control mechanisms in influencing banks' hedging activities. We regress the hedging intensity variables against a variety of corporate governance variables, controlling for bank characteristics. The regression framework is the following:

$$Hedge_{it} = \gamma_0 + \gamma_1 Board_{it} + \gamma_2 ROE_{it} + \gamma_3 CAP_{it} + \gamma_4 MTB_{it} + \gamma_5 TL_{it} + \varepsilon_{it} \quad (3)$$

$Hedge_{it}$ measures the interest-rate or exchange rate hedging intensity of a bank, and $Board_{it}$ is a vector of board-characteristic variables defined earlier. Because the hedging intensity variables are quarterly data and corporate governance variables are annual data, we repeat the annual value for each of the four quarters in each year to form our sample.

We then examine how a bank's hedging intensity and board control affect the idiosyncratic risk of its stock return using the following regression:

$$\psi_{it} = \delta_0 + \delta_1 Hedge_{it} + \delta_2 Board_{it} + \delta_3 ROE_{it} + \delta_4 CAP_{it} + \delta_5 MTB_{it} + \delta_6 TL_{it} + \varepsilon_{it} \quad (4)$$

where ψ_{it} is the logistic transformed relative idiosyncratic volatility generated from equation (2). We include the group of board variables (*Board*) to examine how they matter to bank risk. The independent variable $Hedge_{it}$, is a bank's hedging activities using interest-rate and foreign exchange derivatives. If the bank's hedging activities reduce bank-specific risk above and beyond the board variables, we would expect to see a negative sign on the regression coefficient of $Hedge_{it}$. The control variables may also contribute to the bank's idiosyncratic risk and include *ROE*, defined as the ratio of the market value of equity to total assets and measures bank profitability; *CAP*, defined as the ratio of the market value of equity to total assets and measures bank leverage; *MTB*, the ratio of market equity to book equity measuring the growth opportunity; and *TL*, the ratio of total loans to total assets.

Table 6.1 describes the summary statistics of the main variables for our sample going from 1995 to 2008. On average, the notional amount of interest-rate derivative contracts represents about 20.5 percent of total bank assets. The notional amount of foreign exchange rate derivatives accounts for about 1 percent of bank assets. The average number of directors on the board of U.S. financial institutions is about fifteen. Over three-quarters are considered independent directors not directly affiliated with the bank otherwise. About 67 percent of bank use classified board, and 78 percent of the sample banks employ one executive as the CEO-chairman.

Table 6.1 Summary Statistics

	Sample	*Mean*	*Std Dev*	*Min*	*Max*
Idiosyncratic Risk	4288	0.927	1.147	-1.118	4.368
Interest-Rate Hedging	4288	0.205	0.484	0.000	8.962
Foreign Exchange Hedging	4281	0.010	0.045	0.000	1.095
Board Size	4288	14.58	4.690	1.000	36.00
Classified	4271	0.672	0.470	0.000	1.000
Outside	4288	0.778	0.124	0.000	0.962
Duality	4271	0.774	0.419	0.000	1.000
E-Index	3908	2.801	1.447	0.000	6.000
CAP	4288	0.107	0.073	0.033	1.113
ROE	4288	0.146	0.074	-0.221	0.302
MTB	4288	2.195	0.998	0.172	11.27
TL	4288	0.722	0.208	0.015	1.329

This table reports summary statistics for publicly traded BHCs with total assets greater than $5 billion. The relative measure of idiosyncratic risk is estimated using the market model. *Interest Rate (Foreign Exchange) Hedging* are the quarterly ratios of the notional amounts of hedging positions in interest-rate (foreign exchange) derivatives over the total assets of the banks. *Board Size* is the number of the directors on the board of directors. *Classified* is a dummy variable that equals one if the board is classified, and zero otherwise. *Outside* is the proportion of independent directors on the board. *Duality* is a dummy variable that equals one if the CEO is also the chairman of the board and zero otherwise. *E-Index* is the entrenchment index defined by Bebchuk, Cohen, and Farrell (2009) with higher values indicating more entrenchment. *CAP* is the ratio of the market value of equity to total assets. *ROE* is the ratio of net income to the market value of equity. *MTB* is the ratio of the market value and book value of equity. *TL* is the ratio of total loans to total assets. The sample includes data from 1995 to 2008.

RESULTS AND DISCUSSIONS

We first study the relationship between various aspects of corporate board and CEO characteristics and a bank's hedging intensity. We utilize the Fama-MacBeth (1973) regression methodology to capture the cross-sectional variations in hedge and board control while adjusting for the time series property of the panel data. The dependent variables are the log of the ratios of hedging positions in interest rate and foreign exchange, each divided by total bank assets. The control variables include the return on equity for profitability (ROE), total equity over total asset for leverage (CAP), the market-to-book ratio (MTB), and the total loan-to-assets ratio (TL). The variables of interests are board characteristics including board size, structure, independence, CEO duality, and entrenchment. Tables 6.2 and 6.3 present the regression coefficients and model fit statistics for interest-rate hedging and foreign exchange hedging, respectively, with each board variable appearing one at a time, so we could gauge the maximum possible influence of these variables and remove any concern from multicollinearity.

One dimension of corporate board characteristics frequently examined in empirical literature is board size, the total number of directors on a particular firm's board. Jensen (1993) contends that small boards are more effective. Yermack (1996) finds that firms with smaller boards tend to have higher market valuations. We show that a smaller board also correlates with larger hedging positions against interest-rate risk, but the relation is not statistically significant with interest-rate hedging and only marginally significant with foreign exchange hedging.

Table 6.2 Board Characteristics and Interest-Rate Hedging

	Interest-Rate Hedging									
Board Size	-0.007	(.20)								
Classified			-0.499	(.00)						
Outside					1.068	(.00)				
Duality							0.133	(.02)		
E-Index									-0.133	(.00)
CAP	-17.07	(.00)	-17.58	(.00)	-17.23	(.00)	-17.08	(.00)	-17.78	(.00)
ROE	4.732	(.00)	4.506	(.00)	4.647	(.00)	4.789	(.00)	5.027	(.00)
MTB	-0.301	(.00)	-0.258	(.00)	-0.302	(.00)	-0.289	(.00)	-0.267	(.00)
TL	0.432	(.00)	0.691	(.00)	0.576	(.00)	0.438	(.00)	0.592	(.00)
Constant	-1.567	(.00)	-1.485	(.00)	-2.550	(.00)	-1.820	(.00)	-1.427	(.00)
Sample	4288		4271		4288		4271		3908	
F-Stat	23.34	(.00)	36.73	(.00)	64.05	(.00)	21.30	(.00)	22.86	(.00)
Avg. R^2	0.133		0.160		0.153		0.136		0.182	

This table reports regression coefficients and model fit statistics for Fama-MacBeth regressions of interest-rate hedging intensity. The dependent variable is *Interest-Rate Hedging*, the log of a quarterly ratio defined as the notional amount of hedging position in interest rate derivative to bank total assets. The explanatory variables of interests are board characteristics. Board Size is the number of the directors on the board of directors. *Classified* is a dummy variable that equals one if the board is classified, and zero otherwise. *Outside* is the proportion of independent directors on the board. *Duality* is a dummy variable that equals one if the CEO is also the chairman of the board, and zero otherwise. *E-Index* is the entrenchment index defined by Bebchuk, Cohen, and Farrell (2009) with higher values indicating more entrenchment. The control variables include *CAP*, the ratio of the market value of equity to total assets; *ROE*, net income over the market value of equity; *MTB*, the ratio of the market value to book value of equity; and *TL*, the ratio of total loans to total assets. The sample includes data from 1995 to 2008. Probability values rejecting the null hypothesis of zero regression coefficients or of zero F-Statistics are reported in the parentheses.

Table 6.3 Board Characteristics and Foreign Exchange Hedging

	Foreign Exchange Hedging									
Board Size	-0.020	(.11)								
Classified			-0.453	(.00)						
Outside					0.737	(.27)				
Duality							0.952	(.00)		
E-Index									-0.274	(.00)
CAP	-8.039	(.06)	-7.869	(.05)	-9.699	(.04)	-8.446	(.03)	-8.686	(.04)
ROE	4.003	(.01)	3.758	(.01)	3.790	(.03)	4.145	(.01)	1.997	(.18)
MTB	-0.244	(.05)	-0.235	(.06)	-0.233	(.06)	-0.241	(.05)	-0.135	(.25)
TL	-3.544	(.00)	-3.112	(.00)	-2.980	(.00)	-3.238	(.00)	-3.076	(.00)
Constant	-2.382	(.00)	-2.698	(.00)	-3.443	(.00)	-3.713	(.00)	-2.045	(.00)
Sample	1659		1659		1659		1659		1532	
F-Stat	76.37	(.00)	67.74	(.00)	60.08	(.00)	61.92	(.00)	70.38	(.00)
Avg. R^2	0.250		0.250		0.271		0.275		0.280	

This table reports regression coefficients and model fit statistics for Fama-MacBeth regressions of foreign exchange hedging intensity. The dependent variable is *Foreign Exchange Hedging*, the log of a quarterly ratio defined as the notional amount of hedging positions in foreign exchange derivatives to bank total assets. The explanatory variables of interests are board characteristics. *Board Size* is the number of the directors on the board of directors. Classified is a dummy variable that equals one if the board is classified, and zero otherwise. Outside is the proportion of independent directors on the board. *Duality* is a dummy variable that equals one if the CEO is also the chairman of the board, and zero otherwise. *E-Index* is the entrenchment index defined by Bebchuk, Cohen, and Farrell (2009) with higher values indicating more entrenchment. The control variables include *CAP*, the ratio of the market value of equity to total assets; *ROE*, net income over the market value of equity; *MTB*, the ratio of the market value to book value of equity; and *TL*, the ratio of total loans to total assets. The sample includes data from 1995 to 2008. Probability values rejecting the null hypothesis of zero regression coefficients or of zero F-Statistics are reported in the parentheses.

Board Classification

A classified board is one that reelects only a fraction of directors each year. Faleye (2007) shows that classified boards benefit incumbent management at the expense of shareholders, thus it is an indication of poor corporate governance. In our full sample, 68 percent of banks have classified boards, and they appear to relate to smaller hedging positions ceteris paribus. The results hold consistently with respect to interest-rate and foreign exchange hedging and they are highly statistically and economically significant. All else equal, having a classified board reduces interest-rate hedging by 39 percent, which represents 0.8 times the standard deviation from the mean.

Board Independence

Our measure of board independence is the percentage of outside directors in a particular board. Fama and Jensen (1983) argue that outside directors have an incentive to exert stronger control in an effort to build reputations as experts. Yermack (2004) shows that outside directors receive significant monetary and stock compensation as incentives for performance.

Our regressions indicate that board independence is positively related to hedging intensity in interest rate and foreign exchange, although only the interest-rate coefficient is statistically significant. Holding all other factors at their mean, having an additional independent director relates to an 8 percent increase in interest-rate hedging intensity.

CEO Duality

Shareholder activists and economists have long been concerned about the strength of the board control when the CEO also chairs the board (Jensen 1993, most notably). Pi and Timme (1993) show that when the CEO and chairman are the same person, cost efficiency and asset returns are lower for financial institutions. On the other hand, Brickley, Coles, and Jarrell (1994) show that the costs from splitting the two positions to two persons outweighs the benefits. For example, CEO duality is considered beneficial when the cost of transferring information between the board and the management is relatively high. High complexity of today's financial institutions makes the proprietary information of the CEO valuable to the board. In fact, over three-quarters of CEOs in our sample banks also occupy the chairman of the board position. Particularly, a nonparametric rank test shows that larger banks tend to have dual CEO-chairmen. We find that CEO duality is positively and significantly related to hedging intensity. One possible interpretation of this result is that high levels of information asymmetry improve the cost-benefit tradeoff of having a dual CEO-chairman, and that the information advantage outweighs the agency cost of entrenchment, but we welcome alternative interpretations of the results.

Overall Measure of Board Entrenchment

We use Bebchuk, Cohen, and Ferrell's (2009) executive entrenchment index as a measure of agency costs. The entrenchment index includes six components, and banks score one for each of

(1) Board is classified.
(2) Company adopts shareholder right plans (poison pills).
(3) Company has golden parachutes in place.
(4) Supermajority votes are required for bylaw amendments.

(5) Supermajority votes are required for charter amendments.
(6) Supermajority votes are required to approve a merger.

The e-index for our sample banks rank from zero to six, with an average of 2.8.

The entrenchment index is negatively and significantly related to hedging intensity, indicating a lower hedge ratio associated with more degree of entrenchment controlling for bank characteristics. The results are consistent for both interest-rate and foreign exchange hedging. This result lends another support to our main hypothesis that better board control and stronger outside shareholder rights relate to more hedging activities. The effect is economically significant. Having one additional item of supermajority requirement or other entrenchment provision reduces interest-rate hedging by 12 percent (or 0.25 times standard deviation from sample mean) and foreign exchange hedging by 24 percent (or five times standard deviation from sample mean), holding all other variables constant.

To summarize, we find a strong association between better board control and bank hedging with interest-rate and exchange rate derivatives.

Board Characteristics, Hedging Intensity, and Idiosyncratic Risk

The previous results suggest that strong corporate governance encourages banks to engage in hedging activities to manage their exposure to interest-rate and foreign exchange rate risk. The first regression of Table 6.4 reported in the first column shows that such board control reduces the idiosyncratic risk of bank stock returns. Particularly, when we include all five measures of board control in Fama-MacBeth regressions to explain bank idiosyncratic risk, we find that a higher proportion of independent directors and dual-positioned CEOs relate to reduced bank risk at less than 1 percent statistical significance. Somewhat surprisingly, we find that larger board size and classified boards reduce idiosyncratic risk, although the coefficient on classified boards is statistically insignificant.

We then examine how hedging and board control jointly affect bank risk. The next two columns of Table 6.4 report the Fama-MacBeth procedure of regressing bank idiosyncratic risk on interest-rate hedging intensity and governance control variables.[5] If hedging acts as the channel through which corporate governance control reduces idiosyncratic risk, then we would expect to see the regression coefficients of hedging intensity variables become insignificant in the presence of board control characteristics. Alternatively, if hedging and board control complement each other in reducing bank risk, we should see them both significant in the regressions. The significance of hedging intensity in interest-rate and foreign exchange derivatives remains, and the signs and magnitude of the coefficients on board control also stay about the same compared

Table 6.4 Board Characteristics, Hedging Intensity, and the Idiosyncratic Risk

	Idiosyncratic Risk					
Interest-Rate Hedging			-0.074	(.00)		
Foreign Exchange Hedging					-0.031	(.02)
Board Size	-0.012	(.00)	-0.011	(.01)	-0.022	(.00)
Classified	-0.062	(.17)	-0.100	(.04)	0.117	(.19)
Outside	-0.697	(.00)	-0.720	(.00)	-0.751	(.01)
Duality	-0.266	(.00)	-0.272	(.00)	-0.181	(.06)
E-Index	0.016	(.30)	0.009	(.50)	0.039	(.20)
CAP	3.442	(.01)	0.381	(.67)	2.735	(.11)
ROE	-1.068	(.01)	-0.849	(.04)	-2.353	(.00)
MTB	-0.115	(.00)	-0.110	(.00)	0.012	(.75)
TL	-0.161	(.12)	-0.037	(.68)	-0.412	(.02)
constant	2.052	(.00)	2.011	(.00)	1.702	(.00)
Sample	3874		3874		1532	
F-Stat	17.74	(.00)	15.30	(.00)	8.56	(.00)
Avg. R^2	0.240		0.278		0.524	

This table reports regression coefficients and model fit statistics for Fama-MacBeth regressions of bank idiosyncratic risk on interest-rate and foreign exchange hedging intensity and board characteristics. The dependent variable is relative idiosyncratic risk estimated using the market model. The explanatory variable of interest is *Interest-Rate (Foreign Exchange) Hedging*, the log of a quarterly ratio defined as the notional amount of hedging position in interest-rate (foreign exchange) derivative over bank total assets. *Board Size* is the number of the directors on the board of directors. *Classified* is a dummy variable that equals one if the board is classified, and zero otherwise. *Outside* is the proportion of independent directors on the board. *Duality* is a dummy variable that equals one if the CEO is also the chairman of the board, and zero otherwise. *E-Index* is the entrenchment index defined by Bebchuk, Cohen, and Farrell (2009) with higher values indicating more entrenchment. The control variables include *CAP*, the ratio of the market value of equity to total assets; *ROE*, net income over the market value of equity; *MTB*, the ratio of the market value to book value of equity; and *TL*, the ratio of total loans to total assets. The sample includes data from 1995 to 2008. Probability values rejecting the null hypothesis of zero regression coefficients or of zero F-Statistics are reported in the parentheses.

to the results on the left side of Table 6.4. These results suggest that bank's hedging activities and better board control serve as complements in reducing bank-specific idiosyncratic risk.

CONCLUSIONS AND POSSIBLE EXTENSIONS

We find positive and significant relationships between measures of good board control and the intensity of banks' hedging activities. In addition, larger hedging positions and better boards serve as complements in reducing the idiosyncratic risk of bank stocks. Our results are consistent with DeMarzo and Duffie (1991, 1995); Froot, Scharfstein, and Stein (1993); Smith and Stulz (1985); and others who find the risk-reduction effect of hedging; and with Ferreira and Laux (2007) that stronger corporate control reduces idiosyncratic risk. In addition, we establish a link between stronger board control and hedging, and argue that better corporate governance contributes to higher market valuation of financial institutions through increased hedging intensity, which reduces idiosyncratic risk.

Weak board control at large financial institutions may be a contributing factor to financial crises because firms with weak boards hedge less, which exposes them to higher idiosyncratic risk. Hedging is but one mechanism that links corporate governance to risk management. Further research is needed to identify other mechanisms. These mechanisms can signal the quality of boards to outside investors.

NOTES

1. "Rubin, Under Fire, Defends His Role at Citi," *Wall Street Journal*, November 29, 2008.
2. For example, Federal Reserve Chairman Ben Bernanke spoke about the necessity to "begin thinking about the reforms to the financial architecture [. . .] that could help prevent a similar crisis from developing in the future" at the Council on Foreign Relations, Washington, DC, March 10, 2009, in "Financial Reform to Address Systemic Risk."
3. We wish to note that one exception to this line of argument is Saunders, Strock, and Travlos (1990), who find that banks with larger insider stock ownership assume higher risk than those controlled by managers with small ownership fractions.
4. Most derivative positions at large commercial banks result from market-making activity. Our data exclude such derivatives.
5. The last two regressions of Table 6.4 raise the concern of possible multicollinearity between the hedging variables and board characteristics. We therefore regress hedging on all board characteristics and controls and calculate the residuals from such regressions. We then rerun the regressions using the hedging residual and board characteristics, and the results are nearly identical.

BIBLIOGRAPHY

Allayannis, G., and J.P. Weston. 2001. "The Use of Foreign Currency Derivatives and Firm Market Value." *Review of Financial Studies* 14:243–276.

Bebchuk, Lucian, Alma Cohen, and Allen Ferrell. 2009. "What Matters in Corporate Governance?" *Review of Financial Studies* 22:783–827.

Brickley, J.A., J.L. Coles, and G. Jarrell. 1997. "Corporat Leadership Structure Separating the CEO and Chairman of the Board." *Journal of Corporate Finance* 3: 189–220.

DaDalt, P., G.D. Gay, and J. Nam. 2002. "Asymmetric Information and Corporate Derivative Use." *Journal of Futures Markets* 22:241–267.

DeMarzo, Peter, and Darrell Duffie. 1991. "Corporate Financial Hedging with Proprietary Information." *Journal of Economic Theory* 53:261–286.

———. 1995. "Corporate Incentives for Hedging and Hedge Accounting." *Review of Financial Studies* 8:743–771.

Diamond, D.W. 1984. "Financial Intermediation and Delegated Monitoring." *Review of Economic Studies* 51:393–414.

———. 1991. "Debt Maturity Structure and Liquidity Risk." *Quarterly Journal of Economics* 106:709–737.

Dionne, Georges, and Thouraya Triki. 2005. "Risk Management and Corporate Governance: The Importance of Independence and Financial Knowledge for the Board and the Audit Committee." HEC Montreal Working Paper No. 05–03.

Esty, Benjamin. 1998. "The Impact of Contingent Liability on Commercial Bank Risk Taking." *Journal of Financial Economics* 47:189–218.

Faleye, Olubunmi. 2007." Classified Boards, Firm Value, and Managerial Entrenchment." *Journal of Financial Economics* 83:501–529.

———. 2009. "Classified Boards, Stability, and Strategic Risk Taking." *Financial Analysts Journal* 65 (1): 54–65.

Fama, Eugene, and Kenneth French. 1992. "The Cross-Section of Expected Stock Returns." *Journal of Finance* 25:427–465.

Fama, Eugene, and Michael Jensen. 1983. "Separation of Ownership and Control." *Journal of Law and Economics* 26:301–325.

Fama Eugene, and James MacBeth 1973. "Risk, Return, and Equilibrium: Empirical Tests." *Journal of Political Economy* 81(3):607–636.

Ferreira, Miguel, and Paul Laux. 2007. "Corporate Governance, Idiosyncratic Risk, and Information Flow." *Journal of Finance* 62(2):951–990.

Froot, K.A., D.S. Scharfstein, and J.C. Stein. 1993. "Risk Management: Coordinating Corporate Investments and Financing Policies." *Journal of Finance* 5:1629–1658.

Guay, W., D. Haushalter, and B. Minton. 2002. "The Influence Corporate Risk Exposures on the Accuracy of Analysts' Forecasts." Working Paper, University of Pennsylvania.

Houston, J., and C. James. 1995. "CEO Compensation and Bank Risk: Is Compensation in Banking Structured to Promote Risk Taking?" *Journal of Monetary Economics* 36:405–431.

Jensen, Michael. 1993. "The Modern Industrial Revolution, Exit, and the Failure of Internal Control Systems." *Journal of Finance* 48 (3): 831–880.

John, Kose, Lubommir Litov, and Bernard Yeung. 2008. "Corporate Governance and Risk Taking." *Journal of Finance* 63:1679–1728.

Laeven, Luc, and Ross Levine. 2009. "Bank Governance, Regulation and Risk Taking." *Journal of Financial Economics* 93(2):259–275.

Lel, Ugur. 2009. "Currency Hedging and Corporate Governance: A Cross-Country Analysis." Working Paper, Indiana University.

Markowitz, H. 1952. "Portfolio Selection." *The Journal of Finance* 7(1):77–91.

Morck, R., A. Shleifer, and R.W. Vishny. 1988. "Management Ownership and Market Valuation—an Empirical-Analysis." *Journal of Financial Economics* 20:293–315.

Morck, Randall, Bernard Yeung, and Wayne Yu. 2000. "The Information Content of Stock Markets: Why Do Emerging Markets Have Synchronous Price Movements?" *Journal of Financial Economics* 25:215–260.

Pi, L., and S.G. Timme. 1993. "Corporate Control and Bank Efficiency." *Journal of Banking and Finance* 20:515–530.

Saunders, A., E. Strock, and N.G. Travlos. 1990. "Ownership Structure, Deregulation, and Bank Risk Taking." *Journal of Finance* 45:643–654.

Smith, C., and R. Stulz. 1985. "The Determinants of Firms' Hedging Policies." *Journal of Financial and Quantitative Analysis* 28:391–405.

Whidbee, David A., and Mark Wohar. 1999. "Derivative Activities and Managerial Incentives in the Banking Industry." *Journal of Corporate Finance* 5 (3): 251–276.

Yermack, D. 1996. "Higher Market Valuation of Companies with a Small Board of Directors." *Journal of Financial Economics* 40:185–211.

———. 2004. "Remuneration, Retention, and Reputation Incentives for Outside Directors." *Journal of Finance* 59:2281–2308.

7 Tail Dependence of Major U.S. Stocks

Long Kang and Simon Babbs

INTRODUCTION

Much work has been done by researchers and practitioners to explore non-normal properties of multiple asset returns. Among these properties, tail dependence measures the dependence structure of random variables in an extreme environment. With a volatile financial environment, tail dependence becomes more important for asset allocation and risk management. For instance, to increase risk-adjusted returns, risk managers typically pursue diversification strategies by exploiting positive and negative correlations of various asset returns. However, this diversification strategy will become less effective or even fail in the extreme environment and result in significant portfolio losses. Hence, one task faced by researchers and practitioners is to precisely quantify tail dependence of considered assets and find a proper model that captures different tail dependence patterns well in a multivariate setting.

To the best of our knowledge, there has not been any work focusing on estimating tail dependence coefficients (TDCs) for a wide range of individual U.S. stocks. Papers such as Dobric and Schmid (2005), Schmidt and Stadtmueller (2006), and Frahm et al. (2005) mainly focus on deriving and comparing properties of TDC estimators, and only apply the estimation methods to a very limited set of data for illustration purposes. Other research work only uses tail dependence as a specific property of the data for which their time series model needs to account (e.g., Fortin and Kuzmics 2002). To fill this gap, we conduct an empirical investigation on tail dependence of nine major sectors of U.S. stocks. We have three aims. The first is to establish the "stylized facts" about tail dependence among major U.S. stocks. The second is to compare the "stylized facts" with TDCs implied by a multivariate Student's *t* copula model so as to assess its ability of capturing tail dependence patterns of a large set of assets. The third is to explore the accuracy of estimates of value at risk (VaR) and expected shortfall (ES) when a multivariate Student's *t* copula is used to capture tail dependence.

We first give a brief overview on estimation methods of TDCs and compare their finite-sample performance by a simulation study. The first method we consider is semiparametric estimation, by which we estimate the whole range of data by trying a set of copula forms and then choose the one with the highest likelihood for TDC calculations. As the second method, we use extreme value theory (EVT), specifically peaks-over-threshold (POT) models, to estimate a particular EV copula in the tail region in order to derive TDCs. The third method is nonparametric estimation. Our simulation study shows that the first and third methods yield quite satisfactory estimation accuracy for a range of assumed tail dependence patterns, whereas the second method yields significant estimation biases.

We select forty-five U.S. stocks from nine S&P sectors for our empirical analysis. The time span is about ten years ranging from December 22, 1998, to November 17, 2008. Besides focusing on the whole data set, we also investigate three subperiods for possible regime changes. Moreover, our estimations are conducted based on both raw returns and GARCH-filtered returns. Semiparametric and nonparametric methods lead to very similar point estimates for most cases. As for nine sectors, Financials, Energy, Materials, and Utilities consistently feature very high TDCs with Financial being the highest for all periods and distribution assumptions. Among the low TDC sectors are Consumer Staples, Industrial, Health, and Technology. Meanwhile, the TDC estimates across sectors are at the lowest level. As for the three subperiods, results show the last subperiod featuring the current financial crisis generates significantly higher TDCs than the others.

Moreover, we find that the GARCH-filtered returns have significantly lower TDCs than the raw returns, which suggests that failure to account for heteroskedasticity can affect TDC estimates. Put it another way, TDC based on the raw returns is unconditional, whereas that based on GARCH-filtered returns is conditional. The raw returns are assumed to be *i.i.d.* when directly used to estimate TDCs. So large absolute returns in periods of higher conditional variance will exaggerate TDC estimates based on raw returns. It suggests that in practice we should account for the time-varying variance of returns when estimating TDCs.

It is widely observed for index returns in previous literature that the lower TDC is significantly higher than the upper one. However, we show that this asymmetry pattern may not be true for all pairs of individual stocks. For some pairs, the difference of upper and lower TDCs is insignificant. And to the contrary, the upper TDC is even significantly higher than the lower one for some stock pairs during the recent financial crisis.

With TDC estimates of forty-five selected U.S. stocks as a benchmark, we estimate a multivariate Student's t copula model to assess its ability of simultaneously capturing various tail dependence patterns of the forty-five stocks. We pursue two estimation schemes. With the first one, we estimate both the correlation matrix and the degree-of-freedom parameter of the copula in one step; we call the resulting model "unrestricted." With the second, we arbitrarily set the degree-of-freedom parameter as four to add more probability in the tails and then estimate only the correlation matrix, which leads to a "restricted" model. The "restricted" model is investigated here to account for significantly high TDCs of some stock pairs. Comparing TDCs generated by the Student's *t* copula model with our empirical estimates, we find that the "unrestricted" model tends to understate tail dependence in some cases (e.g., TDCs between financial firms), whereas the "restricted" model tends to overstate in certain cases due to the smaller degree-of-freedom parameter. We conclude that the multivariate Student's *t* copula model has limited flexibility to capture various tail dependence patterns of included assets and more flexible copula structures (e.g., variants of Student's *t* copulas) may be needed to improve the fit of data in the tails.

This chapter is organized as follows. The next section briefly reviews theories of tail dependence, a variety of estimation methods, and the performance of different TDC estimators. The third section reports the data source and estimation results for the nine sectors of U.S stocks. The fourth section compares the TDC estimates with those generated from a multivariate Student's *t* copula model, and investigates its implications for risk measure calculations. The final section concludes.

ESTIMATION METHODOLOGY

Theory on Tail Dependence

Tail dependence describes how two random variables are correlated in the tail. Let X and Y be two random variables with F_X and F_Y as their distribution functions respectively. Then the upper and lower TDCs, λ_U and λ_L, can be defined as:

$$\begin{aligned} \lambda_U &= \lim_{q\to 1^-} \Pr\left(X > F_X^{-1}(q) \middle| Y > F_Y^{-1}(q) \right), \\ \lambda_L &= \lim_{q\to 0^+} \Pr\left(X \le F_X^{-1}(q) \middle| Y \le F_Y^{-1}(q) \right), \end{aligned} \tag{2.1}$$

where F_X^{-1} and F_Y^{-1} are inverse distribution functions for X and Y respectively. TDC tells at what probability X will do the same, when random variable Y goes to extremes. It is well known that TDC is governed only by the copula of the joint distribution and can be expressed as:

$$\lambda_U = \lim_{u\to 1^-} \frac{1-2u+C(u,u)}{1-u}, \text{ and } \lambda_L = \lim_{u\to 0^+} \frac{C(u,u)}{u}, \tag{2.2}$$

where C is the copula[1] for the bivariate joint distribution.[2]

Parametric Estimation

Semiparametric Estimation with a Full Range of Data

Most commonly, we can estimate TDCs by estimating parametric copulas of the joint distribution. We estimate the full set of data by a variety of copula candidates and choose the one with the best overall goodness of fit for calculating TDC estimates. To estimate copula functions, we need to correctly specify marginal distributions for each individual variable, as misspecified marginals automatically lead to a wrong joint distribution. A variety of procedures are available for estimating parametric copulas. We use the canonical maximum likelihood (CML) method, where marginal distributions are estimated by their empirical versions and then parametric copulas are estimated by ML estimation.[3] This semiparametric estimation procedure avoids specifying a specific parametric form for marginal distributions and thus possible misspecifications.[4]

The log-likelihood of a joint distribution is "additively separable" with respect to its marginals and copula. Let X_1 and X_2 be two *i.i.d.* returns or GARCH-filtered returns, then with estimated marginals, the copula can be estimated by maximizing its log-likelihood,

$$\max_{\theta \in \Theta} L = \sum_{t=1}^{T} \log c(\widehat{F}_{X_1}(x_{1,t}), \widehat{F}_{X_2}(x_{2,t})) \tag{2.3}$$

where $\widehat{F}_{X_1}$ and $\widehat{F}_{X_2}$ are empirical distributions, c is a copula density, and θ denotes a set of copula parameters. Hu (2006) shows that this ML estimator is consistent and has asymptotical normality.

Our copula candidates include a variety of frequently used bivariate copulas and Table 7.1 shows their functional forms and corresponding TDCs. Among those candidates, normal, Student's *t*, and Frank are symmetric and have equal upper and lower TDCs. Normal and Frank both feature zero TDCs and Student's *t* has positive ones. The other copulas feature asymmetric dependence. Clayton and Gumbel and their rotated versions feature a positive TDC for one tail and a zero TDC for the other. Mixed copula is specified as a weighted mixture of Clayton and Gumbel, which generates positive but unequal TDCs.

We use log-likelihood to measure overall goodness of fit and choose the copula with the highest log-likelihood to estimate TDCs.[5] TDC estimates are calculated based on the estimated copula parameters and their corresponding TDC functions. From the standard ML estimation theory,[6] this TDC estimator is consistent and has asymptotical normality. Thus, standard errors can be derived by using a delta method and confidence intervals can also be constructed accordingly. Alternatively, we can also resort to bootstrapping methods to derive the distribution of TDC estimators when the sample size is not large enough.

Parametric Estimation Using EVT

TDCs can also be estimated parametrically by using EVT. In particular, TDC estimates are calculated through an estimated extreme value (EV) copula of the joint distribution. According to multivariate EVT, a copula has to satisfy the scaling property $C(u_1^t,...,u_d^t) = C^t(u_1,...,u_d)$ for $t > 0$in order to be an EV copula. Note that there is no single parametric family that includes all the EV copulas.[7] Gumbel copula is an EV copula and we use it and its rotated version in this chapter to estimate upper and lower TDCs respectively.

To estimate bivariate EV copulas, we use ML estimation, which includes only observations over (or below) certain thresholds, assuming that all the included observations have the dependence structure of the chosen EV copula. As the first step, we estimate marginal distributions by using POT models from univariate EVT. Accordingly, the limiting excess distribution (over or below a threshold) follows a general Pareto distribution (GPD). It is a two parameter distribution with the following function form.

$$G_{\xi,\beta}(x) = \begin{cases} 1-\left(1+\frac{\xi x}{\beta}\right)^{-\frac{1}{\xi}} & \xi \neq 0 \\ 1-\exp\left(-\frac{x}{\beta}\right) & \xi = 0 \end{cases}, \ \beta > 0,\ x \geq 0 \text{ if } \xi \geq 0,\ 0 \leq x \leq -\tfrac{\beta}{\xi} \text{ if } \xi < 0. \quad (2.4)$$

Let X_i and u_i for i = 1,2 be returns and upper thresholds for two assets. Then the cumulative distribution of returns when they are greater than the thresholds can be derived as:

$$F_{X_i}(x_i) \simeq (1 - F_{X_i}(u_i))G_{\xi_i,\beta_i}(x_i - u_i) + F_{X_i}(u_i),\ x_i > u_i,\ \text{for } i = 1,2. \quad (2.5)$$

Based on (2.5), $F_{Xi}(x_i)$ can be estimated by plugging the estimates of $F_{Xi}(u_i)$ and $G_{\xi i,\beta i}$, where $F_{Xi}(u_i)$ can be estimated by its empirical version and $G_{\xi i,\beta i}$ by ML estimation. Let $n_{u_i}^U$ be the number of observations exceeding u_i for i = 1,2 and N be the sample size. Thus, $F(x_i)$ can be estimated by[8]:

$$\widehat{F}_{X_i}(x_i) = 1 - \frac{n_{u_i}^U}{N}\left(1 + \hat{\xi}_i \frac{x_i - u_i}{\widehat{\beta}_i}\right)^{-\frac{1}{\hat{\xi}_i}},\ \text{for } i = 1,2. \quad (2.6)$$

where $\hat{\xi}_i$ and $\widehat{\beta}_i$ are the estimated parameters of GPDs. Finally, the chosen Gumbel copula can be estimated by ML estimation and its log-likelihood is:

$$L = \sum_{i=1}^{T} \log c^{Gumbel}(\widehat{F}_{X_1}(x_{1,t}), \widehat{F}_{X_2}(x_{2,t})) \quad (2.7)$$

where c^{Gumbel} is the density function of Gumbel copula. Upper TDC estimates can be calculated accordingly and confidence intervals can be derived by either asymptotical normality or bootstrapping methods. Lower TDCs can be estimated similarly.

Nonparametric Estimation

Because there exists no general finite-dimensional parametric distribution that covers all possible dependence structures in the tail, we can estimate TDCs nonparametrically to avoid possible misspecification of parametric distributions. Nonparametric TDC estimators can be constructed via either empirical copulas introduced by Deheuvels (1981) or tail copulas,[9] and we pursue the former approach in this chapter. First, an empirical copula is defined as follows.

Definition 1 *Let* $\mathbf{z} = \{(z_{1,t}, z_{2,t})\}_{t=1}^{N}$ *denote a sample of size N from a continuous bivariate distribution. The empirical copula is the function* $\hat{C}$ *defined by*

$$\hat{C}\left(\frac{i}{N},\frac{j}{N}\right)=\frac{1}{N}\sum_{t=1}^{N}\mathbf{1}(z_t \le z_{(i)}, z_t \le z_{(j)}), \tag{2.8}$$

where $\mathbf{1}(\cdot)$ *is the indicator function, and* $z_{(i)}$ *and* $z_{(j)}$ *for* $1 \le i, j \le N$ *are the order statistics of the sample.*

Deheuvels (1981) shows that empirical copula converges uniformly to the underlying true copula. By using the equations in (2.2), we can directly estimate TDCs by replacing the equations with their empirical versions. Thus we have the nonparametric estimators as:

$$\hat{\lambda}_U = \frac{1-\frac{2(N-k)}{N}+\hat{C}\left(\frac{N-k}{N},\frac{N-k}{N}\right)}{1-\frac{N-k}{N}}, \text{ and } \hat{\lambda}_L = \frac{\hat{C}\left(\frac{k}{N},\frac{k}{N}\right)}{\frac{k}{N}}. \tag{2.9}$$

where k is the threshold to be chosen. Dobric and Schmid (2005) show that as $k \approx \sqrt{N}$ and $N \to \infty$, these estimators are asymptotically unbiased. However, with $k \approx \sqrt{N}$ their nonparametric TDC estimates are significantly biased with finite samples. Schmidt and Stadtmueller (2006) show weak convergence, asymptotic normality, and strong consistency for these estimators by a functional delta method, assuming that $k \to \infty$ and $k/N \to 0$ as $N \to \infty$. To choose an optimal k, the authors use a plateau-finding algorithm supported by the homogeneity property of tail copulas. They derive the variance of nonparametric estimators and suggest that it be approximated by a known parametric copula. With finite samples, their estimates tend to be biased with small underlying TDCs. In this chapter, we also adopt the plateau-finding algorithm to find the optimal k and we can also derive the estimator variance by bootstrapping methods.

Evaluations of TDC Estimators

Before estimating real TDCs, we evaluate finite-sample performance of the proposed TDC estimators by a simulation study. Following Frahm et al. (2005), we simulate one thousand random samples with a sample size equal to one thousand for each assumed true bivariate distribution. Due to the fact that TDC is solely determined by copula forms, we carry out our simulation study only with copula functions without touching modeling issues of marginal distributions. To cover most possible tail dependence patterns, we assume five true underlying copula functions. They are normal, Student's *t*, Clayton, Gumbel, and mixed copula (Clayton-Gumbel) copulas.

To evaluate the performance of estimators, we need to evaluate both estimation bias and standard deviation. We use two statistical measures to quantify our evaluations. The first measure is the root mean squared errors (RMSE). Let λ and $\hat{\lambda}_{n,i}$ be the true TDC and the TDC estimate from the i th sample of size n respectively. Then the estimated RMSE is given by:

$$\widehat{\text{RMSE}}(\hat{\lambda}_n) = \sqrt{\frac{1}{1000}\sum_{i=1}^{1000}\left(\hat{\lambda}_{n,i} - \lambda\right)^2}. \tag{2.10}$$

The second measure is called mean error to standard error (MESE) and its estimates are given by:

$$\widehat{\text{MESE}}(\hat{\lambda}_n) = \frac{\left|\hat{\mu}(\hat{\lambda}_n) - \lambda\right|}{\hat{\sigma}(\hat{\lambda}_n)}. \tag{2.11}$$

MESE essentially measures the bias of an estimator adjusted by its standard deviation. By using this measure, we can detect the misleading situation with small standard deviation but a large bias. For instance, if we only use standard deviation to rank the estimators, an estimator with smaller standard deviation may be favored. However, if this estimator has a large bias, the corresponding interval estimators will still suggest a misleading result. In this case, MESE tends to be very large.

We evaluate the performance of our proposed estimators with our five simulated dependence patterns and Table 7.2 reports the true underlying TDCs, and the mean, bias, standard deviation, RMSE, and MESE of the three estimators. The parametric estimation using EVT (Method 2 in Table 7.2) yields significantly large bias, RMSE, and MESE, whereas the other two methods yield satisfactorily low bias, RMSE, and MESE. Specifically, semiparametric estimation with a full range of data generates the lowest bias, RESE, and MESE for most simulation cases. Note that all the assumed underlying distributions are among the copula candidates in our semiparametric estimation procedure, which helps generate superior TDC estimates. In reality, when the underlying true distribution is unknown, semiparametric estimation may not generate such decent estimates. On the other hand, nonparametric estimation methods are free of distribution assumptions and can still lead to quite good estimation results. Therefore, we drop parametric estimation using EVT, retaining semiparametric and nonparametric methods to estimate real TDCs.

AN EMPIRICAL INVESTIGATION

Data

We base our data on the nine S&P sectors. These sectors are: Consumer Discretionary, Consumer Staples, Energy, Financials, Health Care, Industrials, Technology, Materials, and Utilities. We choose five individual stocks from each sector, and each selected stock accounts for a major holding in the SPDR ETF of its sector. Table 7.3 shows names and symbols of the SPDR ETFs and selected individual stocks. The data are daily log returns and range from December 22, 1998, to November 17, 2008, consisting of 2,493 observations. Returns are total returns based on the adjusted close stock prices from http://finance.yahoo.com. Figure 7.1 shows plots of daily log returns of the nine SPDR ETFs. It turns out that all the nine returns series consistently experience regimes of different degrees of volatility. Therefore, we divide our data set into three typical subperiods, where the first (from December 22, 1998, to March 10, 2003) features a high volatility due to burst Internet bubbles and terrorist attacks, the second (from March 11, 2003, to July 19, 2007) is of low volatility, and the last one (from July 20, 2007, to November 19, 2008) features an unprecedented high volatility due to the current financial crisis. Besides estimating TDCs using the whole data set, we also investigate TDCs estimates for each subperiod with a caution that TDCs may vary significantly during different regimes.[10]

Table 7.4 shows descriptive statistics for log returns of the nine sector ETFs, where the mean, standard deviation, skewness, and kurtosis are reported for the whole period and three subperiods. For most sectors (except Technology [XLK]), the average of daily returns is positive for the periods 1 and 2 and negative for period 3. Periods 1 and 3 have high volatilities, whereas period 2 has a significantly low volatility. All the returns are either slightly left- or right-skewed and have kurtosis greater than three, clearly indicating fat tails.

Empirical Results

Our estimation of TDCs is conducted for different time periods and with different distribution assumptions. We first assume that the raw asset returns are *i.i.d.* and can be directly used for the TDC estimation. Besides the three subperiods, we still estimate TDCs of the raw returns for the full period, although plots in Figure 7.1 clearly show different volatilities for the three subperiods. More plausibly, we also fit a GARCH(1,1) specification to the raw data and then estimate the TDCs of the fitted residuals, which are assumed to be *i.i.d.* under the GARCH specification. Again, we conduct estimations for both the full period and three subperiods, where even though different volatilities can be captured to some extent by GARCH specifications, we still suspect that TDCs of the fitted residuals can be significantly different across the three subperiods.

Table 7.5 reports the average of TDC estimates within sectors and across sectors for different subperiods considered. The average is calculated based on estimated TDCs of all the stock pairs within and across sectors. The first part of the table reports the results for the raw returns and the second part for the GARCH-filtered returns. Tables 7.6 and 7.7 show TDC estimates of only filtered returns for selected stock pairs from each sector and cross-sectors. Specifically, we estimate upper and lower TDCs using both semiparametric and nonparametric methods (the first and third methods described earlier). In Tables 7.6 and 7.7, the italic values are standard errors, which are calculated by MLE and bootstrapping for the two methods respectively.

There are some main observations on Tables 7.5 to 7.7. First, semiparametric and nonparametric methods generate very close estimates for most cases in both individual and average tables. It implies that the two estimation methods likely lead to more precise TDC estimates. For cases where the two methods give significantly different estimates, we are less confident about either of the estimates and maybe the average of the two can be used as a compromise estimate.

Second, for raw returns in Table 7.5, even though period 1 features high volatilities, TDC estimates tend to be lower for period 1 than all the other periods. This is due to the fact that with raw returns the TDC estimations for the three subperiods are based on distributions with different variances. Period 3 generates the highest TDC estimates, indicating the current financial crisis features significantly higher tail dependence among assets. We observe high TDC estimates for the full period, although for raw returns the estimates for the full period appear not to be quite relevant. On the other hand, for GARCH-filtered returns, TDC estimates tend to be very close between the first two subperiods. Even with GARCH-filtering in Table 7.5, period 3 still stands out with significantly higher TDC estimates. Moreover, the GARCH-filtered returns have significantly lower TDCs than the raw returns, which indicates different assumptions about the return data may lead to quite different TDC values. The raw returns are assumed to be *i.i.d.* when directly used to estimate TDCs. Then large co-movements of returns mostly due to the higher conditional variance will exaggerate the TDC estimates.

Thirdly, the sectors of Financials, Energy, Materials, and Utilities consistently feature very high TDCs with Financials being the highest for all periods and distributions assumptions. This observation is consistent with the features of these sectors. Especially for Financial and Energy, they are usually driven by common factors and even more correlated when in extreme market conditions. Among the low TDC sectors are Consumer Staples, Industrial, Health, and Technology. For Consumer Staples and

Health, they tend to be less sensitive to the business cycles. Together with Industrial and Technology, they are driven by less common factors and are less correlated when in extreme market conditions. Meanwhile, the TDC estimates across sectors are also close to the lowest level.

As widely observed in previous literature for index returns,[11] the lower TDC is noticeably higher than the upper one. However, this dependence asymmetry is not significant for all the pairs of individual stocks considered in our chapter.[12] For some pairs, the upper and lower TDCs are very similar. In sharp contrast, the upper TDC is markedly higher than the lower one for some stock pairs at the financial crisis. For instance, in Table 7.6, the upper TDC between U.S. Bank and JP Morgan (USB-JPM) tends to be low for the two periods and becomes around 0.5 for the third period, leaving the full period at around 0.2. However, their lower TDC estimate for the third period is only around 0.2. The short time length and special features of the financial crisis period may be the reason for the inconsistent patterns. In the crisis, we observe that some stocks' prices steadily decrease for a few days and then suddenly shoot up dramatically. This phenomenon may skew the data to the upper tail.

IMPLICATIONS FOR RISK MANAGEMENT

Multivariate Student's t Copula Model

In previous sections we have estimated TDCs among the selected stocks within and across nine main sectors and these estimates can serve as the "stylized facts" about tail dependence of the asset considered. We can compare those TDC estimates with TDCs generated by risk models to assess their ability of capturing various tail dependence patterns. The selected risk model here is a Student's *t* copula model, which is a general framework to model the joint distribution of a large number of assets with nonnormal properties, and is a popular choice to model multivariate time series for asset allocation or risk management purposes. To construct a Student's *t* copula model, we first model the marginal distribution of each individual asset and then nest all the marginal distributions in a Student's *t* copula.[13]

The group of assets we test in this section are the forty-five selected stocks used in previous sections. We first filter a GARCH (1,1) specification to each individual time series of returns and then model the marginal distribution of filtered residuals by its empirical distribution. In the second step, we estimate the parameters of the Student's *t* copula with estimated marginal distributions plugged in. Besides estimating the correlation matrix and degree-of-freedom parameter simultaneously, which we call an "unrestricted" approach, we also estimate a "restricted" *t* copula where the degree-of-freedom parameter is arbitrarily set to four and only the correlation matrix is to be estimated. The "restricted" model is investigated here to account for significantly high TDCs of some stock pairs. Finally, the implied TDCs can be calculated directly from the parameter estimates of the *t* copula.

Tables 7.8 and 7.9 show the comparison of TDC estimates generated by the Student's *t* copula model with those generated by pair-wise, semiparametric, and nonparametric estimations for selected stock pairs within and across the nine sectors. First, we observe that TDCs generated from "unrestricted" Student's *t* copulas are universally very close to zero. These low TDCs result from the high value of degree-of-freedom parameter estimates, which makes Student's *t* copula approach to normal copula. Then with "restricted" *t* copula where degree-of-freedom parameter is set as four, the generated TDCs, ranging from 0.1 to 0.2, become significantly higher. Finally, comparing with pair-wise estimates, we find that our "unrestricted" *t* copula model tends to understate TDCs of some stock pairs featuring high tail dependence, whereas "restricted" *t* copula model overstates TDCs for certain pairs. This observation implies that our Student's *t* copula model has limited flexibility to capture the tail dependence of all included asset pairs, especially with a large number of modeled assets. More flexible copula structures (e.g., variants of Student's *t* copulas) may be used to improve the fit of data in the tails.

Calculation of Risk Measures

We illustrate in this section the implications of tail dependence of underlying risk factors for risk measure calculations of certain portfolios. The general framework used to calculate risk measures of portfolios here consists of a multivariate time series model capturing the dynamics of underlying risk factors and price functions linking the portfolio values to underlying factors. Basically, the time series models provide us with a predicted joint distribution of future risk factors, and with the pricing function, which can be linear or nonlinear, we can derive the risk measures, VaR, or ES for investigated portfolios. Under this framework, the accuracy of risk measures depends on accuracies of both predicted joint distributions of underlying factors and pricing functions, where pricing functions determine which areas of joint distributions are more important in forming the risk measures.

We have just showed that the Student's *t* copula model has limited flexibility to capture tail dependence of all pairs of underlying risk factors. This finding indicates that the investigated multivariate copula model generates inaccuracies in certain tail areas of predicted joint distributions. Accordingly, portfolios heavily relying on those inaccurate tail areas may be affected with respect to risk measure calculations.

We conduct simple simulation exercises to show how different modeling specifications of tail dependence may affect risk measure calculations. As TDCs measure pair-wise tail dependence, we first construct our portfolios by summing up a pair of selected stocks with equal weights. We choose four pairs. The first two pairs are drawn from the Financial and Energy sectors respectively: U.S. Bank (USB) and JP Morgan (JPM), and Exxon Mobil Corp. (XOM) and ConocoPhillips (COP). For the other two pairs, each pair is drawn from different sectors. We have McDonald's (MCD) and Wal-Mart Stores Inc. (WMT), and Exxon Mobil Corp. (XOM) and Merck & Co. Inc.

(MRK). We estimate GARCH-filtered residuals using both "unrestricted" and "restricted" *t* copula models and then simulate actual returns using the estimated copulas and standard deviations governed by GARCH specifications.[14] For "restricted" the copula degree-of-freedom parameter is set as four and for the "unrestricted" copula it is estimated at 26.0933. Table 7.10 shows simulated VaR and ES (99 percent) featuring different volatilities of three subperiods. Specifically, VaR and ES are calculated based on "unrestricted" and "restricted" *t* copula models and empirical distributions. Percentage change of risk measures between different models is also calculated.

Table 7.10 shows that risk measures are significantly higher in periods 1 and 3 than in period 2. Specifically, the two pairs drawn from the Financial and Energy sectors generate the highest risk measures due to heavy tail dependence. With respect to the percentage change of risk measures between different risk models, we find that for the pair of MCD and WMT, the "restricted" *t* copula model generates 8.77 percent higher of risk measures (ES) in absolute value than the empirical distribution. If empirical distributions are treated as the true distribution, it means we have 8.77 percent higher risk measures in terms of ES. One possible explanation is that by setting the degree-of-freedom parameter to four, the "restricted" t copula brings heavier tail dependence than it should for this pair of stocks. Moreover, "restricted" and "unrestricted" copulas tend to generate higher risk overcharges in ES than in VaR.

We also simulate returns for portfolios consisting of more than two equal-weighted stocks. In Table 7.11, each of the first three portfolios consists of five stocks from one sector (i.e., five from Financials, five from Energy, five from Consumer Staples). The last two portfolios consist of nine stocks from nine different sectors. Periods 1 and 3 generate significantly higher risk measures due to higher volatility than in period 2. In addition to high volatility, the Financial and Energy sectors feature the highest risk measures, most likely due to the heavy tail dependence. Note that in this case we need to generalize the tail dependence concept to the multivariate case in order to describe the joint tail behavior of multiple variables. Finally, compared with risk measures generated by empirical distributions, "restricted" *t* copula models can generate overcharges as high as 12 percent.

In our simulations for simple portfolios, our *t* copula models lead to overstated risk measures due to the larger probability mass assigned to the tails. Overstated risk measures are considered "safer" with respect to risk management. However, it is worthwhile to note that when our *t* copula model assigns more probability in the tail, it will automatically assign less in other area of the joint density, which may lead to understated risk measures for a particular portfolio.

CONCLUSION

We conduct a comprehensive empirical investigation on tail dependence of major U.S. stocks in this chapter. After reviewing a variety of TDC estimators, we assess their finite-sample performance by a simulation study. By both semiparametric and nonparametric estimations, we find that sectors such as Financials and Energy have consistently higher TDCs than other sectors such as Health Care and Industrials, and the current period of crisis features a regime of significantly higher tail dependence. Moreover, we show that the Student's t copula model may overstate or understate tail dependence of certain asset pairs, which may affect risk measure calculations.

There are a few issues in this chapter that are worthwhile to explore further. First, we have not used any statistical tests to test tail independence, due to some subtle issues on tail independence. But it may be beneficial to first indentify a reliable independence test and then apply it to the data. Second, concerning the asymmetry of tail dependence, we only compare the point estimates of TDCs. Instead, we may resort to statistical tests to judge whether the TDCs are statistically symmetric or not. Third, we may test the effect of predicted density inaccuracy on more sophisticated portfolios. Finally, to improve the ability of Student's t copula models to capture tail dependence, we may resort to more flexible copula forms (e.g., skewed t copula). We leave these topics for future research.

APPENDIX

Choosing Threshold *k* for the Nonparametric Estimation

Following Schmidt and Stadtmueller (2006), and Frahm et al. (2005), we choose the "optimal" threshold k by detecting the plateau that is induced by the homogeneity property in the tails. To illustrate the procedure, we concentrate on the lower TDC. The procedure is the same with the upper TDC. First, we use a simple box kernel to smooth the mapping $k \mapsto \hat{\tau}^{L}(k)$ with a bandwidth $b \in N$. Averaging the successive $b + 1$ points of all the mapping points $\hat{\tau}_1^{L},\ldots,\hat{\tau}_n^{L}$ leads to a set of new averaging points $\bar{\tau}_1^{L},\ldots,\bar{\tau}_{n-b}^{L}$. The bandwidth b is chosen as $b = \lfloor pn \rfloor$ where p assigns the percentage of the data included for the moving averaging calculation. We define a plateau of length b as a vector $p_l = (\bar{\tau}_l^{L},\ldots,\bar{\tau}_{l+b-1}^{L})$, $l = 1,\ldots, n-2b+1$. Then the searching algorithm starts from $l = 1$ and stops until the following condition is met:

$$\sum_{i=l+1}^{l+b-1} \left|\bar{\tau}_i - \bar{\tau}_l\right| \le h\sigma \tag{2.12}$$

where σ is the standard deviation of new averaging points $\bar{\tau}_1^{L},\ldots,\bar{\tau}_{n-b}^{L}$ and h is a scaling constant. Accordingly, the TDC estimator is given by:

$$\hat{\tau}^{L}(l^*) = \frac{1}{b}\sum_{i=1}^{b} \bar{\tau}_{l^*+i-1}. \tag{2.13}$$

where l^* is the found optimal index. We set $l^* = 1$ if no satisfactory plateau is found. We need to decide on the values of p and h for this plateau-finding algorithm.[15] Moreover, we may resort to bootstrapping method to calculate the confidence intervals of the TDC estimators.

Student's *t* Copula Model

We briefly introduce a multivariate Student's t copula model estimated in this chapter. Let $X_t = [x_1,\ldots,x_{n,t}]'$ be a vector of $n$asset returns at time t. The individual distribution is modeled by a GARCH(1,1) with a Student's t distribution. For i=1,...,n , the first two conditional moments of $x_{i,t}$ is given as:

$$x_{i,t} = \mu_i + \sigma_{i,t}\varepsilon_{i,t},$$

$$\sigma_{i,t}^2 = \alpha_{i,0} + \alpha_{i,1}\sigma_{i,t-1}^2 + \alpha_{i,2}\sigma_{i,t-1}^2\varepsilon_{i,t-1}^2$$

where $\varepsilon_{i,t}$ follows a standardized t distribution with zero mean and unitary variance. The joint distribution of $\varepsilon_t = [\varepsilon_{1,t},\ldots,\varepsilon_{n,t}]'$ is constructed by a Student's t copula as:

$$F(\varepsilon_{1,t},\ldots,\varepsilon_{n,t}) = C(u_{1,t},\ldots,u_{n,t})$$

where $u_{i,t} = F_i(\varepsilon_{i,t})$ and C(.) is the Student's t copula.

As for the estimation, the log-likelihood is given by:

$$L(\Theta) = \sum_{t=1}^{T} \log c(u_{1,t},\ldots,u_{n,t}) + \sum_{t=1}^{T}\sum_{i=1}^{n} \log f_i(\varepsilon_{i,t}),$$

where $c(\cdot)$ and $f(\cdot)$ are densities of copulas and residuals respectively. As the log-likelihood is "additive separable" with respect to copulas and marginals, we can usually estimate the model in two steps, where marginal distributions and copulas are estimated sequentially. In our case, we are only interested in the copula form, and then we estimate the marginal distribution by its empirical version.

Simulation of Risk Measure Calculations

In the filtered case, $\hat{\varepsilon}_t = [\hat{\varepsilon}_{1,t},\ldots,\hat{\varepsilon}_{n,t}]'$ is assumed to be *i.i.d.* Therefore, in our simulations for risk measure calculations, $\hat{\varepsilon}_t$ consists of the empirical distribution from which we draw and construct each realized return vector. In simulating the t copulas, after $u_{1,t},\ldots,u_{n,t}$ are drawn by using the parametric copula function, the realized returns are determined still by empirical distribution of individual $\varepsilon_{i,t}$.

Table 7.1 A List of Frequently-Used Copulas and the Corresponding Functional Forms of Tail Dependence Coefficients

Copula	*Functional forms (bivariate case)*	*Range of parameters*	λ_L	λ_U
Normal	$C_\rho(\mathbf{u}) = \Phi_\rho(\Phi^{-1}(u_1),\dots,\Phi^{-1}(u_n))$,	$\rho \in [-1,1]$	0	0
Student	$C_{v,\rho}(\mathbf{u}) = t_{v,\rho}(t_v^{-1}(u_1),\dots,t_v^{-1}(u_n))$,	$\rho \in [-1,1], v > 2$	$2\bar{t}_{v+1}\left(\sqrt{\frac{(v+1)(1-\rho)}{1+\rho}}\right)$	$2\bar{t}_{v+1}\left(\sqrt{\frac{(v+1)(1-\rho)}{1+\rho}}\right)$
Frank	$C_F(u_1,u_2) = -\frac{1}{\theta}\ln\left(1+\frac{(e^{-\theta u_1}-1)(e^{-\theta u_2}-1)}{e^{-\theta}-1}\right)$	$\theta \in \mathbb{R} \setminus \{0\}$	0	0
Clayton	$C_C(u_1,u_2) = \left(u_1^{-\theta}+u_2^{-\theta}-1\right)^{-1/\theta}$	$\theta \in [-1,\infty) \setminus \{0\}$	$2^{-\frac{1}{\theta}}$	0
Rotated Clayton	$C_{RC}(u_1,u_2) = 1-u_1-u_2+C_C(u_1,u_2)$	$\theta \in [-1,\infty) \setminus \{0\}$	0	$2^{-\frac{1}{\theta}}$
Gumbel	$C_G(u_1,u_2) = \exp\left(-[(-\ln u_1)^\theta+(-\ln u_2)^\theta]^{1/\theta}\right)$	$\theta \in [1,\infty)$	0	$2-2^{\frac{1}{\theta}}$
Rotated Gumbel	$C_{RG}(u_1,u_2) = 1-u_1-u_2+C_G(u_1,u_2)$	$\theta \in [1,\infty)$	$2-2^{\frac{1}{\theta}}$	0
Mixed	$C_{Mixed}(u_1,u_2) = \omega C_C(u_1,u_2;\theta_1)+(1-\omega)C_G(u_1,u_2;\theta_2)$	$\omega \in [0,1]$.	$\omega 2^{-\frac{1}{\theta_1}}$	$(1-\omega)(2-2^{\frac{1}{\theta_2}})$

This table gives a list of frequently used bivariate copula functions, their parameter ranges and formulas of their implied TDCs. Φ_ρ is bivariate standard normal distribution with correlation p, Φ^{-1} is inverse of standard normal distribution, $t_{v,\rho}$ is bivariate t distribution with degree-of-freedom v and correlation p, With t_v^{-1} is inverse of t distribution with degree-of-freedom v and $\bar{t}_{v+1} = 1-t_{v+1}$.

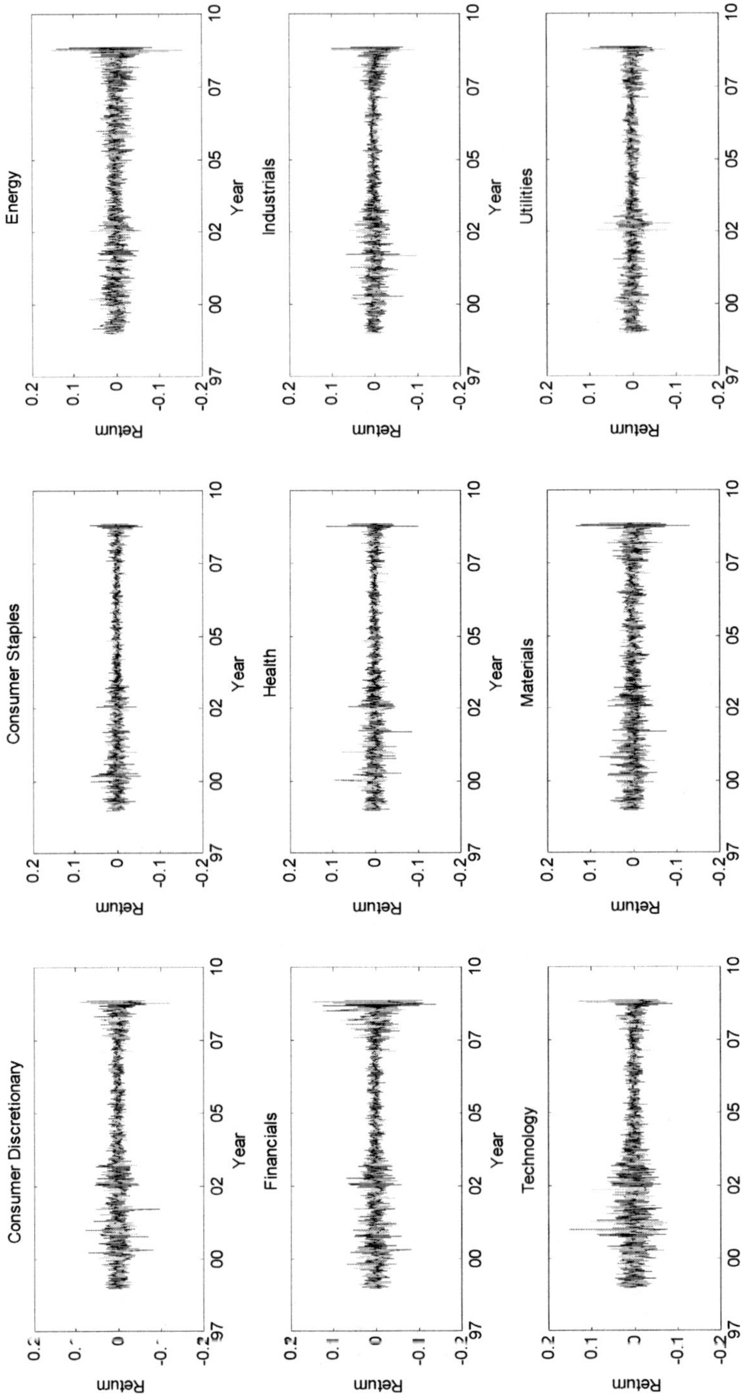

Figure 7.1 Plots of daily log returns of nine sector ETFs.

Table 7.2 Simulation Results for the Three Estimation Methods

		$\mu(\hat{\lambda})$		Bias($\hat{\lambda}$)		$\sigma(\hat{\lambda})$		RMSE		MESE	
		Upper	Lower	Upper	Lower	Upper	Lower	Upper	Lower	Upper	Lower
Gaussian	Method 1	0.010	0.009	0.01	0.009	0.044	0.035	0.045	0.036	0.236	0.249
$\lambda_U = 0$	Method 2	0.549	0.546	0.549	0.546	0.042	0.043	0.551	0.548	13.045	12.595
$\lambda_L = 0$	Method 3	0.091	0.090	0.091	0.090	0.110	0.109	0.142	0.142	0.824	0.827
Student	Method 1	0.462	0.456	0.017	0.011	0.045	0.057	0.048	0.058	0.370	0.194
$\lambda_U = 0.445$	Method 2	0.672	0.673	0.227	0.228	0.034	0.035	0.229	0.230	6.758	6.459
$\lambda_L = 0.445$	Method 3	0.452	0.457	0.007	0.012	0.181	0.167	0.181	0.168	0.038	0.070
Clayton	Method 1	0.008	0.756	0.008	-0.085	0.015	0.250	0.016	0.264	0.532	0.338
$\lambda_U = 0$	Method 2	0.569	0.851	0.569	0.010	0.045	0.018	0.570	0.021	12.648	0.540
$\lambda_L = 0.84$	Method 3	0.020	0.820	0.02	-0.021	0.057	0.096	0.061	0.099	0.346	0.218
Gumbel	Method 1	0.305	0.007	0.009	0.007	0.034	0.016	0.036	0.018	0.286	0.429
$\lambda_U = 0.296$	Method 2	0.606	0.555	0.31	0.555	0.044	0.060	0.313	0.558	7.121	9.179
$\lambda_L = 0$	Method 3	0.277	0.022	-0.019	0.022	0.172	0.058	0.173	0.062	0.106	0.375
Mixed	Method 1	0.143	0.635	-0.005	0.000	0.040	0.097	0.040	0.097	0.128	0.004
$\lambda_U = 0.148$	Method 2	0.634	0.778	0.486	0.143	0.046	0.029	0.488	0.146	10.643	4.896
$\lambda_U = 0.635$	Method 3	0.148	0.652	0.000	0.017	0.145	0.150	0.145	0.150	0.003	0.112

This table reports simulation results for the three estimation methods. Method 1: semiparametric with a full range of data. Method 2: parametric EVT. Method 3: nonparametric. $\mu(\hat{\lambda})$, Bias($\hat{\lambda}$), $\sigma(\hat{\lambda})$, RMSE, and MESE are respectively sample mean, bias, standard deviation, root mean square errors, and mean error to standard error of the upper and lower TDC estimators. The TDC values on the left column are the true underlying TDCs.

Table 7.3 Symbols and Names of Selected ETFs and Stocks of Nine Sectors

Sector	Consumer Discretionary	Consumer Staples	Energy
ETF	XLY	XLP	XLE
Stock	MCD: McDonald's HD: Home Depot DIS: Walt Disney Co. TGT: Target LOW: Lowe's	WMT: Wal-Mart Stores Inc. PG: Procter & Gamble Co. KO: Coca-Cola Co. WAG: Walgreen Co. MO: Altria Group Inc.	XOM: Exxon Mobil Corp. CVX: Chevron Corp. COP: CONOCOPHILLIPS. DVN: Devon Energy Corp. SLB: Schlumberger Limited
Sector	Financials	Health Care	Industrials
ETF	XLF	XLV	XLI
Stock	C: Citigroup Inc. BAC: Bank of America Corp. JPM: JPMorgan Chase & Co. USB: U.S. Bancorp WFC: Wells Fargo & Co.	JNJ: JOHNSON & JOHNSON PFE: Pfizer Inc. ABT: ABBOTT LABORATORIES MRK: Merck & Co. Inc. AMGN: Amgen Inc.	GE: General Electric Co. UNP: Union Pacific Corp. UTX: United Technologies Corp. MMM: 3M Co. BA: Boeing Co.
Sector	Technology	Materials	Utilities
ETF	XLK	XLB	XLU
Stock	T: AT&T Inc. MSFT: Microsoft Corp. IBM: International Business Machines Corp. CSCO: Cisco Systems Inc. HPQ: Hewlett-Packard Co.	NEM: Newmont Mining Corp. DD: E.I. DuPont de Nemours & Co. DOW: Dow Chemical Co. ROH: Rohm & Haas Co. PX: Praxair Inc.	EXC: Exelon Corp. FE: FirstEnergy Corp. PPL: PPL Corporation FPL: FPL Group Inc. DUK: Duke Energy Corp.

Table 7.4 Descriptive Statistics of Returns on Sector ETFs

	Consumer Discretionary (XLY)				*Consumer Staples (XLP)*				*Energy (XLE)*			
	Full Period	*Period 1*	*Period 2*	*Period 3*	*Full Period*	*Period 1*	*Period 2*	*Period 3*	*Full Period*	*Period 1*	*Period 2*	*Period 3*
Mean	-0.0001	0.0002	0.0003	-0.0024	0.0000	0.0000	0.0001	-0.0005	0.0003	0.0007	0.0005	-0.0014
Std. Dev.	0.0154	0.0177	0.0123	0.0227	0.0107	0.0144	0.0084	0.0128	0.0184	0.0162	0.0147	0.0322
Skewness	-0.2452	0.0336	-0.0993	-0.3271	0.0147	0.1136	-0.0691	-0.0470	-0.3407	0.2421	-0.3289	-0.2456
Kurtosis	8.2059	4.8233	7.6140	6.7061	7.0342	4.6593	5.8594	7.6432	12.8596	3.3544	4.0456	8.8579
	Financial (XLF)				*Health Care (XLV)*				*Industrials (XLI)*			
	Full Period	*Period 1*	*Period 2*	*Period 3*	*Full Period*	*Period 1*	*Period 2*	*Period 3*	*Full Period*	*Period 1*	*Period 2*	*Period 3*
Mean	-0.0002	0.0003	0.0002	-0.0035	0.0000	0.0003	0.0002	-0.0011	0.0000	0.0005	0.0003	-0.0020
Std. Dev.	0.0199	0.0233	0.0123	0.0359	0.0126	0.0148	0.0107	0.0161	0.0137	0.0137	0.0118	0.0203
Skewness	0.5821	1.8642	0.1180	0.0824	0.0145	0.5115	-0.4506	0.1195	-0.1737	-0.1720	-0.2566	0.1142
Kurtosis	27.2790	43.5853	6.7129	5.5976	12.3543	7.7759	8.4958	16.8680	9.2360	4.6390	8.7646	7.8119
	Technology (XLK)				*Materials (XLB)*				*Utilities (XLU)*			
	Full Period	*Period 1*	*Period 2*	*Period 3*	*Full Period*	*Period 1*	*Period 2*	*Period 3*	*Full Period*	*Period 1*	*Period 2*	*Period 3*
Mean	-0.0003	-0.0003	0.0000	-0.0019	0.0001	0.0002	0.0005	-0.0021	0.0001	0.0002	0.0003	-0.0010
Std. Dev.	0.0196	0.0247	0.0170	0.0216	0.0163	0.0172	0.0131	0.0257	0.0134	0.0131	0.0119	0.0194
Skewness	0.3592	0.3523	0.2989	0.5148	0.0324	0.5268	-0.0617	0.0228	0.1548	0.0891	-0.2967	0.7574
Kurtosis	7.5723	5.6643	6.7524	9.9504	9.3410	4.2375	5.0879	8.1661	10.8817	3.5413	11.0743	9.9232

(Full period: December 22, 1998–November 17, 2008; Period 1: December 22, 1998–March 10, 2003; Period 2: March 11, 2003–July 19, 2007; Period 3: July 20, 2007–November 19, 2008.)

Table 7.5 Averages of (upper/lower) TDC Estimates Across Sectors and within Each Sector.

Raw returns

	Upper								*Lower*							
	Full period		*Period 1*		*Period 2*		*Period 3*		*Full period*		*Period 1*		*Period 2*		*Period 3*	
Pairs	*Semi-para*	*Non-para*	*Semi-para*	*Non-para*	*Semi-para*	*Non-para*	*Semi-para*	*Non-para*	*Semi-para*	*Non-para*	*Semi-para*	*Non-para*	*Semi-para*	*Non-para*	*Semi-para*	*Non-para*
Consumer Discretionary	0.24	0.24	0.11	0.17	0.22	0.17	0.43	0.62	0.22	0.24	0.08	0.14	0.17	0.22	0.26	0.24
Consumer Staples	0.20	0.19	0.04	0.06	0.14	0.12	0.29	0.57	0.20	0.10	0.06	0.04	0.13	0.11	0.27	0.21
Energy	0.33	0.38	0.06	0.16	0.28	0.29	0.45	0.69	0.33	0.44	0.06	0.09	0.27	0.32	0.52	0.69
Financials	0.46	0.47	0.13	0.24	0.40	0.38	0.61	0.47	0.46	0.42	0.11	0.21	0.40	0.37	0.44	0.46
Health	0.24	0.25	0.17	0.20	0.22	0.18	0.34	0.52	0.24	0.15	0.08	0.09	0.20	0.22	0.30	0.26
Industrials	0.23	0.19	0.09	0.10	0.23	0.20	0.36	0.43	0.22	0.30	0.04	0.09	0.20	0.28	0.32	0.26
Technology	0.26	0.22	0.13	0.14	0.26	0.25	0.31	0.45	0.26	0.15	0.14	0.08	0.26	0.10	0.36	0.36
Materials	0.25	0.23	0.13	0.16	0.20	0.23	0.35	0.39	0.25	0.27	0.05	0.10	0.19	0.24	0.30	0.32
Utilities	0.29	0.37	0.17	0.15	0.27	0.31	0.45	0.68	0.31	0.32	0.26	0.29	0.28	0.25	0.41	0.35
Cross-Sector	0.15	0.17	0.15	0.15	0.05	0.07	0.03	0.04	0.13	0.14	0.13	0.10	0.27	0.42	0.28	0.27

Filtered returns

	Upper								*Lower*							
	Full period		*Period 1*		*Period 2*		*Period 3*		*Full period*		*Period 1*		*Period 2*		*Period 3*	
Pairs	*Semi-para*	*Non-para*	*Semi-para*	*Non-para*	*Semi-para*	*Non-para*	*Semi-para*	*Non-para*	*Semi-para*	*Non-para*	*Semi-para*	*Non-para*	*Semi-para*	*Non-para*	*Semi-para*	*Non-para*
Consumer Discretionary	0.12	0.12	0.08	0.14	0.12	0.08	0.33	0.33	0.10	0.12	0.08	0.13	0.10	0.13	0.20	0.11
Consumer Staples	0.09	0.05	0.05	0.06	0.11	0.03	0.16	0.16	0.10	0.08	0.04	0.04	0.07	0.10	0.16	0.08
Energy	0.21	0.20	0.07	0.19	0.19	0.16	0.34	0.34	0.21	0.29	0.07	0.14	0.19	0.26	0.42	0.50
Financials	0.26	0.32	0.09	0.17	0.23	0.21	0.51	0.57	0.26	0.27	0.09	0.16	0.23	0.28	0.27	0.43
Health	0.15	0.12	0.12	0.13	0.13	0.10	0.21	0.21	0.14	0.11	0.06	0.07	0.14	0.11	0.21	0.14
Industrials	0.15	0.07	0.07	0.07	0.19	0.04	0.23	0.26	0.15	0.15	0.04	0.06	0.18	0.16	0.20	0.17
Technology	0.16	0.09	0.10	0.07	0.18	0.08	0.23	0.17	0.14	0.10	0.13	0.04	0.12	0.11	0.23	0.16
Materials	0.17	0.13	0.14	0.14	0.14	0.10	0.29	0.20	0.14	0.12	0.05	0.10	0.12	0.17	0.24	0.14
Utilities	0.21	0.18	0.08	0.08	0.22	0.17	0.25	0.38	0.25	0.28	0.13	0.17	0.25	0.24	0.30	0.19
Cross-Sector	0.07	0.06	0.04	0.05	0.07	0.04	0.17	0.18	0.08	0.07	0.03	0.03	0.07	0.08	0.16	0.11

Averages of (upper/lower) TDC estimates across sectors and within each sector for different time periods. The average is calculated based on estimated TDCs of all the stock pairs within and across sectors. Especially, "cross-sector" refers to the average of TDC estimates across all the nine SPDR ETFs. "Semi-para" and "Non-para" refer to semiparametric and nonparametric estimation methods (the first and third methods in estimation methodology).

Table 7.6 Estimated TDCs for Selected Stock Pairs in Financial, Energy, Materials, Utility and Technology

Filtered returns

		Upper								*Lower*							
		Full period		*Period 1*		*Period 2*		*Period 3*		*Full period*		*Period 1*		*Period 2*		*Period 3*	
	Pairs	*Semi-para*	*Non-para*	*Semi-para*	*Non-para*	*Semi-para*	*Non-para*	*Semi-para*	*Non-para*	*Semi-para*	*Non-para*	*Semi-para*	*Non-para*	*Semi-para*	*Non-para*	*Semi-para*	*Non-para*
Financials	USB-JPM	0.249	0.219	0.090	0.027	0.303	0.115	0.605	0.563	0.249	0.284	0.090	0.349	0.269	0.338	0.159	0.231
		0.045	*0.066*	*0.098*	*0.072*	*0.028*	*0.061*	*0.045*	*0.176*	*0.045*	*0.071*	*0.098*	*0.159*	*0.031*	*0.099*	*0.052*	*0.182*
	JPM-C	0.291	0.372	0.017	0.553	0.245	0.256	0.557	0.598	0.291	0.402	0.017	0.303	0.245	0.413	0.557	0.623
		0.056	*0.071*	*0.110*	*0.143*	*0.093*	*0.082*	*0.064*	*0.169*	*0.056*	*0.072*	*0.110*	*0.150*	*0.093*	*0.092*	*0.064*	*0.201*
	C-BAC	0.313	0.338	0.022	0.146	0.298	0.132	0.566	0.629	0.313	0.284	0.022	0.026	0.298	0.278	0.566	0.573
		0.042	*0.077*	*0.154*	*0.119*	*0.048*	*0.051*	*0.097*	*0.149*	*0.042*	*0.075*	*0.154*	*0.081*	*0.048*	*0.098*	*0.097*	*0.196*
Energy	XOM-CVX	0.390	0.446	0.176	0.560	0.353	0.320	0.613	0.794	0.390	0.365	0.176	0.307	0.353	0.335	0.613	0.523
		0.050	*0.072*	*0.170*	*0.154*	*0.071*	*0.081*	*0.081*	*0.134*	*0.050*	*0.083*	*0.170*	*0.164*	*0.071*	*0.108*	*0.081*	*0.218*
	COP-CVX	0.307	0.308	0.008	0.238	0.294	0.224	0.478	0.493	0.307	0.342	0.008	0.251	0.294	0.334	0.478	0.592
		0.058	*0.067*	*0.066*	*0.135*	*0.080*	*0.081*	*0.183*	*0.155*	*0.058*	*0.073*	*0.066*	*0.163*	*0.080*	*0.091*	*0.183*	*0.209*
	CVX-SLB	0.086	0.135	0.007	0.097	0.072	0.093	0.485	0.383	0.086	0.194	0.007	0.131	0.072	0.166	0.173	0.442
		0.062	*0.053*	*0.045*	*0.091*	*0.078*	*0.057*	*0.056*	*0.155*	*0.062*	*0.073*	*0.045*	*0.138*	*0.078*	*0.108*	*0.063*	*0.217*
Materials	DD-PX	0.214	0.217	0.043	0.178	0.230	0.161	0.389	0.518	0.214	0.173	0.043	0.013	0.230	0.264	0.254	0.136
		0.040	*0.064*	*0.077*	*0.148*	*0.053*	*0.076*	*0.061*	*0.188*	*0.040*	*0.065*	*0.077*	*0.052*	*0.053*	*0.091*	*0.070*	*0.155*
	NEM-PX	0.027	0.049	0.025	0.013	0.024	0.025	0.219	0.052	0.027	0.082	0.000	0.000	0.024	0.130	0.219	0.000
		0.013	*0.038*	*0.046*	*0.072*	*0.014*	*0.026*	*0.066*	*0.115*	*0.013*	*0.051*	*0.012*	*0.005*	*0.014*	*0.081*	*0.066*	*0.031*
	PX-ROH	0.220	0.166	0.114	0.178	0.369	0.152	0.343	0.281	0.220	0.109	0.114	0.194	0.254	0.269	0.259	0.000
		0.045	*0.056*	*0.087*	*0.154*	*0.028*	*0.072*	*0.058*	*0.199*	*0.045*	*0.053*	*0.087*	*0.144*	*0.031*	*0.098*	*0.067*	*0.067*

Utility	DUK-EXC	0.225	0.180	0.006	0.083	0.225	0.181	0.289	0.277	0.291	0.232	0.006	0.238	0.301	0.315	0.282	0.046
		0.022	*0.063*	*0.051*	*0.099*	*0.028*	*0.079*	*0.065*	*0.180*	*0.025*	*0.077*	*0.051*	*0.177*	*0.032*	*0.116*	*0.075*	*0.093*
	EXC-FE	0.214	0.198	0.167	0.107	0.224	0.184	0.320	0.398	0.325	0.221	0.326	0.044	0.300	0.239	0.379	0.046
		0.022	*0.067*	*0.046*	*0.110*	*0.028*	*0.073*	*0.063*	*0.203*	*0.025*	*0.067*	*0.053*	*0.078*	*0.032*	*0.092*	*0.070*	*0.083*
	FE-FPL	0.244	0.297	0.157	0.030	0.261	0.317	0.302	0.517	0.298	0.369	0.366	0.381	0.253	0.178	0.302	0.156
		0.023	*0.076*	*0.049*	*0.071*	*0.029*	*0.093*	*0.215*	*0.225*	*0.026*	*0.083*	*0.056*	*0.166*	*0.033*	*0.093*	*0.215*	*0.172*
Technology	MSFT-IBM	0.205	0.071	0.058	0.039	0.320	0.142	0.000	0.000	0.205	0.112	0.286	0.059	0.154	0.151	0.000	0.000
		0.032	*0.036*	*0.045*	*0.079*	*0.027*	*0.061*	*0.000*	*0.124*	*0.032*	*0.057*	*0.052*	*0.095*	*0.030*	*0.084*	*0.000*	*0.031*
	IBM-CSCO	0.165	0.122	0.197	0.131	0.192	0.112	0.195	0.162	0.165	0.122	0.247	0.000	0.192	0.110	0.195	0.286
		0.041	*0.051*	*0.046*	*0.123*	*0.046*	*0.064*	*0.179*	*0.163*	*0.041*	*0.060*	*0.056*	*0.020*	*0.046*	*0.068*	*0.179*	*0.198*
	HPQ-T	0.122	0.073	0.014	0.039	0.019	0.000	0.295	0.237	0.138	0.096	0.052	0.085	0.019	0.102	0.295	0.206
		0.021	*0.044*	*0.040*	*0.071*	*0.022*	*0.017*	*0.071*	*0.178*	*0.024*	*0.059*	*0.042*	*0.095*	*0.022*	*0.066*	*0.071*	*0.209*

Estimated TDCs for Selected Stock Pairs in Financial, Energy, Materials, Utility and Technology. The italic values are standard errors. "Para" and "Non-para" refer to semiparametric and nonparametric estimation methods (the first and third methods in estimation methodology).

Table 7.7 Estimated TDCs for Selected Stock Pairs in Consumer Discretionary, Industrials, Consumer Staples, Health, and Cross-Sector

Filtered returns

		Upper								*Lower*							
		Full period		*Period 1*		*Period 2*		*Period 3*		*Full period*		*Period 1*		*Period 2*		*Period 3*	
	Pairs	*Semi-para*	*Non-para*	*Semi-para*	*Non-para*	*Semi-para*	*Non-para*	*Semi-para*	*Non-para*	*Semi-para*	*Non-para*	*Semi-para*	*Non-para*	*Semi-para*	*Non-para*	*Semi-para*	*Non-para*
Consumer Discretionary	MCD-LOW	0.167	0.080	0.096	0.000	0.000	0.018	0.275	0.307	0.064	0.041	0.161	0.192	0.000	0.019	0.244	0.006
		0.022	*0.042*	*0.048*	*0.069*	*0.000*	*0.025*	*0.059*	*0.149*	*0.029*	*0.031*	*0.051*	*0.158*	*0.000*	*0.024*	*0.072*	*0.075*
	LOW-HD	0.253	0.309	0.098	0.431	0.248	0.206	0.663	0.655	0.253	0.276	0.098	0.348	0.248	0.266	0.097	0.162
		0.055	*0.069*	*0.186*	*0.139*	*0.063*	*0.075*	*0.047*	*0.127*	*0.055*	*0.077*	*0.186*	*0.177*	*0.063*	*0.094*	*0.052*	*0.183*
	DIS-TGT	0.089	0.042	0.020	0.131	0.200	0.108	0.332	0.187	0.089	0.152	0.020	0.083	0.159	0.150	0.332	0.156
		0.028	*0.026*	*0.024*	*0.118*	*0.027*	*0.060*	*0.103*	*0.133*	*0.028*	*0.062*	*0.024*	*0.106*	*0.031*	*0.081*	*0.103*	*0.171*
Industrials	UNP-MMM	0.215	0.049	0.159	0.120	0.215	0.012	0.000	0.156	0.140	0.142	0.035	0.000	0.152	0.146	0.000	0.086
		0.022	*0.033*	*0.048*	*0.114*	*0.027*	*0.023*	*0.001*	*0.149*	*0.030*	*0.061*	*0.081*	*0.024*	*0.034*	*0.084*	*0.001*	*0.131*
	MMM-GE	0.197	0.051	0.031	0.059	0.192	0.085	0.384	0.421	0.197	0.146	0.031	0.059	0.192	0.169	0.384	0.187
		0.031	*0.029*	*0.038*	*0.092*	*0.043*	*0.045*	*0.111*	*0.185*	*0.031*	*0.068*	*0.038*	*0.079*	*0.043*	*0.085*	*0.111*	*0.158*
	GE-UTX	0.189	0.116	0.207	0.193	0.172	0.105	0.377	0.156	0.189	0.207	0.026	0.017	0.172	0.184	0.377	0.373
		0.033	*0.052*	*0.047*	*0.140*	*0.044*	*0.061*	*0.098*	*0.132*	*0.033*	*0.072*	*0.051*	*0.066*	*0.044*	*0.084*	*0.098*	*0.226*

Consumer Staples	WMT-WAG	0.220	0.085	0.049	0.000	0.264	0.101	0.000	0.236	0.195	0.037	0.049	0.063	0.076	0.090	0.000	0.006
		0.020	*0.048*	*0.064*	*0.068*	*0.027*	*0.051*	*0.000*	*0.213*	*0.025*	*0.040*	*0.064*	*0.093*	*0.033*	*0.057*	*0.000*	*0.064*
	WAG-PG	0.069	0.089	0.054	0.166	0.071	0.011	0.305	0.236	0.069	0.042	0.054	0.131	0.071	0.018	0.156	0.000
		0.025	*0.049*	*0.040*	*0.127*	*0.031*	*0.021*	*0.064*	*0.213*	*0.025*	*0.032*	*0.040*	*0.132*	*0.031*	*0.023*	*0.073*	*0.060*
	KO-MO	0.145	0.052	0.108	0.039	0.199	0.000	0.003	0.292	0.136	0.061	0.000	0.000	0.006	0.074	0.003	0.066
		0.021	*0.039*	*0.046*	*0.078*	*0.027*	*0.017*	*0.048*	*0.250*	*0.025*	*0.047*	*0.001*	*0.001*	*0.010*	*0.056*	*0.048*	*0.128*
Health	MRK-JNJ	0.218	0.113	0.000	0.006	0.176	0.046	0.235	0.302	0.233	0.061	0.000	0.240	0.229	0.031	0.235	0.027
		0.022	*0.054*	*0.000*	*0.070*	*0.027*	*0.038*	*0.097*	*0.185*	*0.025*	*0.066*	*0.000*	*0.163*	*0.031*	*0.030*	*0.097*	*0.140*
	ABT-PFE	0.120	0.130	0.000	0.000	0.150	0.118	0.043	0.421	0.120	0.147	0.000	0.000	0.150	0.119	0.043	0.142
		0.034	*0.051*	*0.000*	*0.069*	*0.037*	*0.058*	*0.162*	*0.230*	*0.034*	*0.066*	*0.000*	*0.011*	*0.037*	*0.084*	*0.162*	*0.170*
	AMGN-ABT	0.051	0.082	0.081	0.083	0.045	0.065	0.093	0.046	0.051	0.079	0.020	0.024	0.045	0.047	0.368	0.298
		0.023	*0.040*	*0.042*	*0.105*	*0.028*	*0.040*	*0.052*	*0.125*	*0.023*	*0.048*	*0.034*	*0.063*	*0.028*	*0.040*	*0.065*	*0.189*
Cross-Sector	MCD-WMT	0.046	0.038	0.237	0.002	0.000	0.000	0.252	0.181	0.046	0.069	0.000	0.039	0.000	0.057	0.281	0.148
		0.022	*0.027*	*0.045*	*0.065*	*0.000*	*0.018*	*0.058*	*0.145*	*0.022*	*0.049*	*0.000*	*0.041*	*0.000*	*0.058*	*0.069*	*0.178*
	WMT-XOM	0.053	0.065	0.133	0.000	0.161	0.082	0.257	0.187	0.053	0.099	0.000	0.000	0.037	0.098	0.139	0.052
		0.021	*0.037*	*0.047*	*0.073*	*0.028*	*0.049*	*0.063*	*0.133*	*0.021*	*0.059*	*0.000*	*0.000*	*0.028*	*0.069*	*0.073*	*0.153*
	BAC-ABT	0.106	0.094	0.026	0.000	0.102	0.098	0.000	0.236	0.208	0.026	0.138	0.045	0.231	0.044	0.000	0.006
		0.020	*0.052*	*0.043*	*0.065*	*0.026*	*0.064*	*0.000*	*0.223*	*0.024*	*0.021*	*0.052*	*0.087*	*0.030*	*0.039*	*0.000*	*0.055*

Estimated TDCs for Selected Stock Pairs in Consumer Discretionary, Industrials, Consumer Staples, Health, and Cross-Sector. The italic values are standard errors. "Para" and "Non-para" refer to semiparametric and nonparametric estimation methods (the first and third methods in estimation methodology).

Table 7.8 Selected Upper/Lower TDCs within Each Sector Generated (or estimated) by Student's *t* Copula Models, Semiparametric and Nonparametric Models

	Upper				*Lower*			
Pairs	*Unres. t cop*	*Res. t cop*	*Semi-para*	*Non-para*	*Unres. t cop*	*Res. t cop*	*Semi-para*	*Non-para*
MCD-LOW	0.001	0.160	0.167	0.080	0.001	0.160	0.064	0.041
MCD-HD	0.001	0.163	0.023	0.066	0.001	0.163	0.023	0.055
MCD-DIS	0.001	0.145	0.000	0.028	0.001	0.145	0.000	0.085
MCD-TGT	0.001	0.163	0.025	0.028	0.001	0.163	0.025	0.063
WMT-WAG	0.003	0.197	0.220	0.085	0.003	0.197	0.195	0.037
WMT-PG	0.001	0.164	0.145	0.055	0.001	0.164	0.174	0.093
WMT-KO	0.001	0.159	0.030	0.047	0.001	0.159	0.030	0.128
WMT-MO	0.000	0.122	0.000	0.078	0.000	0.122	0.000	0.054
XOM-COP	0.044	0.374	0.284	0.350	0.044	0.374	0.284	0.335
XOM-CVX	0.079	0.462	0.390	0.446	0.079	0.462	0.390	0.365
XOM-DVN	0.012	0.276	0.137	0.157	0.012	0.276	0.137	0.193
XOM-SLB	0.014	0.292	0.132	0.197	0.014	0.292	0.132	0.310
USB-JPM	0.018	0.310	0.249	0.219	0.018	0.310	0.249	0.284
USB-C	0.014	0.289	0.198	0.276	0.014	0.289	0.198	0.168
USB-BAC	0.023	0.327	0.254	0.311	0.023	0.327	0.254	0.258
USB-WFC	0.024	0.336	0.265	0.297	0.024	0.336	0.265	0.297
MRK-JNJ	0.004	0.216	0.218	0.113	0.004	0.216	0.233	0.061
MRK-AMGN	0.001	0.155	0.082	0.053	0.001	0.155	0.082	0.048
MRK-ABT	0.003	0.201	0.086	0.084	0.003	0.201	0.086	0.076
MRK-PFE	0.010	0.266	0.218	0.257	0.010	0.266	0.218	0.103

UNP-MMM	0.002	0.186	0.215	0.049	0.002	0.186	0.140	0.142
UNP-GE	0.002	0.178	0.184	0.053	0.002	0.178	0.127	0.089
UNP-BA	0.001	0.167	0.137	0.068	0.001	0.167	0.109	0.103
UNP-UTX	0.003	0.207	0.084	0.080	0.003	0.207	0.084	0.144
MSFT-IBM	0.005	0.216	0.205	0.071	0.005	0.216	0.205	0.112
MSFT-HPQ	0.003	0.199	0.250	0.098	0.003	0.199	0.111	0.085
MSFT-CSCO	0.008	0.251	0.274	0.122	0.008	0.251	0.248	0.109
MSFT-T	0.001	0.162	0.043	0.047	0.001	0.162	0.043	0.083
DD-NEM	0.000	0.102	0.009	0.000	0.000	0.102	0.009	0.044
DD-DOW	0.023	0.331	0.353	0.318	0.023	0.331	0.241	0.211
DD-PX	0.013	0.298	0.214	0.217	0.013	0.298	0.214	0.173
DD-ROH	0.016	0.296	0.357	0.238	0.016	0.296	0.218	0.168
DUK-EXC	0.008	0.257	0.225	0.180	0.008	0.257	0.291	0.232
DUK-FE	0.008	0.254	0.125	0.155	0.008	0.254	0.125	0.287
DUK-FPL	0.014	0.284	0.129	0.142	0.014	0.284	0.129	0.243
DUK-PPL	0.011	0.271	0.243	0.144	0.011	0.271	0.290	0.321

Selected Upper/Lower TDCs within each sector generated (or estimated) by Student's t copula models (unrestricted and restricted versions), semiparametric and nonparametric methods.

Table 7.9 Selected Upper/Lower TDCs Across Sectors Generated (or estimated) by Student's *t* Copula Models, Semiparametric and Nonparametric Models

	Upper				*Lower*			
Pairs	*Unres. t cop*	*Res. t cop*	*Semi-para*	*Non-para*	*Unres. t cop*	*Res. t cop*	*Semi-para*	*Non-para*
MCD-WMT	0.001	0.154	0.046	0.038	0.001	0.154	0.046	0.069
MCD-XOM	0.000	0.128	0.063	0.024	0.000	0.128	0.149	0.108
MCD-USB	0.001	0.158	0.002	0.048	0.001	0.158	0.002	0.060
MCD-MRK	0.000	0.132	0.000	0.053	0.000	0.132	0.000	0.011
MCD-UNP	0.000	0.135	0.014	0.004	0.000	0.135	0.014	0.059
MCD-MSFT	0.000	0.137	0.083	0.024	0.000	0.137	0.169	0.061
MCD-DD	0.001	0.155	0.000	0.035	0.001	0.155	0.000	0.113
MCD-DUK	0.000	0.128	0.092	0.108	0.000	0.128	0.118	0.003
WMT-XOM	0.000	0.145	0.053	0.065	0.000	0.145	0.053	0.099
WMT-USB	0.003	0.198	0.000	0.032	0.003	0.198	0.000	0.066
WMT-MRK	0.001	0.150	0.064	0.045	0.001	0.150	0.064	0.066
WMT-UNP	0.001	0.166	0.000	0.002	0.001	0.166	0.000	0.108
WMT-MSFT	0.002	0.180	0.178	0.069	0.002	0.180	0.196	0.107
WMT-DD	0.002	0.185	0.036	0.055	0.002	0.185	0.036	0.140
WMT-DUK	0.000	0.134	0.003	0.034	0.000	0.134	0.003	0.057
XOM-USB	0.001	0.161	0.059	0.067	0.001	0.161	0.059	0.087
XOM-MRK	0.001	0.149	0.038	0.094	0.001	0.149	0.038	0.067
XOM-UNP	0.001	0.162	0.154	0.078	0.001	0.162	0.065	0.089
XOM-MSFT	0.001	0.153	0.126	0.120	0.001	0.153	0.157	0.113
XOM-DD	0.002	0.193	0.079	0.187	0.002	0.193	0.079	0.196
XOM-DUK	0.001	0.176	0.139	0.126	0.001	0.176	0.149	0.130

USB-MRK	0.001	0.146	0.000	0.012	0.001	0.146	0.000	0.007
USB-UNP	0.001	0.169	0.049	0.106	0.001	0.169	0.049	0.095
USB-MSFT	0.001	0.162	0.126	0.008	0.001	0.162	0.222	0.068
USB-DD	0.002	0.193	0.191	0.114	0.002	0.193	0.208	0.095
USB-DUK	0.001	0.158	0.009	0.119	0.001	0.158	0.009	0.072
MRK-UNP	0.000	0.140	0.000	0.052	0.000	0.140	0.000	0.002
MRK-MSFT	0.001	0.139	0.123	0.043	0.001	0.139	0.150	0.018
MRK-DD	0.001	0.150	0.127	0.148	0.001	0.150	0.161	0.074
MRK-DUK	0.000	0.129	0.070	0.090	0.000	0.129	0.137	0.071
UNP-MSFT	0.001	0.154	0.141	0.013	0.001	0.154	0.153	0.058
UNP-DD	0.004	0.231	0.103	0.123	0.004	0.231	0.103	0.123
UNP-DUK	0.000	0.134	0.023	0.022	0.000	0.134	0.023	0.073
MSFT-DD	0.001	0.166	0.089	0.077	0.001	0.166	0.089	0.113
MSFT-DUK	0.000	0.126	0.072	0.052	0.000	0.126	0.145	0.032
DD-DUK	0.001	0.159	0.157	0.133	0.001	0.159	0.058	0.021

Selected Upper/Lower TDCs across sectors generated (or estimated) by Student's t copula models (unrestricted and restricted versions), semiparametric, and nonparametric methods.

Table 7.10 Simulated Risk Measures (VaR and ES) for Equal-Valued Selected Stock Pairs

			USB-JPM	*XOM-COP*	*MCD-WMT*	*XOM-MRK*
Period 1		S.D. 1	2.78%	1.80%	2.29%	1.80%
		S.D. 2	2.92%	2.14%	3.21%	1.81%
	VaR	Unres. t copula	-6.59%	-4.84%	-5.47%	-3.89%
		Res. t copula	-6.63%	-4.88%	-5.51%	-3.99%
		Emp. Distr.	-6.56%	-4.84%	-5.59%	-3.98%
	Percentage Change	Res. t/Unres. t	0.60%	0.84%	0.69%	2.42%
		Res. t/Emp.	1.10%	0.80%	-1.45%	0.09%
		Unres. t/Emp.	0.50%	-0.04%	-2.13%	-2.28%
	ES	Unres. t copula	-8.92%	-5.89%	-6.76%	-6.04%
		Res. t copula	-9.12%	-5.98%	-7.06%	-6.31%
		Emp. Distr.	-8.77%	-5.77%	-6.53%	-5.95%
	Percentage Change	Res. t/Unres. t	2.20%	1.46%	4.53%	4.50%
		Res. t/Emp.	3.97%	3.62%	8.15%	6.14%
		Unres. t/Emp.	1.73%	2.14%	3.46%	1.57%
Period 2		S.D. 1	0.93%	1.00%	1.87%	1.00%
		S.D. 2	0.92%	1.31%	1.28%	1.42%
	VaR	Unres. t copula	-2.14%	-2.84%	-3.18%	-2.65%
		Res. t copula	-2.15%	-2.86%	-3.21%	-2.71%
		Emp. Distr.	-2.12%	-2.86%	-3.11%	-2.69%
	Percentage Change	Res. t/Unres. t	0.61%	0.84%	0.78%	2.46%
		Res. t/Emp.	1.35%	0.07%	3.13%	1.05%
		Unres. t/Emp.	0.73%	-0.76%	2.34%	-1.38%

	ES	Unres. t copula	-2.91%	-3.46%	-4.03%	-4.35%
		Res. t copula	-2.97%	-3.50%	-4.18%	-4.52%
		Emp. Distr.	-2.86%	-3.38%	-3.86%	-4.27%
	Percentage Change	Res. t/Unres. t	2.17%	1.41%	3.80%	3.73%
		Res. t/Emp.	3.86%	3.54%	8.28%	5.68%
		Unres. t/Emp.	1.65%	2.10%	4.32%	1.88%
Period 3		S.D. 1	4.61%	2.36%	1.73%	2.36%
		S.D. 2	7.53%	3.86%	1.80%	2.13%
	VaR	t copula	-14.18%	-7.69%	-3.50%	-4.83%
		Res. t copula	-14.24%	-7.75%	-3.54%	-4.94%
		Emp. Distr.	-14.56%	-7.78%	-3.53%	-5.01%
	Percentage Change	Res. t/Unres. t	0.44%	0.78%	0.87%	2.32%
		Res. t/Emp.	-2.18%	-0.38%	0.07%	-1.34%
		Unres. t/Emp.	-2.60%	-1.16%	-0.80%	-3.58%
	ES	t copula	-18.71%	-9.37%	-4.36%	-7.35%
		Res. t copula	-19.11%	-9.49%	-4.56%	-7.69%
		Emp. Distr.	-18.31%	-9.20%	-4.20%	-7.23%
	Percentage Change	Res. t/Unres. t	2.10%	1.29%	4.63%	4.68%
		Res. t/Emp.	4.32%	3.10%	8.77%	6.38%
		Unres. t/Emp.	2.17%	1.79%	3.95%	1.63%

Simulated risk measures (99% VaR and ES) for equal-valued selected stock pairs. "S.D. 1" and "S.D. 2" refer to the selected standard deviations the stock pairs in each period. The risk measures are expressed in terms of log returns. For percentage change, "Res. t/Unres. t" means percentage increase of risk measures (in terms of absolute losses here) using restricted t copula model compared with unrestricted ones. The same interpretations apply for other designations.

Table 7.11 Simulated Risk Measures (VaR and ES) for Equal-Valued Portfolios Containing More Stocks

			5 Financials	*5 Energy*	*5 Consumer Staples*	*9 different sectors*	*9 different sectors*
Period 1	VaR	t copula	-5.87%	-5.14%	-4.45%	-4.21%	-3.86%
		Res. t copula	-5.91%	-5.17%	-4.49%	-4.26%	-3.92%
		Emp. Distr.	-5.82%	-5.30%	-4.32%	-4.02%	-3.92%
	Percentage Change	Res. t/t	0.78%	0.65%	0.97%	1.24%	1.56%
		Res. t/Emp.	1.57%	-2.47%	4.10%	6.09%	-0.04%
		t/Emp.	0.78%	-3.10%	3.10%	4.79%	-1.58%
	ES	t copula	-7.77%	-6.36%	-5.84%	-5.53%	-4.87%
		Res. t copula	-8.03%	-6.56%	-6.27%	-5.94%	-5.30%
		Emp. Distr.	-7.39%	-6.47%	-5.56%	-5.20%	-4.79%
	Percentage Change	Res. t/t	3.38%	3.26%	7.22%	7.46%	8.78%
		Res. t/Emp.	8.65%	1.42%	12.72%	14.09%	10.46%
		t/Emp.	5.10%	-1.78%	5.13%	6.17%	1.55%
Period 2	VaR	t copula	-1.94%	-2.91%	-1.84%	-1.93%	-1.67%
		Res. t copula	-1.96%	-2.92%	-1.85%	-1.95%	-1.71%
		Emp. Distr.	-1.93%	-2.99%	-1.78%	-1.91%	-1.73%
	Percentage Change	Res. t/t	0.89%	0.60%	0.83%	1.32%	2.14%
		Res. t/Emp.	1.39%	-2.35%	4.39%	2.18%	-1.03%
		t/Emp.	0.50%	-2.94%	3.54%	0.85%	-3.10%

	ES	t copula	-2.55%	-3.59%	-2.41%	-2.53%	-2.08%
		Res. t copula	-2.64%	-3.70%	-2.59%	-2.74%	-2.28%
		Emp. Distr.	-2.44%	-3.66%	-2.27%	-2.39%	-2.10%
	Percentage Change	Res. t/t	3.54%	3.25%	7.29%	8.13%	9.89%
		Res. t/Emp.	8.16%	1.29%	14.23%	14.64%	8.68%
		t/Emp.	4.47%	-1.91%	6.47%	6.02%	-1.10%
Period 3	VaR	t copula	-16.28%	-6.98%	-3.04%	-4.07%	-4.83%
		Res. t copula	-16.41%	-7.02%	-3.07%	-4.12%	-4.93%
		Emp. Distr.	-15.90%	-7.18%	-2.92%	-4.02%	-4.96%
	Percentage Change	Res. t/t	0.78%	0.58%	0.98%	1.35%	2.08%
		Res. t/Emp.	3.20%	-2.13%	5.04%	2.62%	-0.62%
		t/Emp.	2.40%	-2.69%	4.02%	1.25%	-2.65%
	ES	t copula	-21.29%	-8.60%	-4.04%	-5.37%	-5.92%
		Res. t copula	-22.01%	-8.88%	-4.33%	-5.77%	-6.45%
		Emp. Distr.	-20.40%	-8.78%	-3.83%	-5.17%	-6.02%
	Percentage Change	Res. t/t	3.37%	3.19%	6.96%	7.47%	8.96%
		Res. t/Emp.	7.89%	1.16%	12.91%	11.74%	7.14%
		t/Emp.	4.37%	-1.97%	5.56%	3.97%	-1.67%

Simulated risk measures (99% VaR and ES) for equal-valued portfolios containing more stocks. The first three portfolios contain five stocks from one sector, and the last two contain nine stocks from different sectors each. The standard deviations are determined by those of a particular day from each period. The risk measures are expressed in terms of log returns. For percentage change, "Res. t/Unres. t" means percentage increase of risk measures (in terms of absolute losses here) using restricted *t* copula model compared with unrestricted ones. The same interpretations apply for other designations.

NOTES

1. See Nelsen (1999) and Joe (1997) for a formal treatment of copula theory. See Bouye et al. (2000); Cherubini, Luciano, and Vecchiato (2004); and Embrechts, McNeil, and Straumann (2002) for applications of copulas in finance.
2. TDC can also be defined via tail copulas. Tail copulas are functions that describe dependence structures of a multivariate distribution in the tail and they generalize TDCs. See Schmidt and Stadtmueller (2006) for definitions of tail copulas.
3. See Cherubini, Luciano, and Vecchiato (2004) for a nice review of these estimation procedures.
4. Frahm et al. (2006) mention that their simulations show roughly the same MSE related to CML method and inference for the margin (IFM) method, where with IFM method, the marginal distributions are estimated parametrically in the first stage.
5. It is worth noting that with this approach the copula with the best overall goodness of fit may not give the best description of the tails. Another approach of choosing the "true" copula is through statistical tests on goodness of fit. However, this approach may not result in definitive selection decisions. With a view that all copula forms are only approximations to the "true" underlying distribution, our approach gives a clear-cut procedure for selecting the "true" copula. Of course, we could also focus on the goodness of fit in the tails instead of overall fit.
6. See Greene (2008).
7. See Pickands (1981) for a general representation of bivariate EV copulas.
8. See McNeil (1999) for details.
9. Schmidt and Stadtmueller (2006) derive nonparametric TDC estimators through both tail copulas and empirical copulas, and show that their derived asymptotic properties hold for both approaches. Moreover, see Dobric and Schmid (2005) for alternative nonparametric estimators.
10. Even though GARCH models can account for time-varying volatility, we still suspect that the true data-generating process has certain regime shifts. In this chapter, we estimate TDCs based on both raw log returns and GARCH-filtered returns.
11. Usually, the asset returns are more correlated in the market downturn than upturn, and, accordingly, lower tail dependence is larger than the upper one.
12. We may resort to statistical tests for a more rigorous treatment on asymmetries of tail dependence, which we leave for future research.
13. See Demarta and McNeil (2005) for a nice review on Student's *t* copula.
14. Note that after the uniform marginals are simulated from the estimated copula, the empirical GARCH residuals are used to back out the simulated GARCH residuals instead of using the estimated Student's *t* distribution. See Appendix 6.1 for details.
15. In this chapter, we set p=0.01 and h = 8 based an ad hoc simulation study.

BIBLIOGRAPHY

Bouye, E., V. Durrleman, A. Nikeghbali, G. Riboulet, and T. Roncalli. 2000. *Copulas for Finance: A Reading Guide and Some Applications.* Paris: Groupe de Recherche Operationelle Credit Lyonnais.

Cherubini, U., E. Luciano, and W. Vecchiato. 2004. *Copula Methods in Finance. Wiley Series in Financial Engineering*. Chichester, UK: Wiley.

Deheuvels, P. 1981. A non parametric test for independence, Publ. Inst. Statist. Univ. Paris 26, 29–50.

Demarta, S., and A.J. McNeil. 2005. "The t Copula and Related Copulas." *International Statistical Review* 73 (1): 111–129.

Dobric, J., and F. Schmid. 2005. "Nonparametric Estimation of the Lower Tail Dependence in Bivariate Copulas." *Journal of Applied Statistics* 32 (4): 387–407.

Embrechts, P.M.E., A.J. McNeil, and D. Straumann. 2002. "Correlation and Dependency in Risk Management: Properties and Pitfalls." In *Risk Management: Value at Risk and Beyond*, ed. M. Dempster, 176–223. Cambridge: Cambridge University Press.

Fortin, I. and C. Kuzmics. 2002. "Tail-Dependence in Stock-Return Pairs," *Economics Series* 126. Institute for Advanced Studies.

Frahm, G., M. Junker, and R. Schmidt. (2005). "Estimating the tail-dependence coefficient: Properties and pitfalls." *Insurance: Mathematics and Economics* 37:80–100.

Greene, William H. (2008). "Econometric Analysis," 6th ed. Prentice Hall.

Hu, L. 2006. "Dependence Patterns across Financial Markets: A Mixed Copula Approach." *Applied Financial Economics* 16:717–729.

Joe, H. 1997. *Multivariate Models and Dependence Concepts*. London: Chapman and Hall.

McNeil, A.J. 1999. *Extreme Value Theory for Risk Managers. Internal Modelling and CAD I*. London: RISK Books, 93–113.

Nelson, R.B. 1999. *An Introduction to Copula*. New York: Springer-Verlag.

Pickands, J. 1981. "Multivariate Extreme Value Distributions." *Bulletin of the International Statistical Institute, Proceedings of the 43rd Session, Buenos Aires* 859–878.

Resnick, S. 1987. *Extreme Values, Regular Variation, and Point Processes*. New York: Springer-Verlag.

Schmidt, R., and U. Stadtmueller. 2006. "Non-Parametric Estimation of Tail Dependence." *Scandinavian Journal of Statistics* 33:307–335.

8 Investors' Cognitive Profile and Herding

Beatriz Fernández, Teresa García-Merino, Rosa Mayoral, Valle Santos, and Eleuterio Vallelado

INTRODUCTION

The efficient market hypothesis holds that information is equally accessible to all investors and that these investors interpret the information in an unequivocally rational way. Rational investors combine different sources of information by using Bayes' rule: the weights placed on the different pieces of information should be proportional to their respective precision (Daniel and Titman 1999). The classic approach in finance is that only outcomes matter. Consequently, following this approach, asset prices incorporate all the existing information at all moments in time because behavioral biases are independent across individuals and cancel out in the aggregate as they are either averaged out or are corrected for by rational arbitrage.

However, certain limitations to this approach have been highlighted in the financial literature. On the one hand, investors cannot possibly digest the vast amount of information present in markets (Simon 1957). They are often not aware of all the information signals, and are frequently unable to analyze all the information they receive (Wärneryd 2001). Individuals have limited processing ability and hence use vague ad hoc rules to translate the information they receive into estimates of cash flows and company valuations. Investors must perforce base much of their analysis on hunches or feelings, which can easily be influenced by behavioral biases (Daniel and Titman 1999). Moreover, people are likely to bias in valuing securities for which information is sparse (Hirshleifer and Luo 2001). If as a consequence of uncertainty or ability limitations people share heuristics, then individuals have the same biases, which imply that errors are not independent across them (Hirshleifer 2001). On the other hand, Barberis and Thaler (2003) argue that arbitrage cannot eliminate all the effects of behavioral biases in financial markets due to: fundamental risk, noise trader risk, or implementation costs. Finally, even if we accept the classic approach it would still prove valuable to discriminate between individuals who are affected to a greater or lesser extent by behavioral biases (Oechssler, Roider, and

Schmitz 2008) because market behavior may at times be extreme and seemingly irrational.

As investors use biases to handle information, it is possible to identify biased behaviors in financial markets. In this chapter, we analyze one such behavior, herding, and we identify the environmental and individual factors that account for it. Investors sometimes opt to imitate the observed actions of others or market movements, rather than following their own beliefs and information to cope with the informational limitations in the markets (Wang 2008). When many such investors imitate at the same time herding appears. In fact, Devenow and Welch (1996) indicate that independent decision making across market participants is a fiction. Many influential market participants emphasize that their decisions are highly influenced by other market participants. Herding is among the most mentioned but least understood terms in the financial lexicon.

Herding in capital markets can be defined as the tendency of a group of investors to buy (sell) certain stocks at the same time, compared to what would be expected were investors to be working independently (Lakonishok, Shleifer, and Vishny 1992). One group of investors adopts the same decisions as other investors, ignoring their own information (Bikhchandani, Hirshleifer, and Welch 1992; Avery and Zemsky 1998), even if they are not sure that other investors have made the right decision (Banerjee 1992).

Devenow and Welch (1996) argue that herding implies behavior patterns that are correlated across individuals. It requires a coordination mechanism that can be either a signal or an ability to observe other decision makers. Such behavior becomes relevant when the volatility induced by herding increases the fragility of financial markets and destabilizes the broader market system (Bikhchandani and Sharma 2001; Chari and Kehoe 2004).

The main consensus is that herding can be construed as either a rational (Banerjee 1992; Bikhchandani, Hirshleifer, and Welch 1992; Welch 1992) or irrational (Keynes 1936; Hirshleifer 2001) form of investor behavior. Devenow and Welch (1996) define the rational view of herding as one centered on externalities. Thus, optimal decision making is distorted by information difficulties or incentive issues.[1] The nonrational view of herding centers on investor psychology. Agents behave following one another blindly, forgoing rational analysis. Finally, the intermediate view holds that decision makers are nearly rational, economizing on information processing or information acquisition costs by using heuristics.

A large number of analyses on herding focus on the question of whether, dependent upon available information, herding is evident in the market or not. Many studies into the origin of this phenomenon focus on the behavior of fund managers and analysts. In this case, authors focus on rational herding as they consider compensation systems and concern for reputation to be responsible for the presence of herding (Scharfstein and Stein 1990;

Zeckhauser, Patel, and Hendricks 1991; Bikhchandani and Sharma 2001). Nevertheless, few researchers have sought to explain the origin of herding by exploring human nature (Graham 1999; Cipriani and Guarino 2005, 2007; Bernardo and Welch 2001).

This research falls into the last nonrational group. Our approach is to consider investor psychology vis-à-vis the reliability of their information as the element that precipitates herding. The literature recognizes that an investor's feeling that other investors are better informed than they are is decisive in encouraging them to ignore their own information and to imitate other investors' decisions. Investors who imitate do not know the quality of other investors' information, financial market trends thus being based on the mood of investors and not on rational responses (Parker and Prechter 2005). Therefore, investors' cognitive profile becomes an important explanatory factor in the herding phenomenon.

One aim of our research is to explore in greater depth the nonrational factors that drive herding behavior in capital markets and to analyze whether investors' cognitive profiles determine their herding behavior. Specifically, the research hinges on a central proposition that postulates the existence of an interaction between uncertainty (lack of information) and investors' cognitive profile, and that this interaction impacts herding.

Studying this phenomenon proves complex because the researcher must identify how investors treat different types of information, and also discriminate between "true or intentional herding" and so-called "spurious herding." Intentional herding occurs when one group of investors consciously copies the decisions of another; spurious herding occurring when decision makers are faced with similar information and problems and make the same decisions without necessarily observing each other (Bikhchandani and Sharma 2001). The method used in this research includes an experiment to study this question empirically. This technique is appropriate because it allows the researcher to observe individuals' behavior in a controlled manner.

The results of the experiment show that uncertainty is more important than the individual cognitive profile in explaining herding among investors. However, as the level of uncertainty diminishes due to the increase in the volume of information available, investors' cognitive profile can account for why individuals show different imitation propensities in identical informational contexts.

This chapter is organized as follows. After the introduction, the next section reviews the determinants of herding. Specifically, it presents the hypotheses concerning the influence of uncertainty and investors' cognitive profile on investor decision making. The third section then describes the design of the empirical analysis and the laboratory experiment carried out. The fourth section looks at the results of the analysis. Finally, the fifth section discusses the main conclusions of the work and its implications for future research.

INFORMATION, BEHAVIORAL BIAS, AND HERDING

Information Uncertainty and Herding

Investors' decisions are surrounded by uncertainty, not only because of the informational limitations in the markets themselves but also because of individuals' cognitive limitations. There is uncertainty not only surrounding the real value of the securities being traded, but also concerning the quality of the information available. In uncertain contexts, investors tend to think that other investors are better informed and have important information that they lack. Thus, investors try to deduce what information other investors have by observing their decisions.

Investors might use herding as a means to protect themselves from uncertainty when behaving irrationally. Moreover, herding becomes relevant when such behavior is able to persist through time. Two related criteria must be considered to justify behavior persistence (Daniel and Titman 1999). The first criterion is that biases would remain were they able to yield benefits that cannot be eliminated over a long period of time by natural selection; the second criterion is that biases that systematically make individuals less successful when investing should not play a role in setting securities prices. Herding complies with both criteria. In the presence of herding we observe offsetting benefits because it is related with cycles. Furthermore, when investors herd, so do all individuals, thus avoiding any comparison between the most and least successful.

Were individuals to have access to public and private information of equal value in predicting the asset's intrinsic value, they would place equal weight on private and public signals. When individuals know that others have also observed the same public signal, the public signal is a better predictor of average opinion. They will attach greater weight to the public signal than to the private signal. If individuals' willingness to pay for an asset is related to their expectations of average opinion, asset prices will outweigh public compared to private information (Allen, Morris, and Shin 2006). A number of authors have noted that agents will not act on private information if they do not expect private information to be reflected in asset prices at the time they sell the asset (Froot, Scharfstein, and Stein 1992). Further, there is no guarantee that financial decision problems will be presented to individuals in a manner that leads to the most accurate decisions being made (Hirshleifer 2001).

In short, information available to investors is linked to the degree of uncertainty they perceive and how the information is presented. Thus, the first hypothesis is:

H_1: Herding behavior is more frequent in high-uncertainty contexts.

UNCERTAINTY, INVESTORS' COGNITIVE PROFILE, AND HERDING

Human heterogeneity and idiosyncrasy play a role in the development of major financial events. Researchers have identified systematic patterns in financial markets, patterns that are financial anomalies or biases. The rational economic paradigm (the way the world should be) and behavioral tendencies (the way the world actually is) will always be at odds with each other. However, the introduction of psychological antecedents into the analysis of financial anomalies is by no means a negation of the rational economic paradigm that needs to grow to account for observed reasons for behavior.

Uncertainty is inherently an emotion with negative valence because people are averse to uncertainty. Tactics to reduce uncertainty, such as identification of patterns, serve an important motivational function (Raghubir and Das 1999), and ability attenuates information-processing biases. Experts are thus less prone to nonnormative information processing, more normative decisions being possible with less time pressure (Raghubir and Das 1999).

Subjects evidence less regret when the bias affects a large amount of people (regret bias). Consequently, herding behavior will depend not only on the uncertainty present in the market, but also on each investor's individual perception of the level of uncertainty surrounding them. Thus, for example, in the same informational context, investors who are more insecure and less confident about their sources of information will display a greater tendency to herd. This feeling of uncertainty is a characteristic of each individual, because it will depend on each individual's attitudes, the extent to which they are more or less intuitive in character, their risk propensity, their excess or lack of confidence, their illusion of control, their degree of tolerance towards ambiguity, and so on. All these variables, which are interrelated, make up the investor's cognitive profile, which determines how the individual receives and interprets the different information stimuli they receive from their environment. Consequently, individuals' cognitive profiles will also be determinant in explaining in which circumstances investors decide to ignore their private information and imitate majority decisions in the market.

Having recognized the importance of the cognitive profile in explaining herding behavior, the difficulty now lies in how to measure this profile and consequently represent it in variables. This problem is resolved by using the biases in individuals' behavior and rules of thumb as proxies of the cognitive profile. The literature identifies a wide variety of biases and rules of thumb, springing from individuals' need to simplify their decision problems due to their cognitive limitations and emotions (Hirshleifer 2001).

The current work aims to explain the herding phenomenon on the basis of investors' cognitive profile, and so concentrates on those biases that might be more directly linked to this phenomenon (because they favor or limit herding): illusion of control, overconfidence, self-attribution, and the hot-hand and gambler fallacies. After identifying subjects' cognitive profile, our aim is to analyze whether this profile is responsible for investors' herding behavior (Hirshleifer and Teoh 2003).

Individuals suffering from the *illusion of control* bias think they can control and influence totally random events, leading them to underestimate the role of chance and to perceive games of chance as games of skill (Langer 1975; Kahneman and Riepe 1998). Such individuals believe that other investors are similarly affected. Thus, these investors infer information from the decisions made by other individuals under the assumption that those individuals have made their decisions based on relevant information and not randomly. Consequently, the illusion of control encourages herding.

Overconfidence occurs when subjects systematically overestimate their capacity to resolve situations compared to other individuals, causing them to overvalue their own decisions and overestimate their own knowledge (Daniel, Hirshleifer, and Subrahmanyam 1998; Dittrich, Güth, and Maciejovsky 2005). Overconfidence can lead individuals to place too great an emphasis on their own private information and too little on any other information available (Chuang and Lee 2006). They act following their own private signals and ignore cascades (Bernardo and Welch 2001). Investor overconfidence can generate momentum in stock returns, a momentum that is likely to be stronger in stocks whose valuations require the interpretation of ambiguous information (Daniel and Titman 1999). Experts tend to be more overconfident than relatively inexperienced individuals (Griffin and Tversky 1992). Besides, overconfidence is generally stronger for more diffuse tasks for which feedback is slow than for more mechanical tasks that provide an immediate outcome (Einhorn 1980). Overconfidence conceivably reduces herding behavior.

When individuals look back and assess their estimations and decisions, they are generally affected by a series of biases known as hindsight bias, including *self-attribution*. Self-attribution bias exists when the individual attributes events that validate their actions to their own skill and events that do not validate their actions to external agents (Fischhoff 1982). Thus, individuals affected by self-attribution will not imitate others unless they have had a long run of poor decisions.

The hot-hand and gambler's fallacies are related to the representativeness heuristic (Rabin 1998). According to Chan, Frankel, and Kothari (2002, 1), "almost invariably, the human information processing bias that underlies a given model of market inefficiency is a variation of the representativeness heuristic." The representativeness heuristic occurs when a person establishes the probability of an event with regard to the degree to which it is similar in its essential characteristics to a population (Kahneman and Tversky 1974). The representativeness heuristic plays a larger role in uncertainty. Biases in evidence when using the representativeness heuristic include the gambler's fallacy, whereby the individual assumes that the future random behavior of an asset necessarily depends on its past performance. Specifically, the subject sometimes considers randomness as a self-correcting process in which a deviation in one direction induces a deviation in the opposite direction to restore the equilibrium (Rabin 1998). These individuals consequently have the mistaken belief that random sequences should exhibit systematic reversals (Bar-Hillel and Wagenaar 1991). In other cases, the representativeness heuristic involves people expecting too few lengthy streaks in random sequences and hence thinking that those streaks are not justified by mere chance (hot-hand fallacy). Thus, the hot-hand fallacy encourages herding because after observing various buy (sell) transactions in the market, investors think that the trend will continue and decide to buy (sell) as their predecessors have done. By contrast, the gambler's fallacy inhibits herding because individuals decide to trade in the opposite direction to that of the recent trend (Rabin and Vayanos 2009).

Thus, as the amount of information increases investors will be guided by their emotions and will follow the mood of the market rather than transforming the information into knowledge to avoid regret. Thus, the second hypothesis is as follows:

> H_2: Investors' cognitive profile, defined as the result of a combination of biases, conditions their feeling of uncertainty and their herding behavior.

However, not all biases foster herding. Subjects for whom the illusion of control and the hot-hand fallacy dominate overconfidence and gambler's fallacies are more prone to herding. Thus, we identify five subhypotheses from the expected relation between each bias and herding:

> H_{2A}: Illusion of control bias favors herding.
> H_{2B}: Overconfidence bias reduces herding.
> H_{2C}: Self-attribution bias reduces herding.
> H_{2D}: Hot-hand fallacy encourages herding.
> H_{2E}: Gambler's fallacy inhibits herding.

Finally, investors habitually react disproportionately when they receive new information in the market, *under-* or *overreacting* (DeBondt and Thaler 1985; Hong and Stein 1999). The level of underreaction varies with information uncertainty (Burghof and Prothmann 2009). There is evidence that the initial market reaction to new public information is incomplete. The degree of incompleteness of the market reaction increases monotonically with the level of information uncertainty. If investors underreact to public information, they will underreact even more in cases of greater information uncertainty (Zhang 2006; Hirshleifer 2001). By contrast, Angelini and Guazzarotti (2009) find scarce evidence that higher uncertainty will cause prices to react more slowly to news. Thus, there is no agreement in the literature concerning the relation between information uncertainty and speed of stock price adjustment to news. Further empirical analyses are required to solve the question of underreaction to new public information.

Research thus simultaneously considers uncertainty and investors' cognitive profile to find an empirical answer to the question of investor underreaction to new public information. If individuals imitate their predecessors' decisions buying or selling, they overreact to public information. However, if individuals imitate their predecessors' decision not to act, they are underreacting to public information. Acting or not might be affected by information uncertainty. Thus, the third hypothesis is:

> H_3: Investors' underreaction to new information explains herding conditioned by information uncertainty.

EXPERIMENTAL AIMS AND DESIGN

The herding issue has been analyzed by using either market data and regression analysis or experiments with students (Bikhchandani and Sharma 2001). In our case, we needed to observe individuals' behavior in a controlled way, the empirical application of this research thus being based on an experimental setting. The main advantage of laboratory experiments over market data is that experiments allow control of public and private information, thus making explicit tests of theoretical predictions easier (Alevy, Haigh, and List 2007). Experiments provide a way to investigate behavior, removing many of the confounding effects present in field studies (Brown and Kagel 2009). Moreover, theory-driven experimental analysis will allow clarification among competing explanations and should complement existing empirical paradigms (Raghubir and Das 1999). Finally, experimental inquiry based on psychological theoretical models is the route to follow to complement the inductive explanation of errant data patterns with a deductive prediction of behavior. Theory-driven experimental inquiry has the potential to provide a unique understanding of how people make financial decisions (Raghubir and Das 1999).

Economics recognizes the importance of using experiments to supplement existing normative modeling and descriptive field research (Plott 1991a, 1991b). Laboratory experiments have been used to explore the behavior of financial markets in the fields of economics and psychology (Andreassen 1988; Myagkov and Plott 1997; Noussair, Plott, and Rieman 1995, 1997) although they are yet to become a mainstream exercise in finance. Experimental inquiry is the single most appropriate methodological tool for isolating causes of behavior and for complementing existing empirical paradigmatic approaches in behavioral finance (Raghubir and Das 1999).

Our experiment considers irrational herding because it centers on investor psychology and economizing on information processing by using heuristics. The experimental design rules out imperfect information, concern for reputation and compensation structure issues that Bikhchandani and Sharma (2001) propose to justify rational herding. In our experiment setting, subjects decide while confounding factors are held constant across different information settings. This allows us to differentiate behaviors that are otherwise difficult to disentangle (Bloomfield, Maureen, and Saar 2005). We focus on a transaction that is easily categorized as having a positive impact on the price of the stock and occurs fairly frequently.

The experiment consisted of two sessions. The first sought to analyze the relation between information and herding behavior, whereas the second examined the influence of behavioral biases on herding behavior under different levels of information.

The two sessions of the experiment took place at our laboratory premises. A total of fifty-six people participated in each session, all of whom were university students studying Business Administration. Subjects were recruited using a public announcement and were rewarded in relation to their performance by being given tickets. Subjects received a total of 21,041 tickets, the best performer being given 1,166 tickets and the worst seventeen. First prize was a laptop computer worth €700, whereas the remaining prizes were cash sums of €100, €50, and €10. Prizes were assigned through a random lottery with all the participants' tickets. Those with more tickets had a greater chance of winning the best prizes, as proved to be the case. The average payment to participants was €38.

Bikhchandani and Sharma (2001) argue that to examine herd behavior, a group of participants that trade actively and act similarly must be found. Our sample consisted of Business Administration students in the last two years of their degree. Such a condition aims to find subjects who possess basic finance knowledge and are familiar with trading in financial markets.

It could be argued that market professionals might provide a better sample for our purposes. However, Alevy, Haigh, and List (2007) indicate that market professionals are less Bayesian than students. Students are much more likely to be Bayesian in symmetric treatment. Using students does not therefore bias the results in favor of nonrational herd behavior. In short, the rate of cascade formation is not significantly different for students and for market professionals (Alevy, Haigh, and List 2007). It is true that market professionals learn from experience more than students do (Menkhoff, Schmidt, and Brozynski 2006). However, experience is not an issue in our experiment.

Alevy, Haigh, and List (2007) present evidence on the prevalence of non-Bayesian decision heuristics, an area in which the two pools of subjects, professionals and students, display similarities. Our sample of Business Administration students thus provides a nice fit for our experiment because our subjects are more Bayesian than professionals, have basic finance knowledge, and understand how financial markets work.

SESSION I: INFORMATION UNCERTAINTY AND HERDING

Cognitive biases are the object of study in experimental psychology. Several studies have shown that those biases diminish if information is expressed in numerical frequencies or posed in visual formats. However, there is no guarantee that financial decisions problems will be presented to individuals in a manner that favors the most accurate decisions (Hirshleifer 2001). Investors may herd if they ignore their private information signals when deciding (Hirshleifer and Teoh 2003), such behavior possibly showing up as: whether to participate in the market; what securities to trade; and/or whether to buy or sell. People may be looking for trends in data where no trends exist because trends imply the future is predictable, enabling control thereof as well as over future outcomes and thereby reducing uncertainty.

In our experiment subjects are paid more if they behave rationally, meaning that they acknowledge changes in prices are random. Moreover, because additional public information may encourage individuals to fall into a cascade sooner (Hirshleifer and Teoh 2003) we have identified three levels of public information. As the public pool of information grows, individuals' actions become less sensitive to private signals. However, if the public pool of information is uninformative, actions are sensitive to private signals (Hirshleifer and Teoh 2003).

To test the hypothesis concerning the relation between uncertainty and the herding phenomenon, the authors established three treatments that differ in the amount of public information available. Each of the treatments reproduces different levels of public information (see Table 7.1). In the three treatments, participants must decide whether they wish to buy or sell a stock or do nothing, given the current market price and the public and private information provided in each of the situations, known as rounds (see Appendix 7.1 for the instructions). Subjects do not act sequentially. Thus, information concerning previous decisions made by the other investors is provided by the experiment manager. This information is generated randomly. Using this design, our aim was to analyze subjects' behavior in the experiment vis-à-vis different types of information to identify who herds in each scenario. Subjects receive no feedback on their actions so as to avoid influencing our results with learning experience.

In each treatment there are forty rounds. Each round can have from three to ten transactions because at least three transactions are needed to observe imitation among investors, whereas ten transactions might be enough to reach the equilibrium point in the stock market price. Each of the fifty-six subjects acts only in the final transaction of each round. The decision in each round is independent of the decisions made in the other rounds in order to isolate herding behavior.

The underlying value of the stock in each round can be either zero or one hundred ducats, which is decided randomly before each round of transactions begins. There is a 50 percent chance that the stock will be worth zero ducats, and a 50 percent chance that it will be worth one hundred ducats. It should be stressed that the subjects do not know for certain the underlying value of the stock at any time and that they only have market price information. The price in each transaction is calculated through Bayes' Law. However, subjects receive no explanation about this procedure when fixing their prices. They are informed that the price of the stock changes from transaction to transaction according to the investor's decision, as occurs in capital markets. When individuals buy a stock, the price rises, when they sell, the price falls, and when they do nothing, the price remains the same.

One objective of the session is to analyze the presence of herding among the investors, the researchers thus designing the experiment so as to give subjects information that will enable them to make the same decisions as other individuals. The public information is different in each of the three treatments in the experiment. In the first treatment—"high uncertainty"—participants must decide whether to buy, sell, or do nothing, when they know the current price of the stock and its prices in previous periods (transactions). In the second treatment—"moderate uncertainty"—the investors have public information about the prices in the previous transactions and about the investors' actual decision: bought, sold, or did nothing. These two treatments differ in the stimuli used to provide the same information. Finally, in the "low-uncertainty" treatment the investors have public information about the prices in the previous periods, the transactions carried out, and the analysts' consensus recommendations. These recommendations are generated randomly because the relevant point is the availability of information provided by financial experts. The analysts' experience in the market may mean that the participants perceive them to be a source of reliable knowledge. Uncertainty diminishes from treatment to treatment as the public information available to the subjects increases.

To prevent the possible presence of spurious herding from contaminating the results, private information is introduced as a filter (Cipriani and Guarino 2005). Private information given to participants in the experiment informs them about the intrinsic value of the stock (market price is the public information) and is the same in all three treatments. This private information will be favorable if the underlying value of the security is one hundred ducats, and unfavorable if the underlying value is zero ducats. To reproduce investors' insecurity about the reliability of their information, participants do not know for certain at any time if the private information they hold is true or not, because this information may come from either a "Truth-teller" or a "Fibber," each with equal probability. Truth-tellers give reliable information in 70 percent of cases, whereas Fibbers give reliable information in only 30 percent of cases. Our goal is to evidence that a subject who acts rationally will find that there is the same likelihood of the information being either true or false. It then depends on a subject's cognitive profile whether they believe the information to be true or false.

Thus, when both types of information—public and private—induce the individual to make the same decision, it is impossible to determine what type of information has had the greatest weight in the individual's decision making. In other words, it is impossible to know whether the individual has imitated the other investors' decision or followed their own private information. These situations only act as a control, allowing the researchers to ensure that participants respond coherently. They cannot consider them in the subsequent analysis of herding. Only when the public and private information induce the investor to make opposite decisions and the investor decides to follow the public information and ignore their private information can intentional herding be said to exist.

In order to analyze the relation between herding behavior and level of uncertainty, each individual's proportion of imitation in each treatment was calculated, taking into account only those situations that exclude the possibility of spurious herding.

The HERD1, HERD2, and HERD3 variables measure the level of herding propensity for each subject in the three treatments in the analysis: high, moderate, and low uncertainty. This is followed by difference of means tests and Wilcoxon signed-ranks tests to accept or reject the first hypothesis that the level of uncertainty accounts for investors' herding behavior.

SESSION II: INFORMATION UNCERTAINTY, BEHAVIORAL BIAS, AND HERDING

The second session of the experiment aims to detect the presence of certain biases in the individual's behavior. The aim of this stage in the experiment is to analyze the effect on herding behavior of the following cognitive profile variables (see Table 8.1): illusion of control (ILC), gambler's fallacy (GF), overconfidence (OC), self-attribution (SA), and hot-hand fallacy (HHF). The research considers how underreaction to new information (UR) influences herding conditioned by information uncertainty. To identify how subjects present the proposed biases, we designed the test of preferences questionnaire (see Appendix 8.1) based on the works of Kahneman and Riepe (1998), Kahneman and Tversky (1974, 2000), and Montier (2002). Some of the questions included in our test of preferences are a selection of questions included in the papers quoted, modified to take account of the environment and culture of Spain. The remaining questions are new and seek to introduce theoretical considerations related to our chapter. This test thus presents participants with different real-life situations, forcing them to decide which of the proposed actions they would take.

In order to gain a deeper insight into the relation between the variables measuring behavioral biases and herding behavior, the researchers first carried out an analysis of variance (ANOVA) and then a binary logistic regression (LOGIT). We are aware that the cognitive variables are not mutually exclusive, and for this reason the latter analysis allows us to consider the interrelations between the cognitive variables chosen in the present study. The researchers observed the reaction of the subjects in those situations in which private information contradicts public information in order to calculate the extent to which each individual imitates. From the original variables (HERD1, HERD2, and HERD3) the researchers then build new dummy variables (G-HERD1, G-HERD2, and G-HERD3) to divide the subjects into two groups: high herding intensity and low herding intensity, for each of the information treatments. Specifically, the frequency distribution of the original variables is split into two blocks depending on whether the value of the variable exceeds the median or not.[2] Block 1 contains individuals that show a low intensity of imitation behavior, whereas Block 2 contains individuals who show a high intensity of imitation behavior. Thus, there are now three variables, one for each treatment, with two possible values that place each individual in either Block 1 or Block 2. Logit analysis is used to study whether the variables measuring behavioral biases can account for this grouping.

Table 8.1 Experiment Sessions and Variables

Session I: Uncertainty and herding		
TREATMENT 1	*TREATMENT 2*	*TREATMENT 3*
Public information: · Price history	**Public information:** · Price history · Transaction history	**Public information:** · Price history · Transaction history · Consensus recommendations
Private information: Initial stock price: · Favorable: 100 Ducats · Unfavorable: 0 Ducats	**Private information:** Initial stock price: · Favorable: 100 Ducats · Unfavorable: 0 Ducats	**Private information:** Initial stock price: · Favorable: 100 Ducats · Unfavorable: 0 Ducats
Session II: Uncertainty, behavioral bias, and herding		
Behavioral bias: · Illusion of control (ILC) · Overconfidence (OC) · Self-attribution (SA) · Underreaction (UR) · Hot-hand fallacy (HHF) · Gambler's fallacy (GF)		

RESULTS

Information Uncertainty and Herding

In the first stage of the analysis, herding gradually diminishes as uncertainty falls (see Table 8.2). Thus, the average individual's imitation values observed in the high-uncertainty treatment (HERD1) is 0.31, falling to 0.29 in the moderate-uncertainty treatment (HERD2), and to 0.27 in the low-uncertainty treatment (HERD3). The test of mean differences shows that the fall in herding between the high- and low-uncertainty treatments is statistically significant at the 90 percent level (t = 1.793; see Table 8.2). The results from the Wilcoxon signed-rank test confirm these results because they show a statistically significant difference in herding between the high- and low-uncertainty treatments (see Table 8.2). Hypothesis H_1, which postulates that herding behavior is more frequent in contexts of higher levels of uncertainty, is thus accepted.

INFORMATION UNCERTAINTY, BEHAVIORAL BIAS, AND HERDING

The second stage of the analysis focuses on the dependence relations between individual behavioral biases (explanatory variables) and herding in each of the three information treatments (dependent variable).

The results show that the interaction relations between the variables measuring behavioral bias and herding occur mainly in the low-uncertainty treatment. Thus, for the high- and moderate-uncertainty treatments, the variables measuring the cognitive profile evidence hardly any explanatory power, whereas the significance of the variables improves considerably in the low-uncertainty treatment.

Table 8.2 Mean Imitation Values, Difference of Means Test and Wilcoxon Signed-Rank Test

TREATMENT 1 *High uncertainty*	*TREATMENT 2* *Moderate uncertainty*			*TREATMENT 3* *Low uncertainty*	
0.3103	0.2856			0.2738	
	Difference of means t test			Wilcoxon signed-rank test	
	Mean	t	(Sig.)	Z	(Asympt. sig.)
High uncert. - Mod. uncert.	0.0246	1.324	(0.019)	-1.966	(0.049)-
High uncert. - Low uncert.	0.0365	1.793	(0.079)	1.832	(0.067)
Mod. uncert. - Low uncert.	0.0118	0.583	(0.563)	-0.057	(0.954)

Logit analysis confirms the dependence relation between the cognitive profile variables and herding in the low-uncertainty treatment. Specifically, the dependent variable is the variable measuring the block to which individuals are allocated depending on their low or high imitation intensity. This variable is available for each of the three treatments considered (G-HERD1, G-HERD2, and G-HERD3). The procedure used was stepwise estimation, allowing the researcher to detect the most important independent variables.

The results obtained in the logit analysis for the high- and moderate-uncertainty treatments show that the behavioral bias variables have little explanatory power, meaning the model cannot be estimated (Table 8.3). These results show that the power of uncertainty to provoke herding behavior prevails over the individual's characteristics.

Table 8.3 Uncertainty, Behavioral Bias, and Herding Logit Analysis

Model *HERD=b0+b1ILC+b2OC+b3SA+b4HHF+b5GF+b6UR*

Estimation: High-uncertainty treatment

	B	T.E.	Wald	df	Sig.	Exp(B)
Constant	.143	.268	.285	1	.593	1.154

-2 log L0: 77.347

Estimation: Moderate-uncertainty treatment

	B	T.E.	Wald	df	Sig.	Exp(B)
Constant	.143	.268	.285	1	.593	1.154

-2 log L0: 77.347

Estimation: Low-uncertainty treatment

	B	T.E.	Wald	df	Sig.	Exp(B)
ILC	8.637	3.604	5.742	1	.017	5634.965
OC	8.538	4.659	3.358	1	.067	5102.887
SA	-6.678	2.186	9.329	1	.002	.001
UR	2.893	1.308	4.893	1	.027	18.053
Constant	2.355	1.426	2.727	1	.099	10.535

-2 log L0*: 60.687

-2 log L1: 34.889

C: 25.798**

* Model including only one constant.

** Maximum likelihood ratio test: C = - 2 log L0/L1 = - 2 (log L0 – log L1); chi-square with as many degrees of freedom as number of variables evaluated.

In the low-uncertainty treatment, however, logit analysis results are statistically significant. Here the cognitive profile variables are statistically significant and allow estimation of the empirical model. The maximum likelihood ratio test confirms the goodness of fit of the model, because its value exceeds the chi-square with four degrees of freedom at the most demanding confidence levels. Hence the deduction is that the allocation of individuals to the high- or low-intensity imitation block is explained by the behavioral bias variables considered in the analysis (cognitive profile). Four of the variables are significant: illusion of control (ILC), self-attribution (SA), underreaction (UR), and overconfidence (OC). The associated signs indicate that the individuals allocated to the high-intensity imitation block show higher levels in illusion of control, overconfidence, and underreaction, and a lower level of self-attribution. In other words, in the low-uncertainty treatment the illusion of control, overconfidence, and underreaction biases have a positive relation with the herding phenomenon, whereas the self-attribution bias has an inverse relation with this behavior.

Contrary to what was expected, the hot-hand and the gambler's fallacies are not significant in the logit analysis. Several reasons may account for this. These variables may not be accurately measuring the bias as intended, or their effect may interact with some of the other variables in the analysis. On the other hand, in low-uncertainty contexts, individuals with a tendency to underreact and be overconfident might behave unexpectedly. In this type of situation, these individuals interpret that the other investors have no difficulty in making decisions, given the variety of stimuli and information sources available, and consequently accept the trading observed in the transaction history as ideal. Hence, they imitate the other investors, letting themselves get carried along by the investors' mood predominating over individual biases, contrary to herding behavior. This is common in periods of bubbles in financial markets when prices keep rising irrationally, and there is nothing to counter the rise, not even the individual biases that counteract herding behavior. This finding could explain why speculative bubbles form in financial markets despite the fact that overconfident individuals should prevent them from appearing or slow them down if they do appear. The current results might indicate that in a low-uncertainty environment, individuals who show biases that counter herding let themselves be carried along by other individuals and imitate, thereby favoring the creation of bubbles. In short, even behavioral biases differ depending upon the uncertainty.

Globally, the current results confirm the influence of behavioral biases on the phenomenon of herding, thus providing support for Hypothesis H_2. However, this relation is more than a simple dependence relation because it only becomes apparent in low-uncertainty contexts. Specifically, the results show that in uncertain contexts the weight of the uncertainty generates herding regardless of differences amongst individuals.

This confirms that the weight of the uncertainty hides the influence of the individual behavioral biases. Yet, in low-uncertainty contexts, in which the general tendency to herd is lower, it is the interindividual differences that can explain different individuals' herding propensities. Thus, the results show that both environmental uncertainty and individuals' behavioral biases are determinants of the herding phenomenon, in addition to which the two determinants interact with each other. In other words, the fall in the level of uncertainty exposes the effect of the biases on herding behaviors. This confirms the complexity of the relations that exist between the determinants of herding behavior.

CONCLUSIONS

Investors' herding behavior in financial markets stems from informational limitations: either the investors lack part of the information or are unable to process the information available and turn it into knowledge. In an uncertain environment, where perfect information does not exist, the feeling of uncertainty leads individuals to think that others are better informed. The greater the investors' sense of uncertainty, the more they question their own information. Consequently, in uncertain environments investors try to obtain information by observing the financial decision making of other participants in the market. The deduction that follows from this is that the higher the level of uncertainty, the higher the investors' propensity to imitate other individuals' decisions.

Along with the uncertainty in financial decision making, individuals are also affected by cognitive limitations and are subject to the influence of their own beliefs, attitudes, and cognitive profile. Thus, they will not always behave as homogenous and perfectly rational agents. Consequently, responses to market signals vary considerably from one investor to the next. This makes it necessary to study how investors' individual profiles affect their herding behavior. The current work analyzes whether the presence of biases in individuals' behavior affects the intensity of their herding behavior.

Results from the experiment carried out here offer new evidence concerning the factors intervening in the herding phenomenon in financial markets. On the one hand, findings show that uncertainty, and consequently informational limitations, favor herding among investors. The results demonstrate that herding behavior reaches a peak in environments with a higher level of uncertainty and that in moderate- and high-uncertainty treatments, personal differences cannot account for the different intensity levels of imitation among individuals. A rise in uncertainty homogenizes individual behavior with regard to the herding phenomenon. Yet, as uncertainty falls, individuals' cognitive profiles become more important in explaining herding behavior. Moreover, the nature of the individual biases that affect herding behavior also changes as uncertainty falls. This helps to account for why, for example, in the final moments of bubbles in financial markets, as the influence of the elements that counteract market irrationality weakens, asset prices accelerate upwards far above their real value. Two conclusions may thus be drawn from this research: firstly, the dependence relation between the feeling of uncertainty, investors' behavioral biases, and the herding phenomenon, and, secondly, that the determinants of herding—information and behavioral biases—are interrelated. Specifically, the presence of high levels of uncertainty favors herding behaviors, regardless of the interindividual differences. Only when the level of uncertainty falls is the effect of the behavioral biases determinant in investors' herding behavior.

In short, the current findings confirm that the herding phenomenon is complex because factors of an extremely diverse nature intervene. Future research should examine further how best to measure the individual cognitive profile and its interaction with information processing in financial markets.

APPENDIX 8.1 EXPERIMENT DETAILS

First Session: Instructions to Participants

Stage 1

Operations simulating the buying and selling of various stocks by several investors are presented. You must decide in each situation whether to buy or sell a particular stock, or do nothing. The intrinsic initial value of the share may be only zero or one hundred ducats, and it will be determined randomly before each round of transactions begins. There is a 50 percent likelihood that the stock will take one of these two values.

Although you will not know the intrinsic value of the stock obtained, you will be given certain private information regarding it. This private information will be favorable if the initial intrinsic value is one hundred ducats, but will be unfavorable if the initial intrinsic value is zero ducats. The problem is that you will not know for certain at any time whether the private information you have been provided with is accurate or not, as it is just as likely to come from one of two sources of information: a "Truth-Teller" or a "Fibber." A Truth-Teller shows a 70 percent degree of reliability in the information provided, whereas a Fibber only supplies news that is accurate 30 percent of the time.

The asset price will change from transaction to transaction depending on the decisions taken by investors. When subjects buy the share, the price rises, and when they sell it, the price falls. If investors do not trade, the price remains the same.

You will be faced with a variety of situations in which you must make a decision based on the current market price, the private information you have been provided with, and the stock's prices in previous transactions.

The nature of the private information available to you (favorable or unfavorable) appears next to the number of the round in which you must decide. The stock's prices in previous periods are shown in brackets together with the corresponding transaction number. The price at which you may trade is shown next to the box in which you must indicate your decision to buy, sell, or not trade.

Example

In round X you are the eighth participant who must decide. You should observe the stock's price over the last seven transactions and take into account whether the private information available to you is favorable, suggesting that the price of the stock is one hundred ducats (remember that you do not know from which of the two sources, Truth-Tellers or Fibbers, the information comes).

Bearing in mind all the information, you must decide whether to buy or sell the stock at seventy ducats (the price shown on the left of the last box in the column corresponding to round X), or do nothing. If you decide to *buy* the stock you should put a C in the right of the last box of the column for round X, meaning that you are willing to pay seventy ducats for a share that may be worth zero or one hundred ducats.

Table 8.4 Stage 1 Example

TRANSACTION	*ROUND X* *Favorable private information*	
1	(50 ducats)	
2	(70 ducats)	
3	(84 ducats)	
4	(70 ducats)	
5	(84 ducats)	
6	(93 ducats)	
7	(84 ducats)	
8	70 ducats	C

Stage 2

At this stage of the experiment, the decisions you are faced with are similar to those in the previous stage, although now you will be given information you did not have in stage 1. Now, you will be able to know whether the previous investors bought, sold, or did not trade, as well as the price at which each of these transactions occurred. Therefore, when making your decisions, you must take into account the current market price, the private information, and the new public information available.

Example

In round X you are the eighth person who has to decide. You should observe the prices at which the seven previous investors traded together with the decision they made. You should also take into account whether the private information available to you is favorable, indicating that the price of the stock is one hundred ducats (remember that you do not know from which of the two sources, Truth-Tellers or Fibbers, the information comes).

Having examined all this information, you must decide whether to buy or sell the stock at seventy ducats (the price shown on the left of the last box in the column corresponding to round X), or do nothing. If you decide to *buy* the stock you should put a C in the right of the last box of the column for round X, meaning that you are willing to pay seventy ducats for a share that may be worth zero or one hundred ducats.

Stage 3

At this stage of the experiment, the decisions you are faced with are similar to those in the previous stage, although now you will be given information

Table 8.5 Stage 2 Example

TRANSACTION	*ROUND X* *Favorable private information*	
1	Bought (50 ducats)	
2	Bought (70 ducats)	
3	Sold (84 ducats)	
4	Bought (70 ducats)	
5	Bought (84 ducats)	
6	Sold (93 ducats)	
7	Sold (84 ducats)	
8	70 ducats	C

you did not know in stage 2. Now, you will be informed of the recommendations of certain analysts. When making your decisions, you should therefore take into account the current market price, the private information, the public information available, and the analysts' recommendations.

Example

In round X you must decide in sixth position. You should observe the prices at which the five previous investors traded and the decisions they made. You should also take into account whether the private information available to you is favorable, indicating that the price of the stock is one hundred ducats (remember that you do not know from which of the two sources, Truth-Tellers or Fibbers, the information comes) and you should bear in mind that analysts recommend selling the stock if it is at a price of fifty ducats or more.

Having seen all of this information, you should decide whether to buy or sell the stock at seventy ducats (the price that appears on the left of the last box of the column corresponding to round X), or do nothing. If you opt to *buy* the stock you should put a C on the right of the last box in the column for round X, thus indicating that you are willing to pay seventy ducats for this stock.

Second Session: Preferences Test

Now mark with an arrow the response which most closely reflects how you would behave in the following situations:

1. You go to a casino to play roulette. When placing your bet:
    a. You take into account the numbers that have been coming up in the previous spins, as you think that a number that has already won is less likely to win again.

Table 8.6 Stage 3 Example

TRANSACTION	*ROUND X* *Favorable private information* *Recommendation: Sell above 50 ducats.*	
1	Bought (50 ducats)	
2	Bought (70 ducats)	
3	Sold (84 ducats)	
4	Bought (70 ducats)	
5	Sold (84 ducats)	
6	70 ducats	C

b. You take into account the numbers that have been coming up in the previous spins because you think that if a number has won more than once it is more likely to win again.
c. You choose the number that appeals to you most at each spin.
d. You keep betting on the same number because you think that it must win eventually.

2. You want to invest in an investment fund. You have sought information about fund X and expect to it go up in the future, and as a result you consider investing in it.
   2. a. A friend in the same situation recommends fund Y to you.
      i. You decide to seek information about fund Y to confirm what your friend has told you and then make a decision.
      ii. Your information about X is excellent and you feel it isn't worth wasting more time finding out about Y.
      iii. You feel you might be wrong and so decide to trust more in your friend's information and so invest in Y.
   2. b. Finally you decided not to investigate further and invested in X. Your fund is now performing extremely badly due to the fact that one of its assets is suffering heavy losses following a financial scandal involving one of the firm's managers. What do you think in this case?
      i. You should perhaps have listened to your friend.
      ii. I made the right decision because if it hadn't been for that scandal, the fund would now be returning a profit.
   2. c. You decide to maintain your investment in fund X because you think that it will turn around. However, the fund continues to return losses over the following months. You think:
      i. I made a mistake. I should not have maintained my investment in X.
      ii. I don't understand how the fund is still making a loss. The scandal has been cleared up and the firm in question has a new management team with an excellent reputation.
      iii. I am sure the fund will now start to pick up.
   2. d. You invested in X and your friend in Y. Your friend's fund is suffering huge losses due to an unexpected change in the law in the sector to which several of the assets in the fund belong. You think:
      i. Luckily I didn't listen to my friend. He was wrong and I wasn't.
      ii. Perhaps my friend made the right choice and was just unlucky with the changes in current legislation.

3. You held a stock that yielded surprisingly high returns over a period of several months but that has recently been showing a constant series

of relatively small losses. Over the last week, however, the losses have become substantial.

i. You think: my stock has always shown a good price. If I wait for this bad patch to blow over, the price is bound to go up again. I won't even listen to analysts' recommendations.
ii. A renowned analyst warns you that the price of your share is likely to continue falling. You decide to sell the share.
iii. The analyst warns you that the share will continue to fall but you decide to keep it because selling the share now means that you will make a loss.

4. The daily mean price of a particular share in recent weeks has been: 23, 20, 20, 21, 26, 26, 24, 20, 23, 22, 23, 28. You:
    a. Decide to invest in the stock as it shows a general upward trend.
    b. Decide to invest because over the last few days its share price has been going up.
    c. Do not invest because you see no clear trend in the share price.

5. You hold fifty shares in a company that is rumored to be considering a share issue due to the healthy state of the firm. You:
    a. Decide to buy more shares in the firm before its price rises.
    b. Ignore it when making your decision as it is only a rumor.

6. You think that after finishing your university studies in order to find a job in line with your qualifications:
    a. It will take you longer than most of your fellow graduates.
    b. It will take you less time than most of your fellow graduates.
    c. It will take you around the same time as most of your fellow graduates.

7. You decide to purchase a lottery ticket for the following Saturday's draw.
    a. You go to the lottery ticket office and ask for a number ending in "your lucky number."
    b. At the lottery ticket office you ask for a ticket without specifying any particular number.
    c. Before going to the lottery ticket office you find out which numbers have been winning over the last few weeks.
    d. You always buy the same number.

8. When deciding which assets to invest in, you prefer:
    a. Stocks recommended by financial analysts.
    b. Stocks that many investors are currently investing in.
    c. Stocks about which you have gathered good information.

9. Pablo is thirty-five, single, extremely brilliant, and determined. After completing his university degree and several years training plus hard work, he was appointed to a post in a bank's portfolio management department. You think Pablo is more likely to be:
   a. A graduate in Business Studies with a master's degree in Financial Markets.
   b. A graduate in Business Studies.

10. You go to a car dealer to buy a new car. You have been gathering information on the Duero and Ebro models. A mechanic you know and trust thinks that the Ebro model is a compact MPV more suited to your needs, and specialized magazines seem to indicate the same, but you prefer the sportier Duero model.

    When you visit the showroom the dealer shows you the Tajo jeep, a new vehicle coming onto the market in a few weeks but which you have heard nothing about. However, it seems to offer excellent value for money. You:
    a. Decide to buy the Duero model, the one you had first thought of.
    b. Buy the Ebro model.
    c. Wait until you have more information about the Tajo model.
    d. Buy the Tajo model that very day.

11. You hold fifty shares in a firm about which rumors have been circulating to the effect that it is in serious financial difficulties. You:
    a. Decide to sell before the rumors are confirmed, even if it means making a loss on the price you paid for them.
    b. Ignore it when making a decision as they are just rumors.

12. Christmas is coming and you decide to purchase a lottery ticket for the Big Christmas Draw. When purchasing your ticket you see a sign listing the numbers that have won first prize in previous years (from 2005 to 1999): 20085, 54600, 42473, 08103, 18795, 49740, 65379.
    a. Without stopping to read the above information you ask for a ticket ending in the number you already had in mind.
    b. Ask for a ticket ending in 5, 0, 3, or 9, as these are the numbers that have won in recent years.
    c. Ask for a number ending in an even number or in 7, as these are the ticket number endings that have not won in recent years.
    d. Buy any number.

13. You hold eighty shares in a firm about which bad rumors have been spreading. You:
    a. Decide to sell the shares in the company before the price falls.
    b. As it is only a rumor, you ignore it when making your decisions.

14. When doing the weekly shopping at the supermarket, you:
   a. Always buy products whose quality you are sure of and you are reluctant to try new ones.
   b. Buy articles that are on offer.
   c. Buy articles recommended to you by friends and family.

NOTES

1. See Bikhchandani and Sharma's (2001) survey of herding as rational investor behavior. According to these authors, rational herding is related to imperfect information, concerns for reputation, and compensation structures.
2. The peculiar frequency distribution in the original variables prevents the blocks from capturing exactly 50 percent of each variable.

BIBLIOGRAPHY

Alevy, J.E., M.S. Haigh, and J. List. 2007. "Information Cascades: Evidence from a Field Experiment with Financial Market Professionals." *Journal of Finance* 62 (1): 151–180.

Allen, F., S. Morris, and A. Postlewaite. 1993. "Finite Bubbles with Short Sale Constraints and Asymmetric Information." *Journal of Economic Theory* 61:206–229.

Allen, F., S. Morris, and H.S. Shin. 2006. "Beauty Contests and Interacted Expectations in Asset Markets." *Review of Financial Studies* 19 (3): 719–752.

Andreassen, P.B. 1988. "Explaining the Price Volume Relationship: The Difference between Price Changes and Changing Prices." *Organization Behavior and Human Decision Processes* 41 (3): 371–389.

Angelini, P., and G. Guazzarotti. 2009. "Information Uncertainty and the Reaction of Stock Prices to News." *SSRN* 13:426–472.

Avery, C., and P. Zemsky. 1998. "Multidimensional Uncertainty and Herd Behavior in Financial Markets." *American Economic Review* 88 (4): 724–748.

Banerjee, A.V. 1992. "A Simple Model of Herd Behavior." *Quarterly Journal of Economics* 107 (3): 797–817.

Barberis, N., and R. Thaler. 2003. "A Survey of Behavioral Finance." In *Handbook of the Economics of Finance*, ed. H.M. Constantinides and R. Stulz, 1051–1121. New York: Elsevier Science B.V.

Bar-Hillel, M., and W.A. Wagenaar. 1991. "The Perception of Randomness." *Advances in Applied Mathematics* 12 (4): 428–454.

Bernardo, A.E., and I. Welch. 2001. "On the Evolution of Overconfidence and Entrepreneurs." *Journal of Economics and Management Strategy* 10 (3): 301–330.

Bikhchandani, S., D.A. Hirshleifer, and I. Welch. 1992. "A Theory of Fads, Fashion, Custom and Cultural Change as Informational Cascades." *Journal of Political Economy* 100 (5): 992–1026.

Bikhchandani, S., and S. Sharma. 2001. "Herd Behavior in Financial Markets: A Review." *IMF Staff Papers* 47 (3): 279–310.

Bloomfield, R.J., O. Maureen, and G. Saar. 2005. "The Limits of Noise Trading: An Experimental Analysis." NYU Working Paper no. FIN-05–015. Available at http://ssrn.com/abstract=1294151.

Brown, A.L., and J.H. Kagel. 2009. "Behavior in a Simplified Stock Market: The Status Quo Bias, the Disposition Effect and the Ostrich Effect." *Annals of Finance* 5:1–14.

Burghof, H.P., and F. Prothmann. 2009. "The 52 Week High Strategy and Information Uncertainty." *SSRN* 13:747–762.

Chari, V.V., and P.J. Kehoe. 2004. "Financial Crises as Herds: Overturning the Critiques." *Journal of Economic Theory* 119:128–150.

Chan, W.S., R.M. Frankel, and S.P. Kothari. 2002. "Testing Behavioral Finance Theories Using Trends and Sequences in Financial Performance." MIT Sloan School of Management Working Paper 4375–02. Available at http://ssrn.com. abstract=316999.

Chen, Q., and W. Jiang. 2006. "Analysts' Weighting of Private and Public Information." *Review of Financial Studies* 19 (1): 319–355.

Chuang, W.I., and B.S. Lee. 2006. "An Empirical Evaluation to the Overconfidence Hypothesis." *Journal of Banking and Finance* 30 (9): 2489–2515.

Cipriani, M., and A. Guarino. 2005. "Herding and Price Convergence in a Laboratory Financial Market." *American Economic Review* 95 (5): 1427–1443.

———. 2007. "Transaction Costs and Informational Cascades in Financial Markets: Theory and Experimental Evidence." ECB Working Paper no. 736. Available at http://ssrn.com/abstract=965422.

Daniel, K., D. Hirshleifer, and A. Subrahmanyam. 1998. "Investor Psychology and Security Market Over- and Underreactions." *Journal of Finance* 53:1839–1885.

Daniel, K., and S. Titman. 1999. "Market Efficiency in an Irrational World." *Financial Analysts Journal* 55 (6): 28–40.

DeBondt, W.F., G. Muradoglu, H. Shefrin, and S.K. Staikouras. 2008. "Behavioral Finance: Quo Vadis?" *Journal of Applied Finance* 19:1–15.

DeBondt, W.F., and R.H. Thaler. 1985. "Does the Stock Market Overreact?" In *Advances in Behavioral Finance*, ed. Richard H. Thaler, 249–264. New York: Russell Sage Foundation.

Devenow, A., and I. Welch. 1996. "Rational Herding in Financial Economics." *European Economic Review* 40:603–615.

Dittrich, D., W. Güth, and B. Maciejovsky. 2005. "Overconfidence in Investment Decisions: An Experimental Approach." *European Journal of Finance* 11 (6): 471–491.

Einhorn, H.J. 1980. "Overconfidence in Judgement." *New Directions for Methodology in Social and Behavioural Sciences* 4 (1): 1–16.

Fischhoff, B. 1982. "For Those Condemned to Study the Past: Heuristic and Biases in Hindsight." In *Judgement under Uncertainty: Heuristics and Biases*, ed. D. Kahneman, P. Slovic, and A. Tversky, 335–354. Cambridge: Cambridge University Press.

Froot, K., D. Scharfstein, and J. Stein. 1992. "Herd on the Street: Informational Inefficiencies in a Market with Short Term Speculation." *Journal of Finance* 47 (4): 1461–1484.

Graham, J.R. 1999. "Herding among Investment Newsletters: Theory and Evidence." *Journal of Finance* 54:237–268.

Griffin, D., and A. Tversky. 1992. "The Weighing of Evidence and the Determinants of Confidence." *Cognitive Psychology* 24:411–435.

Hirshleifer, D. 2001. "Investor Psychology and Asset Pricing." *Journal of Finance* 56:1533–1598.

Hirshleifer, D., and G.Y. Luo. 2001. "On the Survival of Overconfident Traders in A Competitive Securities Market." *Journal of Financial Markets* 4:73–84.

Hirshleifer, D., and S.H. Teoh. 2003. "Herd Behavior and Cascading in Capital Markets: A Review and Synthesis." *European Financial Management* 9 (1): 25–66.

Hong, H., and J.C. Stein. 1999. "A Unified Theory of Underreaction, Momentum Trading and Overreaction in Asset Markets." *Journal of Finance* 54:2143–2184.

Kahneman, D., and M.W. Riepe. 1998. "Aspects of Investor Psychology." *Journal of Portfolio Management* 24:52–65.

Kahneman, D., and A. Tversky. 1974. "Judgment under Uncertainty: Heuristics and Biases." *Science* 185:1124–1131.

———. 2000. *Choices, Values and Frames.* Cambridge: Cambridge University Press.

Keynes, J.M. 1936. *The General Theory of Employment, Interest and Money.* London: MacMillan.

Lakonishok, J., A. Shleifer, and R.W. Vishny. 1992. "The Impact of Institutional Trading on Stock Prices." *Journal of Financial Economics* 32:23–43.

Langer, E. 1975. "The Illusion of Control." *Journal of Personality and Social Psychology* 32:311–328.

Menkhoff, L., U. Schmidt, and T. Brozynski. 2006. "The Impact of Experience on Risk Taking, Overconfidence and Herding of Fund Managers: Complementary Survey Evidence." *European Economic Review* 50:1753–1766.

Montier, J. 2002. *Behavioral Finance: Insights into Irrational Minds and Markets.* Chichester, UK: Wiley.

Myagkov, M., and C.R. Plott. 1997."Exchange Economies and Loss Exposure: Experiments Exploring Prospect Theory and Competitive Equilibria in Market Environments." *American Economic Review* 87 (5): 801–828.

Noussair, C., C.R. Plott, and R.G. Rieman. 1995. "An Experimental Investigation of the Patterns of International Trade." *American Economic Review* 85 (3): 462–491.

———. 1997. "The Principles of Exchange Rate Determination in an International Finance Experiment." *Journal of Political Economy* 105 (4): 822–861.

Oechssler, J., A. Roider, and P.W. Schmitz. 2008. "Cognitive Abilities and Behavioral Biases." *Journal of Economic Behavior and Organization* 72(1): 147–152.

Parker, W.D., and R.R. Prechter. 2005. "Herding: An Interdisciplinary Integrative Review from a Socioeconomic Perspective." Presented at the International Conference on Cognitive Economics, Sofia, Bulgaria. August 5–8.

Plott, C.R. 1991a. "Economics in 2090: The Views of an Experimentalist." *Economic Journal* 101:88–93.

———. 1991b. "Will Economics Become Experimental Science?" *Southern Economic Journal* 57 (4): 909–919.

Rabin, M. 1998. "Psychology and Economics." *Journal of Economic Literature* 36:11–46.

Rabin, M., and D. Vayanos. 2009. "The Gambler's and Hot-Hand Fallacies: Theory and Applications." *Review of Economic Studies* 77:730–778.

Raghubir, P., and S.R. Das. 1999. "A Case for Theory-Driven Experimental Inquiry." *Financial Analysts Journal* 55 (6): 56–79.

Scharfstein, D.S., and J.C. Stein. 1990. "Herd Behavior and Investment." *American Economic Review* 80 (3): 465–479.

Simon, H.A. 1957. *Models of Man: Social and Rational.* New York: Wiley.

Wang, D. 2008. "Herd Behaviour towards the Market Index: Evidence from 21 Financial Markets." Working paper WP-776 IESE Business School, University of Navarra.

Wärneryd, K-E. 2001. *Stock-Market Psychology: How People Value and Trade Stocks*. Cheltenham, UK: Edward Elgar Publishing.
Welch, I. 1992. "Sequential Sales, Learning, and Cascades." *Journal of Finance* 47:695–732.
Zeckhauser, R., J. Patel, and D. Hendricks. 1991. "Nonrational Actors and Financial Market Behavior." *Theory and Decision* 31:257–287.
Zhang, X.F. 2006. "Information Uncertainty and Stock Returns." *Journal of Finance* 61 (1): 105–136.

9 Sample Tangency Portfolio, Representativeness, and Ambiguity

Impact of the Law of Small Numbers

Ghislain Yanou

INTRODUCTION

An investor making an optimal decision needs to know the true parameters under the asset returns. But the true parameters are unknown by the decision maker and have to be estimated. Under the framework of Markowitz (1952), the investor cares only about expected returns and volatility of static portfolio and should hold the tangency portfolio on the efficient frontier.

Following Tobin (1958) and Sharpe (1964), the optimal portfolio for the investor is the mix between the tangency portfolio and the risk-free asset (see Brandt 2004 for a survey of the academic literature about the mean-variance framework). To implement this portfolio in practice one needs to estimate both expected returns and covariance matrix from the time series. The standard estimators used by practitioners and academics for this purpose are the sample mean for the expected returns and the sample covariance matrix for the covariance matrix.

However, Mandelbrot (1963) pointed out the insufficiency of the normal distribution for modeling assets returns. As a result, the sample tangency portfolio obtained from the Sharpe (1964) model, due to estimation errors in the sample mean and sample covariance matrix, produces extreme weights that fluctuate substantially over time and perform poorly *out-of-sample* (see Michaud 1989; Best and Grauer 1991; Litterman 2003). But as Meucci (2005) stated, the sample tangency portfolio remains the most important benchmark model because the sample parameters are nonparametric estimators as well as maximum likelihood estimators.

Two approaches[1] have been developed by literature for dealing with the poor performances of the sample tangency portfolio: the *plug-in* method and the decision theory. Whereas the *plug-in* method consists in specifying parameters of the data-generating process and plugs them into the Markowitz framework, the aim of the decision theory is to build a portfolio allocation process consistent with the subjective view or preferences of investor.

It is well known that the expected returns are more difficult to estimate than the covariance matrix (see, for instance, Merton 1980), and that errors into the sample mean have a larger impact in the expected *out-of-sample* performances than errors into the sample covariance matrix; see Chopra and Ziemba (1993). Following Brandt (2004), it seems that the uncertainty about the estimation of the expected returns tends to increase the posterior variance of the distribution, and the uncertainty about the estimation of the variance tends to fatten the tails of the posterior distribution. Therefore, a well estimator of the covariance matrix is helpful for taking into account the deviation of asset returns from the normal distribution.

From the *plug-in* view, several approaches have been proposed to deal with the problem of estimating the elements into the covariance matrix. One approach consists of imposing some good properties into the sample estimator of the covariance matrix by shrinking the empirical covariance matrix. Ledoit and Wolf (2004b) propose a weighted average estimator of the covariance matrix between the sample covariance and the identity matrix having a better condition number. Fan, Fan, and Jiang (2007) use a similar approach for giving a stationary property to a time-domain estimator of the covariance matrix.

A second approach consists in giving some structural properties to the covariance matrix by imposing a portfolio norm constraint (see Frost and Savarino 1988; Chopra 1993). DeMiguel *et al.* (2009) suggest imposing a norm constraint on the portfolio allocation program and showing some analytical relations between this constraint and the shortage threshold that can be supported by investor. Following Jagannathan and Ma (2003), it seems this approach rewards shrinking the sample covariance matrix.

Several empirical evidences call into question the one factor model (see Fama and French 2004) and show that except the market factor, others risk factors exist and should be taken into account (see Black, Jensen, and Scholes 1972), this is at the origin of the multifactor models. Some statistical methods like the principal component analysis have been used by the literature to extract factors into the historical returns, but this approach does not allow for distinguishing factors that contain real information from the noise. The Random matrix theory developed by physicians in order to understand the energy process for which sources are unknown (see Edelman 1989), gives a solution for filtering noise. Laloux *et al.* (1999) show some empirical evidences justifying the use of the Random matrix theory in finance. Following Edelman's thesis (1989), Plerou *et al.* (2002) perform a study of the Random matrix theory to understand cross-correlation of the high-frequency financial returns. Recent work on the Random matrix theory applied in finance comes from Potters, Bouchaud, and Laloux (2005), Conlon, Ruskin, and Crane (2008), and Yanou (2008).

An alternative method to understand moments of a distribution is obtained by a linear combination of order statistics named L-moments (see Hosking 1990; Serfling and Xiao 2007). Introduced by Sillitto (1951) and popularized by Hosking, Wallis, and Wood (1985), L-moments can be interpreted, like classical moments, as simple descriptors of the shape of a general distribution and they offer a number of advantages over conventional moments (see

Hosking 1986, 1989, 1990; Hosking and Wallis 1987). Serfling and Xiao (2007) developed co-L-moment in a multivariate framework. Yanou (2008) proposes an estimator of the covariance matrix for the global minimum variance portfolio, based on the L-moments and shows how the Random matrix theory may be used to extract information from noise.

Another approach to estimate the covariance matrix consists in using robust statistics as M-estimators or S-estimators (see, for instance, DeMiguel and Nogales 2009), or the minimum determinant covariance matrix (see Rousseeuw and Van Driessen 1999).

The estimation methods in the preceding only focus on the estimation of the covariance matrix without take into account the subjective view or preference of the investor. The decision theory is another literature dealing with the poor properties of the sample tangency portfolio. Brandt (2004) lists three ways to achieve this goal. We only list two ways because of the similarity of one among them with the *plug-in* approach.

The first way consists in eliminating dependence of the optimization process with the true parameters by replacing them with a subjective view or a prior distribution of investor. This is a Bayesian approach,[2] widely used by literature for dealing with the estimation errors into the sample tangency portfolio. Following Brown (1978), the sample tangency portfolio, or more specifically the two-fund rule, which is the mix between the sample tangency and the risk-free asset, is generally outperformed by the Bayesian decision rule under a diffuse prior. Kan and Zhou (2007) give a theoretical demonstration of this result and show that a large class of two-fund rules is outperformed by the Bayesian rule. They propose a three-fund rule, which is a mix between the two-fund rule and the global minimum variance portfolio. It seems that this approach outperforms the Bayesian rule. However the three-fund rule of Kan and Zhou (2007) has some limits. Actually authors do not deal with the case where there is a short sale constraint in the optimization process. Following Frost and Savarino (1988) and Jagannathan and Ma (2003), we know that the introduction of a short sale constraint in the portfolio optimization program improves the performances of the sample covariance matrix. In addition, Kan and Zhou (2007) remain in an ideal framework where returns follow an *i.i.d.* normal distribution.

The second way comes from the behavioral finance literature where the aim consists in explaining financial puzzles or inefficiency on the markets by assuming that some agents are not fully rational. Following some psychological beliefs[3] of investors, the Von-Neumann and Morgenstern (1944) approach based on the maximization of the expectation of a utility function has been rejected. Several nonexpected utility models have been proposed for explaining the behavior of investors under uncertainty when the probability relative to the outcomes of investor choices is known. We may cite among them the disappointment theory (see Gul 1991; Chauveau and Nalpas 2009), the regret theory (see Loomes and Sugden 1982), and the prospect theory of Kahneman and Tversky (1979). The prospect theory is popular in the financial literature because of its ability to explain some financial puzzles, but in the case of decision making, Savage (1964) proposes a subjective expected utility approach where the investor weighted the utility function by his (her) subjective probability. But the experiment of Ellsberg (1961) calls into question this model by introducing an ambiguity aversion of people into the gamble. For instance, an investor hoping for the tangency portfolio and using the sample estimators for this purpose, may take into account the non-Gaussian nature of asset returns and the finite-sample-size character of the investment universe, and then the nature of information. Following Kahneman and Tversky (1974), it seems that people often use the representativeness heuristic, well explained in Cont (1998), in the case of estimation of parameters in finance. One of the biases of the representativeness heuristic is the sample size neglect or the law of small numbers (see Rabin 2002), where investors think that small samples will reflect the properties of the parent distribution.

The aim of this chapter is to propose a model for explaining the impact of the sample size neglect when an investor hopes for the tangency portfolio and uses for this purpose the sample covariance matrix. We build a set of covariance matrices characterizing the ambiguity that investors may have. We then derive some specific covariance matrices and show the existence of an equilibrium among them. This equilibrium is not obtained by the criterion widely used by literature and based on the maximization of the expected utility. Our approach seems to be an alternative approach to the Robust control (or *maxmin* approach) literature (see Gilboa and Schmeidler 1989; Hansen and Sargent 2001).

Our main findings are the following:

1. Following our specification of ambiguity, there is a part of the risk aversion coming from the size of the investment universe. An investor having the maximum ambiguity reliance on the sample tangency portfolio will ask a relative risk premium higher than the one asked by an investor with the minimum ambiguity.
2. We derive a set of covariance matrices characterizing the ambiguity of investor. It seems that the most ambiguous investor will shrink the sample covariance matrix than the less ambiguous investor. The expected loss obtained from our covariance matrices is better than the expected loss of the sample covariance matrix. Among our covariance matrices, the one with the better expected loss is obtained under the *maxmin* approach decision criterion.
3. The *maxmin* approach based on the expected utility is a conservative but not an optimal decision approach when there is a short sale constraint in the optimization program. In this case, the optimal decision is obtained by a multi-criteria *maxmin* approach where the aim is to find a compromise between the less and the most ambiguous investors.
4. Using the S&P500 universe, we show the superiority of the corresponding tangency portfolio using the sample mean as an estimator of the expected returns. This result is just the opposite of the conclusion of Jagannathan and Ma (2003) who stated that, the estimation errors into the

sample mean are so high that a robust estimator of the covariance matrix is not helpful to improve the performance of the tangency portfolio.

5. The model is consistent with the specifications of ambiguity (see kahn and Sarin (1988)). This ambiguity actually comes from the sample size neglect and follows a power law distribution with a parameter almost equal to 0.58.

The remainder of this chapter is organized as follows. The next section presents the general framework. In the third section, after explaining the theoretical process, we provide an expression for the covariance matrix and show some properties of this one. In the fourth section, we provide some specific covariance matrices and highlight the representativeness heuristic of the investor. We provide an equilibrium state in the fifth section and show that the ambiguity comes from the size of the investment universe. In the sixth section, we show the consistency of the model with the market structure by using assets from the S&P500 universe and apply the model to the portfolio optimization. We conclude the chapter in the final section.

THE GENERAL FRAMEWORK

We start by defining some notations and hypothesis. Consider the standard portfolio choice problem of an investor who cares only about the expected returns and the volatility of his (her) portfolio from a universe of N risky assets. Let x the vector of portfolio weights invested in the N risky assets available in the investment universe. We assume that μ and Ω denote respectively the true $N \times 1$ vector of expected returns and the true $N \times N$ covariance matrix from the excess returns[4] universe $\mathbf{R}$ of size $T \times N$. We assume that the elements of the vector of expected returns are different of zero,[5] and the optimal portfolio weight x^* invested in the risky assets is obtained by the maximization of the following utility function:

$$U(x) = x^{\mathrm{T}}\mu - \frac{\gamma}{2}x^{\mathrm{T}}\mathbf{\Omega}x \tag{1}$$

where γ denotes the relative risk aversion of investor higher than zero.[6] The solution of the maximization of the utility function is given as follows:

$$x^* = \frac{1}{\gamma}\mathbf{\Omega}^{-1}\mu \tag{2}$$

And by replacing the expression of the optimal portfolio into the utility function, one obtains the utility function of investor:

$$U(\mathbf{\Omega}) = \frac{1}{2\gamma}\mu^{T}\mathbf{\Omega}^{-1}\mu \tag{3}$$

However, the true covariance matrix is unknown and need to be estimated. Following the estimator of the investor, there will be an expected loss coming from the use of an estimated covariance matrix instead of the true one. Kan and Zhou (2007) follow this idea in order to compare several investment strategies in terms of their expected loss function. We do not follow this approach here.

Our aim consists in analyzing the impact of the law of small number in the estimation of the tangency portfolio when the sample covariance matrix is used and the expected returns vector is assumed known. Our idea is as follows: assume the investor plugs the sample covariance matrix into the expression of the tangency portfolio without any ambiguity on his (her) estimator. This is a case of the sample size neglect, where people think that small sample will reflect the properties of the parent distribution. Following the belief of such an investor, his (her) optimal utility is as follows:

$$U(\hat{\mathbf{\Omega}}_s) = \frac{1}{2\gamma}\mu^{T}\hat{\mathbf{\Omega}}_s^{-1}\mu \tag{4}$$

where $(\hat{\Omega}_s)$ denotes the sample covariance matrix.

However, there are investors on the market although using the sample covariance matrix in order to compute their tangency portfolio, are aware about the sample covariance matrix because of the finite sample property of data returns. These investors have an ambiguity about their resulting portfolio.

Our aim consists in introducing several ambiguity profiles of the investors when the sample covariance matrix is used as the true parameter. The less ambiguous investors will use the resulting portfolio without any ambiguity; unlike the investors aware of the finite sample property of the data returns will adjust their portfolio with respect to their respective ambiguity. Depending on the ambiguity profile of each investor, they will have a specific covariance matrix. The next section introduces the theoretical process and the set of covariance matrices obtained.

THE SET OF COVARIANCE MATRICES FOR THE TANGENCY PORTFOLIO

The Theoretical Process

When the investors use the sample covariance matrix as the true parameter, there is a mistake on the utility function, defined as follows:

$$\rho\left(\mathbf{\Omega},\hat{\mathbf{\Omega}}_s\right)=U(\mathbf{\Omega})-E\left[U(\hat{\mathbf{\Omega}}_s)\right] \tag{5}$$

In order to define the set of covariance matrices characterizing the ambiguity profile of the investors, we follow the idea of the Random Matrix Theory (see Laloux et al. (1999) for details about the intuition behind the use of the Random matrix theory in Finance). Basically, the idea is as follows: since the theoretical distribution of eigenvalues is obtained under a wrong hypothesis in Finance, the eigenvalues which may contain information deviates from the theoretical distribution (Plerou et al. (2002) perform a study of the Random matrix theory to understand cross-correlation of the high frequency financial returns).

In the case the identity matrix is set as the true parameter, which is a wrong hypothesis regarding the market structure of returns, one may compute the mistake on the utility function when using the covariance matrix:

$$\rho\left(\mathbf{I},\hat{\mathbf{\Omega}}_s\right)=U(\mathbf{I})-E\left[U(\hat{\mathbf{\Omega}}_s)\right] \tag{6}$$

From the expression of the utility function of the investor, we have:

$$U(\mathbf{I})=\frac{1}{2\gamma}\mu^{\mathrm{T}}\mu \tag{7}$$

and:

$$E\left[U(\hat{\mathbf{\Omega}}_s)\right]=\frac{1}{2\gamma}\mu^{\mathrm{T}}E(\hat{\mathbf{\Omega}}_s^{-1})\mu \tag{8}$$

The following proposition gives the expected mistake on the utility function under the wrong hypothesis:

Proposition 1. Under the wrong hypothesis, the expected mistake on the utility function when using the sample covariance matrix is as follows:

$$\rho=-\frac{(\mu^{\mathrm{T}}\mu)(N+2)}{2\gamma(T-N-2)} \tag{9}$$

Proof. See Appendix 9.1.

Since the wrong hypothesis is not consistent regarding the market structure of returns, one may compute a covariance matrix such as its difference in terms of utility with the sample covariance matrix is the inverse of the expected mistake in the utility function under the wrong hypothesis.

Another way for understanding our idea is as follows: we compute a covariance matrix such as the mistake with the sample covariance matrix in terms of the utility increases in the case the expected mistake decreases under a wrong hypothesis and vice versa. We are then looking for a covariance matrix $\tilde{\Omega}$ such as:

$$U(\tilde{\Omega}) = U(\hat{\Omega}_s) - \frac{1}{\rho} \tag{10}$$

The equation above may be interpreted as follows: an investor aware of the finite sample property of the data returns will adjust his (her) utility depending on the behavior of the sample covariance matrix with respect to the identity matrix. The challenge is now to find such a covariance matrix. This is the aim of the next sub-section. From now on, the term covariance matrix will be used to characterize the estimation of the covariance matrix derived from (10). In the next subsection, we provide an expression of the covariance matrix.

An Expression of the Covariance Matrix: The General Case

The following proposition gives an expression of the covariance matrix:

Proposition 2. A candidate $\tilde{\Omega}$ for the covariance matrix is defined as follows:

$$\begin{cases} \tilde{\Omega}^{-1} = \hat{\Omega}_s^{-1} + \alpha \Lambda_{\_} \\ \alpha = \dfrac{4\gamma^2 (T - N - 2)}{N^2 (N+2)(\mu^{\mathrm{T}} \mu)} \end{cases} \tag{11}$$

where $\Lambda_{\_}$ is the inverse of each elements of the matrix Λ of size $N \times N$ obtained from the vector of expected returns μ:

$$\Lambda = \mu \otimes \mu^{\mathrm{T}}$$

with the sign $\otimes$ denoting the Kronecker product. Then the covariance matrix is defined as follows:

$$\tilde{\Omega} = \hat{\Omega}_s - \alpha \hat{\Omega}_s \Lambda_{\_} \left(\mathbf{I} + \alpha \hat{\Omega}_s \Lambda_{\_} \right)^{-1} \hat{\Omega}_s \tag{12}$$

Proof. See Appendix 9.2.

Notice that we choose the candidate of the covariance matrix taking into account the correlation between assets. Actually there is another candidate for the covariance matrix with Λ stated as a diagonal matrix, which remains a case of null hypothesis where only the elements into the diagonal of the sample covariance matrix are modified. We do not consider this solution.

It is straightforward to see that the matrix of expected returns Λ is a symmetric matrix. As a result, $\tilde{\Omega}$ remains a symmetric matrix. We will see later in the paper that, since the sample covariance matrix is a positive defined matrix, our covariance matrix is also a positive defined matrix.

Notice that the covariance matrix obtained is not a linear combination between the sample one and a target matrix as for the shrinkage covariance matrices of Ledoit and Wolf (2003, 2004-a and 2004-b). According to the value of the parameter α, the covariance matrix may increase or reduce its elements towards the sample covariance matrix. The parameter α depends on two parameters: the relative risk aversion parameter α, and the size of the investment universe. As a result, according to the risk profile of the investor, there is an unique covariance matrix and there is an infinite number of covariance matrices corresponding to the infinite number of the risk profile of the investors. In the next sub-section, we focus on the behavior of the utility of the investor with respect to the relative risk aversion parameter and the size of the investment universe.

The Utility and the Expected Utility Functions of the Covariance Matrix

The utility obtained from the covariance matrix is the sum between the utility obtained from the sample covariance matrix and a parameter taking into account the size of the investment universe and the relative risk aversion profile of the investor:

$$U(\tilde{\Omega}) = U(\hat{\Omega}_s) + \frac{2\gamma(T-N-2)}{(\mu^{\mathrm{T}}\mu)(N+2)} \tag{13}$$

and the expected utility from the covariance matrix is defined as follows:

$$E\left[U(\tilde{\Omega})\right] = E\left[U(\hat{\Omega}_s)\right] + \frac{2\gamma(T-N-2)}{(\mu^{\mathrm{T}}\mu)(N+2)} \tag{14}$$

Since our aim consists in estimating true covariance matrix, we set the following:

$$E\left[U(\hat{\Omega}_s)\right] = \frac{T}{T-N-2} U(\tilde{\Omega}) \tag{15}$$

By replacing the expected utility expression for $\hat{\Omega}_s$, we then obtain:

$$E\left[U(\tilde{\Omega})\right] = \frac{T}{T-N-2} U(\tilde{\Omega}) + \frac{2\gamma(T-N-2)}{(\mu^{T}\mu)(N+2)} \tag{16}$$

We have another expression for the expected utility of the covariance matrix by replacing $U(\tilde{\Omega})$ by its expression:

$$E\left[U(\tilde{\Omega})\right] = \frac{T}{T-N-2} U(\hat{\Omega}_s) + \frac{2\gamma(2T-N-2)}{(\mu^{T}\mu)(N+2)} \tag{17}$$

By construction the expected utility from the sample covariance matrix is lower than the expected utility from the covariance matrix for the same level of relative risk aversion. We now know that the covariance matrix depends on the relative risk aversion parameter and the size of the investment universe. In the next section, we introduce the representativeness heuristic and the ambiguity of the investors.

REPRESENTATIVENESS HEURISTIC AND AMBIGUITY

The sample size neglect is one of the biases of the representativeness heuristic. Because, the covariance matrix depends on the relative risk aversion of the investor and the size of the investment universe, the covariance matrix takes into account these two facts. In this section, we propose to highlight the relation between the sample size neglect (therefore, the size of the investment universe), the relative risk aversion of the investor, and his (her) ambiguity reliance on the sample tangency portfolio.

Following Kahn and Sarin (1988), we know some implications about the ambiguity of people under uncertainty: (a) decision makers consider ambiguity when making choices under uncertainty, (b) the attitude of people towards ambiguity varies, (c) people are willing to pay for difference in ambiguity, (d) the mean and variance alone may not account completely for choices.

The implications (a), (b), and (c) of Kahn and Sarin (1988) about ambiguity depend on the relative risk aversion of the investor. We propose to point out these implications from our model by computing some relative risk aversions depending on the behavior of investor reliance on the CAPM. We have from investors two extreme behaviors (disappointment and elation). The disappointment behavior characterizes an investor having the maximum ambiguity for the Sharpe model when using the sample covariance matrix, and the elation behavior characterizes an investor having the minimum ambiguity. We may also have some investors with a relative ambiguity. In the next subsection, we compute the relative risk aversion characterizing these behaviors.

The Covariance Matrix for Investor with the Maximum Ambiguity

The covariance matrix changes with the level of the relative risk aversion parameter. The higher the relative risk aversion parameter, the more risk averse the investor. By minimizing the utility function with respect to the relative risk aversion parameter, we then obtain the covariance matrix characterizing the most ambiguous investor, hoping for the tangency portfolio and using in this context the sample covariance matrix. Our aim is to find the relative risk aversion parameter for which the utility function is the worst. The following expression denotes the first derivative of $U(\tilde{\Omega})$ with respect to γ:

$$D_\gamma\left[U(\tilde{\boldsymbol{\Omega}})\right] = -\frac{\mu^{\mathrm{T}}\hat{\boldsymbol{\Omega}}_s^{-1}\mu}{2\gamma^2} + \frac{2(T-N-2)}{(\mu^{\mathrm{T}}\mu)(N+2)} \tag{18}$$

Following (16), we know that the expected utility function increases with respect to the utility function; as a result, this behavior is consistent with the *maxmin* approach. The *maxmin* approach is more a conservative decision approach than an optimal decision approach.

The utility function being a decreasing function with respect to the risk aversion parameter, the first derivative of $U(\tilde{\Omega})$ with respect to the relative risk aversion parameter is then negative. When $(N + 2) < T$, the first derivative is negative whether the following is true:

$$-\frac{\mu^{\mathrm{T}}\hat{\boldsymbol{\Omega}}_s^{-1}\mu}{2\gamma^2} \leq \frac{-2(T-N-2)}{(\mu^{\mathrm{T}}\mu)(N+2)} \tag{19}$$

which means:

$$\frac{2\gamma(T-N-2)}{(\mu^{\mathrm{T}}\mu)(N+2)} \leq \frac{\mu^{\mathrm{T}}\hat{\boldsymbol{\Omega}}_s^{-1}\mu}{2\gamma} \tag{20}$$

and by adding $U(\hat{\Omega}_s)$ on both of the sides, we obtain the following proposition:

Proposition 3. The uncertainty in the utility function for an investor having the maximum ambiguity is characterizes as follows:

$$U(\hat{\boldsymbol{\Omega}}_s) \leq U(\tilde{\boldsymbol{\Omega}}_g) \leq 2U(\hat{\boldsymbol{\Omega}}_s) \tag{21}$$

where $\hat{\Omega}_g$ denotes the covariance matrix of such an investor.

Proof. The proof comes from (20).

As a result, such an investor will ask a relative risk premium for counterbalancing this uncertainty. Notice that when the number of historical returns ($\boldsymbol{T}$) goes to infinite, the utility obtained from $\tilde{\Omega}_g$ is not the same than the one obtained from the sample covariance matrix which is unbiased in this context. Therefore, even the true covariance matrix is used in the Sharpe model, the most ambiguous investor remains ambiguous. This observation is consistent with the implication (d) of Kahn and Sarin (1988) for which the mean and variance alone may not account completely for choices. Although the expected returns vector is assumed known and the sample covariance matrix is the true one, it remains an ambiguity.

The following expression denotes the second derivative of $\tilde{\Omega}_g$ with respect to γ:

$$D_\gamma^2\left[U(\tilde{\Omega})\right] = \frac{\mu^{\mathbf{T}}\hat{\Omega}_s^{-1}\mu}{\gamma^3} \tag{22}$$

which is positive. As a result, the relative risk aversion γ_g of an investor with the maximum ambiguity is obtained by minimizing the utility function; we obtain the following expression of the relative risk aversion:

$$\gamma_g = \frac{1}{2}\sqrt{\frac{(\mu^{\mathbf{T}}\mu)(\mu^{\mathbf{T}}\hat{\mathbf{\Omega}}_s^{-1}\mu)(N+2)}{T-N-2}} \tag{23}$$

and the resulting inverse of the covariance matrix is defined as follows:

$$\begin{cases} \tilde{\mathbf{\Omega}}_g^{-1} = \hat{\mathbf{\Omega}}_s^{-1} + \alpha_g \Lambda_- \\ \begin{cases} \alpha_g = \dfrac{4\gamma_g^2(T-N-2)}{N^2(N+2)(\mu^{\mathbf{T}}\mu)} \\ \quad = \dfrac{\mu^{\mathbf{T}}\hat{\mathbf{\Omega}}_s^{-1}\mu}{N^2} \end{cases} \end{cases} \tag{24}$$

By simple transformation, one obtains the resulting covariance matrix:

$$\begin{aligned} \tilde{\mathbf{\Omega}}_g &= \hat{\mathbf{\Omega}}_s - \alpha_g \hat{\mathbf{\Omega}}_s \mathbf{\Lambda}_- \left(\mathbf{I} + \alpha_g \hat{\mathbf{\Omega}}_s \mathbf{\Lambda}_-\right)^{-1} \hat{\mathbf{\Omega}}_s \\ &= \frac{1}{2}\hat{\mathbf{\Omega}}_s \end{aligned} \tag{25}$$

Therefore, an investor with the maximum ambiguity will shrink the elements of the sample covariance matrix by half. This result is true when $(N + 2) < T$; otherwise γ_g will not exist. The resulting utility function is defined as follows:

$$U(\tilde{\Omega}_g) = U(\hat{\Omega}_s) + \sqrt{\frac{(\mu^{\mathrm{T}}\hat{\Omega}_s^{-1}\mu)(T-N-2)}{(\mu^{\mathrm{T}}\mu)(N+2)}} = 2\sqrt{\frac{(\mu^{\mathrm{T}}\hat{\Omega}_s^{-1}\mu)(T-N-2)}{(\mu^{\mathrm{T}}\mu)(N+2)}} \tag{26}$$

and the expected utility function is defined as:

$$E\left[U(\tilde{\Omega}_g)\right] = \frac{T}{T-N-2}U(\hat{\Omega}_s) + \frac{2T-N-2}{\sqrt{N+2}}\sqrt{\frac{(\mu^{\mathrm{T}}\hat{\Omega}_s^{-1}\mu)}{(\mu^{\mathrm{T}}\mu)(T-N-2)}} = (3T-N-2)\sqrt{\frac{(\mu^{\mathrm{T}}\hat{\Omega}_s^{-1}\mu)}{(\mu^{\mathrm{T}}\mu)(T-N-2)(N+2)}} \tag{27}$$

In the next subsection, we focus on an investor having a relative ambiguity.

The Covariance Matrix for Investors with a Relative Ambiguity

We propose now to build among the set of covariance matrices, the one having the less uncertainty between the utility and the expected utility. Let $\tilde{U}$ the uncertainty between the expected utility and the utility of $\tilde{\Omega}$:

$$\tilde{U} = E\left[U(\tilde{\Omega})\right] - U(\tilde{\Omega}) = \frac{(\mu^{\mathrm{T}}\hat{\Omega}_s^{-1}\mu)(N+2)}{2\gamma(T-N-2)} + \frac{2\gamma T}{(\mu^{\mathrm{T}}\mu)(N+2)} \tag{28}$$

Let $\tilde{\Omega}_u$ the covariance matrix minimizing the uncertainty between the expected utility and the utility. By minimizing $\tilde{U}$ with respect to the relative risk aversion parameter γ, it is straightforward to compute $\tilde{\Omega}_u$. The first derivative of $\tilde{U}$ with respect to γ is defined as follows:

$$D_\gamma\left(\tilde{U}\right) = -\frac{(\mu^{\mathrm{T}}\hat{\Omega}_s^{-1}\mu)(N+2)}{2\gamma^2(T-N-2)} + \frac{2T}{(\mu^{\mathrm{T}}\mu)(N+2)} \tag{29}$$

When $(N + 2) < T$, the first derivative is negative if the following condition is true:

$$\left(\frac{2T}{(\mu^{\mathrm{T}}\mu)(N+2)} \le \frac{(\mu^{\mathrm{T}}\hat{\mathbf{\Omega}}_s^{-1}\mu)(N+2)}{2\gamma^2(T-N-2)}\right) \Leftrightarrow \left(\frac{2\gamma(T-N-2)}{(\mu^{\mathrm{T}}\mu)(N+2)} \le \frac{(\mu^{\mathrm{T}}\hat{\mathbf{\Omega}}_s^{-1}\mu)(N+2)}{2\gamma T}\right) \quad (30)$$

and by adding $U(\hat{\Omega}_s)$ on both of the sides of the inequality, we have the following condition:

$$U(\hat{\mathbf{\Omega}}_s) \le U(\tilde{\mathbf{\Omega}}_u) \le \frac{T+N+2}{T} U(\hat{\mathbf{\Omega}}_s) \quad (31)$$

which is true following Proposition 3. We then have a distance in the efficient frontier between an investor having a relative ambiguity and the sample tangency portfolio. Let C_u the distance, we have:

$$C_u = \frac{T+N+2}{T} \quad (32)$$

Because $(N + 2) < T$, the factor C_u is lower than the factor C_g obtained in the case of an investor having the maximum ambiguity. As a result, an investor having the maximum ambiguity will ask a higher risk premium than an investor with a relative ambiguity. Following this observation, it seems that the implication (c) of Kahn and Sarin (1988), where people are willing to pay for difference in ambiguity, is true. The higher the ambiguity reliance on the sample tangency portfolio, the higher the risk premium asked by the investor.

The second derivative of $\tilde{U}$ with respect to γ is defined as follows:

$$D_\gamma^2\left(\tilde{U}\right) = \frac{(\mu^{\mathrm{T}}\hat{\mathbf{\Omega}}_s^{-1}\mu)(N+2)}{\gamma^3(T-N-2)} \quad (33)$$

Because $(N + 2) < T$, the second derivative of $\tilde{U}$ with respect to γ is positive. That is, there is a minimum for $\tilde{U}$ obtained by setting $D_\gamma(\tilde{U})$ equal to zero. We obtain the following relative risk aversion parameter:

$$\begin{aligned} \gamma_u &= \frac{1}{2}\sqrt{\frac{N+2}{T}}\sqrt{\frac{(\mu^{\mathrm{T}}\mu)(\mu^{\mathrm{T}}\hat{\mathbf{\Omega}}_s^{-1}\mu)(N+2)}{(T-N-2)}} \\ &= \sqrt{\frac{N+2}{T}}\gamma_g \end{aligned} \quad (34)$$

By replacing γ_u in the expression of $\tilde{\Omega}^{-1}$, one obtains:

$$\begin{cases} \tilde{\mathbf{\Omega}}_u^{-1} = \hat{\mathbf{\Omega}}_s^{-1} + \alpha_u \Lambda_- \\ \begin{cases} \alpha_u = \dfrac{4\gamma_u^2(T-N-2)}{N^2(N+2)(\mu^{\mathrm{T}}\mu)} \\ \quad = \dfrac{(N+2)(\mu^{\mathrm{T}}\hat{\mathbf{\Omega}}_s^{-1}\mu)}{N^2 T} \end{cases} \end{cases} \quad (35)$$

By simple transformation, one may compute an expression of the covariance matrix in this context:

$$\tilde{\mathbf{\Omega}}_u = \hat{\mathbf{\Omega}}_s - \alpha_u \hat{\mathbf{\Omega}}_s \mathbf{\Lambda}_- \left(\mathbf{I} + \alpha_u \hat{\mathbf{\Omega}}_s \mathbf{\Lambda}_-\right)^{-1} \hat{\mathbf{\Omega}}_s \\ = \frac{T}{T+N+2} \hat{\mathbf{\Omega}}_s \tag{36}$$

The utility from $\tilde{\Omega}_u$ is defined as follows:

$$U(\tilde{\mathbf{\Omega}}_u) = U(\hat{\mathbf{\Omega}}_s) + \sqrt{\frac{(T-N-2)(\mu^{\mathrm{T}} \hat{\mathbf{\Omega}}_s^{-1} \mu)}{T(\mu^{\mathrm{T}} \mu)}} \\ = \frac{T+N+2}{\sqrt{T(N+2)}} \sqrt{\frac{(\mu^{\mathrm{T}} \hat{\mathbf{\Omega}}_s^{-1} \mu)(T-N-2}{(\mu^{\mathrm{T}} \mu)(N+2)}} \tag{37}$$

The expected utility of $\tilde{\Omega}_u$ is then defined as follows:

$$E\left[U(\tilde{\mathbf{\Omega}}_u)\right] = \frac{T}{T-N-2} U(\hat{\mathbf{\Omega}}_s) + \frac{2T-N-2}{\sqrt{T}} \sqrt{\frac{\mu^{\mathrm{T}} \hat{\mathbf{\Omega}}_s^{-1} \mu}{(T-N-2)(\mu^{\mathrm{T}} \mu)}} \\ = \frac{T^2 + (N+2)(2T-N-2)}{\sqrt{T(N+2)}} \sqrt{\frac{\mu^{\mathrm{T}} \hat{\mathbf{\Omega}}_s^{-1} \mu}{(\mu^{\mathrm{T}} \mu)(N+2)(T-N-2)}} \tag{38}$$

and the minimum uncertainty $\tilde{U}_{\min}$ of the model is defined as follows:

$$\tilde{U}_{\min} = 2\sqrt{T} \sqrt{\frac{\mu^{\mathrm{T}} \hat{\mathbf{\Omega}}_s^{-1} \mu}{(\mu^{\mathrm{T}} \mu)(T-N-2)}} \tag{39}$$

We then have the covariance matrix for an investor hoping for the tangency portfolio with a relative ambiguity. The next proposition gives the behavior of the expected utility obtained from the latter covariance matrix:

Proposition 4. The expected utility of an investor with a relative ambiguity is higher than the expected utility of an investor with a maximum ambiguity reliance on the sample tangency portfolio.

Proof. See Appendix 9.3.

In the next subsection, we focus on the second extreme behavior of an investor facing uncertainty. This is the case of an investor having the minimum ambiguity reliance on the sample tangency portfolio.

The Covariance Matrix for an Investor with the Minimum Ambiguity

In order to characterize an investor having an elation profile reliance on the sample tangency portfolio, we minimize the gap between the expected utility and the sample utility function. We then need to compute the relative risk aversion parameter minimizing the following expression:

$$\hat{U} = E\left[U(\tilde{\mathbf{\Omega}})\right] - U(\hat{\mathbf{\Omega}}_s) \\ = \frac{(\mu^{\mathrm{T}}\hat{\mathbf{\Omega}}_s^{-1}\mu)(N+2)}{2\gamma(T-N-2)} + \frac{2\gamma(2T-N-2)}{(\mu^{\mathrm{T}}\mu)(N+2)} \tag{40}$$

Let $\tilde{\Omega}_t$ the resulting covariance matrix. By minimizing $\hat{U}$ with respect to the relative risk aversion parameter γ, it is straightforward to compute $\tilde{\Omega}_t$. The first derivative of $\hat{U}$ with respect to γ is defined as follows:

$$D_\gamma\left(\hat{U}\right) = -\frac{(\mu^{\mathrm{T}}\hat{\mathbf{\Omega}}_s^{-1}\mu)(N+2)}{2\gamma^2(T-N-2)} + \frac{2(2T-N-2)}{(\mu^{\mathrm{T}}\mu)(N+2)} \tag{41}$$

When $(N + 2) < T$, the first derivative is negative whether the following is true:

$$\left(\frac{2(2T-N-2)}{(\mu^{\mathrm{T}}\mu)(N+2)} \le \frac{(\mu^{\mathrm{T}}\hat{\mathbf{\Omega}}_s^{-1}\mu)(N+2)}{2\gamma^2(T-N-2)}\right) \Leftrightarrow \left(\frac{2\gamma(T-N-2)}{(\mu^{\mathrm{T}}\mu)(N+2)} \le \frac{(\mu^{\mathrm{T}}\hat{\mathbf{\Omega}}_s^{-1}\mu)(N+2)}{2\gamma(2T-N-2)}\right) \tag{42}$$

and by adding $U(\hat{\Omega}_s)$ on both sides of the inequality, we have the following condition:

$$U(\hat{\mathbf{\Omega}}_s) \le U(\tilde{\mathbf{\Omega}}_t) \le \frac{2T}{2T-N-2}U(\hat{\mathbf{\Omega}}_s) \tag{43}$$

which is true following Proposition 3. As earlier, we have a measure of the distance in the efficient frontier between the sample tangency portfolio and the tangency portfolio for an investor with an elation profile. Let C_t the factor of distance, we have:

$$C_t = \frac{2T}{2T-N-2} \tag{44}$$

The second derivative of $\hat{U}$ with respect to γ is defined as follows:

$$D_\gamma^2\left(\hat{U}\right) = \frac{(\mu^{\mathrm{T}}\hat{\mathbf{\Omega}}_s^{-1}\mu)(N+2)}{\gamma^3(T-N-2)} \tag{45}$$

Because $(N + 2) < T$, the second derivative of $\hat{U}$ with respect to γ is positive. That is, there is a minimum for $\hat{U}$ obtained by setting $D_\gamma(\hat{U})$ equal to zero. We obtain the following risk aversion parameter:

$$\gamma_t = \frac{1}{2}\sqrt{\frac{N+2}{2T-N-2}}\sqrt{\frac{(\mu^{T}\mu)(\mu^{T}\hat{\Omega}_s^{-1}\mu)(N+2)}{(T-N-2)}} = \sqrt{\frac{N+2}{2T-N-2}}\gamma_g$$

Because $(N + 2) < T$, we have $\gamma_t < \gamma_g$, as a result γ_t is a relevant relative risk aversion parameter. By replacing γ_t in the expression of $\tilde{\Omega}^{-1}$, we obtain the inverse of the covariance matrix in this case:

$$\begin{cases} \tilde{\Omega}_t^{-1} = \hat{\Omega}_s^{-1} + \alpha_t \Lambda_- \\ \begin{cases} \alpha_t = \dfrac{4\gamma_t^2(T-N-2)}{N^2(N+2)(\mu^{T}\mu)} \\ \quad = \dfrac{(N+2)(\mu^{T}\hat{\Omega}_s^{-1}\mu)}{N^2(2T-N-2)} \end{cases} \end{cases} \tag{47}$$

By simple transformation, we may compute an expression of the covariance matrix:

$$\tilde{\Omega}_t = \hat{\Omega}_s - \alpha_t\hat{\Omega}_s\Lambda_-\left(\mathbf{I} + \alpha_t\hat{\Omega}_s\Lambda_-\right)^{-1}\hat{\Omega}_s = \frac{2T-N-2}{2T}\hat{\Omega}_s \tag{48}$$

The utility from $\tilde{\Omega}_t$ is defined as follows:

$$U(\tilde{\Omega}_t) = U(\hat{\Omega}_s) + \sqrt{\frac{(\mu^{T}\hat{\Omega}_s^{-1}\mu)(T-N-2)}{(\mu^{T}\mu)(N+2)}}\sqrt{\frac{N+2}{2T-N-2}} = \frac{2T}{\sqrt{(N+2)(T-N-2)}}\sqrt{\frac{(\mu^{T}\hat{\Omega}_s^{-1}\mu)(T-N-2)}{(\mu^{T}\mu)(N+2)}} \tag{49}$$

The expected utility of $\tilde{\Omega}_t$ is then defined as follows:

$$E\left[U(\tilde{\Omega}_t)\right] = \frac{T}{T-N-2}U(\hat{\Omega}_s) + \sqrt{(N+2)(2T-N-2)}\sqrt{\frac{(\mu^{T}\hat{\Omega}_s^{-1}\mu)}{(\mu^{T}\mu)(N+2)(T-N-2)}} = \frac{(T+N+2)\sqrt{2T-N-2}}{\sqrt{N+2}}\sqrt{\frac{(\mu^{T}\hat{\Omega}_s^{-1}\mu)}{(\mu^{T}\mu)(N+2)(T-N-2)}} \tag{50}$$

and the minimum uncertainty $\hat{U}_{\min}$ between the expected utility and the utility from the sample covariance matrix is defined as follows:

$$\hat{U}_{\min} = 2\sqrt{\frac{N+2}{2T-N-2}}\sqrt{\frac{(\mu^{T}\hat{\Omega}_s^{-1}\mu)(N+2)}{(\mu^{T}\mu)(T-N-2)}} \tag{51}$$

Our model is relevant whether investor having the minimum ambiguity reliance on the sample tangency portfolio, will have the highest expected utility than other investors. We state this result in the next proposition:

> **Proposition 5.** The expected utility of an investor having the minimum ambiguity with the sample mean-variance framework is higher than the expected utility of an investor having a relative ambiguity.
>
> **Proof.** See Appendix 9.4.

Because the covariance matrix depends on the relative risk aversion of the investor, our model is consistent with the implication (b) of Kahn and Sarin (1988) for which the attitude of the investors toward ambiguity varies. We introduce the following proposition:

> **Proposition 6.** The uncertainty in the utility function of an investor with the minimum ambiguity is lower than the uncertainty for an investor with a relative ambiguity, which is lower than the one for an investor with the maximum ambiguity. As a result, the investor will ask a relative risk premium for counterbalancing their respective uncertainty.
>
> **Proof.** See appendix 9.5.

Following Proposition 6, the higher the ambiguity of the investor, and the higher the risk premium asked, which confirms the implication (c) of Kahn and Sarin (1988) for which people are willing to pay for difference in ambiguity. Because the risk aversion parameter of the investor with the minimum ambiguity reliance on the sample tangency portfolio is not equal to zero, we know that the implication (a) of Kahn and Sarin (1988) for which decision makers always consider ambiguity when making choice under uncertainty is true.

Put simply, we pay attention at two extreme profiles of the investors. The first one is the most ambiguous investor who is aware of the finite sample size of the investment universe used for computing the sample covariance matrix. The relative risk aversion of such an investor is the highest and the expected utility is the lowest because of his (her) ambiguity. As a result, for a level of risk, he (she) will ask a higher risk premium than others. The second profile is the less ambiguous, this investor is not at all aware about the finite sample property of the investment universe. Such an investor has the lowest relative risk aversion and his (her) expected utility is the highest because of his (her) elation. We also introduce a third investor profile having a relative ambiguity reliance of his (her) tangency portfolio. Figure 9.1 shows the mean-variance efficient frontiers obtained from the three profiles:

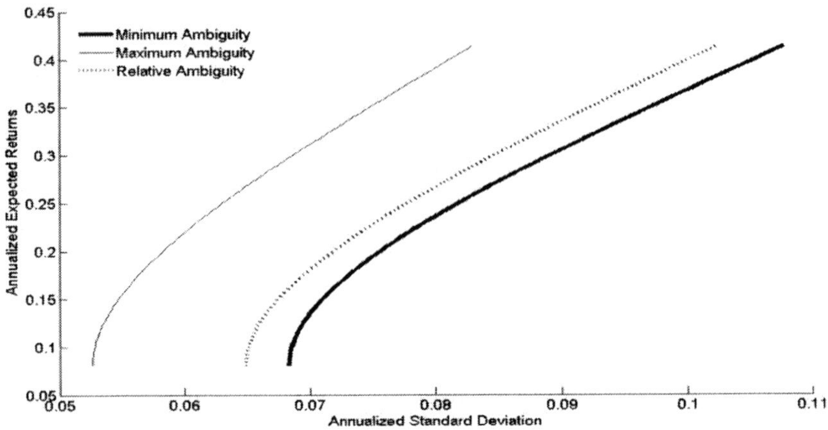

Figure 9.1 The mean-volatility efficient frontiers.

Source: Datastream, mean-variance efficient frontiers, 324 assets from the S&P500 universe, from 01/1985 to 03/2009, no completion need, weekly frequency, no short sale constraint, covariance matrices have been calibrated such as the covariance matrix obtained from the minimum ambiguity is the same than the sample covariance matrix, computation by the author.

Notice that the covariance matrices have been calibrated for having the covariance matrix used by the less ambiguous investor $\tilde{\Omega}_l$ equal to the sample covariance matrix $\hat{\Omega}_s$, therefore we consider the following covariance matrices for computing the efficient frontiers :

$$\begin{cases} \tilde{\Omega}_l \equiv \hat{\Omega}_s \\ \tilde{\Omega}_g \equiv \dfrac{2T}{2T-N-2}\left(\dfrac{1}{2}\hat{\Omega}_s\right) \\ \tilde{\Omega}_u \equiv \dfrac{2T}{2T-N-2}\left(\dfrac{T}{T+N+2}\hat{\Omega}_s\right) \end{cases} \tag{52}$$

From the picture, one may see that for each level of volatility, the investor with the most ambiguous profile will ask a higher return (therefore a higher risk premium). As a result, the corresponding efficient frontier is above the one obtained from the relative profile which is above the sample efficient frontier.

In the next sub-section, we propose to compare the sample covariance matrix with ours in terms of the expected loss function.

A Comparison of the Covariance Matrices in terms of the Expected Loss

We now introduce a proposition for showing that our covariance matrices are better than the sample covariance matrix in terms of the expected loss function. The expected loss function is the loss in the utility function when an estimated parameter is used instead of the true parameter. Equation (2) is the expression of the optimal portfolio under the true parameter. Assume the family of covariance matrices $(k\hat{\Omega}_s)$ obtained as the sample covariance matrix weighted by a parameter k such as $0 < k < 1$. Our covariance matrices defined above belong to this family and the resulting expected loss ξ_k is defined as follows:

$$\xi_k = U(\boldsymbol{\Omega}) - \left[x^{*\mathrm{T}} \mu - \frac{\gamma}{2} x^{*\mathrm{T}} E\left(k\hat{\boldsymbol{\Omega}}_s\right) x^* \right] \tag{53}$$

where x^* denotes the true optimal portfolio. We introduce the following proposition:

Proposition 7. Lower the parameter k and lower the expected loss when the family of covariance matrices $(k\hat{\Omega}_s)$ is used, in comparison with the expected loss when using the sample covariance matrix. As a result, the expected loss of the ambiguous investor is lower than the expected loss of the relative ambiguous investor, which is lower than the expected loss of the less ambiguous investor, which is lower than the expected loss when using the sample covariance matrix.

Proof. See Appendix 9.6.

As a final result, it is straightforward to show that, as the number of historical returns goes to the infinite, except the covariance matrix from the most ambiguous investors, the others covariance matrices are equal to the sample one, and then are unbiased. One may explain the behavior of the covariance matrix of the most ambiguous investor, by an ambiguity linked to the model and not only to the estimation of the covariance matrix.

The next section focuses on the inception of the ambiguity. By construction, we know that, the ambiguity comes actually from the sample size neglect. We show this by running a simulation.

THE EQUILIBRIUM STATE AND THE INCEPTION OF AMBIGUITY

The extreme behaviors of investors are characterized by the covariance matrices $\tilde{\Omega}_g$ for the investor having the maximum ambiguity and $\tilde{\Omega}_l$ for the investor having the minimum ambiguity reliance on the Sharpe model. In order to explain the inception of ambiguity, we need to build an equilibrium state between the two extreme behaviors.

The Equilibrium State

Kan and Zhou (2007) state that, under uncertainty, the *out-of-sample* expected loss function generates a loss in the *out-of-sample* performance. They propose to use the global minimum variance portfolio, which has some estimation errors not correlated with the estimation errors into the sample tangency portfolio. Because we are able to find an optimal combination between the sample tangency portfolio and the global minimum variance portfolio, we may expect higher *out-of-sample* performance. They show this strategy dominates several approaches, among which are the two-fund portfolio rule, the Bayesian approach, and the shrinkage estimators under an *i.i.d.* normal multivariate framework.

The covariance matrix $\tilde{\Omega}_g$ corresponds to an investor having the maximum ambiguity; as a result, the weight of the risk-free asset in his (her) tangency portfolio is higher than the weight of the risk-free asset in the portfolio of an investor having a minimum ambiguity reliance on the Sharpe model. In the case there is an equilibrium on the market, it is between the two extreme behaviors. Let $\tilde{\Omega}_{gt}^{\beta}$ the covariance matrix obtained from a linear combination between the two extreme covariance matrices $\tilde{\Omega}_g$ and $\tilde{\Omega}_t$:

$$\tilde{\mathbf{\Omega}}_{gt}^{\beta} = \beta\tilde{\mathbf{\Omega}}_g + (1-\beta)\tilde{\mathbf{\Omega}}_t \tag{54}$$

with $0 < \beta < 1$. We introduce the following proposition:

Proposition 8. The expected utility of the investor having a relative ambiguity is lower than the expected utility of any investor whose risk profile is characterized by the covariance matrix $\tilde{\Omega}_{gt}^{\beta}$:

$$E\left[U(\tilde{\mathbf{\Omega}}_u)\right] \leq E\left[U(\tilde{\mathbf{\Omega}}_{gt}^{\beta})\right] \tag{55}$$

Proof. See Appendix 9.7.

Therefore, among the infinite ambiguity profile of investors between the extreme behaviors, the expected utility of investors having a relative ambiguity is the lowest. We introduce the following proposition:

Proposition 9. The utility function of the investor having a relative ambiguity is lower than the utility function of any investor whose risk profile is characterized by the covariance matrix $\tilde{\Omega}_{gt}^{\beta}$:

$$U(\Omega_u) \leq U(\Omega_{gt}^{\beta}) \tag{56}$$

Proof. See Appendix 9.8.

Following Proposition 8 and Proposition 9, the covariance matrix $\tilde{\Omega}_u$ characterizes a conservative approach under the utility function criterion and the expected utility function criterion among the combinations obtained from the extreme profiles. As a result, by using $\tilde{\Omega}_u$, one may expect in an *out-of-sample* framework, a better behavior. The optimal parameter β^* is defined by the following proposition:

Proposition 10. The optimal parameter β^* for the linear combination between investors having the maximum ambiguity and investors having the minimum ambiguity reliance on the Sharpe model is defined as follows:

$$\beta^* = \sqrt{\frac{N+2}{T}} \frac{\sqrt{2T-N-2}-\sqrt{T}}{\sqrt{2T-N-2}-\sqrt{N+2}} \tag{57}$$

Proof. See Appendix 9.9.

We may now derive the inception of ambiguity. This is the aim of the next subsection.

The Inception of Ambiguity

Figure 9.2 shows the shape of the optimal parameter depending on the size of the investment universe:

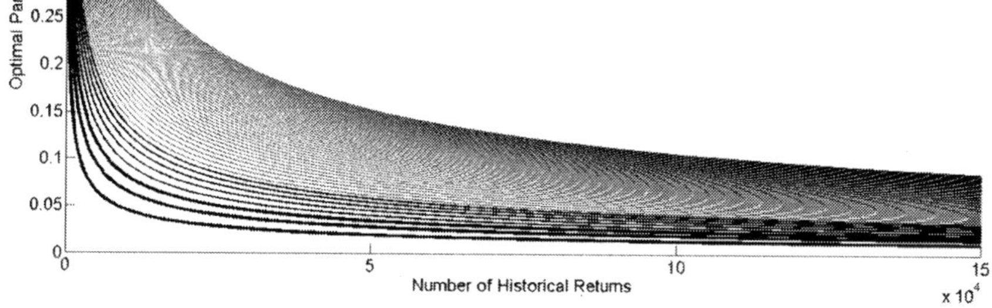

Figure 9.2 The shape of the optimal parameter.

Source: Evolution of the optimal parameter with respect to the number of historical returns, bolder the line and higher the number of assets, the first window size is obtained by adding three to the number of assets, computation by the author.

From N equal to 200, we compute the optimal parameter β^*, from T equal to $N + 3$ until 150,000. We then plot the shape of the optimal parameters obtained with respect to the number of historical returns T. Next, we increment N of 200, the number of assets is now equal to 400, and we compute the optimal parameters and plot them with respect to T. We renew the algorithm fifty times.

Following the picture, it seems that the optimal parameter decreases with respect to the number of historical returns. As a result, the higher the number of historical returns in the investment universe, the lower the weight of the covariance matrix characterizing the maximum ambiguity reliance on the Sharpe model. Notice that the bolder the curve then the higher the number of assets considered. As a result, the higher the number of assets in the investment universe, the lower the decrease of the optimal parameter. This observation means that the weight of the covariance matrix characterizing the maximum ambiguity decreases slowly with respect to the number of historical returns, when the number of assets considered increases. Therefore, the inception of ambiguity of investors actually comes from the size of the investment universe.

It seems that the optimal parameter that characterizes the ambiguity follows a power law distribution with a parameter almost equal to 0.58. In order to confirm this observation, we show in Figure 9.3 the shape of the optimal parameters (in logarithm) with respect to the ratio N/T (in logarithm).

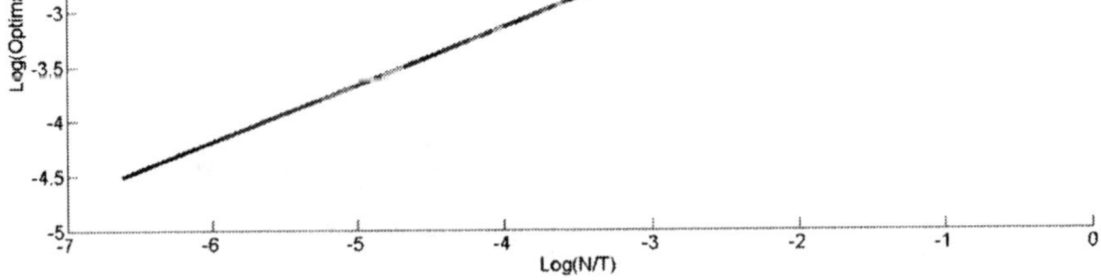

Figure 9.3 Illustration of the power law character of the ambiguity.

Source: Evolution of the optimal parameter with respect to the size of the investment universe in logarithm, the colors denote the shape for a given number of assets, the first window size is obtained by adding three to the number of assets, the slope of the straight lines is around equal to 0.58, computation by the author.

For all the combinations, the shapes of the optimal parameters coincide and correspond to a mix of several increasing straight lines. As a result there are some scale effects in the evolution of the optimal parameter with respect to the size of the investment universe characterized by the ratio N/T. The slope of these lines provides the parameter of the resulting power law distribution, which is almost equal to 0.58.

In the next section, we run an empirical study in the S&P 500 universe for showing the consistency of our model.

THE EMPIRICAL STUDY

We use three databases from the S&P 500 universe. Database 1 is constituted of 250 excess returns[11] in a daily frequency from January 1, 1980, to March 11, 2009. Database 2 is constituted of 250 excess returns in a weekly frequency from January 1, 1980, to March 11, 2009. Database 3 is constituted of 324 excess returns in a weekly frequency from December 22, 1988, to December 18, 2008. Returns are all expressed in U.S. dollars. There is no selection, we only take into account all assets completely available in the financial database between the first and the last dates considered. As a result, there is no completion of returns in our databases. The financial database used for extracting returns is Datastream.

Database 1 and Database 2 are used for showing the consistency of the model. We use Database 3 for an application of our model to the portfolio optimization because it contains more assets than the two others.

The Consistency of the Model

In order to show the consistency of the model, we propose to compute the volatility of the relative risk aversion parameter. The first estimation window for the weekly frequency contains $N + 3$ (which is equal to 253) historical returns. For the daily frequency, we consider a number of historical returns corresponding to the same sample dates than the sample window consider for the weekly frequency. We then compute the relative risk aversion parameter and increase the window size of one day for the daily frequency and one week for the weekly frequency. The next picture (Figure 9.4) shows the dynamic of the relative risk aversion parameter γ_u.

Following the picture, the relative risk aversion parameter decreases as the number of historical returns increases. The decrease is more important with the weekly frequency. However, even there is a decrease of the relative risk aversion parameter, we notice some variations of its values through time. The next picture shows the variation of the relative risk aversion parameter and the volatility of the S&P500 index in a daily frequency (Figure 9.5).

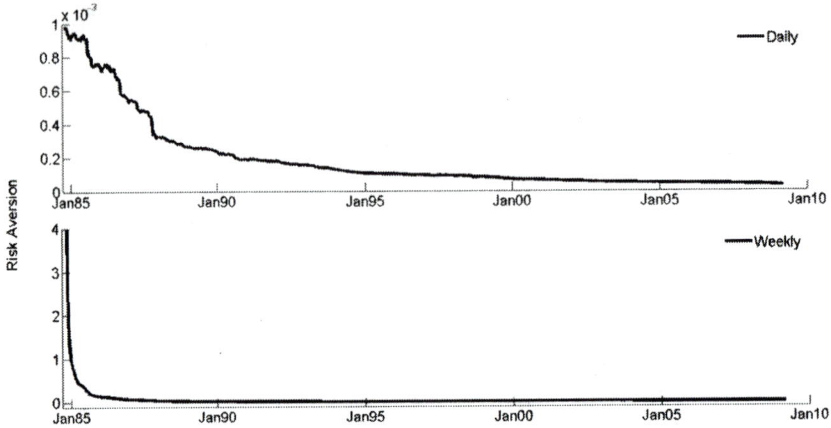

Figure 9.4 The dynamic of the relative risk aversion parameter.

Source: Datastream, dynamic of the relative risk aversion parameter with respect to the size of the investment universe, 250 assets from the S&P 500 universe, 253 historical returns for the first estimation window when considering the weekly frequency; the number of historical returns for the daily frequency is obtained by considering the same window date as for the weekly frequency, the sample window increases by one frequency until the end date, computation by the author.

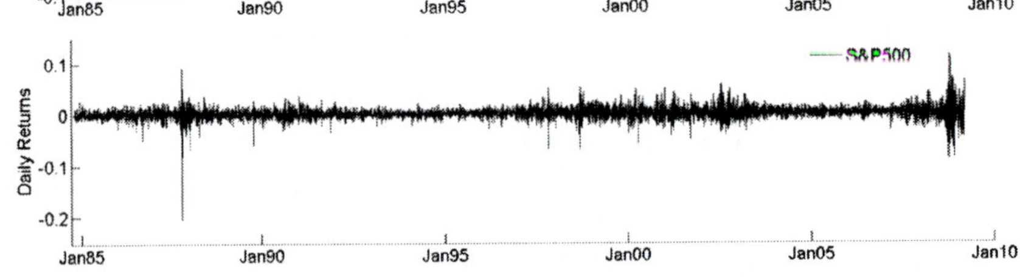

Figure 9.5 The comparison between the volatility of the relative risk aversion parameter and the S&P 500 index in a daily frequency.

Source: Datastream, volatility of the relative risk aversion parameter, and volatility of the S&P 500 index from January 1985 to March 2009, 250 assets from the S&P 500 universe, daily frequency, computation by the author.

We notice the same behavior between the volatility of the relative risk aversion parameter and the volatility of the market index. The relative risk aversion parameter characterizes the behavior of an investor facing the uncertainty. As a result, its variations should catch the volatility properties on the market. When the relative risk aversion of investors knows some turbulence, the S&P 500 index knows some turbulence. When the volatility of the relative risk aversion of investors is low, the S&P 500 index knows a period of low volatility. When considering weekly frequency, we obtain the picture in Figure 9.6.

Although the fit is not as obvious as for the daily frequency, we observe the same behavior. Notice that for both frequencies, the shape of the variation of the relative risk aversion parameter, although the same as the shape of the volatility of the market index, decreases with the time. Actually, the expression of the relative risk aversion parameter obtained from the model is just the share of the whole risk aversion coming from the sample size neglect. Figure 9.7 shows how the ambiguity of investors explains a part of the volatility on the market.

We have on the same picture the S&P 500 index returns and the volatility of the relative risk aversion in daily frequency on the top, and in weekly frequency on the bottom. It seems that the ambiguity of the investors explains a part of the volatility of the market. With the same trend, as the number of historical returns increases, the volatility of the relative risk aversion decreases. This means that the impact of the ambiguity on the market volatility decreases. An investor having the maximum ambiguity will therefore

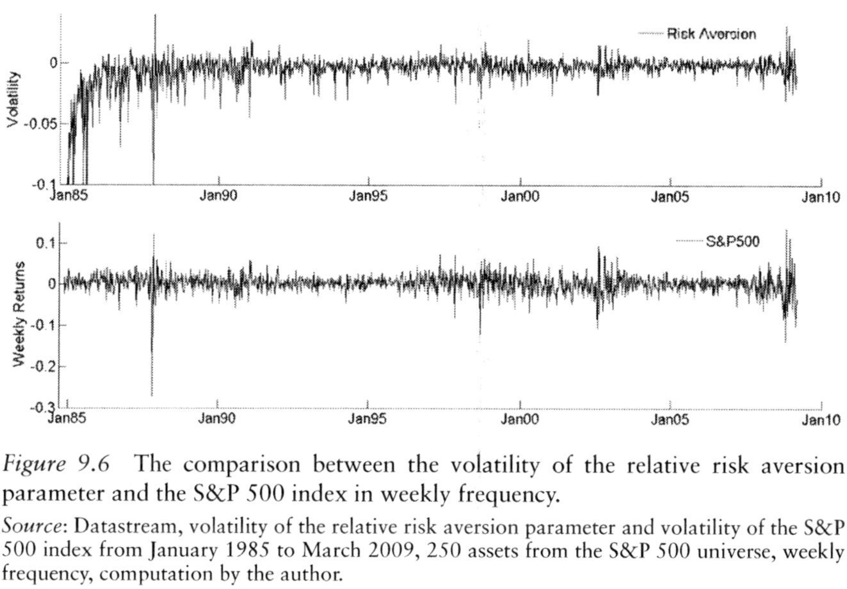

Figure 9.6 The comparison between the volatility of the relative risk aversion parameter and the S&P 500 index in weekly frequency.

Source: Datastream, volatility of the relative risk aversion parameter and volatility of the S&P 500 index from January 1985 to March 2009, 250 assets from the S&P 500 universe, weekly frequency, computation by the author.

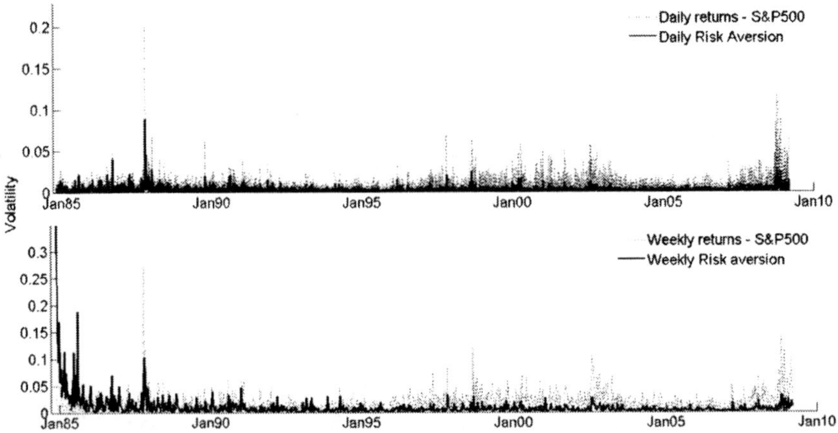

Figure 9.7 The contribution of the sample size neglect to the market volatility.

Source: Datastream, volatility of the relative risk aversion parameter, and volatility of the S&P 500 index from January 1985 to March 2009, 250 assets from the S&P 500 universe, the daily frequency on the top, the weekly frequency on the bottom, computation by the author.

ask a higher risk premium and he (she) will only support the part of the market volatility not explained by his (her) ambiguity. As a result, the use by this investor of the sample covariance matrix yields fewer errors in the estimation of the risk. In the same manner, an investor having the minimum ambiguity is not aware of this risk. The investor will ask a lower risk premium, and the use of the sample covariance matrix yields many estimation errors of the risk.

As seen in the preceding, the approach based on risk management requires the use of the covariance matrix characterizing well the risk depending on the ambiguity of investor. Concerning an allocation process under uncertainty, the existence of several profiles of investors in relation to ambiguity has for a consequence the need to aggregate the ambiguity on the market. Using Database 3, in the next subsection we run an application to the portfolio optimization.

An Application to the Portfolio Optimization

Usually, academic literature uses an *out-of-sample* approach with a rolling estimation window in order to keep constant the ratio between the number of historical returns and the number of assets into the investment universe. We know that the sample estimators of the expected returns and the covariance matrix perform better with the increase of the number of historical returns. In order to take into account the effect of the sample size neglect through time, we consider a conservative approach for our covariance matrices, by using an increasing estimation window for building the *out-of-sample* portfolio.

The Portfolio Allocation Process

The optimization program when there is a short sale constraint consists in maximizing the Sharpe ratio:

$$\begin{cases} \underset{(x_p)}{Max} \dfrac{x_p^{\mathrm{T}} \hat{\mu}_s}{x_p^{\mathrm{T}} \hat{\boldsymbol{\Omega}} x_p} \\ s.t. \begin{cases} x_p^{\mathrm{T}} \mathbf{1} = 1 & (C1) \\ x_{p_i} \geq 0,\ i = 1,\ldots,N & (C2) \end{cases} \end{cases} \tag{58}$$

where $\hat{\mu}_s$ denotes the sample expected returns and $\hat{\Omega}$ one of the covariance matrices among $\hat{\Omega}_s$, $\tilde{\Omega}_g$, $\tilde{\Omega}_t$, and $\tilde{\Omega}_u$. The first estimation window goes from December 22, 1998, to March 16, 1995. That is, we have 324 assets with 326 historical returns. We then compute the optimal tangency portfolio and buy it. One week later, we increase the number of historical returns of one period; we thus have a new estimation window from December 15, 1988, to March 23, 1995, that means 324 assets and 327 historical returns. We compute the new optimal tangency portfolio and rebalance the allocation by selling or buying assets from the last allocation in order to match with the new allocation. We perform the algorithm until the end date. We obtain four *out-of-sample* tangency portfolios from March 23, 1995, to December 18, 2008, depending on the estimator of the covariance matrix used, and compute their respective Sharpe ratios.

Next, we consider one thousand random linear combinations between the tangency portfolios obtained from $\tilde{\Omega}_g$, $\tilde{\Omega}_t$ and compute their respective Sharpe ratios. Figure 9.8 shows the Sharpe ratio of all the tangency portfolios considered.

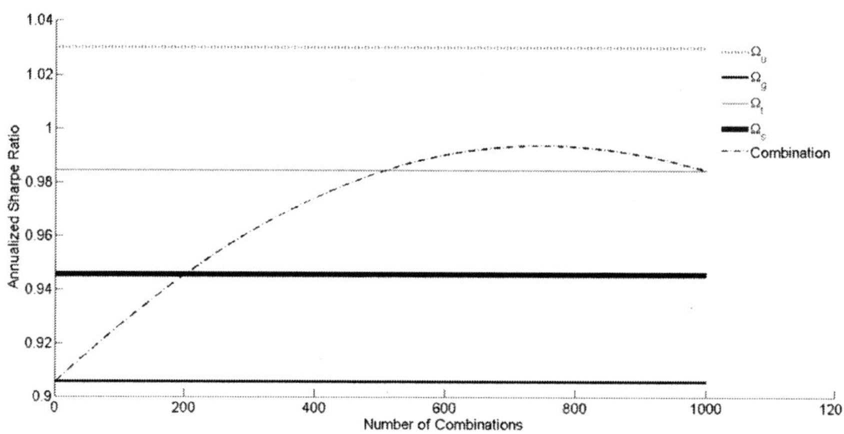

Figure 9.8 Sharpe ratio of tangency portfolios.

Source: Datastream, annualized Sharpe ratios of the *out-of-sample* tangency portfolios, the sample window increases from 326 to 1,004 historical returns, 717 periods of estimation window, 324 assets of the S&P 500 universe, no completion need, weekly frequency, computation by the author.

Comments

From Figure 9.8, it appears that the Sharpe ratio[12] of the sample tangency portfolio equal to 0.94 is higher than the one in the tangency portfolio obtained from the *maxmin* decision approach characterized by the covariance matrix $\tilde{\Omega}_g$ (equal to 0.9). However, it remains lower than the Sharpe ratio obtained from the covariance matrix $\tilde{\Omega}_t$ (equal to 0.98). The covariance matrix $\tilde{\Omega}_u$ is the one characterizing the equilibrium state between the most and the least ambiguous investors. The empirical result seems testify our theoretical result; the Sharpe ratio of the tangency portfolio obtained from the covariance matrix $\tilde{\Omega}_u$ (equal to 1.03) is higher than the Sharpe ratio obtained from the covariance matrix having the highest expected utility and, then, a fortiori than the Sharpe ratio of the sample tangency portfolio.

We know that the covariance matrix $\tilde{\Omega}_u$ is actually a linear combination between $\tilde{\Omega}_g$ and the matrix $\tilde{\Omega}_t$ with the optimal parameter β^*. In order to see if there is a naive approach allowing us to build a tangency portfolio with a higher Sharpe ratio than the one obtained from the covariance matrix $\tilde{\Omega}_u$, we also represent in Figure 9.8 the Sharpe ratios of one thousand random tangency portfolios obtained from several linear combinations between $\tilde{\Omega}_g$ and the matrix $\tilde{\Omega}_t$. From Figure 9.8, it seems that there are some combinations having a lower and others having a higher Sharpe ratio than the sample tangency portfolio. We also observe some combinations having a higher Sharpe ratio than the tangency portfolio obtained from $\tilde{\Omega}_t$. However, these combinations do not provide a higher Sharpe ratio than the one obtained from the equilibrium covariance matrix $\tilde{\Omega}_u$.

CONCLUDING REMARKS

We developed a model for understanding the impact of the sample size neglect when the investors hope for the tangency portfolio. After computing an expression of the covariance matrix characterizing the ambiguity behavior of the investors, the impact of the sample size neglect has been shown. It seems that an investor not aware on the finite sample size of the investment universe will ask a lower risk premium than another one. We derive an analytical expression of the part of the risk aversion coming from the sample size neglect say as the relative risk aversion parameter.

An equilibrium state has been built in order to deal with the problem of allocation decision under uncertainty. The equilibrium shows that the ambiguity of the investor comes actually from the finite sample property of the investment universe and follows a power law distribution with respect to the ratio between the number of assets and the number of historical returns, with a parameter almost equal to 0.58. An empirical study seems confirm the relevance of the covariance matrix derived from the equilibrium state.

We show empirically the consistency of the model. We also show that the model is consistent with the literature dealing with the ambiguity. Our approach has the advantage to link the behavior of the investors with a specific expression of the covariance matrix, therefore even in the case of no short sale, we are able to compute an allocation for the investor.

The model also shows the limit of the *maxmin* approach when a short sale constraint is imposed to the portfolio optimization program, and may be viewed as a multi-criteria *maxmin* approach[13] unlike the traditional *maxmin* approach where the lowest expected utility from a pool is considered. In our approach, we consider several criteria, the utility function, the expected utility function and the difference between both. Facing to the conflict between the most ambiguous and the less ambiguous investors reliance to the Sharpe model, our equilibrium state is a way to find a compromise for the allocation decision.

Because our results have been obtained under the condition that the true expected returns is known, our equilibrium covariance matrix may be used into the Black and Litterman model (1990, 1992), where the aim is to estimate the expected returns from a starting point (the Capital Asset Pricing Model) by taking into account the views of the investors on future returns. This will avoid considering into the Black-Litterman model, the uncertainty parameter reliance to the Sharpe model[14] because our equilibrium covariance matrix already takes into account the aggregate uncertainty.

APPENDICES

Proofs of Proposition and Corollary

Appendix 9.1 Proof of Proposition 1

Proposition 1. Under the wrong hypothesis, the expected mistake on the utility function when using the sample covariance matrix is as follows:

$$\rho = -\frac{(\mu^{\mathrm{T}}\mu)(N+2)}{2\gamma(T-N-2)}$$

Proof.

The expected mistake on the utility function of the sample covariance matrix is defined as follows:

$$\begin{aligned} \rho_{Id}\left(\mathbf{I},\hat{\mathbf{\Omega}}_s\right) &= U(\mathbf{I}) - E\left[U(\hat{\mathbf{\Omega}}_s)\right] \\ &= \frac{1}{2\gamma}\mu^{\mathrm{T}}\mu - \frac{1}{2\gamma}\mu^{\mathrm{T}}E(\hat{\mathbf{\Omega}}_s^{-1})\mu \end{aligned} \tag{A.1.1}$$

The sample covariance matrix $\hat{\Omega}_s$ has the following distribution:

$$\hat{\boldsymbol{\Omega}}_s \equiv W_N(T-1,\mathbf{I})/T \qquad \text{(A.1.2)}$$

where $W_N(T-1, \mathbf{I})$ denotes a Wishart distribution with $T-1$ degree of freedom. Following Muirhead (1982) for small size $T < (N+2)$ we know under the null hypothesis that:

$$E(\hat{\boldsymbol{\Omega}}_s^{-1}) = \frac{T}{T-N-2}\mathbf{I}^{-1} \qquad \text{(A.1.3)}$$

We obtain a new expression for $\rho(\mathbf{I},\hat{\Omega}_s)$:

$$\begin{aligned}\rho\left(\mathbf{I},\hat{\Omega}_s\right) &= \frac{1}{2\gamma}\mu^{\mathrm{T}}\mu - \frac{1}{2\gamma}\frac{T}{T-N-2}\mu^{\mathrm{T}}\mu \\ &= \frac{\mu^{\mathrm{T}}\mu}{2\gamma}\left(1-\frac{T}{T-N-2}\right)\end{aligned} \qquad \text{(A.1.4)}$$

and the development of (A.1.4) gives the following expression in terms of distance:

$$\rho_{Id}\left(\mathbf{I},\hat{\boldsymbol{\Omega}}_s\right) = -\frac{(\mu^{\mathrm{T}}\mu)(N+2)}{2\gamma(T-N-2)} \qquad \text{(A.1.5)}$$

We thus obtain the result.

■

Appendix 9.2 Proof of Proposition 2

Proposition 2. A candidate $\tilde{\Omega}$ for the covariance matrix is defined as follows:

$$\begin{cases}\tilde{\boldsymbol{\Omega}}^{-1} = \hat{\boldsymbol{\Omega}}_s^{-1} + \alpha\boldsymbol{\Lambda}_- \\ \alpha = \dfrac{4\gamma^2(T-N-2)}{N^2(N+2)(\mu^{\mathrm{T}}\mu)}\end{cases}$$

where Λ_- is the inverse of each elements of the matrix Λ of size $N \times N$ obtained from the vector of expected returssns μ:

$$\boldsymbol{\Lambda} = \mu \otimes \mu^{\mathrm{T}}$$

with the sign $\otimes$ denoting the kronecker product. Then the covariance matrix is defined as follows:

$$\tilde{\boldsymbol{\Omega}} = \hat{\boldsymbol{\Omega}}_s - \alpha\hat{\boldsymbol{\Omega}}_s\boldsymbol{\Lambda}_-\left(\mathbf{I} + \alpha\hat{\boldsymbol{\Omega}}_s\boldsymbol{\Lambda}_-\right)^{-1}\hat{\boldsymbol{\Omega}}_s$$

Proof.

Since the following equality holds:

$$U(\tilde{\mathbf{\Omega}}) = U(\hat{\mathbf{\Omega}}_s) - \frac{1}{\rho} \tag{A.2.1}$$

one obtains:

$$\mu^{\mathrm{T}}\tilde{\mathbf{\Omega}}^{-1}\mu = \mu^{\mathrm{T}}\hat{\mathbf{\Omega}}_s^{-1}\mu + \frac{4\gamma^2}{\mu^{\mathrm{T}}\mu}\frac{T-N-2}{N+2} \tag{A.2.2}$$

and a candidate for which the latter is true is defined as follows:

$$\tilde{\mathbf{\Omega}}^{-1} = \hat{\mathbf{\Omega}}_s^{-1} + \frac{4\gamma^2(T-N-2)}{N^2(N+2)(\mu^{\mathrm{T}}\mu)}\mathbf{\Lambda}_- \tag{A.2.3}$$

with:

$$\Lambda = \mu \otimes \mu^{\mathrm{T}}$$

To show this result, we have to compute the utility function of the candidate for the covariance matrix:

$$\begin{aligned} U(\tilde{\mathbf{\Omega}}) &= \frac{1}{2\gamma}\mu^{\mathrm{T}}\tilde{\mathbf{\Omega}}^{-1}\mu \\ &= U(\hat{\mathbf{\Omega}}_s) + \frac{1}{2\gamma}\mu^{\mathrm{T}}\left[\frac{4\gamma^2(T-N-2)}{N^2(N+2)(\mu^{\mathrm{T}}\mu)}\mathbf{\Lambda}_-\right]\mu \\ &= U(\hat{\mathbf{\Omega}}_s) + \frac{2\gamma(T-N-2)}{N^2(N+2)(\mu^{\mathrm{T}}\mu)}\mu^{\mathrm{T}}\mathbf{\Lambda}_-\mu \end{aligned} \tag{A.2.4}$$

We know that the matrix Λ is equal to the Kronecker product between μ and μ^{T}. Therefore:

$$\mu^{\mathrm{T}}\mathbf{\Lambda}_-\mu = \mu^{\mathrm{T}}\left(\mu \otimes \mu^{\mathrm{T}}\right)_-\mu \tag{A.2.5}$$

Remember, μ is the expected returns vector of size $N \times 1$. Assume we have two assets in the investment universe ($N = 2$), we then have:

$$\begin{aligned} \mu^{\mathrm{T}}\mathbf{\Lambda}_-\mu &= (\mu_1, \mu_2)\left(\begin{pmatrix}\frac{1}{\mu_1} \\ \frac{1}{\mu_2}\end{pmatrix} \otimes \left(\frac{1}{\mu_1}, \frac{1}{\mu_2}\right)\right)\begin{pmatrix}\mu_1 \\ \mu_2\end{pmatrix} \\ &= (\mu_1, \mu_2)\begin{pmatrix}\frac{1}{\mu_1^2} & \frac{1}{\mu_1\mu_2} \\ \frac{1}{\mu_1\mu_2} & \frac{1}{\mu_2^2}\end{pmatrix}\begin{pmatrix}\mu_1 \\ \mu_2\end{pmatrix} \\ &= \left(\frac{2}{\mu_1}, \frac{2}{\mu_2}\right)\begin{pmatrix}\mu_1 \\ \mu_2\end{pmatrix} \\ &= 2 + 2 = 2 \times 2 = 2^2 \end{aligned} \tag{A.2.6}$$

We assume now this result is true when there is *N* assets in the investment universe. We then have:

$$\mu^{\mathrm{T}}\Lambda^{-1}\mu = \underbrace{N+N+N+\ldots+N}_{N \text{ times}} = N \times N = N^2 \tag{A.2.7}$$

By recurrence, we show it remains true when we consider N + 1 assets in the investment universe. We then have $\mu = (\mu_i)_{i=1,\ldots,N+1}$ and Λ of size (N + 1) × (N + 1):

$$\begin{aligned}\mu^{\mathrm{T}}\Lambda\_\mu &= (\mu_i)^T_{i=1,\ldots,N+1}\left[(\mu_i\_)_{i=1,\ldots,N+1} \otimes (\mu_i\_)^{\mathrm{T}}_{i=1,\ldots,N+1}\right](\mu_i)_{i=1,\ldots,N+1} \\ &= \left[(\mu_i)^T_{i=1,\ldots,N}\left[(\mu_i\_)_{i=1,\ldots,N} \otimes (\mu_i\_)^{\mathrm{T}}_{i=1,\ldots,N+1}\right](\mu_i)_{i=1,\ldots,N}\right] \\ &+ \left[(\mu_i)^T_{i=1,\ldots,N+1}\begin{pmatrix} \mathbf{0}_{(i,j)_{i,j=1,\ldots,N}} & \Lambda\_{(i,N+1)_{i=1,\ldots,N}} \\ \Lambda\_{(N+1,j)_{j=1,\ldots,N}} & \Lambda\_{(N+1,N+1)} \end{pmatrix}(\mu_i)_{i=1,\ldots,N+1}\right]\end{aligned} \tag{A.2.8}$$

As a result, we have the following expression:

$$\begin{aligned}\mu^{\mathrm{T}}\Lambda\_\mu &= N^2 + \left[\left((\mu_{i\_})^{\mathrm{T}}_{i=1,\ldots,N}, \begin{matrix} N+1 \\ \mu_{N+1}\end{matrix}\right)(\mu_i)_{i=1,\ldots,N-1}\right] \\ &= N^2 + \underbrace{1+1+1+\ldots+1}_{N \text{ times}} + (N+1) \\ &= \underbrace{N+N+N+\ldots+N}_{N \text{ times}} + \underbrace{1+1+1+\ldots+1}_{N \text{ times}} + (N+1) \\ &= \underbrace{(N+1)+(N+1)+(N+1)+\ldots+(N+1)}_{N \cdot 1 \text{ times}} \\ &= (N+1)\times(N+1) = (N+1)^2\end{aligned} \tag{A.2.9}$$

Therefore, if we assume *N* assets in the investment universe, we have:

$$\begin{aligned}U(\tilde{\Omega}) &= \frac{1}{2\gamma}\mu^{\mathrm{T}}\tilde{\Omega}^{-1}\mu \\ &= U(\hat{\Omega}_s) + \frac{2\gamma(T-N-2)}{N^2(N+2)(\mu^{\mathrm{T}}\mu)}\left(\mu^{\mathrm{T}}\Lambda\_\mu\right) \\ &= U(\hat{\Omega}_s) + \frac{2\gamma N^2(T-N-2)}{N^2(N+2)(\mu^{\mathrm{T}}\mu)} \\ &= U(\hat{\Omega}_s) + \frac{2\gamma(T-N-2)}{(N+2)(\mu^{\mathrm{T}}\mu)}\end{aligned} \tag{A.2.10}$$

Because we obtain the same level of noise between the sample covariance matrix and the true one from the candidate, the candidate is actually the covariance matrix.

The covariance matrix $\tilde{\Omega}$ is then obtained by inverting $\tilde{\Omega}^{-1}$. Using the following matrix identity, with **A** and **B** invertible, **C** and **D** generic com fortable matrix:

$$(\mathbf{A}+\mathbf{CBD})^{-1}=\mathbf{A}^{-1}-\mathbf{A}^{-1}\mathbf{C}\left(\mathbf{I}+\mathbf{BDA}^{-1}\mathbf{C}\right)\mathbf{BDA}^{-1} \tag{A.2.11}$$

By setting:

$$\begin{cases}\mathbf{A}=\tilde{\mathbf{\Omega}}^{-1}\\ \mathbf{B}=\mathbf{D}=\mathbf{I}\\ \mathbf{C}=\alpha\mathbf{\Lambda}_{-}\end{cases}$$

one obtains:

$$\tilde{\mathbf{\Omega}}=\hat{\mathbf{\Omega}}_s-\alpha\hat{\mathbf{\Omega}}_s\mathbf{\Lambda}_{-}\left(\mathbf{I}+\alpha\hat{\mathbf{\Omega}}_s\mathbf{\Lambda}_{-}\right)^{-1}\hat{\mathbf{\Omega}}_s$$

■

Appendix 9.3 Proof of Proposition 4

Proposition 4. The expected utility of an investor with a relative ambiguity is higher than the expected utility of an investor with a maximum ambiguity reliance on the sample tangency portfolio.

Proof.

To show this result, we find the relative risk aversion parameters for which the expected utility of $\tilde{\Omega}$ is higher than the expected utility of any covariance matrix $\tilde{\Omega}_u$. Let the following inequality:

$$\left(E\left[U(\tilde{\mathbf{\Omega}}_u)\right]< E\left[U(\tilde{\mathbf{\Omega}})\right]\right)\Rightarrow(I) \tag{A.3.1}$$

with:

$$(I)\equiv\frac{T^2+(N+2)(2T-N-2)}{\sqrt{T(N+2)}}\sqrt{Z}<\frac{T(\mu^{\mathrm{T}}\hat{\mathbf{\Omega}}^{-1}\mu)}{2\gamma(T-N-2)}+\frac{2\gamma(2T-N-2)}{(\mu^{\mathrm{T}}\mu)(N+2)} \tag{A.3.2}$$

where Z is defined as follows:

$$Z=\frac{\mu^{\mathrm{T}}\hat{\mathbf{\Omega}}^{-1}\mu}{(\mu^{\mathrm{T}}\mu)(T-N-2)(N+2)} \tag{A.3.3}$$

We then obtain:

$$\begin{aligned}(I)\Rightarrow\ 0&<\gamma^2\left[\frac{2(2T-N-2)}{(\mu^{\mathrm{T}}\mu)(N+2)}\right]-\gamma\left[\frac{T^2+(N+2)(2T-N-2)}{\sqrt{T(N+2)}}\sqrt{Z}\right]+\left[\frac{T(\mu^{\mathrm{T}}\hat{\mathbf{\Omega}}^{-1}\mu)}{2(T-N-2)}\right] \\ \Rightarrow\ 0&<\mathbf{P}(\gamma)\end{aligned} \tag{A.3.4}$$

where $\mathbf{P}(\gamma)$ denotes an order two polynomial defined as follows:

$$\mathbf{P}(\gamma) = A\gamma^2 + B\gamma + C \tag{A.3.5}$$

with:

$$\begin{cases} A = \dfrac{2(2T-N-2)}{(\mu^{\mathrm{T}}\mu)(N+2)} \\ B = \dfrac{T^2+(N+2)(2T-N-2)}{\sqrt{T(N+2)}}\sqrt{Z} \\ C = \dfrac{T(\mu^{\mathrm{T}}\hat{\mathbf{\Omega}}^{-1}\mu)}{2(T-N-2)} \end{cases} \tag{A.3.6}$$

In order to study the sign of $\mathbf{P}(\gamma)$, we must compute the determinant of the polynomial:

$$\begin{aligned} \Delta &= B^2 - 4AC \\ &= \frac{Z\left[T^2+(N+2)(2T-N-2)\right]^2}{T(N+2)} - 4\left[\frac{2(2T-N-2)}{(\mu^{\mathrm{T}}\mu)(N+2)}\right]\left[\frac{T(\mu^{\mathrm{T}}\hat{\mathbf{\Omega}}^{-1}\mu)}{2(T-N-2)}\right] \\ &= \frac{Z\left[T^2+(N+2)(2T-N-2)\right]^2}{T(N+2)} - 4ZT(2T-N-2) \\ &= \frac{Z}{T(N+2)}\left[\left(T^2+(N+2)(2T-N-2)\right)^2 - 4T^2(N+2)(2T-N-2)\right] \\ &= \frac{ZD}{T(N+2)} \end{aligned} \tag{A.3.7}$$

where D is defined as follows:

$$\begin{aligned} D &= \left(T^2+(N+2)(2T-N-2)\right)^2 - 4T^2(N+2)(2T-N-2) \\ &= T^2 + 2T^2(N+2)(2T-N-2) + (2T-N-2) - 4T^2(N+2)(2T-N-2) \\ &= T^2 - 2T^2(N+2)(2T-N-2) + (2T-N-2) \\ &= \left(T^2-(N+2)(2T-N-2)\right)^2 \end{aligned} \tag{A.3.8}$$

We then have:

$$\sqrt{\Delta} = \left(T^2-(N+2)(2T-N-2)\right)\sqrt{\frac{Z}{T(N+2)}} \tag{A.3.9}$$

and we know that $\mathbf{P}(\gamma)$ has two roots γ_1 and γ_2 defined as follows:

$$\begin{cases} \gamma_1 = \dfrac{1}{2}\sqrt{\dfrac{N+2}{T}}\sqrt{\dfrac{(\mu^{\mathrm{T}}\mu)(\mu^{\mathrm{T}}\hat{\mathbf{\Omega}}_s^{-1}\mu)(N+2)}{(T-N-2)}} \\ \gamma_2 = \dfrac{1}{2}\dfrac{T^2}{2T-N-2}\sqrt{\dfrac{(\mu^{\mathrm{T}}\mu)(\mu^{\mathrm{T}}\hat{\mathbf{\Omega}}_s^{-1}\mu)(N+2)}{(T-N-2)}} \end{cases} \tag{A.3.10}$$

We observe that γ_1 is actually equal to the relative risk aversion parameter corresponding to the covariance matrix with the minimum uncertainty:

$$\begin{cases} \gamma_1 = \sqrt{\dfrac{N+2}{T}}\gamma_g \\ \gamma_2 = \dfrac{T^2}{2T-N-2}\gamma_g \end{cases} \tag{A.3.11}$$

We know that $\mathbf{P}(\gamma)$ has the opposite sign of A inside the roots and the same sign than A outside the roots.

We show now that γ_1 is lower than γ_2. Because $T > 1$, the following inequality is true:

$$\begin{aligned} (T^2 - 2T > 0) &\Rightarrow (T^2 - 2T + N + 2 > 0) \\ &\Rightarrow 2T - N - 2 < T^2 \\ &\Rightarrow 1 < \frac{T^2}{2T-N-2} \\ &\Rightarrow 1 < \gamma_2 \\ &\Rightarrow \gamma_g < \gamma_2 \end{aligned} \tag{A.3.12}$$

Because $(N + 2) < T$, we have $\gamma_1 < 1$, and as a result $\gamma_1 < \gamma_2$.

Because γ_g is the highest relative risk aversion, because of the decreasing of the first derivative of the utility function $U(\tilde{\Omega})$ with respect to γ, we cannot have a relative risk aversion parameter higher than γ_g. Because $\gamma_g < \gamma_2$, the relative risk aversion parameter γ_2 is not relevant. We have the following behavior:

$$\begin{cases} E[U(\tilde{\Omega})] < E[U(\tilde{\Omega}_u)] & \text{for} \quad \gamma_1 < \gamma \\ E[U(\tilde{\Omega}_u)] < E[U(\tilde{\Omega})] & \text{for} \quad \gamma < \gamma_1 \end{cases} \tag{A.3.13}$$

Finally, we know that:

$$\gamma_1 = \sqrt{\frac{N+2}{T}}\gamma_g \tag{A.3.14}$$

and Because $(N + 2) < T$, we have $\gamma_1 < \gamma_g$. As a result, we have:

$$E[U(\tilde{\Omega}_g)] < E[U(\tilde{\Omega}_u)] \tag{A.3.15}$$

We thus obtain the result.

■

Appendix 9.4 Proof of Proposition 5

Proposition 5. The expected utility of an investor having the minimum ambiguity with the sample mean-variance framework is higher than the expected utility of an investor having a relative ambiguity.

Proof.

We just have to compare the relative risk aversion for the covariance matrix $\tilde{\Omega}_t$ with γ_1 because of the following inequality obtained from Proposition 4:

$$\begin{cases} E\left[U(\tilde{\Omega})\right] < E\left[U(\tilde{\Omega}_u)\right] & \text{for} \quad \gamma_1 < \gamma \\ E\left[U(\tilde{\Omega}_u)\right] < E\left[U(\tilde{\Omega})\right] & \text{for} \quad \gamma < \gamma_1 \end{cases} \tag{A.4.1}$$

Remember, the corresponding relative risk aversion parameters are defined as follows:

$$\begin{cases} \gamma_1 = \sqrt{\dfrac{N+2}{T}}\gamma_g \\ \gamma_t = \sqrt{\dfrac{N+2}{2T-N-2}}\gamma_g \end{cases} \tag{A.4.2}$$

Because $(N + 2) < T$, it is straightforward to see that $T < (2T - N - 2)$. As a result we have:

$$(\gamma_t < \gamma_1) \Rightarrow \left(E\left[U(\tilde{\Omega}_u)\right] < E\left[U(\tilde{\Omega}_t)\right]\right) \tag{A.4.3}$$

We thus obtain the result.

■

Appendix 9.5 Proof of Proposition 6

Proposition 6. The uncertainty in the utility function of an investor with the minimum ambiguity is lower than the uncertainty for an investor with a relative ambiguity, which is lower than the one for an investor with the maximum ambiguity. As a result, the investor will ask a relative risk premium for counterbalancing their respective uncertainty.

Proof.

To show that, we must compare C_g, C_u and C_t with:

$$\begin{cases} C_u = \dfrac{T+N+2}{T} \\ C_g = 2 \\ C_t = \dfrac{2T}{2T-N-2} \end{cases} \tag{A.5.1}$$

Because $(N + 2) < T$, we have $C_t < C_g$.

We assume now that $C_u < C_t$, we have the following equation:

$$\begin{aligned} C_u < C_t \;&\Rightarrow \frac{T+N+2}{T} < \frac{2T}{2T-N-2} \\ &\Rightarrow \frac{T+N+2}{T} < \frac{2T}{2T-N-2} \\ &\Rightarrow (T+N+2)(2T+N+2) < 2T^2 \\ &\Rightarrow T < N+2 \end{aligned} \tag{A.5.2}$$

which is wrong. Therefore we have $C_t < C_u$.

■

Appendix 9.6 Proof of Proposition 7

Proposition 7. The lower the parameter k, and the lower the expected loss when the family of covariance matrices $(k\hat{\Omega}_s)$ is used, in comparison with the expected loss when using the sample covariance matrix. As a result, the expected loss of the ambiguous investor is lower than the expected loss of the relative ambiguous investor, which is lower than the expected loss of the less ambiguous investor, which is lower than the expected loss when using the sample covariance matrix.

Proof.

The expected loss ξ_k when using the covariance matrix matrices $(k\hat{\Omega}_s)$ instead of the true covariance matrix is defined as follows:

$$\begin{cases} \xi_k = U(\boldsymbol{\Omega}) - \left[x^{*\mathbf{T}}\mu - \dfrac{\gamma}{2} x^{*\mathbf{T}} E(k\hat{\boldsymbol{\Omega}}_s) x^* \right] \\ = U(\boldsymbol{\Omega}) - \left[x^{*\mathbf{T}}\mu - \dfrac{\gamma}{2} x^{*\mathbf{T}} k E(\hat{\boldsymbol{\Omega}}_s) x^* \right] \end{cases}$$

Since $0 < k < 1$, the following holds:

$$
\begin{cases}
\left[\frac{\gamma}{2}x^{*\mathrm{T}}kE\left(\hat{\boldsymbol{\Omega}}_s\right)x^* < \frac{\gamma}{2}x^{*\mathrm{T}}E\left(\hat{\boldsymbol{\Omega}}_s\right)x^*\right] \Rightarrow \left[-\frac{\gamma}{2}x^{*\mathrm{T}}E\left(\hat{\boldsymbol{\Omega}}_s\right)x^* < -\frac{k\gamma}{2}x^{*\mathrm{T}}E\left(\hat{\boldsymbol{\Omega}}_s\right)x^*\right] \\
\Rightarrow \left[x^{*\mathrm{T}}\mu - \frac{\gamma}{2}x^{*\mathrm{T}}E\left(\hat{\boldsymbol{\Omega}}_s\right)x^* < x^{*\mathrm{T}}\mu - \frac{k\gamma}{2}x^{*\mathrm{T}}E\left(\hat{\boldsymbol{\Omega}}_s\right)x^*\right] \\
\Rightarrow \left[U(\Omega) - \left[x^{*\mathrm{T}}\mu - \frac{\gamma k}{2}x^{*\mathrm{T}}E\left(\hat{\boldsymbol{\Omega}}_s\right)x^*\right] < U(\Omega) - \left[x^{*\mathrm{T}}\mu - \frac{\gamma}{2}x^{*\mathrm{T}}E\left(\hat{\boldsymbol{\Omega}}_s\right)x^*\right]\right] \\
\Rightarrow \xi_k < \xi_s
\end{cases}
$$

where ξ_k denotes the expected loss when using the sample covariance matrix. It is straightforward to see that lower the parameter k and lower the expected loss when using the family matrices $\left(k\hat{\boldsymbol{\Omega}}_s\right)$ in comparison to the expected loss when using the sample covariance matrix. The conclusion comes from Proposition 6.

■

Appendix 9.7 Proof of Proposition 8

Proposition 8. The expected utility of the investor having a relative ambiguity is lower than the expected utility of any investor whose the risk profile is characterized by the covariance matrix $\boldsymbol{\Omega}^{\beta}_{gt}$:

$$E\left[U(\tilde{\boldsymbol{\Omega}}_u)\right] \leq E\left[U(\tilde{\boldsymbol{\Omega}}^{\beta}_{gt})\right]$$

Proof.

If we assume the opposite of the result we are trying to show, we then have:

$$
\begin{aligned}
E\left[U(\tilde{\boldsymbol{\Omega}}^{\beta}_{gt})\right] < E\left[U(\tilde{\boldsymbol{\Omega}}_u)\right] &\Leftrightarrow \gamma_u < \gamma^{\beta}_{gt} \\
&\Leftrightarrow \gamma_u < \beta\gamma_g + (1-\beta)\gamma_t \\
&\Leftrightarrow \gamma_u - \gamma_t \leq \beta(\gamma_g - \gamma_t) \\
&\Leftrightarrow \frac{\gamma_u - \gamma_t}{\gamma_g - \gamma_t} \leq \beta \\
&\Leftrightarrow \frac{\sqrt{T(N+2)(2T-N-2)} - \sqrt{N+2}}{\sqrt{2T-N-2} - \sqrt{N+2}} \leq \beta
\end{aligned}
$$

Because $(N + 2) < T$, we know that:

$$\sqrt{2T-N-2} < T(N+2)(2T-N-2)$$

As a result we have:

$$\left(1 < \frac{\sqrt{T(N+2)(2T-N-2)} - \sqrt{N+2}}{\sqrt{2T-N-2} - \sqrt{N+2}} \leq \beta\right) \Leftrightarrow (1 < \beta)$$

which cannot happened, because $0 < \beta < 1$. We then have the following result:

$$E\left[U(\tilde{\mathbf{\Omega}}_u)\right] < E\left[U(\tilde{\mathbf{\Omega}}_{gt}^{\beta})\right]$$

We thus obtain the result.

■

Appendix 9.8 Proof of Proposition 9

Proposition 9. The utility function of the investor having a relative ambiguity is lower than the utility function of any investor whose the risk profile is characterized by the covariance matrix $\tilde{\mathbf{\Omega}}_{gt}^{\beta}$.

$$U(\tilde{\mathbf{\Omega}}_u) \leq U(\tilde{\mathbf{\Omega}}_{gt}^{\beta})$$

Proof.

From Proposition 8, the expected utility obtained from any combination between $\tilde{\Omega}_g$ and $\tilde{\Omega}_t$ is higher than the one obtained from the covariance matrix $\tilde{\Omega}_u$:

$$(III) \equiv \left(E\left[U(\tilde{\mathbf{\Omega}}_u)\right] < E\left[U(\tilde{\mathbf{\Omega}}_{gt}^{\beta})\right]\right) \tag{A.8.1}$$

Remember, the expression for the expected utility depends on the expression for the utility:

$$E\left[U(\tilde{\mathbf{\Omega}})\right] = \frac{T}{T-N-2} U(\tilde{\mathbf{\Omega}}) + \frac{2\gamma(T-N-2)}{(\mu^{\mathrm{T}}\mu)(N+2)} \tag{A.8.2}$$

We then have from (A.8.1):

$$(III) \Leftrightarrow \left[\frac{T}{T-N-2} U(\tilde{\mathbf{\Omega}}_u) + \frac{2\gamma_u(T-N-2)}{(\mu^{\mathrm{T}}\mu)(N+2)} < \frac{T}{T-N-2} U(\tilde{\mathbf{\Omega}}_{gt}^{\beta})\right.$$

$$\Leftrightarrow U(\tilde{\mathbf{\Omega}}_u) - U(\tilde{\mathbf{\Omega}}_{gt}^{\beta}) < \frac{2(T-N-2)^2}{T(\mu^{\mathrm{T}}\mu)(N+2)}\left(\gamma_{gt}^{\beta} - \gamma_u\right)$$

$$\left. + \frac{2\gamma_{gt}^{\beta}(T-N-2)}{(\mu^{\mathrm{T}}\mu)(N+2)}\right] \tag{A.8.3}$$

Because (III) is true, we also have $\gamma_{gt}^{\beta} < \gamma_u$, which means $\gamma_{gt}^{\beta} - \gamma_u < 0$. As a result:

$$\left[U(\tilde{\Omega}_u)-U(\tilde{\Omega}^{\beta}_{gt})<\frac{2(T-N-2)^2}{T(\mu^{\mathrm{T}}\mu)(N+2)}\left(\gamma^{\beta}_{gt}-\gamma_u\right)<0\right] \Leftrightarrow U(\tilde{\Omega}_u)<U(\tilde{\Omega}^{\beta}_{gt}) \quad \text{(A.8.4)}$$

We thus obtain the result.

■

Appendix 9.9 Proof of Proposition 10

Proposition 10. The optimal parameter β^* for the linear combination between investors having the maximum ambiguity and investors having the minimum ambiguity reliance on the Sharpe model is defined as follows:

$$\beta^* = \sqrt{\frac{N+2}{T}}\,\frac{\sqrt{2T-N-2}-\sqrt{T}}{\sqrt{2T-N-2}-\sqrt{N+2}}$$

Proof.
Because $\tilde{\Omega}_u$ is the optimal combination between $\tilde{\Omega}_g$ and $\tilde{\Omega}_t$, the following equality allows for finding the optimal β:

$$\begin{aligned}
\left[\tilde{\Omega}^{\beta}_{gt}=\tilde{\Omega}_u\right] &\Leftrightarrow \left[\beta^*\tilde{\Omega}_g+(1-\beta^*)\tilde{\Omega}_t=\tilde{\Omega}_u\right]\\
&\Leftrightarrow \beta^*\gamma_g+(1-\beta^*)\gamma_t=\gamma_u\\
&\Leftrightarrow \beta^*\gamma_g+(1-\beta^*)\gamma_g\sqrt{\frac{N+2}{2T-N-2}}=\sqrt{\frac{N+2}{T}}\gamma_g \qquad \text{(A.10.1)}\\
&\Leftrightarrow \beta^*\left(1-\sqrt{\frac{N+2}{2T-N-2}}\right)=\sqrt{\frac{N+2}{T}}-\sqrt{\frac{N+2}{2T-N-2}}\\
&\Leftrightarrow \beta^*\left(\frac{\sqrt{2T-N-2}-\sqrt{N+2}}{\sqrt{2T-N-2}}\right)=\sqrt{N+2}\left(\frac{\sqrt{2T-N-2}-\sqrt{T}}{\sqrt{T(2T-N-2)}}\right)\\
&\Leftrightarrow \beta^*=\sqrt{\frac{N+2}{T}}\left(\frac{\sqrt{2T-N-2}-\sqrt{T}}{\sqrt{2T-N-2}-\sqrt{N+2}}\right)
\end{aligned}$$

We thus obtain the result.

■

NOTES

1. We may cite alternative approaches as the resampling method of Michaud (1998) and Michaud and Michaud (2008), but this approach is so computational that it makes it impossible to explain the behavior of the investor. Concerning robust portfolio allocation rules, see Goldfarb and Iyengar (2003)

and Garlappi, Uppal, and Wang (2007). For a portfolio with moment restrictions, see, for instance, MacKinlay and Pástor (2000).

2. For a purely statistical approach, see, for instance, Barry (1974) and Bawa, Brown, and Klein (1979). For an approach based on shrinkage estimators, see, for instance, Jobson, Korkie, and Ratti (1979); Jobson and Korkie (1980); and Jorion (1985, 1986). For the estimation of expected returns, see Ledoit and Wolf (2003, 2004a) for the estimation of the covariance matrix. For an approach that relies on an asset-pricing model for establishing a prior, see, for instance, Pástor (2000) and Pástor and Stambaugh (2000).
3. For details about these beliefs, see Barberis and Thaler (2003).
4. The excess returns are obtained by removing from the asset returns the risk-free rate.
5. By this assumption, we avoid a Gaussian distribution for returns.
6. We will show later in the chapter that γ is not the whole risk aversion of an investor, but the share characterizing the risk linked to the finite-sample property of the investment universe.
7. However, DeMiguel *et al.* (2009) show that the sample-based mean-variance strategy and its extensions need around three thousand months for a portfolio with twenty-five assets and six thousand months for a portfolio of fifty assets to outperform the naive strategy. Their results indicate that the use of the identity matrix is simply optimal or at least more optimal than strategies developed by literature. Actually, in their empirical study, the authors use simulated data from the one factor model, data corresponding to several sectorial indices and data coming from the Fama and French (1993) portfolios. In the one factor model, noise into the naive allocation is simply the deviation of the market weights of the underlying assets from the average. The beta of each asset characterizing their risks and their cross-correlations are not at all taken into account. The identity matrix does not contain cross-correlation errors, and as a result may be a better estimator of the covariance matrix than several estimators in this case. Furthermore, it is well known that sectorial indices are less correlated than stocks, and by considering only sectorial indices, authors design data for which the identity matrix may be the true covariance matrix—the constant-correlation model of Elton and Gruber (1973) may be used for building a good estimator of the covariance matrix in this case. We can use the same argument when considering many portfolios from Fama and French (1993), which correspond to different factors that are by design statistically independent.
8. This is true because of the positivity of the relative risk aversion parameter.
9. As Ledoit and Wolf (2003) state, when the number of assets N is of the same order of magnitude as the number of historical returns T, the elements into the sample covariance matrix tend to take EVs and contain a lot of errors.
10. A little change of the elements into the sample covariance matrix leads to a big change in the optimal portfolio.
11. We use the federal funds rate as the risk-free rate.
12. This is an annualized Sharpe ratio.
13. It seems there is a literature corresponding to this approach named Multi-Criteria Decision Analysis (MCDA); see Hallerbach and Spronk (2002).
14. There is a disagreement in the literature dealing with the Black-Litterman model about the value of this parameter.

BIBLIOGRAPHY

Barberis, N., and R. Thaler. 2003. "A Survey of Behavioral Finance." In *Handbook of the Economics of Finance*, ed. *G.M. Constantinides, M. Harris, and R. Stulz.*

Barry, C.B. 1974. "Portfolio Analysis under Uncertain Means, Variances, and Covariances." *Journal of Finance 29*:515–522.

Bawa, V.S., S. Brown, and R. Klein. 1979. *Estimation Risk and Optimal Portfolio Choice. Amsterdam.*

Best, M.J., and R.R. Grauer. 1991. "On the Sensitivity of Mean-Variance-Efficient Portfolios to Changes in Asset Means: Some Analytical and Computational Results." *Review of Financial Studies 4*:315–342.

Black, F., M.C. Jensen, and M. Scholes.1972. "The CAPM: Some Empirical Tests." In *Studies in the Theory of Capital Markets, ed. M.C. Jensen, 79–121. New York: Praeger Publishers.*

Black, F., and R. Litterman. 1990. "Asset Allocation: Combining Investor Views with Market Equilibrium." *Working Paper, Goldman Sachs, Fixed Income Research.*

———. 1992. "Global Portfolio Optimization." *Financial Analyst Journal 48(5)*: 28–43.

Brandt, M. 2004. "Portfolio Choice Problems." In *Handbook of Financial Econometrics, ed. Y. Ait-Sahalia and L.P. Hansen. Amsterdam: Elsevier Science.*

Brown, S.J. 1978. "The Portfolio Choice Problem: Comparison of Certainty Equivalence and Optimal Bayes Portfolios." *Communications in Statistics-Simulation and Computation 7*:321–334.

Chauveau, T., and N. Nalpas. 2009. "A Theory of Disappointment." *ESC-Toulouse Working Papers.*

Chopra, V.K. 1993. "Improving Optimization." *Journal of Investing 8*:51–59.

Chopra, V.K., and W.T. Ziemba. 1993. "The Effects of Errors in Means, Variances and Covariances on Optimal Portfolio Choice." *Journal of Portfolio Management 19*:6–11.

Conlon, T., H.J. Ruskin, and M. Crane. 2008. "Random Matrix Theory and Fund of Funds Portfolio Optimisation." Working Paper, *Dublin City University.*

Cont, R. 1998. "Empirical Properties of Assets Returns: Stylized Facts and Statistical Issues." *Quantitative Finance 1*:223–236.

DeMiguel, V., L. Garlappi, F.J. Nogales, and R. Uppal. 2009. "A Generalized Approach to Portfolio Optimization: Improving Performance By Constraining Portfolio Norms." *Management Science 55(5)*: 798–812.

DeMiguel, V., L. Garlappi, and R. Uppal. 2009. "Optimal versus Naive Diversification: How Inefficient Is the 1/N Portfolio Strategy?" *Review of Financial Studies 22(5)*: 1915–1953.

DeMiguel, V., and F.J. Nogales. 2009. "Portfolio Selection with Robust Estimation of Risk." *Operations Research 57(3)*: 560–577.

Disatnik, D., and S. Benninga. 2007. "Shrinking Covariance Matrix—The Simpler Is Better." *Journal of Portfolio Management 33*:56–63.

Edelman, A. 1989. "Eigenvalues and Condition Numbers of Random Matrices." *PhD thesis, Department of Mathematics, Massachusetts Institute of Technology.*

Ellsberg, D. 1961. "Risk, Ambiguity, and the Savage Axioms." *Quarterly Journal of Economics 75*:643–669.

Elton, E., and M. Gruber. 1973. "Estimating the Dependence Structure of Share Prices." *Journal of Finance 28*:1203–1232.

Fama, E.F., and K.R French. 1993. "Common Risk Factors in the Returns of Stock and Bonds." *Journal of Financial Economics 33*:3–56.

———. 2004. "The Capital Asset Pricing Model: Theory and Evidence." *Journal of Economic Perspectives 18*:25–46.

Fan, J., Y. Fan, and J. Jiang. 2007. "Dynamic Integration of Time- and State Domain Methods for Volatility Estimation." *Journal of American Statistical Association 102*:618–631.

Frost, P., and J. Savarino. 1988. "For Better Performance Constrain Portfolio Weights." *Journal of Portfolio Management 15*:29–34.

Garlappi, L., R. Uppal, and T. Wang. 2007. "Portfolio Selection with Parameter and Model Uncertainty: A Multi-Prior Approach." *Review of Financial Studies 20*:41–81.

Gilboa, I., and D. Schmeidler. 1989. "Maxmin Expected Utility with Non-Unique Prior." *Journal of Mathematical Economics 18*:141–153.

Goldfarb, D., and G. Iyengar. 2003. "Robust Portfolio Selection Problems." *Mathematics of Operations Research 28*:1–38.

Gul, F. 1991. "A Theory of Disappointment in Decision Making Under Uncertainty." *Econometrica 59*:667–686.

Hallerbach, W., and J. Spronk. 2002. "The Relevance of the MCDM for Financial Decisions." *Journal of Multi-Criteria Decision Analysis 11*:187–195.

Hansen, L.P., and T.J. Sargent. 2001. "Robust Control and Model Uncertainty." *American Economic Association 91(2)*: 60–66.

Hosking, J. 1986. "The Theory of Probability Weighted Moments." *Research Report RC12210. IBM Research Division.*

———. 1989. "Some Theoretical Results Concerning L-Moments." *Research Report RC14492. IBM Research Division.*

Hosking, J., and J. Wallis. 1987. "Parameter and Quantile Estimation for the Generalized Pareto Distribution." *Technometrics 29*:339–349.

Hosking, J., J. Wallis, and J. Wood. 1985. "Estimation of the Generalized Extreme-Value Distribution by the Method of Probability-Weighted Moments." *Technometrics 27*:251–261.

———. 1990. "L-moments: Analysis and Estimation." *Journal of the Royal Statistical Society Series B 52*:105–124.

Jagannathan, R., and T. Ma. 2003. "Risk Reduction in Large Portfolios: Why Imposing the Wrong Constraints Helps." *Journal of Finance 54*: 1651–1683.

Jobson, J.D., and R. Korkie. 1980. "Estimation for Markowitz Efficient Portfolios." *Journal of the American Statistical Association 75*:544–554.

Jobson, J.D., R. Korkie, and V. Ratti. 1979. "Improved Estimation for Markowitz Portfolios Using James-Stein Type Estimators." *American Statistical Association 41*:279–292.

Jorion, P. 1985. "International Portfolio Diversification with Estimation Risk." *Journal of Business 58*:259–278.

———. 1986. "Bayes-Stein Estimation for Portfolio Analysis." *Journal of Financial and Quantitative Analysis 21*:279–292.

Kahn, B.E., and R.K. Sarin. 1988. "Modeling Ambiguity in Decisions under Uncertainty." *Journal of Consumer Research 15*:265–272.

Kahneman, D., and A. Tversky. 1974. "Judgment under Uncertainty: Heuristics and Biases." *Science 185*:1124–1131.

———. 1979. "Prospect Theory: An analysis of Decision under Risk." *Econometrica 47*:263–291.

Kan, R., and G. Zhou. 2007. "Optimal Portfolio Choice with Parameter Uncertainty." *Journal of Financial and Quantitative Analysis 42*:621–656.

Laloux, L., P. Cizeau, J.-P. Bouchaud, and M. Potters. 1999. "Noise Dressing of Financial Correlation Matrices." *Physical Review Letter 83*:14–69.

Ledoit, O., and M. Wolf. 2003. "Improved Estimation of the Covariance Matrix of Stock Returns with an Application to Portfolio Selection." *Journal of Empirical Finance 10*:603–621.

———. 2004a. "Honey, I Shrunk the Sample Covariance Matrix." *Journal of Portfolio Management 31*:1–22.

———. 2004b. "A Well-Conditioned Estimator for Large Dimensional Covariance Matrices." *Journal of Multivariate Analysis 88*:365–411.

Litterman, R. 2003. *Modern Investment Management: An Equilibrium Approach*. New York: *Wiley*.
Loomes, G., and R. Sugden. 1982. "Regret Theory: An Alternative Theory of Rational Choice Under Uncertainty." *Economic Journal* 92:805–824.
MacKinlay, A.C., and L. Pástor. 2000. "Asset Pricing Models: Implications for Expected Returns and Portfolio Selection." *Review of Financial Studies 13*:883–916.
Mandelbrot, B. 1963. "The Variation of Certain Speculative Prices." *Journal of Business* 36:392–317.
Markowitz, H. 1952. "Mean-Variance Analysis in Portfolio Choice and Capital Markets." *Journal of Finance* 7:77–91.
Merton, R. 1980. "On Estimating the Expected Return on the Market: An Exploratory Investigation." *Journal of Financial Economics 8 (4)*: 323–361.
Meucci, A. 2005. *Risk and Asset Allocation. New York: Springer-Verlag.*
Michaud, R.O. 1989. "The Markowitz Optimization Enigma: Is 'Optimized' Optimal?" *Financial Analysts Journal* 45:31–42.
———. 1998. *Efficient Asset Management: A Practical Guide to Stock Portfolio Optimization*. Oxford: *Oxford University Press*.
Michaud, R.O., and R. Michaud. 2008. "Estimation Error and Portfolio Optimization: A Resampling Solution." *Journal of Investment Management 6 (1)*: 8–28.
Muirhead, R.J. 1982. *Aspects of Multivariate Statistical Theory*. New York: Wiley.
Pástor, L. 2000. "Portfolio Selection and Asset Pricing Models." *Journal of Finance 55*:179–223.
Pástor, L., and R.F. Stambaugh. 2000. "Comparing Asset Pricing Models: An Investment Perspective." *Journal of Financial Economics* 56:335–381.
Plerou, V., P. Gopikrishnan, B. Rosenow, L.A.N. Amaral, T. Guhr, and H.E. Stanley. 2002. "A Random Matrix Approach to Cross-Correlations in Financial Data" *Physical Review E 65*.
Potters, M., J.-P. Bouchaud, and L. Laloux. 2005. "Financial Applications of Random Matrix Theory: Old Laces and New Pieces." *Acta Physica Polonica B 36 (9)*: 2767–2784.
Rabin, M. 2002. "Inference by Believers in the Law of Small Numbers." *Quarterly Journal of Economics 117*:775–816.
Rousseeuw, P.J., and K. Van Driessen. 1999. "A Fast Algorithm for the Minimum Covariance Determinant Estimator." *Technometrics 41*:212–223.
Savage, L. 1964. *The Foundations of Statistics*. New York: *Wiley*.
Serfling, R., and P. Xiao. 2007. "A Contribution to Multivariate L-Moments: L-Comoment Matrices." *Journal of Multivariate Analysis 98*:1765–1781.
Sharpe, W. 1963. "A Simplified Model for Portfolio Analysis." *Journal of Management Science* 9:277–293.
———. 1964. "Capital Asset Prices: A Theory of Market Equilibrium under Conditions of Risk." *Journal of Finance 19 (3)*: 425–442.
Sillitto, G. 1951. "Interrelations between Certain Linear Systematic Statistics of Sample from any Continuous Population." *Biometrika 38*:377–382.
Tobin, J. 1958. "Liquidity Preferences as Behavior towards Risk." *Review of Economics Studies 25*:65–86.
Von-Neumann, J., and O. Morgenstern. 1944. *Theory of Games and Economic Behavior*. Princeton, NJ: *Princeton University Press*.
Yanou, G. 2008. "Extension of Random Matrix Theory to the L-moments for Robust Portfolio Allocation." Working Paper, *University of Paris-1*.

Part III

Legal and Regulatory Dimensions of Corporate Governance and Risk Management

To generate wealth in a free economy, the survival of honest, responsible and open enterprises are essential. Over the last decade, there has been a dramatic erosion of confidence in the truthfulness and transparency of public and private organizations worldwide. During this period, organizations have been, and continue to be, engulfed by major debacles such as product recalls, accounting and insider trading scandals, unforeseen public policy risks, catastrophic bankruptcies, major shifts in markets (which were missed or seen too late), and increasingly complex ecological, ethical and business changes often not recognized by leaders.

In our view, the broader costs (economic and social) associated with the proliferation of corporate malfeasance (Enron, Paramalat and Worldcom, etc.) on the very future of the free market system have been grossly underestimated. The opportunity costs of such ethical violations far exceed the nominal depletion in the asset values of the enterprises engulfed by them and monies squandered away by their top managers.

Knowing the principles and practices of sound, responsible corporate governance can be an important deterrent to unethical behavior. Specifically, one must understand:

- the role and responsibilities of the board of directors and audit committees,
- the basic codes of conduct and conflicts of interest rules,
- the role of corporate compliance,
- the role of public accountants and legal counsel, and, finally,

- the complex interdependencies between corporate governance and other institutions such as the stock exchanges and regulatory bodies.

This understanding is an important factor in successfully managing risk, observing corporate compliance and preserving and enhancing reputation. It should help responsible leaders avoid some of the ethical pitfalls of recent history that remain, as yet, largely unchecked. In the final section of this book, we focus on the timely issues of legal and regulatory compliance in risk management and corporate governance.

In a recent survey of enterprise-wide risk management and corporate governance, Simkins and Ramirez (2008) carefully review the full spectrum of enterprise-wide risk management practices and affirm their beneficial contributions to the financial performance of the firm. Simultaneously, these authors document in detail existing corporate governance mandates to highlight the gap between current legal and regulatory requirements regarding risk management and the practice of risk management by non-legal financial professionals. Their analysis leads to an evaluation of what legal and regulatory additions and modifications are needed for an optimal integration of risk management functions and corporate governance practices.

Given the myriad regulations to which banks, both public and private, must adhere, good corporate governance practices are recognized as essential to the industry. Yet, the financial crisis brings to light questions regarding the force and efficacy of existing banking regulations. Also in question is banks' commitment to continual improvement of the mechanisms and practice of governance in the industry. In, "Corporate Governance of Banks," Peter O. Mülbert asks whether the worldwide, general discussion of corporate governance should include ideas taken from within the banking sector, given its recent failures and the idiosyncrasies of its governance mechanisms. Mülbert first examines what differentiates banks' corporate governance practices from those of generic firms. He then surveys banks' incentives for good governance before offering some lesson-learned regarding governance in the wake of the crisis. A key question for Mülbert is whether banking can stand as an exemplar in the realm of governance improvement.

In the next chapter, Erik Gerding's "'Complexity,' Information Failures in the Financial Crisis" is a response to critiques recently leveled at mandatory securities disclosure by legal scholars. Whereas the critics of disclosure see ineffectuality, Gerding sees an opportunity to enhance the dissemination and understanding of information through technology. Gerding acknowledges that asymmetries of information played a hand in the financial crisis. He however, disagrees with several legal scholars who believe that securities disclosure regulation should be relaxed because it both leads to information overload for investors and fails to adequately convey the complexities of the instruments used in today's financial markets. Rather than ceding that the glut of information and its complexity cannot be overcome, Gerding proposes a remedy. He argues that advances in the general areas of information systems and computer software, and the Open Source software movement, in particular, could be applied to securities disclosure to reduce complexity and provide robust, manageable information to investors. Gerding surveys the types of technologies and their applications that he believes would be beneficial to investors and would aid firms in complying with current mandatory disclosure regulations. He also offers analysis of the costs and risks associated with adopting the technology.

The proliferation of technology into business and society is largely responsible for the ascendancy of commerce to heights once unimaginable. The dark side of the story is that personal and corporate identity information is abundant and susceptible to theft by individuals and organizations intent on profiting from it. Businesses that suffer a breach of customer or corporate identity data face a host of negative impacts, including legal liability, loss of customer goodwill, and the disruption of normal operations. With "Data Integrity Preservation and Identity Theft Prevention: Operational and Strategic Imperatives to Enhance Shareholder and Consumer Value," Kevin Govern and John Winn offer a survey of infrastructure risks that businesses face, a summary of the legal and regulatory landscape that businesses must navigate, and a primer of best-practices that businesses can use in a post-breach emergency.

In the next chapter, "Credit Derivatives and Corporate Governance: A Review of Corporate Theory," P.M. Vasudev argues that despite having "state of the art" governance structures, the firms at the heart of the credit crisis failed to act responsibly. For Vasudev, this raises the question of how much influence public policy should have on corporate governance. After a survey of the shaping of current corporate theory and today's complex credit derivatives, Vasudev analyzes how the mechanisms of corporate governance in place functioned in the lead-up to the credit crisis. The article concludes with a call for specific regulatory definitions and reporting.

Yuki Masujima explores how the current global financial crisis has affected global banks' management of risk associated with lending activity in "Lending Currency Mix of Globalized Banks: A Potential Risk for Foreign Affiliates via Internal Fund Transfer." The paper investigates what determines the growth of foreign bank loans by currency in the Indonesian banking sector, where foreign banks disburse loans in both foreign and local currency. Thus, the author does not emphasize the generality of results for other countries. However, if both foreign banks' presence and the share of foreign currency lending are high, Masujima urges us to pay attention to the currency mix of lending to understand the lending channel of shock transmission accurately.

As this volume was being assembled, the United States Supreme Court handed down a landmark decision in Citizens United v. FEC, elevating the

First Amendment rights of corporations to speak (i.e., make contributions to political campaigns from corporate treasuries). In her paper, "Corporate Political Spending & Shareholders' Rights: Why the U.S. Should Adopt the British Approach," Ciara Torres-Spellicy questions whether the corporations' or the shareholders' money is actually being spent when firms support or oppose a candidate for office through direct financial contributions. Corporations are not obligated to inform their shareholders of political spending. Torres-Spellicy objects that the shareholders have no right of either consent or objection to such corporate expenditures. Furthermore, she cites evidence that political spending can be detrimental to corporations. She, therefore, calls on managers to join with advocates of campaign finance reform in reducing the overall levels of firms' political contributions. As a remedy, she proposes a change to U.S. securities law modeled on U.K. law that requires corporations to notify their shareholders of all political spending. The law would also make all corporate political expenditures subject to shareholder authorization. In an epilogue, written after the *Citizens United* decision, Torres-Spellicy discusses the presentation of her proposal and other legislation to Congress.

REFERENCES

Simkins, Betty J. and Ramirez, Steven A., Enterprise-Wide Risk Management and Corporate Governance (March 1, 2008). *Loyola University Chicago Law Journal*, Vol. 39, 2008. Available at SSRN: http://ssrn.com/abstract=1657036.

10 Corporate Governance of Banks

Peter O. Mülbert

INTRODUCTION

The economics and functions of banks differ from those of industrial firms. Because of these differences, banks are subject to stringent prudential regulation of their capital and risk. Moreover, these differences are reflected in corporate governance practices observed in the banking sector and in theoretical works on the "good corporate governance of banks." With respect to corporate governance practices, a particularly striking feature of mostly large commercial and investment banks has been the prevalence of remuneration schemes that provide high-powered incentives, not only for executive directors/officers (i.e., members of the management board in a two-tier system), but also for senior managers at lower levels, and even for more junior employees in some functions, in particular the trading and sales function. In turn, at least some theoretical works suggest that good corporate governance of banks requires a somewhat different framework from that for industrial firms. At an even more fundamental level, even the notion of "good corporate governance of banks" is somewhat ambiguous. Some participants in the debate, in particular banking supervisors, use this term in a way that reflects their particular supervisory concerns but deviates from the general understanding. Hence, quite a number of proposals and ideas for further improvements of corporate governance in the banking sector are bank-specific and, at a first glance, do not easily fit in with the general debate on good corporate governance. However, more recently, some elements, such as risk management and compliance, have started to become an important issue in the general corporate governance debate as well. From this perspective, good corporate governance of banks shows the way forward for good corporate governance in general.[1]

Against this backdrop, the rest of this chapter is organized as follows: The next section briefly explores the diverging usage of the term *corporate governance* in the context of banks. The third section identifies previous work on banks' corporate governance and describes the extent to which the recent turbulence on the financial markets has been attributed to deficient corporate governance practices. The fourth section outlines what is special about banks compared to a generic firm, explores the consequences flowing from these particularities in a principal-agent approach, and, in part as a contrast, describes the supervisors' ideas and concepts for the good corporate governance of banks. Against this backdrop, the fifth section presents the results of empirical studies of the (un)importance of banks' corporate governance for the financial crisis and outlines the numerous reforms already implemented or, at least, under way as well as some ideas for even further reforms in this area. Finally, the sixth section offers some concluding remarks.

CONCEPTS OF CORPORATE GOVERNANCE

A generally accepted definition of corporate governance has not yet evolved. Traditional concepts describe corporate governance as a complex set of constraints that shape the ex post bargaining over the quasi rents generated by a firm[2] or as every device, institution, or mechanism that exercises power over decision making within a firm.[3] Put differently, corporate governance deals with the decision making at the level of the board of directors and top management (i.e., the management board in a two-tier system), and the different internal and external mechanisms that ensure that all decisions taken by the directors and top management are in line with the objective(s) of a company and its shareholders, respectively.

The OECD Principles of Corporate Governance, inter alia referred to in the EU Commission's Action Plan on Company Law and Corporate Governance,[4] take a slightly broader view:

> Corporate governance involves a set of relationships between a company's management, its board, its shareholders and other stakeholders. Corporate governance also provides the structure through which the objectives of the company are set, and the means of attaining those objectives and monitoring performance are determined. Good corporate governance should provide proper incentives for the board and management to pursue objectives that are in the interests of the company and its shareholders, and should facilitate effective monitoring.[5]

This definition goes beyond the definitions cited earlier mainly insofar as a company's objective(s) and the mechanism for setting the objective(s) are treated as a corporate governance issue, not as endogenously given. Put succinctly, corporate governance "deals with the ways in which suppliers of finance to corporations assure themselves of getting a return on their investment."[6]

By contrast, a much broader definition describes corporate governance as encompassing the standards for decision making within a company, the duties of board members and officers, the internal structure of the firm (enterprise), and the relationship between the corporation and its shareholders and other stakeholders.[7] Such a concept of corporate governance goes beyond even the OECD's definition in two respects: first by implying that corporate governance also deals with substantive management issues and the pertinent decision making by the board and top management, for example, by requiring them to set up an independent compliance function and a risk management system, and second by dealing with the internal structure of the firm (i.e., with internal structures below the level of the company's board and officers).

This much broader concept is very much in line with the banking supervisors' understanding of corporate governance as embodied in the Basel Committee on Banking Supervision's guidance entitled "Enhancing Corporate Governance for Banking Organisations." The guidance paper states that from:

> a banking industry perspective, corporate governance involves the manner in which the business and affairs of banks are governed by the board of directors and senior management which, *inter alia*, affects how they
>
> - set corporate objectives;
> - operate the bank's business on a day-to-day basis;
> - meet the obligation of accountability to their shareholders and take into account the interests of other recognized stakeholders [including, inter alia, supervisors, governments and depositors];
> - align corporate activities and behavior with the expectation that banks will operate in a safe and sound manner, and in compliance with applicable laws and regulations; and
> - protect the interests of depositors.[8]

THE RISING INTEREST IN BANKS' CORPORATE GOVERNANCE

From the Asian Crisis in 1997 to the Financial Crisis

The particularities of banks' corporate governance first became of some interest during and after the Asian crisis in 1997.[9] From then on, in line with a more general trend, listed banks and even nonlisted institutions worldwide started to publicly emphasize that good corporate governance is of vital concern for the company, and even to adopt individualized corporate governance codices.

More specifically, the Basel Committee on Banking Supervision published the first edition of its aforementioned guideline "Enhancing Corporate Governance for Banking Organisations" in 1999 and, building on the OECD's thoroughly reviewed *Principles of Corporate Governance* of 2004,[10] a revised version of its guideline in 2006.[11] Some national banking supervisors even published rules detailing the corporate governance structures and features required by banks, in particular the Swiss Financial Market Supervisory Authority (FINMA; formerly Swiss Banking Supervisory Authority)[12] and the Banca d'Italia.[13] At the international level, the World Bank Group, as a direct consequence of the experiences during the Asian crisis, has taken up the issue of banks' corporate governance from several angles. The World Bank itself, taking the Basel Committee's guideline as a starting point, developed a corporate governance methodology in order to assess the legal and regulatory framework for banks' corporate governance on a country level. In contrast, the International Finance Corporation (IFC) concentrates on the corporate governance of individual financial institutions because the IFC bases its decision whether to invest in a particular bank partly on an in-depth due diligence of the bank's corporate governance.[14]

Finally, research into banks' corporate governance had picked up even before the onset of the financial crisis, as is evidenced by the publication of an increasing number of empirical studies[15] and theoretical works[16] as well.

Mood Swings in the Financial Crisis

Phase 1: Irrelevance of Banks' Corporate Governance

After the beginning of the financial turbulence in summer 2007, the issue of banks' corporate governance, with the notable exception of remuneration, went out of focus for some time.

To be sure, the Banca d'Italia only published its aforementioned decree[17] in spring 2008 and in mid-2008 Switzerland's UBS moved to modernize its corporate governance structures mainly by introducing a clear separation of the roles and responsibilities between the board of directors and executive management and a strengthening of the oversight role of the board through the operation of its committees.[18]

On the other hand, numerous reports, documents, and statements published in 2008 dealing with the causes and consequences of the financial crisis do not even mention the corporate governance of banks. This holds true, inter alia, for the reports prepared by the (U.S.) President's Working Group on Financial Markets,[19] the Financial Stability Board (FSB; formerly known as FSF),[20] the International Monetary Fund (IMF),[21] the Institute of International Finance (IIF),[22] the G-20 Study Group,[23] the Declaration of the Washington Summit of the G-20 proposing the "Action Plan to Implement Principles for Reform,"[24] and the German Council of Economic Experts.[25] Specifically, the report by the Senior Supervisors Group mentions that in November 2007 the national supervisors belonging to the group met with the senior management of selected banks to elicit their perspective on how well or how poorly key elements of their corporate governance had worked up to that point in time.[26] The respondents could not have reported any more serious problems because subsequently the document does not refer to corporate governance anymore. Arguably an exception to the rule is the report of the CRMPG III with its particular emphasis on the adequate status of key control personnel, in particular on their independence from frontline business units, and on risk monitoring and risk management.[27]

By way of exception, banks' remuneration practices attracted much interest from the outset of the crisis. Even without any hard evidence being available so far, the heavily incentivized, short-term-oriented remuneration structures, together with a fair amount of greed on the part of bankers were seen as a major or even the single most important cause of the financial turbulence. As a consequence, proposals for reform of this area soon abounded at the international as well as at the national level, resulting in the meantime in rather detailed regulation by many banking supervisory authorities.[28]

Phase 2: Banks' Corporate Governance as a Major Cause of the Crisis

During the second year of the financial crisis, the issue of banks' corporate governance began to resurface with a vengeance, starting with the OECD. The OECD Steering Group on Corporate Governance, based on the premise that corporate governance problems of banks are not fundamentally different from those of generic corporations, first commissioned a fact-finding study with respect to four areas of corporate governance (remuneration, risk management, board practices, and exercise of shareholder rights).[29] Based on those findings, the Steering Committee recently published a full report on the key results and main lessons inside and outside of the banking industry, finding, in particular, that there is no immediate call for a revision of the OECD Principles, but a need for a more effective implementation of standards already agreed upon.[30] The G-20, at its London summit in April 2009, acknowledged the importance of the issue as well, albeit somewhat indirectly.[31] At the European level, former EU Commissioner McCreevy declared his commitment to rethink the roles of directors, managers, and shareholders of financial institutions with a view to strengthening the role of nonexecutive directors and shareholders, and to prioritizing long-term shareholder value over short-term bonus payments.[32] And the High-Level Group on Financial Supervision in the EU, chaired by Jacques de Larosière, stated flatly in its report that banks' corporate governance "is one of the most important failures in the present crisis."[33] At the level of EU member states, very similar assessments are voiced in the UK, in particular. The Association of Chartered Certified Accountants (ACCA) "believes that the credit crunch can ... be viewed, in large part, as a failure in corporate governance."[34] For Sir David Walker, charged with an independent review of corporate governance in the UK banking industry by the UK government, the "need is now to bring corporate governance issues to center stage" because serious deficiencies in prudential oversight and financial regulation in the period before the crisis were accompanied by major governance failures within banks.[35] Even the Financial Services Authority (FSA), albeit somewhat reluctantly, probably due to its own track record in this area, states that "poor governance [as] ... only one of many factors contributing to the crisis ... has widely been acknowledged to have been an important one."[36]

Not surprisingly, the changed perception of the interrelationship between the crisis and banks' corporate governance is also reflected in recent empirical studies[37] and theoretical works.[38]

BANKS' CORPORATE GOVERNANCE: THEORY

Differences between Banks and the Ordinary Firm

Banks differ substantially from a generic firm in several important respects. Foremost among the well-known differences is the liquidity-producing function of banks based on a maturity mismatch between the two sides of a bank's balance sheet. More technically, a bank's core business is to accept, voluntarily, a mismatch in the term structure of its assets and its liabilities. As a corollary, the existence of banks depends, crucially, on continuous access to liquidity, be it deposits, short-term funding on the interbank market, funding on secured financing markets, or funding from a central bank as the liquidity provider of last resort. The importance of banks' access to liquidity was forcefully demonstrated in the financial crisis, when all possible sources of liquidity dried up at the same time for all banks in (most) Western countries and central banks had to intervene to prevent a collapse of the banking systems in the countries affected. Hence, for regulators, one of the important lessons of the crisis is to provide for more demanding, prudential regulation pertaining to banks' liquidity risk and its management.[39]

Second, banks are highly leveraged institutions. Banks are compensated for accepting a maturity mismatch by a premium charged to creditors (i.e., a bank's creditors have to pay a higher interest rate than the bank pays for its refinancing). Hence, ceteris paribus, a bank's profit increases directly in proportion with the volume of lending to creditors. The upper bound for an increase in lending is derived from the marginal cost of a bank's refinancing, given that an increase of the bank's leverage will increase its probability of default, and depositors as well as other debt holders will demand a higher risk premium as compensation for the higher risk of insolvency, and from minimum capital requirements provided for by prudential regulation.

Third, banks' balance sheets are notoriously more opaque than those of generic firms (i.e., firms in other sectors of the economy).[40] The quality of bank loans is not readily observable whereas the quality of assets of industrial firms, in particular physical assets such as machinery, plants, etc., is much more easily discernable by third parties. The same holds true for other assets banks invest in, such as securities like Asset-Backed Securities (ABSs), Collateralized Debt Obligations (CDOs), and Credit-Default Swaps (CDSs). In fact, to a large extent, the financial turbulence in the autumn of 2008 was caused by these difficulties. After the collapse of Lehman Brothers, the interbank market virtually crashed even for (very) short-term lending because, all of a sudden, an all-out distrust prevailed among banks about the quality of other banks' assets. Put differently, even banks themselves find it difficult to assess the riskiness of other banks accurately.[41] This hypothesis is not only supported by the recent financial turbulences, but, for example, also by two studies that found that analysts disagree more with respect to the quality of bonds issued by banks than with the quality of bonds issued by other firms.[42] As a response to the problem of banks being arguably more opaque than generic firms, Pillar 3 of the Revised Framework of the Basel Committee on Banking Supervision (Basel II) sets out disclosure requirements covering quantitative and qualitative aspects of overall capital adequacy and capital allocation, as well as risk exposure and assessment, all with a view to promoting market discipline (i.e., better informed monitoring and controlling activities by market participants).[43]

Fourth, banks do a substantial and/or even a major part of their business with other banks. More technically, banks are highly interconnected among themselves. Important elements of the interbank business are, inter alia, activities on the interbank market, the OTC derivates market, and the foreign exchange market. Hence, unlike the situation in other industries, from a bank's perspective, competitors are also important business partners and, hence, pose a major counterparty risk. Moreover, the banking system is prone to contagion: problems at one bank will spread to other banks and systemwide at a very fast rate.

Fifth, in contrast to the typical nonfinancial firm, a bank holding a substantial portfolio of derivatives and securities with embedded options is subject to sharp changes in its risk profile even if the bank does not take new positions. The possibility arises from the fact that complex derivatives often have exposure to risk factors that are extremely sensitive to market conditions and, thus, even incremental changes on the market may effect a drastic change in the value of the derivative.[44]

Sixth, because of the mismatch in the term structure of assets and liabilities banks are subject to creditor runs.[45] Because, in the case of a run, readily available liquidity reserves will be exhausted very rapidly and most of a bank's assets will not be readily liquidated, only the very first creditors to withdraw their money will receive a payout (in time and in full). Because dispersed creditors (i.e., depositors, bondholders, other banks) face a classic prisoner's dilemma, even a solvent bank can become the victim of a collective action problem in the form of a run. Ideally, a run can be started either by (small) depositors, by bondholders, or by other banks in the interbank market. As a practical matter, once a bank runs into financial distress all three groups of creditors will withdraw their money. Still, whereas the run on UK's Northern Rock can be seen more as a "classical" run of (small) depositors, the downfall of Lehman Brothers and the takeover of Merrill Lynch were more the result of an (imminent) run by other banks in the interbank market. Of course, depository insurance can substantially mitigate the danger of bank runs. However, its effectiveness in this respect, crucially, depends on the details of the protection accorded. In particular, not only the maximum amount protected but also the kind of deposits protected can be of pivotal importance. Prior to the events in autumn 2008, most mandatory depository insurance protection schemes worldwide were geared only to protect (small) depositors.[46] The "trust crisis" in the wake of Lehman Brothers' insolvency, however, caused most countries soon to raise the maximum coverage under existing deposit protection schemes and, even more quickly, to establish additional insurance and guarantee schemes that enabled banks to issue state-backed new debt. For example, the EU amended Directive 94/19/EC on deposit-guarantee schemes to the effect that member states will have to raise the existing minimum coverage level of twenty thousand euros to fifty thousand euros by June 30, 2009, and to one hundred thousand euros by December 31, 2010.[47] And in the U.S., the Federal Deposit Insurance Corporation (FDIC) raised the minimum coverage level of one hundred thousand U.S. dollars, temporarily (i.e., through December 31, 2013), to a hefty 250,000 U.S. dollars. Prime examples among the second type of initiatives are the U.S. Temporary Liquidity Program (TLGP) set up by the FDIC, which allowed U.S. banks to issue certain senior unsecured debt guaranteed by the FDIC,[48] and the German program that allows participating German banks to issue new bonds guaranteed by the German SoFFin (*Sonderfonds Finanzmarktstabilisierung*).[49]

Seventh, because of their systemic importance[50] on the one hand and their vulnerability to runs on the other hand, banks are heavily regulated and supervised entities. Basically, banking regulation:

- limits the amount of risk a bank may take, in particular, under Pillar 1 of the Revised Framework of the Basel Committee on Banking Supervision (Basel II) by stipulating risk-adjusted minimum capital requirements (i.e., by linking the required regulatory capital for a bank's assets in a rather sophisticated approach to the adjusted risk weight of the different assets)
- limits a bank's exposure to a single creditor or group of creditors
- addresses the risk from disruptions in the access to sufficient liquidity by setting standards for liquidity management

In addition, as a lesson from the market turmoil, regulators and supervisors have very recently committed themselves to introducing an additional backstop ceiling—similar to, but not identical with, existing U.S. regulations—that would limit a bank's non-risk-adjusted total exposure to an arbitrary multiple of its capital.[51] Such a leverage ratio serves as a safety valve for the weaknesses and shortcomings of risk-weighted requirements, in particular for underestimation of risk. However, in order to prevent some countries' banks from being put at a competitive disadvantage, the accounting rules for measuring the capital base will have to be harmonized at an international level. On an even more fundamental level the leverage ratio concept is the exact opposite of the Basel II philosophy in that a bank's leverage is limited on a non-risk-adjusted basis. This may create additional incentives for banks to seek more risky assets with a higher yield in order to compensate the "losses" due to business restrictions imposed by the leverage ratio ceiling. Hence, the leverage ratio will have to be supported by additional risk-adjusted safeguards, which, in turn, may raise doubts as to the efficiency of the whole concept.

Principal–Agent Analysis

In important respects, the particularities of banks just described impact their corporate governance. For a more detailed analysis of these problems, agency theory provides a suitable framework.[52] After all, corporate governance concerns agency conflicts among different stakeholders, in particular the principal–agent conflict between shareholders and directors/managers and about how to solve possible conflicts among them. Treating the corporation (i.e., banks) as a nexus of explicit or implicit contracts among the different stakeholders acting as agents for each other allows us to identify possible agency conflicts as well as possible solutions to these conflicts.

The following analysis starts with a brief overview of the different types of agents, agency conflicts, and solutions to these conflicts in general before taking up the implications for banks in particular.

Agents, Conflicts, and Solutions

The different stakeholders that may act as an agent in the context of firms are well known:

- shareholders, owning a large stake (i.e., blockowners) or small stakes (i.e., dispersed shareholders)
- directors (i.e., members of the board performing the supervisory function, fruitfully discriminated according to the two mutually nonexclusive qualifications of inside/outside directors and nonindependent/independent directors)

- officers/executive directors or managers/members of the management board (i.e., the persons performing the management function at top level)
- creditors (i.e., employees, bondholders, depositors, commercial creditors, the state, etc.)

Possible agency conflicts fall into three categories, each comprising two major subcategories:

- Type 1: The conflict between shareholders and managers/directors resulting from the separation of ownership and control: (a) managers show a higher degree of risk aversion than diversified shareholders because "pure" managers have most of their wealth tied up in the firm and, hence, are less diversified; (b) managers are underperformers with respect to their managerial tasks because of a preference for empire building, shirking, and/or wasting the company's assets for personal expenses.
- Type 2: The conflict between blockowners and dispersed shareholders: (a) blockowners will prefer to receive payouts from the firms in the form of private benefits instead of dividends because the latter payments would also benefit other (dispersed) shareholders; (b) blockowners very often will show a comparatively higher degree of risk aversion because, typically, a higher percentage of their wealth is tied up in the firm.
- Type 3: The conflict between shareholders and creditors (bondholders/depositors): (a) creditors in general, and bondholders/depositors in particular, are more risk averse than shareholders given that the former are only interested in their claims being paid back in full on time and, hence, in the firm choosing the least risky strategy possible, whereas shareholders are interested in a riskier business strategy with a higher expected return; (b) specifically, shareholders benefit from ex post opportunism on the part of the firm (i.e., from a firm's subsequent shift to a riskier business strategy and/or from a subsequent distribution of company assets to its owner).

Numerous solutions for mitigating these agency conflicts have been identified, as well as possible costs ensuing from each of these mechanisms. Most important and probably best known are the following:

- Type 1 conflicts: (a) Blockholders have a high(er) incentive to monitor management closely whereas, on the other hand, the presence of a blockowner creates or intensifies type 2 agency conflicts; (b) activist shareholders exercise a more active monitoring function, but their incentives for monitoring are either less pronounced than those of blockowners or are detrimental to the company for other reasons (e.g., strike suits); (c) performance-based compensation, in particular equity-based compensation such as stock options and share grants, may effectively align the interest of managers and shareholders, provided that a remuneration scheme achieves the long-term alignment of these interests; (d) takeovers or, more, precisely, the threat of an unfriendly takeover may incentivize management to pursue the goal in shareholder value maximization in order to discourage any attempt at an unfriendly takeover.

- Type 2 conflicts: (a) Independent directors may serve to protect minority interests at the board level, even though such directors, precisely because of their independence, may have less experience with the firm's business and, as a consequence, may cause substantial opportunity costs for the company; (b) minority self-help, either by means of a shareholder agreement with a larger blockowner or, more realistically, by making use of legal remedies provided for by mandatory corporate law.
- Type 3 conflicts: (a) Creditor/bondholder self-help based on pertinent covenants agreed with the company; (b) providing for (financially) disinterested directors (i.e., decoupling directors' remuneration from the stock price development); (c) public intervention and supervision to ensure that a firm takes creditors' interests into proper account.

Agency Conflicts in Banks

The particularities of banks described in the preceding have a substantial impact on the agency conflicts present in banks by changing the incentive structures as well as the spectrum of solutions available for mitigating these conflicts.

1. To begin with, banks hold a portfolio of financial assets (i.e., debt claims and securities) that due to their composition and corresponding risk profile can be altered much faster than the assets of, for example, a car manufacturer, who will make more firm-specific and, hence, less readily marketable investments in production equipment and property.[53] The technique of securitization even allows banks to liquidate easily long-term debt claims (e.g., mortgages and securities) lacking a viable secondary market by transforming them into tradable assets and investing the proceeds in new assets with a very different risk profile. In fact, Citigroup's rapidly growing investment in CDOs following Charles O. Prince's taking office as CEO in 2003[54] can serve as a good example of a bank's ability to rapidly change its risk profile. Many more banks followed the same pattern, in particular UBS[55] and some of the German state-controlled public sector banks (*Landesbanken*), including WestLB, HSH Nordbank, BayernLB, and Landesbank Baden-Württemberg (LBBW).

   Depending on the situation, the management or shareholders will benefit from the greater flexibility in risk shifting. Managers, whose remuneration is (partly) performance based, will find it easier to change the bank's risk profile in order to meet the agreed performance targets. This holds true, in particular, for more short-term performance targets. Shareholders, on the other hand, will find it easier to exploit depositors and other debt holders by an opportunistic (ex post) switch to a riskier business strategy.

Additional factors act to exacerbate both problems even more.

2. Due to the greater opaqueness of banks' balance sheets, incentive contracts with managers will be (even) less effective in aligning the interests of managers and shareholders.[56] The board of directors will find it difficult to observe whether management did actually meet their performance targets and whether this resulted from the shift to a riskier business strategy than expected and anticipated. By the same token, outside monitoring by shareholders, depositors, and other debt holders will be much more difficult and, thus, less effective.
3. If a substantial part of management's total remuneration is equity based in order to align managers and shareholder interests more closely, managers will focus on short-term results. In addition, they will have an excessively low risk aversion because a riskier business strategy will increase the stock price. Specifically, managers have an incentive to increase the bank's leverage, which, in turn, gives an incentive to increase the bank's leverage even more, and so on and so forth.
4. Dispersed shareholders face even stronger incentives for a bank to operate with a high leverage than managers with equity-based remuneration. Prudential regulation stipulating minimum capital requirements acts as an upper bound to such tendencies. From a shareholder's perspective, such regulation has the effect of exacting a higher investment in the bank than they would make otherwise and, hence, acts as an incentive to favor a riskier business strategy as compensation for the higher investment.[57] Admittedly, this effect only holds true if minimum capital requirements are not risk-sensitive (i.e., if they only reflect the nominal value but not the riskiness of the bank's assets). Hence, the risk-based Basel II framework should have eliminated this effect to a large degree.
5. Deposit insurance is often said to weaken the incentives for outsider control[58] and, as a corollary, to cause banks to take on more risk by pursuing a riskier business strategy (e.g., by offering higher interest rates for deposits).

   As regards explicit deposit insurance, however, this effect may well be of only limited importance in practice. Mandatory insurance coverage is often limited to a certain (low) amount. Given a rather low cap, deposit insurance eliminates incentives for control only for small depositors, and, very often, these are nonexperts and would not serve as capable monitors anyway. In addition, the deposit insurer may serve as a substitute for small depositors, provided that the insurance charges paid by banks are risk adjusted and the insurer is provided with sufficient monitoring rights. Moreover, before the intervention of states during the financial crisis,[59] large creditors, and in particular expert monitors, faced undiminished incentives to monitor because deposit insurance protected neither bondholders nor other banks. The upshot, then, is that the distortional impact of mandatory, explicit deposit insurance is mostly relevant for small banks because small depositors will play a, comparatively, much more important role for small banks' refinancing. If, in addition, a bank is also member of a voluntary protection scheme, the incentives will change depending on the scope of a bank's liabilities protected and the amount protected. For example, if—as is at present the case with German cooperative banks and savings banks (*Sparkassen*)—other banks will have to step in to prevent a member bank from becoming insolvent, all depositors and debt holders are covered and their monitoring incentives will be rather small, at best.

The situation is very different with respect to implicit deposit guarantees by central banks, states, or other public entities resulting from the "too big to fail" dilemma. Such implicit guarantees are very often interpreted by market participants as extending to all claims on a bank and, hence, will distort the incentives of all actors (i.e., those of depositors and other debt holders, as well as those of the banks themselves).

6. The market for control functions less well than for other industries, at least within the EU. Whereas the merger market for nonpublicly traded small and medium banks is quite active, for example, in Germany with respect to savings banks and cooperative banks, the situation is different regarding large listed banks and cross-border takeovers in particular. Among the reasons are the higher opaqueness of banks' balance sheets and the potential large-scale loss of human capital (investment bankers).[60] With respect to cross-border takeovers in particular, two additional factors act as additional impediments: the fit and proper requirement for large shareholders, mandated by EU law, and some EU member states' protectionist inclinations,[61] which, in turn, are (partly) due to the large banks' systemic importance for the economy as a whole.
7. To sum up, the particularities of banks described in the preceding act to exacerbate the multiple agency conflicts present within banks and to reduce the effectiveness of some of the mechanisms for mitigating these conflicts. The overall effect is for banks to take on more risk than a generic firm would do.

Consequences

Shareholders' Perspective

From a shareholder's perspective, the holy grail of banks' corporate governance is to check management's short-term orientation without creating incentives for choosing a suboptimal low level of risk. With a view to that goal, remuneration should be structured to include a higher, not a lower, amount of equity compensation (i.e., stock, not stock options), and to require managers to hold such stock on a long-term basis (restricted stock).

The well-known downside of such a remuneration arrangement is that the company and, hence, ultimately the shareholders, in absolute numbers, will have to pay a higher total amount of remuneration. By accepting a higher amount of stock, (less diversified) managers take on an additional firm-specific risk, and they will require compensation in the form of an additional nonvariable cash component: the more stock (options) the company grants, the higher will be the amount of additional nonvariable compensation demanded by managers—an economic logic supported, indeed, by some anecdotal evidence from the banking industry.

Depositors'/Other Debt Holders' Perspective

Depositors and other debt holders are only interested in a bank's ability to pay its debts when they fall due. Consequently, the management remuneration structure preferred by creditors is very different from the one favored by shareholders. If remuneration includes performance-based elements at all, performance criteria should not be volume based (e.g., not on sales volume) and should discourage taking on risk as much as possible. Specifically, compensation should not include any equity or any equity-related element or, at the very least, the fraction of equity-based compensation should be as small as possible.[62]

The presence of large shareholders, and of powerful large shareholders in particular, is an ambiguous mechanism for mitigating any conflicts between depositors/other debt holders and management.[63] On the one hand, large shareholders will typically be more risk averse and have higher incentives for monitoring management. On the other hand, large shareholders will be interested in extracting private benefits, thus reducing the value of their higher monitoring activities. Empowering large shareholders further increases the risk that a blockowner will extract private benefits to the detriment of depositors and other debt holders, even though small shareholders are hurt more by such behavior.

As a corollary, with respect to directors' qualifications, requiring some or even all directors to be independent from large shareholders is ambiguous, too. Whether depositors and other debt holders benefit from the presence of directors that are independent from a large blockowner depends, ceteris paribus, on whether, on balance, the positive effects of a blockowner's more intense monitoring activities are greater than the costs associated with his extraction of private benefits. By contrast, the presence of financially independent directors (i.e., directors whose remuneration is not equity related in any form) is beneficial to depositors and other debt holders because they lack the incentive to exercise their monitoring and controlling functions with a view to stock price development.[64]

A more general mechanism for mitigating the conflict between depositors/other debt holders and shareholders is to expand corporate governance with a view to encompass debt governance. The more sweeping approach is to substitute shareholder supremacy by stakeholder supremacy either by substituting the shareholder-only-oriented goal of value maximization by that of depositor-restrained value maximization, or, slightly less far-reaching, by requiring the (board of) directors—and possibly even officers/executive directors—to take the interests of depositors and other debt holders into account.[65] A somewhat less sweeping approach is to empower the supervisor to appoint one or, to uphold the balance in case of a board subject to codetermination, even two members to the board of directors.[66]

Finally, depositors and other debt holders will favor the existence of a powerful supervisor with far-reaching powers to regulate, to monitor, and to control a bank's activities in the interest of financial stability.

Supervisors' Perspective

Financial Stability Concerns

The supervisors' taking on the issue of banks' corporate governance is sometimes referred to as a financial stability perspective.[67] Indeed, supervisors, in pursuing their primary objective of maintaining and even enhancing the stability of the financial sector, are concerned with the financial soundness of all banks, even the smallest ones. Put differently, supervisors, with a view to financial stability, seek to prevent the collapse of even a single small bank, regardless of whether that event results from criminal or disloyal behavior by directors or top managers, or from the bank taking on too much risk. With respect to the latter, the role of banking supervisors is sometimes said to complement regulations to further limit excessive risk taking.[68] However, their primary responsibility is to enforce existing prudential regulation and, if the legislator vested them with the power to promulgate pertinent binding rules, to promulgate such prudential regulation.

Enhancing Corporate Governance with a View to Fostering Financial Stability

The Basel Committee on Banking Supervision's Guidance

The supervisors' perspective on the issue of banks' corporate governance has been articulated most comprehensively by the Basel Committee on Banking Supervision in its guideline "Enhancing Corporate Governance for Banking Organisations." In a nutshell:

Supervisors (and governments) as stakeholders have a keen interest in sound corporate governance because effective oversight of a bank's business and affairs by its board and senior management contributes to the maintenance of an efficient and cost-effective supervisory system and, in addition, permits the supervisor to place more reliance on the bank's internal processes.[69] In order to assist supervisors and banking organizations worldwide with the implementation of such sound practices, the guidance paper presents eight high-level principles accompanied by more detailed standards and explanatory passages. These guidelines, in principle, apply to all types of banking organizations regardless of their legal form, regardless of the board structure (one/two-tier), regardless of the ownership structure, and regardless of whether they are publicly listed or not, but, on the other hand, should be applied in proportion to the size, complexity, structure, economic significance, and risk profile of the bank and banking group, respectively.[70]

The eight principles, accompanied by some more details, are as follows:

1. *Board members* should be qualified for their positions, have a clear understanding of their role in corporate governance, and be able to exercise sound judgment about the affairs of the bank. Because the board of directors is ultimately responsible for the operations and financial soundness of the bank, the board, inter alia, should understand the bank's risk profile; approve its overall business strategy, including the overall risk policy and risk management procedures; select, monitor, and, where necessary, replace key executives; provide oversight of the senior management; and meet regularly with senior management and internal auditors. In addition, with respect to board structure, the board should include an appropriate number of independent directors (qualified nonexecutive directors), have an adequate collective knowledge of each of the types of material activities of the bank, and establish specialized committees. At a minimum, large banks should have an audit committee, with a majority of its members being independent and having a firm understanding of the role of the audit committee in the bank's risk management and governance.
2. The *board* of directors should approve and oversee the bank's strategic objectives and corporate values that are communicated throughout the banking organization. Setting the professional and ethical "tone at the top" requires the board to ensure that the bank has adequate policies and procedures in place for identifying, avoiding, and, where unavoidable, managing all types of conflicts throughout the bank (e.g., by establishing information barriers and providing for separate reporting lines and internal controls), as well as rules prohibiting or limiting related-party transactions.
3. The *board* of directors should set and enforce clear lines of responsibility and accountability throughout the organization (i.e., on a groupwide basis).
4. The *board* should ensure that there is appropriate oversight by senior management consistent with board policy. In particular, senior

management should establish an effective system of internal controls, including the compliance and legal functions.

5. The *board* and *senior management* should effectively utilize the work conducted by the internal audit function, external auditors, and internal control functions. The bank, inter alia, has to have sound internal control functions, including an effective compliance function, which, in appropriate situations, reports directly to the board of directors, and an internal audit function, which, as sound practice, should report to the board of directors through an audit committee or an equivalent structure.
6. The *board* should ensure that compensation policies and practices are consistent with the bank's corporate culture, long-term objectives and strategy, and control environment. In particular, the remuneration of nonexecutive directors should not be unduly related to the short-term performance of the bank, and performance-related remuneration of executive directors and senior managers should be set, within the scope of general business policy, in such a way that incentives do not overly depend on short-term performance, such as short-term trading gains.
7. The *bank* should be governed in a transparent manner. Timely, accurate, and in-depth disclosure of a broad set of corporate governance–related items should assist market participants and other stakeholders in monitoring the soundness of the bank, thereby facilitating market discipline.
8. The *board* and *senior management* should understand the bank's operational structure, including where the bank operates in jurisdictions, or through structures, that impede transparency (i.e., "know-your-structure"). In particular, the bank's use and/or sale of transparency-impeding structures (i.e., complex financial structures such as special purpose vehicles and corporate trusts), instruments, and products should be governed by appropriate policies established by the board.

Characteristics of the Basel Committee's Approach

The Basel Committee's approach to banks' corporate governance is driven exclusively by supervisors' concerns. The eight principles, discussed elsewhere in more detail,[71] aptly reflect this perspective. To summarize the pertinent aspects:

The board has to take the interests of depositors, not just those of shareholders into account.[72]

The principles focus on the board of directors and, albeit to a much more limited extent, on top management, in particular on executive directors. The role of shareholders and that of the market for corporate control (external governance) is relegated to the sideline. Indeed, supervisors whose focal concern is the soundness of a bank will be primarily interested in the soundness of a bank's business practices, and in particular in a bank having effective risk management, control, compliance, and audit functions. By the very nature of these functions, it is up to the board and top management to take all the actions necessary to realize this goal (i.e., to establish and implement adequate policies, as well as internal structures and mechanisms).

The principles are partly concerned with internal firmwide structures below the board level, (i.e., below the level of the supervisory function and the management function), for example, by requiring an internal control function, including the compliance and legal functions, and an internal audit function.

The principles focus very much on the duties of the board and/or individual board members and, although to a lesser degree, on the duties of top management and top managers. Particularly striking in this respect is an extensive list—albeit not intended to be a "checklist"—detailing activities of the board and its members that the committee has observed to contribute to enhancing the financial soundness of a bank.[73] Indeed, given supervisors' prime concern of keeping a bank safe and sound, corporate governance is about business management practices, in particular management decisions dealing with the structure of the organization and with the mechanism of managing and controlling all kinds of risk. As the Banca d'Italia succinctly puts it: "Banks' organizational and corporate governance structures must not only respond to the corporate interest but also ensure conditions of sound and prudent management, the essential objective of regulation and supervisory controls."[74]

The upshot, then, is that from a supervisor's perspective the purpose of banks' corporate governance is less to safeguard the integrity of the promises made by corporations to investors,[75] but to safeguard the promises made to depositors and other debt holders.

Implementation of the Basel Committee's Approach through EU Law

The implementation of the eight principles detailed in the Basel Committee's guidance paper has been most comprehensive in the EU so far. Largely, the principles are derived from Pillar 2 (entitled: "Supervisory Review Process") of the Basel II framework.[76] The EU has introduced the whole Basel II framework for all banks through the Capital Requirements Directive, which, in turn, comprises the recast Banking Directive[77] and the recast Capital Adequacy Directive.[78] In contrast, the U.S. has opted for a more restrictive implementation. Only some large international banks are required—whereas other qualifying banks may opt in—to use an internal ratings-based approach or other methodologies to calculate risk-based capital requirements for credit risk and advanced measurement approaches to calculate risk-based capital requirements for operational risk.[79]

In addition, the Committee of European Banking Supervisors (CEBS), as part of its Lamfalussy level 3–activities to coordinate member states' application of EU law, has published guidelines containing, inter alia, a list of requirements regarding the internal governance of a bank that, according to CEBS, are to be derived from the recast Banking Directive.[80]

Functional Relationship between Corporate Governance and Banking Regulation/Supervision

Functionally, the relationship between corporate governance and banking regulation/supervision is often seen either as substitutive or as complementary. However, the antithetical characterizations relate to the practical effects from the existence of banking regulation and supervision at the level of banks' boards and top management. For example, the existence of a powerful supervisor may allow shareholders to tolerate a lower level of remuneration and of incentive-based compensation at the level of top management as well as a lower level of remuneration at the level of the board, the latter being a well-documented feature of U.S. banks in the 1990s.[81]

On a theoretical level, the relationship between bank's corporate governance and banking regulation/supervision is more intricate. For a fruitful analysis, one has to distinguish between debt holder governance and equity governance.

With respect to debt holder governance, the supervisor's interest in maintaining the financial stability of individual banks parallels the perspective of a bank's depositors and its other debt holders. Indeed, the banking supervisory authority is often regarded as a functional substitute to debt governance of banks (i.e., the monitoring activities of depositors and other debt holders).[82] Even more to the point, banking regulation/supervision serves as a necessary fill in for deficiencies in depositor/debt holder governance that result from depositor/debt holder monitoring of a bank's risk taking:

- being difficult because of banks' opaqueness
- being a public good encouraging free-riding
- being disincentiviced by the existence of deposit insurance

Hence, with respect to the latter, banking regulation and supervision have to compensate the adverse effects on depositors' and other debt holders' incentives to monitor a bank's risk taking.

The impact of banking regulation/supervision on equity governance is very different because the interests of shareholders and supervisors are not fully aligned. Both shareholders and the supervisor want banks to have high-quality corporate governance mechanisms, structures, and procedures in place. In particular, both are interested that banks design effective internal control systems and observe effective risk management practices, that banks' boards are staffed with members who boast pertinent experience and sufficient time for board work, and that banks' boards function effectively (e.g., by setting up an appropriate committee structure).

However, one fundamental difference remains: the supervisor is interested in the long-term existence of the bank whereas shareholders are interested in high stock returns, and with well-diversified shareholders, the divergence is even more pronounced. As a consequence, with respect to corporate governance standards for substantive issues (i.e., a bank's objective and the criteria for decisions taken by senior management or the board) a supervisor will favor rather different standards. Prudential regulation (e.g., arbitrary limits on leverage and requirements for liquidity) is a case in point. In addition, a supervisor's notion of good corporate governance will be different with respect to corporate governance mechanisms that have an indirect bearing on the substantive standards for decision making by the board or top management. The most important area in this respect is the structure of remuneration systems. Pay arrangements that would be preferred by shareholders are by no means identical to those that are preferred by the supervisor as a socially optimal solution.[83] Tellingly, the restrictions for banks' remuneration structures recently designed or even implemented by regulators/supervisors are much tougher than the incentive structures in place before the crisis, which served the (short-term) interests of shareholders rather well.

BANKS' CORPORATE GOVERNANCE AFTER THE FINANCIAL CRISIS: EVIDENCE AND REFORMS

Evidence

Whether and to what extent corporate governance failures can be considered to be a cause of the financial crisis seems easily answered by a resounding "yes, we matter." Banking supervisors Sir David Walker and Nestor Advisors, to name a few, can point to numerous examples of unsound corporate governance practices before the crisis and undoubtedly, over time, even more anecdotal evidence will come to light. Still, even egregious cases of unsound corporate governance practices do not support the claim that major governance failures were one important or even the most important cause for the crisis, and, more generally, neither will any amount of anecdotal evidence serve as proof. Proof of widespread corporate governance failure at banks can only come from empirical studies.

Systematic empirical studies, so far, do not provide strong support for the corporate governance failure hypothesis. For example, Beltratti and Stulz found no evidence that banks with better governance, when governance is measured with data used in the well-known Corporate Governance Quotient (CGQ score), performed better during the crisis, but found strong evidence that banks with more shareholder-friendly boards performed worse in terms of stock return performance during the crisis and better in 2006 before the crisis.[84] Similarly, Erkens, Hung, and Matos, studying

296 financial firms from thirty countries, arrive at the conclusion that their results obtained are inconsistent with the hypothesis that the firms losses suffered during the financial crisis were the result of lax oversight by boards and investors. Rather, firms with more independent boards and greater institutional ownership were not only more likely to replace their CEOs for poor performance, but also experienced worse stock returns and recognized larger write-downs during the crisis.[85]

Arguably, these results should not serve as an all-out argument against any reforms designed to improve bank's corporate governance even more. Some areas, most notably risk management, indeed warrant substantial improvement, albeit to a widely varying degree with different banks. On the other hand, the deficiencies highlighted, inter alia, by supervisors often relate to faulty management practices, not to the ways shareholders assure themselves of getting a return on their investment. A case in point is the overreliance on value at risk (VaR) or other quantitative risk measures as a means to assess the firm's current risk position. Moreover, even if all banks had followed exemplary corporate governance practices because of the incentives created by states (e.g., prudential regulation), central banks (e.g., very low interest rates), and supervisors in all probability, the crisis would have erupted anyway within a few years.[86] For example, if boards were not involved in setting the risk appetite of a firm it does not follow that level of risk appetite would have been any different from the one chosen by the board if the latter had been involved. Theory suggests that, depending on the situation, executive managers/officers will chose a suboptimal low level of risk just as likely as a suboptimal high level of risk.

Risk Management

Apart from remuneration,[87] risk management has attracted the most interest in the debate on lessons to be learned from the crisis with a view to improve banks' corporate governance.

The list of causes advanced to explain the sometimes almost complete failure of risk management at some banks, at least, is long.[88] Risk management focused more on measuring instead of identifying risks; the riskiness of structured products such as CDOs, ABSs, and others was not fully realized;[89] areas of risk concentration were not properly identified below top management level (silo structures); risk stress tests were performed using past events instead of identifying new risks and looking at possible new scenarios respectively; boards relied too much on quantitative risk models (daily VaR and similar techniques) and failed to see the "fat" risks that should be a board's foremost concern and even failed to understand the firm's current risk position relative to its risk appetite. In particular, a key lesson from the crisis is said to be that the directors on banks' boards should not take false comfort from their regulatory capital ratios.[90]

For the boards to take on a more active role in risk management presupposes not only that (some) members have adequate financial expertise or, at the very least, a background that enables them to learn to understand the tools and concepts for risk management used by the firm quickly. It also presupposes that the board is presented with information on the firm's risk position in a way and to an extent that allows the board to participate in setting the firm's risk appetite and to assess its current total risk position in relation to the goals set.[91]

By contrast, improving the organization of risk management responsibility at the top level seems to be less warranted. Whereas the Walker review strongly recommends the establishment of a stand-alone risk committee (i.e., a risk committee apart from the audit committee that focuses on the current and forward-looking aspects of risk exposure)[92] the existence of such a committee may be advisable but not indispensable.[93] Indeed, the key lesson seems to be for a bank to have a comprehensive and independent[94] risk management function under the direct responsibility of a (totally independent)[95] chief risk officer (CRO) at the highest level of top management (executive director/*Mitglied des Vorstands*)[96] who has direct access (reporting)[97] to the board or, where a risk committee or an audit committee exists, to the committee, and who as an individual, possesses the authority and standing to impress the importance of sound risk management practices throughout the organization, thus vesting the risk function with the necessary authority and organizational powers.

Requirements for Board Members

With respect to the qualification of board members, a relatively higher proportion of independent directors does not affect performance in either way. More surprising is another finding that distinguishes banks' boards from those at other firms. The financial industry expertise of the chairman of the board is positively related to bank performance, and this holds true regardless of whether the chairman is a former chief executive of the bank or has acquired his/her expertise at another institution.[98] This finding has an obvious bearing on whether for financial firms, the independency requirement stipulated by law or enshrined in corporate governance codes should be construed more strictly or, as is increasingly argued, more loosely.[99]

The role and the qualifications of the nonexecutive directors on boards, in particular, are of major concern for the Walker review, in particular given that several banks on both sides of the Atlantic, the strategies of which appear to have been determined by long-entrenched executives with little external input to their internal decision making, seem to have fared materially worse than those where there was opportunity for effective challenge within the boardroom.[100] The review calls for nonexecutive directors to deviate from the "accepted convention" by demonstrating greater readiness to test and challenge the plans, strategies, and ideas presented by the executive board members.[101] With a view to this transition, the review recommends more stringent qualifications for nonexecutive directors, both in terms of knowledge, expertise, and experience, and in character[102]; the ability to allot more time to board activities[103]; and the implementation of procedural safeguards designed to ensure that nonexecutive directors will be able to comply with the higher standards (e.g., the availability of internal support[104]; the existence of a program for induction, training, and development[105]; and a more active role of the FSA).[106]

Remuneration

Whether the industrywide remuneration structures creating high-powered incentives for short-term risk taking are an important or even the major cause for the financial crisis is still open to debate. However, regulators, politicians, and society at large are united in favoring tough new rules on remuneration issues at banks, in particular, and, albeit to somewhat lesser extent, at large and/or listed companies in general.

Empirical Evidence

So far, empirical studies do not offer clear-cut support for the claim that the high-powered short-term remuneration structures were a (major) cause for the crisis. Whereas some early studies found that high executive compensation was prevalent for the riskiest financial institutions,[107] others did not find any correlation between remuneration structures and risk.[108] Studying ninety-eight U.S. banks, Fahlenbrach and Stulz found that banks led by a CEO whose interests were better aligned with the bank's interests had worse stock returns and a worse return on equity (ROE) during the crisis but performed significantly better before the outbreak of the crisis.[109] Even more to the point, they claim that lack of alignment of bank CEO incentives with shareholder interests cannot be blamed for the credit crisis or the performance of banks during that crisis because CEOs did not sell shares ahead of the crisis.[110]

In response to this argument—which, incidentally, reflects a broader consensus among many observers—Bebchuk, Cohen, and Spamann recently showed that the five top executives at Bear Stearns and Lehman Brothers, respectively, derived cash flows from cash bonuses and equity sales during the period 2000–2008 that substantially exceeded the value of the executives' initial holdings at the beginning of the period and, thus, the executives' net payoffs for the period were decidedly positive. Hence, they correctly point out, the large paper losses that the executives suffered when their companies collapsed should not provide a basis for either dismissing or accepting the claim that the prevailing remuneration structures acted as an important cause of the financial crisis. Still more importantly, the top executives' proven inability to foresee the crisis does not rule out the possibility that their decisions were in fact influenced by their heavily incentivized short-term-oriented remuneration packages.[111] But, then, the study by Fahlenbrach and Stulz found that the amount of stock options and cash bonuses granted had no effect on a bank's performance, either in terms of stock returns or in terms of accounting ROE.

Reform Initiatives before and after the G20 Pittsburgh Summit

1. The FSB "Principles of Sound Compensation Practices" of September 25, 2009,[112] prepared by the FSB for the Pittsburgh Summit on September 24–25, 2009, following a request from the G-20, marks a turning point in the effort of numerous countries to limit bankers' pay and, at the same time, serve as a useful point of reference for categorizing the numerous initiatives at the international and national level.

By setting internationally agreed minimum standards, the principles ended any attempts at an international race to the bottom in regulating banks' remuneration practices. Before that, draft regulations published by national regulators were usually watered down before final implementation as a result of severe criticism by interested parties. In particular, this held true for the UK FSA's code of remuneration practices[113] and the FINMA's circular (*Rundschreiben*) on remuneration arrangements,[114] respectively.

By contrast, the Basel Committee on Banking Supervision's recently published assessment methodology for compensation principles and standards,[115] in detailing the principles and rules suggested by the FSA, in part goes even further than the FSB. Similarly, in August 2009, the German Federal Financial Services Supervisory Authority (*Bundesanstalt für Finanzdienstleistungsaufsicht*; BaFin) first published a revised version of its circular "Minimum Requirements for the Risk Management of Credit Institutions,"[116] providing for rather generic rules broadly in line with the FSF "Principles for Sound Compensation Practices" of April 2, 2009,[117] and the CEBS's "High-Level Principles for Remuneration Policies" of April 20, 2009.[118] In December, then, BaFin stipulated much more detailed and stringent requirements in its Circular "Supervisory Requirements for Remuneration Systems at Financial Institutions."[119] Finally, the EU Commission Recommendation on remuneration policies of April 30, 2009,[120] provides for less detailed "rules" than the proposal for a so-called Capital Requirements Directive III (CRD III), which amends Annex V of the Capital Requirements Directive by introducing a new Section 11 with a view to obliging credit institutions and investment firms to have remuneration policies that are consistent with effective risk management.[121]

By way of exception, in the U.S., Title II of the Wall Street and Consumer Protection Act of 2009[122] introduced in Congress in December incorporates the Draft Corporate and Financial Institution Compensation Fairness Act of 2009[123] introduced in Congress in July without making the substantive rules on remuneration at large financial institutions substantially stricter.

2. In addition to these initiatives directly targeting remuneration at large and/or listed banks and, sometimes, at other financial institutions some national legislatures have tightened corporate law provisions on remuneration issues or, at least, are in the process of introducing new rules.[124] For example, the German legislature, referring to the financial crisis and the misincentives from short-term-oriented remuneration structures tightened the criteria for the statutorily mandated Appropriateness (*Angemessenheit*) of management board remuneration enshrined in Sect. 87(1) of the Stock Corporation Act through the Act on the Appropriateness of Management Board Remuneration (*Gesetz zur Angemessenheit der Vorstandsvergütung—VorstAG*)[125] coming into force on August 4, 2009, and, following the regime in place in the UK, extended the power of the general meeting by introducing the possibility of a nonbinding vote on the remuneration system for the executive board (Sect. 120(4) of the Stock Corporation Act). Similarly, the Draft Wall Street and Consumer Protection Act of 2009, with respect to issuers, provides for a nonbinding annual vote of approval on the compensation of executive officers (Sect. 2002) and for the requirement that all members of a compensation committee or, in the absence of such committee, all board members must be independent (i.e., apart from in their capacity as board members must not accept any consulting, advisory, or other compensatory fee from the issuer; Sect. 2003).

Overview of Substantive Issues

As regards substantive issues covered by the numerous initiatives, the following areas should be distinguished:

- field of application
    - type, size, etc., of financial institutions covered
    - persons covered: board members, top executives, individual risk takers, others
- governance structures
    - committee at board level
    - remuneration committee at the top management level
    - "say on pay" by shareholders
- substantive rules on remuneration systems
- disclosure
- prudential regulation

1. Field of application: Some new rules or guidelines target only a particular set of financial institutions, for example, only significant financial institutions (FSB Principles) or financial institutions with assets of more than $1 billion (Sect. 2004 of the Draft Wall Street and Consumer Protection Act of 2009).

In addition, some of the substantive rules target only particular, relevant subsets of the employees at the institutions covered, such as:

- senior executives and other employees whose actions have a material impact in the risk exposure of the firm (FSB Principles; BaFin Circular 22/2009 [BA]) or, in a very similar definition, those categories of staff, including senior management, whose professional activities have a material impact on the risk profile of the said credit institution (Annex V Sect. 11 Point 23 of Directive 2006/48/EC [Banking Directive] as amended by the Proposal for a CRD III—Presidency compromise)
- employees in the risk and compliance function (FSB Principles)

2. Governance structures: A remuneration committee should exist with the power, inter alia, to oversee the compensation systems' design and operation (FSB Principles). Alternatively, given the particularities of the two-tier system, the supervisory board should be responsible for the remuneration system of the management board members whereas the management board should design the remuneration system for lower-level employees, whereas a remuneration committee composed of top executives and employees from different functions (e.g., the compliance function) should supervise such a system (BaFin Circular 22/2009 [BA]).

In addition, as already mentioned, corporate law sometimes provides for a voluntary or even mandatory vote on the compensation of top executive/management board members (UK, Germany, U.S.).[126]

3. Substantive rules on remuneration systems target staff whose professional activities have a material impact on the risk exposure of the firm and who also have a risk and compliance function.

With respect to the first group, the overarching goal of all substantive rules is to foster compensation practices that reduce employees' incentives to take excessive risk. Well-known mechanisms to achieve this goal include the linking of remuneration to levels of residual risk and the calculation of bonuses based on long-term performance through the choice of appropriate performance measures (risk adjustment, time horizon), deferred payout of variable compensation, malus components/clawback provisions, payout of a substantial portion (> 50 percent) of the variable compensation in shares or share-linked instruments, and the prohibition of guaranteeing bonuses for more than one year, etc. (e.g., Basel Committee[127]; Annex V Sect. 11 Point 23 of Directive 2006/48/EC [Banking Directive] as amended by the Proposal for a CRD III—Presidency compromise).

For employees in the risk and compliance function remuneration should be independent of other business areas and, as a corollary, performance-based remuneration should be based solely on the achievement of the objectives of their functions (FSB Principles; Annex V Sect. 11 Point 23[da] of Directive 2006/48/EC [Banking Directive] as amended by the Proposal for a CRD III—Presidency compromise).

4. Disclosure: An annual report on compensation is to be mandated including, inter alia, information on the decision-making process, with details on the remuneration committee, the most important design characteristics of the compensation system, and aggregate quantitative information on compensation (FSB Principles; BaFin Circular 22/2009 [BA]; Annex 12, Part 2, Point 15 of Directive 2006/48/EC [Banking Directive] as amended by the Proposal for a CRD III—Presidency compromise).
5. Prudential Oversight: Financial institutions have to be obliged to have remuneration policies and practices that are consistent with and promote sound and effective risk management (Art. 22[1] Directive 2006/48/EC [Banking Directive] as amended by the Proposal for a CRD III).

Supervisors should be empowered to take measures to address problems arising from ill-designed or ill-operated remuneration systems, either by requiring the firm to make appropriate changes with regard to its remuneration system ("qualitative requirement") and/or by requiring the firm to hold additional own funds against the operational risk ("quantitative requirement") (Art. 54[2] Directive 2006/48/EC [Banking Directive] as amended by the Proposal for a CRD III—Presidency compromise). In all probability, supervisors will prefer the first approach. Within the risk-based Basel II framework requiring a bank to hold additional own funds presupposes the possibility of somehow quantifying a firm's risks due to a given remuneration system (i.e., the probability and the amount of unexpected losses the firm will suffer because of the incentives created by a particular remuneration structure). Given the emerging empirical evidence, such a calculation would amount to a formidable challenge, at best.

Dampening Banks' Risk Appetite by Corporate Law Mechanisms?

Requiring a Bank to Act in the Interest of Depositors/Other Debt Holders, Too

From a corporate law perspective, two strategies primarily exist for requiring a bank to act in the interest of depositors/other debt holders: incorporate these interests into a bank's corporate objective by mandatory law or stipulate a fiduciary duty of directors and officers to depositors, and even to other debt holders.

Regarding the first approach, one may want to point to the blurred line between equity and debt resulting from the existence of hybrid debt (i.e., subordinated debt or even loss-taking debt). Moreover, banks are of systemic importance and perform a general interest function. Finally, the acute information asymmetry and complexity present in banks is only to be overcome by explicitly taking the interests of other stakeholders into account as well. However, the counterarguments should prevail.[128] First, hybrid debt can protect its interest through self-help, in particular by requiring adequate contractual protection in the form of covenants. Second, firms outside of the banking sector can be of systemic importance as well, whereas small and medium-size banks cannot, by virtue of their size, carry such risk. Put differently, the systemic importance criterion fails to clearly distinguish banks from other firms and to explain why (all) banks should be subject to a unique legal regime. Third, and most important, stakeholder instead of shareholder supremacy does not provide for a higher degree of depositor protection, at least not in practice. German banks are arguably subject to a stakeholder regime.[129] Nevertheless, anecdotal evidence from the current financial crisis strongly suggests that, all in all, German listed banks did not fare any better than their competitors in the UK or even Switzerland.[130] The theoretical argument for preferring a monistic corporate goal is very well known: stakeholder supremacy allows directors/officers an unbridled pursuit of their own interests in the guise of balancing the interests of different stakeholders.

The second strategy is to assert that directors and officers also have a fiduciary duty towards depositors,[131] and to require that banks' (executive) directors pursue a less risky business strategy than their counterparts at other firms.[132] Such an approach begs the question why corporate law should intervene over and above the standards for an acceptable level of risk taking established by prudential regulation. In response, one may want to point out that regulators are less suited to the task of setting pertinent standards because of informational asymmetries, time lags in processing the information received, and acting on it because of, inter alia, limited resources, etc.[133] Indeed, "a key lesson from the recent crisis is that directors of banks' boards should not take false comfort from their regulatory capital ratios."[134] Still, defining the (lower) level of risk taking that is still acceptable from the point of view of depositors and other debt holders will always be an arbitrary decision for which no ready-made yardstick exists. Moreover, if a deposit insurance scheme does exist, at best, a fiduciary duty should extend to the insurer but not to depositors.

Applying a Higher Standard of Care to Directors/Officers of Banks

The alternative to requiring directors and officers to act in the interest of depositors, too, is to subject their actions to a higher standard of care than would apply in a generic firm. The most sweeping approach is not to apply the business judgment rule or its national equivalents (e.g., Sect. 93[1][2] German Stock Corporation Act). A somewhat less intrusive measure would be an expanded application of the bad faith exception of the business judgment rule and, if a director or officer failed to take any action because of a lack of adequate information or a deficient reporting system, to concentrate on the lack of a business decision (business judgment rule not applicable) instead of on the deficiencies in the information-gathering process (business judgment rule applicable).

However, even in the U.S., with the notable exception of New York,[135] most courts nowadays apply the business judgment rule to directors and officers of banks in the same way as to those of other corporations. The arguments advanced in favor of stricter standards—the relationship of directors and officers with depositors is close to a fiduciary relationship, and because of deposit insurance, directors and officers put taxpayers' money on the line[136]—cannot refute the main argument in favor of applying the business judgment rule in full: banks are entrepreneurial risk takers just like any generic corporation, and the objective of the business judgment rule is precisely to reflect the particular problems that face a director or officer taking an entrepreneurial decision under risk.

CONCLUDING REMARKS

Banks' corporate governance differs from that of generic firms. Given banks' high leverage, debt holders, such as depositors and bondholders, as well as a bank's management will prefer the firm to take on substantially less risk than diversified shareholders. However, deposit insurance and prudential regulation, although aimed at compensating for deficits in the monitoring and control of banks, weaken debt holder monitoring and control. Highly incentive-based remuneration can neutralize management's aversion to take on more risk, in particular if a substantial part is in the form of short-term cash bonuses.

Banking regulators'/supervisors' interest in maintaining financial stability parallels the interest of debt holders and, hence, the monitoring and controlling activities of supervisors act as a substitute for poor debt holder monitoring and control. It follows that, with respect to banks' corporate governance, their activities will affect shareholders and debt holders unevenly. Both groups will benefit from improvements in corporate governance mechanisms, structures, and procedural standards (i.e., from rules designed to improve internal control systems and risk management practices, as well as the expertise of board members and the board structure). In contrast, shareholders will benefit less from substantive rules on decision making (i.e., from rules that prescribe financial-stability-oriented decision making). This also holds true with respect to mechanisms, etc., that serve to induce a bank's management to make decisions that are in line with the supervisor's financial stability interests. Banking regulations prescribing substantive standards for remuneration systems are of particular relevance in this respect.

Against this backdrop, banks' corporate governance should not provide a generalized way forward for corporate governance. In particular, whereas advances with respect to risk management practices and internal controls may serve as a model for firms of similar size and complexity outside the financial sector, the shortcomings of bank corporate governance does not warrant public intervention in generic firms through either setting standards or prescribing even detailed rules for the structure and substantive contents of remuneration systems.[137]

NOTES

1. Cf. the position of the OECD Steering Group on Corporate Governance (notes 29–30).
2. Luigi Zingales, "Corporate Governance," in *The New Palgrave—Dictionary of Economics*, ed. Steven N. Durlauf and Lawrence E. Blume, 250 (Basingstoke: Macmillan, 2008).
3. Jonathan R. Macey, *Corporate Governance* (Princeton, NJ: Princeton University Press, 2008), 2.
4. See Communication from the Commission to the Council and the European Parliament, "Modernising Company Law and Enhancing Corporate Governance in the EU" (COM(2003)284), 10 n. 10, http://ec.europa.eu/internal_market/company/modern/index_en.htm.
5. OECD, *Principles of Corporate Governance* (Paris: OECD, 2004), 11. Also available online at www.oecd.org/daf/corporateaffairs/principles/text.
6. Andrei Shleifer and Robert W. Vishny, "A Survey of Corporate Governance," *Journal of Finance* 52 (1997): 737.
7. See Stefan Grundmann and Peter O. Mülbert, "Corporate Governance: European Perspectives," *International and Comparative Corporate Law Journal* 2 (2000): 415–422.
8. Basel Committee on Banking Supervision, "Enhancing Corporate Governance for Banking Organisations" (Basel: BIS, 2006), 4 n. 10, http://www.bis.org/publ/bcbs122.htm. See Peter O. Mülbert, "Bankenaufsicht und Corporate Governance—Neue Organisationsanforderungen im Finanzdienstleistungsbereich," *BKR (Zeitschrift für Bank- und Kapitalmarktrecht)* 6 (2006): 349–360; Jan-Velten Große and Karl-Heinz Boos, "2005—ein Fortschritt bei den Corporate Governance-Regeln?" *WM (Zeitschrift für Wirtschafts- und Bankrecht)* 60 (2006): 1177–1183; Klaus J. Hopt, "Corporate Governance von Banken—Überlegungen zu den Grundsätzen des Basler Ausschusses für Bankenaufsicht vom Februar 2006," in *Entwicklungslinien im Bank- und Kapitalmarktrecht—Festschrift für Gerd Nobbe*, ed. Mathias Habersack et al., 853–882 (Cologne: RWS Verlag, 2009).
9. See, e.g., Simon Johnson et al., "Corporate Governance in the Asian Financial Crisis," *Journal of Financial Economics* 58 (2000): 141–186.
10. OECD, *Principles of Corporate Governance.*
11. Basel Committee, "Enhancing Corporate Governance," 4 n. 10.
12. Eidgenössische Bankenkommission, "Überwachung und interne Kontrolle," EBK-RS 06/06 (2006), http://www.finma.ch/archiv/ebk/d/regulier/rundsch/

index.html. See Jean-Baptiste Zufferey, "Private Banking Governance," *Zeitschrift für Schweizerisches Recht* 126, no. 1 (2007): 235–257.

13. Banca d'Italia, "Supervisory Provisions Concerning Banks' Organization and Corporate Governance" (Decree of March 4, 2008), http://www.bancaditalia.it/vigilanza/banche/normativa/disposizioni/provv. See Renzo Costi and Francesco Vella, "Banche governo societario e funzioni di vigilanza," *Quaderni di Ricerca Giuridica* 62 (2008): 8–38, http://www.bancaditalia.it/pubblicazioni/quarigi/qrg62/qrg_62.
14. For more information see IFC World Bank, "Corporate Governance Financial Institution," http://www.ifc.org/ifcext/corporategovernance.nsf/Content/CGTools_FinancialInstitutions.
15. See, inter alia, Kose John and Yiming Qian, "Incentive Features in CEO Compensation in the Banking Industry," *FRBNY Economic Policy Review* 9 (2003): 109–121; Renee B. Adams and Hamid Mehran, "Is Corporate Governance Different for Bank Holding Companies?" *FRBNY Economic Policy Review* 9 (2003): 123–142; Kenneth R. Spong and Richard J. Sullivan, "Corporate Governance and Bank Performance" (SSRN Working Paper, Federal Reserve Bank of Kansas City, August 31, 2007), http://ssrn.com/abstract=1011068; Eduardus Tandelilin, Hermeindito Kaaro, Putu Anom Mahadwartha, and Supriyatna, "Corporate Governance, Risk Management, and Bank Performance: Does Type of Ownership Matter?" (EADN Working Paper no. 34, 2007), http://www.eadn.org/eduardus.pdf; Luc Laeven and Ross Levine, "Bank Governance, Regulation, and Risk Taking" (SSRN Working Paper, 2008), http://ssrn.com/abstract=1142967; Pablo de Andres Alonso and Eleuterio Vallelado Gonzalez, "Corporate Governance in Banking: The Role of the Board of Directors," *Journal of Banking and Finance* 32 (2008): 2570–2580.
16. See, inter alia, Stephen Prowse, "The Corporate Governance System in Banking: What Do We Know?" *Banca del Lavoro Quarterly Review* (March 1997): 11–40; Penny Ciancanelli and José A. Reyes-Gonzalez, "Corporate Governance in Banking: A Conceptual Framework" (SSRN Working Paper, Department of Accounting and Finance, University of Strathclyde, Glasgow, 2000), http://ssrn.com/abstract=253714; Jonathan R. Macey and Maureen O'Hara, "The Corporate Governance of Banks," *FRBNY Economic Policy Review* 9 (2003): 91–107; Ross Levine, "The Corporate Governance of Banks: A Concise Discussion of Concepts and Evidence" (World Bank Policy Research Working Paper no. 3404, 2004), http://www-wds.worldbank.org; Johan Devriese, Mathias Dewatripont, Dirk Heremans, and Grégory Nguyen, "Corporate Governance, Regulation and Supervision of Banks," in *Financial Stability Review 2004*, ed. National Bank of Belgium, 95–120 (Brussels: National Bank of Belgium, 2004), http://nbb.be/pub/06_00_00_00_00/06_03_00_00_00/06_03_02_00_00/FSR_20040602.htm?l=en; Heinz Christian Hafke, "Anmerkungen zur Corporate Governance in der Kreditwirtschaft," in *Festschrift für Walther Hadding*, ed. Franz Häuser, Horst Hammen, Joachim Hennrichs, Anja Steinbeck, Ulf R. Siebel, and Reinhard Welter, 863–874 (Berlin: de Gruyter, 2004); Peter Nobel, "Corporate Governance im Bankbereich: Rechtliche Grundlagen und Compliance," in *Liber Amicorum Guy Horsmans*, ed. Bruylant, 819–842 (Brussels: Bruylant, 2004); Andy Mullineux, "The Corporate Governance of Banks," *Journal of Financial Regulation and Compliance* 14 (2006): 375–382; Kern Alexander, "UK Corporate Governance and Banking Regulation: The Regulators Role as Stakeholder," *Stetson Law Review* 33 (2004): 991–1034; Kern Alexander, "Corporate Governance and Banks: The Role of Regulation in Reducing the Principal–Agent Problem," *Journal of Banking Regulation* 7

(2006): 17–40; Kern Alexander, Rahul Dhumale, and John Eatwell, *Global Governance of Financial Systems* (Oxford: Oxford University Press, 2006), 239–250; Zufferey, "Private Banking Governance," 235–257; Mülbert, "Bankenaufsichtsrecht und Corporate Governance," 349–360; Große and Boos, "2005—ein Fortschritt bei den Corporate Governance-Regeln?"; Andrea Polo, "Corporate Governance of Banks: The Current State of the Debate" (SSRN Working Paper, Said Business School, University of Oxford, 2007), http://ssrn.com/abstract=958796; Dirk Heremans, "Corporate Governance Issue for Banks: A Financial Stability Perspective" (SSRN Working Paper, Center for Economic Studies, Catholic University of Leuven, 2007), http://ssrn.com/abstract=1024693; Birgit Sauerzopf, "Corporate Governance and Credit Institutions," in *Financial Stability Report No. 16*, ed. Oesterreichische Nationalbank, 135–148 (Vienna: Oesterreichische Nationalbank, 2008), http://www.oenb.at/en/presse_pub/period_pub/finanzmarkt/finanzmarktstabilita/financial_stability_report.jsp; Vasile Cocris and Maria-Cristina Ungureanu, "Why Are Banks Special? An Approach from the Corporate Governance Perspective" (Scientific Annals—Al.I.Cuza University of Iasi, Economics Series, 2007), http://ssrn.com/abstract=1090291; Costi and Vella, "Banche governo societario," 8–38; Maria-Cristina Ungureanu, "Banks: Regulation and Corporate Governance Framework," *Journal of Ownership and Control* 5 (2008): 449–458; Hopt, "Corporate Governance von Banken."

17. See note 13.
18. See UBS, investor release of July 1, 2008, http://www.ubs.com/1/e/investors/releases?newsId=144611.
19. The President's Working Group on Financial Markets, "Policy Statement on Financial Markets," March 2008, http://www.ustreas.gov/press/releases/reports/pwgpolicystatemktturmoil_03122008.pdf.
20. Financial Stability Forum, "Report of the Financial Stability Forum on Enhancing Market and Institutional Resilience," April 7, 2008, http://www.financialstabilityboard.org/list/fsb_publications/page_3.htm.
21. IMF, "The Recent Financial Turmoil—Initial Assessment, Policy Lessons, and Implications for Fund Surveillance," April 9, 2008, http://www.imf.org/external/np/pp/eng/2008/040908.pdf.
22. IIF, "Final Report of the IIF Committee on Market Best Practices: Principles of Conduct and Best Practices Recommendations," July 2008, http://www.iif.com/download.php?id=Osk8Cwl08yw=.
23. G-20 Study Group, "Report on Global Credit Market Disruptions," October 2008, http://www.g20.org/pub_further_pubs.aspx.
24. G-20 Declaration of the Summit in Financial Markets and the World Economy, November 15, 2008, http://www.g20.org/pub_communiques.aspx.
25. Sachverständigenrat zur Begutachtung der gesamtwirtschaftlichen Entwicklung, *Die Finanzkrise meistern—Wachstumskräfte stärken, Jahresgutachten 2008/09* (Wiesbaden: 2008), 116–191. Also available online at http://www.sachverstaendigenrat-wirtschaft.de/gutacht/ga-content.php?gaid=53.
26. Senior Supervisors Group, "Observations on Risk Management Practices during the Recent Market Turbulences," March 6, 2008, http://www.financialstabilityboard.org/list/fsb_publications/page_3.htm.
27. Counterparty Risk Management Policy Group III, "Containing Systemic Risk: The Road to Reform," August 6, 2008, 9–12, 71–74, 77–101, http://www.crmpolicygroup.org/.
28. For more detail see sections Risk Management and Requirements for Board Members under Bank's Corporate Governance After the Financial Crisis: Evidence and Reforms.

29. See Grant Kirkpatrick, "The Corporate Governance Lessons from the Financial Crisis," *Financial Market Trends* (2009): 1–30. Also available online at http://www.oecd.org/document/48/0,3343,en_2649_34813_42192368_1_1_1_1,00.html.
30. OECD, "Corporate Governance and the Financial Crisis: Key Findings and Main Messages," June 2009, 7, http://www.oecd.org/document/48/0,3343,en_2649_34813_42192368_1_1_1_1,00.html. As to a follow-up report, see OECD, "Corporate Governance and the Financial Crisis: Conclusions and Emerging Good Practices to Enhance Implementation of the Principles," February 24, 2010, http://www.oecd.org/document/48/0,3343,en_2649_34813_42192368_1_1_1_1,00.html.
31. G-20 Working Group 1, "Enhancing Sound Regulation and Strengthening Transparency," March 25, 2009, http://www.internationalepolitik.de/ip/dossiers/g20/enhancing-sound-regulation-and-strengthening-transparency.html.
32. Charlie McCreevy, "Address to the Association of European Journalist," December 8, 2008, http://ec.europa.eu/ireland/press_office/speeches-press_releases/mccreevy-aej-speech_en.htm.
33. "Report of the High-Level Group on Financial Supervision in the EU, February 2009," no. 110, http://ec.europa.eu/internal_market/finances/committees/index_en.htm#delarosierereport.
34. ACCA, "Corporate Governance and the Credit Crunch," November 2008, 4, http://www.accaglobal.com/economy/analysis/acca.
35. David Walker, "A Review of Corporate Governance in UK Banks and other Financial Industry Entities—Final Recommendations," November 26, 2009, 9, http://www.hm-treasury.gov.uk/walker_review_information.htm.
36. FSA, "Effective Corporate Governance" (Consultation Paper 10/3, January 2010), http://www.fsa.gov.uk/pubs/cp/cp103.pdf.
37. Nestor Advisors, *Banks Boards and the Financial Crisis* (London: Nestor Advisors, 2009); Renee B. Adams, "Governance and the Financial Crisis" (ECGI Finance Working Paper no. 248/2009, April 2009), http://ssrn.com/abstract=1398583.
38. Peter O. Mülbert, "Corporate Governance von Banken," *ZHR (Zeitschrift für das gesamte Handels- und Wirtschaftsrecht)* 173 (2009): 1–11; Gottfried Wohlmannstetter, "Corporate Governance von Banken," in *Handbuch Corporate Governance*, ed. Peter Hommelhoff, Klaus J. Hopt, and Axel von Werder, 779–804 (Cologne: Otto Schmidt, 2009); cf. Eddy Wymeersch, "Corporate Governance and Financial Stability" (Financial Law Institute Working Paper 2008–11, Ghent University, October 2008), http://ssrn.com/abstract=1288631.
39. See Basel Committee on Banking Supervision, *Principles for Sound Liquidity Risk Management and Supervision* (Basel: BIS, 2008), http://www.bis.org/publ/bcbs144.htm; Basel Committee on Banking Supervision, "International Framework for Liquidity Risk Measurement, Standards and Monitoring" (consultative document, December 2009), http://www.bis.org/publ/bcbs165.htm. At the level of the EU, see the directive amending Directives 2006/48/EC and 2006/49/EC as regards banks affiliated to central institutions, certain own fund items, large exposures, supervisory arrangements, and crisis management, *OJ* 2009 L 302/07 (known as Capital Requirements Directive [CRD] II), providing for changes to Annexes V and XI of the original CRD; CEBS, "Consultation Paper on Liquidity Buffers & Survival Periods" (Consultation Paper 28, July 2009), www.c-ebs.org/Publications/Consultation-Papers/All-consultations/CP21–CP30/CP28.aspx.
40. Succinctly developed by Mullineux, "Corporate Governance of Banks," 377–378. For a contrary assessment based on bank stocks' trading behavior, see

Mark J. Flannery, Simon H. Kwan, and M. Nimalendran, "Market Evidence on the Opaqueness of Banking Firms' Assets," *Journal of Financial Economics* 51 (2004): 419–460; for further references, see Bhanu Balasubramanian and Ken B. Cyree, "Market Monitoring of Banks: Do Short Sellers Monitor Banks?" (SSRN Working Paper, Emporia State University, Emporia, Kansas, January 2008), 7–8, http://ssrn.com/abstract=1089865.

41. But see Craig H. Furfine, "Banks as Monitors of other Banks: Evidence from the Overnight Federal Funds Market," *Journal of Business* 74 (2001): 54. The price of a federal funds loan reflects, in part, the credit risk of the borrowing institution.
42. Donald P. Morgan, "Rating Banks: Risk and Uncertainty in an Opaque Industry," *American Economic Review* 92 (2002): 874–888; Giuliano Iannotta, "Testing for Opaqueness in the European Banking Industry: Evidence from Bond Credit Ratings" (SDA Bocconi Working Paper no. 122/04, June 2004), http://ssrn.com/abstract=570483.
43. Basel Committee on Banking Supervision, *International Convergence of Capital Measurement and Capital Standards: A Revised Framework*, updated November 2005 (Basel: BIS, 2005), 184–200 nn. 808–825, http://www.bis.org/publ/bcbs118.htm.
44. See, e.g., Rene Stulz, "Risk Management Failures: What Are They and When Do They Happen?" *Journal of Applied Corporate Finance* 20, no. 4 (2008): 39–48. Also available at http://ssrn.com/abstract=1317102.
45. See, e.g., Macey and O'Hara, "Corporate Governance of Banks," 97.
46. Voluntary schemes, i.e., schemes set up by banks on a voluntary basis are often different. For example, in Germany, each of the three pillars of the German banking sector—private banks, cooperative banks, and public sector banks—has created an additional scheme on a voluntary basis. Cooperative banks are protected as such by the other members of the scheme, i.e., a cooperative bank will not become insolvent, and the same holds basically true for savings banks (*Sparkassen*) whereas each depositor of a private bank is protected to a maximum of 30 percent of the liable capital of said bank; as to more details, see Ute Brunner-Reumann, "Deposit Protection and Investor Compensation," in *Banking Regulation in Germany*, ed. Peter Scherer and Sven Zeller, 209–225 (Frankfurt: German Law Publishers, 2009). However, it remains to be seen whether the EU Commission will intervene against those German voluntary protection schemes that protect the bank as such on the grounds of a violation of EU competition rules.
47. Directive 2009/13/EC amending Directive 94/19/EC on deposit-guarantee schemes as regards the coverage level and the payout delay, *Official Journal* 2009 L 68/3.
48. For details, see Federal Deposit Insurance Corporation, "Temporary Liquidity Guarantee Program," http://www.fdic.gov/regulations/resources/TLGP/index.html.
49. For details, see Bundesanstalt für Finanzmarktstabilisierung, "Leistungen—Guarantien," http://www.soffin.de/leistungen_garantien.php?sub=3.
50. Systemic importance (risk) is not a unique characteristic of banks although large firms in other sectors of the economy are less likely to pose a systemic risk; see Devriese et al., "Corporate Governance," 98. With respect to the insurance sector the (U.S.) "monoliners," e.g., FSA, AMBAC, MBIA et al., and AIG may serve as prime examples of systemically important companies. Whether (large) insurance firms are of systemic importance in general is a different question. For an answer mostly to the negative—only noncore activities of insurers could have the potential for systemic relevance—see Geneva Association, "Systemic Risk in Insurance—An Analysis of Insurance and Financial Stability"(March 2010), 31–63, http://www.genevaassociation.org.

51. For more details, see Basel Committee on Banking Supervision, "Strengthening the Resilience of the Banking Sector," (consultative document, December 2009), no. 202–238, http://www.bis.org/publ/bcbs164.htm. For a rather critical assessment of an additional non-risk-adjusted leverage ratio, see, e.g., Bundesverband deutscher Banken, "Positionspapier des Bankenverbandes zu Maßnahmen für eine angemessene Ausstattung der Eigenkapitalvorschriften" (July 15, 2009), 5–8, http://www.bankenverband.de/bundesverband-deutscher-banken/presse/presse-informationen/basel-ii-nicht-in-frage-stellen-aber-anpassen.
52. Critical, however; see Ciancanelli and Reyes-Gonzalez, "Corporate Governance in Banking."
53. This situation is to be distinguished from even sharper involuntary changes in a bank's risk profile that result from changes in the value of its portfolio of derivatives and securities with embedded options. See note 44 and accompanying text.
54. See Eric Dash and Julie Creswell, "Citigroup Saw No Red Flags Even as It Made Bolder Bets," *New York Times*, November 23, 2008. Also available online at http://www.nytimes.com/2008/11/23/business/23citi.html.
55. UBS, "Shareholder Report on UBS's Write-Downs," April 18, 2008, 12–16, http://www.ubs.com/1/g/investors/releases.html?newsId=140340.
56. Levine, "Corporate Governance of Banks," 7–8.
57. Laeven and Levine, "Bank Governance, Regulation, and Risk Taking," 15.
58. See, e.g., Levine, "Corporate Governance of Banks," 10–11; Macey and O'Hara, "Corporate Governance of Banks," 98–99; Devriese et al., "Corporate Governance," 98.
59. See notes 47–49 and accompanying text.
60. For additional reasons from a U.S. perspective, see Adams and Mehran, "Is Corporate Governance Different?" 126.
61. Banca d'Italia's handling of attempted cross-border acquisitions of Italian banks even prompted the EU to adopt a Directive 2007/44/EC of the European Parliament and of the Council of September 5, 2007, amending Council Directive 92/49/EEC and Directives 2002/83/EC, 2004/39/EC, 2005/68/EC, and 2006/48/EC as regards procedural rules and evaluation criteria for the prudential assessment of acquisitions and increase of holdings in the financial sector; see *Official Journal* 2007 L 247/1.
62. See, e.g., John and Qian, "Incentive Features," 110; cf. from a banking stability perspective, Devriese et al., "Corporate Governance," 100.
63. Cf. from a banking stability perspective, Devriese et al., "Corporate Governance," 100.
64. Cf. Heremans, "Corporate Governance Issue for Banks," 19; cf. from a banking stability perspective, Devriese et al., "Corporate Governance," 106.
65. In favor of the latter approach, see Macey and O'Hara, "Corporate Governance of Banks," 102–103; Mullineux, "Corporate Governance of Banks," 375; cf. from a banking stability perspective, note 82 and accompanying text.
66. See Wohlmannstetter, "Corporate Governance von Banken," 795–796.
67. See, e.g., Devriese et al., "Corporate Governance," 95.
68. Ibid., 99.
69. Basel Committee on Banking Supervision, "Enhancing Corporate Governance," 4 n. 11.
70. Ibid., 5 n. 14 et seq., 2 nn. 3, 5. With regard to fundamental issues of corporate governance that are specific to listed companies, such as effective shareholder rights, the guidance paper refers to the OECD *Principles of Corporate Governance* (see ibid., 2 n. 5).
71. Mülbert, "Bankenaufsichtsrecht und Corporate Governance," 354–360; Hopt, "Corporate Governance von Banken," 860–880.

72. Basel Committee on Banking Supervision, "Enhancing Corporate Governance," 9 n. 25, 19 n. 59; Devriese et al., "Corporate Governance," 107.
73. Basel Committee on Banking Supervision, "Enhancing Corporate Governance," 6 n. 17.
74. Banca d'Italia, "Supervisory Provisions," 1.
75. See Macey, *Corporate Governance*, 2.
76. Basel Committee on Banking Supervision, *International Convergence*, 162–183 nn. 719–807 .
77. Directive 2006/48/EC of the European Parliament and of the Council of June 14, 2006, relating to the taking up and pursuit of the business of credit institutions (recast); see *Official Journal* 2006 L 177/1.
78. Directive 2006/49/EC of the European Parliament and of the Council of June 14, 2006, on the capital adequacy of investment firms and credit institutions (recast); see *Official Journal* 2006 L 177/201.
79. As to the U.S. implementation of the Basel II advanced approaches framework, see Federal Register, December 7, 2007, vol. 72, no. 235: final rule and supplementary information by the Office of the Comptroller of the Currency (OCC), the Board of Governors of the Federal Reserve System (Board), the Federal Deposit Insurance Corporation (FDIC), and the Office of Thrift Supervision (OTS). The final rule became effective April 1, 2008.
80. See CEBS, "Guidelines on the Application of the Supervisory Review Process under Pillar 2" (January 25, 2006), 11–20, http://www.c-ebs.org/Publications/Standards-Guidelines.aspx.
81. See Adams, "Governance and the Financial Crisis," 11; David A. Becher, Terry L. Campbell, and Melissa B. Frye, "Incentive Compensation for Bank Directors: The Impact of Deregulation," *Journal of Business* 78 (2005): 1753–1777.
82. Devriese et al., "Corporate Governance," 95–98; Heremans, "Corporate Governance Issue for Banks," 8.
83. The point is most forcefully developed by Lucian A. Bebchuk and Holger Spamann, "Regulating Bankers' Pay," *Georgetown Law Journal* 98, no. 2, 247–287. Also available online at http://ssrn.com/abstract=1410072.
84. Andrea Beltratti and Rene M. Stulz, "Why Did Some Banks Perform Better during the Credit Crisis?" (Charles A. Dice Center Working Paper no. 2009–12, Ohio State University, July 2009), http://ssrn.com/abstract=1433502.
85. David Erkens, Mingyi Hung, and Pedro P. Matos, "Corporate Governance in the 2007–2008 Financial Crisis: Evidence from Financial Institutions Worldwide" (ECGI—Finance Working Paper no. 249/2009, December 2009), http://ssrn.com/abstract=1397685 (equating independent directors with non-executive directors).
86. For a very similar assessment see Brian R. Cheffins, "Did Corporate Governance 'Fail' during the 2008 Stock Market Meltdown? The Case of the S&P 500" (ECGI Law Working Paper no. 124/2009, July 2009), http://ssrn.com/abstract=1396126.
87. See Risk Management and Requirements for Board Members under Bank's Corporate Governance After the Financial Crisis: Evidence and Reform.
88. As to the following, see Nestor Advisors, *Banks Boards and the Financial Crisis*, 46–92; Kirkpatrick, "Corporate Governance Lessons," 6–12; Basel Committee on Banking Supervision, "Enhancements to the Basel II Framework" (Basel: BIS, 2009), http://www.bis.org/publ/bcbs157.htm. Cf. Senior Supervisors Group, "Risk Management Lessons from the Global Banking Crisis of 2008" (October 21, 2009), 20–28, http://www.financialstabilityboard.org/list/fsb_publications/page_1.htm; ACCA, "Corporate Governance and

the Credit Crunch," 8–9. For an informative survey on sources and causes of risk management failures drawing in part on the observations from the recent crisis, see Stulz, "Risk Management Failures?"

89. See Kirkpatrick, "Corporate Governance Lessons," 8; CDO investments far exceeded (some) banks' understanding of the risks inherent in such instruments.
90. Nestor Advisors, *Banks Boards and the Financial Crisis*, 10.
91. For more detail, see Senior Supervisors Group, "Risk Management Lessons," 23–24; Basel Committee on Banking Supervision, "Enhancements," 14–15 nn. 22–24.
92. Walker, "A Review," 93–94 nn. 6.10–6.12 (for more details see 96–98 nn. 6.16, 6.18–6.20).
93. See Nestor Advisors, *Banks Boards and the Financial Crisis*, 37–40.
94. CEBS, "High Level Principles for Risk Management" (February 16, 2010, no. 9), 25, http://www.c-ebs.org/Publications/Standards-Guidelines.aspx.
95. Walker, "A Review," 98–99 nn. 6.21–6.22; "Report of the High-Level Group on Financial Supervision in the EU," 123; OECD, "Corporate Governance and the Financial Crisis," 15 n. 40.
96. OECD, "Corporate Governance and the Financial Crisis," 15 n. 40; but see Basel Committee on Banking Supervision, "Enhancements," 13 n. 19; CEBS, "High Level Principles," 21; Walker, "A Review," 99 n. 6.22; "Report of the High-Level Group on Financial Supervision in the EU," 123. CRO may report to the CFO or CEO.
97. Basel Committee on Banking Supervision, "Enhancements," 13 n. 19; CEBS, "High Level Principles," 21; Walker, "A Review," 98 n. 6.22; "Report of the High-Level Group on Financial Supervision in the EU," 123; OECD, "Corporate Governance and the Financial Crisis," 15 n. 40.
98. Nestor Advisors, *Banks Boards and the Financial Crisis*, 19–21, 28.
99. See Walker, "A Review," 44 n. 3.10; Adams, "Governance and the Financial Crisis."
100. Walker, "A Review," 37 n. 2.12. Hau und Thum present corroborative evidence in a study of the twenty-nine largest German banks (private banks and state-controlled public sector banks, i.e., *Landesbanken*). They find that the level of financial expertise at the supervisory board correlates with crisis performance at a 5 percent statistical significance level by linking the comparatively higher losses suffered by *Landesbanken* (controlling for size, on average their losses were twice as large as those of their private competitors) to a lower level of financial expertise of supervisory board members of *Landesbanken*. See Harald Hau and Marcel P. Thum, "Subprime Crisis and Board (In-)Competence: Private vs. Public Banks in Germany" (CESifo Working Paper Series no. 2640 and ECGI Finance Working Paper no. 247/2009, April 2009), http://ssrn.com/abstract=1360698.
101. Walker, "A Review," 55 n. 4.11.
102. Ibid., 55 n. 4.11.
103. Ibid., 47–49 nn. 3.19–3.23.
104. Ibid., 47 nn. 3.17–3.18.
105. Ibid., 46 n. 3.16.
106. Ibid., 49–50 nn. 3.24–3.25.
107. See Audit Integrity, "Insights," September 2008, http://www.researchrecap.com/index.php/2008/09/22/poor-corporate-governance-highlights-risk-of-bank-failure/. As to the predictive value of the governance rating produced by Audit Integrity, AGR, see Robert Daines, Ian D. Gow, and David F. Larcker, "Rating the Ratings: How Good Are Commercial Governance Ratings" (Stanford Law and Economics Olin Working Paper no. 360, Stanford

University, September 2009), 48, http://ssrn.com/abstract=1152093: "we find some relation between AGR and both future operating performances and excess returns"; for older studies that found a lower pay-performance sensitivity for banks' CEOs compared to those of other firms' CEOs, see John and Qian, "Incentive Features"; Adams and Mehran, "Is Corporate Governance Different?" 131–132.

108. Nestor Advisors, *Banks Boards and the Financial Crisis*, 95–98; Kirkpatrick, "Corporate Governance Lessons," 13–14.
109. Rüdiger Fahlenbrach and Rene M. Stulz, "Bank CEO Incentives and the Credit Crisis" (Charles A. Dice Center Working Paper no. 2009–13, Ohio State University, and ECGI Finance Working Paper no. 256/2009, December 2009), http://ssrn.com/abstract=1439859.
110. Ibid., 25.
111. Lucian A. Bebchuk, Alma Cohen, and Holger Spamann, "The Wages of Failure: Executive Compensation at Bear Stearns and Lehman 2000–2008" (Working Paper, Harvard Law and Economics Discussion Paper no. 657, Harvard Law School, November 2007), http://ssrn.com/abstract=1513522.
112. FSB, "Principles of Sound Compensation Practices—Implementation Standards" (September 25, 2009), http://www.financialstabilityboard.org/list/fsb_publications/index.htm; for a less detailed prior version, see "FSF Principles for Sound Compensation Practices" (April 2, 2009), http://www.financialstabilityboard.org/list/fsb_publications/page_2.htm.
113. Compare FSA, "Reforming Remuneration Practices in Financial Services" (Policy Statement 09/15, August 2009), http://www.fsa.gov.uk/pubs/policy/ps09_15.pdf, to FSA, "Draft Code on Remuneration Policies" (March 2009), http://www.fsa.gov.uk/pubs/other/remuneration.pdf. See also FSA, "Reforming Remuneration Practices in Financial Services" (consultation paper 09/10, March 2009), http://www.fsa.gov.uk/pages/Library/Policy/CP/2009/09_10.shtml.
114. Compare FINMA, "Rundschreiben 10/1: Vergütungssysteme—Mindeststandards für Vergütungssysteme bei Finanzinstituten" (November 11, 2009), http://www.finma.ch/d/aktuell/Seiten/mm-rs-verguetungssysteme-20091111.aspx, to FINMA, "Rundschreiben 2009/. . .: Vergütungsssteme—Mindeststandards für Vergütungssysteme bei Finanzinstituten" (March 6, 2009), http://www.finma.ch/d/aktuell/Seiten/mm-rs-verguetungssysteme-20090603.aspx.
115. Basel Committee on Banking Supervision, "Compensation Principles and Standards—Assessment Methodology" (Basel: BIS, 2010), http://www.bis.org/publ/bcbs166.htm.
116. Bundesanstalt für Finanzdienstleistungsaufsicht, "Rundschreiben 15/2009 (BA)—Mindestanforderungen an das Risikomanagement—MaRisk" (August 14, 2009), http://www.bafin.de.
117. See note 112.
118. CEBS, "High-Level Principles of Remuneration Policies" (April 2009), http://www.c-ebs.org/Publications/Standards-Guidelines.aspx.
119. Bundesanstalt für Finanzdienstleistungsaufsicht, "Rundschreiben 15/2009(BA)—Aufsichtsrechtliche Anforderungen an die Vergütungssysteme von Instituten" (December 21, 2009), http://www.bafin.de.
120. Commission Recommendation on remuneration policies in the financial services sector; see *Official Journal* 2009 L120/22.
121. See Commission Proposal for a Directive of the European Parliament and of the Council amending Directives 2006/48/EC and 2006/49/EC as regards capital requirements for the trading book and for resecuritizations, and the supervisory review of remuneration policies, COM(2009)362 final, http://

eur-lex.europa.eu/LexUriServ/LexUriServ.do?uri=CELEX:52009PC0362:EN:NOT; for the text of the Presidency compromise see Proposal for a Directive of the European Parliament and of the Council amending Directives 2006/48/EC and 2006/49/EC as regards capital requirements for the trading book and for resecuritizations, and the supervisory review of remuneration policies (Interinstitutional File: 2009/0099 [COD] 14732/09, October 28, 2009), http://register.consilium.europa.eu/pdf/en/09/st14/st14732.en09.pdf.

122. Wall Street Reform and Consumer Protection Act of 2009, HR 4173, 111th Cong., 1st sess., http://thomas.loc.gov/cgi-bin/query/D?c111:1:./temp/~c111wFzEm6:.
123. Corporate and Financial Institution Compensation Fairness Act of 2009, HR 3269. 111th Cong., 1st sess., http://www.thomas.gov/cgi-bin/query/z?c111:H.R.3269:.
124. For a comprehensive overview, see Guido A. Ferrarini, Niamh Moloney, and Maria-Cristina Ungureanu, "Understanding Directors' Pay in Europe: A Comparative and Empirical Analysis" (ECGI Law Working Paper no. 126/2009, August 2009), http://ssrn.com/abstract=1418463.
125. For the newly introduced appropriateness criteria, see, e.g., Daniela Weber-Rey, "Änderungen des Deutschen Corporate Governance Kodex 2009," *WM (Zeitschrift für Wirtschafts- und Bankrecht)* 63 (2009): 2257–2260.
126. Given the UK experience, the effectiveness of a nonbinding shareholder vote in curbing remuneration excesses is doubtful, at best. See, e.g., Cheffins, "Did Corporate Governance 'Fail?'" 41; Jeffrey N. Gordon, "'Say on Pay': Cautionary Notes on the UK Experience and the Case for Shareholder Opt-In" (Columbia Law School Working Paper no. 343, August 2009), http://ssrn.com/abstract=1331482.
127. See, in particular, Basel Committee on Banking Supervision, "Compensation Principles and Standards," 11–23 nn. 36–67.
128. In the same sense, see Walker, "A Review," 137.
129. See, e.g., Uwe Hüffer, *Aktiengesetz*, 8th ed. (Munich: C.H. Beck, 2008), § 76 n. 12a et seq.; but see also Peter O. Mülbert, "Shareholder Value aus rechtlicher Sicht," *ZGR (Zeitschrift für Unternehmens- und Gesellschaftsrecht)* 26 (1997): 147–156; Peter O. Mülbert, "Soziale Verantwortung von Unternehmen im Gesellschaftsrecht," *AG* (Die Aktiengesellschaft) 54 (2009): 770–772.
130. See the table "Share Price Trough as a % of Share Price Peak," in Nestor Advisors, *Banks Boards and the Financial Crisis*, 3.
131. See note 65 and accompanying text.
132. Macey and O'Hara, "Corporate Governance of Banks," 102.
133. But see Walker, "A Review," 31 n. 2.8, for a somewhat nuanced assessment: "even the most experienced and disciplined board is likely to be less well-placed than the regulator to assess the implications of new risks that may be building up in the financial system at large."
134. Nestor Advisors, *Banks Boards and the Financial Crisis*, 10.
135. See, very critically, Joel B. Harris and Charles T. Caliendo, "Who Says the Business Judgment Rule Does Not Apply to Directors of New York Banks?" *Banking L.J.* 118 (2001): 493 et seq.
136. See William M. Fletcher, *Fletcher Cyclopedia of the Law of Corporations* (Eagan, MN: West Group, 2002), § 1042.10.
137. In the same sense, see Bebchuk and Spamann, "Regulating Bankers' Pay," 40.

11 Disclosure 2.0

Leveraging Technology to Address "Complexity" and Information Failures in the Financial Crisis

Erik Gerding

INTRODUCTION

Recent legal scholarship has continued the tradition of critiquing mandatory disclosure, but with two modern twists. Rather than argue that disclosure is superfluous, several scholars have contended that disclosure is either:

- counterproductive given the cognitive limitations of investors
- losing effectiveness because the complexity of modern financial instruments prevents investors from adequately understanding those instruments

Professor Troy Paredes (now a commissioner of the Securities Exchange Commission [SEC]) has put forth the first argument; he posits that required securities disclosure overloads investors with too much information and, therefore, disclosure requirements should be scaled back.[1] Professor Steven Schwarcz has articulated a second argument; he argues securities disclosure has lost effectiveness in the face of "complexity," which frustrates the ability of investors to understand and evaluate various financial instruments such as Asset-Backed Securities (ABSs) and derivatives.[2] In light of disclosure's decreased effectiveness, Schwarcz argues that policy makers should focus attention on regulations other than disclosure, such as third-party certification of securities.[3]

Although Paredes's and Schwarcz's respective criticisms of disclosure are separate, they may be seen as two sides of the same coin. This chapter places these two arguments together and labels them as the "complexity critique," which might be paraphrased as follows: disclosure cannot help investors adequately understand complex financial instruments and, even if it attempted to do so, investors could not process the additional information in any event. This complexity critique may have a certain seductiveness in light of the current financial crisis, in which ordinary citizens still struggle to understand the complex financial instruments at the heart of the market meltdown.

Nevertheless, the arguments of Paredes and Schwarcz have a number of limitations, which this chapter outlines. Moreover, their general attacks on disclosure should now be evaluated in light of the current financial crisis, which was exacerbated by information failures. These failures included the following:

- the difficulty investors face in identifying the ultimate cash-producing assets that underlay ABSs and derivatives
- the destruction of information regarding underlying assets as those assets are securitized
- the additional progressive information destruction as the resultant ABSs are then resecuritized or hedged with credit default swaps (which information destruction worsens further when the products of those new securitizations or swaps are themselves securitized or hedged)
- the intermittent disclosure that comes with periodic financial reporting, which obscures changes in a company's balance sheet and risk profile between reporting periods and enables accounting gamesmanship
- the lack of granular information on a company's investments, which can mask dangerous homogeneity among the portfolios of various companies
- the opacity of models used to price ABSs and derivatives, set firm risk management policies, which opacity hides faulty assumptions, gamesmanship of models, and dangerous homogeneity in risk management
- the limitations in using firm specific disclosure to uncover systemic problems such as those created by either excessive homogeneity in investment portfolios, trading strategies, risk management, and risk exposures or complex market interactions among the portfolios and trading strategies of separate firms

Each of these information failures is described in more detail in this chapter.

These information failures mean that regulators should consider enhancing securities disclosure requirements and not merely prune them, as Paredes argued before the crisis, or turn to other regulatory solutions, as Schwarcz has argued since the onset of the crisis. Merely adding a new list of required disclosure items to U.S. securities regulation, however, is not necessarily the answer. Although the complexity critique has severe limitations, it nonetheless serves a valuable role in highlighting the deep tension that disclosure requirements must negotiate. On the one hand, securities disclosure must present financial information in sufficient detail and nuance to enable investors to understand the intricate risks and rewards embedded in complex financial products and the byzantine ways in which those instruments interact in modern financial markets. On the other hand, disclosure must take into account the cognitive limitations of investors and the costs they incur in sifting through massive amounts of information.

What is needed then is a fundamental rethinking of the approach of securities disclosure, not merely the content. Computer science, software, and information systems have long grappled with similar tensions between users demand for access to volumes of information and their need to navigate through information easily and focus on potential areas of concern. This chapter sketches out a number of technological advances in software and information systems that might play a key role in enhancing securities disclosure and disclosure regulations. This chapter discusses the following technologies and technological insights that can enhance disclosure:

- the SEC's XBRL initiative that requires firms to include data tags on electronic disclosure to allow investors to download disclosure items into spreadsheets and other analytical software
- affixing data tags to assets that underlay ABSs and derivatives to allow investors to trace which assets underlay which financial instruments
- real-time financial disclosure
- "open source" risk models
- interactive disclosure that allows users to change certain assumptions or accounting methods to see how financial disclosure would change
- software designs that improve the look and feel of computer programs through drag-down menus and other devices

This chapter explores some of the potential benefits of each of these technologies, as well as a few of their costs. The aim is to provoke thought and to structure a later, more extensive cost-benefit analysis of these technologies and a survey of potential investor demand for them.

This chapter proceeds as follows: the next section outlines the arguments of Professors Paredes and Schwarcz. The third section offers a critique of the complexity critique. The fourth section offers a typology of three kinds of complexity that may afflict complex financial instruments—contractual complexity, derivative complexity, and systemic complexity. The fifth section elaborates on the information failures in the current financial crisis that disclosure must address. The sixth section provides details on the possible technological enhancements to disclosure listed earlier that might begin to address the information failures of the crisis. The seventh section outlines some of the potential costs and risks involved with these technological enhancements. The final section concludes by advocating for experimental testing of the effectiveness of new disclosure technologies in improving the understanding of investors.

THE "COMPLEXITY CRITIQUE"

Mandatory securities disclosure has endured periodic attacks by legal scholars that have focused on whether required disclosure adds any information that investors and financial markets cannot demand or otherwise obtain.[4] In the past five years, several legal scholars have revived this critique, but added novel twists. First, in 2003, Professor Troy Paredes argued that securities disclosure overloads investors with too much information.[5] The cognitive limitations and behavioral biases of investors and the costs of processing massive amounts of financial disclosure, Paredes argued, meant that securities disclosure has not only become less effective in informing the investing public, but also counterproductive.[6] Investor decision making can become suboptimal, Paredes contended, as investors take mental shortcuts to sift through the massive amount of information a securities issuer is required to disclose.[7] Investors inevitably select only a portion of any issuer's disclosure to process and on which to base their investment decisions. Often, investors pick the wrong information.[8]

Paredes recognized that less sophisticated investors may free-ride off more sophisticated investors who can better process voluminous securities disclosure. Yet he responded with arguments that sophisticated investors can also face information overload from disclosure.[9] He also recognized that the Efficient Markets Hypothesis (EMH) suggests that it does not matter that certain individual investors may be overwhelmed by information; the marketplace collectively will process information.[10] He responded to the EMH overall in part by noting that behavioral finance has shown that there are limitations to the EMH, and many securities markets are sometimes not informationally efficient.[11] Paredes concluded from his findings that policy makers should consider pruning securities regulations on disclosure to reduce information overload and improve investor decisions.[12]

Professor Stephen Schwarcz added a second side to this complexity critique in a series of articles that argued that securities disclosure failed to capture the "complexity" of modern financial instruments and markets. In 2004, he argued that the Enron fraud revealed a larger failure of securities disclosure to remedy information asymmetries in securitizations, derivatives, and other structured finance transactions because of the growing complexity of those transactions.[13] In a similar vein as Paredes, Schwarcz argued that markets and policy makers should not necessarily take comfort from the ability of sophisticated institutional investors and their experts to process complex information; he cited data that institutional investors do not hire sufficient experts and that experts themselves are subject to behavioral biases and cognitive limitations.[14] Like Paredes, Schwarcz also cited evidence that the EMH may have limited application to many markets, such as ABSs markets.[15] Moreover, Schwarcz contended that the complexity of structured finance transactions may prevent a critical mass of sophisticated investors from sufficiently understanding particular transactions and driving market prices to an efficient level.[16] After the financial crisis took root, Schwarcz reiterated his arguments in a 2008 article.[17] Schwarcz concludes that because complexity decreases the effectiveness of mandatory disclosure, policy makers should focus attention on regulations other than disclosure, such as third-party certification of securities.[18]

Although Paredes and Schwarcz's respective criticisms of disclosure are separate, they may be seen as two sides of the same coin. This chapter places these two arguments together and labels them as the "complexity critique," which might be paraphrased as follows: disclosure does not help investors adequately understand complex financial instruments and, even if it attempted to do so with additional disclosure, investors could not process the new information in any event.

CRITIQUING THE CRITIQUE

The arguments of both Paredes and Schwarcz have significant limitations, raise additional questions, and demand further refinement. The Paredes critique does not specify how much information is optimal and how much is overload. Professor Paredes, in fact, admits that empirical evidence would be necessary to determine which items of financial disclosure are helpful for investors and which are superfluous or counterproductive.[19] Paredes also recognizes that this in turn begs the question of how to address the demands of different investors for different kinds of information.[20]

The Schwarcz critique also needs refinement. Schwarcz offers a very general definition of "complexity."[21] This general definition has the benefit of being comprehensive, but forecloses the development of ways to measure complexity and generate testable hypotheses. Further definitional clarity would allow empirical evidence to be gathered to evaluate Schwarcz's thesis—that complexity of certain financial instruments renders disclosure less effective. Several definitions and metrics for complexity are discussed in the following section.

TYPES OF COMPLEXITY

The importance of the EMH and the role that sophisticated investors play in analyzing disclosure and setting the market price argues for creating a more refined definition of "complexity" and breaking it into several components. This chapter argues that ABSs, derivatives, and other structured products may exhibit at least three kinds of complexity. First, these financial products may exhibit *contractual complexity* (or "structural complexity") in that they may have numerous contractual terms that define the rights of investors under the products. These terms may include rights to payments and collateral that may vary, in the case of ABSs, for different tranches of securities of the same issuer.[22] Contractual complexity might be measured by the number of tranches of securities being issued or the presence or absence of particular contractual structures.

Second, these products may exhibit *derivative complexity* in that ABSs, derivatives, and other structured products derive their value from underlying assets. For example, mortgage-backed securities pay out according to payments received on the mortgages that underlay the securities. Often, ABSs may be backed by other securities, which might in turn be backed by a third layer of securities. This layering of securitization of securitization has analogues in derivatives, as a counterparty to a derivative contract can hedge various risks by entering into a second derivative contract with yet another counterparty.[23] Derivative complexity increases with (a) the number of layers of assets underlying a particular financial instrument, (b) the diversity of assets in each layer, and (c) the complexity of each of those underlying assets (as measured along the dimensions of the three kinds of complexity mentioned in this section).

Third, these financial products may exhibit *systemic* complexity. The value and risks of any product depend not only on underlying assets (and the value and risks of those assets) and the contractual terms governing the product, but also changes in the marketplace. Most basically, the financial instrument may have a market price, which may depend in part on the market prices of substitute instruments. Potential losses from changes in market price are often labeled as market risk, but financial instruments are also subject to liquidity risk (the risk that the number of willing buyers for a particular product will suddenly plummet causing the market to dry up) and systemic risk (the risk of marketwide losses). Systemic complexity captures all of these forms of risk, which are difficult to evaluate and model. Systemic complexity increases when the value of a financial instrument or security is more heavily dependent on the price movements of many other financial instruments (other than underlying assets).

Of these three forms of complexity, sophisticated investors may have the least difficulty navigating contractual complexity. Retail investors may have difficulty reading through a prospectus and indenture for an ABS, but sophisticated investors are likely to have considerable experience with the contractual terminology and structures involved in such a security.

INFORMATION FAILURES IN THE GLOBAL FINANCIAL CRISIS

Sophisticated investors might face greater difficulty in evaluating financial instruments with greater derivative or systemic complexity. It does not follow, however, that the antidote to greater complexity is less disclosure. The current financial crisis was exacerbated by a series of information failures. This section will outline a few of these failures, several of which relate closely to derivative or systemic complexity, and the next section will discuss how disclosure could be improved with the aid of technological advances to address these failures.

Securitization, Derivatives, and the Destruction of Information

As noted earlier, ABSs often derive their value from several layers of underlying assets. In other words, because ABSs are themselves securitized and used to back new ABSs, any class of ABSs may be several securitizations removed from the ultimate underlying cash-producing assets, such as mortgages or other loans. Similarly, derivatives may be used to hedge the risks of other derivatives. For example, credit derivatives may be used to hedge the risk of default on ABSs (or other derivatives). To value ABSs and derivatives investors need information on the value and risks associated with underlying assets. This becomes complicated when those values and risks in turn require information on assets underlying those underlying assets. Investors may have difficulty identifying through layers of securitization and derivatives the ultimate underlying assets.[24]

There are, of course, substitutes for direct information on those ultimate underlying assets. However, investors cannot necessarily rely on the parties involved in earlier securitizations and derivatives to pass on high-quality information on underlying assets earlier in the chain. Often these parties lack incentives to pass on accurate and detailed information. For example, lenders who sold the mortgages and other loans they originated to be securitized had diminished incentives to ensure the creditworthiness of borrowers. This created the problem of low-documentation and zero-money-down loans.[25] Unable to trace back to the ultimate underlying assets, investors might also resort to shortcuts, such as relying on the ratings assigned to underlying assets by credit rating agencies. Rating agencies, however, have a poor track record of evaluating credit risk as evidenced by sudden massive downgrades of higher rated securities. Many scholars attribute this poor performance to conflicts of interest caused by those firms being paid by the issuers of the securities they are rating.[26]

Perverse incentives and the cost of passing on information on underlying assets contributed to what economists have called the progressive destruction of information with each layer of securitization or derivatives.[27] This information destruction can lead to serious errors in valuing risk. Economists have also noted that securitizing and resecuritizing assets like mortgages in multiple layers exacerbates the risk of errors; small errors in measuring the risk of underlying assets, like mortgages, are magnified at each subsequent level of securitization or hedging. This can lead to large errors in valuing the financial instruments at the end of a chain of securitizations and derivatives.[28] One particular error merits special attention. When losses on assets become highly correlated,[29] losses on one asset are no longer offset by continued profits on other assets; losses then occur in waves.[30] When the correlation of losses on underlying assets exceeds expectations even slightly, valuations on the ABSs or derivatives that are backed by or based on those assets can exhibit spectacular errors.[31] In short, a failure to identify the ultimate assets that affect an ABS or derivative increases the likelihood of serious errors in valuing that security or derivative.

Financial Institution Risk Models and Model Risk

These same errors can afflict the models that various parties (such as investors, rating agencies, derivative counterparties, bond insurers, sponsors of securitizations) use to price ABSs and derivatives. These pricing models exhibited phenomenal failures in measuring risk in the current financial crisis, as did the models that financial institutions relied on to price loans, manage investment portfolios, set overall firm risk management policies, and even establish regulatory capital.[32] These models failed in part because of faulty assumptions that were largely hidden from the public due to the opacity of the models.[33] Opacity of risk models has other negative consequences. It hides potential gamesmanship of models by individuals within a financial institution. For example, traders in financial institutions have been faulted for engaging in trading strategies that involve low-probability but high-magnitude risks to evade detection by their firm's risk models (a practice called "stuffing risk into the tails").[34] In addition, the fact that the details of any financial institution's risk models remain largely secret prevents other financial institutions from adequately evaluating their counterparty risk to that institution.[35] The marketplace cannot necessarily rely on regulators to police risk modeling and risk management, as regulators may lack necessary resources and expertise. Moreover, regulators may lack motivation; from an international perspective, one nation's regulators may wish to allow their home country financial institutions to use looser models to take on more risk, earn greater profits, and gain a competitive advantage over institutions in other countries.[36] Opacity of risk models and regulatory auditing of those models obscures the failures of regulators and can undermine international efforts to ensure minimum standards across countries for financial institution regulation.[37]

In addition, opacity of risk models hide potentially dangerous levels of homogeneity in the risk modeling and risk management of financial institutions. If financial institutions employ similar investment and risk management strategies, they may purchase the same assets at the same time (causing prices to surge) and sell those assets simultaneously (causing prices to plummet). There is some indication that this homogeneity exacerbated the current financial crisis, as many financial institutions began suffering losses and selling assets at the same time.[38]

Firm-Specific Disclosure and Systemic Exposures

The problem of excessive homogeneity in risk models, risk management, and investment strategies points to a broader informational problem: investors need to understand systemic risks, but securities disclosure is firm-specific. For example, investors may want to know if different financial institutions have concentrated risk exposure to the same borrowers or the same types of loans or investments. To find this information, investors would have to compare the SEC filings of multiple institutions. Differences in the way in which firms report financial information frustrate this comparison. Although regulations on financial statement disclosure are designed to ensure common yardsticks of financial performance, securities and accounting rules are replete with examples of disclosure that gives issuers discretion to pick among various methodologies for calculating financial results or different disclosure formats.[39]

The Granularity of Disclosure

In addition, investors seeking to uncover worrisome homogeneity among the investment portfolios and exposures of different firms need fairly granular information about the specific assets and liabilities in a firm's balance sheet. When too many firms have similar balance sheets, similar risk exposure, and similar investment and risk management strategies, systemic risk can mushroom. To detect excessive homogeneity among firms, investors would need fairly detailed information on the balance sheets, risk exposures, and risk management strategies of individual firms.[40] This detailed information is also necessary for investors to back-test the quality of a firm's risk modeling (and whether a firm is faithfully describing its modeling and risk management practices). Disclosure rules that require firms simply to list borrowers that represent the largest source of credit risk are inadequate if the firm has numerous smaller loans to multiple borrowers that present similar risk exposures (such as exotic mortgages that would experience a jump in default rates if interest rates rose and housing prices stagnated, to pick a fanciful example). Regulations can add requirements to disclose specific exposures (such as exposure to mortgages or mortgage-backed securities), but this poses two problems. First, regulators must anticipate the next investment fad that will cause multiple securities issuers to have similar exposures. Alternatively, regulators could put the onus on issuers to determine emerging areas of dangerous homogeneity. But this would require firms to gather information on the specific practices and portfolios of competitors, and the necessary data may not be publicly available.

Intermittent Disclosure and Periodic Reporting

Securities disclosure can also be gamed because financial reporting is periodic and intermittent. Scholars have noted how periodic reporting may facilitate earnings management (and even manipulation) and may be gamed to boost executive compensation.[41] Periodic reporting may also obscure changes in a firm's balance sheet and risk profile that occurred in the period between financial statements. For example, accounting research demonstrates that firms tend to close securitization transactions immediately before a financial quarter ends.[42] This timing may mask risk that firms face for most of a financial quarter, but that disappears magically right before the date of the quarterly balance sheet. For example, a firm may originate numerous mortgages at the beginning of a financial quarter and then sell them to be securitized right before quarter's end. The firm is exposed to the credit risk of the mortgages defaulting for most of the quarter, but this risk evaporates when the mortgages are sold. An investor can trace through the financial statements (such as the income and cash flow statements) to find that the transactions occurred. A snapshot of risk exposures as of the quarter end, however, does not reveal the risk to the firm for most of the quarter. This becomes a problem if the firm is unable in the future to unload its mortgages at the end of quarter for any reason (e.g., because of the collapse of the securitization market or a liquidity freeze). In that event, risk would suddenly materialize in the form of impaired loans on the balance sheet.

TECHNOLOGICAL REMEDIES TO INFORMATION FAILURES: UPGRADING DISCLOSURE

The information failures outlined in the previous section prevent the marketplace from fully understanding the risks faced by both individual financial institutions and by the financial sector as a whole. Because the financial crisis stemmed in large measure from information failures, it would be perverse and potentially disastrous to dilute securities disclosure on account of its failure to prevent the crisis.

The Deep Tension between Nuance and Accessibility

Current disclosure is clearly inadequate. The complexity critique has been used to argue for pruning disclosure requirements (in the case of Paredes) or that the disclosure paradigm has been undermined (in the case of Schwarcz). The arguments of these two scholars may prove useful not in undermining disclosure rationales but also in highlighting areas in which disclosure needs improvement. In particular, the two sides of the complexity critique bring to the surface a deep tension that disclosure must negotiate. On the one hand, securities disclosure must present financial information in sufficient detail and nuance to enable investors to understand the complex risks and rewards embedded not only in complex financial products but even in the plain vanilla securities of modern firms operating in a dynamic marketplace. On the other hand, disclosure must take into account the cognitive limitations of investors and the costs they incur in sifting through massive amounts of information. Any enhancements to disclosure must make disclosure accessible and user-friendly,[43] while still allowing investors to access information they would value in sufficient scope and detail and with sufficient timeliness.

Technological Innovations

Computer science, software, and information systems have long grappled with similar tensions, and insights from these fields can vastly improve securities disclosure. More particularly, technological advances in software and information systems can play a key role in enhancing securities disclosure and disclosure regulations. This subsection outlines several key technologies or technological insights that can improve disclosure and remedy some of the information failures outlined earlier.[44]

XBRL

The SEC's XBRL initiative,[45] which is already being implemented, provides a useful launching point for using technology to enhance and reform disclosure.[46] The XBRL initiative builds off the decades-old SEC EDGAR regulations, which require firms and individuals that must make filings with the SEC to do so in an electronic format that would be searchable and available on the SEC's online EDGAR database.[47] The XBRL rules now require SEC registrants to begin embedding data "tags" in their electronic filings. These tags would identify key items (called "elements" in the relevant regulatory language) in financial statements and allow investors to download these separate pieces of information directly into spreadsheets or other analytical software. Investors can then make side-by-side comparisons of financial information—for example, loans that are more than ninety days delinquent—from different issuers.

Tagging Assets in Securitization and Derivatives

This same XBRL technology can be expanded to affix data tags to specific mortgages,[48] ABSs, and derivatives. This could dramatically lower the cost to investors in tracing back to the assets that underlay specific ABSs and derivatives even through multiple layers of securitization and hedging.[49] This tracing would improve the ability of investors to map the web of securitizations and hedging in a nuanced fashion. By understanding underlying assets, investors could analyze how underlying risks—including credit and market risk—on underlying assets course through the system all the way to the securities they purchase. The SEC should consider expanding the XBRL initiative to require data tags on various underlying assets.

Access to Underlying Financial Data

Data tags on specific mortgages, ABSs, and derivatives can also ultimately enable investors to see specific assets and liabilities in a firm's balance sheet. Required disclosure of specific assets and liabilities would uncover information that is hidden by aggregated information. More granular information would allow investors to spot risks or accounting gamesmanship in a firm's financial statements that would be masked by more aggregated information. It would also allow investors to comb through balance sheets of individual firms and then make comparisons among firms. These comparisons might uncover potentially dangerous areas of homogeneity lurking in the balance sheets and risk profiles of multiple firms.

Real-Time Reporting

Advances in information systems will enable more rapid and frequent disclosure than current quarterly and other periodic reports. It is conceivable that certain financial disclosure could be made practically in real time.[50] This would mimic how exchange trades are reflected in real-time stock quotes.[51] More frequent disclosure would curtail the accounting gamesmanship of many issuers noted earlier that is facilitated by the periodic, intermittent nature of current disclosure.

Open Source Models

As noted earlier, the models that firms use to price ABSs and derivatives and to set investment and risk management strategies are dangerously opaque. Regulators should require that issuers, particularly financial institutions, disclose much greater detail on the methodologies and assumptions behind these models. More radically, an open source approach could force disclosure of the algorithms in these models. This would allow investors to analyze the models in greater detail and spot limitations, "bugs," and the potential for dangerous homogeneity among the models of different firms.[52]

Interactive Disclosure and Calculators

Firms will likely resist disclosing information on their risk models and financial statements in too much detail. As an alternative to this detailed disclosure, issuers could present interactive disclosure—either online or embedded in an electronic document—that would allow users to change certain assumptions or accounting methods and see how financial disclosure would change accordingly. This technology resembles the interactive calculators that many financial firm websites now offer and that the Obama administration has endorsed as part of its reform of consumer financial regulations.[53]

Layout of Disclosure

If disclosure would be increasingly delivered in electronic and interactive formats, this would allow regulators, issuers, and securities lawyers to rethink the overall presentation of disclosure to make it more accessible, malleable, and "user-friendly." Behavioral economists and legal scholars have explored how research on the cognitive limitations, behavioral biases, and heuristics can be used to improve the decision making of investors and other individuals.[54] One strand of this literature focuses on using regulations to improve the "menu design" for consumer and investment choices available to individuals.[55] This approach on improving individual decisions can also be applied to improving disclosure to consumers. The "menu" metaphor is quite apt, as software designers have gleaned valuable experience on making software more user-friendly. Drop-down "menus" and other interactive devices have been introduced and progressively improved in software since the advent of the graphical user interface (GUI). These devices allowed software to perform more complex tasks and be used by more consumers at the same time.[56]

CHALLENGES

Employing these technologies to advance a brave new world of securities disclosure will involve costs, pose risks, and generate opposition. This section sketches some of these challenges.

Privacy

Regulators and issuers would need to take care that either tagging individual mortgages or consumer loans or more granular financial disclosure on underlying assets does not lead to the personal information of individuals being made public.

Proprietary Information

As noted earlier, many firms would fiercely resist requirements that they produce open source risk models or disclose granular and real-time information on individual assets and liabilities. These firms would have legitimate concerns, as this information would give competitors access to proprietary models, which might dull the incentives of firms to invest in better models. Moreover, disclosure on investment portfolios and strategies would allow other investors to trade against the firm and reap a profit. Nevertheless, even if open source models and granular and real-time financial disclosure are not fully realized, as ideals for useful disclosure to investors they provide a valuable starting point for policy discussion.

Investor "Processing Speed"

Technologically enhanced disclosure, particularly more frequent or real-time disclosure, will challenge the ability of investors to process information carefully. On the positive side, higher speed of disclosure promotes market efficiency, but it also raises questions, including:

> *Would disclosure be sufficiently audited?* Audit firms could not realistically audit financial information disclosed in real time, i.e., as transactions occur. Some information may be important enough to merit slower disclosure to enable auditors to catch potential accounting errors, whether deliberate or intentional.
>
> *Would higher speed disclosure promote greater market volatility?* Under even the weak form of the EMH, real-time disclosure would have immediate effects on the market price of an issuer's securities. This could make prices more volatile and exacerbate noise trading.
>
> *Would higher volatility be gamed by issuers, market intermediaries, and sophisticated traders?* Instantaneous disclosure, higher volatility, and higher levels of noise trading could allow sophisticated players in the marketplace to take advantage of retail investors by using superior access to information to trade ahead of the market, engage inside trading, or manipulate prices.
>
> *Would higher volatility lead to greater automated trading?* Faster disclosure times may push more sophisticated institutional traders looking to gain a competitive advantage further into automated trading. Several episodes in the last two decades in financial markets, beginning with the 1987 stock market crash, have demonstrated that widespread use of automated trading can lead to unexpected market crises and place the risk management of financial institutions on autopilot.[57]

BETA TESTING DISCLOSURE

As noted earlier, Professor Paredes acknowledged that more empirical evidence would be needed to identify when investors are overloaded with information, which investors are overloaded, and which pieces of information are critical for which investors. The possibility of information overload and questions on the effectiveness of disclosure given the cognitive limitations and behavioral biases of investors indeed point to a need for rigorous testing of technologically enhanced disclosure. The reforms outlined in the preceding, for example the "menu" redesigns mentioned earlier, should be thoroughly tested through experiments to determine their effect on the comprehension level of various types of investors. Legal scholars have increasingly advocated using methodologies from experimental economics to test the effectiveness of various legal rules.[58] This chapter continues in that vein. Research from psychology and neuroeconomics can be used to test the effectiveness of different disclosure technologies and approaches. Sophisticated experimental devices, such as functional MRI, can also be employed.

This chapter has argued that technology can remedy information failures and create enhanced disclosure that would improve the comprehension of investors. Like most software, the actual 2.0 version of securities disclosure should be rigorously beta tested.

NOTES

1. Troy A. Paredes, "Blinded by the Light: Information Overload and its Consequences for Securities Regulation," *Washington University Law Quarterly* 81 (2003): 417.
2. Steven L. Schwarcz, "Rethinking the Disclosure Paradigm in a World of Complexity," *University of Illinois Law Review* (2004): 1; Steven L. Schwarcz, "Disclosure's Failure in the Subprime Mortgage Crisis," *Utah Law Review* (2008): 1109.
3. Schwarcz also proposes supplementing disclosure requirements with other regulations, such as requiring originators in securitization transactions to provide guaranties, developing private sector or government certifications of complex financial transactions, and enhancing corporate governance rules to mitigate conflicts of interest in those transactions. Schwarcz, "Rethinking the Disclosure Paradigm," 22–35; See also Schwarcz, "Disclosure's Failure," 20–21. Schwarcz considers banning excessively complex structured finance transactions a suboptimal option. Schwarcz, "Rethinking the Disclosure Paradigm," 20–22.
4. For an earlier volley in the debate on whether mandatory securities law was justified, compare Frank H. Easterbrook and Daniel R. Fischel, "Mandatory Disclosure and the Protection of Investors," *Virginia Law Review* 70 (1984): 669 (questioning many justifications for mandatory disclosure) with John C. Coffee Jr., "Market Failure and the Economic Case for a Mandatory Disclosure System," *Virginia Law Review* 70 (1984): 717 (supporting mandatory disclosure).
5. Paredes, "Blinded by the Light."
6. Ibid., 441–443.
7. Ibid., 440–442.
8. Ibid., 442–443.
9. Ibid., 453–458.
10. For a germinal work in legal scholarship on the applications of the EMH to law, see Ronald J. Gilson and Reinier H. Kraakman, "The Mechanisms of Market Efficiency," *Virginia Law Review* 70 (1984): 549.
11. Paredes, "Blinded by the Light," 480–483.
12. Ibid., 484.
13. Schwarcz, Rethinking the Disclosure Paradigm, *supra* note Error! Bookmark not defined..
14. Ibid., 13–15.
15. Ibid., 18.
16. Ibid.
17. Schwarcz, "Disclosure's Failure."
18. See note Error! Bookmark not defined. and accompanying text.
19. Paredes, "Blinded by the Light," 473–474.
20. Ibid., 459–460.

21. Schwarcz, "Rethinking the Disclosure Paradigm," 2 n. 3 ("I use the term 'complexity' in its ordinary meaning: the state of being complicated").
22. For a summary of some of the structural features of ABSs, see Leon T. Kendall, "Securitization: A New Era in American Finance," in *A Primer on Securitization*, ed. Leon T. Kendall and Michael J. Fishman, 1 (Cambridge, MA: The MIT Press, 1997); Steven P. Baum, "The Securitization of Commercial Property Debt," in *A Primer on Securitization*, ed. Leon T. Kendall and Michael J. Fishman, 45, 49 (Cambridge, MA: The MIT Press, 1997) (describing commercial mortgage-backed securities).
23. For a discussion of the layering of securitizations and credit derivatives, see Joshua Coval, Jakub Jurek, and Erik Stafford, "The Economics of Structured Finance," *Journal of Economic Perspectives* 23 (2009): 3.
24. Erik F. Gerding, "Code, Crash, and Open Source: The Outsourcing of Financial Regulation to Risk Models and the Global Financial Crisis," *Washington Law Review* 84 (2009): 127, 165.
25. Ibid., 181–182.
26. Frank Partnoy, "The Siskel and Ebert of Financial Markets?: Two Thumbs Down for the Credit Rating Agencies," *Washington University Law Quarterly* 77 (1999): 619; Frank Partnoy and David A. Skeel Jr., "The Promise and Perils of Credit Derivatives," *University of Cincinnati Law Review* 75 (2007): 1019; Frank Partnoy, "How and Why Credit Rating Agencies Are Not Like Other Gatekeepers," in *Financial Gatekeepers: Can They Protect Investors*, ed. Yasuuki Fuchita and Robert E. Litan, 59 (Washington, DC: Brookings Institution Press, 2006).
27. Willem H. Buiter, "Lessons from the 2007 Financial Crisis," *Centre for Economic Policy Research Policy Insight* 18, nos. 2–3 (December 2007), http://www.cepr.org/pubs/PolicyInsights/PolicyInsight18.pdf.
28. Coval, Jurek, and Stafford, "Economics of Structured Finance."
29. Losses on mortgages and securities can become increasingly correlated due to spillover effects (for example, the default on one mortgage lowering surrounding property values and increasing the probability of default on other mortgages) and feedback loops (for example, widespread defaults on mortgages constricting lending, which increases interest rates, which leads to a new round of defaults). Martin Hellwig, "Systemic Risk in the Financial Sector: An Analysis of the Subprime-Mortgage Financial Crisis," Max Planck Inst. Res. on Collective Goods Bonn 2008/4316 (November 2008), http://papers.ssrn.com/sol3/papers.cfm?abstract_id=1309442.
30. Gerding, "Code, Crash, and Open Source," 172.
31. Coval, Jurek, and Stafford, "Economics of Structured Finance."
32. Gerding, "Code, Crash, and Open Source," 164–167. Under the Basel II Accord, certain large banks are now allowed to set their own regulatory capital requirements according to internal risk models (ibid., 154–157). The SEC extended this privilege to several large investment banks under its now defunct Consolidated Supervised Entity program (ibid., 158–159).
33. Gerding, "Code, Crash, and Open Source," 182–184.
34. Joe Nocera, "Risk Mismanagement," *NY Times Magazine*, January 2, 2009, 46.
35. Gerding, "Code, Crash, and Open Source," 182–183.
36. Ibid., 185.
37. Ibid.
38. Gerding, "Code, Crash, and Open Source," 165, 184.
39. E.g., Robert M. Bowen, Shivaram Rajgopal, and Mohan Venkatachalam, "Accounting Discretion, Corporate Governance, and Firm Performance," *Contemporary Accounting Research* 25 (2008): 351.

40. See Gerding, "Code, Crash, and Open Source," 184.
41. Meredith M. Stead, "How Incentive Pay for Executives Isn't—and What We Can Do about It," *NYU Law Review* 80 (2005): 722.
42. Patricia M. Dechow and Catherine Shakespeare, "Do Managers Time Securitization Transactions to Obtain Accounting Benefits?" *Accounting Review* 84 (2009): 99.
43. The SEC has long recognized this need, which animated a number of reform initiatives including the SEC's initiatives in the late 1990s requiring that disclosure be written "Plain English." Final Rule: Plain English Disclosure, Securities Act Release No. 33–7494, 63 Fed. Reg. 6370 (January 28, 1998).
44. Other scholars have recently advocated other uses of technology to streamline disclosure to reduce costs for securities issuers. E.g., Joseph A. Grundfest and Alan L. Beller, "Reinventing the Securities Disclosure Regime: Online Questionnaires as Substitutes for Form-Based Filings" (Stanford University Law and Economics Olin Working Paper no. 361, August 4, 2008, http://papers.ssrn.com/sol3/papers.cfm?abstract_id=1235082) (advocating replacing SEC form filings with Internet-based questionnaires for companies required to file with the SEC).
45. See Interactive Data to Improve Financial Reporting, Securities Act Release No. 33–2461 (January 30, 2009) (17 C.F.R. Parts 229, 230, 232, 239, 240, and 249 [2009]). XBRL reporting was previously an entirely voluntary pilot project. See Final Rule: XBRL Voluntary Financial Reporting on the EDGAR System, Securities Act Release No. 33–8,529, Exchange Act Release, 34–51,129, 70 Fed. Reg. 6,556 (February 3, 2005).
46. Commentators in the press have already lauded the potential of the XBRL Rule to increase transparency in financial markets and allow an "army of citizen regulators" to police risk in financial markets, e.g., Daniel Roth, "Road Map for Financial Recovery: Radical Transparency Now!" *Wired*, February 23, 2009, 81.
47. The EDGAR system was first created as a pilot program in the 1980s. See Securities Act Release No. 33–6977 (February 23, 1993) (explaining the EDGAR system generally and setting forth SEC rules and procedures that apply to electronic submissions). On December 19, 1994, the SEC required all domestic issuers to make Exchange Act filings electronically via the EDGAR system. Rulemaking for EDGAR System, Securities Act Release No. 33–7122 (December 19, 1994).
48. Chris Murphy, "The Fed CIO Agenda: Should Every Mortgage Have a Data Tag?" *Information Week Global CIO Blog*, http://www.informationweek.com/blog/main/archives/2009/03/the_fed_cio_age.html;jsessionid=P3FCQFYVFNZVVQE1GHPCKHWATMY32JVN.
49. SEC officials appear to be actively considering at least tagging ABSs and derivatives. See Nicholas Rummell, "Tagging, Tracking of ABSs 'Urgent': SEC—Commission Says XBRL Formatting of the Securities Could be Done within a Year," *Financial Week*, October 15, 2008, http://www.financialweek.com/apps/pbcs.dll/article?AID=2008810159987.
50. Other legal commentators have explored the costs and benefits of moving from periodic to real-time disclosure. For example, Erick D. Prohs, "Periodic Reporting: A Relic of the Past?" *Journal of Corporate Law* 27 (2002): 481.
51. Ken Bamberger notes that developments in information systems may now allow for real-time reporting and monitoring of "governance, risk, and compliance" issues; see Kenneth A. Bamberger, "Technologies of Compliance: Risk and Regulation in a Digital Age," *Texas Law Review* 88 (2010): 669, 697–698.
52. Gerding, "Code, Crash, and Open Source," 190–191.

53. U.S. Department of Treasury, *Financial Regulatory Reform: A New Foundation* 65 (2009). These current calculators are designed to help consumers and investors calculate financial needs not to show financial disclosure under different scenarios and assumptions.
54. This academic movement was popularized in Richard H. Thaler and Cass R. Sunstein, *Nudge: Improving Decisions about Health, Wealth, and Happiness* (New Haven, CT: Yale University Press, 2008).
55. E.g., Ian Ayres, "Menus Matter," *University of Chicago Law Review* 73 (2006): 3.
56. For a thumbnail sketch of how the GUI and drop-down menus made computer operating systems more user-friendly, see Linda Null and Julia Lobur, *The Essentials of Computer Organization and Architecture* (Sudbury, MA: Jones and Bartlett, 2006), 414.
57. See Gerding, "Code, Crash, and Open Source," 167–168.
58. See Jennifer Arlen and Eric Talley, eds., *Experimental Law and Economics* (Aldershot, Hants, England: Edward Elgar Publishing, 2008)(surveying emergent field); Erik F. Gerding, "Laws Against Bubbles: an Experimental-Asset-Market Approach to Analyzing Financial Regulation," Wisconsin Law Review (2007): 977 (arguing for using experimental asset market research to test securities regulations).

12 Data Integrity Preservation and Identity Theft Prevention

Operational and Strategic Imperatives to Enhance Shareholder and Consumer Value

Kevin Govern and John Winn

INTRODUCTION

Today, more than ever before in the history of modern commerce, businesses find themselves acquiring, using, and protecting personal and corporate identity information. At the same time, identity theft and identity fraud crimes have "grown to epidemic proportions, [especially] theft of sensitive, non-public protected information."[1] Consumers needing access to diverse goods and essential services increasingly turn over more and more identity data. *Forbes Magazine* has noted the existence of an increasingly acute market tension as "companies and the public sector grow more aggressive in gathering and using information," while increasing the risk of identity theft and fraud.[2]

Given the current risk environment, businesses are obligated to do their utmost to protect systems and ensure consumer confidentiality. Unfortunately, even the prudent and vigilant business entities may still be susceptible to data theft or other outside system intrusion. In this respect, sound corporate governance should include some degree of planning and preparation for worst-case scenarios. There are several fundamental questions that every business should consider in order to effectively prepare for a breach of cybersecurity and ensure the integrity of stored data. For instance, in the event of a major system compromise, who bears the cost of system restoration or reimbursement? What about negative publicity, loss of goodwill, and lawsuits? What constitutes due diligence before and after a data compromise? What steps should management consider postbreach? What are the legal consequences to our business, customers, and other stakeholders, and should we purchase cyberinsurance?

This chapter seeks to provide answers to those questions, as well as to offer valuable suggestions for both individual private consumers and business entities on how to best protect electronic information. The first section of the chapter, "Part I," addresses current infrastructure risks and the challenges associated with cyberinsurance underwriting. The next section, "Part II," will attempt to summarize the increasingly complex legal and regulatory landscape inherent in preserving data integrity and preventing identity theft. Finally, the last section, "Part III," of this chapter will address the concept of "due diligence" and emphasize the importance of postbreach best practices that seek to protect revenue streams and customer goodwill while minimizing business disruptions and legal liability.

PART I: THE CYBER-RISK CLIMATE AND CYBER INSURANCE

The Internet has been the greatest boon in history for interpersonal communications, international commerce, and, unfortunately, the perpetuation of criminal theft and fraud. In 2007, market-leader Microsoft Inc. announced in a "Data Privacy Imperative" that "as advances in technology simplify and accelerate the flow of information, concerns about the collection and use of personal data, widely publicized security and data breaches, and growing alarm about online fraud and identity theft threaten to erode public confidence in the computing ecosystem and digital commerce."[3]

As businesses assess their operational as well as legal responsibilities, a culture of risk management should transcend mere risk mitigation and shareholder value. Jeffrey Liesendahl, CEO of Accertify, advises e-security is more than "cutting fraud losses and fraud-related complaints. It's about increasing accuracy, efficiency, and productivity of fraud-fighting efforts so the issue doesn't damage profitability, expansion plans, or brand reputation."[4] In assessing cyberthreats confronting the U.S., the FBI notes threats to commerce as emanating from two distinct areas: "(1) [T]raditional criminal activity that has migrated to the Internet, such as fraud, identity theft, child pornography, and trade secret theft; and (2) Internet-facilitated activity, such as terrorist attacks, foreign intelligence threats, and criminal intrusions into public and private networks for disruption of theft."[5]

The loss of private customer data to unauthorized third parties—such as Social Security numbers, credit card numbers, birthdates, and other confidential information—presents a daunting set of challenges as well as legal obligations for affected businesses. Identity theft has been America's "fastest growing crime" since at least 1989, and, although actual cost data is difficult to gauge, various studies estimate direct domestic losses to the U.S. business community at between fifty-six and one hundred billion dollars per year.[6] These rather staggering figures do not include significant additional tangential costs such as the criminal prosecution and incarceration of offenders.[7]

According to the Association of Certified Fraud Examiner's (ACFE) *2006 Report to the Nation on Occupational Fraud*, U.S. organizations lose an estimated 5 percent of their annual revenues due to fraud.[8] When applied to the estimated 2006 GDP, those losses added up to approximately $653 billion.[9] Organizations with antifraud programs—such as fraud hotlines, internal audit departments, and antifraud training—lost approximately half as much as those without such programs.[10]

Identity theft, and the resulting aftermath of a stolen identity, costs private consumers over two billion dollars and one hundred million hours of time each year. The Privacy Rights Clearinghouse, a nonprofit consumer organization, reported over eight million individual victims of identity theft in 2007 alone.[11] Also reported that year were nine hundred business-related data breaches in the United States alone, involving the compromise of over 245 million records containing personal information.[12] In just the past two years, hackers, disaffected employees, and other cybercriminals have compromised data networks at TJ Maxx/Marshalls, Barnes & Noble, Bank of America, Wells Fargo, Stanford University, Princeton University, the Veterans Administration, Fannie Mae, and the City of San Francisco.[13] According to the Department of Justice, reports of data breaches increased even more dramatically in 2008, with 656 reported breaches, an increase of 47 percent over the preceding year's total of 446.[14] This includes a total of 35,691,255 stolen of otherwise compromised identities. According to that same study, only 2.4 percent of all breaches occurred while encryption or other strong protection methods were in use, and 8.5 percent of reported breaches had password protection.[15] Considering the enormity of these incidents, there is no way to be certain "how many other retailers, who might not be quite as careful, are already being breached."[16] As dependence upon data access—especially wireless applications—continues to grow, new vulnerabilities will be further exploited.

Cybercrooks perpetrate criminal theft and fraud over the Internet to obtain goods, services, and cash impersonally while exploiting time lags in discovery and investigation. Cybercrooks also seek out valuable non-ID-specific business data including executive emails, engineering and marketing data, bid sheets, and trade secrets. In the financial services sector, the vast majority of credit card, debit card, and ATM transactions—even mortgage transactions—occur online in virtual anonymity without the risks normally associated with in-store, face-to-face transactions. Cybertheft is usually nonviolent, has high profit margins, and incurs little or no risk of detection or prosecution. In ideal circumstances, identity theft can go undetected for months—or may never be detected at all. The 2003–2004 breach at TJ Maxx/Marshalls, which compromised over 94,000,000 Visa and MasterCard accounts, remained undiscovered for nearly two years.[17]

Journalist Sandra Block recently wrote about the insidious and persistent nature of such cybercrimes, noting their ability to haunt victims for months.[18] At particular risk are young adults, of whom about 5.3 percent aged eighteen to twenty-four self-identify as victims of identity theft within the past twelvemonths in 2007 (up from 4.5 percent in 2006), according to Javelin Strategy and Research.[19] The same study also found that 3.7 percent of all adults were victimized, down from 4 percent a year earlier.[20] Yet, when only a single individual is victimized, the loss of private information is usually attributable to theft by another family member, friends, or "data-mining" via home waste (i.e., "dumpster-diving"), or scams such as data "phishing." Out-of-pocket consumer costs in these instances rarely exceed one hundred dollars because the business community absorbs most individual account losses associated with consumer data theft.[21] Federal consumer protection laws under Title 15 of the U.S. Code limit liability for most losses—such as unauthorized electronic fund and credit card charges—to a maximum of fifty dollars per account.[22] The Electronic Funds Transfer Act also limits consumer liability for unauthorized ATM or debit card transactions.[23] Of course, this does not take into account the difficulties, aggravations, and expenses entailed in canceling compromised accounts and activating new ones.

Despite the significant burdens placed on individual victims of cybertheft, it is rare for the perpetrators to find themselves faced with sanctions. Although convictions for cyber-related theft and fraud may carry substantial criminal penalties under existing statutes such as the False Identification Crime Control Act and the Internet False Identification Act, few law enforcement agencies have the time, expertise, or even inclination to pursue online criminals.[24] Because identity theft crimes take place in "cyberspace," police must often coordinate with other state, federal, or even international agencies in what can easily become a cross-jurisdictional and diplomatic three-ring circus. Even when jurisdictional issues are capable of resolution, normally only high-profile or careless offenders face actual criminal prosecution by federal, state, or local authorities.

Private consumers are not the only ones burdened by cybertheft, as many businesses also have private and valuable information to protect. In many respects, businesses have become even easier targets for identity theft than private consumers. Almost anyone can obtain a business's tax identification number (i.e., the business' Social Security number). A merchant's basic financial information, including back account numbers, may be known to hundreds of wholesale customers and suppliers. Data access can be exploited by numerous employees. Such insider theft and fraud is often difficult to detect, especially when carried out by trusted individuals. Businesses virtually never review their own credit information for fraud and may not be as careful as they should be in shredding or disposing of documents. Few businesses ensure the bona fides of their commercial waste shredding contractor and even fewer conduct background checks of in-house or contract cleaning staff.[25] Businesses are also slow to upgrade data security. One commentator noted that, in his experience, most retail data systems are "put together with baling wire and packing tape . . . as retailers move from dial-up or proprietary networks to open networks and wireless connectivity, the risks go up exponentially."[26]

In the business sector, however, data compromises usually involve an in-house or organic information network.[27] Such business-specific data-breach operational risks may include:

> Hundreds, if not thousands, of separate consumers, business partners, as well as other stakeholders. In addition to costs for indemnifying individual consumer accounts, business must also absorb indirect remediation expenses such as making contact with affected customers, coordination with credit report agencies, and assisting law enforcement. There may also be business disruption expenditures to upgrade compromised information systems and litigation expenses. Indirect remediation costs may easily exceed the costs attributable to consumer reimbursement alone.[28]

To deal with traditional risks such as fire, flood, and thefts, businesses purchase blanket or umbrella insurance policies. Unlike individual consumers who may purchase relatively low cost (and usually unnecessary) "identity theft" insurance, commercial identity theft and data intrusion coverage is quite expensive, and, in some instances, remains unavailable. In fact, insuring business losses associated with cybercrime has been a singular challenge to the entire insurance industry worldwide. Currently, less than a third of U.S. companies have cyber-indemnification for data theft, hacking, business disruption, or customer reimbursement.[29]

Because threats to IT systems change almost daily, predicting loss scenarios, the frequency of cyberattacks, or victim financial outcomes on an actuarial basis are extremely difficult. It is generally conceded by IT professionals that 100 percent security is impossible to achieve and IT security is almost entirely reactive. In fact, "penetrate and patch" is the term most widely used in the cybersecurity field.[30] Not surprisingly, even when available, cyberinsurance may incorporate a myriad of confusing definitions, preconditions, limitations, and exclusions. Premiums for even small and mid-size businesses often begin at ten thousand dollars, and rapidly escalate to a point at which they rival the cost of predicated losses. Deductibles are also high, sometimes only beginning coverage after the first twenty-five thousand dollars in documented losses.[31]

Some policies mandate expensive third-party IT system audits, which, by necessity, allow unfettered access by strangers to proprietary data such as budgets, security, or trade secrets. Not surprisingly, most businesses have determined that preventative measures are a more efficient allocation of resources than cyberinsurance. When purchased, however, some cyberinsurance policies do cover legal and public relations expenses. In one instance, a cyber-risk insurer indemnified a policyholder for payments made to settle threats from a web-based extortionist.[32] Even the best cyberinsurance policies, however, do not indemnify for lost customer trust and goodwill.

Certain industries that are particularly susceptible to cybertheft have responded by developing their own specific defenses and procedures. A specific partial response to network vulnerabilities in the credit card industry is the Payment Card Industry Data Security Standard (PCI-DSS) initiated by Visa and MasterCard and even more recently by several other major credit card companies.[33] PCI-DSS requirements are part of a global network that requires participating merchants (or service providers) to establish and maintain rigorous standards related to network security, encryption, and access controls. PCI-DSS also requires continuous monitoring and testing of system vulnerabilities, including wireless networks. Merchant compliance may be validated by third-party industry-certified auditing terms, self-assessment for small merchants, or network scanning.[34]

PART II IDENTITY THEFT AND THE CYBERLAW LANDSCAPE

In light of substantial media coverage of identity theft, especially upon individual consumers, the cyberlaw regulatory climate has changed substantially. Virtually all states have new "information privacy" laws on their books. And whereas most other new state legislation focuses upon criminal actors, penalties, and restitution (following California's lead), at least forty-four states have also enacted customer notification laws.[35]

In the federal sector, the focus has shifted somewhat from criminal enforcement to regulation. The Federal Trade Commission (FTC) in particular has imposed heavy fines for rule violations and requires affected businesses to self-report data breaches. In November of 2004, the FTC filed a civil enforcement action against Nationwide Mortgage for its failure to protect private mortgage data under the Gramm-Leach-Bliley (GLB) Act Safeguards Rule.[36] Sunbelt Lending Services was cited the next year for similar violations.[37] In 2005, the FTC held that BJ's Wholesale Club created unnecessary risks by: (a) storing information longer than thirty days; (b) allowing anonymous employee access to consumer accounts; (c) failing to encrypt data; (d) failing to secure wireless access portals; and (e) failing to detect intrusions or conduct follow-up security investigations.[38] As part of the settlement in this case, BJ's agreed to allow FTC supervision for twenty years and third-party verification of security procedures. BJ's was also forced to write off sixteen million dollars in claims for reimbursement from related fraudulent credit card purchases.[39] Both of these cases indicate the level of precaution a business entity must take in order to protect electronic data, at the risk of paying the expenses of potential fraudulent misuse of that information.

Another important challenge for businesses to consider is the risk of class action lawsuits by disaffected and angry customers. Even in light of recent limiting legislation, including the Class Action Reform Act of 2005 (aka Class Action Fairness Act),[40] identity theft victims are probably much more likely than other litigants to share a jurisdictional "commonality of issues" requirement.[41] For large businesses especially, consumer losses from data theft could easily exceed the five-million-dollar threshold, triggering exclusive federal jurisdiction for class actions.[42] In addition to extensive litigation costs, class actions also expose businesses to intrusive and disruptive pretrial discovery processes, including the possibility of punitive or even trebled damages.

In this complex and dangerous environment it is therefore of critical importance to be aware of the most important federal laws affecting business and industry interests. A lack of understanding about current regulation could result in a heavy fine, in addition to the loss of customer trust and the creation unnecessary risks for the business' financial future. The following is a brief overview of relevant and evolving identity theft and cyberlaws.

Identity Theft and Assumption Deterrence Act (ITADA)

Primary among cyber-related federal criminal statutes is the Identity Theft and Assumption Deterrence Act of 1998 (ITADA).[43] The ITADA distinguishes identity theft from other crimes such as wire fraud by encompassing theft of data and mandating significant fines and imprisonment, even for certain first offenders. The ITADA encompasses businesses or persons that seek access to personal records via banks, state and federal agencies, or insurance companies. Federal criminal jurisdiction, however, requires an underlying felony (such as fraud or conspiracy) and must involve an "identification document" that either: (a) is purportedly issued by the United States, (b) is used or intended to defraud the United States, (c) is sent through the mail, or (d) is used in a manner that affect interstate or foreign commerce.[44]

Fair and Accurate Credit Transactions Act of 2003 (FACTA)

The Fair and Accurate Credit Transactions Act of 2003 (FACTA)[45] established a national fraud detection system to preempt fraud and theft as early as possible with or without subsequent law enforcement investigation. The final rules were effective January 1, 2008. They require financial institutions and creditors to develop and implement an Identity Theft Prevention Program (ITPP) to mitigate the risk of identity theft from customer accounts.[46] The compliance deadline was May 1, 2009. Approximately two million financial institutions, credit unions, and creditors had until May 1 to adopt security updates to their ITPPs.[47]

Due to FACTA, a consumer may alert all three major credit reporting agencies of purported criminal misuse of financial data or accounts via phone or email. FACTA also led to the creation of the well-known "free" annual credit report regime, additionally requiring mortgage lenders to provide actual FICO credit scores (not just credit account data) if that score could be used to determine interest rates for home loans.[48] For additional consumer protection, FACTA also mandates that merchants leave off all but the last five digits of credit card numbers on store receipts. It also established a nationwide fraud alert system to "red flag" suspicious requests for consumer data and allow military personnel to "freeze" credit files while they are deployed overseas.[49] Whereas individual consumers may not have the sophistication or wherewithal to perform a detailed red flag approach, one suggested corporate strategy from the Jefferson Wells Corporation recommends the following:

Key Activities

Phase 1: Perform an IT risk assessment: Analyze the current environment for risks, including redundancies, inefficiencies, and insufficient and nonexistent controls. Identify current process and procedures related to identity theft and incident response.

Phase 2: Develop the appropriate identity theft program: Set up a framework and integration plan with the participation of senior leadership. Create a mitigation plan for identity theft risks, develop or update security policy and procedures, and create a security awareness program.

Phase 3: Implement the policy and procedures: Execute a mitigation plan for identity theft risks and train the organization on the identity theft and security awareness program.

Phase 4: Perform regular review and analysis of identity theft program: Update the risk assessment related to identity theft, re-evaluate the legislation, and modify the policy and procedures to reflect the requirements.

Key Results

Phase 1: Risk assessment.

Phase 2: Identity theft policy and procedures, mitigation plan, implementation plan, and documented security awareness program.

Phase 3: High-performing identity theft process.

Phase 4: Update risk assessment policy and procedure.

Consumer "red flags" include actual fraud alerts from a reporting business that has identified either a data breach, unusual patterns in credit usage, suspicious documentation, credit usage after long periods of inactivity, known mail drop addresses, or other anomalies.[50] FACTA enables consumers to place either an "initial" alert or "extended" alert to prevent credit grantors from opening new accounts. An "initial alert" is for individuals who suspect they are victim of an ID theft, and an "extended alert" are for those individuals who are confident they have been victimized and have filed a police report. The extended alert remains in place for up to seven years. As part of the extended alert package, credit agencies must also exclude the consumer's name from prescreened credit or insurance offers for five years. A third option is available to members of the U.S. military, who may also place an "active duty alert" during active duty or assigned when they are assigned to service away from the usual duty station.[51]

According to FACTA, not only must businesses shred documents containing employee data, but those that supply or facilitate consumer credit must also secure or destroy consumer information. The so-called "disposal rule" requires reasonable and appropriate destruction of all information derived from a consumer credit report before disposal. Failure to comply with destruction requirements (i.e., shredding) may be charged penalties of up to $2,500 per violation.[52] Proper destruction prior to disposal may consist of burning, pulverizing, or shredding papers as well as electronic files. There is an implied obligation within the FACTA disposal rule to conduct due diligence in hiring or contracting out data disposal including audits, reference checking, and physical inspection of licenses or certificates.

Notable FACTA developments include the October 30, 2009, decision in the related case of order by U.S. District Court Judge Reggie B. Walton regarding the American Bar Association's seeking to enjoin the FTC from applying its "Red Flags Rule" to practicing attorneys. Judge Walton granted the ABA's motion in a partial summary judgment, holding that the FTC had exceeded its authority by interpreting the term "creditor" to include attorneys engaged in the practice of law. That same day, the FTC issued a press release announcing that it was delaying enforcement of the rule until June 1, 2010, a decision welcomed by the American Institute of Certified Public Accountants (AICPA).[53]

The AICPA has filed a lawsuit against the FTC challenging the applicability of the "Red Flags Rule" to Certified Public Accountants. The lawsuit follows on the heels of FTC's recent decisions to delay the enforcement of the rule for the fourth time.[54] The rule, promulgated by the FTC in November 2007 to comply with the FACTA of 2003, requires financial institutions and creditors to develop and implement written identity theft programs to help identity, detect and respond to patterns, practices, or specific activities—known as "red flags"—that could indicate identity theft. It was originally set to take effect on November 1, 2008, but after the latest extension, it is now set to become effective June 1, 2010.

Fair Credit Reporting Act (FCRA)

Victims of identity theft may also bring legal action against businesses under the Fair Credit Reporting Act (FCRA).[55] FCRA requires reporting businesses and agencies to adopt reasonable procedures to maintain and report consumer data with confidentiality, accuracy, relevancy, and reasonable security. Credit reporting businesses must ensure "reasonable procedures to assure maximum possible accuracy of the information concerning the individual about whom the report relates."[56]

Consumer victims may sue for willful or negligent failure to verify the accuracy of disputed information or correct inaccurate information resulting from a stolen identity. Consumers who report errors or fraudulent transactions are entitled to a "reasonable investigation" by the reporting business and an expectation that discovered errors will be corrected and reported back promptly. The statute provides for attorney's fees and punitive damages for willful violations under the act. Under FCRA, victims of identity theft may authorize law enforcement agencies to obtain their credit reports and other records without the necessity of obtaining a subpoena at no additional cost. FCRA, however, imposes a two-year statute of limitations that begins when an inaccurate disclosure or report is filed, not when the consumer actually becomes aware of the inaccuracies.[57]

Similar to FACTA, the FCRA also includes a "disposal rule" requiring any business that has access to or that utilizes consumer reporting information (usually credit reports) to dispose of this sensitive information properly. The FCRA disposal rule is broader than the FACTA disposal rule however and encompasses any company that complies, sells or purchases any reports containing private personal or medical information. This includes employment agencies, banks, private investigators, landlords, auto dealers, insurance agents, claims adjusters, and others. This particular disposal rule applies to the disposal of information in any format, requiring it to be done using a method that renders the documents or information unreadable or incapable of reconstruction.

GRAMM-LEACH-BLILEY ACT (GLBA)

Additional consumer credit information safeguards for financial institutions are found in the GLBA of 1999. GLBA instructs eight federal regulatory agencies and the states to administer and enforce the Financial Privacy Rule and the Safeguards Rule, to ensure the financial institutions prevent unauthorized disclosure of consumer financial information. Within the category of unauthorized disclosure is fraudulent access, a crime that financial institutions are instructed to prevent by implementing appropriate policies, procedures, and controls. Also known as the Financial Services Modernization Act of 1999, GLBA defines financial institutions as a "business significantly engaged in providing financial services or products for personal, family, or household use."[58] This encompasses both traditional banks and credit unions, but also includes check-cashing and payday loan services, nonbank lenders, real estate appraisers, tax preparers, debt collectors, financial advisors, and insurance agents and brokers. GLBA prohibits "pretexting" by identity thieves or others seeking consumer data via financial institution or other listed quasi-financial institutions.[59]

Right to Financial Privacy Act (RFPA)

The Right to Financial Privacy Act of 1978 (RFPA) falls under the auspices of the Federal Deposit Insurance Corporation (FDIC) and targets industrial loan companies, trust companies, saving associations, building and loan companies, credit unions, and consumer finance institutions.[60] RFPA creates statutory Fourth Amendment protection for personal bank records by stating that:

> No government authority [state or federal] may have access to or obtain copies of, or the information contained in the financial records of any customer from a financial institution unless the financial records are reasonably described and:
>
> 1. the customer authorizes access;
> 2. there is an appropriate administrative subpoena or summons;
> 3. there is a qualified search warrant;
> 4. there is an appropriate judicial subpoena; or
> 5. there is an appropriate written request from an authorized government authority.[61]

In addition, RFPA prohibits banks and other covered entities from requiring customers to release financial records as a condition of doing business and mandates banks provide customers with access to records of all disclosures made to third parties.[62]

Health Insurance Portability and Accountability Act (HIPAA)

Health care systems are extremely dependent upon computer-based or electronic medical records. Medical staff and other users are also heavy users of hand-held data units, laptops, home-computer links, Smart Phones, Smart Cards, USB "flash drives," and BlackBerries, as well as other Personal Digital Assistant (PDA) technology. Medical data is transmitted and stored among a myriad of computerized patient record networks. Doctors and others are moving very rapidly to paperless "E-Prescribe" systems linking them directly to pharmacies via laptops and hand-held wireless devices such as BlackBerries.

Health care networks implement varying security systems, practices, and policies but within the context, all "covered entities" that collect or retain private health information in paper or electronic form must comply with privacy provisions of the HIPAA of 1996.[63] HIPAA, which is administered by the U.S. Department of Health and Human Services (HHS), establishes nationwide security standards for electronic health care information. This so-called HIPAA "security rule"[64] requires all covered entities to be compliant with specific administrative, technical, and physical security standards and procedures for electronic data. HIPAA rules apply not only to doctors, clinics, hospitals, pharmacies, and laboratories, but may also apply to certain collection agencies, health insurers, and lawyers. HIPAA rules also apply to any businesses that maintain self-insure employee health care plans.

Under HIPAA, cyberdata is labeled as "electronic protected health information" or "EPHI."[65] EPHI is of particular value to identity thieves because health care data is truly the "mother lode" of private information. Included in the category of EPHI are names, addresses, birthdates, Social Security numbers, insurance information, bank and credit card data, and records of past and present medical treatment. HIPAA also requires covered entities to only do business with secondary organizations that also adequately and appropriately safeguard EPHI. A more detailed discussion of HIPAA's complex requirements is outside the ambit of this analysis—but like any data loss the consequences of medical identity theft, besides direct financial costs, include negative publicity, loss of customers, and potential civil liability.

PART III OPTIONAL AND REQUIRED SAFEGUARDS FOR BUSINESSES

Good protection equates to good preservation and promotion of shareholder value, consumer confidence, and operational efficiency. Any effort to ensure the integrity of online data requires an effective combination of administrative, physical, and technical safeguards. Access to data should always be limited to the absolute minimum number of persons with a valid need for access. Employees with access to data must be properly screened, trained, supervised, and disciplined as necessary. In the event of resignation, suspension, or termination of employees, human resources departments must be diligent to ensure that systems and infrastructure are firewalled from further access. Risks assessment must be uncompromising and include the possibility of audits of system administrator functions by trusted outside agents.

Working partnerships and similar business arrangements with third parties must be based upon a shared commitment to data privacy, safeguards, and systems oversight. Security policies must be created in accordance to the highest reasonably assessed risk. In this respect, pinching pennies is a poor business strategy if any significant system compromise yields a "zero" return on cybersecurity. There is a wealth of best practices information available to business manages and leaders via the Internet Security Alliance (ISA).[66] ISA provides a twelve-step security program for small businesses at no cost.[67] Similar secure networking information is available from the National Cyber Security Alliance (NCSA), the Chamber of Commerce, and the United States FTC.[68]

Proper protection does not end at preventative measures. A business that believes it is facing a criminal compromise of IT data or systems should call their local police department immediately. The sooner law enforcement officials become involved, the more effective their efforts at assistance can be. In many instances, local police agencies may additionally seek the assistance of the FBI or U.S. Secret Service. Financial institution fraud (FIF) continues to be a significant "white-collar crime" problem throughout the country.[69] Since 9/11, the FBI has refocused its FIF program and is now investigating higher-priority cases to a much greater degree. Large-scale mortgage fraud and identity theft operations, many perpetrated by organized criminal enterprises, also continue to plague the United States.[70]

The Secret Service has concurrent jurisdiction with the Justice Department for financial crimes and primary jurisdiction for crimes involving financial infrastructure and bank payment systems. This includes both domestic and international access device fraud, theft of debit and credit information, identity theft, false identification, and computer fraud. As part of the U.S. Patriot Act of 2001, the Secret Service was mandated to establish a nationwide Electronic Crimes Task Force (ECTF).[71] The ECTF network coordinates with federal, state, and local law enforcement agencies to prevent, detect, and mitigate threats to financial infrastructures.[72] The benefit of agencies at different levels sharing information can be seen in certain instances such as mail-related fraud, or the theft of information from the mail, where local authorities will coordinate their investigative efforts with the Office of the Postal Inspector at the federal level.

Proper communication procedure requires not only the notification of law enforcement agencies, but also the notification of those affected by the crime. Section 609(e) of the FCRA requires businesses to provide copies of transactions records to victims of identity theft (and law enforcement) upon request.[73] Victims of identity theft may in turn authorize law enforcement agencies to obtain records free of charge within thirty days of receiving the request in writing. There is no requirement for a subpoena under these circumstances as long as the agency in question has a victim's written permission.[74] Required records may include invoices, credit applications, or account statements. Businesses should be careful to avoid making matters worse by requesting victims or law enforcement agencies to provide affidavits or police reports before complying with such requests.

Further, a proper response to identity theft also requires communication with other businesses that may be impacted. Identity theft from one business frequently impacts other businesses, especially banks, credit card issuers, and credit reporting agencies. For this reason, it is critical that every business that may need to monitor a customer's accounts (for subsequent fraudulent activity) be notified as soon as possible. This is especially important if names or Social Security numbers are compromised, in which case all three major credit bureaus should be advised of the situation as soon as possible. A quick response and direct communication better prepares these agencies to facilitate customer requests for fraud alerts and account freezes.

Throughout the process of responding to an identity theft, businesses must be sure to protect any information that may be helpful for criminal prosecution. Safeguarding the evidentiary digital "chain of custody" for future prosecution of wrongdoers is often difficult. This process may require the assistance of a computer forensics specialist, or someone who is capable of preserving computer data in the proper format. Thus, when cases finally get to court, records will be properly admitted under the "business records" exception to the hearsay rules.[75] One case from 2003 demonstrates what happens if this information is not properly protected. In that case, a cyber-extortionist threatened to expose customer data from 350,000 credit cards obtained from CD Universe Inc. In the subsequent investigation, law enforcement officials (including the FBI) admitted that failure to properly preserve the electronic evidence "virtually eliminated the possibility of prosecution."[76]

Despite past difficulties in criminal enforcement, advances in the process and law enforcement capabilities are still being made. For example, an important change in the prosecution of cybercrime and identity theft came about in October 2008 via the Identity Theft Enforcement and Restitution Act (ITERA).[77] This act allowed for the prosecution of even more cybercrimes than previously allowed, eliminating the past requirement that prosecutors show the illegal activity caused at least five thousand dollars in damages before they can bring charges for unauthorized access to a computer. As this act amends Title 18's Crimes and Criminal Procedure,[78] it is now a felony, during any one-year period, to damage ten or more protected computers used by or for the federal government or a financial institution. The act also directs the U.S. Sentencing Commission to review its guidelines and consider increasing the penalties for those convicted of identity theft, computer fraud, illegal wiretapping, or breaking into computer systems.[79]

Avoidance and Prevention

Due diligence measures address the problem of cybertheft or identity theft before it happens, and may include some or all of the following practices.

- Compile a list of state and federal regulations affecting or applicable to your business.
- Develop policies, procedures, and training to ensure compliance with applicable rules and regulations.
- Review confidentiality agreements with business partners, IT vendors, and archive services (if applicable).

- Appoint a qualified and trusted employee as an information security officer.
- Set and enforce strict access and encryption policies including rules describing what data can be printed, emailed, or copied.
- Limit, monitor, or block employees from disclosing confidential information (or inadvertently downloading malware) via social networking and blogging sites.
- Strengthen password and authentication regimes via onetime password generation, smart cards, or a combination of these technologies plus electronic access badges.
- Test systems to ensure they are able to detect and prevent intrusions and inappropriate usages.
- Consistent with legal requirements, contractual obligations, and corporate values, prepare contact lists of persons and entities (including credit reporting agencies) that should be notified in the event of a data breach.
- Ensure your corporate governance, including board members, are cognizant of your IT security planning. (Note: Sarbanes-Oxley standards require that accurate reporting systems and sufficient internal controls are in place).[80]
- Ensure human resources departments document all employee security training.
- Promulgate a policy requiring employees to report lost or stolen laptops, smartphones, and other PDAs immediately.
- Monitor reports of data theft and other incidents via organizations such as the nonprofit Identity Theft Resource Center.
- Audit janitorial, waste disposal, and shredding services to ensure compliance with applicable disposal rules.
- Develop a continuity plan to protect critical business processes in emergency or disaster scenarios (including plans for database failure or physical loss).
- Designate and train a postincident/postdetection "Computer Incident Response Team" (CIRT) composed of IT professionals and appropriate managers.
- Consider adding information security and privacy to your business or corporate code of conduct.

Postcompromise Measures:

- Review state and federal disclosure and notification regulations.
- Ensure adequate information is provided to customers, law enforcement, and other stakeholders regarding how the breach may affect them and what steps your organization is taking.
- Designate one member of the CIRT as primary point of contact (person and office) within your organization for information dissemination to customers, police, and press inquiries.

- Prepare an informative press release to reassure the public that appropriate measures are in place to minimize any disruptions to customers or service. Be sure to provide the same information via your home webpage.
- Notify customers promptly via mail that their private customer data may be compromised and advise them of the appropriate steps they should take to protect their accounts from further misuse, obtain refunds, etc.
- Keep affected customers and others updated as information develops or mitigation strategies are put in place.
- Consider engaging the services of a qualified IT consulting company to provide customers with professional ID monitoring and restoration services such as TheftSmart or LifeLock at no personal cost.[81]
- File a complaint with the FTC using the online complaint form, the Identity Theft Hotline, or the nongovernmental Privacy Rights Clearinghouse to provide information that can help law enforcement officials across the nation track down identity thieves and stop them, and for referrals to other government agencies and companies for further action.[82]

CONCLUSION

This has been the most elemental of surveys regarding one of the most increasingly pervasive threats to business entities and individuals in the twenty-first century. In reviewing this assessment, managers and leaders should consider the need to integrate both preventative security and post-breach survivability into IT planning, and communicate their proactive strategies to their shareholders and consumers alike to build their confidence—as well as market confidence—in the soundness of their efforts. In other words, implement data security prospectively, but don't neglect strategic planning for worst-case scenarios, and keep a simultaneous focus on the security of day-to-day operations. As present and future opportunities for IT-based commerce grows, both private and governmental entities must also heighten their appreciation and anticipation of future infrastructure risks and the cyber-risk climate, and adapt corporate and public policies and laws not just to resist but to more effectively prevent and combat cybercrime and identity theft.

NOTES

1. Institute of Fraud Risk Management, *Critical Need for Certified Identity Theft Risk Management Specialists*, http://www.tifrm.net/content.aspx?id=91.
2. Kevin Allison and Michael Peel, "Devil in the Details: Why Personal Data Are Ever More Open to Loss and Abuse," *Forbes*, December 11, 2007, 45.

3. Data Privacy Imperative, *Microsoft's Approach to Helping Protect Personal Information in the Digital Ecosystem*, February 2007, 1, http://download.microsoft.com/download/c/0/d/c0ddb7d5–287d-4b65–88d4–c0ee1b94adbb/Microsoft percent20Data percent20Privacy percent20Imperative.doc.
4. Jeffrey Liesendahl, "Ask the Information Security Experts," *Washington Post, Media Planet: 2 Information Security Supplement* (2009): 8.
5. Federal Bureau of Investigation Strategic Plan 2004–2009, 16, http://www.fbi.gov/filelink.html?file=/publications/strategicplan/strategicplanfull.pdf.
6. See *Identity Theft: Is There Another You?* Joint Hearing before the House Subcommittees on Telecommunications, Trade, and Consumer Protection, and on Finance and Hazardous Materials, 106th Cong. 16 (1999), Serial No. 106–16, December 7, 2009. See also GAO-02–363, *Identity Theft: Prevalence and Cost Appear to Be Growing*, March 2002, http://www.gao.gov/new.items/d02363.pdf.
7. Ibid.
8. ACFE, *2006 ACFE Report to the Nation on Occupational Fraud and Abuse* (2009), 8–9 http://www.acfe.com/documents/2006–rttn.pdf (2009).
9. Ibid.
10. See, e.g., *Managing the Business Risk of Fraud: A Practical Guide*, cited with authority on Corporate Governance Website (July 2008), http://corpgov.net/news/archives2008/july.html.
11. Privacy Rights Clearing House, *Reducing the Risk of Identity Theft*, http://www.privacyrights.org/fs/fs17–it.htm.
12. Privacy Rights Clearing House, *A Chronology of Data Breaches*, http://www.privacyrights.org/ar/ChronDataBreaches.htm.
13. Ibid.
14. The Identity Theft Resource Center (ITRC), Report Database 1/2/2009, 1, 201, http://www.idtheftcenter.org/BreachPDF/ITRC_Breach_Report_2008_final.pdf.
15. Ibid.
16. Evan Shuman, "Data Theft Began in 2005; Data Taken from 2003," *E-Week.com*, http://www.eweek.com/c/a/Security/TJX-Data-Theft-Began-in-2005–Data-Taken-from-2003.
17. See Shuman, "Data Theft Began in 2005." See also, e.g., Allison McGevna and Mike Levine, *Three Indicted in Largest Corporate Identity Theft Case in History* (August 17, 2009), available at http://www.foxnews.com/story/0,2933,540060,00.html.
18. Sandra Block, "Identity Thefts a Big Pain, but Protecting Yourself Needn't Be," *USA Today*, February 6, 2007, C1.
19. Javelin Strategy and Research Study, *U.S. Identity Theft Losses Fall*, February 1, 2007, http://www.privacyrights.org/ar/idtheftsurveys.htm#Jav2007.
20. Ibid.
21. GAO, *Identity Theft*, at 9.
22. 15 USC §1643.
23. 15 USC §1693g.
24. False Identification Crime Control Act, Pub. L. No. 97–396, 96 Stat. 2009 (December 31, 1982); Internet False Identification Act, Pub. L. No. 106–578, 114 Stat. 3075.
25. See Shuman, "Data Theft Began in 2005."
26. Ibid.
27. U.S. Secret Service, "Identity Fraud Trends and Patterns: Building a Data-Based Foundation for Proactive Enforcement," *Center for Identity Management and Information Protection* 67 (October 2007), http://www.utica.edu/academic/institutes/ecii/publications/media/cimip_id_theft_study_oct_22_noon.pdf.

28. *National Security: Cyber Infrastructure Risk, Operational Risk Management*, November 22, 2009, http://operationalrisk.blogspot.com.
29. Russ Wiles, "Cybercrime Insurance Growing," *Arizona Republic*, September 15, 2004, http://www.azcentral.com/arizonarepublic/business/articles/0915insure15.html.
30. David Maynor, "Why the 'Penetrate and Patch' Idea Is Not Only Great, but also Essential," *Errata Security* (April 21, 2008), http://erratasec.blogspot.com/2008/04/why-pentrate-and-patch-idea-is-not-only.html.
31. Dan Briody, "Full Coverage: How to Hedge Your Cyber Risk," *Inc.com* (April 1, 2007), http://www.inc.com/magazine/20070401/technology-insurance.html.
32. 2006 CSI/FBI Computer Crime and Security Survey, http://i.cmpnet.com/gocsi/db_area/pdfs/fbi/FBI2006.pdf.
33. PCI Security Standards Council, *The Prioritized Approach to Pursue PCI-DSS Compliance* (March 31, 2009), https://www.pcisecuritystandards.org/education/docs/Prioritized_Approach_PCI_DSS_1_2.pdf.
34. Ibid.
35. State Security Breach Notification Laws, National Conference of State Legislatures (NCSL), http://www.ncsl.org/programs/lis/cip/priv/breachlaws.htm.
36. FTC website, http://www.ftc.gov/os/caselist/0423153/0423153.htm.
37. In re: Sunbelt Lending Services, FTC File No.:042 3153, January 7, 2005.
38. Thomas Claburn, "BJ's Wholesale Club Settles FTC Data—Protection Complaint," *Information Week*, June 26, 2005.
39. FTC: In the Matter of BJ's Wholesale Club, Inc. File No. 042 3160, *Analysis of Proposed Consent Order to Aid Public Comment*, http://www.ftc.gov/os/caselist/0423160/050616anal0423160.pdf.
40. Class Action Fairness Act, Public Law 109–2, 119 Stat. 4 (2005).
41. Federal Rule of Civil Procedure 23(a)(2) lists "questions of law or fact common to the class" as a prerequisite to bringing a class action.
42. Office of the Clerk, U.S. House of Representatives, 105th Congress, Second Session, March 5, 1998, http://commdocs.house.gov/committees/judiciary/hju59921.000/hju59921_cf.htm.
43. 18 USC §1028(a)(7).
44. Ibid.
45. FACTA of 2003 (FACT Act or FACTA, Pub. L. 108–159).
46. Ibid.
47. Ibid.
48. Ibid.
49. FTC, *Agencies Issue Final Rules on Identity Theft Red Flags and Notices of Address Discrepancy* (October 31, 2007), http://www.ftc.gov/opa/2007/10/redflag.shtm.
50. FACTA §§114, 335.
51. 15 USC §1681c.
52. FACTA §216.
53. *American Bar Association v. FTC*, C.A. No. 09 1636 (RBW) October 20, 2009.
54. "FTC Extends Deadline for 'Red Flags' ID Theft Rule," *WebCPA*, November 2, 2009, http:///www.webcpa.com/news/FTC-Extends-Deadline-Red-Flags-ID-Theft-Rule-52277–1.html.
55. FCRA, 15 USC §1681.
56. Ibid., §1681e(b).
57. *TRW Inc. v. Andrews*, 122 S. Ct. 441 (2001).
58. GLB Act, Pub. L. 106–102, 113 Stat. 1338 (1999).
59. 15 USC §§6821, 6823
60. RFPA, 12 USC §3401 (1978).

61. Ibid.
62. Ibid.
63. HIPAA, Pub. L. 104–191, 110 Stat. 1936 (1996) (as amended).
64. U.S. HHS, 45 Code of Federal Regulations (CFR) Part 160—General Administrative Requirements, and 45 CFR Part 164—Security and Privacy (2009).
65. See HIPAA, note Error! Bookmark not defined..
66. ISA, *Articulating the Value of Cyber Security* (2010), www.isalliance.org.
67. Ibid.
68. Chamber of Commerce, United States FTC, NCSA.
69. Internal Revenue Service, *Financial Institution Fraud- Criminal Investigation (CI): Overview* (November 3, 2009), http://www.irs.gov/compliance/enforcement/article/0,,id=117522,00.html (describing their program designed to combat FIF as addressing "criminal violations involving fraud against banks, savings and loan associations, credit unions, check cashers, and stockbrokers").
70. FBI Strategic Plan 204–2009, 4, see note 5.
71. Uniting and Strengthening America by Providing Appropriate Tools Required to Intercept and Obstruct Terrorism (U.S. Patriot) Act of 2001, Pub. L. No. 107–56, 84 Stat. 1116.
72. Ibid.
73. FCRA, 15 USC §1681 et seq. (1978).
74. Ibid.
75. FRE §803(6).
76. Mike Brunker, "CD Universe Evidence Compromised," *ZDNet*, June 8, 2000, http://news.zdnet.com/2100–9595_22–96132.html.
77. ITERA 2008, amending Title 18, Part II, Chapter 232, § 3663 (2008).
78. Ibid.
79. Ibid.
80. Public Company Accounting Reform and Investor Protection Act of 2002, Pub. L. 107–204, 116 Stat. 745 (2002).
81. See http:www.lifelock.com; https://www.idtheftsmart.com/default.aspx.
82. FTC website, *DEFEND: Recover from Identity Theft*, http://www.ftc.gov/bcp/edu/microsites/idtheft/consumers/defend.html. The FTC website provides a link to the online complaint form at https://www.ftccomplaintassistant.gov/; it provides the FTC's Identity Theft Hotline toll-free number as: 1–877-THEFT (438–4338); TTY: 1–866–653–4261; and provides the address to write to the Identity Theft Clearinghouse, Federal Trade Commission, 600 Pennsylvania Avenue, NW, Washington, DC, 20580.

13 Credit Derivatives and Corporate Governance

A Review of Corporate Theory

P.M. Vasudev

> [T]here are so many [derivatives] and some of them so esoteric that the risk involved may not be properly understood even by the most sophisticated investor, and I'm supposed to be one.
>
> George Soros (1994)[1]

INTRODUCTION

The recent events in the financial markets, usually termed the "credit crisis," throw up serious issues of corporate governance. There have been significant failures at major corporations in the financial sector—American International Group (AIG), Bear Sterns, and Lehman Brothers, to name the more prominent. This chapter examines the events of the credit crisis from the perspective of corporate governance in the post-Enron, Sarbanes-Oxley world.

Current corporate theory conceives governance as a two-tier structure. Managers or full-time executives of the corporations would be responsible for day-to-day management and for making the operational decisions. The managers would be under the oversight of a board of directors, which is charged with the task of monitoring the executives. To promote the integrity of the structure corporate theory has, in the recent past, stressed the "independence" of the directors, who would have an arm's-length relationship with the managers. In addition, audit by independent professionals is conceived as an external check on the management, although the scope of the audit exercise is quite limited.

The chapter examines how the governance framework, outlined in the preceding, functioned in the events that led to the credit crisis. It approaches good governance as an endogenous feature in corporations, rather than a product of the legal regime and the threat of sanction that is implicit in public regulation. This is consistent with:

- the open structure of the law of corporations and its minimally intrusive character
- the idea that the governance must be more a concern of the corporations, rather than regulation[2]

It is significant that the recent failures have happened in what could be called the Sarbanes-Oxley world. The Sarbanes-Oxley Act of 2002[3]was enacted in response to serious lapses at the turn of the century. It can be interpreted as a product of increased recognition of the idea that public policy has a meaningful role in corporate governance. The Sarbanes-Oxley, which imposes some standards on public corporations, was presented as a measure to promote corporate responsibility. U.S. President George Bush, while commending the legislation in New York in 2002, stood against the backdrop of a banner with the words "corporate responsibility" prominently printed on it and spoke about the "difference between ambition and destructive greed, between justified risk and irresponsibility."[4]

For their part, most corporations in the recent times position themselves as responsible companies and stress that they treat their corporate citizenship with seriousness. For example, AIG stated in its annual report for 2006:

> Truly excellent companies not only deliver superior results, they do so in a way that respects the dignity and uniqueness of individuals while observing responsible and sustainable business practices. At AIG, we believe that being a good corporate citizen protects the interests of our shareholders, customers and employees, and is essential for long-term success.[5]

The corporations involved in the credit crisis had "state-of-the-art" governance structures—with independent directors, audit committees, governance charters, and so on. The chapter argues that these trappings of good governance and a stated commitment to the principle of responsible governance made little difference to the outcome. The experience, once again, brings to the fore the question how far the good governance of public corporations ought to be a concern of public policy.

Considering the latest round of failures, the chapter proposes regulatory definition of the functional responsibilities of the directors of public corporations. This would expand the role of the directors beyond the limited, and largely undefined, monitoring task that is assigned to them in economic theory, and can potentially promote greater deliberation in determining corporate policy and developing business strategies. The chapter also recommends mandatory risk assessment as a means of monitoring corporate health and sustainability on an ongoing basis.

The chapter is divided into six sections. The second section discusses the important credit derivatives developed in the recent times—namely, Collateralized Debt Obligations (CDOs) and Credit Default Swaps (CDSs), which were at the center of the crisis. The third section provides an overview of the development of corporate theory and outlines the considerations that have shaped its development. The fourth section examines how a new line of business—such as credit derivatives—would be typically handled in the prevailing framework of governance. It discusses how the various elements in the current theory of corporate governance played out in the failures seen during the credit crisis. The fifth section examines the case for a more expansive role for the boards of directors in public corporations. It explores the question of defining the functional responsibilities of the directors, and mandatory risk assessment and reporting for the corporations. The final section concludes with proposals for regulatory definition of the functional responsibilities of the directors and for submission of reports by the directors.

CREDIT DERIVATIVES

Credit derivatives—mainly CDOs and CDSs—played an important role in the recent crisis.[6] These have been developed recently, and have complex characteristics. This part provides an overview of CDOs and CDSs, which have been at the center of the crisis.

Collateralized Debt Obligations

A CDO is a pool of debt consisting of a number of debt securities or loans. The level of risk in the individual loans or securities, which could range from treasury securities and corporate bonds to subprime mortgages, would be quite diverse, and the return from them would also vary significantly. CDOs were developed by Drexel Burnham Lambert, a now defunct investment bank.[7] The theory is that by combining a number of debt securities with varying degrees of risk—ranging from treasury bonds to credit card debt—it would be possible to obtain higher yields without significantly increasing the overall credit risk.

Understandably, the pools of debt in CDOs would be more complex than simple lending transactions between a borrower and a lender, or even conventional debt securities issued by a single borrower. The following are some important characteristics of CDOs.

- In the financial industry, CDOs were generally treated as a single consolidated pool of debt, rather than a collection of individual debts.
- The method of credit rating applied to CDO reflected this idea of consolidated debt. Adopting a collective approach, the portfolio of debt would be normally ranked into three broad categories or "tranches":
    - equity or residual, which had the highest risk
    - junior or subordinated or mezzanine, with moderate risk
    - senior, which would have minimum risk

- Tranching of CDOs would be done on the basis of the creditworthiness of the subgroups of debt securities and the risk perceived in each of them. Typically, the senior tranche would consist of "AAA" rated debt securities.
- Understandably, credit rating had a major function in the CDOs business. The tranches in a CDO would be based on the respective grades of risk identified by the professional credit rating agencies.[8]
- The return model in CDO is quite different from conventional debt. Here, the focus would be on the total cash flows from the portfolio, which would be the aggregate of the interest and principal receipts over the entire tenor or duration of the debt securities in the CDO. Unlike conventional debt, interest and principal repayments would not be treated separately.
- The cash flow from a CDO would be allocated among the three levels or tranches, and prioritized among the senior, junior, and equity levels in that order. This is the return for the investors. The senior tranche, with the lowest risk, would have the lowest return. The return to the middle level, or junior, would be greater and the "equity" category with the highest risk would receive the highest return.
- The incentive to invest in CDOs was the promise of a return above London Inter-Bank Offered Rate (LIBOR). The incremental return, termed a "spread," would be the highest for the equity tranche and lowest for the senior segment.
- CDOs were marketed among investors as having defined risk and reward computed according to complex mathematical models. CDOs were sold to investors on the basis of these models that defined the risk in each tranche and the relative reward.[9]

These were the major characteristics of "cash" CDOs, which were fully funded and relatively straightforward. In cash CDOs, an investment bank would arrange for the transfer of a group of debt securities from a bank or a lending institution to a Special Purpose Entity (SPE). The money raised by the SPE from the investors would be equivalent to the par value of the debt securities to be acquired, and this amount would be paid to the originating bank or lending institution for assigning or transferring the securities to the SPE.

Normally, the originating bank or lending institution would transfer all the debt securities in a CDO to the SPE, except the equity or residual tranche. The bank would retain the residual tranche, and any defaults in this segment will be borne by the bank. The bank's retention of this most risky element, usually about 5 percent of the total value of a CDO, was used a selling point for marketing the other tranches among investors.

A CDO would help a bank eliminate sizable debt, or loan portfolios, from its balance sheet. The transfer of debt and attendant credit risk, and the consequent reduction in the level of regulatory capital applicable were the incentives for the banks to support and encourage CDO. In the cash model of CDOs, the SPE, being fully funded, would acquire the credit risk in the portfolio from the lender by paying it off. The credit risk is merely transferred from the lender to the SPE, and no new risk or enhanced risk would be created in the process. For these reasons, cash CDO would not engender significant systemic risk or instability.

The following figure explains the relatively simple cash CDO model, also known as the balance sheet model because it removed the debt portfolio from the balance sheets of the banks. The figure shows the hierarchy among the CDO holders—equity, subordinate, and senior tranches.

There is another variety of CDOs—synthetic—in which the originating bank would merely transfer the credit risk to the SPE, rather than the debt securities themselves. The bank would retain the debt with itself. Normally synthetic CDO would be partially funded, which means that the amount of money raised from the investors in the CDO would be only a fraction of the par value of the underlying debt portfolio. Obviously, this variety of CDO is more volatile and engenders greater risk. In synthetic CDOs the originating bank, as noted earlier, would not transfer the underlying debt to the SPE. The debt would continue with the bank or other lending institution. The SPE, which assumes the risk, would purchase credit protection, in the form of CDSs, for the "reference" portfolio of debt.[11] This would be the safeguard against risk.

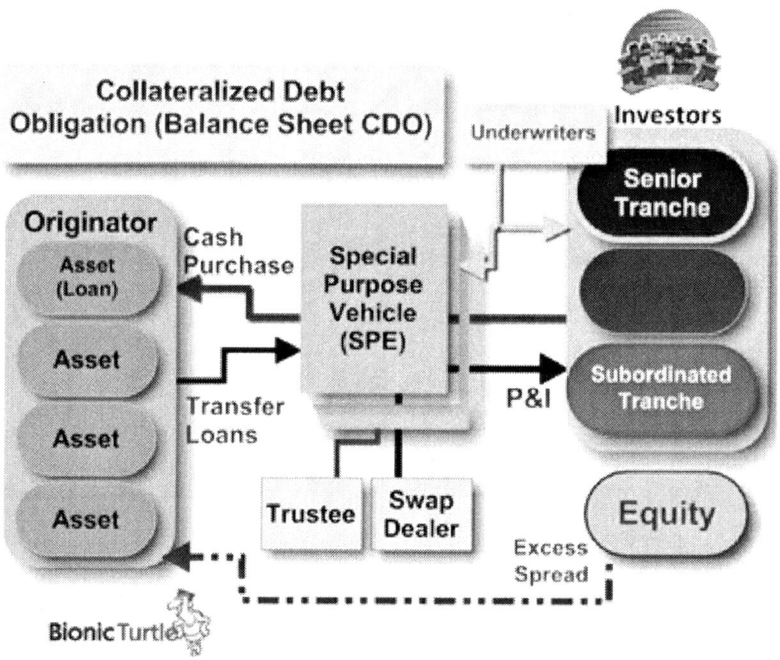

Figure 13.1 Cash or balance sheet CDOs.[10]

The case of BISTRO, which was the earliest partially funded synthetic CDO, is illustrative. It was promoted by JP Morgan in 1997, and had a funded component of $700 million against a total value of the reference portfolio at $10 billion.[12] The funding, which was just 7 percent of the total, was raised from the investors.[13] Apparently the remaining 93 percent, or $9.3 billion of the reference portfolio, would be covered by CDSs. For BISTRO, the swaps were provided by Morgan Guaranty Trust Company of New York.

If any default occurred in the reference debt portfolio covered by a synthetic CDO, the seller of the CDSs must make good the loss. The final liability will, therefore, be on the agency providing the swaps. The structure of a partially funded synthetic CDO is shown in Figure 13.2.

The synthetic or partially funded CDO appears foolproof in design—until there are large-scale defaults. Investors stand to gain as long as the premium for the default swaps is lower than the spread on their tranche of the CDOs. They simply pocket the difference without exposing themselves to any risk, as they are protected by the swaps. For the CDSs seller, the premium income would almost be a bonus as there is hardly any risk in the

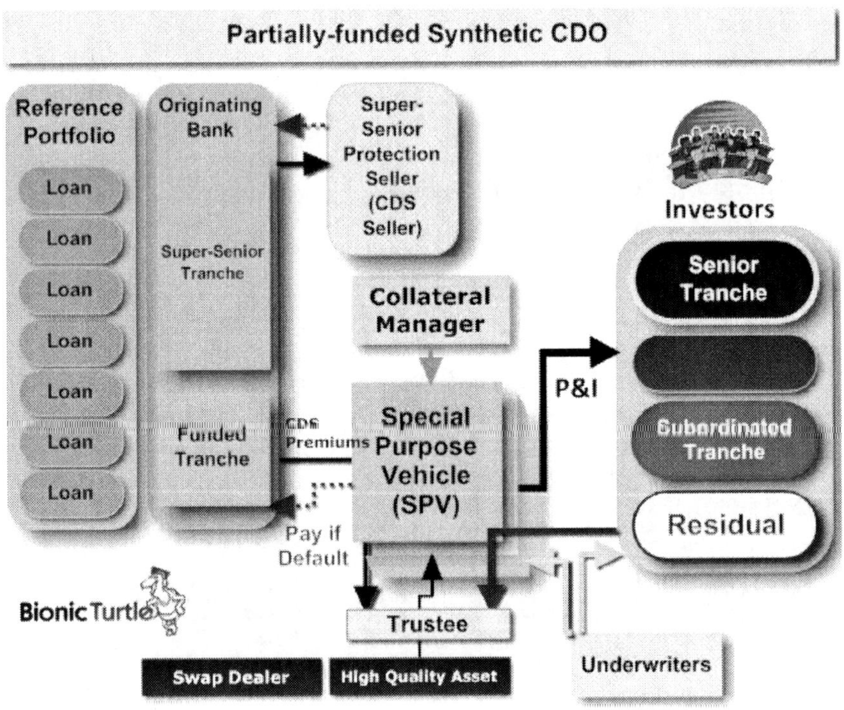

Figure 13.2 Partially-funded Synthetic CDO.
Source: www.bionicturtle.com

transaction. The debt securities covered by the CDSs are supposedly rated by professional agencies and, in theory, there is hardly any risk.

The synthetic CDOs framework, outlined earlier, had substantial economic legitimacy. It served to transfer or disperse risk, without creating additional risk or breeding systemic risk. This was, however, not the end of the story. Synthetic CDOs underwent another stage of development, and the financial industry developed CDOs that did not even assume the risk from the bank or the original lender, but simply purchased CDSs for the reference portfolios.

Obviously in this variety of synthetic CDOs, investors would simply bet on defaults in the reference portfolios, and would stand to gain if the defaults actually occurred. They would have a vested interest in default, and can compel the CDSs seller to pay. Synthetic CDOs of this variety are almost entirely speculative, and lack substantive economic justification. It was at the center of the meltdowns witnessed in the credit crisis of 2007–2008.

Credit Default Swaps

CDSs have been described as a "major risk-transferring instrument developed in the past few years."[14] In substance, they are similar to credit insurance, which has been a feature of the insurance industry landscape for a long time. CDSs have been in use since the early 1990s and were, arguably, "the most highly utilized type of credit derivative."[15] PIMCO, a large bond fund manager, explained the characteristics of CDS:

> In its most basic terms, a credit default swap *is similar to an insurance contract, providing the buyer with protection against specific risks* . . . CDS contracts can mitigate risks in bond investing by transferring a given risk from one party to another without transferring the underlying bond or other credit asset. Prior to credit default swaps, there was no vehicle to transfer the risk of a default or other credit event, such as a downgrade, from one investor to another. (*Bond Basics*; emphasis added)

In a CDS, one party "sells" risk and the counterparty "buys" that risk. The "seller" of credit risk—who also tends to own the underlying credit asset—pays a periodic fee to the risk "buyer." In return, the risk "buyer" agrees to pay the "seller" a set amount if there is a default (technically, a credit event).[16]

Like in insurance contracts, CDSs would provide protection against risk for a specified period of time and the CDS provider gets a fee from the other party for providing the cover. The CDS provider would be liable to make a payment on the happening of the "credit events" defined in the contract. The basic trigger would be simple default by the "reference entity," which would be the borrower.[17] But most CDS contracts also named other credit events such as the borrower filing for bankruptcy or resorting to restructuring of debts.[18] The sellers of CDSs must make either cash settlement or physical settlement when the credit event occurs.

- Cash Settlement: The CDS provider will pay the difference between the par value of the underlying debt security—the "reference obligation"—and its present value, determined in the manner specified in the contract. Cash settlement would be less onerous for the CDS provider when the debt security is assessed to have *some* value.
- Physical Settlement: Here, the CDS provider must purchase, at par, the debt security covered by the swap. Then, presumably, the CDS provider would be free to deal with the security as it pleases,[19] subject to any restrictions that might be applicable.

There are, however, important differences between regular insurance contracts and CDSs as they were developed. For instance a purchaser of CDSs, unlike an insured person, need not have an "insurable interest" in the asset. Insurable interest is an essential element in insurance contracts and it promotes the integrity of the transaction. There is a real and subsisting economic risk for the purchaser of insurance, which the insurance provider attempts to cover.

In some synthetic CDOs, as noted earlier, the debt portfolio would not be actually acquired by or transferred to the SPE. Therefore, it is questionable how far a SPE that operates a synthetic CDOs has an economic interest in the debt portfolio for it has purchased default swaps. There are reports of multiple default swaps for a reference obligation, which is evidence of financial speculation.[20] The issue is about the legitimacy of a person or an entity seeking protection against risk when there is no real and substantial economic interest in the risk. This is from the point of the buyer of CDSs.

There can, however, be little doubt about the *similarity* of the risk assumed by insurers and sellers of CDSs. The credit risk carried by the swap provider, a periodic fee for providing the cover, and making a settlement on default all underscore the similarities between CDSs and insurance policies. In other words, the seller of a default swap is in effect selling credit insurance.

The International Swaps and Derivatives Association (ISDA) argued, during the peak of the credit derivatives era, that CDSs are not in the nature of insurance contracts. This argument is quite understandable; ISDA was keen to keep CDSs business outside the net of the well-developed and fairly stringent regulation applicable to insurance. In *Aon Financial Products, Inc. v. Societe Generale*,[21] the court examined the character of CDSs. ISDA participated in the action as *amicus* and argued that they were different from insurance contracts. It was successful in persuading the court to make the following observation:

> CDS agreements are thus significantly different from insurance contracts. As amicus correctly points out, they "do not, and are not meant to, indemnify the buyer of protection against loss. Rather, CDS

> contracts allow parties to 'hedge' risk by buying and selling risks at different prices and with varying degrees of correlation." (qtd. from 476 F. 3d 90)

The case was decided in 2007—before the onset of the credit crisis—and the interpretation is open to question. It remains to be seen how the courts will deal with issues related to default swaps in the post-AIG world. In any case, the point made here is that the risk a CDS provider assumes is similar to the risk incurred by an insurer.

Other than making settlements on default, often CDS providers must also provide collateral when there is any decline in the market value of the debt portfolio covered by the swap. This could be a continuing obligation triggered by each fall in the market value of the CDO. This feature of default swaps makes them more onerous than insurance contracts. In its filing for 2007, AIG has explained the situation arising from its obligation to post collateral for declines in the market value of debt securities covered by the CDSs it had sold:

> AIG's liquidity may be adversely affected by requirements to post collateral. Certain of the credit default swaps written by AIGFP contain collateral posting requirements. The amount of collateral required to be posted for most of these transactions is determined based on the value of the security or loan referenced in the documentation for the credit default swap. Continued declines in the values of these referenced securities or loans will increase the amount of collateral AIGFP must post which could impair AIG's liquidity.[22]

The litigation between Paramax Capital, a small hedge fund, and UBS, the Swiss banking group, brings out the ramifications of the collateral requirement. Paramax created a SPE with a relatively meager capital of $4.6 million for providing default swaps for a debt portfolio of $1.31 billion. Soon the debt portfolio started falling in value due to defaults and downgrades, and Paramax had to provide additional collateral.

On demand from UBS, which had purchased the CDS, Paramax provided further collateral of $29.3 million. In all, it furnished collateral of $33.9 million against the debt portfolio of $1.31 billion for which it had provided credit protection under the swap. After this, Paramax refused demands from UBS for more collateral and the parties went to court.[23] Undercapitalization of CDS sellers, in this case Paramax, illustrates the dangers in unregulated financial markets and the larger systemic risks they can breed.

CORPORATE THEORY AND ITS DEVELOPMENT—AN OVERVIEW

The recent crisis saw some significant failures in corporate governance. AIG's assumption of unmanageable risk in the CDSs it sold and the volume of the unsustainable CDOs business in Citigroup are particularly glaring instances. In all these companies, the business decisions involved the application of corporate power. This section examines how current theory deals with corporate power and how far it regulates the exercise of the power.

Michael Jensen and William Meckling, in their famous article on agency costs, described a corporation as "a 'black box' operated so as to meet the relevant marginal conditions with respect to inputs and outputs, thereby maximizing profits."[24] This is a purely economic interpretation of business corporations and their governance. It does not pay sufficient attention to the law under which the corporations are organized and its underlying theory. The legal framework is designed to facilitate corporations to be efficient in their economic function and, at the same time, satisfy some normative criteria. The analysis in this part is concerned with both the dimensions—the economic as well as the normative.

To better understand current corporate theory, this section traces its development over time. The overview is helpful in juxtaposing the events in the credit crisis against the governance structure that has been conceived in corporate theory. The legal theory of corporate governance is influenced by a number of factors, such as corporate law, securities law, and stock exchange regulations. Each of them influences how listed companies are managed, and do so in different and significant ways.

The analysis of corporate theory is in part is with reference to each of the elements in the regulatory framework of governance—namely:

- corporate law
- governance codes
- securities law
- stock exchange regulations
- audit

Corporate Law

The formation of business corporations under general incorporation statutes began around the mid-nineteenth century.[25] At the time, business corporations were essentially conceived as vehicles for pooling capital.[26] Since the late nineteenth century, however, the legal framework as it developed recognized a proprietary position for the shareholders who had contributed the risk capital. Adolf A. Berle and Gardiner C. Means reflected this idea when they described the theory of corporate law:

> Corporations were originally groups of investors pooling their individual contributions of risk capital to organize and carry on an enterprise. Since they had saved their earnings or gains and had risked them in

> the undertaking, they were assimilated to the owner of the land, who cleared and cultivated it, and sold its products.[27]

For the management or the governance of these entities, the law adopted the principle of democracy as it had developed in the political arena. The shareholders were assimilated to the citizens in a society, and were given voting rights in proportion to the capital they had contributed.[28] They would elect the directors who derived their management powers from the statutes.

The rules on annual meetings of the shareholders and election of the directors were consistent with the democratic idea. Corporations were conceived as collective bodies that held periodic deliberations and the shareholder-owners would elect the directors as their representatives to manage the business and affairs, within the sphere allocated to them in the law of corporations. Corporate statutes reserve specific nonoperational decisions, such as amendments to the articles of incorporation, for the shareholders. This framework of the relationship between shareholders and directors is usually represented in economic theory in the principal–agent idiom.

The corporate statutes traditionally vested management powers in the board of directors, who would be elected by the shareholders. They also authorize the directors to delegate their powers to the "officers" or the executives, subject limited exceptions. Having done so, the corporate statutes with their open structure make no further intervention in the internal arrangements in corporations. The directors and executives are quite free to develop the governance structures and systems. Other than placing some restrictions on the powers of the directors to delegate their functions, the statutes provide little guidance to the corporations on the division of powers among the two groups—directors and executives—or define their respective areas of responsibility.

The idea that the directors, as elected representatives of the shareholders, would manage the corporations remained, more or less, intact as the twentieth century progressed. There were, however, other significant strands in the story of business corporations as it unfolded. One was the fact that the directors, who were nominally the elected surrogates of the shareholders, proved to be more powerful in the corporate framework. The shareholders were, in fact, ineffective. This development, since termed "separation of ownership and control," was the theme of the celebrated work of Adolf Berle and Gardiner Means, *The Modern Corporation and Private Property*, published originally in 1932.

Two major factors shaped the separation of ownership and control. One was the growing popularity of investments in shares by the general public and the rise of retail shareholders.[29] These investors fitted poorly in the proprietary position that shareholders had in corporate law. For all practical purposes, the retail investors did not possess the proprietary interest imputed to them in corporate theory and their interest was mostly confined to the stream of dividend income and potential capital gains from rise in share prices. Dispersal of shareholding and the emergence of passive retail shareholders undermined the legal model that shareholders would elect the directors and oversee them.

The other factor was the rise of large industrial corporations whose operations were immense in scale and complexity. These corporations required expert managers who worked full-time and had intimate knowledge of the business.[30] The senior executives who managed the corporations were also mostly on their boards. Their intimate knowledge of the business and the lack of any meaningful oversight by the shareholders made the manager-directors, in particular the CEOs, very powerful. Managerial power was almost unquestionable.

Berle and Means, whose work included a significant empirical component, found that the directors of large corporations had become entrenched. The directors were also able to perpetuate their positions, or, alternatively, determine their successors. In these processes the shareholders, contrary to the theory of corporate law, played no meaningful role. The term "managerial capitalism" was coined later to describe the new reality. The reality that the directors of large corporations do not, in fact, have a role in their management has also been recognized by the courts. There has been a general reluctance of the courts to hold the directors accountable for lapses by the corporations.[31]

Understandably, the concentration of economic power in the corporate directors generated controversy given the ingrained American suspicion of power and elite groups considered to have special privileges. The political argument against the concentration of economic power was stated eloquently by scholars such as Berle and Means (1932) and J.K. Galbraith (1967).[32] There were also complaints that many of the business decisions made by the corporate managers were motivated by self-interest.[33] In any event, the concern about corporate managers and their potential for abuse is a long-standing one. It can be traced all the way back to Adam Smith (1787) and his skepticism.[34]

Near-absolute control of the corporations by their full-time managers and the reality of managerial power raised the issue of regulating the executives. Here again, corporate theory resorted to the practices and ideas of the political democracy. As a result, it adopted the political instrument of "checks and balances" applied in constitutional law.

The debate on corporate power took on the idiom of "insiders" and "outsiders" on the boards of directors of public corporations. To counter the power of the insiders who were in control, in 1940 William Douglas proposed the appointment of "public interest directors" who would oversee the managements.[35] To be clear, independent directors have been around in Anglo-American business enterprises since at least the early nineteenth century,[36] and Douglas's proposal for public interest directors represented continuity with the tradition. Given the reality of shareholder inefficacy, it was believed that the outside directors would act as an effective check on the insiders.

Control of corporations by their executives, especially the CEOs, was again highlighted by Myles Mace in 1970.[37] By doing so, Mace reinforced the thesis of Berle and Means (1932) about entrenched and self-perpetuating directors who wielded enormous and unchecked power. The work of Myles Mace kept alive the issue about corporate boards and their composition, and encouraged public corporations to appoint independent or outside directors.

Analyzing the complexion of boards since 1950, Jeffrey Gordon divided the directors into three classes—inside, affiliated, and independent.[38] There can be little doubt about the first two classes; they would be naturally representatives of so-called managerial capitalism. The last group in Jeffrey Gordon's classification—"independent" directors—was conceived as a salutary influence on corporate managements and their power—a check on managerial capitalism, if you will. The idea was that the independent directors would have no relationship with the companies or their managers, and would be in a position to restrain managerial power. In addition, they would bring in greater objectivity in the governance of public corporations. The changes in the complexion of corporate boards between 1950 and 1980 are captured in Figure 13.3.

The pattern in the chart can be interpreted as a response to the growing sense of opposition to the concentration of corporate power in the managers. The three decades from 1950 to 1980 saw a fall in the ratio of inside and affiliated directors, and an increase in independent directors. The rise in independent directors has been particularly pronounced since 1970.

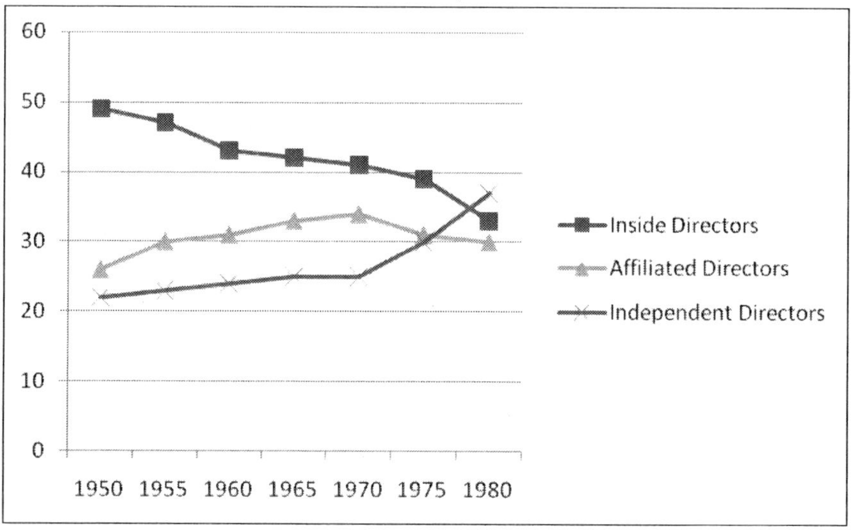

Figure 13.3 Board composition, 1950–1980.[39]

The "checks-and-balances" approach to governance and the prevailing ideas about outside directors also shaped the thinking about the function of boards. Given the dominance of insiders, the emphasis gradually shifted to the monitoring of managers by the directors. The role of the directors, especially the outside directors, moved from managing the corporations towards monitoring the managers. The trend towards monitoring boards is also evident from the decline in the ratio of inside directors.

These developments meant that the earlier model of management by the directors lost much of its validity. In the new setup, the directors would no longer manage the companies, but merely supervise or oversee the full-time managers. The statute law recognizes the concept of supervisory boards, and authorizes the directors to delegate many of their powers to the executives.[40]

In the model that emerged, the business and affairs of the corporations would be managed by full-time executives, and the boards would only play a monitoring role. This management structure was articulated by Mel Eisenberg in 1976.[41] Eisenberg compared the monitoring board with other possible models—(a) full-time directors, (b) boards made up fully of corporate managers, and (c) professional directors—and concluded that monitoring boards are the most practical and effective choice. In advocating this, Eisenberg stressed the importance of director independence and freeing them from the influence of the managers.

There is some evidence that the independent directors were discouraged from being active. In 1973 Arthur Goldberg, a former associate judge of the Supreme Court, resigned simultaneously from the boards of eight major corporations, protesting against their reluctance to provide the support needed for effective functioning.[42] More recently, Steve Jobs of Apple Computers withdrew his invitation to Arthur Levitt to be an independent director of the company when Jobs learned that Levitt planned to be active in his role.[43]

Corporate Governance Codes

Numerous codes of corporate governance have been developed in the recent years.[44] They are yet another significant influence on companies. These codes are designed to guide the corporations and provide a more concrete shape to the structure of governance. They elaborate the bare outline provided in the corporate statutes. The codes, as it were, provide flesh and blood to the skeletal structure laid out in the statutes. The codes are usually voluntary in application, and they do not have the effect of so-called "black-letter law." Yet they are important both for as evidence of the prevailing ideas on governance and for their influence on corporate practices.

The codes on corporate governance mostly formalize the structure outlined earlier—namely, management powers with the CEO and his /her team of executives, and oversight by the directors. *OECD Principles of*

Corporate Governance (2004), developed by the Organisation for Economic Co-operation and Development (OECD), can be cited as an example of voluntary codes. It is based on the monitoring board concept, and the section on boards' responsibilities begins with the following:

> The corporate governance framework should ensure the strategic guidance of the company, the effective monitoring of management by the board, and the board's accountability to the company and the shareholders.[45]

The OECD *Principles* stress the monitoring function of the boards. They also reflect the democratic principle in corporate law and the position of the directors as the representatives of the shareholders. OECD *Principles* identify eight "key functions" of boards of directors and the first two, extracted in the following, provide guidance on the scope of board oversight of business.

1. Reviewing and guiding corporate strategy, major plans of action, risk policy, annual budgets, and business plans; setting performance objectives; monitoring implementation and corporate performance; and overseeing major capital expenditures, acquisitions, and divestitures.
2. Monitoring the effectiveness of the company's governance practices and making changes as needed.
3. Selecting, compensating, monitoring, and, when necessary, replacing key executives and overseeing succession planning.
4. Aligning key executive and board remuneration with the longer term interests of the company and its shareholders.
5. Ensuring a formal and transparent board nomination and election process.
6. Monitoring and managing potential conflicts of interest of management, board members, and shareholders, including misuse of corporate assets and abuse in related party transactions.
7. Ensuring the integrity of the corporation's accounting and financial reporting systems, including the independent audit, and that appropriate systems of control are in place, in particular, systems for risk management, financial and operational control, and compliance with the law and relevant standards.
8. Overseeing the process of disclosure and communications.[46]

These prescriptions suggest a trend of expanding board responsibilities. The monitoring role is no longer restricted to passive oversight, or restraining the managers from abusing their powers. It is increasingly conceived and presented in more positive terms. The directors' function extends to playing a more active role in corporate business and policies. This development can, to some extent, be interpreted as promoting convergence between theory and practice by placing the directors in a closer relationship with the corporations. This is quite appropriate considering the fact that corporate law vests very substantial corporate powers in the directors.

The framework conceived in the OECD *Principles* reflects the model of governance adopted in most public corporations, including those in the financial sector. AIG's governance charter can be cited as evidence of this fact. At the material time, AIG's charter read:

> The business of AIG is conducted by management under the oversight of the Board. The roles of the Board and management are related, but distinct. AIG's business strategy is developed and implemented under the leadership and direction of the Chief Executive Officer by its officers and other employees . . . In performing its general oversight function, *the Board reviews and assesses AIG's strategic and business planning as well as management's approach to addressing significant risks and challenges facing AIG.* [T]he Board reviews and discusses reports regularly submitted to the Board by management with respect to AIG's performance, as well as significant events, issues and risks that may affect AIG's business or financial performance. [T]he Board and its members will maintain frequent, active and open communication and discussions with the Chief Executive Officer and the management of AIG. (emphasis added)[47]

The wording of the charter suggests a board of directors that is reasonably active. Its function is not confined to passive oversight of the managers, but something more. The board would engage with the managers regularly and provide guidance on business policies and strategies.

Securities Law

Federal securities law is the third element in the web of corporate governance regulation. Securities law has traditionally applied disclosure as the principle of regulation.[48] The idea is that compelling public corporations to make disclosures about their operations and financial results would be effective in achieving the desired results. This is, in turn, is based on the theory that:

1. When corporations are aware that they must make disclosures, they will adopt healthy and responsible practices. In other words, the disclosure regime has the potential to steer corporations towards good governance.
2. Alternatively (or cumulatively), mandatory disclosure will put the investors on alert, so they can avoid investing in the shares of corporations that have less-than-desirable standards of governance. The corporations would be eager to make themselves attractive to investors in the stock

market, and this is the incentive for them to adopt good governance, even if they are not persuaded merely by the need to disclose.

In the words of Louis Loss and Joel Seligman, "substantive regulation has its limits. But '[t]he truth shall make you free.'"[49] With this philosophy regulation, until recently, stopped with mandating disclosure. It required the corporations to disclose not only what had happened, but also what they expected to happen, including the risk factors.

The Sarbanes-Oxley Act, which was enacted in 2002 in the wake of the scandals at Enron, WorldCom, et al., went beyond mere disclosure. It makes what, in the traditional sense, would be considered an intrusion in corporate governance—dictating the composition of boards of directors and qualifications of independent directors. Public corporations must now have independent directors, or rather, audit committees consisting of independent directors.[50] The Sarbanes-Oxley Act requirement for independent directors is thus indirect. Rooted as it is in the scandals about financial disclosures by corporations, the Sarbanes-Oxley's concern is mainly with disclosures and promoting the integrity of the process. To achieve this, it requires the corporations to have audit committees which would oversee financial reporting and the committees must only have independent directors.

Stock Exchange Regulations

In the recent years, the stock exchanges as self-regulating organizations have made some significant inroads into the governance of listed companies. Post-Enron, the New York Stock Exchange (NYSE) compiled a set of governance standards applicable to the corporations listed on it.[51] The rules framed by NYSE can be traced to the Securities Exchange Act of 1934, and it is possible to identify a regulatory source for them.[52] The governance standards developed by NYSE are quite extensive, and the principal provisions are summarized in the following.

There is considerable depth and breadth in the corporate governance standards developed by NYSE. The standards are also refreshingly "organic" or institutional in approach. They are not designed on the conventional "command-and-control" principle. Rather, they seek to put in place agencies and systems that can promote the responsible and ethical governance of business corporations.

In the framework that is evolving, there is significant reliance on committees of the board of directors. NYSE governance standards, for example, are replete with references to the committees. The increasing reliance on committees is in recognition of the limitations of full boards—a relatively larger body—in carrying out specific tasks, such as ensuring the integrity of the financial statements or monitoring the business risks facing a company. To address this systemic issue, the device of committees

Table 13.1 New York Stock Exchange Corporate Governance Standards Summary

Section Reference	*Requirement*	*Remarks*
303A.01	Listed companies must have a majority of independent directors.	Extensive of definition of "independence" is included in the Standards.
303A.03	Outside directors must hold regular meetings with executives, in the absence of management directors.	The procedure would promote internal transparency in companies, and provide an opportunity for the executives to bring any issues to the notice of the outside directors.
303A.04	Listed companies must have a Nominating/Corporate Governance Committee consisting entirely of independent directors and a charter that spells out the responsibilities of the committee.	The standards provide guidance on the contents of the charter and the functional methods of the Committee. Evaluation of the committee's performance is mandatory.
303A.05	Mandatory Compensation Committees made up of independent directors, and the Committee must have a charter.	Companies are provided guidance on preparing the charter, similar to Nominating/Corporate Governance Committee
303A.06	Audit Committee with only independent directors, and must have a charter.	Additional requirements are specified for Audit Committees.
303A.08	Shareholder approval is mandatory for equity compensation plans for executives.	Guidance is provided on the applicability of the rule requiring shareholder approval for equity compensation.
303A.09	Listed companies must have Corporate Governance Guidelines.	Guidance is provided on the contents of the Guidelines
303A.10	Listed companies must have Code of Business Conduct and Ethics	Guidance is provided on the contents of the Code. Issues i nclude conflict of interests, corporate opportunity and confidentiality.
303A.12	CEOs must provide annual certification about non-violation of the governance standards.	The exercise is meant to ensure that companies regularly monitor compliance with the standards.

(continued)

Table 13.1 (continued)

Section Reference	*Requirement*	*Remarks*
303A.13	There can be a public remand by NYSE for violation of the standards.	This is a "soft" penal provision for enforcing the mandatory governance standards.
303A.14	Listed companies must have a website that fulfils the specified conditions and has the requisite contents.	The device would promote transparency by providing the public easy access to key corporate information.

is increasingly adopted in regulation, and specific responsibilities are assigned to the committees.

The committee system and its application can be seen in AIG whose board had a total of six committees at the material time. In the recent times, risk management has emerged as a major issue and it is recognized as such in corporate governance. Risk and its management were particularly relevant for the credit derivatives business. Among the committees of AIG's board, two—namely, the Audit Committee and the Finance Committee—had risk management as a part of their function. The Audit Committee's charter had, at the material time, the following among the "Other Duties and Responsibilities" of the committee:

> The Committee shall discuss the guidelines and policies governing the process by which senior management of AIG and the relevant operations of AIG assess and manage AIG's exposure to risk, as well as AIG's major financial risk exposures, and the steps management has taken to monitor and control such exposures. The Committee is not the sole body responsible for oversight of AIG's risk assessment and management. AIG manages and assesses its risk through multiple mechanisms other than the oversight of the Committee, including the oversight of other committees of the Board.[53]

The Finance Committee, which is the other committee involved in risk management, has a more direct responsibility. Its "Duties and Responsibilities" included:

> *Risk Management*
>
> Management shall review with the Committee, as the Committee may deem appropriate, reports concerning AIG's exposures to market, liquidity, credit and operational risks in so far as those

> exposures relate to financial, transactional and other matters considered by the Committee as part of its duties and responsibilities under this Charter.[54]

The rationale for having board committees, as noted earlier, is that they are more compact bodies better suited for handling specific tasks or responsibilities. Considering the recent experience with the financial corporations and credit derivatives, it is an open question how far the board committee mechanism has fulfilled the expectations about their contribution to promoting good governance.

Audit

Financial reporting and audit are requirements under the federal securities law, and this legal history defines the ethos of the reporting and audit exercises. In its origin in America, financial reporting by public corporations was understood as the means for facilitating the determination of fair prices for the securities traded in the stock market. Adolf A. Berle was an influential figure who argued for the adoption of the informational regime in securities regulation. Writing in 1932, just before the enactment of the securities statutes and in the aftermath of the Great Crash of 1929, Berle explained the principle:

> In a word, a respectable open market appraisal, based on a compromise between the opinions of willing buyers and willing sellers was what was actually required.
>
> Appraisal necessarily turns on information. If the open market view was to approximate a judgment of worth, it became essential that some material for such judgment should be provided.[55]

Price discovery in the stock market was thus understood as the goal of regulation in requiring corporations to publish periodic financial reports. Audit was introduced in America along with the rule on corporate reporting. It was conceived as a supplement to the disclosure regime. At the time of its introduction corporate reporting was restricted, more or less, to submitting financial statements, and audit was conceived as the instrument for ensuring the integrity and accuracy of the financial reports furnished by the corporations.[56] The Securities Exchange Act of 1934 mandates listed corporations to have their reports audited by an independent firm.[57]

The scope of audit and regulatory intervention in the subject has gradually expanded since the Securities Exchange Act of 1934 was enacted more than several decades ago.[58] By and large, the integrity and accuracy of financial reports have continued as the major concerns of the audit process. After Enron and other scandals in the early 2000s, there is evidence of some change in the thinking about the scope of the audit of public corporations. The new regime introduced under the Sarbanes-Oxley Act is more elaborate in outlining the scope of the audit exercise. Other than detecting "illegal acts" and "identify[ing] related party transactions," audit must now include:

> an evaluation of whether there is substantial doubt about the ability of the issuer to continue as a going concern during the ensuing fiscal year.[59]

The new requirement pays greater attention to the business aspect. Audit is no longer merely about detecting illegality or conflicts of interests. Equally, the process must examine the business conditions and determine the viability and sustainability of the enterprise for the next year. These broader terms of reference extend the scope of audit to detection of business risks and threats. This can be interpreted as graduating step for the audit exercise—as an instrument for strengthening the governance structure in public corporations. This is consistent with the trend of expansion in the responsibilities of the boards of directors, discussed a little earlier.

The Corporate Governance Process

In the model of corporate governance outlined earlier, business decisions would be made by the managers, subject to review by senior managers, board committees, and finally the board itself. In addition, there would be audit by an independent firm. This framework with its numerous layers can be understood as a linear process and the product would, or ought to, be good governance.

The reference to "good governance" raises definitional issues. Defining good governance, as a concept, is important considering the apparent differences in the perceptions about the corporate objective or goal. In the recent times, economic theory has emphasized shareholder value as the goal. Another school, however, treats the nonshareholder groups, or the stakeholders, as equally important.

At a minimum, good governance would consist of a management structure and a set of practices that foster the growth of a company's business, in a sustainable manner, with due regard to all the stakeholders including shareholders, and without causing significant externalities. This framework recognizes the shareholders as the "residual claimants," who will derive the ultimate benefit from a company's success, but equally respects the other constituencies such as employees, suppliers, and communities.

The governance model with its various elements can be understood as a liner process. The process and its outcome—namely, good governance—are shown in Figure 13.4.

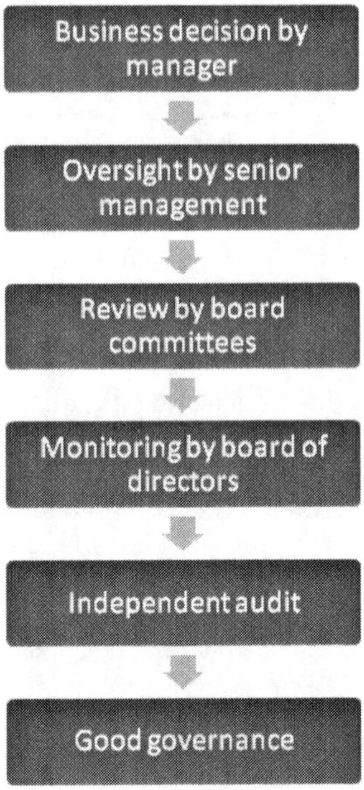

Figure 13.4 Corporate governance as a linear process.

John C. Coffee has recently included other agencies, such as lawyers, securities analysts, credit rating agencies, and investment banks, also in the governance framework. They are termed "gatekeepers" who would monitor the corporations.[60] At present, however, there is little recognition of these gatekeepers in the framework of corporate governance. No clear or precise role has been conceived for them in governance as a continuing process. For this reason, they are not included in the model discussed here.

THE CREDIT DERIVATIVES BUSINESS AND THE CORPORATE GOVERNANCE PROCESS

The experience with the credit derivatives business in major corporations in the financial sector must be evaluated against the governance structure and process discussed in the third section of this chapter. The question is whether the framework with its various devices and mechanisms—oversight by senior managers, review by board committees, board monitoring, and independent audit—was effective in delivering the results expected in corporate theory.

There are at least two dimensions to the credit derivatives business:

- level of engagement of the various layers in the business
- appreciation of the risks involved

This is a complex question of fact. As an empirical issue, it would require a detailed examination of the process of management oversight in the individual companies, the proceedings of board committees, and the proceedings of the boards of the corporations during the relevant period. In general, information on these issues is not publicly available, and it is not possible to come to concrete conclusions about the respective roles played by the agencies comprised in the governance structure.

However, the outcome—namely, business failure—is quite clear unambiguous. Considering the result, it would be reasonable to conclude that there *are* deficiencies in the present multilayer monitoring and oversight model of corporate governance, which lays little stress on responsible governance or individual accountability.

Derivatives have been controversial since they made their appearance more than two decades ago. They have been in the news. This is an important fact in determining the level of awareness of the directors about the credit derivatives business in the respective companies and the risks perceived in the business. The continual debate on derivatives and knowledge about the debate would be relevant both as a matter of fact and in providing objective standards for streamlining the engagement of senior managers and directors in major corporate decisions.

In 1992, Representative Edward J. Markey directed the General Accounting Office (GAO) to study the risks in derivatives, and the report published by GAO in 1994 identified "significant gaps and weaknesses" in the regulatory oversight of derivatives.[61] In the late 1990s Brooksley E. Born, chief of the Commodity Futures Trading Commission (CFTC), made efforts to regulate derivatives, but was unable to make progress.[62]

In 1994, George Soros testified before the House Banking Committee and issued warnings about derivatives.[63] He stated that some derivatives "appear to be specifically designed to enable institutional investors to take gambles which they would not otherwise be permitted to take."[64] In 2003, Warren Buffett famously described derivatives "as time bombs, both for the parties that deal in them and the economic system."[65] Buffett stated:

> Large amounts of risk, particularly credit risk, have become concentrated in the hands of relatively few derivatives dealers, who in addition trade extensively with one other. The troubles of one could quickly infect the others.
>
> On top of that, these dealers are owed huge amounts by non-dealer counter-parties. Some of these counter-parties are linked in ways that could cause them to run into a problem because of a single event, such

> as the implosion of the telecom industry. Linkage, when it suddenly surfaces, can trigger serious systemic problems.[66]

There can be little doubt that derivatives were right in the middle of the debate in financial and regulatory circles. This background, as noted earlier, is relevant in evaluating the business decisions made by the companies that engaged in credit derivatives business, especially from the perspective of corporate governance, monitoring, and oversight. It would be difficult to argue that the top managers and directors of the companies lacked knowledge about the business and its complexities, or the risk it carried. This idea informs the following discussion on the corporate governance structure and contemporary practices.

Undeniably, credit rating agencies played a role in the decisions that were made in the credit derivatives business. Assessment of credit risk by the professional agencies is presented as a crucial factor both in marketing the CDOs among the investors and in selling the default swaps. But this cannot justify laying the entire blame on the rating agencies, and by implication, absolving the actors in the corporations charged with the responsibility for their governance. As just seen, there were sufficient warning signals about credit derivatives and the corporate actors cannot purport to have placed complete faith in the credit rating exercise.

The experience with the credit derivatives business of many large financial corporations points towards some significant weaknesses in the present model of corporate governance based on multilayer oversight. These include (a) lack of clarity about the responsibilities of boards of directors, (b) the absence of a reporting procedure for the directors, and (c) inadequate scope of audit.

Role of the Board and Its Responsibilities

In corporate theory the task of the directors, as representatives of the shareholders, is to oversee the managers. This principle is, in fact, applied in most corporations. For example, it found affirmation in AIG's Corporate Governance Guidelines, which, at the material time, stated that the directors' duty was to "act as advisors and counsellors to the Chief Executive Officer and senior management and oversee management's performance on behalf the shareholders."[67]

The monitoring role of the directors is quite adequate as a statement of principle. But its deficiencies become obvious when there are specific questions—such as the board's involvement in starting a new line of business and overseeing it. In current theory, there is no specific need for the directors to engage at this level of detail. It is difficult to gauge the level of involvement of the directors in the credit derivatives business. The regulatory reports published by the corporations do not indicate whether the credit derivatives business was, in fact, placed before the board for its consideration. Indeed, they need not do so. Hence, it is superfluous to raise questions about the decision of the board of a given corporation on the issue or any guidance the board might have given the management about the business or its risks.

In the case of Citigroup there is a report that Robert Rubin, an influential director, played a role in promoting the ill-fated credit derivatives business of the company.[68] According to the report, Rubin encouraged the then CEO, Charles Prince, to expand the business. Rubin and Prince were both on the board of Citigroup, but there is no clarity about the opinions of the other directors on the credit derivatives business. If it was that two directors were able to make major business decisions without a more comprehensive and deliberative exercise by the board, it only underscores the need for fine-tuning the board culture and practices in public corporations.

The monitoring model is incomplete without sufficient clarity on the decisions or issues that a board must monitor. This would be equally true whether the function of the board is understood as considering discrete transactions—for example, decision to start a new business or close a plant—or exercising general and continuing oversight. The experience highlights the need for better articulation of the functions and responsibilities of the directors of public corporations.

It is, of course, possible to treat the role of the board as purely advisory, but that would be erroneous. It would negate the principle of corporate law that vests the primary power of management with the directors. Treating the directors merely as advisors would also eliminate accountability. It is not desirable, either for the shareholders or for other stakeholders, to have directors who are not accountable. It is a sad reflection that corporate law in America, particularly in Delaware, has developed precisely along these lines.

Reporting Procedure for the Directors

The next issue is about reporting by the directors of business corporations. As noted, it is generally accepted that the directors represent the shareholders and their interests; most companies specifically recognize this in their corporate governance charters. There is, however, no requirement that the directors must submit any kind of reports. This is a gap in the existing arrangement. The omission is particularly striking when we consider the complementary requirement in corporate statutes for annual meetings of the shareholders. Annual meetings would be more meaningful and complete if there was also a report from the directors for the shareholders to consider at the meetings.

Specifically in the context of the credit derivatives, a question is whether the directors of the corporations that took up the business were aware, or ought to have been aware, that the companies had entered the business. At least some details about the business are available in the statutory reports of the companies, which are public documents. Based on them, would it be possible to impute the directors with knowledge about the credit derivatives business and make efforts to hold them accountable? For a number of reasons, this would be difficult.

The statutory filings under the Securities Exchange Act represent "management's discussion" of the business. They are not reports of the directors, and this is a lacuna in American corporate law. In comparison, English company law requires the directors to submit annual reports to the shareholders, and this compels the directors to go on record regularly with comments about the companies' business and affairs. In that framework, the directors of companies not only oversee the managers, but they must also submit a report to the shareholders.[69] The reporting requirement ensures that there is a document by which the directors can be held to account.

There is no similar requirement in the United States. The duty of the directors ends with oversight, although the principle is the same in both jurisdictions—that the directors are representatives of the shareholders and oversee the managers in that capacity. The cycle of oversight would be complete and the structure would be more efficacious if the directors are also required to submit a report to the shareholders.

Audit and Its Scope

Audit, as noted, was developed originally as a mechanism to promote the integrity and accuracy of corporate financial reports. Although the scope of audit has been gradually expanded, it mostly retains loyalty to the original principle—misfeasance and inaccurate reporting. The development of audit has been driven almost entirely by corporate failures and scandals, punctuated by efforts from the private sector to ward off public regulation through assurances about self-regulation.

An overview of the process of development of audit over the last several decades reveals two strands that are complementary.[70] One is the emphasis on a policing approach. Audit has been mostly concerned with policing, or detecting, misfeasance after it has occurred, rather than analysis of structural or business issues, or areas of potential risk. In general, the concern for promoting the integrity of management practices, as distinct from the integrity of financial reports, has been secondary or subordinate at best and nonexistent at worst.

This trend is exemplified by the audit committees and their terms of reference. Audit committees became a part of the regulatory landscape in 1978 through the collaborative action of the Securities and Exchange Commission (SEC) and NYSE. In the wake of Enron and other financial reporting scandals which broke out at the turn of the century, audit committees are now compulsory under the Sarbanes-Oxley Act. The policing approach that permeates the audit committee mechanism is evident from the "minimum" purposes that are currently specified by NYSE for the committees. Audit committees must ensure:

(1) the integrity of financial statements
(2) compliance with legal and regulatory requirements
(3) independent auditor's qualifications and independence
(4) performance of the internal audit function and independent auditors[71]

These purposes leave little doubt about the substantive end that audit committees are supposed to attain. The underlying notions define the limited nature of the audit exercise in public corporations.

The other strand in the development of audit is the focus on illegal or criminal acts by the persons in control of corporations. With this as the starting point, audit regulation has understandably been mostly of the "command-and-control" variety. Regulation has been more ready to punish misfeasance, ex post, and less ready to concern itself with business issues. Historically, there has been little effort to detect business risks and report on them or to influence behavior in a positive manner. The latest Sarbanes-Oxley Act provisions on criminal liability for misstatements are consistent with this trend.

In the Sarbanes-Oxley, the focus was as much on auditor integrity as it was on corporate integrity. In Enron, the company's relationship with its auditor, Arthur Andersen, was at the center of the scandal. Audit was, therefore, an important element in the Sarbanes-Oxley reforms. Reflecting this concern, the principle of auditor independence has now been given statutory status. The issue of auditor integrity is of fairly longstanding. In 2000, the SEC intervened, and initiated reform by laying down some standards for determining auditor independence. SEC classified some nonaudit services which an auditor could provide without risking loss of independence.

Regulation has generally stayed away from issues such as defining the scope of audit, or the standards to be applied in the audit process. Sarbanes-Oxley took the first step here by setting up a statutory agency—the Public Company Accounting Oversight Board (PCAOB). PCAOB, which is charged with the responsibility to develop audit standards for public corporations,[72] has developed Audit Standard No. 5. The standard deals with the "audit of internal control over financial reporting that is integrated with an audit of financial statements."[73] The title reveals the limited scope of the audit exercise.

Under the PCAOB standard, audit would not be concerned with any business issues including risk. It would not be the auditor's job to examine documents like derivatives contracts, determine the risks in them, or report on the risks. Presently, the auditor's duty is limited to reporting *after* a risk has materialized, and not while it is still latent. The audit exercise is not concerned with evaluating the risks in a company's business or reporting on them.

The limitations of this approach are evident from the experience with AIG. In early 2008, the company's independent auditor, PricewaterhouseCoopers (PwC), reported "a material weakness in internal control over *financial reporting related* to the AIGFP super senior credit default swap portfolio valuation process and oversight thereof."[74] By this time, AIG had been in the credit derivatives business for many years and the risks that blew up were recorded in the contracts concluded by the company in the earlier years.

Again, PwC's complaint was limited to "financial reporting" on the valuation of the CDS portfolio; it had little to say about the business itself or the underlying risks. In doing so, PwC acted entirely according to the applicable norms—namely, Auditing Standard No. 5, or the recently superseded Auditing Standard No. 2.[75]

Under the current standards, auditors do not have to be concerned with anything other than financial reporting, and control and oversight of the reporting process. The audit exercise, as now conceived, has proved to be inadequate. The issue about the scope of independent audit has received regulatory attention. In 1998, SEC set up a Panel on Audit Effectiveness (PAE) to consider the question "whether public company audits were adequately serving and protecting the interests of investors." PAE was an initiative of Arthur Levitt, then chairman of SEC. The Panel, which published its report in 2000, confined itself to the conventional path and focused mostly on frauds and earnings misstatements. Its recommendations said little about business issues or risks, which would be vital for investor protection.[76]

There is a case for a review of the scope of the audit of public companies. The issue is about the adequacy of current framework, and the standard certification that financial statements "present fairly, in all material respects, the financial position" of a corporation. The expanded terms of reference for audits now included in the Securities Exchange Act, referred to earlier, suggest greater sensitivity to the issue, and they can potentially define the path of reform.

Consequences for Corporate Governance

The structural weaknesses in the present model of corporate governance, discussed in the preceding, played a role in the failures seen recently in the financial sector. The expectation that the multilayer oversight model, shown in Figure.15. 3, would lead to good governance has not been fulfilled. Apparently, the oversight and monitoring mechanisms at different levels did not make a significant difference to the outcome. Omissions at each level fed the other, and the result was that a cycle of unsustainable business—credit derivatives—went on for a number of years before it imploded. The process is shown in Figure 13.5.

Figure 13.5 Cycle of governance weaknesses.

To be clear, the weaknesses in the corporate governance structure are independent of external factors, such as deficiencies in credit rating or change of accounting rules. The issue raised here is about the adequacy and effectiveness of the prevailing model in achieving the goal of responsible, sustainable, and healthy corporate governance. If, at different levels in the companies, greater attention had been paid to the credit derivatives business and efforts made to develop appropriate risk models, the external factors would have been less relevant.

THE WAY FORWARD

The experience with credit derivatives and corporate governance offers valuable lessons. It stresses the need for a transition to a new model based on responsibility. This must be the basic principle or the *grundnorm*, to paraphrase Hans Kelsen.[77] If this approach is adopted, the following are some possibilities:

- treating the directors as corporate stewards rather than monitors, and developing a list of their functional responsibilities

- mandatory reporting by corporate directors
- revisiting the subject independent audit and the scope of the audit exercise

These directional possibilities for refining corporate theory and regulation are explored in the following.

Minimum Board Responsibilities

The monitoring board is now standard among public corporations. Successive corporate failures and the challenges posed by the globalized markets of the present times warrant a review of the governance framework based on narrow notions of monitoring. Such a monitoring board might be adequate as well as appropriate in a period of growth and prosperity. In that setup, the corporations would be delivering economic value and the limited concern would be to keep in check the powers of the actors who controlled them. This was the background of the monitoring board idea developed in the 1970s, based on the experience of the earlier decades.

The notions about monitoring and the consequent emphasis to the independence of the directors have gained considerable traction. The ratio of outside directors—defined as affiliated and independent—on the boards of public corporations has zoomed in the last two decades, as shown from the graph in Figure 13.6.

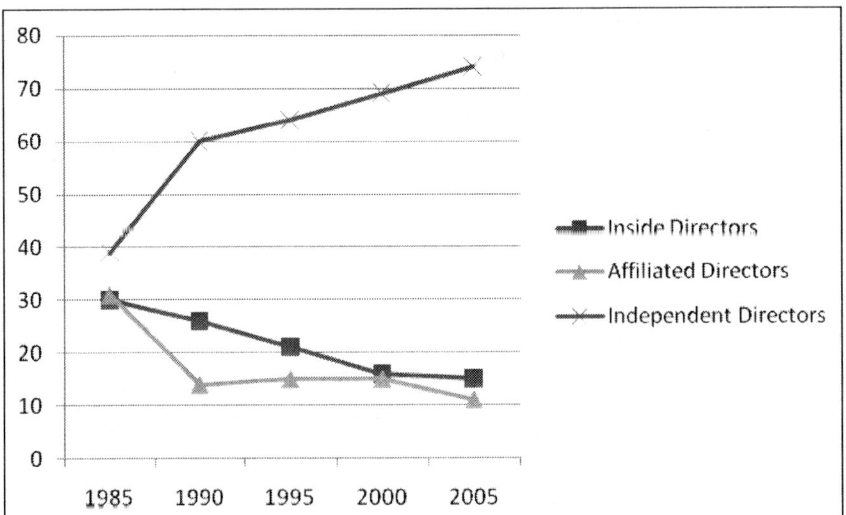

Figure 13.6 Board composition, 1985–2005.

In keeping with the increase in the ration of outside directors, there has been a decline in inside and affiliated directors. Both these trends are in continuity with the events of 1950–1980, discussed earlier.[78] Indeed, the recent years have seen a strengthening of the trend. As a result, most public corporations now have quite a small presence of insiders and an overwhelming contingent of outsiders—affiliates and independents. The issue is whether this is an appropriate arrangement. Is it desirable that most of the directors of public corporations have limited knowledge about the enterprises and equally limited involvement in their business and affairs?

The directors of public companies have been the subject of critical analysis in the recent years. They came under scrutiny in the wake of the corporate failures at the turn of the century. A report on Enron, prepared by the U.S. Senate, was critical of the directors of the company who apparently affirmed many of the questionable decisions made by the management.[79] Paul MacAvoy and Ira Millstein have made various recommendations for making corporate boards more proactive and to streamline their functioning. Their recommendations include charging the boards with the "responsibility for the company's strategy, risk management, and financial reporting based on sufficient knowledge of the company's business environment, challenges and opportunities."[80] MacAvoy and Millstein were, however, skeptical about the adoption of their recommendations in legal regulation.

As noted earlier, the ideas about insiders and outsiders on corporate boards were developed during a period of economic growth when corporate enterprises were quite competitive and profitable. The landscape is now quite different. The present times are characterized by the issues of industrial decline, unemployment, and globalized markets. The corporations are now under significant competitive pressures, quite different in substance from the earlier times. The present environment calls for a more relational version of the corporations. A more relational environment can facilitate better collaboration among the various groups or constituencies in the corporations and help in attaining business success that is sustainable.

The directors *are* the repositories of corporate power. There can be little dispute with this proposition. Unified command is essential for defining the direction of the enterprise and for promoting its efficiency. Having stated this, there is a case for more clearly articulating the institutional position of the directors and their substantive role. As noted, the recent trend has been to expand the directors' functions and charge them with more specific responsibilities. This trend is evident in the various codes of corporate governance that have been developed and the charters of individual companies.

In 2003, the Task Force on Corporate Responsibility constituted by the American Bar Association (ABA) referred to a need to "more clearly delineate the oversight responsibility of directors generally, and the unique role that independent directors play in discharging that responsibility in public company settings."[81] The "specific oversight matters" identified by the task force include "reviewing, approving, and monitoring fundamental financial and business strategies and the performance of the company relative to those strategies; assessing major risks facing the company; and ensuring that reasonable processes are in place to maintain the integrity of the company and the corresponding accountability of senior management."[82] The ABA Task Force Report is one more piece of evidence of the increased attention that is being paid to directors and their functions.

In the United Kingdom, the move in the recent years has been towards what Chris Riley termed the "juridification of corporate governance"[83]—a process by which the governance of companies would be progressively placed in a legal framework that is more elaborate and nuanced. While predicting juridification, Riley cautioned that "much [ ] depends upon the precise form that juridification takes," and argued in favor of "making at least some [ ] structural provisions more rule-like."[84]

Redefining the directors' role and clearer articulation of their functions advocated here are in keeping with the trend of juridification of corporate governance. These measures have the potential to strengthen the governance framework of public corporations by enhancing director engagement and greater deliberation in decision making. The current political and economic climate and instances of corporate failure provide an opportunity for reform. Sarbanes-Oxley took a step towards direct intervention in governance by requiring public corporations to have audit committees consisting of independent directors. A possible next step would be for regulation to specify the issues that corporate boards must monitor—in other words, a list of "minimum board responsibilities."

The consequences of not having clearly delineated responsibilities for the boards of public corporations were evident recently *In Re Citigroup Inc. Shareholder Derivative Litigation.*[85] The action was specifically in the context of the credit derivatives business of Citigroup. Referring to the charge made against the directors about investments in Special Investment Vehicles (SIV) "that were unable to pay off maturing debt," the Delaware Chancery Court observed:

> Plaintiffs do not adequately plead that the asset purchases or the investments in SIVs were the result of board action rather than inaction.[86]

Minimum board responsibilities would be different from the codification of *standards* for directors' duties, which has been completed in Britain in the Companies Act 2006.[87] In essence the standards, such as the duties of loyalty and care, now included in the statute provide guidance to the directors on *how* to perform their duties; they do not spell out the duties themselves. It is now time to consider developing a set of specific responsibilities for the boards of directors of public companies.

The concept of minimum board responsibilities is not quite radical. It would not detract from the widely accepted two-tier model of governance; the decisions will still be made by the management, but subject to express board approval. To provide flexibility, provision can be made for ex post approval in specified circumstances. In this framework, decisions such as starting a new business or discontinuing an existing one would be appropriate as board responsibilities. The requirement of board approval for major decisions can streamline governance, facilitate better deliberation, and promote accountability. More analysis and consultation would be needed for determining the elements that can be included among the functional responsibilities of the directors of public corporations.

Reporting by Directors

Placing the directors of public corporations under a duty to submit periodic reports would complement and complete the board responsibility regime outlined earlier. In the new framework, the directors would not only handle specific functions or tasks, but also report on them. A reporting requirement specifically for the directors ought to be a key element in developing a model that recognizes the central role of corporate boards in corporate governance.

Unfortunately, American corporate law has not shown much seriousness about reporting in general.[88] Indeed, comparing the Massachusetts corporate statute of 1882 with the new one enacted in 1903, E. Merrick Dodd complained that the reporting requirements had been significantly diluted in the latter statute.[89] James Hurst found that as late as 1965, only twenty-two out of the fifty-one American jurisdictions (including the District of Columbia) imposed any kind of reporting requirements on the corporations.[90]

It is not clear whether the reporting duty in the corporate statutes applies specifically to the directors or to the corporations in general. This is significant because there is evidence of awareness about the theory of the reporting rule in the law of business corporations. Adolf Berle and Frederick Fisher pointed out in 1932 that the rule "is designed to show the proprietor the property . . . what happened to the property interests which were in the hands of someone else."[91] This was a reference to shareholders and directors, assimilated to the principal–agent model of relationship.

The position in the United States, as pointed out earlier, presents a striking contrast to Britain. Traditionally in UK company law, the principal–agent idea has been prominent, and the directors are under a duty to provide annual reports to the shareholders. In comparison, the reporting rule in federal securities law had its origin in a different principle—namely, facilitating efficient price discovery for shares.[92] This stock market–centric approach of federal securities law is logical, but it would be quite inadequate in developing a framework of responsible corporate governance.

The need, as stated earlier, is for a more institutional approach to law. Regulation would set out the functional responsibilities of the directors; having done so, it would place them under a duty to report, periodically, on how they have handled their responsibilities. An argument that can be made against this proposal is its potential impact on business confidentiality. It is not suggested here that the report must be so elaborate or detailed that it compromises the business interests of the corporation. The content of the report and developing a standard template are matters of detail, which must be worked out. In any case, the reporting rule in UK company law has functioned quite well for a long time now without serious hitches.

The Audit Exercise, Business, and Its Risks

The audit exercise, as currently designed, is quite limited. A major challenge is to make audit more meaningful in the framework of corporate governance, and do so without significantly increasing either the cumbersome nature of the task or the attendant costs. There is a case to examine how far the audit procedure can be concerned with the business of the corporations and the potential risks in it.

Risk has emerged as a serious issue in the recent times—financial risk being the most significant.[93] The subprime crisis in the United States and its reverberations worldwide are proof of the interconnectedness of national economies and corporations, and, equally, the apparent fragility of the arrangements. In this environment, it is understandable that risk management has become an important subject. Indeed, it is now an independent discipline.[94]

Securities laws have mandated disclosures on risks for a long time, and managements must include warnings about business risks in their reports. This arrangement appears to be quite inadequate if the recent events are any indication. Mandatory risk assessment and reporting procedures for public corporations can be useful in gaining a better understanding the risks they face and in highlighting them. In turn, these can help developing appropriate safeguards against the risks.

The two options in developing a better risk management system are:

- risk reports prepared by experts
- risk assessment as a part of audit

The trend in the development of audit, discussed earlier, has been one of broadening of its terms of reference. Continuing with this trend, risk assessment can be included in audit. This would make it a single comprehensive external verification process, and avoid the difficulties in having numerous piecemeal exercises. From the perspective of accountability also, it would be better if the responsibility for verifying and certifying the level of diligence in corporations is centralized in a single agency.

Either option would involve cost. Whether a corporation engages independent risk experts or the job is made a part of the audit exercise, there would undoubtedly be an expense. The question is whether the cost would be prohibitive. However, considering the seriousness of the issue and the recent experience, it would be more appropriate to steer the debate towards containing the cost at reasonable levels. Developing an internal system for risk assessment and management can make the task of external experts easier and consequently less expensive. Procedures designed for reducing risk, and enhancing the integrity and sustainability of corporations, must not end up undermining business competitiveness.[95] Equally, we must be wary of arguments about cost being used as a tactical weapon to ward off justifiable regulatory intervention.

CONCLUSION

Learning from the experience during the credit crisis, this chapter proposes charging the directors of public corporations with a set of functional responsibilities and for regulatory definition of the responsibilities. Logically, the directors would be under a duty to provide regular reports about their functions. The chapter also proposes a risk assessment procedure. These measures can improve the quality of governance of public companies and their capability to handle risk in the complex, interconnected, and uncertain world in which we live.

Of course, the proposals made here would take corporate governance in the direction of juridification—but with an important difference. They are not based on the "command-and-control" principle. The measures are based on an organic or structural approach, and seek to promote interdisciplinary regulation of corporate governance. In this model, legal regulation would adopt techniques and practices from finance and business management, and incorporate them in the institutional framework of public companies.

An equally important issue is about the source of regulation. In *In Re Citigroup Shareholders Derivative Litigation*, discussed earlier, the Delaware court recently ruled that directors were not under a duty to regulate the business decisions made by the managers, even if the directors had general awareness about deteriorating market conditions and the enhanced business risks. Given this approach and the trend in federal securities regulation, it would be more realistic to look to the Congress and the SEC for meaningful action. It is encouraging that the SEC has commenced an inquiry into the role of the boards in the credit crisis.[96]

NOTES

1. Cited in Edward Chancellor, *Devil Take the Hindmost: A History of Financial Speculation* (New York: Farrar, Strauss, and Giroux, 1999), 334.
2. See, e.g., Norman Veasey, "Should Corporate Law Inform Aspirations for Good Corporate Governance Practices—or Vice-Versa?" *University of Pennsylvania Law Review* 149 (2001): 2179.

3. Pub. L. 107–204, 116 Stat. 745.
4. George Bush's speech to the Association for a Better New York, online: http://custom.marketwatch.com/custom/earthlink-net/mw-news.asp?guid= percent7b78BC1B28–6171–4DD8–B7D7–0C10F6577E88 percent7d. The Sarbanes-Oxley Act has been criticized for its "efficiency" and the costs its requirements impose on the corporations. See, e.g., Larry E. Ribstein, "Market vs. Regulatory Responses to Corporate Fraud: A Critique of the Sarbanes-Oxley Act of 2002," *Journal of Corporate Law* 28 (2003): 1.
5. American International Group, Annual Report for 2006, 6, http://www.aig-corporate.com/investors/annualreports_proxy.html.
6. For a comprehensive discussion of CDOs and CDSs, see Janet M. Tavakoli, *Structured Finance and Collateralized Debt Obligations: New Developments in Cash and Synthetic Securitization* (Hoboken, NJ: John Wiley and Sons, 2008).
7. Mark Pittman, "Bear Sterns Fund Collapse Sends Shock through CDO Market" *Bloomberg*, June 21, 2007, http://www.bloomberg.com/apps/news?pid =newsarchive&sid=aoPvUyNqWvdA.
8. For a critical discussion on the credit rating of CDO, see Frank A. Partnoy and David A. Skeel Jr., "The Promise and Perils of Credit Derivatives," *University of Cincinnati Law Review* 75 (2007): 1019.
9. For a discussion on the pricing of CDO tranches, see Leif B.G. Andersen and Jakob Sidenius, "CDO Pricing with Factor Models: Survey and Comments," Journal of Credit Risk 1 (2005): 71. Available at http://jakobsidenius.com/papers/factormodels2.pdf.
10. *Source*: www.bionicturtle.com.
11. The term "reference" indicates that the underlying portfolio of debt securities is not actually held by the SPE. The debt portfolio in a synthetic CDO is, in essence, notional.
12. *The J.P. Morgan Guide to Credit Derivatives* (Risk Publications, n.d.), http://www.investinginbonds.com/assets/files/Intro_to_Credit_Derivatives.pdf.
13. If the bank or other original lender retained the "equity" tranche, it would be adequate if the amount raised was even less than $700 million. To the extent of the equity tranche, also known as "toxic waste," the bank would have no credit protection in any case.
14. Dezhong Wang, Svetlosar T. Rachev, and Frank J. Fabozzi, "Pricing Tranches of a CDO and a CDS Index: Recent Advances and Future Research" (2006), www.statistik.uni-karlsruhe.de/download/doc_secure1/workshop_final.pdf.
15. *Bond Basics* (June 2006), 1, http://media.pimco-global.com/pdfs/pdf/Bondpercent20Basics-percent20Creditpercent20Defaultpercent20Swaps percent20US.pdf?WT.cg_n=PIMCO-US&WT.ti=Bondpercent20Basics-percent20Credit percent20Default percent20Swaps percent20US.pdf.
16. Ibid.
17. The term "reference" is used here in the same sense as in "reference portfolio," explained earlier. It indicates the notional character of the transaction, and the absence of actual transfers of assets or liabilities among the contracting parties.
18. Geoff Chaplin, *Credit Derivatives: Risk Management, Trading and Investing* (Hoboken, NJ: John Wiley and Sons, 2005), 61.
19. This would be the right of subrogation available to an insurer in the law of insurance.
20. See, e.g., Michael Gibson, "Credit Derivatives and Risk Management," *Economic Review* 92 (2007): 39. Available at. http://www.frbatlanta.org/filelegacydocs/erq407_gibson.pdf.
21. 476 F. 3d 90 (2d Cir. 2007).

22. American International Group, Statutory filing in Form 10-K for 2007 at 17. Available at: http://www.aigcorporate.com/investors/annualreports_proxy.html.
23. Morgen Gretchenson, "First Comes the Swap, Then It's the Knives," *New York Times*, June 1, 2008.
24. "Theory of the Firm: Managerial Behavior, Agency Costs and Ownership Structure," *Journal of Financial Economics* 3 (1976): 306–307.
25. For an account of this development, see James W. Hurst, *The Legitimacy of the Business Corporation in the Law of the United States, 1780–1970* (Charlottesville: University Press of Virginia, 1970).
26. For a summary of the Massachusetts incorporation statute in the 1880s, see E. Merrick Dodd, "Statutory Developments in Business Corporation Law, 1886–1936," Harvard Law Review 50 (1937): 27.
27. *The Modern Corporation and Private Property* (New York: Harcourt, Brace, and World, 1968), xiv–xv.
28. See, e.g., Bruce Welling, *Canadian Corporate Law: The Governing Principles* (Toronto: Butterworths, 1984), 443.
29. On this development, see generally Lawrence E. Mitchell, *The Speculation Economy: How Finance Triumphed over Industry* (San Francisco: Berrett-Koehler, 2007).
30. For an account of this development, see Alfred D. Chandler, *Visible Hand: The Managerial Revolution in American Business* (Cambridge, MA: Belknap Press, 1977).
31. See generally Jennifer Arlen, "The Story of Allis-Chalmers, Caremark, and Stone: Directors' Evolving Duty to Monitor," in *Corporate Law Stories*, ed. J. Mark Ramseyer, http://lsr.nellco.org/cgi/viewcontent.cgi?article=1164&context=nyu_lewp, accessed August 11, 2011.
32. *The New Industrial State* (London: Hamish Hamilton, 1967).
33. See, e.g., Robin Marris, *The Economic Theory of Managerial Capitalism* (London: Macmillan, 1964); and William Baumol, *Business Behavior, Value and Growth* (New York: Harcourt, Brace, and World, 1967).
34. Adam Smith, *An Enquiry into the Nature and Causes of the Wealth of Nations* (New York: The Modern Library, 1937), 700.
35. *Democracy and Finance* (1940).
36. See George Herberton Evans, *British Corporation Finance 1775–1850: A Study of Preference Shares* (Baltimore, MD: The Johns Hopkins University Press, 1936). For an account of the recent developments relating to independent directors on the boards of American corporations, see Jeffrey N. Gordon, "The Rise of Independent Directors in the United States, 1950–2005: Of Shareholder Value and Stock Market Prices," *Stanford Law Review* 59 (2007): 1465.
37. *Directors: Myth and Reality* (Boston: Harvard Business School, 1970).
38. Jeffrey Gordon, "Rise of Independent Directors."
39. Based on ibid., appendix. Gordon has provided multiple data sets for 1970 and 1980, referring to different sources. In Table 15.1, I have adopted the lower of the values as they are consistent with the trends noted by Gordon for the three groups in the fifty-five-year period until 2004. The data for the subsequent years are presented a little later.
40. See, e.g., Del. Code Ann. Title 8, Delaware General Corporation Law, §141.
41. *The Structure of the Corporation: A Legal Analysis* (Boston: Little, Brown, 1976).
42. See Douglas M. Branson, "Corporate Governance 'Reform' and the New Corporate Social Responsibility," *University of Pittsburgh Law Review* 62 (2001): 605.

43. Arthur Levitt, *Take on the Street: What Wall Street and Corporate America Don't Want You to Know* (New York: Pantheon Books, 2002).
44. A comprehensive database of corporate governance codes in various jurisdictions is available online: http://www.ecgi.org/codes/all_codes.php.
45. OECD, *Principles of Corporate Governance* (2004), 24, http://www.oecd.org/dataoecd/32/18/31557724.pdf.
46. Ibid., 24–25.
47. AIG Corporate Governance Guidelines, http://ir.aigcorporate.com/phoenix.zhtml?c=76115&p=irol-govguidelines.
48. For the history of the adoption of the disclosure regime in the securities law, see Joel Seligman, *The Transformation of Wall Street: A History of the Securities and Exchange Commission and Modern Corporate Finance* (Boston: Houghton Mifflin, 1982).
49. Louis Loss and Joel Seligman, *Fundamentals of Securities Regulation*, 5th ed. (Frederick, MD: Aspen Publishers, 2004), 8.
50. Sarbanes-Oxley Act, §301.
51. New York Stock Exchange Listed Company Manual, Section 303A.00, Corporate Governance Standards, http://nysemanual.nyse.com/lcm/.
52. 15 USC §78a et seq., Section 19.
53. AIG Audit Committee Charter, http://ir.aigcorporate.com/phoenix.zhtml?c=76115&p=irol-govcommcomp.
54. AIG Finance Committee Charter, http://ir.aigcorporate.com/phoenix.zhtml?c=76115&p=irol-govcommcomp.
55. Adolf A. Berle and Gardiner C. Means, *The Modern Corporation and Private Property* (New York: Macmillan Company, 1932), 293.
56. For a recent account of the development of audit in the United States and the attendant issues, see John Coffee Jr., *Gatekeepers: The Professions and Corporate Governance* (New York: Oxford University Press, 2006).
57. Securities Exchange Act, §13(b).
58. Loss and Seligman, *Fundamentals*, 190–194, have explained the expansion in the scope of the audit of public corporations in this period.
59. Securities Exchange Act, Section 10A(a).
60. John C. Coffee, *Gatekeepers.*
61. Peter Goodman, "Taking Hard New Look at a Greenspan Legacy," *New York Times*, October 9, 2008.
62. Anthony Faiola, Ellen Nakashima, and Jill Drew, "What Went Wrong?" *Washington Post*, October 19, 2008. For the developments on regulation of derivatives, see also Nelson Schwartz and Julie Creswell, "What Created this Monster?" *New York Times*, March 23, 2008.
63. Chancellor, *Devil Take the Hindmost.*
64. Ibid.
65. Warren Buffett, Excerpts from Buffett's letter to the shareholders of Berkshire Hathaway for 2002, http://www.fintools.com/docs/Warren percent20-Buffet percent20on percent20Derivatives.pdf.
66. Ibid.
67. AIG Corporate Governance Guidelines, 1.
68. See Eric Dash and Julie Creswell, "The Reckoning: Citigroup Saw No Red Even as It Made Bolder Bets," *New York Times*, November 23, 2008.
69. Companies Act 2006 (UK), Ss. 415–419.
70. Loss and Seligman, Fundamentals.
71. NYSE Listed Company Manual, §303A.07(c)(i)(A).
72. Sarbanes-Oxley Act, §101–109.
73. Public Company Accounting Oversight Board, http://www.pcaobus.org/Standards/Standards_and_Related_Rules/Auditing_Standard_No.5.aspx.

74. AIG Statutory Report for 2007, 129.
75. Public Company Accounting Oversight Board, http://www.pcaobus.org/Rules/Rules_of_the_Board/Auditing_Standard_2.pdf.
76. Panel on Audit Effectiveness, *Report and Recommendations* (2000), http://www.pobauditpanel.org/downloads/prefatory.pdf.
77. Hans Kelsen, *General Theory of Law and State* (Cambridge, MA: Harvard University Press, 1945).
78. Ibid.
79. *The Role of the Board of Directors in Enron's Collapse* (2002), U.S. Senate, Committee on Governmental Affairs, Permanent Subcommittee on Investigations, http://news.findlaw.com/hdocs/docs/enron/senpsi70802rpt.pdf.
80. *The Recurrent Crisis in Corporate Governance* (Stanford, CA: Stanford University Press, 2004), 128–129.
81. ABA, *Report of the Task Force on Corporate Responsibility* (2003), 32, http://www.abanet.org/buslaw/corporateresponsibility/final_report.pdf.
82. Ibid., 33.
83. Chris Riley, "The Juridification of Corporate Governance," in *The Reform of United Kingdom Company Law*, ed. John de Lacy (London: Cavendish Publishing, 2002), 179–202.
84. Ibid., 201.
85. Civil Action no. 3388–CC, decided on February 24, 2009, http://law.du.edu/documents/corporate-governance/governance-cases/citigroup-in-re.pdf.
86. Ibid., 50 n. 96.
87. There was opposition even to the codification of standards. See John Birds, "The Reform of Directors' Duties," in *The Reform of United Kingdom Company Law*, ed. John de Lacy (London: Cavendish Publishing, 2002), 149–178.
88. Lawrence Mitchell, *Speculation Economy*, has discussed how business corporations tended to be secretive until federal securities law introduced mandatory financial reporting and audit in the 1930s.
89. E. Merrick Dodd, "Statutory Developments."
90. Hurst, *Legitimacy*, 90.
91. "Elements of the Law of Business Accounting," *Columbus Law Review* 32 (1932). 573.
92. See note 21.
93. See generally Raghuram G. Rajan, "Has Financial Development Made the World Riskier?" (NBER Working Paper No. W11728, November 2005), http://ssrn.com/abstract=842464.
94. See, e.g., Michael Power, *The Risk Management of Everything: Rethinking the Politics of Uncertainty* (London: Demos, 2004).
95. In answering this question, law-and-economics tools such as Pareto optimality and Kaldor-Hicks efficiency can be helpful. These issues are, however, a story for another day. The logistics and the cost of risk assessment are outside the scope of this chapter.
96. Zachary A. Goldfarb, "SEC to Examine Boards' Role in Financial Crisis," *Washington Post*, February 20, 2009, D01.

14 Lending Currency Mix of Globalized Banks

A Potential Risk for Foreign Affiliates via Internal Fund Transfer

Yuki Masujima

INTRODUCTION

Global banks played a significant role in the transmission of the current crisis to emerging-market economies, because the U.S. liquidity shocks to developed-country banking have reduced lending in local markets through contractions in cross-border lending to banks and private agents and also through contractions in parent banks' support of foreign affiliates (Cetorelli and Goldberg 2009). As banks are more globalized, their lending activities are affected by shocks across countries. How are shocks transmitted? What are the determinants of global banks' lending in the emerging markets? Does foreign banks' lending stabilize or destabilize credit supply in the emerging market?

This empirical chapter investigates global bank lending channeled through local branches (i.e., internal transfer channel) as a shock transmission path between home (a country where globalized banks' headquarters are located) and host (Indonesia as the emerging market). I extend the interstate banking model of Morgan, Rime, and Strahan (2004) to the international banking model between home and host by considering capital immobility in local currency lending under the undeveloped foreign exchange market. Internal capital transfer is often discussed in the context of multinational banks' asset and cash management in developed economies; owing to a lack of data, most of the literature focuses not on foreign banks' lending via local branches, but rather on cross-border lending, in which global banks' headquarters directly provide loans to firms in other countries. Thus, this chapter contributes further insight into the shock transmission through internal capital and provides a connection between these strands of literature through the case of a developing country.

Shocks to foreign banks' home economy and their parent bank's capital could matter for local businesses through the lending channel in a host country, whereas their response of local currency lending to shocks is more stable than their response of foreign currency lending. In fact, the foreign banks' foreign currency lending in terms of U.S. dollars did not drop by as much credit as domestic banks did after the crisis (Figure 14.1, right middle)

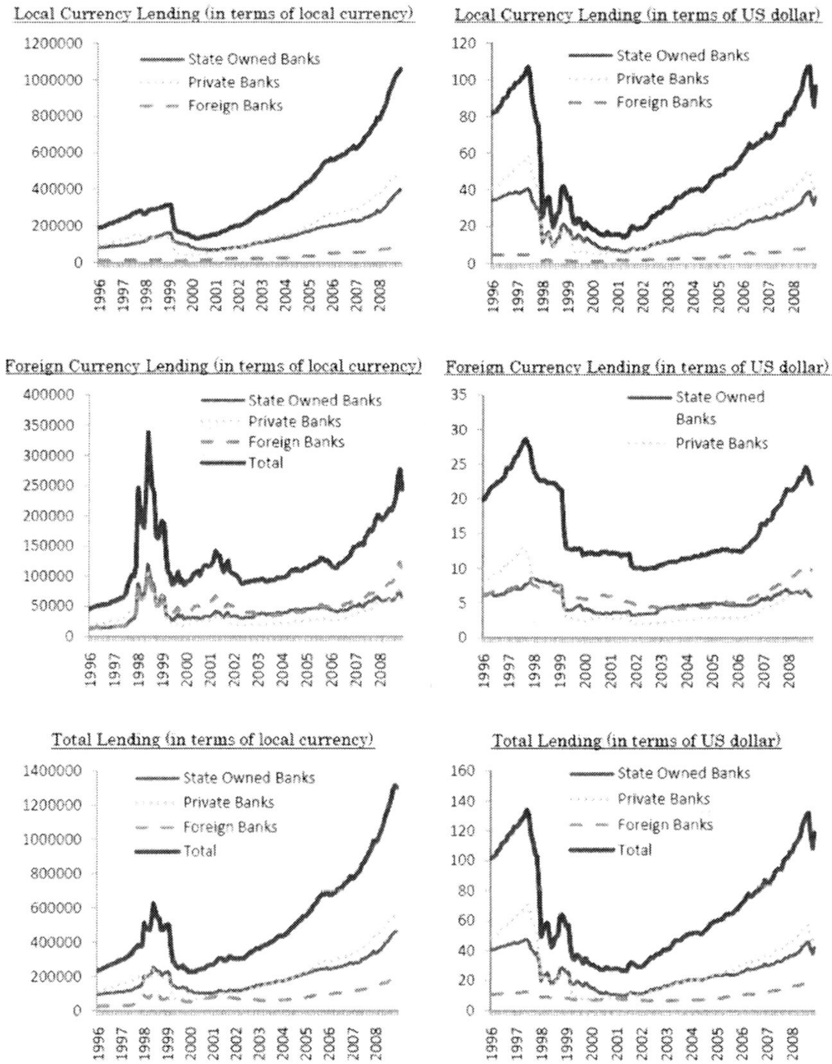

Figure 14.1 Loan outstanding by type of banks.

Note: Local currency lending consists of loans outstanding in Indonesian rupiah; foreign currency lending consists of loans outstanding in any foreign currency; total lending includes both of them. The amount of lending expressed in terms of local currency (billions of Indonesian rupiah) and U.S. dollars (billions of U.S. dollars) is converted by nominal exchange rates (end of the period) in International Financial Statistics.

Source: Bank Indonesia, IFS, and author's estimation

although the Indonesian economy was severely damaged by the Asian crisis of 1997–1998.[1] Some literature finds that binding risk-based capital requirements coupled with the rapid Japanese stock market drop resulted in a decrease in lending by Japanese banks in the United States (Peek and Rosengren 1997), whereas others find evidence that foreign banks, except the Japanese ones, tended to increase their lending to Latin America when economic conditions in their home countries worsened (Martinez Peria, Powell, and Hollar 2002). Shocks to parent bank's capital could also affect foreign currency lending because foreign banks' branches typically rely on a parent bank or financial markets to finance foreign currency (U.S. dollars). Because bank-level data is available, I can distinguish a bank's idiosyncratic effects from a country's fixed effects.

The currency denomination for loans is more important in developing countries than in developed countries. In the developing countries, foreign exchange risk directly reflects the share of foreign currency loans to total loans. This foreign exchange risk is amplified if foreign currency borrowing is a main funding source for banks. In the developed world, however, the currency denomination could relatively be neglected because foreign exchange risk can be hedged by derivatives such as futures, currency options, and currency swaps.

The importance of the currency denomination for loans is enhanced in two ways: capital immobility and foreign exchange rate risk due to limited hedging instruments of foreign exchange rate risk. Under undeveloped foreign exchange markets, local currency lending in a host country can be regarded as immobile capital across countries, whereas foreign currency lending is mobile between a home and host country. Second, the impacts of shocks to bank lending activity might be different between currencies for lending, depending on foreign exchange risk. Thus, Indonesia is one of the most appropriate candidates where foreign banks actively disburse loans denominated in both foreign currency and local currency with limited hedging instruments of foreign exchange risk.

I find the evidence that global banks' internal capital market plays a vital role in transmitting shocks of a parent bank and home stock market, that is, high growth rates in the parent bank's stock price in the home market increase foreign banks' U.S. dollar lending in a host country, but not local currency lending due to the lack of internal capital market.

The structure of this chapter is as follows. In the next section, I review the theoretical background and empirical results of literature. In the third section, data sources and data summary are described. In the fourth section, I move on to the econometric methodologies and results. The final section concludes.

LITERATURE REVIEW

For global bank activity in the emerging markets, there is no comprehensive theory[2] that covers the parent bank's trade-off lending across several countries ("substitution effect") and that supports weak subsidiaries ("support effect") (Cetorelli and Goldberg 2009). In the two-country model, the negative impact of a bank capital crunch in a home country on bank loans is smaller under interstate banking than under unit banking due to capital transfer from a host country to a home country (Morgan, Rime, and Strahan 2004). This model also proves that the negative impact of a firm's capital (collateral) squeezes in a home country on the amount of bank loans in a home country is larger under interstate banking. In the model, a globalized bank's capital is constrained; the bank is risk-neutral and propagates shocks owing to the rebalance of their international credit portfolios in response to country-specific shocks.

Most theoretical mechanisms of relationships between foreign banks entry and a host country's economic stability elaborate on the fact that foreign bank subsidiaries highly depend on the decision of a foreign-based parent bank with an internationally diversified asset portfolio. As positive effects, this parent bank may work as the lender of last resort during crisis periods. It may also manage an internal capital market and centralized treasury operations to allocate capital and liquidity over its subsidiaries (Stein 1997). This system contributes to stable loan supply of foreign banks in a host country when foreign branches have capital shocks. Foreign bank subsidiaries may be able to recover relatively fast, compared to domestic banks.

Foreign branches, however, could suddenly cut their credit supply when a host economy is in recession. In this case, foreign banks' activity in a host country can be pro-cyclical and less stable than credit supply from domestic banks. A reason for such behavior could be that the parent bank reallocates capital over different geographical regions on the basis of expected risks and returns. When economic growth in a particular host country declines, the activities of the foreign branches in this country may be scaled down, compared to other regions. Because few Indonesian banks have global operations, they have a harder time reallocating their portfolio. Thus, this substitution effect is likely to be weak. When home country conditions improve, the opportunity costs of limiting home country lending increase and banks may therefore allocate less capital to their foreign branches (Molyneux and Seth 1998; Moshirian 2001). In this scenario there is thus a negative relationship between the home country business cycle and the foreign subsidiary's credit supply. The latter would be more likely if parent banks are financially healthy and follow the proposition of Morgan, Rime, and Strahan (2004). Yet, the crisis may force banks to change the regime.

Some insist on a stabilizing effect of foreign bank entry on the credit supply in host countries such as Argentina and Mexico (Dages, Goldberg, and Kinney 2000). During the second half of the 1990s foreign banks that had been present in the host country for a relatively long time exhibited stronger and less volatile credit growth than domestic banks. Also, during times of crisis, diversity of ownership has contributed to greater stability of credit as foreign banks showed significant credit growth during crisis periods and thereafter. Moreover, foreign banks did not reduce their credit supply during adverse economic times in the host country (De Haas and Van Lelyveld 2004; Peek and Rosengren 2000; Goldberg 2001; Martinez Peria, Powell, and Hollar 2002). Indeed, they viewed such economic problems as opportunities to expand, by acquisition or by growth of existing subsidiaries. However, domestically owned and foreign-owned banks with low problem loan ratios behave similarly (Dages, Goldberg, and Kinney 2000). Thus, if foreign banks have a relatively long time horizon of their strategies, their lending stabilizes a host's economy.

Meanwhile, under certain circumstances foreign banks may also destabilize the economy and credit market (Goldberg 2005; Williams 2003; De Haas and Van Lelyveld 2006; Rosenberg and Tirpák 2008; Focarelli and Pozzolo 2005; Cerutti, Dell'Ariccia, and Martiez Peria 2007). A positive link between foreign bank presence and economic volatility might tentatively exist (Morgan and Strahan 2003). This is due to foreign banks being relatively sensitive to local business conditions as they are better able to reallocate funds outside the particular host country. Bank lending to emerging countries is positively correlated with the economic cycles in the major industrial countries (Jeanneau and Micu 2002). Thus, worsening home country conditions lead banks to seek external lending opportunities (Moshirian 2001; Calvo, Leiderman, and Reinhart 1992; Hernandez and Rudolph 1997). Yet, the direction of causality of this push relationship depends on in which region foreign branches have activity (Goldberg 2001).

A few papers shed light on currency denomination of loans from the currency mix preferred by firms (Benavente, Johnson, and Morande 2003; Kedia and Mozumdar 2003; Galindo, Panizza, and Schiantarelli 2003; Basso, Calvo-Gonzalez, and Jurgilas 2007) and the deposit dollarization of banks (Bahmani-Oskooee and Domac 2003; Honohan and Shi 2001). Yet, the discussion of currency denomination of loans from the bank side is relatively limited. For example, a two-currency banking model to show that the direction in which dollarization tends to move with macroeconomic shocks is shown to depend on interest rates, exchange rate risk, costly banking, the initial dollarization levels, and so forth (Catao and Terrones 2000). Thus, ignoring currency denomination might lead to missing the part of bank lending activities responding to shocks. Even if it is easier for banks to borrow in local currency in times of crisis than in dollars, the bank will hold a relatively large amount of dollars and a relatively small amount of local currency (Machicado 2008). Thus, the impact of macroeconomic and financial shocks on local currency and foreign currency lending is different. Under high liquidity uncertainty, banks prefer U.S. dollar loans to local currency ones.

Suppose that banks have preference of currency for loans, which depends on various factors, a question is how easily banks can change the currency composition of bank loans as they want, because loans are usually regarded as illiquid assets. Recent innovative financial instruments such as credit derivatives, however, make it possible for banks to transfer loan risk and to sell loans. "Derivatives and the more liquid markets they encourage make possible a new discipline at commercial banks, that of active portfolio management . . . unwanted credit risks can be divested in a variety of forms, through hedges or purchases of insurance as well as outright sales in the secondary markets."[3] Of course, this statement for credit derivative instrument cannot directly be applied to the financial market in emerging economies. Moreover, in the Indonesian case, foreign banks' rupiah loans can be fully financed by their customers' deposits because loan to deposits ratio in rupiah is approximately 100 percent or slightly below that on average (Figure 14.2). Loan and deposit are well balanced as they may be too much concerned about hedging the foreign exchange rate risk from external finance. Consequently, foreign banks' banking activity in rupiah works as if it would be under unit banking.

In contrast, the loan-to-deposit ratio of foreign banks' branches in U.S. dollars clearly exceeds 100 percent. Thus, they must rely on internal borrowing through which shocks from their parent bank and their home country are transmitted (Figure 14.3). To the extent of the preceding, the currency denomination is important. Although foreign banks' activity in rupiah might be constrained, they can change the currency composition of lending by using internal transfer. The strands of literature on internal capital market show that internal capital markets in a global bank relax the credit constraints faced by smaller bank affiliates. This suggests the internal capital market reduces a risk due to diversification effects. However, significant shocks to a parent bank are propagated to foreign branches in host markets. Thus, frictions between global banks and external capital markets could be at the root of investment inefficiencies generated by internal capital markets (Campello 2002; De Haas and Van Lelyveld 2010; Ashcraft and Campello 2007; Ashcraft 2008).

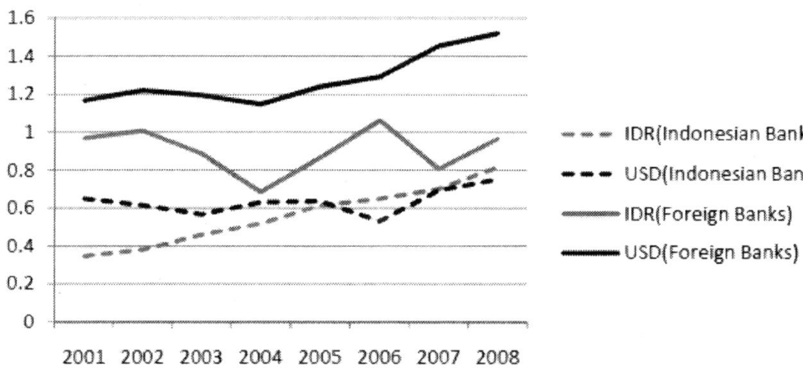

Figure 14.2 Average loan-to-deposit ratio.

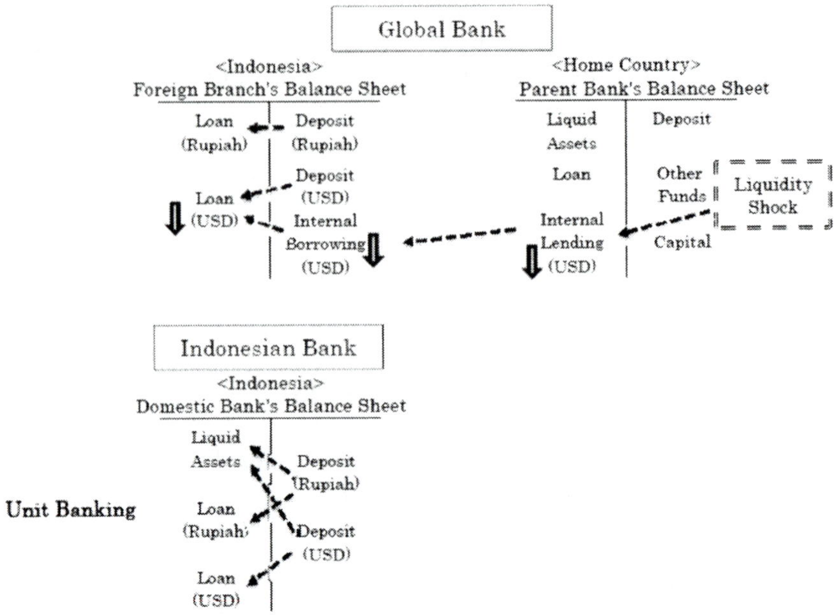

Figure 14.3 Cross-border shock transmission via internal transfer.

DATA AND DESCRIPTIVE STATISTICS

Data Source

Bank Indonesia, not like other countries, discloses the balance sheet and financial statements of most of the local banks including foreign banks' branches every month.[4] I use this novel monthly data set, which on average covers approximately 80 percent of loans outstanding in the Indonesian banking sector from December 2001 to December 2008.[5] The coverage exceeds 95 percent of foreign banks' loans. Thus, the data set covers a significant share of the Indonesian Banking sector, especially for foreign banks. Moreover, I use host lending rates and host deposit rates available at Bank Indonesia's website.[6] The advantage of this data set is the availability of interest rates by type of banks and type of use by currency. I decide to use working capital lending rates and one-month time deposit rates as lending and deposit rates in the host. They are average rates for each type of bank. Thus, there are three lending rates for state-owned banks, domestic private banks, and foreign banks.

Monthly frequency of the data set could capture a response to financial and economic shocks from a parent bank and a home country, which might be unobservable in quarterly and annual data because during the current global crisis, financial institutions are forced to respond to shock

Table 14.1 Indonesian Banking Sector Statistics

	Total lending (billions of USD)	Loan Growth Rate	Market Share	Market Share Growth Rate	Lending Rate	Deposit Rate	Loan/Deposit Ratio
Local Currency Lending							
Foreign Bank	4.5	20.5%	8.0%	-4.8%	15.5%	5.7%	90.6%
State Owned Bank	20.4	25.0%	37.3%	-1.2%	15.8%	8.3%	63.9%
Domestic Private Bank	25.4	28.9%	44.8%	1.8%	15.5%	7.2%	60.0%
Foreign Currency Lending							
Foreign Bank	2.7	10.1%	39.9%	-1.4%	8.6%	2.8%	130.4%
State Owned Bank	4.9	8.6%	35.3%	-2.8%	9.2%	3.2%	98.1%
Domestic Private Bank	3.5	18.6%	23.5%	6.2%	9.6%	3.1%	52.1%
Total Lending					LC Loan Growth Rate	FC Loan Growth Rate	FC/Total Loan Ratio
Banking Sector	69.4	22.9%			26.6%	11.7%	21.6%

Note: All the values and rates are the average during the sample period (December 2001–December 2008). The sum of market share of each bank type is not 100 percent because regional government banks are excluded. Lending rates are loans for working capital. Deposit rates are for one-year time deposit. LC and FC mean local and foreign currency, respectively.

Source: Bank Indonesia and author's estimation.

much quicker than before the crisis period.[7] Monthly financial and economic data is mostly collected from International Financial Statistics unless specified. Daily exchange rates, stock prices of parent banks, and stock indexes of home countries are collected from Datastream (Thomson Financial). Monthly volatility of stock indexes, stock prices, and exchange rates is calculated as annualized daily volatility by taking the standard deviation of daily returns multiplied by the square root of 252 (total business days in a year).

Indonesian Banking Sector and Descriptive Statistics

The size of the Indonesian banking sector is approximately seventy billion U.S. dollars on average during the sample period (Table 10.1). Domestic credit (including nonbank financial institutions) to GDP ratio is 47.0 percent as of 2005 (World Development Indicator). This is higher than most Latin American countries (e.g., Argentina 38.3 percent, Mexico 35.3 percent), but the lowest of ASEAN four countries (Malaysia 143.7 percent, the Philippines 50.9 percent, Thailand 111.1 percent). Thus, in this financial development measurement Indonesia ranks medium in the emerging markets. The annual loan growth rate is 22.9 percent; local currency loans expand more rapidly than foreign ones. Consequently, the share of foreign currency lending (21.6 percent) tends to decrease during the period. Of the three types of banks, domestic private banks enjoy the highest annual loan growth rates in local currency (28.9 percent) and foreign currency (18.6 percent). Only their market shares increase, accordingly. Foreign banks appear to rely on a parent bank or the financial market to finance foreign currency because average loan-to-deposit ratio exceeds 100 percent.

Indonesia's banking sector was closed before the crisis. Still, the significant expansion of foreign presence after the postcrisis period could be the evidence of bank sector reform (Sato 2005). Although foreign banks have not been the sole owners of any Indonesian bank, foreign investors, sovereign wealth funds, and international organizations have been major shareholders in leading domestic banks. According to Bank International Settlements (BIS), foreign banks are defined as ones with more than 50 percent of foreign shareholders. However, the object of this chapter is to distinguish two types of financial sources such as deposits and internal capital markets. Thus, criterion that I use to distinguish among different types of banks is whether they really manage international portfolios or just manage an Indonesian portfolio.

For example,[8] Standard Chartered Bank (United Kingdom) owned 44.5 percent of PT Bank Permata Tbk as of December 2007.[9] Yet, the management of Standard Chartered emphasized the localized strategies in Indonesia. This implies that Bank Permata still disburses rupiah loans that are fully covered by local customers' deposits and invests in the Indonesian government bonds. Other Indonesian banks that have a high presence of foreign ownership are also in similar situations.

As discussed, the mixed structure of ownership structure made it difficult to evaluate impacts of home factors on the lending activity of Indonesian banks taken over by more than one foreign investor. In-depth analysis of ownership is not the objective of this chapter. In this chapter's definition, therefore, foreign banks do not include banks taken over by foreign investors even if the share of their ownership exceeds 50 percent. I define foreign banks as banks founded by greenfield investment by a foreign parent bank. This means they run the business in Indonesia as branches of foreign banks.[10]

The list of individual banks is available in Appendix 10.1. Although the number of state-owned banks is five, their market share in terms of loans is more than one-third in both the currencies. The number of foreign banks covered in the data set is twenty-five; the number of nationalities of foreign banks is twelve; the loan market share of each foreign bank is under 2 percent except Citibank (2.5 percent). Although total share of foreign banks is 10.4 percent, their share in U.S. dollars is about 40 percent. Thus, the lending market is not dominated by one or a few foreign banks. In the meantime, their foreign currency loan to total loan ratio is much higher than state-owned banks and domestic private banks.[11] Thus, foreign banks have high presence in foreign currency lending. Because almost all the lending in foreign currency is denominated in U.S. dollars, I assume only U.S. dollars would be used for foreign currency lending.[12] This implies that foreign banks except U.S. banks might face foreign exchange rate risk between their home currency and U.S. dollars even if they do not lend loans in the Indonesian rupiah. Growth rates of local currency loan (LC Loan Growth Rates) means growth rates of local currency loans denominated in the Indonesian rupiah. Growth rates of foreign currency loan (FC Loan Growth Rates) means growth rates of foreign currency loans denominated in U.S. dollars. The original data are shown in the Indonesian rupiah. Thus, the value of foreign currency loan is converted to U.S. dollars by the monthly average of exchange rates from IFS.

METHODOLOGY AND RESULTS

Theoretical Base Model: Two-Country International Lending in the Holmstrom and Tirole Model (the HT model)

The basic model consists of firms, banks that have a strategy to monitor firms (monitoring banks), and banks that are unable monitor firms (blind banks).[13] All are risk-neutral. Firms choose between a good project and either of two bad projects. The "good" project succeeds with probability p_H; both "bad" projects succeed with probability p_L. The relative likelihood of success is defined as $p = p_H - p_L > 0$. All of the projects return R (per unit invested) if they succeed and 0 if not. The two bad projects also produce different amounts of private benefit (b); type B bad projects produce a larger private benefit ($B > b$). Monitoring banks can prevent B investments by monitoring, but not b investment. Monitoring cost c per unit of investment. Monitoring banks must invest enough of their own capital in the project to be credible monitors.

Firms borrow from both the monitoring bank (*informed capital*) and the blind bank (*uninformed bank*). If the projects succeed, the firm, monitoring banks, and uninformed blind banks receive Rf, Rm, and Ru. Rf must be large enough to induce the firm to choose the good project ($Rf \geq bI/\Delta p$). Rm must be large enough to induce the monitoring bank to lend ($Rf \geq cI\Delta p$). At equilibrium, the two incentives' constraint and the firm's budget constraint will bind. The maximum pledgeable income, defined by the Holmstrom and Tirole Model (HT) as the maximum expected income per unit of investment that can be guaranteed to uninformed banks without destroying incentives is then equal to $p_H\,(R - (b + c)/\Delta p)$.

Local Currency Lending with No Exchange Hedging Instruments

In local currency lending of global banks as well as local banks' *local* and *foreign currency* lending, I assume that informed capital is completely immobile across home (Source) and host (Destination). Because in this chapter *host* is a developing country, there are no headquarters of global and no hedging exchange instruments for local currency. That immobility means the equilibrium in each state is the same as in the HT one-state model. Let β and γ denote the rates of return required by informed banks and uniformed banks, respectively. Let Kf_H be the aggregate amount of firm capital in a home country where global banks' headquarters are located, Km_H the aggregate amount of informed capital in home, and Ku_H the aggregate supply of uninformed capital in home. The first two are fixed, whereas the third is determined so that the demand for uninformed capital (the sum of the pledgeable expected returns of individual firms, discounted by γ) equals the supply of uninformed capital. Equilibrium in the uninformed capital market in Home requires that:

$$p_H(Kf_S + Km_S + Ku_S)(R - (b + c)/\Delta p)(1/\gamma) = Ku_S.$$

The equilibrium quantity of uninformed capital in Home is determined by:

$$Ku_S\_= (p_H - b - c + R \times \Delta p)(Kf_S + Km_S) / (\,p_H(\,b + c - R \times \Delta p) + \Delta p \times \gamma).$$

The equilibrium rates of return in informed capital markets are defined by:

$\beta_S = p_H \times c(Kf_S + Km_S + Ku_S) / (Kf_S + Km_S \times \Delta p)$.

Foreign Currency Lending with No Exchange Hedging Instruments

By foreign currency lending of global banks, I mean that informed capital *can* move freely to equalize β across home (Source) and host (Destination). Denote π_S as the share of aggregate informed capital ($Km_S + Km_D$) invested in home. Let Ku_S^* and Ku_D^* be the quantities of uninformed capital attracted by firms in home and host (note the superscript * for foreign currency lending of global banks). Equilibrium with the foreign currency lending is determined by these three equations:

$$pH(Kf_S + p_S (Km_S + Km_D) + Ku_S^*)(R—(b + c) /\Delta p) (1/ \gamma) = Ku_S^*;$$

$$pH(Kf_D + (1—\pi_S)(Km_S + Km_D) + Ku_D^*)(R—(b + c) /\Delta p) (1/ \gamma) = Ku_D^*;$$

$$\beta = pH \times c(Kf_S + \pi_S (Km_S + Km_D) + Ku_S^*) / (\Delta p \times \pi_S (Km_S + Km_D))$$

$$= pH \times c(Kf_{SD} + (1—\pi_S)(Km_S + Km_D) + Ku_S^*) / (\Delta p \times (1—\pi_S) (Km_S + Km_D)).$$

The equilibrium quantities attracted by firms in home and host and the share of informed capital invested in home are:

$$Ku_S^* = p_H (-b—c + R \times \Delta p)(Kf_S + Kf_D + Km_S + Km_D) Kf_S$$

$$/ ((p_H(b + c—R \times \Delta p) + \Delta p \times \gamma)(Kf_S + Kf_D)).$$

$$Ku_D^* = p_H (-b—c + R \times \Delta p)(Kf_S + Kf_D + Km_S + Km_D) Kf_D$$

$$/ ((p_H(b + c—R \times \Delta p) + \Delta p \times \gamma)(Kf_S + Kf_D)).$$

$$\pi_S = Kf_S / (Kf_S + Kf_D).$$

Propositions

The following propositions are almost identical to Morgan, Rime, and Strahan (2004) except the fact that I add the assumptions that a parent bank's stock price and the stock market index of home are a linear function of uninformed bank capital and firm capital in a home country, respectively.

Proposition 1: The negative impact of a parent bank capital in home, where a global bank's headquarters exist (a decrease in Ku_S), on the amount of informed and of uninformed capital invested in home, is smaller under foreign currency lending. I assume a parent bank's stock price (P_S) is a linear function of Ku_S: $P_S = f(Ku_S)$, where $\delta P_S / \delta Ku_S > 0$. Thus, a parent bank's stock price (P_S) is $Ku_S = g(P_S)$, where $g(x) = f^1(x)$, $\delta Ku_S / \delta P_S > 0$. Intuitively, the increase in β caused by the bank capital, which could be captured by the parent bank's stock price, leads to bank capital from a host country

(Indonesia). This capital inflow moderates the negative shock to the bank capital on the availability of external finance in two ways. First, the bank capital inflow causes a lower decrease in the amount lent by banks to firms in a home country (e.g., U.S., UK, and Japan). Second, less decrease in the amount of bank loans to firms in a home country results in a smaller reduction in the pledgeable income that can be promised to uninformed banks by firms in a home country. Consequently, we have a smaller reduction in the amount of uninformed capital that firms in a home country can attract. With global banks' *local currency* lending as well as local banks' *local* and *foreign currency* lending, these moderating effects do not happen, because bank capital cannot move across home and host. Formally, Proposition 1 implies that $\delta\pi_S (Km_{SS} + Km_D) / \delta Km_S < \delta Km_S / \delta Km_S$ and $\delta Ku_S^* / \delta Km_S < \delta Ku_S / \delta Km_S$.[14]

Proposition 2: The negative impact of a collateral squeeze in Home (a decrease in Kf_S) on the amount of uninformed and informed capital invested in home is larger for foreign currency lending of global banks. I assume the stock market index of home (V_S) is a linear function of Kf_S: $V_S = f(Kf_S)$, where $\delta V_S / \delta Kf_S > 0$. Thus, the home stock index (V_S) is $Kf_S = g(V_S)$, where $g(x) = f^{1}(x)$, $\delta Kf_S / \delta V_S > 0$. With foreign currency lending of global banks, the decrease in β after the collateral squeeze, which could be captured by the stock market index, drives bank capital from home to host. Two effects are distinguished here. First, the bank capital flight causes a decrease in the amount lent by banks to firms in home. Second, this reduction of the amount lent by banks to firms in home leads to a decrease in the pledgeable income that can be promised to uninformed banks. Consequently, firms in home can attract less uninformed capital. With unit banking (e.g., local banking in developing countries), these amplifying effects do not take place, because bank capital cannot move across home and host.[15]

Empirical Base Models

Following two propositions of the extension of Morgan, Rime, and Strahan (2004), I proposed three hypotheses:

1. High growth rates in the parent bank's stock price in the home market increase foreign banks' U.S. dollar lending in a host country through internal capital market, but not local currency lending.
2. Low performance in the home stock index or other shocks such as high volatility of home stock markets pushes up foreign banks' U.S. dollar lending in a host country.
3. A decrease in the host stock index or other shocks such as high volatility of host stock markets results in an decrease in foreign banks' lending in U.S. dollar in a host country.

In the model, a globalized bank's capital in local currency in host is constrained; the bank is risk-neutral and propagates shocks owing to the rebalance of their international credit portfolios in response to country-specific shocks. The first proposition states that a negative impact to bank capital in a home country on bank loans is smaller under globalized banking than under unit banking due to capital transfer from a host country to a home country. Suppose that the stock price of a foreign bank's parent bank represents shocks to bank capital. Then, a change in the parent bank's stock price positively affects foreign banks' lending in U.S. dollars through internal capital market as we see in Figure 10.3. However, the parent stock price does not directly affect bank lending in rupiah because it works as if it would be under unit banking. Due to the difference of the existence of internal capital markets, the currency denomination plays a vital role in distinguishing shock transmission via internal capital markets from via other channels.

The second proposition states that the negative impact of firms' capital (collateral) squeezes in a home country on the amount of bank loans in a home country is larger under globalized banking (foreign currency lending). Suppose asset prices such as stock market indexes represent shocks to firm capital (collateral). Then, a decrease in the home stock index or other shocks such as high volatility of home stock markets leads to an increase in foreign banks' lending in U.S. dollars in Indonesia. Similarly, a decrease in the host stock index or other shocks such as high volatility of host stock markets leads to a decrease in foreign banks' lending in U.S. dollars in Indonesia. But its impact on rupiah lending via the internal capital market channel should be limited.

In econometric methodology, I modify De Haas and Van Lelyveld (2006, 2010), because they include variables that represent macroeconomic conditions of other host countries. But I follow the original two-country setting (a relationship between host and home) in Morgan, Rime, and Strahan (2004). In the first model, the growth rate of a loan is determined by the foreign branch's specific variables, financial variables in Indonesia (a host country), the parent bank's stock price, and home factors.[16] In the second regression, we introduce two relative home and host factor factors: the difference of stock market returns and lending rates (host minus home). Combining hypothesis (2) with (3), I expect high relative stock returns strongly increase foreign banks' U.S. dollar loans in Indonesia. Furthermore, high relative lending rates increase foreign banks' U.S. dollars in Indonesia lending because of high expected returns for lending. Afterwards, I will investigate the effects of the current crisis on foreign banks' lending, based on the relative factor model.

I follow the selection of variables from De Haas and Van Lelyveld (2006, 2010) as a baseline. They do not focus on the value of the unobserved bank-specific effect μ_i for a particular bank, but rather in making inferences with respect to population characteristics. Thus they estimated the random effects (RE) model. Because I would like to pay more attention to the individual characteristics of banks, I estimate the fixed effects (FE) model.[17]

$$GR_{it} = \alpha_i + \beta_1 \, Host + \beta_2 \, Branch + \beta_3 Home + \beta_4 Parent + \beta_5 \mathbf{Z} + \mu_i + \varepsilon_{it}$$

$$GR_{it} = \alpha_i + \beta_1 \, Host\_ + \beta_2 \, Branch + \beta_3 \, Home\_$$

$$+ \beta_4 Parent + \beta_5 \, Relative\ Host\text{-}Home\ factors + \beta_6 \mathbf{Z} + \mu_i + \varepsilon_{it}$$

where

GR_{it} is percentage loan growth of bank *i* in month *t*;

is the intercept term;

Host consists of $HOST\_LEND_{jt}$ a monthly change in lending rates, $HOST\_FX_t$ a monthly return of a value of Indonesia rupiah per U.S. dollar, $HOST\_FXVOL_t$, a the annualized volatility of daily returns in $HOST\_FX_t$, $HOST\_CPI_t$ a monthly change in inflation rates, $HOST\_SI_t$ a monthly stock index return in Jakarta Stock Exchange, and $HOST\_SIVOL_t$ the annualized volatility of daily returns in the stock index;

Branch consists of *Size* (the loan market share of the Indonesian banking sector by currency), *Profitability* (Return on Asset before income tax), *Efficiency* (interest margin by currency), *Liquidity* (liquidity asset divided by total asset of a bank), and *Solvency* (capital divided by total asset);

Home consists of $HOME\_LEND_{kt}$ a home country's monthly change in lending rates, $HOME\_FX_t$ a monthly return of a value of Indonesia rupiah per U.S. dollar, $HOME\_FXVOL_t$, a the annualized volatility of daily returns in $HOME\_FX_t$, $HOME\_SI_{kt}$ a monthly stock index return in a home country, $HOME\_SIVOL_{kt}$ the annualized volatility of daily returns in the home stock index, $PARENT_{it}$ a monthly stock return of a parent bank in a home country, and $PARENTVOL_{it}$ the volatility of daily returns in the parent bank's stock price;

Parent is a monthly stock return of a parent bank in a home country;

Z consists of seasonal adjustment dummies;

Relative Host-Home factors are HOST-HOME_LENDkt (*the difference of HOST_LENDjt,and HOME_LENDkt*), and *HOST-HOME_SI* (*the difference of HOST_SIt and HOME_SIkt*); *Host_* are Host except HOST_LENDjt,and HOST_SIt;

*Home_* are Home except $HOME\_LEND_{kt}$ and $HOME\_SI_{kt}$;

μ_i is the unobserved, panel-level fixed effect;

ε_{it} is the idiosyncratic error, $\varepsilon_{it} \sim \text{IID}(0; \sigma^2_{\mu})$;

$\beta_1, \ldots, \beta_4$ are the coefficients (or coefficient vectors);

$i = 1, \ldots, N$ where N is the number of banks in the sample;

$j = 1, 2, 3$ where the number is the type of banks (state owned, private national, foreign)

$k = 1, \ldots, M$ where M is the number of foreign bank's nationalities in the sample;

$t = 1, \ldots, Ti$ where Ti is the number of months in the sample for bank i.

Dependant variables consist of two types of loan growth rates: Local Currency Loan Growth (LC Loan Growth Rates) and Foreign Currency Loan Growth (FC Loan Growth Rates). I separately estimate coefficients of explanatory variables for full samples (Panel A) and foreign banks (Panel B) to see a difference between foreign banks and the banking sector as a whole. I expect an increase in *HOST_LEND* positively affects growth rates of loans. Because the outstanding of loans for total lending and local currency is denominated in the Indonesian rupiah in a nominal base, an increase in inflation rates probably expands the nominal loan outstanding. High *HOST_SI* is a positive factor for the Indonesian economy. As a result, I expect it has a positive effect on the loan growth. In the meantime, an increase in *HOST_SIVOL* could dampen an incentive for banks to increase their credit. What's more, I expect the negative sign of the coefficient for *Size* (the loan market share of the Indonesian banking sector by currency) because loan growth rates tend to decline as the market share becomes high; positive for *Profitability* (Return on Asset before income tax); positive for *Efficiency* (interest margin by currency); positive for *Liquidity* (liquidity asset divided by total asset of a bank); positive for *Solvency* (capital divided by total asset). I use one-month lagged value of *Size, Liquidity, and Solvency* to avoid simultaneous bias.

HOST (HOME) includes host country (home country) financial variables that are likely to influence the (relative) attractiveness of expanding credit in a particular host country (home country). These are the average bank lending rate (+), the nominal exchange rate against the U.S. dollar (normally +, during the crisis -), and inflation (-) (expected sign for the host country variables in parentheses). Banks are likely to expand lending if lending rates are higher and inflation is lower. If the local currency depreciates against the U.S. dollar, it would be a chance to expand loans in a host country if foreign exchange markets are well developed. An increase in volatility in home (host) stock markets and home (host) exchange rates generally discourages increasing loans owing to uncertainty in home (host) markets. Consequently, foreign banks tend to increase (decrease) lending in a host country.

Because I assume foreign currency lending is denominated in U.S. dollars, deposit in foreign banks' home countries except U.S. banks cannot be the main financial source of foreign currency lending. Thus, I do not include deposit rates from the host and home factor model.[18] I preassume monthly data are more appropriate to capture a response to the financial shocks from a home country than quarterly data because financial institutions usually reallocate their assets more frequently than quarterly, reflecting a change in exchange rates and asset prices. Moreover, referring to the recent financial crisis triggered by U.S. subprime loans, multinational banks could face difficulties due to the fluctuation of their own stock prices even though they do not newly announce their current financial status.[19] Thus, these factors might lead to the reallocation or repatriation of loans from a host country.

Because there should be a lag to home shocks for headquarters to make a decision on allocation of global assets, I use one-month lagged of average monthly returns in a parent stock price.[20] In Panel A, all the home factors of state-owned banks and private domestic banks are zero, because there is no shock from home for domestic (Indonesian) banks.

First, I analyze the impacts of host and home factors in the first regression (Table 14.2). Because the results of both full samples (Panel A) and foreign bank samples (Panel B) are quite similar, I focus on Panel B unless specified. One percent increase in host lending rate leads to 2.94 percent increase in local currency loans by foreign banks at the 10 percent significant level. Higher host exchange rate volatility dampens local currency lending at the 10 percent significant level; higher host inflation rates decrease growth rates of foreign currency lending. The sign of coefficients of these variables is consistent with prediction.

Next, I move on to the impact of branch factors. The sign of coefficients of *Size* and *Profitability* are as expected and significant for lending in both currencies. As foreign banks are able to receive capital transfer from the headquarters, at the branch level, *Solvency* is not a key determinant of their lending although it is quite important as a holding company. *Liquidity* is significant for only full samples and foreign banks' foreign loans. Because foreign banks' headquarters tend to reallocate host and home assets that are more profitable with relatively low risk, high loan-to-deposit ratio of foreign branches may reflect the fact that high liquidity of assets strongly motivates foreign banks' branches to lend more under high pressure from a parent bank. However, high liquidity is not always associated with banking stability due to the recent financial innovation (Wagner 2007).

Finally, I check the internal capital market hypotheses. If shocks to home and a parent bank are propagated to foreign banks' lending activity through internal capital transfer, only foreign currency loans should

Table 14.2 Impact of Host and Home Factors

	Panel A - Full Samples		Panel B - Foreign Banks	
	(1) LC Loan Growth Rate	(2) FC Loan Growth Rate	(1) LC Loan Growth Rate	(2) FC Loan Growth Rate
Host D.Lending Rate	0.0143 (0.0105)	0.0011 (0.0083)	0.0294* (0.0170)	0.0013 (0.0098)
Home D.Lending Rate	-0.0443** (0.0226)	-0.0283 (0.0276)	-0.0427 (0.0287)	-0.0183 (0.0306)
Host %.Exchange Rate	0.1618 (0.1902)	-0.3743 (0.2289)	0.2813 (0.3174)	-0.4818 (0.3331)
Host Exchange Rate Volatility	-0.1626* (0.0877)	-0.0201 (0.1068)	-0.2479* (0.1444)	-0.0119 (0.1532)
Home %.Exchange Rate	0.0705 (0.2077)	-0.2706 (0.2505)	-0.0637 (0.2720)	-0.1680 (0.2853)
Home Exchange Rate Volatility	0.0786 (0.1022)	-0.0872 (0.1234)	0.1840 (0.2146)	-0.2420 (0.2264)
Host %.Inflation	-0.1606 (0.3394)	-0.7217* (0.3970)	-0.4525 (0.5589)	-1.0851* (0.5756)
Host %.Stock Index	-0.1205 (0.0760)	0.0410 (0.0907)	-0.1755 (0.1300)	0.0380 (0.1407)
Host Stock Index Volatility	-0.0584 (0.0455)	0.1546** (0.0553)	-0.0937 (0.0751)	0.1940** (0.0811)
Home %.Stock Index	-0.1793 (0.1355)	-0.3937*** (0.1130)	-0.1099 (0.1771)	-0.3865** (0.1433)
Home Stock Index Volatility	-0.0099 (0.0558)	0.0434 (0.0624)	-0.0035 (0.0729)	0.0338 (0.0721)
Parent %.Stock Price	0.0812 (0.0603)	0.1710** (0.0568)	0.0667 (0.0765)	0.1869** (0.0631)
Size	-1.5303** (0.6862)	-2.5201*** (0.3463)	-7.2029** (3.3813)	-3.3594*** (0.8222)
Profitability	1.8490*** (0.2912)	1.1658** (0.3619)	2.0047*** (0.3766)	1.3412** (0.4096)
Efficiency	0.0595*** (0.0162)	-0.8052*** (0.1116)	-0.0624** (0.0205)	-3.2488*** (0.2639)
Liquidity	0.0357 (0.0294)	0.0406 (0.0355)	0.0418 (0.0414)	0.0505 (0.0434)
Solvency	-0.0755 (0.0683)	0.1179 (0.0888)	-0.1352 (0.0943)	0.0576 (0.1090)
Observations	2640	2600	1590	1551
R-squared	0.041	0.066	0.049	0.132
Number of Banks	38	37	23	23
Bank Fixed Effect	Yes	Yes	Yes	Yes

Note: All the results are estimated by monthly panel regressions with individual bank's fixed effects. LC Loan Growth Rate means growth rates of total loan and local currency loan denominated in Indonesian rupiah. FC Loan Growth Rate means growth rates of foreign currency loan denominated in U.S. dollars. "D." means the difference between the current rate and the last month's rate. "%." means the monthly growth rates. "X" means interaction terms with type of bank dummies. Exchange Rates of Host and Home are the values of each country's currency per U.S. dollar. Thus, they become higher as the U.S. dollar appreciates. Volatility is calculated by using annualized standard deviation of daily returns of each month. Parent Stock Price means the stock price of a parent bank of foreign banks in a home country. Size is the credit market share of the Indonesian banking sector by currency. Profitability is Return on Asset before income tax. Efficiency is interest margin by currency. Liquidity is liquidity asset divided by total asset of a bank. Solvency is capital divided by total asset. The coefficients of seasonal adjustment dummies are not reported. *, **, and *** denote significance at 10, 5, and 1 percent, respectively.

be significant. The results of the host and home factor models show parent stock prices and home stock index are prominent factors that determine foreign banks' lending. When a parent's stock returns become higher, foreign banks increase foreign currency lending in a host country. The sign of coefficients is also positive in local currency, but it is not significant. This is because the headquarters are not the main financial sources of local currency and foreign banks' rupiah lending works as if it were stand-alone. Thus, when a parent bank is in good condition, foreign banks expand their U.S. dollar loans in a host country.[21] Goldberg (2001) finds that there is substitution between claims on industrialized countries and claims on the United States. Similar effects are observed on emerging Asia. Thus, this finding is consistent with her findings as well as my prediction based on the theoretical framework of Morgan, Rime, and Strahan (2004).

In the second regression I consider relative factors between host and home (Table 10.3). I subtract home factors from host factors for a change in lending rates and monthly stock index return rates because my coefficients from previous regressions suggested similar, opposite effects for some home and host variables, and now I want to check whether one can gain explanatory power by using relative variables. Again, the results of both full samples (Panel A) and foreign bank samples (Panel B) are quite similar. Thus, I report the result of Panel B unless specified.

I start from relative host-home factors. An increase in *HOST-HOME_LEND* and *HOST-HOME_SI* means there is relatively higher profitable opportunity in a host country than in a home country. Therefore, it can increase loan disbursement in a host country. The result indicates that relative host-home lending rates positively affect local currency loan growth rates at 5 percent significant level. Greater relative host-home stock indexes lead to an increase in foreign currency loan growth rates, but to a decrease in local currency growth rates. The result of the foreign currency lending follows the internal capital market hypothesis derived from Morgan, Rime, and Strahan (2004). Then, what happens to local currency lending? One explanation is that firms that need local currency loan shift to direct finance such as the issue of corporate bonds and initial public offering during a good time despite the fact that the Indonesian corporate bond market is still underdeveloped. From the view of the loan supply side, it is in the same line with the strands of literature that economic problems are good opportunities to invest (De Haas and Van Lelyveld 2004; Peek and Rosengren 2000; Goldberg 2001; Martinez Peria, Powell, and Hollar 2002). In this case, we must see the impact of a host stock market as well as a home stock market to conclude it. Although from the view of the loan demand side the concern for foreign banks is relatively limited, I test a robustness of the model by controlling such demand effects.[22]

Table 14.3 Impact of Host and Home Relative Facto

	Full-Sample Period (2002–2008)				Before the Global Crisis (2002–2006)				During the Global Crisis (2007–2008)			
	Panel A - Full Samples		Panel B - Foreign Banks		Panel A - Full Samples		Panel B - Foreign Banks		Panel A - Full Samples		Panel B - Foreign Banks	
	(1) LC Loan Growth Rate	(2) FC Loan Growth Rate	(1) LC Loan Growth Rate	(2) FC Loan Growth Rate	(1) LC Loan Growth Rate	(2) FC Loan Growth Rate	(1) LC Loan Growth Rate	(2) FC Loan Growth Rate	(1) LC Loan Growth Rate	(2) FC Loan Growth Rate	(1) LC Loan Growth Rate	(2) FC Loan Growth Rate
Host-Home	0.0207**	0.0021	0.0557**	0.0024	0.0175	-0.0005	0.0551*	-0.0055	0.0551**	-0.0157	0.0644**	0.0550
D Lending Rate	(0.0095)	(0.0080)	(0.0145)	(0.0094)	(0.0121)	(0.0085)	(0.0196)	(0.0102)	(0.0171)	(0.0252)	(0.0251)	(0.0585)
Host	0.1884	-0.2715	0.5267	-0.2576	0.5128	-0.2420	0.5157	-0.2245	-1.0028**	-0.8605	-1.2592	-0.2846
% Exchange Rate	(0.1759)	(0.2117)	(0.2988)	(0.3156)	(0.2173)	(0.2245)	(0.5729)	(0.5507)	(0.4785)	(0.8488)	(0.8551)	(1.2900)
Host	-0.1668*	0.0055	-0.2572*	0.0482	-0.1498	0.0955	-0.2527	0.2666	0.5895	0.2429	0.7056	0.9566
Exchange Rate Volatility	(0.0860)	(0.1049)	(0.1402)	(0.1495)	(0.1591)	(0.1402)	(0.2286)	(0.2111)	(0.5245)	(0.5858)	(0.5840)	(0.8679)
Home	-0.0188	-0.1995	-0.0925	-0.1265	0.0145	0.0796	-0.0415	0.2179	-0.0810	-0.4545	-0.0175	-0.1562
% Exchange Rate	(0.2109)	(0.2545)	(0.2725)	(0.2846)	(0.2842)	(0.2894)	(0.5721)	(0.5409)	(0.5218)	(0.5602)	(0.4566)	(0.6202)
Home	0.0871	-0.0875	0.1928	-0.2021	-0.0259	-0.0017	-0.1481	-0.0546	0.1997	-0.2090	0.5905	-0.0550
Exchange Rate Volatility	(0.1017)	(0.1229)	(0.2158)	(0.2259)	(0.1543)	(0.1587)	(0.5557)	(0.5088)	(0.1782)	(0.3146)	(0.2846)	(0.4089)
Host	-0.1830	-0.5525	-0.4574	-0.9152	-0.5087	-0.8175**	-0.6885	-1.4225**	5.0787	-5.8168	5.2961	1.9855
% Inflation	(0.3562)	(0.5944)	(0.5605)	(0.5710)	(0.5777)	(0.5756)	(0.6155)	(0.5599)	(2.6791)	(5.0857)	(4.7420)	(7.8820)
Host-Home	-0.2252**	0.1660*	-0.1960*	0.2075*	-0.5180**	0.1951*	-0.2759*	0.1446	0.0945	-0.0255	0.1565	0.4991
% Stock Index	(0.0814)	(0.1007)	(0.1104)	(0.1192)	(0.1056)	(0.1066)	(0.1467)	(0.1558)	(0.1464)	(0.2859)	(0.2146)	(0.5628)
Host	-0.0290	0.1900***	-0.0585	0.2651***	-0.0562	0.0645	-0.0870	-0.0409	-0.0573	0.2094	-0.1546	-0.0206
Stock Index Volatility	(0.0419)	(0.0510)	(0.0701)	(0.0780)	(0.0755)	(0.0760)	(0.1219)	(0.1124)	(0.1270)	(0.2561)	(0.2147)	(0.5828)
Home	0.0251	0.0951	0.0275	0.0669	-0.0157	-0.1140*	0.0019	-0.1075	0.0569	0.4727**	0.0025	0.5104*
Stock Index Volatility	(0.0499)	(0.0614)	(0.0656)	(0.0705)	(0.0641)	(0.0668)	(0.0852)	(0.0785)	(0.0879)	(0.1551)	(0.1501)	(0.1878)
Parent	0.0222	0.1455**	0.0229	0.1605**	0.0109	0.0587	0.0067	0.0650	0.2462**	0.5856**	0.2880**	0.4559**
% Stock Price	(0.0460)	(0.0561)	(0.0685)	(0.0620)	(0.0650)	(0.0543)	(0.0666)	(0.0620)	(0.1025)	(0.1826)	(0.1427)	(0.2054)
Size	-1.5255**	-2.4851***	-7.0607**	-5.2810***	-2.1642**	-1.5156**	-7.7665*	-1.5188	-6.0528	-10.5100***	-32.4987**	-19.8557***
	(0.6855)	(0.5467)	(3.5770)	(0.8225)	(0.9165)	(0.4752)	(4.1455)	(1.0860)	(5.2662)	(0.9851)	(12.5108)	(2.7529)

(continued)

Table 14.3 (continued)

	Full Sample Period (2002–2008)				Before the Global Crisis (2002–2006)				During the Global Crisis (2007–2008)			
	Panel A · Full Samples		Panel B · Foreign Banks		Panel A · Full Samples		Panel B · Foreign Banks		Panel A · Full Samples		Panel B · Foreign Banks	
	(1) LC Loan Growth Rate	(2) FC Loan Growth Rate	(1) LC Loan Growth Rate	(2) FC Loan Growth Rate	(1) LC Loan Growth Rate	(2) FC Loan Growth Rate	(1) LC Loan Growth Rate	(2) FC Loan Growth Rate	(1) LC Loan Growth Rate	(2) FC Loan Growth Rate	(1) LC Loan Growth Rate	(2) FC Loan Growth Rate
Profitability	1.8515***	1.1412**	2.0046***	1.5552**	1.9455***	1.0518**	2.1164***	1.2060**	-4.2105*	1.1627	-4.4879	1.4580
	(0.2910)	(0.3626)	(0.5762)	(0.4100)	(0.5059)	(0.5192)	(0.5896)	(0.5750)	(2.1559)	(3.8259)	(2.9225)	(4.1968)
Efficiency	-0.0615***	-0.8614***	-0.0657**	-5.2425***	-0.0574***	-0.7654***	-0.0600**	-2.9791***	-1.1425***	-0.8880**	-1.2052***	-8.0942***
	(0.0162)	(0.1117)	(0.0208)	(0.2659)	(0.0171)	(0.1027)	(0.0216)	(0.2465)	(0.2152)	(0.4512)	(0.2826)	(1.4188)
Liquidity	0.0560	0.0685	0.0414	0.0475	0.0152	0.0971**	0.0285	0.1060**	0.3522***	-0.0611	0.4712**	-0.0452
	(0.0295)	(0.0656)	(0.0415)	(0.0455)	(0.0560)	(0.0571)	(0.0505)	(0.0469)	(0.0995)	(0.1679)	(0.1485)	(0.2070)
Solvency	-0.0770	0.1385	-0.1582	0.0486	-0.2559**	0.2124**	-0.3739**	0.1552	0.0948	-0.2906	-0.0552	-0.4871
	(0.0682)	(0.0888)	(0.0942)	(0.1090)	(0.0890)	(0.1022)	(0.1254)	(0.1551)	(0.2617)	(0.4616)	(0.3629)	(0.8225)
Observations	2640	2500	1590	1581	1985	1944	1207	1168	657	656	585	583
R-squared	0.041	0.062	0.049	0.129	0.055	0.061	0.067	0.146	0.122	0.215	0.161	0.288
Number of Banks	58	57	25	25	56	56	25	25	55	52	18	18
Bank Fixed Effect	Yes	Yes	Yes	Yes	Yes	Yes	Yes	Yes	Yes	Yes	Yes	Yes

Note: All the results are estimated by monthly panel regressions with individual bank's fixed effects. Total Loan Growth and LC Loan Growth mean growth rates of total loan and local currency loan denominated in Indonesian rupiah. FC Loan Growth means growth rates of foreign currency loan denominated in U.S dollars. "D." means the difference between the current rate and the last month's rate. "Host - Home" means a Host's rate minus a Home's rate. "%." means the monthly growth rates. "X" means interaction terms with type of bank dummies. Exchange Rates of Host and Home are the values of each country's currency per U.S. dollar. Thus, they become higher as the U.S. dollar appreciates. Volatility is calculated by using annualized standard deviation of daily returns of each month. Parent Stock Price means the stock price of a parent bank of foreign banks in a home country. Size is the credit market share of the Indonesian banking sector by currency. Profitability is Return on Asset before income tax. Efficiency is interest margin by currency. Liquidity is liquidity asset divided by total asset of a bank. Solvency is capital divided by total asset. The coefficients of seasonal adjustment dummies are not reported. *, **, and *** denote significance at 10, 5, and 1 percent, respectively.

Next, I move on to the analysis of host factors. Higher host exchange rate volatility dampens local currency lending at the 10 percent significant level, same as the host and home factor model. Because I assume foreign banks deal with only U.S. dollars as foreign currency lending, a home exchange rate and volatility of U.S. banks are set as one and zero. The results indicate that shock (volatility) from the home exchange rates promotes foreign currency lending in a host country. This follows my expectation. The remarkable result comes from the impact of stock index volatility on foreign banks. High stock index volatility encourages them to increase foreign currency one. Actually, in full samples, banks also expand foreign currency loans when the stock market is volatile. This is critical missing information if the currency mix of loans is treated as one currency denomination.

Finally, I check the internal capital market hypotheses. The results of the relative host and home factor models show parent stock price. When a parent's stock returns become higher, foreign banks increase foreign currency lending in a host country. But this internal capital transfer channel is not significant for local currency lending. This result is consistent with the result of host and home models and follows the hypothesis.

Impacts of Crisis

In this section, I try to capture how the global financial crisis of 2007–2008 changed the sensitivity of foreign banks' lending behavior to host and home shocks, including shocks to a parent bank. Figure 10.4 shows the rates of stock returns of major parent banks from six countries and growth rates of lending of their foreign branches in Indonesia.23 During a normal period, correlation between them is very low, at most 0.08. Yet, as the crisis becomes more severe, they synchronize more closely. The correlation of rates of parent stock returns with growth rates of foreign currency lending becomes 0.28 during the crisis. Synchronicity seems to reach the peak in September 2008 when Lehman Brothers went bankrupt. If there is a regime change for banks during a crisis period that is different from during a normal period, policy makers should account for it to tackle crisis. Therefore, it is important to investigate the impact of crisis on banks' behavior.

To estimate the impact of crisis on banks' behavior, I divide samples into precrisis period and crisis period. Then, I run regressions on the relative host and home factor model for subsamples (Table 14.4, middle and right). The results of full samples and the precrisis period look similar, but, remarkably, internal capital market hypotheses do not always work well. In fact, parent stock prices are no more significant for the precrisis period. Thus, parent banks would not face difficulties in accessing external finance or collecting deposits or reserving capital. The impact of home exchange

Table 14.4 Robustness Test (1)

	Panel A - Full Samples		Panel B - Foreign Banks	
	(1)	(2)	(1)	(2)
	LC Loan Growth Rate	FC Loan Growth Rate	LC Loan Growth Rate	FC Loan Growth Rate
Host-Home D.Lending Rate	0.0156	0.0029	0.0343*	0.0014
	(0.0112)	(0.0091)	(0.0181)	(0.0107)
Host-Home D.Lending Rate X Crisis	0.0147	0.0028	-0.0051	0.0367
	(0.0224)	(0.0198)	(0.0329)	(0.0237)
Host %.Exchange Rate	0.2621	-0.1875	0.4648	-0.2858
	(0.1952)	(0.2345)	(0.3361)	(0.3508)
Host %.Exchange Rate X Crisis	-1.0190	-2.0827**	-2.5973**	-0.7651
	(0.6758)	(0.7929)	(1.2861)	(1.3305)
Host Exchange Rate Volatility	-0.0823	0.0129	-0.1575	0.1034
	(0.1126)	(0.1339)	(0.1853)	(0.1928)
Host Exchange Rate Volatility X Crisis	0.4484	0.5747*	1.1519**	0.4107
	(0.2980)	(0.3429)	(0.5754)	(0.5908)
Home %.Exchange Rate	0.0844	0.0036	0.0360	0.0680
	(0.2603)	(0.3108)	(0.3382)	(0.3479)
Home %.Exchange Rate X Crisis	0.0406	-0.7760	0.1215	-0.7809
	(0.4727)	(0.5528)	(0.6113)	(0.6199)
Home Exchange Rate Volatility	0.0695	-0.1339	0.0386	-0.0492
	(0.1092)	(0.1285)	(0.2381)	(0.2458)
Home Exchange Rate Volatility X Crisis	-0.1931	-0.1169	-0.1794	-0.2904
	(0.2243)	(0.2536)	(0.3211)	(0.3263)
Host %.Inflation	-0.2171	-0.7676*	-0.6018	-1.2188**
	(0.3553)	(0.4076)	(0.5861)	(0.5872)
Host %.Inflation X Crisis	1.3090	0.2875	3.0056	5.0284
	(1.7405)	(2.1070)	(3.0138)	(3.2646)
Host-Home %.Stock Index	-0.3117***	0.2169*	-0.2732**	0.1726
	(0.0938)	(0.1127)	(0.1309)	(0.1353)
Host-Home %.Stock Index X Crisis	0.3075	-0.3499	0.0780	0.0416
	(0.2071)	(0.2600)	(0.2923)	(0.3127)
Host Stock Index Volatility	-0.0385	0.0544	-0.0748	0.0222
	(0.0641)	(0.0758)	(0.1054)	(0.1089)
Host Stock Index Volatility X Crisis	-0.1091	0.3070**	-0.1094	0.2757
	(0.1080)	(0.1302)	(0.1835)	(0.1961)
Home Stock Index Volatility	-0.0312	-0.0288	-0.0152	-0.0659
	(0.0562)	(0.0681)	(0.0745)	(0.0782)
Home Stock Index Volatility X Crisis	0.0334	0.2141**	-0.0990	0.3605*
	(0.0861)	(0.0914)	(0.1785)	(0.1859)
Parent %.Stock Price	0.0119	0.0543	0.0081	0.0740
	(0.0498)	(0.0596)	(0.0631)	(0.0653)
Parent %.Stock Price X Crisis	0.1729	0.5922***	0.1999	0.4526**
	(0.1331)	(0.1608)	(0.1733)	(0.1803)
Size	-1.6338**	-3.3564***	-8.1165**	-2.3802**
	(0.6903)	(0.3523)	(3.4272)	(0.8607)
Size X Crisis	-0.1736	-2.3279***	-5.0453	-3.9967***
	(0.2703)	(0.2726)	(3.0939)	(0.8370)
Profitability	1.9282***	1.0442**	2.0868***	1.2190**
	(0.2909)	(0.3563)	(0.3759)	(0.4002)
Profitability X Crisis	-7.6993**	3.2436	-8.5201**	3.7579
	(2.9406)	(3.4852)	(3.9616)	(4.0748)
Efficiency	-0.0618***	-0.7382***	-0.0633**	-3.0691***
	(0.0162)	(0.1103)	(0.0206)	(0.2606)
Efficiency X Crisis	-0.4650*	-2.3557***	-0.6313*	-10.3541***
	(0.2395)	(0.5335)	(0.3270)	(1.4703)
Liquidity	0.0438	0.0798**	0.0442	0.0978**
	(0.0304)	(0.0364)	(0.0433)	(0.0446)
Liquidity X Crisis	0.1314**	0.0636	0.1556*	0.2183**
	(0.0607)	(0.0602)	(0.0841)	(0.0866)

(continued)

Table 14.4 (continued)

	Panel A - Full Samples		Panel B - Foreign Banks	
	(1) LC Loan Growth Rate	(2) FC Loan Growth Rate	(1) LC Loan Growth Rate	(2) FC Loan Growth Rate
Solvency	-0.1206*	0.1507*	-0.1836*	0.1200
	(0.0710)	(0.0913)	(0.0981)	(0.1117)
Solvency X Crisis	0.1844**	-0.2995**	0.2003*	-0.4989***
	(0.0782)	(0.0942)	(0.1051)	(0.1170)
Observations	2640	2600	1590	1551
R-squared	0.055	0.108	0.067	0.186
Number of Banks	38	37	23	23
Bank Fixed Effect	Yes	Yes	Yes	Yes

Note: All the results are estimated by monthly panel regressions with individual bank's fixed effects. LC Loan Growth Rate means growth rates local currency loan denominated in Indonesian rupiah. FC Loan Growth Rate means growth rates of foreign currency loan denominated in U.S. dollars. "D." means the difference between the current rate and the last month's rate. "Host – Home" means a Host's rate minus a Home's rate. "%." means the monthly growth rates. "X" means interaction terms with type of bank dummies and a crisis dummy (= 1 if values are in or after August 2007; otherwise 0). Exchange Rates of Host and Home are the values of each country's currency per U.S. dollar. Thus, they become higher as the U.S. dollar appreciates. Volatility is calculated by using annualized standard deviation of daily returns of each month. Parent Stock Price means the stock price of a parent bank of foreign banks in a home country. The coefficients of seasonal adjustment dummies, Size, Profitability, Efficiency, Liquidity, and Solvency are not reported. *, **, and *** denote significance at 10, 5, and 1 percent, respectively

rates, home inflation, and *Liquidity* also differs. Depreciation of host exchange rates discourages the expansion of local currency lending. Higher host inflation rates have a negative effect on growth rates of foreign currency lending. As foreign banks have more liquidity, they increase foreign currency lending. The sign of coefficients of these variables is consistent with prediction. Relative host-home stock indexes become insignificant for foreign currency lending in Panel B (foreign samples only).

Finally, the regression results of crisis samples suggest that foreign banks could be less sensitive to host and home shocks, but highly sensitive to shocks to a parent bank. Thus, this would be evidence that foreign banks changed their regime during the global crisis. Internal capital market hypothesis does not work for host-home stock indexes. Yet, shocks to a parent bank positively affect local currency lending as well as foreign currency lending. This is because local currency lending works as if it were stand-alone banking under the capital immobility assumption between foreign currency loans and local currency due to the lack of hedging instruments of foreign exchange. However, if a parent bank focuses on short-term funding rather than long-term profit maximization, capital constraint to local currency lending is no more valid, because the foreign exchange market and short-term forward markets for the Indonesia rupiah do exist. Or simply foreign branches did not actively disburse loans because of the dysfunction of a parent bank.

Robustness Test

To estimate the impact of the crisis on banks' behavior in another methodology, I extended the relative host and home factor model (the second regression) by introducing a crisis dummy variable. *Crisis* dummy is 1 for the samples from August 2007 until December 2008 (the end of the sample period). Thus, the coefficients of the interaction term *Host (Home) factors X Crisis* indicate by how much percentage foreign banks' response to host and home factors during the crisis is different from their response during the normal periods.

The results expose differences of banks' behavior during normal and crisis periods and they are consistent with the results of the subsample methodology for precrisis and crisis periods (Table 10.5). The main difference is that a parent bank's stock prices do not affect growth rates of local currency lending. This follows the initial hypothesis. Next, I take a look at home factors. Foreign banks change the reaction to exchange rate movement during a whole sample period, as we see in the previous chapter of this volume. During a crisis period, host currency depreciation dampens local currency lending. Higher inflation rates lead to a decrease in foreign currency lending.

Second, shocks to home such as home exchange rate volatility appear to affect foreign banks' lending behavior significantly during the crisis only. In contrast, relative host-home stock prices affect growth rates of lending during only the precrisis period. Consequently, although policy makers might not have to worry too much about a parent banks' soundness during a normal period, its soundness could turn into a driving force for their lending activity of foreign currency during crisis.

The supply (bank) side of loans is so far emphasized. However, the results of a home factor model may imply that the borrowers' choice of currency could be a dominant factor for growth rates of loans. For example, Turkish investors actively switch between U.S. dollar and Turkish lira assets owing to the high elasticity of substitution between domestic and foreign currency (Bahmani-Oskooee and Domac 2003). This is common for not only institutional investors, but also individuals in Turkey.[24] Moreover, it is observed in highly dollarized countries such as Latin America. Thus, it is necessary to test whether the results of the models are significant even if demand factors that drive loan growth rates are excluded. To do this, I use growth rates of each foreign bank's loan market share instead of growth rates of the loan outstanding. The loan market shares, the local currency, and foreign lending share are calculated by currency. All the explanatory variables are the same as ones in previous sections.

Table 14.5 Robustness Test (2)

	Host and Home Factors		Relative Host and Home Factors		Relative Factors with Crisis	
	(1)	(2)	(3)	(4)	(5)	(6)
Foreign Bank Samples	LC Loan Share Growth Rate	FC Loan Share Growth Rate	LC Loan Share Growth Rate	FC Loan Share Growth Rate	LC Loan Share Growth Rate	FC Loan Shar Growth Rate
Host	0.0542**	-0.0012				
D.Lending Rate	(0.0170)	(0.0098)				
Home	-0.0566	-0.0107				
D.Lending Rate	(0.0286)	(0.0506)				
Host-Home			0.0354**	-0.0006	0.0368**	0.0011
D.Lending Rate			(0.0145)	(0.0094)	(0.0181)	(0.0107)
Host-Home					-0.0085	0.0363
D.Lending Rate X Crisis					(0.0528)	(0.0237)
Host	0.2704	-0.5899*	0.2974	-0.2930	0.3928	-0.4255
%.Exchange Rate	(0.3160)	(0.3329)	(0.2948)	(0.3137)	(0.3357)	(0.3511)
Host					-2.5170*	-0.3834
%.Exchange Rate X Crisis					(1.2843)	(1.3316)
Host	-0.2359	-0.0663	-0.2314*	0.0105	-0.2047	0.0209
%.Exchange Rate Volatility	(0.1457)	(0.1551)	(0.1399)	(0.1494)	(0.1851)	(0.1929)
Host					1.1421**	0.3826
%.Exchange Rate Volatility X Crisis					(0.5746)	(0.5912)
Home	-0.0689	-0.2050	-0.0684	-0.1606	0.0566	0.0886
%.Exchange Rate	(0.2723)	(0.2852)	(0.2719)	(0.2845)	(0.3577)	(0.3482)
Home					0.1013	-0.8965
%.Exchange Rate X Crisis					(0.6105)	(0.6204)
Home	0.1501	-0.2919	0.1557	-0.2442	0.0265	-0.0372
%.Exchange Rate Volatility	(0.2140)	(0.2263)	(0.2153)	(0.2260)	(0.2378)	(0.2460)
Home					-0.1793	-0.3793
%.Exchange Rate Volatility X Crisis					(0.3206)	(0.3266)
Host	-0.5347	-0.5792	-0.5318	-0.3813	-0.6473	-0.6984
%.Inflation	(0.5570)	(0.5753)	(0.5493)	(0.5712)	(0.5854)	(0.5876)
Host					2.1147	6.5004**
%.Inflation X Crisis					(3.0098)	(3.2672)
Host	-0.1974	-0.1151				
%.Stock Index	(0.1341)	(0.1406)				
Home	0.1615	-0.3057**				
%.Stock Index	(0.1318)	(0.1433)				
Host-Home			-0.1788	0.0891	-0.2534*	0.0147
%.Stock Index			(0.1102)	(0.1192)	(0.1308)	(0.1355)
Host-Home					0.0900	0.2117
%.Stock Index X Crisis					(0.2919)	(0.3130)
Host	-0.0505	0.1448*	-0.0429	0.2291**	-0.0564	0.0116
Stock Index Volatility	(0.0762)	(0.0811)	(0.0700)	(0.0750)	(0.1052)	(0.1090)
Host					-0.0982	0.2534
Stock Index Volatility X Crisis					(0.1832)	(0.1963)
Home	0.0007	0.0469	0.0044	0.0845	-0.0293	-0.0228
Stock Index Volatility	(0.0673)	(0.0721)	(0.0654)	(0.0705)	(0.0744)	(0.0783)
Home					-0.1065	0.3353*
Stock Index Volatility X Crisis					(0.1783)	(0.1860)
Parent	0.0389	0.1793**	0.0362	0.1472**	0.0225	0.0640
%.Stock Price	(0.0593)	(0.0651)	(0.0562)	(0.0620)	(0.0630)	(0.0654)
Parent					0.1934	0.4227**
%.Stock Price X Crisis					(0.1730)	(0.1805)
Size	-6.7677**	-3.7515***	-6.7607**	-3.6623***	-7.9395**	-2.6535**
	(3.3747)	(0.8218)	(3.3696)	(0.8225)	(3.4226)	(0.8614)
Size X Crisis					-5.2690*	-4.1381***
					(3.0898)	(0.8376)
Profitability	2.0223***	1.3727***	2.0208***	1.3655***	2.1023***	1.2545**
	(0.3757)	(0.4094)	(0.3755)	(0.4101)	(0.3754)	(0.4005)
Profitability X Crisis					-8.4702**	3.3959
					(3.9564)	(4.0780)
Efficiency	-0.0617**	-3.1837***	-0.0619**	-3.1735***	-0.0615**	-3.0157***
	(0.0205)	(0.2638)	(0.0205)	(0.2640)	(0.0206)	(0.2608)
Efficiency X Crisis					-0.6364*	-10.2421***
					(0.3266)	(1.4715)
Liquidity	0.0350	0.0756*	0.0349	0.0715*	0.0333	0.1179**
	(0.0413)	(0.0433)	(0.0412)	(0.0433)	(0.0432)	(0.0447)
Liquidity X Crisis					0.1549*	0.1888**
					(0.0840)	(0.0867)

(continued)

Table 14.5 (continued)

Foreign Bank Samples	Host and Home Factors		Relative Host and Home Factors		Relative Factors with Crisis	
	(1) LC Loan Share Growth Rate	(2) FC Loan Share Growth Rate	(3) LC Loan Share Growth Rate	(4) FC Loan Share Growth Rate	(5) LC Loan Share Growth Rate	(6) FC Loan Share Growth Rate
Solvency	-0.1214	0.0189	-0.1217	0.0085	-0.1639*	0.0825
	(0.0941)	(0.1089)	(0.0940)	(0.1090)	(0.0980)	(0.1118)
Solvency X Crisis					0.1894*	-0.4899***
					(0.1050)	(0.1171)
Observations	1590	1551	1590	1551	1590	1551
R-squared	0.042	0.127	0.042	0.123	0.059	0.180
Number of Banks	23	23	23	23	23	23
Bank Fixed Effect	Yes	Yes	Yes	Yes	Yes	Yes

Note: All the results are estimated by monthly panel regressions with individual bank's fixed effects. LC Loan Share Growth Rates means growth rates of local currency loan divided by total local currency lending of the Indonesian banking sector. FC Loan Share Growth Rates means growth rates of foreign currency loan divided by total foreign currency lending of the Indonesian banking sector. "D." means the difference between the current rate and the last month's rate. "Host - Home" means a Host's rate minus a Home's rate. "%." means the monthly growth rates. "X" means interaction terms with type of bank dummies and a crisis dummy (= 1 if values are in or after August 2007; otherwise 0). Exchange Rates of Host and Home are the values of each country's currency per U.S. dollar. Thus, they become higher as the U.S. dollar appreciates. Volatility is calculated by using annualized standard deviation of daily returns of each month. Parent Stock Price means the stock price of a parent bank of foreign banks in a home country. The coefficients of seasonal adjustment dummies, Size, Profitability, Efficiency, Liquidity, and Solvency, are not reported. Host Exchange Rate Volatility, Home %Exchange Rate, and Home Exchange Rate Volatility are also not reported. *, **, and *** denote significance at 10, 5, and 1 percent, respectively.

Overall results of loan share growth models are very similar to ones of loan growth models in the previous section. The main difference comes from home stock index and relative host-home stock index. These are not consistent with the earlier results. However, shocks to a parent bank positively affect foreign currency lending only. Thus, a parent bank's shock transmission via internal capital markets is quite robust.

CONCLUSION

This chapter investigates the determinant of growth of foreign bank loans by currency in the Indonesian banking sector, where foreign banks actively disburse loans denominated in foreign and local currency. Globalized banking, coupled with limited hedging instruments in the Indonesian foreign exchange markets, distinguishes the transmission of shocks to foreign currency lending from local currency lending in Indonesia. Extending the theoretical framework of Morgan, Rime, and Strahan (2004), I proposed three hypotheses:

1. High growth rates in the parent bank's stock price in the home market increase foreign banks' U.S. dollar lending in a host country through internal capital market, but this is not observed in local currency lending.

2. Low performance in the home stock index or other shocks such as high volatility of home stock markets pushes up foreign banks' U.S. dollar lending in a host country.
3. A decrease in the host stock index or other shocks such as high volatility of host stock markets results in a decrease in foreign banks' lending in U.S. dollars in a host country.

The first hypothesis is consistently valid and quite robust. The second and the third hypotheses could be valid, but they are not as robust as the first hypothesis, depending on the specification of the model.

In fact, foreign banks' foreign currency lending is highly sensitive to a parent bank's stock returns. When a parent bank's stock price goes up, foreign banks' branches actively increase foreign currency lending in a host country. These effects are more emphasized during the crisis. However, a parent bank's financial condition appears not to affect foreign banks' local currency lending. This is probably because the important financial source of a host's currency (the Indonesian rupiah) is deposit. Thus, local currency banking of foreign banks works as if it were standalone. On the other hand, foreign bank's branches rely on a parent bank to finance U.S. dollars. Thus, foreign banks' branches easily finance U.S. dollars through a parent bank unless the home market is in turmoil. In this case, the internal capital market therefore plays an important role in transmission of shocks to a parent bank.

Foreign banks' foreign currency lending grows when a host's stock market returns increase more rapidly than a home's stock market does. Furthermore, foreign banks change their response to exchange rates and inflation rates during crisis. It dampens during the crisis period. Foreign banks, therefore, can stabilize a host economy during a normal period, whereas their lending activity could be pro-cyclical during the crisis period, because they are likely to change their regime during the global crisis.

A final remark is that there is a significant difference of response to macroeconomic factors between the lending of two currencies. This is derived from the existence of internal capital markets. This is a country study for the Indonesian banking sector. Thus, I do not emphasize too much the generality of results for other countries. However, if both foreign banks' presence and the share of foreign currency lending are high, which is often observed in emerging markets and small developed economies that concentrate on the financial industry, we need to pay attention to the currency mix of lending to understand the lending channel of shock transmission accurately.

Lessons from the findings are: (a) knowing the currency denomination of loans is imperative to monitor foreign banks' response to host and home shocks; (b) during a home crisis, it is important to monitor a parent bank's soundness; (c) monitoring internal capital transfer of global banks is as important as doing so for direct cross-border lending.

APPENDIX 14.1 Statistics of Individual Banks

	Panel A - Full Samples	Bank Name	Natinality	Market Share	FC Loan/ Total	Total Loan Growth	LC Loan Growth	FC Loan Growth	LC Loan/ Depoisit	FC Loan/ Depoisit
1	State Owned Bank	PT Bank Ekspor Indonesia Persero	Indonesia	0.7%	45.7%	5.4%	-0.1%	-1.3%	N/A	N/A
2	State Owned Bank	PT Bank Mandiri Persero	Indonesia	14.8%	11.7%	1.5%	1.8%	0.8%	36.5%	109.2%
3	State Owned Bank	PT Bank Negara Indonesia Persero Tbk	Indonesia	9.7%	10.2%	1.4%	1.7%	0.9%	42.3%	83.8%
4	State Owned Bank	PT Bank Rakyat Indonesia Persero	Indonesia	11.5%	4.1%	1.9%	2.0%	1.0%	68.9%	101.5%
5	State Owned Bank	PT Bank Tabungan Negara Persero	Indonesia	2.5%	0.0%	1.6%	2.1%	N/A	107.8%	N/A
6	Private National Bank	PT Bank Buana Tbk	Indonesia	1.3%	0.9%	2.0%	2.0%	1.9%	73.1%	8.7%
7	Private National Bank	PT Bank CIC International Tbk	Indonesia	0.4%	2.8%	0.8%	2.0%	-4.6%	37.3%	22.5%
8	Private National Bank	PT Bank Central Asia Tbk	Indonesia	7.0%	3.1%	2.4%	2.5%	1.6%	31.8%	41.9%
9	Private National Bank	PT Bank Danamon Indonesia Tbk	Indonesia	5.1%	6.2%	2.2%	2.2%	2.0%	72.1%	59.5%
10	Private National Bank	PT Bank Internasional Indonesia Tbk	Indonesia	2.6%	10.4%	1.7%	2.5%	0.5%	51.5%	45.1%
11	Private National Bank	PT Bank NISP Tbk	Indonesia	1.8%	9.5%	1.9%	1.8%	2.1%	82.0%	79.3%
12	Private National Bank	PT Bank Niaga Tbk	Indonesia	3.7%	16.1%	2.2%	2.8%	0.8%	75.2%	95.6%
13	Private National Bank	PT Bank Permata Tbk	Indonesia	2.5%	6.9%	3.3%	3.5%	2.5%	61.8%	63.3%
14	Private National Bank	PT Lippo Bank Tbk	Indonesia	1.4%	5.5%	2.1%	2.3%	1.4%	33.6%	37.2%
15	Private National Bank	PT Pan Indonesia Bank Tbk	Indonesia	2.5%	11.6%	1.7%	2.3%	0.3%	81.6%	67.4%
16	Foreign Bank	PT ANZ Panin Bank	Australia	0.4%	23.6%	2.1%	2.1%	1.9%	167.3%	64.8%
17	Foreign Bank	PT Bank BNP Paribas Indonesia Tbk	France	0.2%	66.1%	1.0%	3.3%	0.7%	202.0%	282.5%
18	Foreign Bank	Deutsche Bank AG	Germany	0.8%	13.1%	0.1%	0.6%	-0.4%	41.8%	47.8%
19	Foreign Bank	PT Bank Finconesia (commerz)	Germany	0.2%	46.4%	-0.5%	-0.7%	-0.3%	119.5%	164.8%
20	Foreign Bank	PT Bank Daiwa Perdania	Japan	0.5%	52.3%	0.9%	1.4%	0.6%	136.6%	174.9%
21	Foreign Bank	PT Bank Mizuho Indonesia	Japan	0.7%	46.7%	1.6%	1.7%	1.5%	68.1%	140.4%
22	Foreign Bank	PT Bank Sumitomo Indonesia	Japan	0.7%	51.4%	0.8%	2.7%	0.4%	83.2%	111.4%
23	Foreign Bank	PT Bank UFJ Indonesia	Japan	1.1%	66.5%	-4.3%	-2.5%	-4.5%	53.3%	212.7%
24	Foreign Bank	The Bank of Tokyo-Mitsubitshi Ltd	Japan	1.4%	52.3%	1.6%	1.1%	1.7%	125.4%	124.5%
25	Foreign Bank	PT Bank Woori Indonesia	Korea, Rep.	0.2%	39.9%	1.3%	3.1%	1.1%	14.2%	138.2%
26	Foreign Bank	PT Korea Exchange Bank Danamon	Korea, Rep.	0.2%	51.5%	0.7%	0.9%	0.6%	49.6%	150.6%
27	Foreign Bank	PT Bank Maybank Indocorp	Malaysia	0.0%	31.9%	0.0%	0.3%	-0.4%	32.7%	199.8%
28	Foreign Bank	ABN Amro Bank	Netherlands	1.0%	21.4%	0.6%	1.0%	0.3%	58.7%	56.4%
29	Foreign Bank	PT Bank ING Indonesia	Netherlands	0.2%	26.9%	-2.2%	6.0%	-14.3%	146.3%	154.2%
30	Foreign Bank	PT Rabobank Duta Indonesia	Netherlands	0.4%	60.4%	1.3%	2.0%	0.9%	168.0%	274.6%
31	Foreign Bank	PT Bank DBS Indonesia	Singapore	0.8%	29.7%	3.5%	4.1%	2.9%	107.0%	105.3%
32	Foreign Bank	PT Bank OCBC-NISP	Singapore	0.1%	38.6%	3.6%	4.1%	3.4%	39.1%	162.9%
33	Foreign Bank	PT Bank UOB Indonesia	Singapore	0.4%	32.5%	2.4%	3.1%	1.9%	83.4%	96.4%
34	Foreign Bank	PT Bank Chinatrust Indonesia	Taiwan, China	0.4%	43.3%	1.2%	2.6%	0.3%	114.5%	129.1%
35	Foreign Bank	The Bangkok Bank Comp Ltd	Thailand	0.2%	59.1%	2.2%	2.9%	2.0%	101.2%	246.4%
36	Foreign Bank	HSBC	United Kingdom	1.8%	27.8%	1.2%	2.3%	0.5%	78.7%	62.5%
37	Foreign Bank	Standard Chartered Bank	United Kingdom	1.2%	20.0%	1.5%	1.1%	1.7%	69.7%	73.2%
38	Foreign Bank	Bank of America N.A	United States	0.0%	2.9%	4.1%	-2.2%	8.3%	2.6%	5.1%
39	Foreign Bank	Citibank N.A	United States	2.5%	18.7%	1.0%	1.1%	0.8%	95.4%	46.1%
40	Foreign Bank	JP Morgan Chase Bank, N.A.	United States	0.2%	7.5%	0.0%	-0.7%	2.0%	106.4%	34.4%

Note: All the values are average rates in the sample period (December 2001–December 2008). The sample period of each bank varies. Foreign banks do not include banks taken over by foreign investors even if the share of their ownership exceeds 50 percent. Foreign banks consist of Joint Venture and Foreign Banks in the classification of Bank Indonesia. Both are founded by greenfield investment and in reality work as branches of foreign banks.

NOTES

1. In 1998, the real GDP growth rate dropped to -13.2 percent; the inflation rate skyrocketed to 77.6 percent; the Indonesian rupiah per U.S. dollar was depreciated by 85 percent; and nonperforming loans reached almost a half of total lending. Consequently, domestic private banks and state-owned banks cut out half of loans due to write-off.
2. Derviz and Podpiera (2007) try to study theoretically the interdependence of lending decision in different country branches as the propagation caused by delegation and precautionary motives. (Derviz and Podpiera 2007)
3. Standard and Poor's (2003).
4. As of March 29, 2009, individual bank's data is available at the Bank Indonesia's website (http://www.bi.go.id/web/en/Publikasi/Laporan+Keuangan+Publikasi+Bank/Bank/Bank+Umum+Konvensional/).
5. I excluded regional government's banks and private banks that are not permitted to deal with foreign exchanges. If they were included, the coverage would be more than 90 percent in the banking sector. The coverage ratio is stable through the sample period even if the data set is decomposed by type of banks.
6. As of March 29, 2009, this is available at http://www.bi.go.id/web/en/Statistik/Statistik+Ekonomi+dan+Keuangan+Indonesia/Versi+HTML/.
7. Bankscope provided by Bureau van Dijk is one of the most commonly used databases for the research at the level of individual bank activity. The coverage of Bankscope is comprehensive and generally covers approximately 90 percent of total bank assets in each country. Although Bankscope provides the balance sheet and income statement of foreign banks' affiliates, it does not cover foreign banks' branches' because they are usually not reported separately from the headquarters in consolidated financial statements. Moreover, the frequency of data is usually on an annual basis, or, at most, quarterly basis.
8. Comments from management boards are based on the interviews held from January 2007 to June 2007 unless specified.
9. Ownership information is based on Bankscope, hereafter.
10. In the classification of Bank Indonesia, *Joint Venture Bank* and *Foreign Bank* belong to the definition of foreign banks in this chapter.
11. Exception is PT Bank Ekspor Indonesia Persero (state-owned bank). Foreign currency loan ratio is high (45.7 percent) because it is in charge of trade finance.
12. In fact, Bank Indonesia publishes lending and deposit rates in U.S. dollars only.
13. This model is the same as Morgan, Rime, and Strahan (2004), which is based on Holmstrom and Tirole (1997), except the fact that uninformed investors, intrastate banking, and interstate banking are replaced with uninformed banks, foreign currency lending, and local currency lending of foreign banks.
14. See Morgan and Strahan (2003) for the proofs.
15. See Morgan and Strahan (2003) for the proofs, again.
16. I test host factor model by the type of bank, such as state-owned banks, domestic private-owned banks, and foreign banks, that is, all the banks are treated as if they were operating on a stand-alone basis. The growth rate of a loan is determined by the foreign branch's specific variables and financial variables in Indonesia (a host country). However, the results are not significant. This might indicate that home factors are important.

17. The Hausman test indicates that a panel with fixed effects is more appropriate than one with random effects.
18. A model that includes the difference between lending rates and deposit rates as a proxy of interest-rate spread appears not to be significant and the separate inclusion of deposit rates does not change the sign of coefficients of lending rates.
19. An increase in spreads of credit default swap also resulted in a rapid drop in a parent's stock price.
20. Banks' time horizon of investment, which may vary by bank or by country, also determines the length of lags. Although one month seems to be a too simple assumption, it works the best, compared with more lags.
21. I test an impact of the current parent stock price and volatility on growth of loans. However, they are not significant in most cases. Moreover, I check the impacts of the two, three, four, and five months lags. Yet, the results are either insignificant or unstable.
22. See the section "Impacts of Crisis" for details.
23. Rates of stock returns of parent banks are one-month lagged values.
24. In Turkey, more than half of the deposits were denominated due to the high inflation of local currency.

BIBLIOGRAPHY

Ashcraft, Adam B. 2008. "Are Bank Holding Companies a Source of Strength to Their Banking Subsidiaries?" *Journal of Money, Credit and Banking (Blackwell)* 40 (2–3): 273–294.

Ashcraft, Adam B., and Murillo Campello. 2007. "Firm Balance Sheets and Monetary Policy Transmission." *Journal of Monetary Economics* 54 (6): 1515–1528.

Bahmani-Oskooee, Mohsen, and Ilker Domac. 2003. "On the Link between Dollarisation and Inflation: Evidence from Turkey." *Comparative Economic Studies* 45 (3): 306–328.

Basso, Henrique S., Oscar Calvo-Gonzalez, and Marius Jurgilas. 2007. "Financial Dollarization—The Role of Banks and Interest Rates." European Central Bank Working Paper Series no. 748.

Benavente, Jos Miguel, Christian A. Johnson, and Felipe G. Morande. 2003. "Debt Composition and Balance Sheet Effects of Exchange Rate Depreciations: A Firm-Level Analysis for Chile." *Emerging Markets Review* 4 (4): 397–416.

Calvo, Guillermo, Leonardo Leiderman, and Carmen Reinhart. 1992. "Capital Inflows and Real Exchange Rate Appreciation in Latin America: The Role of External Factors." IMF Working Papers no. 92/62.

Campello, Murillo. 2002. "Internal Capital Markets in Financial Conglomerates: Evidence from Small Bank Responses to Monetary Policy." *Journal of Finance* 57 (6): 2773–2805.

Catao, Luis A.V., and Marco Terrones. 2000. "Determinants of Dollarization—The Banking Side." IMF Working Papers no. 00/146.

Cerutti, Eugenio, Giovanni Dell'Ariccia, and Maria Soledad Martiez Peria. 2007. "How Banks Go Abroad: Branches or Subsidiaries?" *Journal of Banking and Finance* 31 (6): 1669–1692.

Cetorelli, Nicola, and Linda S. Goldberg. 2009. "Globalized Banks: Lending to Emerging Markets in the Crisis." Federal Reserve Bank of New York Staff Reports no. 377.

Dages, B. Gerard, Linda S. Goldberg, and Daniel Kinney. 2000. "Foreign and Domestic Bank Participation in Emerging Markets: Lessons from Mexico and Argentina." National Bureau of Economic Research Working Paper Series no. 7714.

De Haas, Ralph, and Iman Van Lelyveld. 2004. "Foreign Bank Penetration and Private Sector Credit in Central and Eastern Europe." *Journal of Emerging Market Finance* 3 (2): 125–151.

———. 2006. "Foreign Banks and Credit Stability in Central and Eastern Europe. A Panel Data Analysis." *Journal of Banking and Finance* 30 (7): 1927–1952.

———. 2010. "Internal Capital Markets and Lending." *Journal of Financial Intermediations* 19(1): 1–25.

Derviz, A., and J. Podpiera. 2007. "Cross-Border Lending Contagion in Multinational Banks." European Central Bank Working Paper Series no. 807.

Focarelli, Dario, and Alberto Franco Pozzolo. 2005. "Where Do Banks Expand Abroad? An Empirical Analysis." *Journal of Business* 78 (6): 2435–2463.

Galindo, Arturo, Ugo Panizza, and Fabio Schiantarelli. 2003. "Debt Composition and Balance Sheet Effects of Currency Depreciation: A Summary of the Micro Evidence." *Emerging Markets Review* 4 (4): 330–339.

Goldberg, Linda S. 2001. "When Is U.S. Bank Lending to Emerging Markets Volatile?" National Bureau of Economic Research Working Paper Series no. 8209.

———. 2005. "The International Exposure of U.S. Banks." National Bureau of Economic Research Working Paper Series no. 11365.

Hernandez, Leonardo, and Heinz Rudolph. 1997. "Sustainability of Private Capital Flows to Developing Countries: Is a Generalized Reversal Likely?" *Cuadernos de Economia* [Latin American Journal of Economics] 34 (102): 237–266.

Holmstrom, B., and Tirole, J. (1997). Financial Intermediation, Loanable Funds, and the Real Sector. *The Quarterly Journal of Economics* 112(3): 663–691.

Honohan, Patrick, and Anging Shi. 2001. "Deposit Dollarization and the Financial Sector in Emerging Economies." World Bank Policy Research Working Paper Series no. 2748.

Jeanneau, Serge, and Marian Micu. 2002. "Determinants of International Bank Lending to Emerging Market Countries." BIS Working Papers no. 112.

Kedia, Simi, and Abon Mozumdar. 2003. "Foreign Currency–Denominated Debt: An Empirical Examination." *Journal of Business* 76 (4): 521–546.

Machicado, Carlos Gustavo. 2008. "Liquidity Shocks and the Dollarization of a Banking System." *Journal of Macroeconomics* 30 (1): 369–381.

Martinez Peria, Maria Soledad, Andrew Powell, and Ivanna Vladkova Hollar. 2002. "Banking on Foreigners: The Behavior of International Bank Lending to Latin America, 1985–2000." World Bank Policy Research Working Paper Series no. 2893.

Molyneux, Philip, and Rama Seth. 1998. "Foreign Banks, Profits and Commercial Credit Extension in the United States." *Applied Financial Economics* 8 (5): 533–539.

Morgan, Donald, Bertrand Rime, and Philip E. Strahan. 2004. "Bank Integration and State Business Cycles." *Quarterly Journal of Economics* 119 (4): 1555–1584.

Morgan, Donald, and Philip Strahan. 2003. "Foreign Bank Entry and Business Volatility: Evidence from U.S. States and Other Countries." National Bureau of Economic Research Working Paper Series no. 9710.

Moshirian, Fariborz. 2001. "International Investment in Financial Services." *Journal of Banking and Finance* 25 (2): 317–337.

Peek, Joe, and Eric S. Rosengren. 1997. "The International Transmission of Financial Shocks: The Case of Japan." *American Economic Review* 87 (4): 495–505.

———. 2000. "Collateral Damage: Effects of the Japanese Bank Crisis on Real Activity in the United States." *American Economic Review* 90 (1): 30–45.

Rosenberg, Christoph B., and Marcel Tirpák. 2008. "Determinants of Foreign Currency Borrowing in the New Member States of the EU." IMF Working Paper no. 08/173.

Sato, Yuri. 2005. "Bank Restructuring and Financial Institution Reform in Indonesia." *Developing Economies* 43 (1): 91–120.

Standard and Poor's. 2003. "Demystifying Banks' Use of Credit Derivatives." December 8. Available at www2.standardandpoors.com/spf/pdf/fixedincome/DemystifyingBank.pdf.

Stein, Jeremy C. 1997. "Internal Capital Markets and the Competition for Corporate Resources." *Journal of Finance* 52 (1): 111–133.

Wagner, Wolf. 2007. "The Liquidity of Bank Assets and Banking Stability." *Journal of Banking and Finance* 31 (1): 121–139.

Williams, Barry. 2003. "Domestic and International Determinants of Bank Profits: Foreign Banks in Australia." *Journal of Banking and Finance* 27 (6): 1185–1210.

15 Corporate Political Spending and Shareholders' Rights

Why the U.S. Should Adopt the British Approach

Ciara Torres-Spelliscy

EXECUTIVE SUMMARY

Money may be the mother's milk of politics, but when corporations spend money in politics, the key question is whose money is really being spent. When a publicly-traded corporation spends money to influence the political process, it may do so in conflict with the values and interests of a portion of its shareholders who would likely be dismayed to learn that the assets they invested in a business have been diverted in manner with which they may disagree, without notice or any effective ability to object.

Roughly half of American households own stocks, many through mutual funds or 401(k) retirement accounts.[1] These American shareholders lack the ability to object or consent to political spending by American corporations. Indeed, because of gaps between corporate and campaign finance law, U.S. corporations can make political expenditures without giving shareholders any notice of the spending either before or after the fact. Technically, "while companies do not have political preferences, their managers do."[2] This is problematic because the political interests of the managers who spend the corporate money may diverge from the political interests of shareholders. This chapter focuses on whether it is proper for an American corporation to use money from investors to pay for political expenditures without full disclosure or consent.

This odd American model where corporate money flows into the political system through obscured channels is not inevitable. We have a counterexample from our peers in England. British companies must seek permission from shareholders in order to make political expenditures under the Political Parties, Elections and Referendums Act and must report such spending to UK shareholders on an annual basis. This chapter fills a gap in the literature because this divergence between U.S. and British corporate law on the question of shareholder consent to corporate political expenditures has been thus far overlooked.

A century's worth of American election laws have prohibited corporate managers from spending a corporation's general treasury funds in *federal* elections.[3] Preexisting laws required corporate managers to make political expenditures via separate segregated funds (SSFs), which are also commonly known as corporate political action committees (PACs),[4] so that shareholders, officers, and managers who would like the corporation to advance a political agenda can designate funds for that particular purpose.[5]

These laws protected both the integrity of the democratic process as well as shareholders. Recognizing the wisdom of this approach, many states followed suit with similar laws. In the twenty-eight states that lack federal-style election rules, however, corporations may give political donations directly from their corporate treasuries, including high-cost states like New York, California, and Illinois, where political campaigns can cost millions of dollars. This money is used in such states to pay for legislative, executive, and judicial elections without consent from or notice to shareholders.[6]

The laws that require corporations to pay for political expenditures only through corporate PACs are under legal attack. Most recently, the Supreme Court heard a rare reargument in September 2009 in *Citizens United v. FEC*. The topics at reargument were whether to overrule *Austin v. Michigan Chamber of Commerce* and *McConnell v. FEC*—two cases that upheld the right of the government to require corporations to conduct political spending through corporate PACs.[7] As predicted by top legal scholars, the Supreme Court used *Citizens United* as an opportunity to expand corporate speech rights by overturning *Austin*'s and *McConnell*'s limits on corporate political spending.[8] The Court turned the clock back to before 1947, the year Congress outlawed corporate and union independent expenditures in federal elections.

This change in law caused by *Citizens United* potentially allowing more corporate money in politics may not be welcome even by corporate managers. Some executives may feel that political spending traps them in a prisoners' dilemma with their competitors: whereas it would be better for the bottom line if every corporation stopped spending money on politics, some corporations persist in the practice because they fear the consequences if they stop giving, worried that benefits will flow to their competitors. This model is based on the misperception that political giving aids the corporate entity and maximizes value. But recent research is beginning to expose the myth.

A recent study of over twelve thousand U.S. firms, "Corporate Political Contributions: Investment or Agency?" by Aggarwal, Meschke, and Wang (2009),[9] found that, in fact, large corporate political expenditures are linked with lower shareholder value and less effective corporate management. In other words, this study suggests that some managers make political expenditures in part because they want to, not because giving will necessarily benefit the corporations they manage.

In this chapter, I will argue that, in light of the evidence that political giving can impact corporations in a negative way, both corporate managers and campaign finance reform advocates share a common interest in reducing corporate political spending. In the first section, "Part I," I will outline the issues surrounding proper regulation of the role of corporate money in

American politics. Then in the second section, "Part II," I will show how the state of law is in flux by exploring both campaign finance law and corporate law. In the section titled "Part III," I will discuss the risks of deregulated corporate political spending. In the section titled "Part IV," I propose a solution, and in "Part V," I anticipate and dismiss critiques of this model. This chapter will argue that one means to greatly increase transparency and accountability would be for the U.S. to adopt a modified version of the British approach to corporate political expenditures by changing the U.S. securities laws. In the first instance, publicly-traded U.S. corporations should disclose their political spending directly to shareholders (as many top firms have already pledged to do), and secondly, they should give shareholders the opportunity to consent to political spending via periodic shareholder votes. These reforms will improve corporate governance and minimize corporate risk.

The need for this reform has become heightened with the Supreme Court's decision in *Citizens United*, now that the ability of managers to spend corporate treasury funds in federal and state elections has expanded markedly. In this new world where corporations can spend an unlimited amount of corporate treasury funds on federal and state elections, shareholders will need new protections to guard against self-interested political spending by corporate managers.

PART I HOW TO REGULATE CORPORATE MONEY IN AMERICAN POLITICS?

The Basic Problem

The appropriate role of corporate money in elections is an ongoing conundrum of American democracy.[10] This chapter offers one vision of how to regulate managers who may not have the corporation's best interests at heart when they spend corporate money on politics. I suggest that shareholders should be given a say about the use of corporate funds because they are the beneficial owners of the corporations. Presently, not only do shareholders have no say over corporate political spending, they may have no idea that such spending has taken place.

Before I proceed further, allow me to define the scope of this chapter. This chapter is about changing the U.S. securities laws to require publicly-traded corporations to report their political spending to their shareholders, as well as to require shareholder authorization for corporate political spending before it is done. For the purposes of this chapter, I will not address the issue of lobbying, which merits an entirely separate chapter.[11] Here, the term "political spending" is meant to include spending that is intended to influence the outcome of any candidate's election or the outcome of a matter on the ballot such as a referendum, initiative, constitutional amendment, or ballot measure. This phrase includes independent expenditures and spending that funds electioneering communications. Furthermore, I will not address all corporations, which could include closely held corporations and single proprietorships; my exclusive focus is publicly-traded corporations.

My proposed policy change is necessary because full disclosure of contributions from corporations to candidates and political causes presently falls into a gap between corporate and campaign finance law.[12] Consequently, shareholders often know very little about the beneficiaries of corporate political expenditures,[13] and they may unwittingly fund political spending at odds with their political philosophies.[14]

As Professor Jill Fisch has explained:

> Political contributions are generally not disclosed to the board or shareholders, nor are political expenditures generally subject to oversight as part of a corporation's internal controls. The lack of oversight makes it difficult for corporate decision makers and stakeholders to evaluate the costs and benefits of political activity.[15]

With even governing boards in the dark about corporate political spending, shareholders have little hope of fully understanding the scope of companies' political expenditures.[16]

Moreover, because so many shareholders hold their shares through intermediaries like mutual funds, corporations and their shareholders are strangers.[17] The shareholder may not know their holdings day-to-day and the corporation does not know who owns it day-to-day. This distance between corporate managers and beneficial owners magnifies corporate agency problems.[18]

Whether shareholders need protecting from corporate manager's political expenditures has been a problem that Americans have grappled with since at least 1905.[19] This was the year when the biggest insurance companies in the country were discovered to have given vast sums of money to the Republican Party using policy holder money. At the time, the policy owners were thought to be the true owners of the companies and thus are analogous to shareholders today. In the press of the day, the managers who made these political expenditures were characterized as embezzlers and thieves,[20] but they were not subject to criminal sanctions. (Had they been, they could have been guilty of grand larceny.[21])

Whereas most internal corporate matters are proprietary and secret—take, for example, the formula for Cola-Cola—political spending is distinguishable because it engages in the public sphere in a way that can impact public policy choices. So whereas secrecy may be appropriate for a trade secret; it is patently inappropriate for a public act like supporting or opposing a candidate for office. Disclosure of corporate political spending should be the norm.

Providing shareholders with notice of corporate political spending is not a simple matter because any reforms would not be written on a blank slate.

There is already a patchwork of campaign finance laws that regulates certain categories of corporate money in politics. These laws are inevitably challenged and the resulting case law has left an internally inconsistent jurisprudence about the First Amendment rights of corporations.

Another challenge in this area is the very structure of corporations and the history of courts' treatment of managerial decisions. The "business judgment rule" insulates managerial decisions from shareholders' objections. As one commentator noted, the Supreme Court has recognized the anticorruption interest to be a compelling one justifying regulation,[22] but thus far it "has not taken the shareholder protection argument seriously because it has failed to appreciate the limited role of shareholders in shaping corporate policy."[23]

Mere disclosure will not fix this problem. If publicly-traded corporations were only required to disclose political spending, shareholders would, in the face of inappropriate expenditures, have but two blunt and unsatisfactory instruments with which to respond: (a) voting out the board or (b) selling their shares. Instead, the investing public needs either prophylactic rules (like FECA's) to prevent corporate managers from spending investor money on politics in the first place, or shareholders need a mechanism through which they can register their consent to corporate political spending.

Reformers like the Center for Political Accountability (CPA)[24] and Common Cause[25] have tried a number of tactics to get individual corporations to behave in a more forthright manner. Ultimately, though, these issues need to be addressed at a broader level with federal legislation so that all publicly traded corporations will be subject to similar requirements.

British law provides a model (see Appendix 15.2) that the United States could emulate that requires disclosure of political contributions to shareholders in the directors' annual reports as well as requiring directors to get shareholders' authorization before making political expenditures above a certain threshold amount.[26] This chapter includes a legislative proposal (see Appendix 15.1) that would give shareholders in American companies the right to know how much corporate money is being spent on political expenses as well as the opportunity to consent.

The Risk of Corporate Money in Politics

There are at least two problems implicated by corporate political spending: (a) first is the potential damage to the polity as public policy choices are made for the benefit of individual corporations or industries; and (b) second, there is the potential negative effect on the corporation as rent-seeking managers waste corporate assets on expenditures that do not benefit the corporation or its shareholders. The paradox of political spending by large corporate entities is that from the corporation's point of view the money spent is tiny, but from that of the democratic process, corporate money comprises a huge portion of political funding.[27]

Corporations have long sought to influence public policy through a variety of strategies. Corporations hire lobbyists to directly propose and oppose policy changes; they join trade associations to magnify their political voice; they form SSFs[28] so that they can contribute to political campaigns; and they pay for state-level political advertising through independent expenditures.[29] They also pay for events surrounding political conventions and inaugurals,[30] and endow institutes and libraries that will carry presidents' or congressional members' names.[31] Corporations frequently make contributions to both political parties in the same election, which is indicative of attempts to curry favor with politicians rather than contributing out of ideological purity or personal loyalty.[32]

The magnitude of corporate PAC spending is undeniable, comprising hefty percentages of overall election giving. Contributions in the 2008 federal election totaled $3.2 billion. Money from corporate PACs comprised one out of every ten federal dollars contributed.[33] Since 2005, 173 corporate donors, "their Political Action Committees, executives and other employees have contributed, under campaign finance law limits, $180 million to federal candidates and political parties, an average of over $1 million per organization."[34] Increasingly, corporations are making anonymous contributions to trade associations and other tax-exempt organizations, which are becoming "proxies for corporate political involvement."[35] Just six major trade associations spent an estimated $107 million on political and lobbying activities in 2004 alone.[36]

The risk to democracy is that political spending will buy policies that are antithetical to the common good, instead benefiting only the company or industry that contributed. Professor Daniel Greenwood has outlined this democratic problem:

> When the pot of [corporate] money enters the political system, it distorts the very regulatory pattern that ensures its own utility. When the pot of money is allowed to influence the rules by which it grows, it will grow faster, thus increasing its ability to influence—setting up a negative feedback cycle and assuring that the political system will be distorted to allow corporations to evade the rules that make them good for all of us (to extract rents, in the economists' jargon).[37]

Corporations' latitude to spend money for political purposes depends on the forum. For example, presently in *federal* elections, corporations are strictly prohibited from giving political contributions from the corporation's general treasury funds to candidates for federal office.[38] Many states also ban corporate contributions directly to candidates.[39] However, other states take a more laissez-faire approach and permit unlimited corporate contributions directly to candidates.[40] An intermediate approach taken by a few states is to limit contributions from those corporations that are state contractors under what are known as "pay-to-play" restrictions.[41] Because so many U.S. corporations are multinational corporations with interests across the world, some of the political spending may go on in countries apart from the U.S.[42] Therefore, the legal ability of corporations to give political contributions depends on the context.[43]

The Rights of Shareholders Implicated by Corporate Political Spending.

At least two key shareholder rights are at stake in corporate political spending. First, there is the shareholders' right to a fair return on their investment. In other words, as the U.S. Solicitor General recently noted, "[founding father] John Hancock pledged his own fortune; when the CEO of John Hancock Financial uses corporate-treasury funds for electoral advertising, he pledges someone else's."[44] Because the shareholder's money is being spent, the shareholders should have more say about whether that money is spent on nonbusiness purposes such as political contributions. Shareholders in the corporate context are less protected than employees in the union context, because unions must refund the portion of agency fees from nonmember employees that are used for political activity.[45]

Second, the shareholder's First Amendment right to remain silent in a political debate or to support a candidate of his or her choosing is also at risk when a manager uses corporate money to support political causes which are antithetical to the shareholder's wishes. As the Congressional sponsors of the Bipartisan Campaign Reform Act (BCRA) wrote, shareholders' First Amendment rights were at stake when the Supreme Court decided to change the law to unleash corporate treasury funds into the political process:

> The tremendous resources business corporations and unions can bring to bear on elections, and the greater magnitude of the resulting apparent corruption, amply justify treating corporate and union expenditures differently from those by individuals and ideological nonprofit groups. So, too, does the countervailing free-speech interest of the many shareholders who may not wish to support corporate electioneering but have no effective means of controlling what corporations do with what is ultimately the shareholders' money.[46]

Using corporate funds traceable to shareholder investments tramples on shareholders' free speech and associational rights by making them unwittingly subsidize speech that they may disagree with.

The Prisoner's Dilemma of Corporate Political Spending

As strange as it may seem at first blush, the sad truth is managers may not be making political expenditures to benefit the corporation or shareholders at all. The current culture of American political contributions places corporations into a "prisoner's dilemma" with their corporate competitors.

Presumably, corporate managers make expenditures supporting politicians in large part because they think such spending will eventually help the bottom line: in the short term, political expenditures are a net loss and, like lobbying expenses, are not tax deductible and must be paid out of after-tax profits.[47] Corporate managers may fear that ending political contributions will cause incumbent politicians to overlook their interests and act favorably towards those competitors that contribute.[48] Consequently, when operating fully out of self-interest, corporation A will avoid limiting its political spending, unless it credibly believes competitor corporations B through Z will also limit their political spending.

As the Committee for Economic Development (CED)[49] explained, corporate managers give to political campaigns in part because they are frightened of the consequences of not giving.

> As past and present executives of some of the nation's largest companies, CED's trustees have direct experience with solicitations for financial support from party leaders, elected officials, and the officials' influential backers. Their experiences teach a simple lesson: corporate participation in elections is more transactional than ideological. It is forced by the competitive need to maintain access to and avoid retribution from elected officials of both parties.[50]

Even the Supreme Court has recently acknowledged that corporate managers are caught in a prisoner's dilemma where they feel compelled to give. As the Court noted, "[b]usiness and labor leaders believe, based on their experience, that disappointed Members [of Congress], and their party colleagues, may shun or disfavor them because they have not contributed."[51]

If all corporations were able to put an end to political contributions, more funds would be available to further the actual purposes of the corporations—to make money for their investors. From a short-term cost-savings perspective, stopping political spending would be in all corporations' best interests. Yet no corporation wants to unilaterally disarm. Federal legislation is necessary to place all publicly traded companies on the same footing. The prisoners' dilemma is rooted in the misperception that lavish political spending is good for the corporate entity. A recent empirical study of corporate political spending seriously undermines this assumption.

In fact, however, corporate political giving may be symptomatic of management problems. Whereas political spending can be motivated by a calculated risk assessment based on the fear that incumbents will reward competitors, political spending by corporations can also be driven by politically ambitious managers as well. The CPA and the Zicklin Center for Business Ethics Research at the Wharton School posited that the danger posed by unfettered corporate treasury funds in federal elections is the risk that "[m]anagers will engage in rent-seeking behavior, spending corporate funds for personal gain or to advance management's personal political preferences."[52] This hypothesis about rent-seeking[53] managers is supported by recent empirical work in the field.

According to a study of over twelve thousand firms conducted by Aggarwal, Meschke, and Wang at the University of Minnesota's Carlson School of Management, political expenditures of firms are likely to be symptomatic of agency problems[54] within the corporation.[55] Political expenditures can represent a form of "perquisite consumption for top managers,"[56] in which managers funnel money to candidates or parties of their personal preferences, to achieve personal access to politicians, or to acquire high-profile political appointments.[57] Moreover, Aggarwal, Meschke, and Wang found that firms who make political expenditures have lower excess returns[58] in the year following an election than firms that did not donate at all.[59]

The Aggarwal study, which included large "soft money" contributions made directly from corporate treasuries pre-BCRA, further found that the more a firm donates, the lower its excess returns.[60] It was only when firms made very large expenditures that this trend would reverse. Firms would have to give $1.89 million in expenditures before they would begin to see a marginal increase in returns for each dollar given and only twenty-six out of 12,105 firms studied were in this high spending category.[61]

Thus, according to this study, firms that give political contributions see a decrease in shareholder value as a general rule.[62] Thus, shareholders' interests are likely not the driving force behind a manager's decisions to make political expenditures.[63] These findings add to the already compelling argument that shareholders should be given more notice of political expenditures and more control over political spending.

PART II THE STATE OF LAW ON CORPORATE POLITICAL SPENDING

A Bridge between Corporate Law and Campaign Finance Law

Now that I have described the problem, in this section I will describe the state of both campaign finance and corporate law to demonstrate that existing approaches fail both democratic norms as well as shareholders' interests. This shared failure is why many corporate managers can agree with campaign finance reformers that reducing the amount of corporate money spent on politics would be preferable to the status quo where too frequently corporate officers feel compelled to financially support politicians.

There is a conceptual gap between corporate managers and campaign finance advocates. Corporate managers are often unaware of the details of campaign finance law. Meanwhile, campaign finance advocates are frequently unfamiliar with the intricacies of corporate law. This chapter is meant to bridge this gap.

The data on how corporate directors view disclosure of political contributions are relatively sparse. However, a 2008 survey of 255 directors at Russell 2000 companies found that 88 percent said corporations should be required to publicly disclose all corporate funds for political purposes.[64] "Significantly, 76 percent agreed that 'corporations should also be required to disclose payments made to trade associations and other tax exempt organizations which are used for political purposes.'"[65]

Directors surveyed thought they knew the requirements of campaign finance laws that applied to their corporations, but "overwhelming majorities of directors *incorrectly* think that all political contributions by corporations, trade associations and non-profits are required to be disclosed [and] [m]ore interestingly is the fact that 63 percent of directors mistakenly think that boards are required to approve and oversee political expenditures."[66]

Why Don't Shareholders Have Information about Corporate Political Spending?

The short answer to why shareholders have so little information about corporate political spending is that neither the Federal Elections Commission (FEC) nor the Securities and Exchange Commission (SEC) requires corporations to disclose political spending directly to their shareholders. Publicly-traded corporations are governed by securities laws,[67] which require detailed public reporting of many aspects of organizational structure and financial status. Political contributions are not one of the categories of required reporting. Firms must also report a catchall category of "material" information to the SEC.[68] However, because of the large size of most publicly traded firms, political contributions—even if they are tens of thousands of dollars—are usually too small from the corporation's point of view to fall into this category.[69]

The FEC requires reporting from candidates, political committees, and parties. Corporate SSFs report their spending directly to the FEC.[70] To track contributions by SSFs, at the federal level, the public would need to know the exact names of the SSFs involved. Tracking spending becomes difficult when an SSF does not contain the "doing business as" name of the corporation at issue. For example, the Abraham Lincoln Leadership Political Action Committee, Americans for the Republic, the Democracy Believers Political Action Committee, and the Freedom and Democracy Fund are largely funded by corporate PACs.[71]

Moreover, federal spending is only one subset of political spending. Corporations may also spend on state elections and ballot initiatives. Any spending in state elections is reportable to each of the fifty states, not to any centralized location. Each state has its own distinct disclosure requirements with its own definitional loopholes and architectural failings. Thus, whereas most corporate political spending is technically reportable to state regulators, state laws are porous and may not capture the full universe of political spending. As the Campaign Disclosure Project has demonstrated, year after year, states fail to achieve meaningful disclosure or accessible databases.[72] Once the specter of political spending in foreign jurisdictions is added into the mix, discerning who gave what to whom can require costly due diligence for even the most careful and active investor. To reconstruct the total amount of reported political spending, shareholders would have to comb through vast volumes of records at the federal and state level—and perhaps even at the international level—to learn how and how much corporations contribute.[73]

Some corporate political spending does not go directly to candidates or parties. Instead, many supporters make independent expenditures that are underreported in most states. One study found that a mere five states make information about independent expenditures readily available to the public. As this report noted, "holes in the laws—combined with an apparent failure of state campaign-finance disclosure agencies to administer effectively those laws—results in the poor public disclosure of independent expenditures. The result is that millions of dollars spent by special interests each year to influence state elections go essentially unreported to the public."[74]

Some political spending falls under the radar, so no matter how much due diligence a shareholder does, the spending remains unknown. For example, trade associations, such as the U.S. Chamber of Commerce, do not divulge the identity of those funding their political activities and most corporations do not divulge how much they have given to trade associations.[75]

Even for the political spending that is properly reported to a government agency, there is no duty to share this information directly with shareholders in an accessible way. Because political spending by corporate entities is not disclosed in a single place like a Form 10-K filed with the SEC, discovering the full extent of the political spending of any corporate entity takes copious research. This basic asymmetry of information needs to be addressed by changing federal securities laws to better protect shareholders.

Corporate Structure

Corporate law provides no panacea for the problem of managers' spending corporate money on politics because courts are very deferential to managers under the business judgment rule. So, the more complex answer to why corporations have not traditionally disclosed political spending to shareholders, nor sought their consent to such spending, lies in the very structure of the way corporations are organized and the very magnitude of many modern corporations. At first blush, many principles of corporate law appear to favor disclosure of political spending as a basic part of overall transparency, a linchpin of good corporate governance.[76] However, other precepts like the business judgment rule make corporate law an unpredictable launching pad for reform. Indeed, any reform based on current corporate law would require corporations to police themselves, and thus differences in disclosures would be expected from one corporation to the next. As will be discussed later, reformers have succeeded in persuading 45 of the S&P 100 companies[77] to make full disclosure of political spending. But thousands of corporations still have not agreed to self-regulate.

Understanding basic corporate structure is key to appreciating this policy problem. Shareholders own a corporation by holding a transferable share interest, but do not manage the corporation day-to-day.[78] The default management structure of a corporation is that the shareholders elect a board of directors.[79] The board delegates business decisions to the officers, who are vested with day-to-day management of the business and affairs of the corporation.[80] The distinction between ownership and control ideally works to reduce the costs of corporate decision making by placing control over most corporate affairs in the hands of elected directors and appointed officers who are better informed than shareholders about the business of the corporation.[81] Conversely, this structure inhibits shareholders from changing or controlling corporate political spending, or even requesting that the spending be disclosed in a particular manner.[82]

Professor Thomas Joo has rightly noted the Supreme Court's detachment from reality when it comes to shareholder input on corporate political speech:

> Dissenting in *Austin*, Justice Scalia dismissed the idea that shareholders might justifiably object to management political speech. According to Justice Scalia, every shareholder "knows that management may take any action that is ultimately in accord with the majority (or a specified supermajority) of the shareholders' wishes, so long as that action is designed to make a profit. That is the deal." This passage suggests that shareholders are entitled to vote on corporate actions, but that is most emphatically *not* the deal with respect to a corporation's election-related spending.[83]

Accordingly, in most American corporations, shareholders have zero say about the corporation's political spending.

The interests of the directors and officers and those of the shareholders may diverge at times.[84] The larger the corporation, the less ability shareholders will have to monitor the performance of the board and officers, and thus corporate law constantly strives to create rules to ensure that the directors and officers will advance the interests of shareholders.[85]

The ability to transfer shares on the open market in publicly traded companies could potentially work to restrain self-serving behavior of corporate managers.[86] But the sale of shares does not give shareholders a way to signal to the managers that it was motivated by the corporation's political spending. Moreover, because nearly all publicly-traded corporations tend to be similarly situated vis-à-vis their treatment of political expenditures, the shareholder has no way of buying shares that give them a greater amount of control over corporate political spending. So long as shareholders invest in American companies,[87] they risk that part of their investment may be used for a political purpose.

Corporate Fiduciary Duties

Directors and officers owe fiduciary duties to the corporation and its shareholders.[88] There are three fiduciary duties: obedience, loyalty, and care. The duty of care is the broadest of the fiduciary duties, reaching all aspects of conduct.[89] The duty of care encompasses the duty to not waste corporate assets. A transaction constitutes a waste of corporate assets if it involves an expenditure of corporate funds for which no or inadequate consideration is received and there is no rational business purpose.[90] Theoretically, if corporate political spending were incredibly high, this could be deemed a waste of corporate assets. Even though corporate directors and officers owe certain duties to shareholders, so far, courts and regulators have not construed these duties to encompass disclosure of political spending.

The Business Judgment Rule

Claims that an action like spending corporate funds on political advertisements constitutes a waste of corporate assets or a breach of a fiduciary duty are likely to be thwarted by the business judgment rule, a judicially created principle that is extremely deferential towards the decisions of directors and officers.[91] The business judgment rule holds that a decision constitutes a valid business judgment if it is (a) made by financially disinterested directors or officers, (b) who have become duly informed before exercising judgment, and (c) who exercise judgment in a good faith effort to advance corporate interests.[92] Courts have traditionally been very hesitant to apply the label of bad faith to decisions made by officers and directors unless they are clearly extreme and irrational.[93]

Shareholder Lawsuits Alleging Breach of Fiduciary Duties

Shareholders have brought suits in the past alleging that decisions of managers constitute a waste of corporate assets. The most common suits alleging waste of corporate assets challenge executive compensation and charitable giving. Courts have been overwhelmingly reluctant to intervene in such decisions.[94]

In *Cort v. Ash*,[95] the Supreme Court held that there was no private right of action for shareholders to peruse derivative suits against corporations for violations of the FECA's ban on the use of corporate treasury funds in federal elections.[96]

In the same year, shareholders brought suit in California specifically claiming that a corporate political contribution to a ballot measure campaign was an improper use of funds.[97] The court rejected the shareholders' claims by specifically characterizing a corporate political contribution as a good faith business decision under the business judgment rule.[98] The court found no restriction in either the corporation's articles of incorporation or state law regarding such a contribution and therefore held that the action was allowable.[99]

Judicial deference to corporate decisions make shareholder suits unlikely to prevail in alleging that corporate political contributions are a waste of corporate assets. Professor Thomas Joo elucidates:

> Shareholders must allege corruption or conduct approaching recklessness in order to even state a claim challenging management actions. This principle of deference is not limited to decisions regarding "business," narrowly defined. Courts have applied business judgment deference to . . . political spending on the ground that management may believe such decisions will indirectly advance the corporation's business.[100]

In sum, courts essentially presume that managers' business decisions are made in good faith and defer to all but the most egregiously negligent or irrational management decisions.[101]

Campaign Finance Law and the Corporation

Corporate law is not the only source of potential reform. Indeed most disclosure of corporate political spending is available because of local, state, and federal campaign finance laws.

The current Supreme Court appears ready to largely deregulate the corporate area of campaign finance law. Where there were limits on or regulations of corporate spending today, they may be lifted tomorrow. In the *Citizens United* case, the Supreme Court turned the clock back to before 1947, the year Congress outlawed corporate and union independent expenditures. To fully understand the breadth of this radical change, the full context of the last one hundred years of federal regulation of corporate political spending is needed.[102]

Statutory Campaign Finance Law

Until very recently, statutory federal campaign finance law has been particularly hostile to corporate political spending.[103] The history of campaign finance regulation of corporations goes back to the turn of the last century. President Theodore Roosevelt was a catalyst for reform after being caught in a political scandal involving expenditures from the largest insurance companies of the day.[104] In his 1905 message to Congress, Roosevelt advocated for reform:

> All contributions by corporations to any political committee for any political purpose should be forbidden by law; directors should not be permitted to use stockholders' money for such purposes. . . . [T]he national and the several State legislatures [should] forbid any officer of a corporation from using the money of the corporation in or about any election.[105]

Congress responded by passing the Tillman Act in 1907, which prohibited corporations from making contributions to candidates for federal office.[106]

The 1925 Corrupt Practices Act extended the Tillman Act by broadening the definition of contribution, extending the ban on corporate contributions to Delegates and Resident Commissioners that were elected to Congress, and punishing the recipient of any illegal contribution in addition to the contributor.[107] Congress passed the Smith-Connally Act in 1943, which extended the Federal Corrupt Practices Act to organized labor.[108] In 1947, Congress passed the Taft-Hartley Act, which prohibited both corporate and union independent expenditures for or against federal candidates.[109] In early 1972, Congress passed FECA, which provided corporations and unions with the ability to establish and administer separate, segregated funds (SSFs or corporate PACs) for the purpose of making political contributions and expenditures.[110]

Watergate provided more fodder for political reformers with the revelation of illegal corporate contributions to presidential candidates.

> For corporate shareholders, one of the most disturbing findings was the large number of illegal corporate campaign contributions. Nineteen companies pleaded guilty to charges by the Watergate special prosecutor that they had violated a federal criminal statue barring corporations from contributing their funds to candidates for federal office.[111]

Post-Watergate, FECA was amended in 1974 to include strict contribution and expenditure limits as well as presidential public financing. Under FECA, corporations and labor unions are prohibited from using their general treasury funds to "make a contribution or expenditure in connection with any election to any political office."[112] FECA, as amended in 1974 was challenged in the landmark case of *Buckley v. Valeo*.[113] The *Buckley* Court invalidated expenditure limits allowed contribution limits so long as they applied to express advocacy, and upheld voluntary public financing.[114] *Buckley* also upheld FECA's disclosure requirements. FECA was amended again in 1976 to take into account the Supreme Court's holdings in *Buckley*.

The next major development in the treatment of corporate money occurred in the wake of corporate accounting scandals such as Enron, when Congress enacted the BCRA of 2002 (also known as McCain-Feingold). BCRA regulates political party use of nonfederal funds (also known as soft money) and prohibits corporate treasury funds from being used to run electioneering communications, which are ads run directly before a federal election that mention a federal candidate and are targeted to the relevant electorate.[115]

Campaign Finance Case Law

The campaign finance case law is particularly jumbled when it comes to corporations. For years, the Supreme Court vacillated between two extremes. On the one hand, it treated corporate political spending as a menace that needed to be tightly regulated, while simultaneously in another line of cases, it granted more speech rights to corporations.[116]

In 1948, in *United States v. Congress of Industrial Organizations*, the Court explained that Taft-Hartley's prohibition of corporate independent expenditures in federal elections, like the Tillman Act's prohibition on corporate contributions, was motivated by two considerations. "First, the necessity for destroying the influence over elections which corporations exercised through financial contribution. Second, the feeling that corporate officials had no moral right to use corporate funds for contribution to political parties without the consent of the stockholders."[117]

In marked departure from precedent, the Court invalidated limits on spending by corporations on ballot measures in *First National Bank of Boston v. Bellotti.*[118] Decided in 1978, *Bellotti* was the first case to find that corporations had political speech rights.[119]

The Court seemingly reversed itself in 1982, when it recognized that states have a compelling interest in seeing that the "substantial aggregations of wealth amassed by the special advantages which go with the corporate form of organization . . . not be converted into political 'war chests' which could be used to incur political debts from legislators."[120]

But four years later, in 1986, the Supreme Court found in *FEC v. Massachusetts Citizens for Life, Inc. (MCFL)* that the prohibition on corporate and union treasury spending on expenditures found in 2 U.S.C. § 441b could only apply to express advocacy,[121] and that ideological nonprofits that do not take corporate or union money cannot be banned from spending their treasury funds on elections.[122] As a result, corporations could use general treasury funds to pay for issue advocacy campaigns in federal elections. Even in *MCFL*, as the Court granted expanded speech rights to political nonprofit corporations, the Court held:

> The resources in the treasury of a business corporation, however, are not an indication of popular support for the corporation's political ideas. They reflect instead the economically motivated decisions of investors and customers. The availability of these resources may make a corporation a formidable political presence, even though the power of the corporation may be no reflection of the power of its ideas.[123]

The Supreme Court's 1990 case, Austin *v. Michigan Chamber of Commerce*, upholding Michigan's ban on corporate independent expenditures, also identifies that states have an interest in preventing: "the corrosive and distorting effects of immense aggregations of wealth that are accumulated with the help of the corporate form and that have little or no correlation to the public's support for the corporation's political ideas."[124]

As Justice William Brennan wrote in his concurring opinion in *Austin*, laws requiring corporations to pay for political expenditures through corporate PACs, "protect dissenting shareholders of business corporations"[125] who object to their money going to political campaigns. As Justice Brennan explained:

> the State surely has a compelling interest in preventing a corporation it has chartered from exploiting those who do not wish to contribute to the Chamber's political message. . . . We have long recognized the importance of state corporate law in "protect[ing] the shareholders" of corporations chartered within the State.[126]

In response to Justice Scalia's assertion that offended shareholders could simply sell their shares, Justice Brennan described the difficulties of keeping perpetual tabs on corporate political spending, stating, "shareholders in a large business corporation may find it prohibitively expensive to monitor the activities of the corporation to determine whether it is making expenditures to which they object."[127]

The Supreme Court reiterated *Austin*'s holding in 2003 in a case called *McConnell v. FEC*, which upheld BCRA's ban on the use of corporate treasury funds to pay for electioneering communications.[128] The *McConnell* Court stated in sweeping terms that "Congress' power to prohibit corporations and unions from using funds in their treasuries to finance advertisements expressly advocating the election or defeat of candidates in federal elections has been firmly embedded in our law."[129]

In 2003, keeping with its pro-regulatory swing, in *FEC v. Beaumont*, the Rehnquist Court held that even political nonprofit corporations could be barred from making any campaign contributions, adding that:

> corporate contributions are furthest from the core of political expression, since corporations' First Amendment speech and association interests are derived largely from those of their members, and of the public in receiving information. A ban on direct corporate contributions leaves individual members of corporations free to make their own contributions, and deprives the public of little or no material information.[130]

The Roberts Court, however, has been deregulatory in its campaign finance jurisprudence.[131] In 2007, it dealt a serious blow to the regulation of election-eve corporate political spending in a 5–4 decision in *FEC v.*

Wisconsin Right to Life (WRTL II).[132] In this case, the Court held that the ban on corporate use of general treasury funds for "electioneering communications" under BCRA was unconstitutional as applied to the advertisements at issue.[133]

WRTL II effectively, although not formally, overruled the part of *McConnell* that upheld BCRA's electioneering restrictions in response to a facial challenge to the law. In *McConnell,* the Court found the "vast majority" of issue ads allowed during preelection periods should be subject to regulation as "functional equivalent[s]" of express advocacy.[134] Post–*WRTL II,* BCRA prohibits corporate use of general treasury funds only for ads that are "susceptible to no reasonable interpretation other than as an appeal to vote for or against a specific candidate."[135] The dissenting justices in *WRTL II* wrote that this ruling allows corporations and unions to circumvent political spending limitations more easily.[136] After *WRTL II,* lower courts have come to conflicting conclusions about what electioneering communications states can regulate.[137]

Given this back-and-forth on the treatment of corporate political spending, it is no wonder that one leading commentator has deemed the Supreme Court's approach to the subject "beyond incoherent."[138]

The Stakes in Citizens United: *Corporate Treasury Money Back in the Mix*

At the end of the 2009 term, the Supreme Court failed to come to a conclusion in the case of *Citizens United v. FEC*. Rather, the Court ordered a rare reargument on two questions:

1. whether to overturn *Austin*, which required corporations to use PACs to pay for independent expenditures in state elections [and]
2. whether to overrule the portion of *McConnell*, which found section 203 of BCRA constitutional, thereby affirming the requirement that corporations pay for federal electioneering communications with PACs.

Simply put, the broad ruling issued on January 21, 2010, in favor of Appellant Citizens United swept away decades of laws limiting corporate expenditures in elections.

During the *Citizens United* reargument on September 9, 2009, the justices and the solicitor general debated whether shareholders can look after their own interests or whether certain laws like the federal corporate treasury bans were necessary. Chief Justice Roberts posited:

> your shareholder protection rationale, isn't it extraordinarily paternalistic for the government to take the position that shareholders are too stupid to keep track of what their corporations are doing and can't [they] sell their shares or object in the corporate context if they don't like it?

Solicitor General Elena Kagan responded:

> [in] a world in which most people own stock through mutual funds, in a world where people own stock through retirement plans in which they have to invest, they have no choice, I think it's very difficult for individual shareholders to be able to monitor what each company they own assets in is doing.[139]

The oral argument made clear that even among the top legal minds of the day, there is fundamental disagreement about how much protection shareholders need. Lacking in Justice Robert's conception, however, is the recognition that shareholder influence is extremely limited in the corporate context. The idea that shareholders could react to political spending about which they are unaware, or that derivative suits might be successful when so far no modern court has punished a manager for political spending, is completely divorced from reality.

It should be noted that *Citizens United* is not a mere repeat of *WRTL II*. *WRTL II* opened a loophole that threatened to swallow the rule barring corporate expenditures in federal elections. In *Citizens United*, in contrast, the Court has done away with the rule against spending corporate treasury funds on federal elections entirely.

It is hard to overstate what a paradigm shift *Citizens United* has caused for both American democracy and American shareholders. In short, overturning *Austin* and *McConnell* has freed corporate managers to spend corporate treasury funds in presidential, congressional and twenty-two additional state elections.[140] Shareholders should be notified of this new spending and should be given the opportunity to rein it in through a shareholder vote.

The Supreme Court's Crimped View of Shareholders' Rights

In *Bellotti*, the Supreme Court rejected a shareholder protection rationale offered by the state of Massachusetts in defending their ban on corporate spending on ballot measures. The Court found Massachusetts's law paternalistic and stated that existing corporate law already provided shareholders with sufficient rights. As the Court explained:

> The overinclusiveness of the statute is demonstrated by the fact that § 8 would prohibit a corporation from supporting or opposing a referendum proposal even if its shareholders unanimously authorized the contribution or expenditure. Ultimately shareholders may decide, through the procedures of corporate democracy, whether their corporation should engage in debate on public issues. Acting through their power to elect the board of directors or to insist upon protective provisions in the corporation's charter, shareholders normally are presumed competent

> to protect their own interests. In addition to intracorporate remedies, minority shareholders generally have access to the judicial remedy of a derivative suit to challenge corporate disbursements alleged to have been made for improper corporate purposes or merely to further the personal interests of management.[141]

More recently, the Supreme Court addressed shareholder rights regarding corporate political spending in *dicta* in a case regarding union dues called *Davenport v. Washington Education Association*.[142] In the *Davenport* lead opinion, Justice Scalia upheld a state requirement that public sector labor unions must receive affirmative authorization from a nonmember before spending that nonmember's agency-shop fees for election-related purposes.[143] When addressing corporate shareholder rights, Justice Scalia specifically distinguished the *Davenport* case finding that: "our campaign-finance cases are not on point."[144] His opinion noted that public sector unions only had these funds because employees were legally compelled to pay them, whereas corporations employed no such coercion in attracting investments.[145] In other words, the restriction is not "how the union can spend 'its' money; it is a condition placed upon the union's extraordinary *state* entitlement to acquire and spend *other people's* money."[146]

Echoing his dissent in *Austin*, Justice Scalia argued in *Davenport* that shareholder protection, on the other hand, would regulate money that is voluntarily in the hands of the corporation and that can be withdrawn at any time by a dissatisfied shareholder.[147] Corporate political spending, according to Justice Scalia, does not raise the same First Amendment issues implicated by unions' mandatory agency-shop fees.[148] In their concurrence, however, Justices Breyer, Roberts, and Alito stated that they did not agree with this particular part of the lead opinion because the shareholder protection argument was raised for the first time in briefs before the Supreme Court.[149] Thus, the fate of shareholder rights under the Roberts Court is unclear. This issue was not clarified in *Citizens United*.[150]

PART III THE RISKS OF DEREGULATED CORPORATE POLITICAL SPENDING

Now that the schizophrenic state of the law has been described, the following are a few of the risks posed by deregulating this area of the law further. The 102 years of regulating corporate political money through the federal election laws may have lulled the corporate law into complacency and left a system of norms that are unprepared for a time when corporate treasury money is widely available for political expenditures. Now that the campaign finance protections have been peeled away, there is a stronger need for fundamental changes like more internal corporate controls of political spending because American corporate political spending does not require board approval.[151] From a management point of view, there is something incredibly strange about corporate money being used for nonbusiness purposes—money that if used badly could negatively impact the corporation—without adequate internal controls. So even if my legislative proposal to empower shareholders is not adopted, corporations, for their own quality control, should independently adopt more internal controls.

The first risk posed by total deregulation is that corporate managers who were restrained by the corporate PAC requirement will spend much more on politics—using the corporate treasury as a personal piggy bank. As Aggarwal, Meschke, and Wang have indicated, shareholder value could be hurt by such wasteful political spending. Furthermore, shareholders' First Amendment rights could be trampled. A third risk is that politicians may change their behaviors based on the new threat of high corporate political spending.[152] Government could shun reforms that look hostile to big donors and favor policies dictated by a few at the expense of the many.

The prisoner's dilemma described earlier in this chapter could become turbocharged. As corporate executives represented by the CED articulated in their Supreme Court brief, if corporate money is allowed back into federal elections and elections in twenty-two states, then the corporate prisoner's dilemma about political giving will become all the more intense:

> Overruling *Austin* or *McConnell* would put corporations in the same prisoner's dilemma that existed when soft-money contributions were permitted [pre-BCRA]. While corporations generally would prefer not to divert their resources from running profitable businesses to funding politics, they would fear the consequences of remaining on the sidelines. The race to the bottom that occurred with direct contributions at the end of the nineteenth century and with soft money in the early 1990s would begin anew. And in addition to forcing corporations to waste overwhelming sums of shareholder wealth on independent electioneering, the new regime would undermine public trust in business by furthering the already extant belief that corporations are in bed with government officials.[153]

So whether the problem is a democratic one or one of corporate management, now that the spigot of corporate political spending is turned on, a policy response is needed to rationalize the flow.

PART IV PROPOSED SOLUTIONS

Now that I outlined the problem and the state of the law, I'll offer some policy responses. Even if the Supreme Court had not used *Citizens United* to rewrite the prohibitions against the use of corporate treasury money to influence federal elections, there is already a significant amount of corporate money that is making its way into politics. Sound public policy demands that reforms be devised to better protect shareholders' interests.

Existing Proposals for Increased Corporate Transparency

Reform groups such as the CPA and Common Cause have tackled the shareholders' rights problem through tactics ranging from public education and rating corporations to encouraging shareholder proposals. They have also partnered with institutional investors to push corporations to change their disclosure practices. Although these shaming techniques are useful to a point, an act of Congress is necessary to fully address the problems of disclosure and consent in all publicly-traded corporations.

The CPA has ably led efforts to expand disclosure of corporate political contributions. For instance, in a 2005 report, the CPA examines the risks of nondisclosure and loose internal controls over soft-money contributions to shareholder value.[154] The report concludes that not only does nondisclosure hide potential conflicts of interest between shareholders and corporations, it sanctions secrecy and all of its associated risks; denies shareholders a complete, accurate picture of a company's expenditures; and denies directors crucial information in fulfilling their fiduciary duties to the corporation.[155] All of these consequences hurt shareholder value. The CPA argues that "[t]he only way to mitigate the problem [of corporate political contributions] and the accompanying risk is to require companies to disclose and explain the business rationale of their contributions."[156]

The CPA also rates corporate transparency through its Political Accountability Rating and Contribution Transparency Rating—which examines corporate policies and procedures around disclosure, approval of contributions, and oversight of contributions.[157] In addition, the CPA's Comparative Giving Assessment compares a company's expenditures with those of its industry peers.

The CPA has developed a model corporate code of conduct for political spending.[158] The CPA advocates including strong political spending provisions in a corporate code of conduct "because it is the final authority governing corporate and employee behavior."[159] To mitigate risks for shareholders, the CPA recommends that corporate codes set out: guidelines on corporate contributions; prior approval of contributions; disclosure of an approving officer or department; executive level oversight; board-level oversight; and public disclosure of contributions.[160]

The CPA helped to file more than twenty-five shareholder resolutions in 2004, urging corporate management to provide reports of all corporate political giving, along with rationales for each contribution, to shareholders, directors, and the public.[161] As of mid-December 2009, CPA reported that seventy companies, forty-eight of which are in the S&P 100, have agreed to disclose all their political spending to shareholders.[162] While this is an impressive feat, there are over thirty-nine hundred companies listed on the New York Stock Exchange alone.[163] The fact that seventy companies are being transparent does not change the state of play for the average stockholder. Furthermore, because these seventy companies are doing this voluntarily, they can rescind these good practices and revert to more secretive ways of doing business at any moment.

Each of these strategies largely draws their power from a corporation's "reputational concern," that is, their concern with creating and maintaining an image agreeable to investors and consumers.[164] Should there not be the political will to change the securities law, the CPA's suggestions remain available alternatives that corporations should voluntarily adopt.

The U.S. Should Follow the British Model of Notice and Consent

Although the CPA and Common Cause's efforts to increase corporate transparency and increase internal corporate controls are laudable, these efforts are undermined by the perpetual prisoner's dilemma mentality outlined earlier. If a corporation feels it must give a political contribution to remain competitive, it will do so no matter how many good government groups pillory them for the practice. Therefore, only a legislative fix at the federal level is likely to have a real impact on how the average corporation discloses its use of shareholder money for political purposes or requires shareholder assent.[165] A second best solution would be to amend the corporate laws in New York, Delaware, and South Dakota because so many corporations are incorporated in these three states.

To be clear, the best policy is the continuation of FECA's ban on the use of corporate treasury funds in federal elections, but now that the ban has been found unconstitutional, proper disclosure and shareholder authorization of corporate political expenditures should be adopted.

The 2000 Amendments to the UK Companies Act

The British provide a useful and elegant legislative model that the United States could emulate because the federal law banning corporate treasury funds in elections has been revoked by the Supreme Court in the *Citizens United* case.[166] The UK allows direct corporate spending to candidates and political parties, yet it does so with transparency.[167] In 2000, the UK adopted an amendment to its Companies Act, which requires British companies to disclose political contributions to its shareholders as well as to seek consent from shareholders before political donations are made.[168]

Like America, the UK has had its share of campaign finance scandals. As a researcher at the House of Commons explained the history of political funding before the 2000 UK reforms:

> The main objections to the [pre-2000] system, where party finances are largely free from any statutory regulation, revolve around suspicions that financial considerations can buy undue influence and improper access. . . . There is now a great deal of support for more openness and transparency in the system. Among the issues perceived as causing most concern are: large donations from individuals and companies, and, more specifically, the correlation between donations and access to Ministers, influence on policy, favourable commercial considerations, and the receipt of honours or other personal appointments.[169]

These atmospherics contributed to the sense that reform was needed in the UK. However, the 2000 changes in British law came about as a direct response to the Fifth Report of the Committee on Standards in Public Life.[170] Lord Neill of Bladen, who chaired the Committee, explained the need for the new approach:

> Many members of the public believe that the policies of the major political parties have been influenced by large donors, while ignorance about the sources of funding has fostered suspicion. We are, therefore, convinced that a fundamentally new framework is needed to provide public confidence for the future, to meet the needs of modern politics and to bring the United Kingdom into line with best practice in other mature democracies.[171]

Consequently, the Neill Committee recommended that a company wishing to make a donation to a political party should have the prior authority of its shareholders.[172]

Under British law, if a company has made a political donation of over £2,000, then the director's annual report to the shareholders must include the donation's recipient and the donation amount.[173] In England, the director's report is equivalent to a company's 10-K annual report in the United States and £2,000 is roughly equal to $3,000 at current exchange rates.[174]

In addition to requiring disclosure, the British law goes further and requires shareholder consent for spending over £5,000 on political expenditures, approximately $8,000.[175] If shareholders in British companies do not approve a political donation resolution, then the company cannot make political contributions during the relevant period.[176] Directors of British public companies who make unauthorized political donations are personally liable to the company for the amount spent plus interest, and must compensate the company for any loss or damage resulting from the unauthorized donation or expenditure.[177] The interest rate charged on unauthorized political expenditures is 8 percent per annum.[178]

In fact, British companies with American businesses actually report their American political expenditures to their British shareholders under the Companies Act.[179] For a sample of such firms, please see Appendix 15.3.

Thus, especially for transnational companies, harmonizing American law to match British law would not require any additional data gathering for these already reporting companies.

Here is a snapshot of how the British system works. The British shareholders do not approve each and every individual political donation. Instead, the managers request a political budget for a year or longer of £100,000, for example, and the shareholders give an up or down vote. If management loses the vote, then the managers cannot spend the money. If the managers make unauthorized political expenditures, then they are liable to the corporation for the cost of the unauthorized expenditures and for any resulting damages.

British Experience after Reform

The Apparent Drop in Corporate Political Expenditures

"UK political donations, once commonplace for listed blue-chip companies, have almost disappeared[,]" according to one British newspaper report in 2008.[180] Although the available data, described in the following, indicates that corporate political expenditures have in fact decreased since the reform, relevant data are limited because there has been little to no empirical research of this topic. Accordingly, future study on the Companies Act's impact on the political behavior of British companies is necessary.

The available data show that, both before and after the reform, most corporate money went to the Conservative Party (aka the Tories).[181] The Labour Party, by comparison, has historically received substantially less corporate money.[182] For example, during the 1995–1996 fiscal year, there were only three corporate donations to the Labour Party totaling £98,000.[183] In contrast, that year the Conservative Party received approximately £2.7 million from 145 companies.[184] Similarly, for the 1997–1998 fiscal year, there were 120 corporate donations worth a total of £2.88 million to the Conservative Party.[185] After the reforms, the total company donations to the Conservatives were down to £1.74 million in 2001 and £1.16 million in 2003.[186]

To be sure, not every British company has foregone large political expenditures.[187] Overall, however, spending by individual companies appears to have dropped after the 2000 reforms. A study of corporate donations from 1987 to 1988 showed twenty-eight companies that had given £50,000 or more.[188] In contrast, a recent sampling of the biggest UK firms reveals that some of the same firms that used to give at the £50,000 level (or higher) have decided to forgo political spending altogether. Others are spending more modest amounts.

UK Proxy Votes to Authorize British Political Spending

The Pensions and Investment Research Consultants Limited (PIRC), an independent British research and advisory firm that provides data on corporate governance to institutional investors, supplied the author with a data set of proxy votes authorizing political spending by firms subject to the Companies Act. The data from PIRC show resolutions dating back to January 1, 2002, for 160 companies subject to the Companies Act—for a total of 638 shareholder resolutions authorizing political corporate spending during eight years.

The PIRC data reveals that most British companies seeking authorization from their shareholders under the Companies Act seek modest political budgets ranging from £12,000 to £250,000 for a year or longer.[189] There were a few exceptions. For example, BP (formerly known as British Petroleum) sought and was granted an authorization for £400,000 for itself and an additional £400,000 for BP International Limited over a four-year period.[190] British American Tobacco sought and was granted an authorization for £1 million over a four-year period, [191] but these larger amounts were outliers.

Disclosure of UK Corporate Political Spending

In terms of recent political spending, companies gave detailed accounts of how the money had been spent. For example, Northumbrian Water Group PLC reported its political activities:

> Includ[ing] attending Party Conferences, as these provide the best opportunity to meet a range of stakeholders, both national and local, to explain our activities, as well as local meetings with MPs, MEPs and their agents. The costs associated with these activities during 2006/07 were as follows: Labour £7,585, Liberal Democrats £2,293, Conservative £2,303 [for a] Total £12,181.[192]

ITV made similarly detailed accounts, reporting "[d]uring the year the Group made the following payments totalling £7,968 (2007: £9,110): Labour Party £3,920; Conservative Party £685; Liberal Democrat Party £2,086 and Plaid Cymru Party £1,277."[193]

Most companies asked for a general authority from their shareholders to make political expenditures in the UK and Europe. However, one company has indicated for several years in a row which political party it intended to benefit. Caledonia Investments PLC sought and was granted authorization to give £75,000 to the Conservative Party for two years.[194]

A review of the recent annual reports by top British firms reveals that many companies are refraining from political spending and have a stated policy against the practice. For example, British Airways states in its most recent annual report that:

> We do not make political donations or incur political expenditure within the ordinary meaning of those words and have no intention of doing

> so. The amount of political donations made and political expenditure incurred in the year to March 31, 2009, was £nil (2008: £nil).[195]

Many firms shared this policy of not making political contributions. For example, HMV, the music retailer, stated in its most recent annual report: "[i]t is Group policy not to make donations to political parties or independent election candidates and therefore no political donations were made during the period."[196] Burberry also shared this approach noting, "[t]he Company made no political donations during the year in line with its policy."[197]

Some of the same firms that have policies against political donations nonetheless have sought shareholder authorizations to avoid inadvertent violations of British law. As GlaxoSmithKline explains:

> GSK has adopted a global policy ending the provision of political contributions in any market in which the company operates. . . . However, in order to protect GSK from any inadvertent violation of the U.K. law (where political contributions are defined very broadly) GSK will continue to seek shareholder approval for political contributions within the EU.[198]

Cadbury shared this precautionary approach:

> The Company has a long standing policy of not making contributions to any political party. . . . neither the Company, nor any of its subsidiaries, made any donation to any registered party . . . . However, the [Companies Act] contains very wide definitions of what constitutes a political donation and political expenditure. Accordingly, as a precautionary measure to protect the Company . . . approval will be sought at the 2009 AGM for the Company to make donations to political organisations . . . of £100,000.[199]

Resistance to UK Corporate Political Spending

Whereas some British pension funds are categorically opposed to corporate political spending and state so in their explanations of their voting philosophies,[200] shareholders generally approve the corporate political budgets requested by British firms.[201]

Shareholders have, however, defeated a corporate political budget.[202] In 2004, for example, shareholders voted against a resolution to authorize £1.25 million in political spending by BAA PLC. This resolution was proposed by a shareholder who was angered by the revelation that BAA had given free airport parking passes to members of Parliament. The shareholder considered these free passes to be political donations, and he therefore sought shareholder approval of the value of the passes.[203] The shareholders voted against this authorization.[204] It is not clear from this result whether shareholders agreed with the motives of the shareholder proposing it or not. Nonetheless, after the shareholder vote, BAA stopped giving free passes to parliamentarians.[205]

The BAA example shows the importance of transparency and the impact of empowered shareholders. When a corporation spends a large sum on politics, shareholders can react to the disclosure by limiting such spending in the future. British shareholders, like those invested at BAA, have this power and so should investors in American companies.

The U.S. should adopt the British approach to political expenditures by (a) providing disclosure of political expenditures directly to shareholders and (b) getting the consent of shareholders before political spending is done. Draft legislation for use at either the federal or state level, based on this British approach, is attached hereto in Appendix 15.1. This approach ensures that shareholders' speech rights are respected and may ensure that less corporate money is wasted on political expenditures.

PART V ANTICIPATING CRITIQUES OF ADOPTING THE BRITISH MODEL

Now that I have offered a policy solution, I will anticipate and address possible criticism of the proposed model.

Apathetic Shareholders

Some may argue that shareholders either do not really care about corporate political spending or that they may be ill-equipped to judge the political spending by corporate managers. However, as Professor Joo explains, this view seems contrary to American democratic norms:

> [T]he extension of business judgment discretion to political decisions expresses norms inconsistent with our self-governing polity. Most shareholders presumably have neither expertise nor interest in making the corporation's routine business decisions. . . . But to presume that shareholders have neither expertise nor interest in matters involving political preference contradicts the basic assumptions of self-government and thereby perverts the meaning of the First Amendment.[206]

It may well be the case that many shareholders will be as apathetic about voting on political spending as they are in choosing a board. But for those that do care about their investments being funneled into the political system, the current U.S. system offers no redress, save selling all stock holdings. As discussed more in the following, this "solution" offers little redress at all.

There is ample evidence that many shareholders do care. A recent survey of shareholders found that shareholders do care about corporate political spending and want greater disclosure.[207] Shareholders have demonstrated their interest in disclosure of corporate political activity by filing shareholder resolutions requesting more corporate transparency on this very topic. As the CED reports, disclosure of political expenditures has become the second most popular shareholder resolution.

> After climate change, the leading category of social issue proposals filed by shareholders in 2007 dealt with political contributions, according to an analysis by the governance rating firm RiskMetrics. Proposals on political contributions usually ask companies to issue semi-annual reports on political contributions and to provide guidelines for making contributions.[208]

In the past few years, there have been numerous shareholder resolutions requesting the disclosure of political expenditures by corporations. In 2006 such resolutions gained the support of 20 percent or more of the vote at eleven major companies, including Citigroup (20 percent), American Financial Group (20.5 percent), Clear Channel Communications (20.5 percent), General Dynamics (21 percent), Washington Mutual (22 percent), Wyeth (25.2 percent), Charles Schwab (27 percent), Marsh and McLennan (30.5 percent), Verizon (33 percent), and Home Depot (34 percent).[209] At Amgen, a political expenditure disclosure resolution received 75.5 percent of the vote following endorsement by the company's directors.[210] At least fifty-six disclosure resolutions were filed during the 2009 proxy season, including at major financial institutions such as Charles Schwab, Goldman Sachs, JPMorgan Chase, Regions Financial, and Wells Fargo.[211] Such resolutions have been strongly supported by major institutional investors, including the New York City pension fund.[212] In 2008, the proxy voting advisory service RiskMetrics Group supported a disclosure resolution calling on AT&T to disclose its political spending, after opposing a similar resolution at AT&T the three previous proxy seasons.[213] For example, a typical resolution requests periodic disclosure of political expenditures including payments to trade associations and other tax exempt organizations.[214]

The Market Alone Cannot Solve This Problem.

Critics of interventions on the shareholder's behalf, like Justices Roberts and Scalia, may argue that the ability to sell shares on the open market solves this problem. But market discipline is not a good enough deterrent and this problem is not self-correcting. As Professor Thomas Joo has explained, the ability to sell shares[215] is actually no remedy at all for the harm of wasting corporate funds on politics:

> [T]he "Wall Street Rule" teaches that if a shareholder disagrees with management, it is more efficient for her to sell her stock than to attempt to change management. . . . [E]ven if the shareholder learns of objectionable election-related spending, "voting with her feet" allows the shareholder only to escape *continued* unauthorized use of the corporate resources. It does not put a stop to the activity or provide any remedy for unauthorized use that has already occurred. Moreover, selling shares because of the corporation's election-related spending is unlikely to have a disciplining effect on management.[216]

Once the money is out the door, in the hands of campaign or political consultants, then the corporation cannot retrieve that money. Selling the shares does not make the corporation or the shareholder whole again.

Why Not Get Consent For Every Single Political Expenditure?

The British system, which serves as a model for the legislative proposal here, requires managers to get shareholder approval for a political budget. The shareholders in Britain and in the suggested model for the U.S. do not approve every single political expenditure. The critique could honestly be leveled that this does not fully address the issue of shareholders' paying for political speech with which they disagree. Under the British model, it is entirely possible for a shareholder who is a Labour Party member to authorize a British company to spend funds that ultimately go to a Tory or vice versa.

The reason I suggest the British model instead of a model where every individual expenditure is subject to a separate shareholder vote is a deep concern about administrability and transaction costs. A system that put every political action of a corporation to a vote would be costly and unwieldy to administer. By contrast, under this proposal, the corporation can simply add an additional question (on the authorization of the political budget) to the list of items that are regularly subject to a shareholder vote at the annual meeting, alongside traditional matters like reelecting the board of directors or appointing auditors. This gives shareholders a say without making the whole process collapse under its own weight.

The worry about administrability merges quickly into concern about constitutionality and how American courts reviewing a new system would react if it is particularly burdensome for corporations to make political speech. Since the Supreme Court has taken the step of allowing corporate treasury funds into candidate elections in the *Citizens United* case, it has embraced a vision of corporations' having strong First Amendment rights to engage in political speech. Now that the Court has granted such a right to corporations, then any regulation that impacts that right will have to be narrowly tailored and minimally burdensome. Merely adding a question to annual proxies that are already being circulated, as suggested here, generates minimal cost to the corporation while providing shareholders a meaningful opportunity to object or consent.

Furthermore, requiring the company to articulate who the corporate political budget will benefit or attack many months in advance of an election may itself generate hostility from the courts. For example, if an annual general meeting (AGM) for a particular company is in early spring and a federal election is in the fall, then the company may not know at the time of the AGM who it will support in the election. Forcing corporations to articulate the recipients months before an election may be viewed by American courts as impermissible.

On the other hand, if the company has already chosen the recipients of its political budget at the time of the AGM, then it would be quite reasonable and appropriate to require the company to articulate to whom the money will be delivered so that shareholders could take this into consideration when voting for or against the authorizing resolution.

Drafting the new law would have to be done carefully to ensure that it did not function as an absolute ban on corporate political speech. This proposal would still have a moderating impact on the flow of corporate money into the political sphere because the very act of articulating a political budget to the shareholders would encourage corporate managers to choose defensibly small political budgets. As the experience in Britain shows, once companies were required to seek authorization from shareholders, many stopped giving to political parties altogether. Another powerful factor is the director liability. By placing liability on directors personally, they have all the more reason to make sure that authorization is complete, proper, and lawful.

Finally, disclosure of past political expenditures empowers the shareholder to anticipate whether future political spending is likely to conform with his or her political views. If a company supports nothing but Democrats, then a Republican shareholder should take that knowledge into account when voting on whether the next political budget should be approved. Or even if a corporation traditionally splits its spending evenly between both parties, each shareholder will have to decide which is more important (that the corporation spends money supporting particular desirable candidates or that the corporation spends money supporting particular undesirable candidates). Some may vote to stop the spending; others may take the contrary view.

Federalism Concerns

Because the legislative fix proposed here creates a federal requirement that impacts internal corporate management, a traditionally state law realm, it could be argued that this proposal raises federalism concerns. In other words, that it might be inappropriate for the federal government to pass laws in this area at all because it has historically been a subject of state law. This objection holds little weight after the recent experience with Sarbanes-Oxley. Congress has the full authority to legislate in the corporate governance sphere of publicly-traded companies using its Commerce Clause power.

Whereas the Public Company Accounting Reform and Investor Protection Act of 2002, which is more popularly known as the Sarbanes-Oxley Act, is synonymous with the "federalization" of corporate law, this characterization is not trenchant constitutional critique. To the contrary, commentators agree that Congress has broad powers to regulate corporate governance and any objections to "federalization" are purely normative. As Professor Stephen M. Bainbridge[217] notes:

> No one seriously doubts that Congress has the power under the Commerce Clause, especially as it is interpreted these days, to create a federal law of corporations if it chooses.[218]

Or as Professor Robert B. Ahdieh[219] put it, "[n]o line of sufficient impermeability to categorically exclude any and all possible federal interventions into corporate law can be identified."[220]

When the Sarbanes-Oxley bill was debated by Congress, few legislators raised concerns about the bill's constitutionality on the record, perhaps due to its quick passage.[221] Representative Ron Paul is the only congressional voice that raised any specter of constitutional challenge in the record.[222] While chiefly objecting to the expansion of "federal power over the accounting profession," as it "preempt[ed] the market's ability to come up with creative ways to hold corporate officials accountable," Representative Paul also argued that the bill, "interfere[ed] in matters the 10th amendment reserves to state and local law enforcement."[223] Despite Representative Paul's predictions, thus far no plaintiff has tried to assert a purely federalism claim against the enforcement of Sarbanes-Oxley.[224]

Picking up on Justice Brandeis's famous "states are the laboratories of democracy" dissent, detractors of Sarbanes-Oxley's federal approach argue that states are better poised to innovate and thereby create more efficient legal regimes. For example, E. Norman Veasey[225] has argued, "[F]ederalism spurs innovation in public policy because of the incremental experimentation afforded by fifty laboratories of states competing for . . . firms."[226] However, Harvard Professor Mark J. Roe counters that this critique is misconceived because there is little serious interstate competition for corporate charters—Delaware is the site of incorporation and thus the only state whose corporate law truly matters—and Delaware's "competition in making corporate law comes . . . not even primarily [] from other states, but also from the federal government," from Congress and the SEC.[227] Similarly, Professor Ahdieh dismisses detractors who decry federalization of corporate law as simply deregulators; he sees that they use arguments about efficiency as mere cover.[228]

Just as Sarbanes-Oxley regulated the independence of boards and other matters that were traditionally state law matters and was not barred by federalism concerns, the legislative proposal articulated here would also not be barred. Rather, Congress would have the power to regulate publicly traded companies and could require disclosure to shareholders as well as shareholder approval of political budgets under the Commerce Clause.

The Corruption Risk Remains

Consent to political spending by shareholders does not eliminate the original problem that motivated the original federal bans on corporate treasury spending: the fear of corporate money corrupting the political system. Hypothetically, shareholders of a highly regulated corporation may authorize unlimited corporate political spending because the shareholders feel that the only way to protect corporate interests is by flooding the political arena with corporate money. This criticism illustrates the limits of the proposed approach to moderate corporate political spending and confirms that Congress's original decision to impose prophylactic rules preventing corporate treasury funds from being used in federal elections is the preferable policy choice. But because *Citizens United* holds these prophylactic rules are unconstitutional, then the instant proposed model has the potential to mitigate the level of corporate political spending by placing more gate keepers in the system.

CONCLUSION

Because the Supreme Court gave corporations carte blanche to engage in more political expenditures at the state and federal level in *Citizens United*, the need for reform of corporate governance has become acute. Shareholders, as well as the investing public, need access to better quality information about corporate political spending. Yet, neither corporate law nor campaign finance law provides shareholders with accessible salient information about the total universe of corporate political spending.

Reformers have turned to two forms of countervailing power to stem corporate political spending—shareholder activism and voluntary improvement in corporate governance. But the prisoner's dilemma mentality that fuels corporate political spending makes it unlikely that corporations will unilaterally disarm and stop spending, nor are the majority likely to either voluntarily disclose their spending to their shareholders or voluntarily seek shareholder consent. A solution to this knotty problem is to pass legislation that clearly requires corporations to disclose corporate political spending to shareholders and the investing public, and gives shareholders the ability to authorize the corporate political spending in the first place.

EPILOGUE

The first draft of this chapter was written in September 2009 shortly after the *Citizens United* reargument before the U.S. Supreme Court. The chapter was subsequently revised in December 2009 after input from peer reviewers.

On January 21, 2010, while this volume was being assembled to go to press, the Supreme Court handed down its decision in *Citizens United*, overturning sixty-three years of federal law and over one hundred years of state law. The Court held that corporations, like human beings, have the right to make unlimited political expenditures in favor of or in opposition to candidates for office.

Writing for the 5–4 majority in *Citizens United*, Justice Anthony M. Kennedy argued that shareholders do not need Congress to protect them from corporate political spending through campaign finance laws because they can protect themselves using corporate governance tools.[229] Although, Justice Kennedy asserts this as a fact, there was an incomplete factual record before the Court. Perhaps, with a full factual record, Justice Kennedy would have agreed that shareholder rights are sharply circumscribed under current state law.

According to Justice Kennedy, the free flow of information empowers shareholders to protect their own interests. As he wrote, "[s]hareholder objections raised through the procedures of corporate democracy can be more effective today because modern technology makes disclosures rapid and informative."[230] His vision is not grounded in reality. In fact, as this chapter has explained, corporate political spending is far from transparent.

Whereas forty-eight corporations in the S&P 100 have decided to voluntarily disclose their political spending,[231] the vast majority of publicly traded companies keep their political activities in the dark and no corporate law requires them to do otherwise. Whereas it is laudable that so many top companies are embracing transparency, there are over thirty-nine hundred companies listed on the New York Stock Exchange alone.[232] Also, there is no indication that any corporation voluntarily gives its shareholders a vote over corporate political spending.

Justice Kennedy's second mistaken assumption is that shareholders who discovered a large or imprudent corporate political expenditure could actually do anything about it.[233] Unfortunately, state-based corporate law gives shareholders little recourse. A suit for breach of fiduciary duties or a waste of corporate assets is likely to be in vain; and attempts to oust the board that oversaw the spending would likely fail. Although shareholders can sell their shares, it could be at a loss. Genuine protections require congressional action or barring that, action by the SEC to adopt a strong disclosure rule on corporate political spending.

Justice Kennedy is correct that knowledge of corporate political spending will help shareholders and voters alike make informed decisions. The world he pictured in *Citizens United* of transparent corporate expenditures does not exist presently, but it should.

Within days of *Citizens United*, the U.S. Congress as well as many state legislatures sprung into action to draft legislation to mitigate the impact of the decision. In the first week of February 2010, Congress held three hearing on the post–*Citizens United* fixes, including the legislative fixes articulated in this chapter: that the U.S. should amend its securities laws to require shareholder consent to corporate political spending and companies should disclose their political spending on an annual basis to shareholders.[234]

At the time this book went to press, Congress had not come to a final decision about which of the many options before it would be adopted. Only time will tell whether improved corporate governance will be a lasting legacy of *Citizens United.*

—Ciara Torres-Spelliscy, New York, NY, February 28, 2010

APPENDIX 15.1 MODEL LEGISLATION TO IMPROVE CORPORATE GOVERNANCE POST-*CITIZENS UNITED*

1. Draft Language of Possible Federal Shareholder Protection Bill[235]

Section 1. Short Title.

This Act may be cited as the "Corporate Political Accountability Act of 2010."

Section 2. Findings and Declarations.

The People find and declare that:

(a) Although corporations cannot vote, corporations make significant political contributions and expenditures that directly or indirectly influence the election of candidates and support or oppose political causes at the state and federal level. Decisions to use corporate treasury funds for political contributions and expenditures are currently made by corporate managers, often without the knowledge or consent of shareholders.
(b) Corporations acting through their managers have a fiduciary duty to conduct business in the best interests of the shareholders. Corporate managers that use corporation funds to support and oppose political candidates, parties, and causes in opposition to the interests of many or all of their shareholders may not be acting in the best interests of the corporation.

(c) Historically, shareholders of corporations that are publicly traded in the United States have not had a way to know of, or to influence, the political activities of corporations they own. Shareholders and the public have a right to know how these corporations are spending their funds to make political contributions or expenditures benefiting candidates, political parties, and political causes.
(d) These corporations should be accountable to their shareholders prior to making political contributions or expenditures affecting local, state, or federal governance and public policy. Requiring the express approval of a corporation's individual public shareholders prior to making political contributions or expenditures will help establish the necessary accountability.
(e) If corporations use corporate general treasury funds for political expenditures, then those funds should be clearly reported to shareholders and shareholders should authorize the use of corporate general treasury funds for political expenditures.

Section 3. Definitions.

As used in this section:

(a) The term "general treasury funds" means those monies in possession of a public corporation in the normal course of business. General treasury funds may include, among others, funds from sales, accounts payable, loans, investments, bonds, or debt instruments.
(b) The term "issue advocacy campaign" means contributions or expenditures for any communication to the general public intended to encourage the public to contact a government official regarding pending legislation, or a government rule or regulation. Issue advocacy campaign does not include expenditures for registered lobbyists employed by the corporation to lobby directly state or federal government officials.
(c) The term "known at the time of the authorization vote" means that at the time the corporation seeks authorization from shareholders to spend corporate funds for political activities, (1) the corporation's officers, directors, or employees have selected a specific candidate, ballot measure, or issue advocacy campaign for the corporation to support or oppose, (2) corporate officers or directors have taken steps to obligate funds to support or oppose a specific candidate, ballot measure, or issue advocacy campaign by signing a contract, promissory note, or loan that would obligate the corporation to pay for a political activity, or (3) the corporation has a regularly scheduled payment to a trade association or nonprofit to pay for a political activity in the next twelve months.

(d) The term "majority of all shareholders" means a vote of shareholders that combined own 50 percent plus one of all outstanding shares. Shareholders not casting votes shall not count toward affirmative authorization under this section.

(e) The term "political activities" means any contributions or expenditures made directly or indirectly to, or in support of or opposition to, any candidate, political party, committee, electioneering communication, ballot measure campaign, or an issue advocacy campaign. Political activities do not include activities defined as lobbying under any local, state, or federal law. For purposes of this section, the term "contribution or expenditure" includes any monetary and nonmonetary political contributions and expenditures not deductible under section 162 (e)(1)(B) of the Internal Revenue Code, including but not limited to contributions to or expenditures on behalf of political candidates, political parties, political committees, and other political entities organized and operating under 26 USC Sec. 527 of the Internal Revenue Code and any portion of any dues or similar payments made to any tax-exempt organization that is used for an expenditure or contribution if made directly by the corporation would not be deductible under section 162 (e)(1)(B) of the Internal Revenue Code, any contribution or expenditure, as those terms are defined in 2 USC Sec. 431, as well as any contribution or expenditure defined under state law, and also includes any direct or indirect payment, distribution, loan, advance, deposit, or gift of money, or any services, or anything of value (except a loan of money by a national or state bank made in accordance with the applicable banking laws and regulations and in the ordinary course of business) to any candidate, campaign committee, or political party or organization, in connection with any election to any office. The term "contribution or expenditure" shall not include:

(1) communications by a corporation to its stockholders and executive or administrative personnel and their families;
(2) nonpartisan registration and get-out-the-vote campaigns by a corporation aimed at its stockholders and executive or administrative personnel and their families;
(3) the establishment, administration, and solicitation of contributions to a separate segregated fund to be utilized for political purposes by a corporation.

(f) The term "separate segregated fund" means a political action committee formed by a corporation for the purpose of making contributions to candidates for office. A "separate segregated fund" that supports federal candidates shall have the same meaning as that found in 2 USC 441b.

Section 4. Shareholder Vote on corporate Political Activities.

Section 14 of the Securities Exchange Act of 1934 (15 USC 78n-2) is amended by adding at the end the following new subsection:

(1) ANNUAL VOTE—

(a) Applicability. Any corporation where proxies are solicited in respect of any security registered under section 12 of the Exchange Act occurring on or after the date that is six months after the date on which final rules are issued under paragraph (5), shall provide for a separate resolution subject to shareholder vote to approve any spending of $10,000 or more by the corporation for any political activity.
(b) Notwithstanding this requirement for an annual shareholder vote to authorize any spending of $10,000 or more by the corporation for any political activity, a corporation may request authorization for spending on political activities on a more frequent basis. Any authorization request by the corporation that is not made during an annual authorization shall be deemed a special authorization.
(c) If the corporation spends less than an aggregate of $10,000 in a twelve-month period for political activities, then it does not have to seek shareholder authorization for such spending.

(2) SHAREHOLDER APPROVAL—

(a) When seeking shareholder authorization for expenditures for political activities, the corporation shall request the authority to spend a maximum dollar amount in the next twelve months.
(b) If known at the time of the shareholder vote (1) the company shall articulate whether the corporate treasury funds so authorized are intended to benefit or defeat specific candidates, ballot measures, or issue advocacy campaigns, or whether it will be paid to specific non-profits or trade associations for political activities.

    (1) To be effective, the authorization vote must garner support from a majority of the corporation's shareholders.
    (2) A vote by the shareholders to approve or disapprove any spending of $10,000 or more by a corporation for a political activity shall be binding on the corporation.
    (3) Notwithstanding the requirement for an annual shareholder vote to authorize any spending of $10,000 or more by the corporation for any political activity, a corporation may request a special authorization for additional spending on political activities, provided that:

(a) All spending on political activities of $10,000 or more must be authorized by a shareholder majority vote.
(b) For any special authorization, the company shall articulate whether the corporate treasury funds so authorized are intended to benefit or defeat candidates, ballot measures, or issue advocacy campaigns, or will be paid to specific nonprofits or trade associations for political activities, at the time the special authorization is requested.

(3) DISCLOSURE OF SHAREHOLDER VOTES—Every institutional investment manager subject to section 13(f) of the Exchange Act shall report at least annually how it voted on any shareholder vote pursuant to paragraphs (1) or (2) of this section, unless such vote is otherwise required to be reported publicly by rule or regulation of the Securities and Exchange Commission.
(4) DIRECTOR LIABILITY—If a corporation makes an unauthorized contribution or expenditure for a political activity, then the directors at the time that the unauthorized contribution or expenditure was incurred are jointly and severally liable to repay to the corporation the amount of the unauthorized expenditure, with interest at the rate of 8 percent per annum.
(5) RULEMAKING—Not later than six months after the date of the enactment of the Corporate and Political Accountability Act of 2010, the Securities and Exchange Commission shall issue final rules to implement this subsection.

Section 5. Notification to Shareholders of Corporate Political Activities.

Section 13 of the Securities Exchange Act of 1934 (15 USC 78m) is amended by adding at the end the following:

SEC. [ ]. NOTIFICATION TO SHAREHOLDERS OF CORPORATE POLITICAL ACTIVITIES.

(a) Notification to Shareholders—

(1). At least quarterly during each fiscal year, public corporations that make contributions or expenditures for political activities must notify shareholders and the Securities and Exchange Commission in writing of the nature of all its political activities, funded by either its separate segregated fund or through its general corporate treasury, including contributions or expenditures made directly or indirectly.

(2) A report made pursuant to this section shall include the following:

(A) the date of the contributions or expenditures
(B) the amount of the contributions or expenditures
(C) the name or identity of the candidate, political party, committee, electioneering communication, ballot measure campaign, or issue advocacy campaign
(D) if the contributions or expenditures were made for or against a candidate, including an electioneering communication, the office sought by the candidate and the political party affiliation of the candidate
(E) if the contributions or expenditures were made for or against a ballot measure, the purpose of the measure and whether the contributions or expenditures were made in support or opposition to the ballot measure
(F) if the contributions or expenditures were made for or against an issue advocacy campaign, the nature of the political issue and whether the contributions were made in support or opposition to the political issue
(G) all expenditures made by a separate segregated fund affiliated with the corporation

(b) Public Disclosure—

(1) The quarterly reports of political activities by a public corporation to shareholders shall be public record as prescribed in Section 24(f) of this Act.
(2) A copy of the reports filed pursuant to subsection (a)(1) shall be posted for at least one year on the corporation's website.

Section 6. Public Disclosure of Corporate Political Activities by the Securities and exchange commission.

Section 24 of the Securities Exchange Act of 1934 (15 USC 78x) is amended by adding at the end the following new subsection:

(f)Public Disclosure—

(1) The quarterly reports of political activities by a public corporation to shareholders shall be made publicly available by the Securities Exchange Commission.
(2) A quarterly report required to be filed under this subsection shall be filed in electronic form, using filing software approved or developed by the Securities Exchange Commission, in addition to filing in any other form that the Securities Exchange Commission may require by regulation.

(3) The Securities Exchange Commission shall ensure that, to the greatest extent practicable, the quarterly reports on political activities are publicly available through the Securities and Exchange Commission's website in a manner that is searchable, sortable, and downloadable.

*Section 7. **Report by the Office of Management and Budget.***

(a) On an annual basis, the Office of Management and Budget shall audit the extent of compliance or noncompliance with the requirements of this Act by public corporations, their management, and shareholders, as well as the effectiveness of the Securities Exchange Commission in meeting the reporting and disclosure requirements of this Act.
(b) Not later than April 1 of each year, the Office of Management and Budget shall submit to the President a report on the review required by subsection (a) for the preceding year.

*Section 8. **Severability.***

If any clause, sentence, subdivision, paragraph, section, or part of this Act should be adjudged by any court of competent jurisdiction to be invalid, such judgment shall not affect, impair, or invalidate the remainder thereof, but shall be confined in its operation to the clause, sentence, subdivision, paragraph, section, or part thereof directly involved in the controversy in which such judgment shall have been rendered.

APPENDIX 15.1 CONTINUED

2. Draft Language of Possible State Shareholder Protection Bill[236]

*Section 1. **Short Title.***

This Act may be cited as the "State [X] Corporate Political Accountability Act of 2010."

*Section 2. **Findings and Declarations.***

The People of State [x] and the Legislature find and declare that:

(a) Although corporations cannot vote, corporations make significant political contributions and expenditures that directly or indirectly influence the election of candidates and support or oppose political causes at the local, state, and federal level. Decisions to use corporate treasury funds for political contributions and expenditures are currently made by corporate managers, often without the knowledge or consent of shareholders.

(b) Corporations acting through their managers have a fiduciary duty to conduct business in the best interests of the shareholders. Corporate managers that use corporate funds to support and oppose political candidates, political parties, and political causes in opposition to the interests of many or all of their shareholders may not be acting in the best interests of the corporation.

(c) Historically, shareholders of corporations in the United States have not had a way to know of, or to influence, the political activities of corporations they own. Shareholders and the public have a right to know how these corporations are spending their funds to make political contributions or expenditures benefiting candidates, political parties, and political causes.

(d) These corporations should be accountable to their shareholders prior to making political contributions or expenditures affecting local, state, and federal governance and public policy. Requiring the express approval of a corporation's shareholders prior to making political contributions or expenditures will help establish accountability.

(e) If corporations use corporate general treasury funds for political expenditures, then those funds should be clearly reported to shareholders and shareholders should be able to authorize the use of corporate general treasury funds for political expenditures.

Section 3. Definitions.

As used in this section:

(a) The term "general treasury funds" means those monies in possession of a corporation incorporated under the laws of state [x] in the normal course of business. General treasury funds may include, among others, funds from sales, accounts payable, loans, investments, bonds, or debt instruments.

(b) The term "issue advocacy campaign" means contributions or expenditures for any communication to the general public intended to encourage the public to contact a government official regarding pending legislation or a government rule or regulation. Issue advocacy campaign does not include expenditures for registered lobbyists or other persons employed by the corporation to lobby directly state or federal government officials.

(c) The term "known at the time of the authorization vote" means that, at the time the corporation seeks authorization from shareholders to spend corporate funds for political activities, (1) the corporation's officers, directors, or employees have identified a specific political activity for the corporation to support or oppose, (2) corporate officers, directors, or employees have taken steps to obligate funds to a political activity, or (3) the corporation has a regularly scheduled payment to a trade association or other entity to pay for a political activity in the next twelve months.

(d) The term "majority of all shareholders" means 50 percent plus one of all outstanding voting securities. Shareholders not casting votes shall not count toward affirmative authorization under this section.

(e) The term "political activities" means any contributions or expenditures made directly or indirectly to, or in support of or opposition to, any candidate, political party, committee, electioneering communication, ballot measure campaign, or an issue advocacy campaign. Political activities do not include activities defined as lobbying under any local, state, or federal law. For purposes of this section, the term "contribution or expenditure" includes any monetary and nonmonetary political contributions and expenditures not deductible under section 162 (e)(1)(B) of the Internal Revenue Code, including but not limited to contributions to or expenditures on behalf of political candidates, political parties, political committees, and other political entities organized and operating under 26 USC Sec. 527 of the Internal Revenue Code and any portion of any dues or similar payments made to any tax-exempt organization that is used for an expenditure or contribution if made directly by the corporation would not be deductible under section 162 (e)(1)(B) of the Internal Revenue Code, any contribution or expenditure, as those terms are defined in 2 USC Sec. 431, as well as any contribution or expenditure defined under state law [insert cross-reference to relevant state law], and also includes any direct or indirect payment, distribution, loan, advance, deposit, or gift of money, or any services, or anything of value (except a loan of money by a national or state bank made in accordance with the applicable banking laws and regulations and in the ordinary course of business) to any candidate, campaign committee, or political party or organization, in connection with any election to any office. The term "contribution or expenditure" shall not include:

(1) communications by a corporation to its stockholders and executive or administrative personnel and their families;
(2) nonpartisan registration and get-out-the-vote campaigns by a corporation aimed at its stockholders and executive or administrative personnel and their families; or
(3) the establishment, administration, and solicitation of contributions to a separate segregated fund to be utilized for political purposes by a corporation.

(f) The term "separate segregated fund" means a political action committee formed by a corporation for the purpose of making contributions to candidates for office or to political parties. A "separate segregated fund" that supports federal candidates shall have the same meaning as that found in 2 USC Sec. 441b.

Section 4. Shareholder Vote on corporate Political Activities.

Section [] of [State Business Law Section [ ]] is amended by inserting after section [ ] the following new [sub]section:

(1) ANNUAL VOTE—

(a) Applicability. Any corporation incorporated in state [x] that spends in the aggregate $10,000 or more of corporate treasury funds on all political activities, must comply with the requirements of this section.
(b) Any proxy or consent or authorization for an annual meeting of the shareholders of a corporation incorporated in state [x] (or a special meeting in lieu of such meeting) where proxies are solicited in respect of any security occurring on or after the date that is six months after the date on which final rules are issued under paragraph (5), shall provide for a separate resolution subject to shareholder vote to approve any spending of $10,000 or more by the corporation for any political activity.
(c) Notwithstanding this requirement for an annual shareholder vote to authorize any spending of $10,000 or more by the corporation for any political activity, a corporation may request authorization for spending on political activities on a more frequent basis. Any authorization request by the corporation that is not made during an annual authorization shall be deemed a special authorization.
(d) If the corporation spends less than an aggregate of $10,000 in a twelve-month period for political activities, then it does not have to seek shareholder authorization for such spending.

(2) SHAREHOLDER APPROVAL—

(a) When seeking shareholder authorization for expenditures for political activities, the corporation shall request the authority to spend a maximum dollar amount in the next twelve months.
(b) If known at the time of the shareholder vote (1) the company shall articulate whether the corporate treasury funds so authorized are intended to benefit or defeat specific candidates, ballot measures, or issue advocacy campaigns, or whether it will be paid to specific nonprofits or trade associations for political activities.

(1) To be effective, the authorization vote must garner support from a majority of the corporation's shareholders.
(2) A vote by the shareholders to approve or disapprove any spending of $10,000 or more by a corporation for a political activity shall be binding on the corporation.
(3) Notwithstanding the requirement for an annual shareholder vote to authorize any spending of $10,000 or more by the corporation for any political activity, a corporation may request a special authorization for additional spending on political activities, provided that:

(a) All spending on political activities of $10,000 or more must be authorized by a shareholder majority vote.
(b) For any special authorization, the company shall articulate whether the corporate treasury funds so authorized are intended to benefit or defeat candidates, ballot measures, or issue advocacy campaigns, or will be paid to specific nonprofits or trade associations for political activities, at the time the special authorization is requested.

(3) DIRECTOR LIABILITY—If a corporation makes an unauthorized contribution or expenditure for a political activity, then the directors at the time that the unauthorized contribution or expenditure was incurred are jointly and severally liable to repay to the corporation the amount of the unauthorized expenditure, with interest at the rate of 8 percent per annum.

(4) RULEMAKING—No later than six months after the date of the enactment of the State [X] Corporate Political Accountability Act of 2010, the [Relevant State Business Authority] shall issue final rules to implement this subsection.

(5) Sole proprietorships excluded. Notwithstanding the foregoing, nothing in the title shall apply a new duty to the owner of a sole proprietorship.

Section 5. Notification to Shareholders of Corporate Political Activities.

[State Business Law Section [ ] is amended by inserting after section [ ] the following new section:

SEC. [ ]. NOTIFICATION TO SHAREHOLDERS OF CORPORATE POLITICAL ACTIVITIES.

(a) Notification to Shareholders—

(3) At least quarterly during each fiscal year, a corporation incorporated in the state of [x] that makes contributions or expenditures

for political activities must notify its shareholders and the [Relevant State Business Authority] in writing of the nature of all its political activities, funded by either its separate segregated fund or through its general corporate treasury, including contributions or expenditures made directly or indirectly.

(4) A report made pursuant to this section shall include the following:

(A) the date of the contributions or expenditures
(B) the amount of the contributions or expenditures
(C) the identity of the candidate, political party, committee, electioneering communication, ballot measure campaign, or issue advocacy campaign
(D) if the contributions or expenditures were made for or against a candidate, including an electioneering communication as defined under federal law [and/or state law (x)], the office sought by the candidate and the political party affiliation of the candidate
(E) if the contributions or expenditures were made for or against a ballot measure, the purpose of the measure and whether the contributions or expenditures were made in support or opposition to the ballot measure
(F) if the contributions or expenditures were made for or against an issue advocacy campaign, the nature of the political issue and whether the contributions were made in support or opposition to the political issue
(G) all expenditures made by a separate segregated fund affiliated with the corporation

(b) Public Disclosure—

(3) The quarterly reports of political activities by a corporation incorporated in the state of [x] shareholders shall be public records.

(4) A copy of the reports filed pursuant to subsection (a)(1) shall be posted for at least one year on the corporation's website, if any.

Section 6. Public Disclosure of Corporate Political Activities by the [Relevant State Business Authority].

Section [] [State Business Law Section [z] is amended by adding at the end the following new subsection:
[] Public Disclosure—

(4) The quarterly reports of political activities by a corporation incorporated in the state of [x] to shareholders shall be made publicly available by the [Relevant State Business Authority].

(5) A quarterly report required to be filed under this subsection shall be filed in electronic form, using filing software approved or developed by the [Relevant State Business Authority], in addition to filing in any other form that the [Relevant State Business Authority] may require by regulation.

(6) The [Relevant State Business Authority] shall ensure that, to the greatest extent practicable, the quarterly reports on political activities are publicly available through the [Relevant State Business Authority]'s website in a manner that is searchable, sortable, and downloadable."

Section 7. Report by the [State inspector general or comparable office].

(a) On an annual basis, [state inspector general or comparable office] shall [audit] the extent of compliance or noncompliance with the requirements of this Act by corporations incorporated in state [x], their management and shareholders, as well as the effectiveness of [Relevant State Business Authority] in meeting the reporting and disclosure requirements of this Act.
(b) Not later than April 1 of each year, the [state inspector general or comparable office] shall submit to the governor a report on the review required by subsection (a) for the preceding year.

Section 8. Board Approval for all corporate political expenditures.

Notwithstanding any other provision of this title, no corporation, or trade, business, or professional association shall make any campaign contribution or expenditure unless specifically authorized to do so whether: by the vote of the board of directors of the corporation, of the executive committee of the trade, business, or professional association at a regular or special meeting thereof; by the president, vice president, secretary, or treasurer of a corporation whom the board has specifically empowered to authorize such contributions or expenditures; or, for a corporation, by any other person designated by resolution of the board of directors of a corporation to authorize contributions or expenditures. No corporation, trade, business, or professional association shall make any contribution or expenditure as defined under federal or state law, other than an in-kind contribution or expenditure, except by check.

Section 9. Applicability of this title to foreign corporations doing a majority of their business in state [x].

(a) A "foreign corporation" as defined in [Section [] of State (x) Business Code] (other than a foreign association or foreign nonprofit corporation but including a foreign parent corporation even though it does not itself transact intrastate business) is subject to the requirements of sections 2 through 7 of this Act inclusively, if:

(1) The average of property, payroll, and sales (as defined in Sections [ ] of State (x) Tax Code) with respect to the foreign corporation is more than 50 percent during its latest full income year.

(2) More than one-half of its outstanding voting securities are held of record by persons having addresses in this state appearing on the books of the corporation on the record date for the latest meeting of shareholders held during its latest full income year or, if no meeting was held during that year, on the last day of the latest full income year. The property factor, payroll factor, and sales factor shall be those used in computing the portion of its income allocable to this state in its franchise tax return or, with respect to corporations the allocation of whose income is governed by special formulas or that are not required to file separate or any tax returns, which would have been so used if they were governed by this three-factor formula. The determination of these factors with respect to any parent corporation shall be made on a consolidated basis, including in a unitary computation (after elimination of intercompany transactions) the property, payroll, and sales of the parent and all of its subsidiaries in which it owns directly or indirectly more than 50 percent of the outstanding shares entitled to vote for the election of directors, but deducting a percentage of the property, payroll, and sales of any subsidiary equal to the percentage minority ownership, if any, in the subsidiary. For the purpose of this subdivision, any securities held to the knowledge of the issuer in the names of broker-dealers, nominees for broker-dealers (including clearing corporations), or banks, associations, or other entities holding securities in a nominee name or otherwise on behalf of a beneficial owner (collectively "nominee holders"), shall not be considered outstanding. However, if the foreign corporation requests all nominee holders to certify, with respect to all beneficial owners for whom securities are held, the number of shares held for those beneficial owners having addresses (as shown on the records of the nominee holder) in this state

and outside of this state, then all shares so certified shall be considered outstanding and held of record by persons having addresses either in this state or outside of this state as so certified, provided that the certification so provided shall be retained with the record of shareholders and made available for inspection and copying in the same manner as is provided in Section 1600 with respect to that record. A current list of beneficial owners of a foreign corporation's securities provided to the corporation by one or more nominee holders or their agent pursuant to the requirements of Rule 14b-1(b)(3) or 14b-2(b)(3) as adopted on January 6, 1992, promulgated under the Securities Exchange Act of 1934, shall constitute an acceptable certification with respect to beneficial owners for the purposes of this subdivision.

(b) Provided however, this section does not apply to any corporation:

(1) with outstanding securities listed on the New York Stock Exchange or the American Stock Exchange
(2) with outstanding securities designated as qualified for trading on the NASDAQ National Market (or any successor thereto) of the NASDAQ Stock Market operated by the NASDAQ Stock Market Inc.
(3) if all of its voting shares (other than directors' qualifying shares) are owned directly or indirectly by a corporation or corporations not subject to this section

(c) Liability. Any party who obtains a final determination by a court of competent jurisdiction that the corporation failed to provide to the party information required to be provided by this subdivision or provided the party information of the kind required to be provided by this subdivision that was incorrect, then the court, in its discretion, shall have the power to include in its judgment recovery by the party from the corporation of all court costs and reasonable attorneys' fees incurred in that legal proceeding to the extent they relate to obtaining that final determination.

Section 10. Severability.

If any clause, sentence, subdivision, paragraph, section, or part of this act should be adjudged by any court of competent jurisdiction to be invalid, such judgment shall not affect, impair, or invalidate the remainder thereof, but shall be confined in its operation to the clause, sentence, subdivision, paragraph, section, or part thereof directly involved in the controversy in which such judgment shall have been rendered.

APPENDIX 15.2 SELECTED PORTIONS OF BRITISH CORPORATE LAW

Reporting requirements to shareholders of UK companies' political spending:

> (1) If—(a) the company . . . has in the financial year—(i) made any donation to any registered party or to any other EU political organisation, or (ii) incurred any EU political expenditure, and (b) the amount of the donation or expenditure, or (as the case may be) the aggregate amount of all donations and expenditure falling within paragraph (a), exceeded £200, the directors' report for the year shall contain the particulars specified in sub-paragraph (2).
>
> (2) Those particulars are—(a) as respects donations falling within sub-paragraph (1)(a)(i)—(i) the name of each registered party or other organisation to whom any such donation has been made, and (ii) the total amount given to that party or organisation by way of such donations in the financial year; and (b) as respects expenditure falling within sub-paragraph (1)(a)(ii), the total amount incurred by way of such expenditure in the financial year. . . .
>
> (3) In this paragraph "contribution," in relation to an organisation, means—(a) any gift of money to the organisation (whether made directly or indirectly); (b) any subscription or other fee paid for affiliation to, or membership of, the organisation; or (c) any money spent (otherwise than by the organisation or a person acting on its behalf) in paying any expenses incurred directly or indirectly by the organisation.[237]

UK Companies must get consent from shareholders to make political expenditures:

> Prohibition on donations and political expenditure by companies. (1) A company must not—(a) make any donation to any registered party or to any other EU political organisation, or (b) incur any EU political expenditure, unless the donation or expenditure is authorised by virtue of an approval resolution passed by the company in general meeting before the relevant time. (2) For the purposes of this section an approval resolution is a qualifying resolution which authorises the company to do either (or both) of the following, namely—(a) make donations to EU political organisations not exceeding in total a sum specified in the resolution, or (b) incur EU political expenditure not exceeding in total a sum so specified, during the requisite period beginning with the date of the resolution. . . . (4) The resolution must be expressed in general terms conforming with subsection (2), and accordingly may not purport to authorise particular donations or expenditure.[238]

Directors who do not get authorization from shareholders are liable: Liability of directors in case of unauthorised donation or expenditure.

(1) This section applies where a company has made a political donation or incurred political expenditure without the authorisation required by this Part.
(2) The directors in default are jointly and severally liable—(a) to make good to the company the amount of the unauthorised donation or expenditure, with interest, and (b) to compensate the company for any loss or damage sustained by it as a result of the unauthorised donation or expenditure having been made.
(3) The directors in default are—(a) those who, at the time the unauthorised donation was made or the unauthorised expenditure was incurred, were directors of the company by which the donation was made or the expenditure was incurred, and (b) where—(i) that company was a subsidiary of a relevant holding company, and (ii) the directors of the relevant holding company failed to take all reasonable steps to prevent the donation being made or the expenditure being incurred.[239]

APPENDIX 15.3 SAMPLE OF BRITISH/AMERICAN COMPANIES REPORTING AMERICAN POLITICAL SPENDING

Company	*Website*	*U.S. Giving Disclosed*
AstraZeneca	http://www.astrazeneca-annualreports.com/2007/business review/governance/other_matters.asp http://www.astrazeneca-annualreports.com/2008/downloads/AZ_AR08_Full.pdf (page 95)	2006: $416,675 2007: $321,645 2008: $815,838 by U.S. entities "to state political party committees, campaign committees of various state candidates affiliated with the major parties in accordance with pre-established guidelines."
GlaxoSmith-Kline PLC	http://www.secinfo.com/d139r2.s3h.htm#n4au	2008: £319,000 2007: £249,000; Glaxo discontinued political contributions as of July 2009 but the GSK PAC continues to give. In 2008 it gave £539,359 and in 2007 it gave £522,172.

(continued)

APPENDIX 15.3 (CONTINUED)

Company	*Website*	*U.S. Giving Disclosed*
Lockheed Martin	http://www.lockheedmartin.com/investor/corporate_governance/PoliticalDisclosures.html	Has PAC, gives soft money to Democratic Governors Association and Republican Governors Association. Total expenditures in 2008: $82,375.
ExxonMobil Corporation	http://www.exxonmobil.com/Corporate/Imports/ccr2008/pdf/community_ccr_2008.pdf	Corporate political contributions—U.S. state campaigns and national 527s: 2005: $340,000 2006: $410,000 2007: $270,000 2008: $450,000
National Grid	http://www.nationalgrid.com/NR/rdonlyres/265D645B-6106-49B4-A20F-4F9AD5747DEE/17808/05DirectorsReports4.pdf http://www.nationalgrid.com/NR/rdonlyres/0D9BEF89-D5EB-43CE-A5FA-9E15DB8ECF7D/34975/5DirectorsReports.pdf	2006–2007: $100,000 from National Grid; $146,706 from National Grid PAC; 2007–2008: $70,000 from National Grid; $56,656 from PAC; Keyspan gave $37,015 2008–2009: $180,000 from National Grid and subs to NYS PACs; $156,975 from National Grid PACs.

NOTES

1. See Joint Economic Committee, 106th Cong., *The Roots of Broadened Stock Ownership* (2000), 1, www.house.gov/jec/tax/stock/stock.pdf; Investment Company Institute, *U.S. Household Ownership of Mutual Funds in 2005*, (2005), 2, http://www.ici.org/pdf/fm-v14n5.pdf; The Investment Company Institute, *2009 Investment Company Fact Book 8*, 49th ed. (2009), http://www.icifactbook.org/pdf/2009_factbook.pdf (noting "[h]ouseholds are the largest group of investors in [investment] funds, and registered investment companies managed 19 percent of households' financial assets at year-end 2008").
2. Rajesh K. Aggarwal, Felix Meschke, and Tracy Wang, *Corporate Political Contributions: Investment or Agency?* (2009), 1, http://papers.ssrn.com/sol3/papers.cfm?abstract_id=972670.
3. The Federal Elections Campaign Act (FECA) prohibits corporations (profit or nonprofit), labor organizations, and incorporated membership organizations from making direct contributions or expenditures in connection with federal elections (2 USC § 441b). The limits have a long vintage. For sixty-two years, since Taft-Hartley, corporations have been banned from spending corporate treasury money to expressively support or oppose a federal candidate and for 102 years, since the Tillman Act, corporations have been

banned from giving contributions directly from corporate treasury funds to federal candidates.

4. The corporate PAC requirement has some harsh and powerful critics. For example, Justice Anthony Kennedy's dissent in *McConnell* called the federal corporate PAC requirement "compulsory ventriloquism" and articulated his long-standing view that it was unconstitutional to require corporations to pay for political speech through corporate PACs. *McConnell v. FEC*, 540 U.S. 93, 333 (2003) (Kennedy, J., dissenting in part and concurring in part).
5. 11 C.F.R. 100.6; Fed. Election Comm'n, SSFs and Nonconnected PACs (May 2008), http://www.fec.gov/pages/brochures/ssfvnonconnected.shtml.
6. Adam Winkler, "*McConnell v. FEC*, Corporate Political Speech, and the Legacy of the Segregated Fund Cases," *Election Law Journal* 3 (2004): 361 (arguing "treasury funds reflect the economically motivated decisions of investors or members who do not necessarily approve of the political expenditures, while segregated funds—such as a political action committee (PAC)—raise and spend money from knowing, voluntary political contributors"); see *FEC v. Beaumont*, 539 U.S. 146, 154 (2003) (explaining "the [corporate treasury spending] ban has always done further duty in protecting 'the individuals who have paid money into a corporation or union for purposes other than the support of candidates from having that money used to support political candidates to whom they may be opposed'"; internal citations omitted).
7. Order for Reargument, *Citizens United v. FEC*, No. 08–205 (June 29, 2009), http://www.supremecourtus.gov/docket/08–205.htm.
8. See Richard L. Hasen, *The Supreme Court Gets Ready to Turn on the Corporate Fundraising Spigot*, Slate.com (June 29, 2009), http://www.slate.com/id/2221753/; Michael Dorf, *Should the Supreme Court Alter Its Approach to Campaign Finance Regulation?*, Findlaw.com (August 12, 2009), http://writ.lp.findlaw.com/dorf/20090812.html ("Unfortunately, there is reason to think that the Supreme Court will make matters worse by overruling *Austin* and/or *McConnell* and holding BCRA § 203 facially invalid. If it does so, the American people could be excused for thinking that the Court too is part of the rigged game"); *Citizens United v. FEC*, No. 08–205, slip op. (2010).
9. Aggarwal, Meschke, and Wang, *Corporate Political Contributions*.
10. See Daniel Greenwood, "Essential Speech: Why Corporate Speech Is Not Free," *Iowa Law Review* 83 (1998): 995, 1055, http://ssrn.com/abstract=794785 ("Corporate speech, then, should be viewed with extreme suspicion. Corporate interference in the political sphere raises an omnipresent specter of impropriety, of a valuable institution stepping out of its proper sphere, of a tool of the people becoming its ruler").
11. For a good exploration of federal lobbying see generally Robert G. Kaiser, *So Damn Much Money: The Triumph of Lobbying and the Corrosion of American Government* (New York: Knopf, 2009).
12. Victor Brudney, "Business Corporations and Stockholders' Rights under the First Amendment," *Yale Law Journal* 91 (1981): 235, 237 (stating "[t]he use of that wealth and power by corporate management to move government toward goals that management favors—with little or no formal consultation with investors—is also a phenomenon that is generally undeniable").
13. Bruce F. Freed and John C. Richardson, "Company Political Activity Requires Director Oversight," *ALI-ABA Course of Study Materials* (December 2005): 478.
14. Ibid., 480; see also Brudney, "Business Corporations," 239–240 (noting "unless investor approval is obtained, the funds of some investors are being used to support views they do not favor").

15. Jill Fisch, "The 'Bad Man' Goes to Washington: The Effect of Political Influence on Corporate Duty," *Fordham Law Review* 75 (2006): 1593, 1613.
16. The lack of board approval is the norm. However, two states (Louisiana and Missouri) do require board approval of political donations before they are made. See La. Rev. Stat. Ann. §18:1505.2(F) (also allowing officers of the corporation to make such contributions if empowered to do so by the board of directors); Mo. Ann. Stat. §130.029.
17. Jennifer S. Taub, "Able but Not Willing: The Failure of Mutual Fund Advisers to Advocate for Shareholders' Rights," *Journal of Corporation Law* 34 (2009):101, 102, http://papers.ssrn.com/sol3/papers.cfm?abstract_id=1066831 ("Approximately 77.7 million individuals in the United States invest in equities through stock mutual funds").
18. Ibid., 105 ("Investors who are the risk-takers are now pushed further away from the decisionmakers, and the agency problem is amplified").
19. Arguably, the problem predates the 1905 scandal. See Marc Hager, "Bodies Politic: The Progressive History of Organizational 'Real Entity' Theory," *University of Pittsburgh Law Review* 50 (1989): 575, 639 ("[C]oncern with corporate power over democratic processes in America grew sharply toward the close of the nineteenth century as concentrations of private capital, in the form of corporations and trusts, reached unprecedented size and power. These huge pools of capital raised the frightening prospect that candidates and elections might actually be bought in systematic fashion").
20. Adam Winkler, "'Other People's Money': Corporations, Agency Costs, and Campaign Finance Law," *Georgetown Law Journal* 92 (June 2004): 871, 893–894.
21. Ibid., 914–915 (one insurance executive involved in the 1905 scandal was charged with grand larceny, but the criminal charges were thrown out by the New York courts).
22. See, e.g., *Buckley v. Valeo*, 424 U.S. 1 (1976).
23. Thomas W. Joo, "Corporate Governance and the Constitutionality of Campaign Finance Reform," *Election Law Journal* 1 (2002): 361, 370.
24. The CPA is a 501(c)(3) organization founded in 2003 "to bring transparency and accountability to corporate political spending." CPA, About Us, http://www.politicalaccountability.net/content.asp?contentid=406.
25. Common Cause is a nonprofit, nonpartisan 501(c)(4) lobbying organization founded to strengthen public participation and faith in government institutions, to ensure that government serves the public interest, to curb the influence of money in political life, to promote fair elections and high standards of conduct for government officials, and to protect civil rights and civil liberties. Common Cause, About Us, http://www.commoncause.org/site/pp.asp?c=dkLNK1MQIwG&b=189955.
26. Political Parties, Elections and Referendums Act, c. 41 §§ 139, 140, sched. 19 (2000), http://www.opsi.gov.uk/Acts/acts2000/ukpga_20000041_en_1.
27. Bruce F. Freed and Karl J. Sandstrom, "Political Money: The Need for Director Oversight," http://www.conference-board.org/publications/publicationdetail.cfm?publicationid=1454.
28. A SSF is a PAC that is formed by a corporation. Unlike other PACs, a SSF cannot solicit contributions from the general public. Rather SSFs can solicit only from the officers, directors, certain employees. and shareholders of the company, along with the families of these four groups. These solicitations by the SSF allow the shareholders the ability to voluntarily contribute and shareholders who give to a SSF know that their money will be used for a political purpose. SSFs are also subject to detailed reporting requirements. This report will not address SSFs, except incidentally. See 11 C.F.R. 100.6; Fed. Election Comm'n, see note 5.

29. Fed. Election Comm'n, *Federal Election Commission Campaign Guide: Corporations and Labor Organizations* (January 2007), http://www.fec.gov/pdf/colagui.pdf.
30. Press Release, Campaign Finance Institute, *Party Conventions' Financiers Have Spent Nearly $1.5 billion on Federal Campaign Contributions and Lobbying Since 2005* (August 20, 2008), http://www.cfinst.org/pr/prRelease.aspx?ReleaseID=203.
31. Elizabeth Drew, *The Corruption of American Politics: What Went Wrong and Why* (New York: Overlook, 2000), 72 (noting the corporate donations to the Trent Lott Leadership Institute).
32. Center for Responsive Politics, 2008 Election Overview, http://www.opensecrets.org/overview/index.php; see also *McConnell*, 540 U.S. at 124–125 (noting "the largest corporate donors often made substantial contributions to both parties. Such practices corroborate evidence indicating that many corporate contributions were motivated by a desire for access to candidates and a fear of being placed at a disadvantage in the legislative process relative to other contributors, rather than by ideological support for the candidates and parties").
33. Center for Responsive Politics, see note 32.
34. Campaign Finance Institute, *Party Conventions' Financiers* (finding these same donors also spent over $1.3 billion to lobby the federal government).
35. Bruce F. Freed and Jamie Carroll, *Hidden Rivers: How Trade Associations Conceal Corporate Political Spending* (2006), 1–2, http://www.politicalaccountability.net/index.php?ht=a/GetDocumentAction/i/932.
36. Ibid., 5. This figure was based on federal tax returns, and as such, does not provide a breakdown of political versus lobbying activities; accordingly, determining the amount of corporate political spending is "guesswork." It is also unclear whether the figure represents political giving and lobbying for federal elections only, or for both state and federal elections.
37. Greenwood, "Essential Speech," 1054 (in sum, arguing that "corporations, not being citizens, cannot be legitimate political actors").
38. 2 USC § 441b(a). This prohibition on corporate expenditures in elections was changed by the Supreme Court in the *Citizens United* case.
39. National Counsel on State Legislatures, *State Limits on Contributions to Candidates* (April 30, 2009), http://www.ncsl.org/print/legismgt/limits_candidates.pdf.
40. Ibid.
41. Craig Holman, *Public Citizen, "Pay to Play" Restrictions on Campaign Contributions from Government Contractors 2008–2009* (2009), http://www.cleanupwashington.org/documents/paytoplay2009.pdf.
42. Herbert E. Alexander, *Financing Politics: Money, Elections and Political Reform* , 4th ed. (Washington, DC: CQ Press, 1992), 20 (reporting the international political spending by U.S. corporations revealed by the Watergate investigation, "millions of dollars [were] known to have been given to politicians in Italy, Korea and other countries").
43. See 2 USC § 441b(a) (banning contributions and expenditures by corporations, banks, and labor unions). State laws vary from allowing unlimited corporate contributions to banning them. National Counsel on State Legislatures, see note 39.
44. Supplemental Reply Brief for Appellee, *Citizens United v. FEC*, No. 08–205 at 7 (2009).
45. *Abood v. Detroit Board of Education*, 431 U.S. 209, 235–236 (1977) (holding "[T]he Constitution requires only that [political] expenditures be financed from charges, dues, or assessments paid by employees who do not object to advancing those ideas").

46. Supplemental Brief of Amici Curiae Senator John McCain, Senator Russell Feingold, Former Representative Christopher Shays, and Former Representative Martin Meehan in Support of Appellee, *Citizens United v. FEC*, No. 08–205 at 2 (2009).
47. Gioia Ligos and David Jones, *Internal Revenue Service, Disallowance of a Deduction Under IRC 162 for Lobbying Expenses* (1995), http://www.irs.gov/pub/irs-tege/eotopicb95.pdf.
48. Alexander, *Financing Politics*, 19 (reporting "[o]fficials of the corporations that donated [pre-Watergate] claimed they did so not to obtain favors, but to avoid possible retaliation by the Nixon administration. . . . Gulf Oil's Claude Wild said he decided to arrange the contribution so that his company 'would not be on a blacklist or at the bottom of the totem pole' when it came time for someone in Washington to return his phone calls"; internal citations omitted).
49. The Committee for Economic Development (CED) is a nonprofit, nonpartisan, and nonpolitical public policy organization directed by approximately two hundred senior corporate executives and university leaders. CED, About CED, http://www.ced.org/about/about-ced.
50. Supplemental Brief of Committee for Economic Development as Amicus Curiae in Support of Appellee, *Citizens United v. FEC*, No. 08–205 at 10 (2009).
51. *McConnell*, 540 U.S. at 125 n. 13.
52. Supplemental Brief of the CPA and the Carol and Lawrence Zicklin Center for Business Ethics Research at the Wharton School as Amici Curiae in Support of Appellee, *Citizens United v. FEC*, No. 08–205 at 4 (2009). Furthermore, political giving comes with the risk of the corporation's being sucked into a future political scandal. "In recent years, some institutional investors have argued that political contributions could come back to haunt companies." Aaron Bernstein, "When Political Giving Doesn't Pay," *Directorship* (June 1, 2008), http://www.politicalaccountability.net/index.php?ht=display/ArticleDetails/i/1416/pid/188.
53. The term "rent-seeking" generally implies the extraction of uncompensated value from others without making any contribution to productivity.
54. As Jennifer Taub explains "agency problems" have been an ongoing issue with the corporate structure. Taub, "Able but Not Willing," 104 ("the prevailing framework [ ] is largely based upon the agency problem recognized in 1932 by Adolf Berle and Gardiner Means [who] saw a shift between the nineteenth- and twentieth-century business enterprises. Persons other than those who [had] ventured their wealth were directing industry. They recognized that the separation of ownership from control would lead to directors or titular managers who can employ the proxy machinery to become a self-perpetuating body, even though as a group they own but a small fraction of the stock outstanding. They identified the agency problem as a conflict between the interest of management and owners, whereby management can serve their own pockets better by profiting at the expense of the company than by making profits for it").
55. Aggarwal, Meschke, and Wang, *Corporate Political Contributions*, 1 (examining four types of corporate political contributions from 1991 to 2004: PAC donations, soft-money donations, donations by individuals affiliated with a company, and donations to 527s).
56. The term "perquisite consumption" is more commonly known as "perks" in the lingua franca. "Perquisite consumption" could include the use of private corporate jets by executives or furnishing an executive office suite lavishly.
57. Aggarwal, Meschke, and Wang, *Corporate Political Contributions*, 13.
58. Excess returns are defined as a firm's one-year buy and hold returns minus their expected return for the year as measured from the Wednesday

following Election Day to the first Monday of November in the following year (ibid., 17).

59. Ibid., 34 (revealing "[e]ven within the top five donating industries, including banking, financial trading, and utilities that have undergone deregulation during our sample period, donors have lower excess returns than non-donors").
60. Ibid., 9 (explaining "[s]oft money donations are unlimited campaign contributions to the national parties for party-building activities such as get-out-the-vote drives and non-party specific advertising. Soft money donations are made directly by the company and its officers using company funds"); see also ibid., 23 (finding "the more a firm donates, the lower the excess returns").
61. Ibid., 21; see also ibid., 39 (noting "[w]e also find that returns to donations are positive for the very largest donors in our sample. To put this in context, this is true for one quarter of one percent of our donating firm-year observations").
62. Ibid., 3–4 (stating "[g]iven the magnitude of the destruction of shareholder value that we document, it is more plausibly the case that corporate political contributions are symptomatic of wider agency problems in the firm"). The Aggarwal study conforms with international studies of the relationships between political connections and shareholder value. Mara Faccio, "The Characteristics of Politically Connected Firms," *American Economic Review 96(1)* (March 2006): 369–386 (finding in forty-seven countries, companies with political connections underperform nonconnected companies); Mara Faccio, Ronald Masulis, and John J. McConnell, "Political Connections and Corporate Bailouts" *Journal of Finance*, 61(6): 2597–2635 (Dec. 2006) (finding in thirty-five countries politically connected firms are significantly more likely to be bailed out than similar nonconnected firms); Paul K. Chaney, Mara Faccio, and David Parsley, The Quality of Accounting Information in Politically Connected Firms" *Journal of Accounting and Economics*, February 2011, 51(1–2): 58–76 (finding in twenty countries, quality of earnings reported by politically connected firms is significantly poorer than that of similar nonconnected firms).
63. Aggarwal, Meschke, and Wang, *Corporate Political Contributions*, 4 (reporting "[w]hile the view that corporate political contributions are not in shareholders' interests may be surprising (at least to us), it is apparently not surprising to shareholder activists").
64. Valentina Judge, "Survey Assesses Director Views on Political Disclosure," *Corporate Social Issues Reporters 5* (March 2008), http://www.investorsagainstgenocide.net/2008-0328CorporateSocialIssuesReport.pdf.).
65. Press Release, CPA, *Directors Strongly Support Corporate Political Spending Disclosure, Question Whether Contributions Help Companies, CPA Poll Finds* (February 28, 2008), http://www.politicalaccountability.net/index.php?ht=a/GetDocumentAction/i/1259.
66. Mason-Dixon Polling and Research, the CPA and Zicklin Center For Business Ethics Research, the Wharton School 2008 Nationwide Survey of Members of Corporate Boards of Directors Attitudes Towards and Awareness of Campaign Finance Laws, Corporate Oversight of Political Spending and Activity, Proposed Reforms (2008), http://cpa.timberlakepublishing.com/files/CPA percent20– percent20Dirs percent20Survey percent20Report percent20– percent2003–20–08.pdf (emphasis added).
67. The laws governing publicly traded companies include the Securities Act of 1933, the Securities Exchange Act of 1934, the Trust Indenture Act of 1939, the Investment Company Act of 1940, the Investment Advisers Act of 1940, and the Sarbanes-Oxley Act of 2002. See SEC, *The Laws That Govern the Securities Industry*, http://www.sec.gov/about/laws.shtml.

68. Joo, "Corporate Governance," 368. Information is considered material if there is "substantial likelihood that a reasonable shareholder would consider it important in deciding how to vote." *TSC Indus. v. Northway, Inc.*, 426 U.S. 438, 449 (1976).
69. Joo, "Corporate Governance," 368.
70. Independent spending and funding of electioneering communications are also reported to the FEC and the FCC, respectively. See Fed. Election Comm'n, Electronically Filed Independent Expenditures (2009), http://fec.gov/finance/disclosure/ie_reports.shtml; FCC, Electioneering Communications Database (ECD) (2009), http://gullfoss2.fcc.gov/ecd/. Spending corporate treasury funds on express advocacy in federal elections was illegal, thus even if it happened, it was unlikely to be reported.
71. Fed. Election Comm'n, *Contributions Received by Abraham Lincoln Leadership Political Action Committee*, http://query.nictusa.com/cgi-bin/com_rcvd/C00357095/; Fed. Election Comm'n, *Contributions Received by Americans for the Republic Inc*, http://query.nictusa.com/cgi-bin/com_rcvd/C00196220/; Fed. Election Comm'n, *Contributions Received by Democracy Believers Political Action Committee*, http://query.nictusa.com/cgi-bin/com_rcvd/C00382036/; Fed. Election Comm'n, *Contributions Received by Freedom & Democracy Fund*, http://query.nictusa.com/cgi-bin/com_rcvd/C00409987/.
72. See Campaign Disclosure Project, *Grading State Disclosure* (2008), http://www.campaigndisclosure.org/gradingstate/index.html. The Campaign Disclosure Project is a collaboration of the UCLA School of Law, the Center for Governmental Studies, and the California Voter Foundation.
73. Susannah Goodman, "Mutual Protection: Why Mutual Funds Should Embrace Disclosure of Corporate Political Contributions" 2 (December 2005), http://www.commoncause.org/atf/cf/%7BFB3C17E2-CDD1-4DF6-92BE-BD4429893665%7D/MUTUAL%20FUND%20REPORT%202-15-05.PDF.
74. Linda King, *National Institute on Money in State Politics, Indecent Disclosure Public Access to Independent Expenditure Information at the State Level* (August 1, 2007), 4, https://www.policyarchive.org/bitstream/handle/10207/5807/200708011.pdf?sequence=1.
75. Freed and Carroll, *Hidden Rivers*, 1.
76. For example, Sarbanes-Oxley imposes increased disclosure and reporting requirements, creates stricter rules concerning the independence of the accounting firms working for publicly traded companies, and imposes additional responsibilities on the directors and officers of public companies. See Excellence in Corporate Governance Online, Legal Issues, http://www.corpgovonline.com/Content/LegalIssues.html; J. Brent Wilkins, "The Sarbanes-Oxley Act of 2002: The Ripple Effects of Restoring Shareholder Confidence," *Southern Illinois University Law Journal* 29 (2005): 339, 349; Scott Harshbarger and Goutam U. Jois, "Looking Back and Looking Forward: Sarbanes-Oxley and the Future of Corporate Governance," *Akron Law Review* 40 (2007): 1, 3.
77. Introduced in 1983 and known by its ticker symbol OEX, the S&P 100 it is made up of one hundred major, blue-chip companies across diverse industry groups. See Standard & Poor's, *S&P 100 Overview*, http://www2.standardandpoors.com/portal/site/sp/en/us/page.topic/indices_100/2,3,2,2,0,0,0,0,0,2,1,0,0,0,0,0.html.
78. William T. Allen and Reinier Kraakman, *Commentaries and Cases on the Law of Business Organization* (New York: Aspen Publishers, 2003), 96.
79. Ibid.
80. Ibid., 100.

81. Ibid.; see also *Dodge v. Ford Motor Co.*, 204 Mich. 459, 507 (1919) (holding "[a] business corporation is organized and carried on primarily for the profit of the stockholders. The powers of the directors are to be employed for that end").
82. The division of ownership and day-to-day management largely collapses in the case of a closely held corporation. A close corporation is often defined simply as one with few shareholders, whose shares are not traded in securities markets. The small number of shareholders means that management and ownership are frequently concentrated in the same hands. See James D. Cox, Thomas Lee Hazen, and F. Hodge O'Neal, *Forms of Business Association: Definitions and Distinctions* (New York: Aspen Law, 2002), § 1.20; Thomas W. Joo, "The Modern Corporation and Campaign Finance: Incorporating Corporate Governance Analysis into First Amendment Jurisprudence," *Washington University Law Quarterly* 79 (2001): 1, 109 ("[E]lection-related spending may in fact constitute shareholder expression in some corporations, such as a corporation owned by a single person, or a closely held corporation actively managed by its shareholders. Those shareholders do not require state protection from management abuses").
83. Joo, "Modern Corporation," 54.
84. Walter Werner and Steven T. Smith, *Wall Street* (New York: Columbia University Press, 1991), 113–114.
85. Allen and Kraakman, *Commentaries*, 97.
86. Ibid., 95.
87. The only way to buy shares in a company that give shareholders more rights over corporate political spending is by investing in an American company that is subject to the British Companies Act of 2006. Companies Act c. 46, §§ 369, 374 (2006), http://www.opsi.gov.uk/acts/acts2006/pdf/ukpga_20060046_en.pdf.
88. Ibid., 31; a fiduciary relationship is one "founded on trust or confidence reposed by one person in the integrity and fidelity of another." See *Black's Law Dictionary*, 7th ed. (New York: West, 1999).
89. Allen and Kraakman, *Commentaries*, 240. The classic formulation of this duty requires a corporate director or officer to perform his or her functions (a) in good faith, (b) in a manner that he or she reasonably believes to be in the best interests of the corporation, and (c) with the care that an ordinarily prudent person would reasonably be expected to exercise in a like position and under similar circumstances. See American Law Institute (ALI), *Principles of Corporate Governance* (Philadelphia, PA: American Law Institute, 1994), § 4.01.
90. Ibid., § 1.42.
91. Allen and Kraakman, *Commentaries*, 252.
92. Ibid., 251.
93. Ibid., 252.
94. Ibid., 288–290.
95. 422 U.S. 66 (1975).
96. Winkler, "Other People's Money," 872.
97. *Marsili v. Pacific Gas & Elec. Co.*, 51 Cal. App. 3d 313, 322 (Cal. Ct. App. 1975).
98. Ibid., 313.
99. Ibid., 324; but compare *McConnell v. Combination Mining & Milling Co.*, 76 Pac. 194, 198 (Mont. 1904) (finding corporate political contributions to be *ultra vires*: "The [political] donation[s] . . . were clearly outside the purpose for which the corporation was created, both being for strictly political purposes").

100. Thomas W. Joo, "People of Color, Women, and the Public Corporation: Corporate Hierarchy and Racial Justice," *St. John's Law Review* 79 (2005): 955, 959 (citation omitted).
101. Joo, "Corporate Governance," 368.
102. Ann B. Matasar, *Corporate PACs and Federal Campaign Finance Laws: Use or Abuse of Power* (Westport, CT: Quorum Books, 1986), 2 (noting "U.S. history is replete with examples of corporate involvement in campaign financing and attempts by Congress to prohibit or to control this activity").
103. *McConnell v. FEC*, 251 F. Supp. 2d 176, 188 (D.D.C. 2003).
104. But see Robert E. Mutch, *Campaigns, Congress, and Courts: The Making of Federal Campaign Finance Law* (Santa Barbara, CA: Praeger Publishers, 1988), 4–8 (arguing Teddy Roosevelt was not a true reformer, but rather that he acted along with Congress in response to organized public support for reform in the wake of the scandal about political contributions from the country's biggest corporations to his campaign in the 1904 election); see also Robert E. Mutch, "Before and After *Bellotti*: The Corporate Contributions Cases," *Election Law Journal* 5 (2006): 293, 319 n. 71 (Roosevelt's contemporaneous personal letters contradicted his public pro-reform stance in 1905).
105. 40 Cong. Rec. 96 (1905).
106. See *United States v. U.S. Brewers Ass'n*, 239 F. 163 (W.D. Pa. 1916) (upholding the Tillman Act and finding "[t]hese artificial creatures [e.g., corporations] are not citizens of the United States, and, so far as the franchise is concerned, must at all times be held subservient and subordinate to the government and the citizenship of which it is composed").
107. *Burroughs v. United States*, 290 U.S. 534, 547–548 (1934) (providing Congress with broad discretion to regulate federal campaign finance); see also *United States v. Classic*, 313 U.S. 299 (1941) (allowing Congress to regulate in primaries).
108. Winkler, "Other People's Money," 928 (recounting that "the Smith-Connolly Act of 1943—popularly known as the War Labor Disputes Act . . . banned union campaign contributions for the remainder of World War II . . . [T]he Taft-Hartley Act of 1947 . . . amended the federal election law to make the union contribution ban permanent").
109. Pub. L. No. 80–101, 61 Stat. 159 (1947); see also Mutch, *Campaigns, Congress, and Courts*, 153–157 (arguing that Republicans in the 80th Congress passed Taft-Hartley to punish organized labor. Truman vetoed the bill but the Republicans joined forces with the Southern Democrats to override the veto).
110. See Mutch, *Campaigns, Congress, and Courts*, 160–163; Winkler, "Other People's Money," 931–934 (PACs were first used by unions but FECA 1971 made it clear that both unions and corporations could spend through PACs). Corporations are permitted to use general treasury funds to establish and administer SSFs, which may accept voluntary contributions from individuals and make contributions to political committees. Press Release, Fed. Election Comm'n, *FEC Confirms that Corporation may Solicit Contributions from Certain Individual Members of its Wholly Owned Subsidiaries* (February 12, 2009), http://www.fec.gov/press/press2009/20090212AO_2008–21.shtml.
111. Michael D. Holt, "Corporate Democracy and the Corporate Political Contribution," *Iowa Law Review* 61 (1975): 545; see also Alexander, *Financing Politics*, 18 (reminding us that "twenty-one companies pleaded guilty to charges—brought against them by Watergate special prosecutor Archibald Cox of making illegal corporate contributions totaling $968,000").
112. 2 USC § 441b.
113. *Buckley v. Valeo*, 424 U.S. 1 (1976).

114. Richard L. Hasen, *The Supreme Court and Election Law Judging Equality from* Baker v. Carr *to* Bush v. Gore (New York: NYU Press, 2003), 105–108.
115. Winkler, "Other People's Money," 935 ("BCRA's new limitation on corporate and union electoral activity further restricts executives' ability to use 'other people's money' by prohibiting expenditures of general treasury funds on parties or sham issue advertising campaigns").
116. Granting corporations political speech rights has been highly controversial. See Robert Monks and Peter Murray, Harvard Law School Forum on Corporate Governance and Financial Regulation, *Is the Supreme Court Determined to Expand Corporate Power?* (August 25, 2009), http://blogs.law.harvard.edu/corpgov/2009/08/25/is-the-supreme-court-determined-to-expand-corporate-power/ (arguing "[t]he notion that artificial legal entities organized to facilitate the transaction of business and the accumulation of wealth should have constitutionally protected rights that the Framers believed came to human beings from their Creator has even less credibility today than in 1978 [the year *Bellotti* was decided]").
117. *United States v. Congress of Industrial Organizations*, 335 U.S. 106, 113 (1948).
118. *First National Bank of Boston v. Bellotti*, 435 U.S. 765, 767–770, 795 (1978); see also Lloyd Hitoshi Mayer, *Breaching a Leaking Dam?: Corporate Money and Elections* (2009), 24, http://papers.ssrn.com/sol3/papers.cfm?abstract_id=1458972 (stating "[w]hile it could also be argued that investors in for-profit corporations do not, at least usually, invest because of the political stands of a for-profit corporation and so are at risk of having their funds 'hijacked' for a political activity not of their choosing, the Court in *Bellotti* rejected such concerns because it found the prohibition at issue in that case both under and over-protected shareholders").
119. Monks and Murray, *Supreme Court*, arguing "Justice Powell's discovery (or invention) of First Amendment rights for corporations in *Bellotti* let a genie out of the bottle"; Kaiser, *So Damn Much Money*, 119–120. (Noting that before Justice Powell was a member of the Supreme Court, he wrote an influential memorandum for the U.S. Chamber of Commerce, arguing "the American business executive is truly the 'forgotten man.'" Therefore, "[political] power must be assiduously cultivated; and when necessary, it must be used aggressively and with determination—without embarrassment and without the reluctance which has been so characteristic of American business." Quoting Lewis F. Powell's 1971 memorandum.); Brudney, "Business Corporations," 242 (asserting until *Bellotti*, "nothing in the Constitution was thought to restrict the state's power to forbid management from wasting corporate assets").
120. *FEC v. National Right to Work Comm.*, 459 U.S. 197, 207 (1982) (NRWC).
121. *FEC v. Massachusetts Citizens for Life, Inc.*, 479 U.S. 238, 249 (1986) (*MCFL*) ("We therefore hold that an expenditure must constitute 'express advocacy' in order to be subject to the prohibition of § 441b").
122. Ibid., 263.
123. Ibid., 257–258 (citations omitted).
124. *Austin v. Michigan Chamber of Commerce*, 494 U.S. 652, 660 (1990); see also Hasen, *Supreme Court and Election Law*, 112–114 (explaining the history of the drafting of the *Austin* opinion).
125. *Austin*, 494 U.S. at 673.
126. Ibid., 675 (citations omitted). But see Jill Fisch, "Frankenstein's Monster Hits the Campaign Trail: An Approach to Regulation of Corporate Political Expenditures," *William and Mary Law Review* 32 (1991): 587, 636 ("The

common law provides several important restrictions on corporate political speech that the Court seemed to overlook in *Austin*"; listing after-the-fact measures such as shareholder derivative suits, breach of fiduciary duty, and board elections).

127. *Austin*, 494 U.S. at 675 n. 5.
128. "Electioneering communications" are "any broadcast that refers to a candidate for federal office and is aired within 30 days of a federal primary election or 60 days of a federal general election in the jurisdiction where that candidate is running"; see 2 USC § 434(f)(3)(A).
129. *McConnell v. FEC*, 540 U.S. 93, 203 (2003).
130. 539 U.S. 146, 161 n.8, 162–63 (2003) (citations omitted).
131. The Roberts' Court invalidated Vermont's contribution and expenditure limits and invalidated BCRA's Millionaires' Amendment. See *Randall v. Sorrell*, 548 U.S. 230 (2006) and *Davis v. FEC*, 554 U. S. ___, 128 S. Ct. 2759 (2008), respectively.
132. 551 U.S. 449 (2007).
133. *Wisconsin Right to Life*, 551 U.S. at 456.
134. 540 U.S. 93 (2003).
135. *Wisconsin Right to Life*, 551 U.S. at 470.
136. Ibid., 536 ("After today, the ban on contributions by corporations and unions and the limitation on their corrosive spending when they enter the political arena are open to easy circumvention, and the possibilities for regulating corporate and union campaign money are unclear").
137. *Human Life of Wash., Inc. v. Brumsickle*, 2009 WL 62144, *17 (W.D. Wash. Jan. 8, 2009), *aff'd* 624 F.3d 990 (9th Cir. 2010) ("Because *WRTL*'s as-applied challenge was limited to the BCRA's corporate speech prohibition, it is unclear whether the opinion's logic extends to lesser burdens on non-express advocacy."); *California Pro-Life Council, Inc. v. Randolph*, 507 F.3d 1172, 1177 (9th Cir. 2007) (*WRTL II* did not reach disclosure); and *Koerber v. Federal Election Com'n*, 583 F. Supp. 2d 740, 746 (E.D.N.C. 2008) ("The *WRTL II* decision makes no mention of the disclosure requirements upheld in *McConnell*"); but see *N.C. Right to Life, Inc. v. Leake* (*NCRL III*), 525 F.3d 274, 317 (4th Cir. 2008) (Only broadcast electioneering communications can be regulated or disclosed); *Broward Coal. of Condominiums, Homeowners Assocs. & Cm'ty Orgs., Inc. v. Browning*, 2008 WL 4791004, *8 (N.D. Fla. Oct. 29, 2008) (striking down disclosure as overbroad).
138. Richard L. Hasen, "Beyond Incoherence: The Roberts Court's Deregulatory Turn in *FEC v. Wisconsin Right to Life*," *Minnesota Law Review* 92 (2008): 1064.
139. Transcript of reargument at 57–59, *Citizens United v. FEC* (September 9, 2009) (No. 08–205), http://www.supremecourtus.gov/oral_arguments/argument_transcripts/08–205 percent5BReargued percent5D.pdf.
140. *Citizens United v. FEC*, No. 08–205, slip op. (2010); Alaska Stat. § 15.13.074(f); Ariz. Const. art. XIV, § 18; Ariz. Rev. Stat. §§ 16–919(A), -920; Colo. Const. XXVIII, § 3(4)(a); Conn. Gen. Stat. § 9–613(a); Iowa Code § 68A.503; Ky. Rev. Stat. § 121.150(20); Mass. Gen. L. ch. 55, § 8; Mich. C. L. S. § 169.254(1); Minn. Stat. § 211B.15; Mont. Code Ann. § 13–35–227; N.C. Gen. Stat. §§ 163–278.15,-278.19; N.D. Cent. Code § 16.1–08.1–03.3; Ohio Rev. Code Ann. § 3599.03(A)(1); Okla. Stat. tit. 21, § 187.2 ch. 62, Appx., 257: 10–1–2(d); 25 Pa. Stat. § 3253(a); R.I. Gen. Laws § 17–25–10.1(h), (j); S.D. Codified Laws § 12–27–18 2a; Tenn. Code Ann. § 2–19–132; Tex. Elec. Code § 253.094; W. Va. Code § 3–8–8; Wis. Stat. § 11.38; Wyo. Stat. § 22–25–102(a).
141. *Bellotti*, 435 U.S. at 793–794; for a contrary view, see Daniel Greenwood, "Should Corporations Have First Amendment Rights," *Seattle University*

Law Review 30 (2007): 875, 875 (arguing that "[c]orporations are the wrong sort of thing to have speech rights").

142. 551 U.S. 177 (2007).
143. Ibid.
144. Ibid., 187.
145. Ibid.
146. Ibid. (emphasis in original).
147. *Davenport v. Wash. Educ. Ass'n*, 551 U.S. 177, 187 (2007).
148. Ibid.
149. Ibid., 191. The concurring opinion stated that these arguments about shareholder protection should be addressed by the lower courts first.
150. *Citizens United v. FEC*, No. 08–205, slip op. at 46, 55 (2010).
151. This is with the exception of Louisiana and Missouri corporations, which do require board approval of political expenditures. See note 16.
152. Ruth Marcus, "'Judicial Activism' on Campaign Finance Law," *Real Clear Politics* (August 3, 2009), http://www.realclearpolitics.com/articles/2009/08/03/judicial_activism_on_campaign_finance_law_97746.html (arguing "[w]e don't want Wal-Mart—at least I don't—using its purchasing power to buy elections, and we don't want Wal-Mart funneling money to a nonprofit proxy").
153. Supplemental Brief of Committee for Economic Development as Amicus Curiae in Support of Appellee, *Citizens United v. FEC*, No. 08–205 at 11 (2009).
154. See Bruce F. Freed and John C. Richardson, *Green Canary: Altering Shareholders and Protecting Their Investments* (2005), 7, http://www.politicalaccountability.net/index.php?ht=a/GetDocumentAction/i/920. The report includes case studies on companies that collapsed for various reasons, and whose large political contributions may have contributed to the collapse and/or signaled unsound business management and practices.
155. Ibid., 22.
156. Ibid.
157. Ibid., 28.
158. Bruce F. Freed and Jamie Carroll, *Open Windows: How Codes of Conduct Regulate Corporate Political Spending and A Model Code to Protect Company Interests and Shareholder Value* (March 2007), 19–29, http://www.politicalaccountability.net/index.php?ht=a/GetDocumentAction/i/611.
159. See ibid., 17.
160. See generally ibid., 11–16.
161. Susannah Goodman, *Common Cause, Mutual Protection: Why Mutual Funds Should Embrace Disclosure of Corporate Political Contributions* (2005), 6, http://www.commoncause.org/atf/cf/ percent7B8A2D1D15–C65A-46D4–8CBB-2073440751B5 percent7D/MUTUAL percent20FUND percent20REPORT percent202–15–05.PDF (a model resolution drafted by the CPA was filed at more than twenty-five companies by several pension funds).
162. Press Release, CPA, *New Companies Bring Political Disclosure to Nearly Half of Trendsetting S&P 100*, http://www.politicalaccountability.net/index.php?ht=a/GetDocumentAction/i/2636.
163. New York Stock Exchange, *Listings Directory* (2009), http://www.nyse.com/about/listed/lc_all_overview.html (noting 3908 US companies are listed on the NYSE).
164. Dana Gold, Solange E. Bitol-Hansen, Charlie Cray, and Bruce Freed, "Protecting the Polity: Strategies for Reform," *Seattle University Law Review* 30 (2007): 991, 1008.

165. See Jill Fisch, "How Do Corporations Play Politics? The Fedex Story," *Vanderbilt Law Review* 58 (2005): 1495, 1565. ("It may also be desirable to incorporate political activity into the disclosure requirements applicable to publicly-traded companies under the federal securities laws. In addition to enabling shareholders to monitor the activities of a corporation's officers and directors, and thereby to police against possible waste or self-dealing, such disclosure would integrate information on political activity with a firm's reporting on the business operations to which the firm's political participation relates.")
166. *Citizens United v. FEC*, No. 08–205, slip op. (2010).
167. Certain authors in Britain have argued corporations should not be able to make political expenditures. Austin Mitchell and Prem Sikka, *Association for Accountancy & Business Affairs, Taming the Corporation* (2005), visar.csustan.edu/aaba/TamingtheCorporations.pdf (arguing "[c]ompanies should be banned from making any political donations to individual politicians or parties").
168. Political Parties, Elections and Referendums Act, §§ 139–140, and sched. 19 (see note 26); see also Explanatory Notes to Political Parties, Elections and Referendums Act (2000), c. 41, http://www.opsi.gov.uk/ACTS/acts2000/en/ukpgaen_20000041_en_1. The Companies Act was amended again in 2006. As a result of the 2006 amendments, donations to trade unions are exempt. In addition, directors are jointly and severally liable for any unauthorized political expenditures plus interest. Companies Act, c. 46, §§ 369, 374 (see note 87); see also Companies Act 2006 Regulatory Assessment (2007), http://www.berr.gov.uk/files/file29937.pdf.
169. Aileen Walker, "Parliament and Constitution Centre House of Commons Library," *The Political Parties, Elections and Referendums Bill—Donations* (January 7, 2000), 9, http://www.parliament.uk/commons/lib/research/rp2000/rp00–002.pdf.
170. Home Department, *The Funding of Political Parties in the United Kingdom: The Government's Proposals for Legislation in Response to the Fifth Report of the Committee on Standards in Public Life 1999–2000*, http://www.archive.official-documents.co.uk/document/cm44/4413/4413–00.htm.
171. Committee on Standards in Public Life, *The Funding of Political Parties in the United Kingdom* (1998), iii, http://www.archive.official-documents.co.uk/document/cm40/4057/volume-1/volume-1.pdf.
172. Ibid., 86.
173. Political Parties, Elections and Referendums Act, § 140 (see note 26); see also Electoral Commission, *Guidance to Companies: Political Donations and Lending* (2007), http://www.electoralcommission.org.uk/__data/assets/electoral_commission_pdf_file/0014/13703/Companies-Guidance-Final1_27776-20443__E__N__S__W__.pdf.
174. The original reporting threshold in the 2000 law was £200. The amount was later raised to £2,000 in 2007 under secondary legislation, the British equivalent of American implementing regulations. See Department for Business Enterprise and Regulatory Reform, *Government Response to Consultation on the Companies Act 2006—Accounting and Reporting Regulations* (2007), http://www.berr.gov.uk/files/file40480.doc.
175. Companies Act, § 378 (see note 87); see also Companies Act 2006: Explanatory Notes (2006), http://www.opsi.gov.uk/acts/acts2006/en/ukpgaen_20060046_en.pdf.
176. Political Parties, Elections and Referendums Act, §§ 139–140, & sched. 19 (see note 26).
177. Companies Act, § 369 (see note 87); see also Travers Smith, *The Companies Act 2006: Political Donation*(2007), 3, http://www.traverssmith.com/

assets/pdf/Legal_Briefings/companies_act_2006_-_political_donations_-_nov_2007.pdf.

178. The Companies (Interest Rate for Unauthorised Political Donation or Expenditure) Regulations 2007, Statutory Instruments 2007 No. 2242 (July 25, 2007), http://www.opsi.gov.uk/si/si2007/uksi_20072242_en_1.
179. See as examples, AstraZeneca, *Directors' Report: Business Review: Corporate Governance: Other Matters*, http://www.astrazeneca-annualreports.com/2007/business_review/governance/other_matters.asp (reporting, "In 2007, AstraZeneca's US legal entities made contributions amounting in aggregate to $321,645 [2006 $416,675] to state political party committees and to campaign committees of various state candidates affiliated with the major parties"); National Grid, *Directors' Report for the Year Ended 31 March 2007* (May 16, 2007), http://www.nationalgrid.com/annualreports/2007/06_dir_reports/dir_report.html. (Reporting, "National Grid USA and certain subsidiaries made political donations of $100,000 [£52,289] during the year. National Grid USA's political action committees, funded partly by voluntary employee contributions, gave $149,709 [£78,282] to political and campaign committees in 2006/07.")
180. Patrick Hosking, "Business Big Shot: Peter Buckley of Caledonia Investments," *The Times*, May 30, 2008, http://business.timesonline.co.uk/tol/business/movers_and_shakers/article4029538.ece.
181. Press Release, Labour Research Department, *Tories Still Get Corporate Millions* (June 2, 2001), http://www.lrd.org.uk/issue.php?pagid=1&issueid=362 ("[t]he Conservative Party has received a total of £1.74 million in company donations since the last election from 62 companies . . . just 12 corporate donations [went] to Labour totalling £191,500"); Labour Research Department, "Party Funding," *Labour Research* 11 (October 2003), http://www.lrd.org.uk/db/downloads/lr0310.pdf (companies gave £1,161,644 to the Conservative Party and £245,690 to the Labour Party in the 2002–2003 election cycle).
182. Lisa E. Klien, "On the Brink of Reform: Political Party Funding in Britain," *Case Western Reserve Journal of International Law* 31 (1999): 1, 13.
183. Committee on Standards in Public Life, Fifth Report § 6.31 (vol. 1 1998) ("CSPL Report I") (noting £47,000 from the Caparo Group, £30,000 from GLC Limited, and £21,000 from the Mirror Group for the Labour Party).
184. Committee on Standards in Public Life, Fifth Report at 52, ¶ 597 (vol. 2 1998) ("CSPL Report II").
185. Press Release, Labour Research Department, *Tory Donations Take a Dive* (November 19, 1998), http://www.lrd.org.uk/issue.php?pagid=1&issueid=330.
186. See note 181.
187. See The Co-operative Group, *Annual Report and Accounts 2008* (2008), 36, http://www.co-operative.coop/Corporate/PDFs/Annual_Report_2008.pdf ("[i]n 2008 an annual subscription of £476,000 [2007: £646,103] was made to the Co-operative Party").
188. Michael Pinto-Duschinsky, "British Party Funding 1913–87," *Parliamentary Affairs* (April 1989): 210 (listing as £50,000 or over donors: George Weston Holdings, British and Commonwealth Holdings, Taylor Woodrow, Rugarth Investment Trust, Hanson Trust, P & O, United Biscuits, Allied Lyons, Trafalgar House, Plessey, Whitbread, Consolidated Goldfields, Racal, Guardian Royal Exchange, Sun Alliance, Willis Faber, Hambros, General Accident, Newarthill, Trust House Forte, Baring, British Airways, General Electric, Glaxo Holdings, Rolls Royce, Royal Insurance, Unigate, and Williams Holdings).
189. For example, the resolution passed at AstraZeneca stated the company could "make donations to political parties; and make donations to political

organisations other than political parties; and incur political expenditure; not exceed[ing] $250,000." AstraZeneca, *AstraZeneca Notice Of Annual General Meeting 2009 and Shareholders' Circular* (2009), 6, http://www.astrazeneca.com/_mshost3690701/content/resources/media/investors/2009–AGM/AZ_NoM_EN.pdf. Other companies had far more modest political budgets. See, for example, 3i Group PLC, *Notice of Annual General Meeting 2007* (2007), 2, http://www.3igroup.com/pdf/AGM_-_notice_of_AGM_2007.pdf (requesting a political budget of £12,000 for a subsidiary); Balfour Beatty, *Annual General Meeting 2009 and Separate Class Meeting of Preference Shareholders*, (2009), 4, http://www.balfourbeatty.com/bby/investors/shinfo/agm/2009/agm09.pdf (requesting a political budget of £25,000 for the coming year).

190. BP PLC, *Notice of BP Annual General Meeting 2007* (2007), 10, http://www.bp.com/liveassets/bp_internet/globalbp/STAGING/home_assets/IC_SHMV07_BP_notice_of_meeting_2007.pdf.
191. British American Tobacco, *Annual General Meeting 2009* (2009), 5, http://www.bat.com/group/sites/uk__3mnfen.nsf/vwPagesWebLive/DO57YMK7/$FILE/medMD7QJMDX.pdf?openelement ("[a]t its Annual General Meeting in April 2005, the Company was given authority to make donations to EU political organisations and incur EU political expenditure . . . for a period of four years and was subject to caps of £1 million on donations to EU political organisations and £1 million on political expenditure during that period").
192. Northumbrian Water Group PLC, *Notice of Annual General Meeting 2007* (2007), 2, http://www.nwg.co.uk/agmnotice07.pdf.
193. ITV PLC, *Report and Accounts 2008* (2008), 44, 2008.itv.ar.ry.com/action/printBasket/?sectionId=26443; see also Tesco PLC, Regulatory News, 30/06/2008, http://www.tescoplc.com/plc/ir/rns/rnsitem?id=1214847200nRn3d9573X&t=popup_rns. "During the year, the Group made contributions of £45,023 (2007—£41,608) in the form of sponsorship for political events: Labour Party £13,040; Liberal Democrat Party £5,850; Conservative Party £5,786; Scottish Labour Party £500; Scottish National Party £2,000; Fine Gael £1,397; Plaid Cymru £450; trade unions £16,000.
194. Caledonia Investments PLC, *Letter from the Chairman and Notice of 2008 Annual General Meeting* (2008), 9, http://www.caledonia.com/docs/AGM08.pdf; see also Caledonia Investments PLC, *Caledonia Investments PLC: Results of Annual General Meeting* (2008), 1, http://www.caledonia.com/docs/Result percent20of percent20AGM percent202008.pdf; Richard Wachman, "Caledonia Set for Revolt on Plan to Donate to the Tories," *The Observer*, July 19, 2009, http://www.guardian.co.uk/business/2009/jul/19/caledonia-investments-political-donations-pirc.
195. British Airways, *2008/09 Annual Report and Accounts* (2009), 57, http://www.britishairways.com/cms/global/microsites/ba_reports0809/pdfs/BA_AR_2008_09.pdf.
196. HMV Group PLC, *Annual Report and Accounts 2009* (2009), 42, http://www.hmvgroup.com/files/1302/HMV_final1.pdf.
197. Burberry Group PLC, *Annual Report 2008/09* (2009), 57, http://smartpdf.blacksunplc.com/burberry2008–09ara/Burberry_2008–09_AnnualReport.pdf.
198. GlaxoSmithKline, *Political Contributions Policy* (2009), 2, http://www.gsk.com/about/corp-gov/Policy-Political-Contributions.pdf.
199. Cadbury PLC, *Annual Report & Accounts 2008* (2009), 55, http://cadburyar2008.production.investis.com/~/media/Files/C/cadbury-ar-2008/pdf/cadbury_ra_13mb_compressed.ashx.

200. See South Yorkshire Pensions Authority, *South Yorkshire Pension Fund Corporate Governance Policy : Voting Guidelines* (2005), 3, http://www.southyorks.gov.uk/embedded_object.asp?docid=1397&doclib (stating the pension's policy is to "[v]ote against all resolutions to approve political donations as this is an inappropriate use of shareholder funds"); London Borough of Bexley Pension Fund, *Statement of Investment Principles* (2008), 35, http://www.yourpension.org.uk/Agencies/Bexley/docs/pdf/SIP percent2008.pdf (stating "[i]t is inappropriate for a company to make such [political] donations"); London Borough of Sutton Pension Fund, *Statement of Investment Principles*, http://www.sutton.gov.uk/CHttpHandler.ashx?id=876&p=0 (stating, "We normally consider any political donations to be a mis-use of shareholders' funds and will vote against resolutions proposing them").
201. See notes 189, 191, 193.
202. See West Midlands Pension Fund, *Corporate Governance Proxy Voting Activity* (2004), 1–2, http://www.wmpfonline.com/pdfs/activity0604_0804.pdf.
203. Ben Webster, "Unhappy Landing for MPs' Parking Perk," *The Times*, July 28, 2004, https://www.timesonline.co.uk/article/0,,2–1193813,00.html.
204. Ibid.
205. See BAA PLC, *Annual Report 2004/05* (2005), 47, http://www.heathrowairport.com/assets//B2CPortal/Staticpercent20Files/BAAAnnualReport2004–05.pdf.
206. Joo, "Modern Corporation," 94 (citation omitted).
207. Press Release, CPA, *Shareholders See Risky Corporate Political Behavior as Threat to Shareholder Value, Demand Reform, CPA Poll Finds* (April 5, 2006), http://www.politicalaccountability.net/index.php?ht=a/GetDocumentAction/i/1267. (Announcing a "poll found a striking 85 percent [of shareholders] agreed that the 'lack of transparency and oversight in corporate political activity encourages behavior' that threatens shareholder value. 94 percent supported disclosure and 84 percent backed board oversight and approval of 'all direct and indirect [company] political spending.'")
208. CED, *Rebuilding Corporate Leadership: How Directors Can Link Long-Term Performance with Public Goals* (2009), 18, http://www.ced.org/images/library/reports/corporate_governance/cgpt3.pdf (citing Carolyn Mathiasen, "2008 Preview: Social Issues," *RiskMetrics Risk & Governance Blog*, March 28, 2008, http://blog.riskmetrics.com/2008/03/2008_preview_social_issuessubm.html).
209. Timothy Smith and Bruce Freed, "Social Investment—Highlights from 2006 Proxy Season," *GreenMoneyJournal.com*, October 10, 2006, http://www.politicalaccountability.net/index.php?ht=d/ArticleDetails/i/373.
210. Ibid.
211. Jeanne Cummings, "Companies Try to Clean Up Their Act," *Politico*, March 24, 2009, http://www.politico.com/news/stories/0309/20401.html.
212. Francesco Guerrera, "Investors Want Facts on Political Donations," *Financial Times*, April 1, 2007, http://www.politicalaccountability.net/index.php?ht=d/ArticleDetails/i/532.
213. CPA, *Key Proxy Advisor Recommends Vote against AT&T Management on Political Contributions Disclosure* (April 21, 2008), http://www.politicalaccountability.net/index.php?ht=a/GetDocumentAction/i/1275.
214. Shareholder Resolution filed by Trillium Asset Management Corporation Requesting Political Contributions by Ford Motor Company (2010), http://www.onlineethicalinvestor.org/eidb/wc.dll?eidbproc~reso~9143 (asking for semi-annual reporting on Ford's political expenditures).
215. Lisa M. Fairfax, "The Future of Shareholder Democracy," *Indiana Law Journal* 84 (Fall 2009): 1259, 1262 n. 11. ("Shareholders also have the

right to sell their shares. This so-called exit right has been viewed by some as particularly important because it facilitates the market for corporate control by enabling the displacement of poorly performing managers. . . . However, scholars have pointed out that the market for corporate control is imperfect. . . . noting that even when shareholders sell their shares and attendant voting rights, management often remains in power." Internal citations omitted.)

216. Joo, "Modern Corporation," 57–58; see also 67–68 ("[t]he law should communicate society's disapproval of the mercenary view by rejecting the presumption that shareholders always value wealth above their political preferences"; citation omitted).
217. Stephen M. Bainbridge is a Professor of Law at UCLA School of Law.
218. Stephen M. Bainbridge, "The Creeping Federalization of Corporate Law," *Regulation* 26 (Spring 2003), http://ssrn.com/abstract=389403; see also Harvard Law Professor Mark J. Roe, "Delaware's Competition," *Harvard Law Review* 117 (2003): 588, 592. ("Federal authorities reverse state corporate law that they dislike and leave standing laws that they tolerate. State power is to jigger the rules in the middle by adopting those rules that Washington does not gear up to reverse.")
219. Professor Law and Director, Center on Federalism and Intersystemic Governance, Emory Law School.
220. Robert B. Ahdieh, "From 'Federalization' to 'Mixed Governance' in Corporate Law: A Defense of Sarbanes Oxley," *Buffalo Law Review* 53 (2005): 721, 731.
221. See Ahdieh, "From 'Federalization,'" 724 ("[t]he brief congressional debate over the Sarbanes-Oxley Act only cursorily addressed issues of corporate governance"). See also Roberta Romano, "The Sarbanes-Oxley Act and the Making of Quack Corporate Governance," *Yale Law Journal* 114 (2005): 1521, 1549–1556 (discussing the lack of debate in both chambers).
222. See H.R. Rep. No. 107–414 (statement of Ron Paul).
223. Ibid.
224. In one case, the defendant health insurance company executive raised an unsuccessful vagueness challenge to the criminal penalties in 18 U.S.C.S. § 1350, which penalizes executives who "willfully certify" a periodic financial report knowing that the report does not comply with the act's requirements. See *United States v. Scrushy*, 2004 U.S. Dist. LEXIS 23820 (N.D. Ala. Nov. 23, 2004). In the second case, the plaintiffs brought a facial challenge to the constitutionality Public Company Accounting Oversight Board, created by Sarbanes-Oxley but classified as a nonprofit rather than a governmental agency; see 15 U.S.C.S. 7211(b), as a violation of the Appointments Clause and the separation of powers. *Free Enter. Fund v. Public Co. Accounting Oversight Bd.*, 537 F.3d 667 (D.C. Cir. 2008). The challenge was rejected by both the district and appellate courts and is currently before the U.S. Supreme Court. See *Free Enter. Fund v. Public Co. Accounting Oversight Bd.*, 129 S. Ct. 2378 (2009) (granting certiorari).
225. E. Norman Veasey is a retired chief justice of the Delaware Supreme Court.
226. E. Norman Veasey, "What Would Madison Think? The Irony of the Twists and Turns of Federalism," *Delaware Journal of Corporate Law* 34 (2009): 35, 43; quoting Roberta Romano, *The Genius of American Corporate Law*, ed. Christopher C. DeMuth (Washington, DC: AEI Press, 1993), 5.
227. See Ahdieh, "From 'Federalization,'" 736 ("[t]here is, for the most part, a national corporate law in the United States; it is simply enacted by the state of Delaware"); Mark Roe, "Delaware's Competition," *Harvard Law Review* 117 (2003): 588, 592.

228. See Ahdieh, "From 'Federalization,'" 740 (those critical of "federalization" "must either rest on a generalized claim of the efficiency of a market dynamic or mean nothing at all").
229. *Citizens United v. FEC*, No. 08–205, slip op. at 46 (2010) (arguing there is "little evidence of abuse that cannot be corrected by shareholders through the procedures of corporate democracy").
230. Ibid., 55.
231. Press Release, CPA, *New Companies Bring Political Disclosure to Nearly Half of Trendsetting S&P 100*, http://www.politicalaccountability.net/index.php?ht=a/GetDocumentAction/i/2636.
232. New York Stock Exchange, *Listings Directory* (2009), http://www.nyse.com/about/listed/lc_all_overview.html (noting 3908 U.S. companies are listed on the NYSE).
233. *Citizens United v. FEC*, slip op. at 55: "With the advent of the Internet, prompt disclosure of expenditures can provide shareholders and citizens with the information needed to hold corporations and elected officials accountable for their positions and supporters. Shareholders can determine whether their corporation's political speech advances the corporation's interest in making profits."
234. Testimony of Ciara Torres-Spelliscy Counsel at the Brennan Center for Justice at NYU School of Law before the Committee on House Administration U.S. House of Representatives (February 3, 2010), http://cha.house.gov/UserFiles/282_testimony.pdf.
235. This model legislation may have to be adapted for use in particular legislative context.
236. This model legislation may have to be adapted for use in particular legislative context.
237. Political Parties, Elections and Referendums Act, §140, & sched. 19 (see note 26).
238. Ibid., sched. 19.
239. Companies Act, § 369 (see note 87).

Contributors

Simon Babbs is Head of Quantitative Risk Management at the Options Clearing Corporation, where he is responsible for the analytics for computing margin requirements. Babbs has put forward a new methodology for determining the size of the OCC's Clearing Fund. Simon began his career at the Bank of England, where he worked in their Mathematical Techniques Group and in Banking Supervision. After specializing in quantitative research in British banks, he headed both the derivatives research and quantitative risk management functions at Bank One. He set up a new strategy at a Chicago-based hedge fund, before joining OCC in October 2007. He has published numerous articles in refereed academic finance journals and other publications. He holds an MA in Mathematics from Oxford University and a PhD in Economics from London University.

Kurt Desender is Affiliated Professor at the Universitat Pompeu Fabra (Barcelona) and at the Universitat Autònoma of Barcelona (UAB). He is currently a PhD candidate in the Department of Business Economics at UAB. His research interests include corporate governance, business economics and risk management, and his research has been published in the *American Journal of Economics and Sociology*.

Beatriz Fernández has been Assistant Professor of Finance and Mathematics at Universidad de Valladolid since 1996. She obtained her PhD Degree in Business Administration at the University of Valladolid. She has published in Behavioral Finance, which is her main research topic. She is a member of the European Academy of Business Administration.

Kathy Fogel, PhD (University of Alberta), is Assistant Professor of Finance at the Sam Walton College of Business, University of Arkansas, Fayetteville, AR. Her research interests include corporate governance, institutional economics, and entrepreneurial finance. Her work focuses on corporate control systems around the world and the interactions between firms' economic behaviors and their external environment comprised of legal and political systems; government and regulatory policies; and the competitive markets of capital, labor, and products.

Teresa García-Merino holds a PhD from the University of Valladolid in Spain. She is currently Associate Professor of strategy at that university, where she teaches courses in management principles and strategic management. Her research concerns strategic management and managerial cognition. She has published widely in scientific journals: *Organization Studies*, *Technovation*, *Journal of Scholarly Publishing*, *Leadership and Organization Development*, and *Journal of Change Management*. By demand, she referees in several journals: *Technological Forecasting and Social Change*, *Baltic Journal of Management*, *Leadership and Organization Development Journal*, and *Management Decision*. She has also participated as a reviewer in international conferences.

Erik Gerding joined the UNM law faculty in 2006 after practicing in the New York and Washington, DC offices of Cleary Gottlieb Steen and Hamilton LLP. His practice at the firm included representing clients in securities offerings, financings, mergers and acquisitions and joint ventures, with a particular focus on cross-border transactions. He also advised clients on securities regulatory and enforcement matters. At the UNM School of Law, Professor Gerding teaches business law courses, including business associations and commercial law, as well as law and economics. Gerding's research interests include securities, banking, and other financial regulation; corporate governance; and community economic development. For the last several years, he has been working on projects involving securities and corporate law during asset price bubbles and periods of market volatility. His current writing and teaching focuses on the causes and cures of the subprime mortgage crisis.

Kevin Govern, Assistant Professor of Law, began his legal career as an Army Judge Advocate. He served twenty years at every echelon during peacetime and war in worldwide assignments involving every legal discipline. He has also served as an Assistant Professor of Law at the United States Military Academy, and currently teaches at Ave Maria School of Law and California University of Pennsylvania. He has published widely and spoken frequently on national security and homeland security law, international, comparative and Islamic law, contracts law, criminal law and corrections law, military operations, and professional ethics. He received a Bachelor of Arts and a Juris Doctor from Marquette University, a Master of Laws with International and Operational Law Specialization from the Judge Advocate Generals School, and a Master of Laws in International and Comparative Law from the University of Notre Dame.

Long Kang is an econometrician at Quantitative Risk Management of the Options Clearing Corporation in Chicago. He received his PhD in economics from Indiana University Bloomington. His research interests include financial econometrics, empirical finance, and monetary economics. He received his MA degree from Humboldt University of Berlin, Germany, and BA degree from Huazhong University of Science and Technology, China.

Yu Flora Kuang, Assistant Professor of Accounting at VU University Amsterdam, obtained her PhD from Tilburg University in 2007. Her research interests are executive compensation, corporate governance, CEO turnover, and earnings management. She has published papers on academic journals including *Journal of Business, Finance and Accounting, British Accounting Review*; and practitioner journals including *Management, Control and Accounting (Journal for Financial Executives).*

Abol Jalilvand is Professor of Finance and Marotta Chair in Free Enterprise at the School of Business Administration, Loyola University Chicago. Formerly, he has served as Dean at two major U.S. and Canadian universities: Dalhousie University, Canada, and Loyola University Chicago, USA. His scholarly work in corporate debt structure, risk management, sovereign debt and international capital flows, mergers and acquisitions, corporate restructuring and initial public offerings have appeared in top refereed journals. Professionally, he has been Editor-in-Chief, *Canadian Journal of Administrative Science*, and President, AACSB Mid-Continent East Division. He has testified on behalf of public and private companies on fair rate-of-return on equity and asset valuation before regulatory agencies. He has also been a turn-around consultant in the higher education field. Dr. Jalilvand received his Ph.D. in Finance from the University of North Carolina at Chapel Hill, a MBA from Oklahoma State University and a B.A. in Banking from the Iranian Institute of Banking.

Esteban Lafuente (MBA and PhD) is Professor at the Fundació Universitat Autònoma de Barcelona (UAB) and he also serves as CEO and researcher in the Romanian Centre for Entrepreneurship and Business Research (CEBR). His research interests include corporate governance, business economics, entrepreneurship, and efficiency analysis. His research documents have been published in *Regional Studies, British Journal of Management, Entrepreneurship and Regional Development*, and *Sociologia Ruralis*.

Yuki Masujima is an economist at the Bank of Japan (BOJ). Before joining the BOJ, he served as a consultant at the World Bank Jakarta Office (2007) and at the Development Economics Research Group (2008–2010). He also worked as an associate at the Nomura Trust and Banking

(1996–2002). His research focuses on international finance, particularly banking, capital markets, financial sector development, and their relation to macroeconomic and financial shocks. Mr. Masujima is a PhD candidate at Brandeis International Business School and earned an MS in International Economics and Finance. He also received an MA in International Development at the International University of Japan, and a BA in Economics at Keio University.

A.G. (Tassos) Malliaris is currently Professor of Economics and Finance and holds the Walter F. Mullady Sr. Chair in Business Administration at Loyola University Chicago. He has authored and co-authored numerous articles in professional journals and has also co-authored with William A. Brock two books on *Stochastic Methods in Economics* and Fin*ance and also Differential Equations, Stability and Chaos in Dynamic Economics.* Another of his books on *Foundations of Futures Markets* was published in 1999. His most recent book is on *Economic Uncertainty, Instabilities and Asset Bubbles*, published by World Scientific. He specializes in financial economics and has made several contributions in the area of futures markets, options markets and risk management. Malliaris is President of the Multinational Finance Society, the Athenian Policy Forum and Past-President of the North American Economic and Finance Association. He has a B.A. in economics from the Athens University of Economics and Business, a Ph.D. in economics from the University of Oklahoma and a second Ph.D. in mathematics from the University of Chicago. He is on the board of directors and a member of investments committees in several organizations and editor or Associate editor in five journals.

Rosa Mayoral obtained her bachelor's degree in Economics and Actuarial Science at the University of Barcelona in 1992. That year she got a Research grant from the Catalonia Regional Government and held posts at the Economic, Financial, and Actuarial Mathematics Department of the University of Barcelona since 1992 until 1998. She earned a PhD in Economics in 1997. Since 1998, she has been Associate Professor of Finance and Accounting at the University of Valladolid where she lectures on Actuarial Mathematics. Her early work was in the area of stochastic valuation models applied to the finance and actuarial fields. More recently her research has focused on Solvency II, Real Options, and Behavioral Finance. She has been director of the Annals of the Spanish Actuaries Institute and acts as regular reviewer in the *Spanish Review of Finance and Accounting.*

Richard McGowan, S.J., is a Professor of the Carroll School of Management and the Economics Department at Boston College. The focus of his research is on the interaction of the Business and Public Policy processes. Professor McGowan has published six books with the latest, entitled *The Gambling Debate*, published by Greenwood Press. He is currently working on books on the privatization process (April 2010) and microfoundations of economic development.

Peter O. Mülbert, Professor of Corporation Law, Capital Market Law, and Banking Law, and Director of the Center for German and International Law of Financial Services, Johannes Gutenberg-Universität, Mainz; member, Panel of Financial Services Experts of the Committee on Economic and Monetary Affairs of the European Parliament; member, Administrative Protest Committee of the Federal Financial Supervisory Authority; Research Fellow, European Corporate Governance Institute; management board, Bankrechtliche Vereinigung e.V—wissenschaftliche Gesellschaft für Bankrecht e.V.; coeditor, "Zeitschrift für das gesamte Handelsrecht und Wirtschaftsrecht"; coeditor, "Neue Zeitschrift für Gesellschaftsrecht"; advisory board, "Wertpapiermitteilungen"; 1976–1981, studies at the Universities of Tübingen and Genf; 1984, doctorate in Law, University of Tübingen; 1994, Habilitation, University of Munich; 1994–present, Professor of Law, Universities of Heidelberg, Trier, and Mainz; visiting professor, Harvard Law School, 2007, University of Tokyo, 2009; books and articles on corporation law, groups of corporation, capital market law, banking law.

Bo Qin, Assistant Professor of Accounting at University of Groningen, obtained his PhD from the same university in 2010. His research interests are executive compensation, corporate governance, and financial reporting quality. He has published papers in academic journals including *British Accounting Review*, and practitioner journals including *Management, Control and Accounting (Journal for Financial Executives).*

Valle Santos holds a PhD from the University of Valladolid (Spain). She is currently Associate Professor at that university, where she teaches courses on strategic management. Her research concerns strategic management, organizational evolution, and cognitive biases. She has published in *Management Decision*, *Organization Studies*, *Technovation*, *Leadership and Organization Development Journal*, *Management International*, *Management Research News*, *Revista de Empresa*, *Cuadernos de Economía y Dirección de Empresa*, and *International Journal of Information Management.* She acts as regular reviewer in national and international conferences as well as in journals: *Journal of Business Environment*, *Cuadernos de Economía y Dirección de Empresa, Revista Europea de Dirección y Economía de la Empresa*; *Leadership and Organization Development Journal*; *Journal of Administrative and Social Sciences.*

Yingying Shao is Assistant Professor of Finance at the College of Business and Economics, Towson University, Towson, MD. Her research interests include financial intermediations, risk management, institutions, and emerging markets. Her current work includes understanding the impact of financial innovations on the stability of financial systems, and how institutions affect financial and economic decisions and outcome.

Ralf Steinhauser, PhD (University of California, Berkeley), is a Research Fellow in the Research School of Economics at the Australian National University. His research interests include Environmental and Behavioral Economics, Applied Econometrics, and Corporate Social Responsibility. His current work focuses on the intersection of Behavioral Economics and Environmental Economics, using findings from Psychology and Economics to inform efficient policy inducing a desired environmental behavior.

Ciara Torres-Spelliscy is an Assistant Professor of Law at Stetson University College of Law. Previously, she was Counsel for the Democracy Program at the Brennan Center for Justice at NYU School of Law, working on campaign finance reform and fair courts. She is the coauthor along with Ari Weisbard of "What Albany Could Learn from New York City: A Model of Meaningful Campaign Finance Reform in Action," *Albany Government Law Review* 1 (2008): 194; *Electoral Competition and Low Contribution Limits* (2009), with coauthors Kahlil Williams and Dr. Thomas Stratmann; and *Improving Judicial Diversity* (2008), with coauthors Monique Chase and Emma Greenman, which was republished by Thompson West Reuters in *Women and the Law* (2009). Ms. Torres-Spelliscy has been published in the *New York Law Journal*, *Roll Call*, *BusinessWeek*, *Forbes*, Salon.com, CNN.com and the *ABA Judges Journal*. She has also been quoted by the media in *The Economist*, *The National Journal*, Sirius Radio, and NPR. She provides constitutional and legislative guidance to lawmakers who are drafting bills. Before joining Stetson, she worked as a corporate associate at the law firm of Arnold and Porter LLP and was a staff member of Senator Richard Durbin.

Eleuterio Vallelado is Associate Professor of Finance at Universidad de Valladolid. Born in Laguna de Duero (Spain), he obtained his bachelor's degree in Economics and Business and his PhD at the University of Valladolid and MBA from New York University. He has published widely in corporate finance, banking and behavioral finance areas. He has authored several books, and his articles can be found in *Journal of Banking and Finance*, *Applied Economics*, *Financial Review*, *Abante*, *Spanish Review of Finance and Accounting*, *Cuadernos de Economía y Dirección de Empresas*, among others. His research interest include: corporate finance, corporate governance in banks, and behavioral finance.

P.M. Vasudev is a Senior Lecturer in the Business School of the University of Auckland, New Zealand. Mr. Vasudev switched to academia recently after having practiced law in Bangalore, India, for many years. He has been at the University of Auckland since January 2008. His main research interests include corporate governance, capital markets, securities regulation, and the philosophy of law. Mr. Vasudev's current research projects include the origin and development of the stakeholder principle in corporate governance; the financial markets and their institutional position in the society; and economic pursuits and human life.

John Winn is an Associate Professor of Business Law at the Harry F. Byrd, Jr. School of Business at Shenandoah University in Winchester, Virginia. Professor Winn also served in the Army Judge Advocate General's Corps from 1985 through 2005. He has a B.A. in History from Guilford College (1981), J.D. from Campbell University (1984), and LL.M from the Judge Advocate General's School (1993). He is also a graduate of Army Command and General Staff College (1996) and is admitted to practice in North Carolina, the Court of Appeals for the Armed Forces, and United States Supreme Court.

Ghislain Yanou teaches finance at Paris-1 University and SciencesPo., Paris. His research interests are behavioral finance, asset allocation, portfolio management, risk management, and information theory. He has been a Research Fellow at the Economic Department of Brown University and is a member of the American Finance Association. Ghislain serves as a referee for several journals. Ghislain also has experience in the financial industry. He received an MS in Telecommunication from a "Grande Ecole d'Ingénieur," an MS in Economics and Finance and his BE in Mathematics at Paris-1 University in France, where he is close to defending his PhD in Finance.

Timothy Yeager is Associate Professor at the Sam Walton College of Business, University of Arkansas, Fayetteville, AR. He also serves as the Arkansas Bankers Association Chair. Prior to joining the University in January 2006, he was an Assistant Vice President over the Supervisory Policy Analysis unit of the Federal Reserve Bank of St. Louis. Recently, his articles have been published in the *Journal of Money, Credit and Banking, Journal of Financial Services Review, Journal of Banking and Finance*, and *Journal of Economics and Business.* Yeager earned both a PhD and an MA in Economics from Washington University.

Rodrigo Zeidan Rodrigo Zeidan works in Applied Finance and Economics. He is Associate Professor of Economics & Finance at Fundação Dom Cabral and affiliated Assistant Professor at Nottingham University Business School China. He has had works published in relevant journals such as *Review of Industrial Organization, Economics Letters*, and the *European Journal of Health Economics.* He also has participated in many conferences around the world and served as the keynote speaker at the First Conference on Social Entrepreneurship, Systems Thinking, and Complexity.

Index

Note: Page numbers ending in "f" refer to figures. Page numbers ending in "t" refer to tables.